RELIGION AND LAW
IN
INDEPENDENT INDIA

Religion and Law in Independent India

(Second Enlarged Edition)

edited by
ROBERT D. BAIRD

MANOHAR
2005

First published 1993
Second edition 2005

© Robert D. Baird, 1993, 2005

All rights reserved. No part of this publication may be
reproduced or transmitted, in any form or by any means,
without prior permission of the editor and the publisher

ISBN 81-7304-588-7

Published by

Ajay Kumar Jain for
Manohar Publishers & Distributors
4753/23 Ansari Road, Daryaganj
New Delhi 110 002

Printed at

Lordson Publishers Pvt. Ltd.
Delhi 110 007

Contents

Preface	vii
Contributors	ix
Robert D. Baird *Introduction*	1
Robert D. Baird *Religion and Law in India: Adjusting to the Sacred as Secular*	7
P.N. Bhagwati *Religion and Secularism Under the Indian Constitution*	35
Harold G. Coward *India's Constitution and Traditional Presuppositions Regarding Human Nature*	51
Robert D. Baird *On Defining "Hinduism" as a Religious and Legal Category*	69
Gerald J. Larson *Mandal, Mandir, Masjid: The Citizen as Endangered Species in Independent India*	87
Gregory C. Kozlowski *Muslim Personal Law and Political Identity in Independent India*	103
Tahir Mahmood *Interaction of Islam and Public Law in Independent India*	121
Kavita R. Khory *The Shah Bano Case: Some Political Implications*	149
N. Gerald Barrier *Sikhs and the Law: A Century of Conflict over Identity and Authority*	167
John H. Mansfield *The Personal Laws or a Uniform Civil Code?*	207

V.S. Rekhi
  *Religion, Politics and Law in Contemporary India:
  Judicial Doctrine in Critical Perspective* — 247

Vasudha Dhagamwar
  *Women, Children and the Constitution: Hostages to
  Religion, Outcaste by Law* — 283

Kay K. Jordan
  *Devadasi Reform: Driving the Priestesses or the
  Prostitutes Out of Hindu Temples?* — 325

Vasudha Narayanan
  Renunciation and Law in India — 347

Robert N. Minor
  Auroville and the Courts in India: Religion and Secular — 361

Ronald W. Neufeldt
  *To Convert or Not to Convert: Legal and Political
  Dimensions of Conversion in Independent India* — 381

Robert J. Stephens
  *Conflict in the Courts: Cates and Religious Conversion
  In the Indian Secular State* — 401

Brian K. Smith
  *How Not to Be a Hindu: The Case of the
  Ramakrishna Mission* — 425

Michael C. Baltutis
  *Recognition and Legislation of Private Religious
  Endowments in Indian Law* — 443

Richard W. Lariviere
  A Persistent Disjunction: Parallel Realms of Law in India — 469

Jonathan M. Lindsay and Richard Gordon
  *Reflections on Law and Meaningfulness in a
  North Indian Hindu Village* — 479

INDEX OF CASES — 505

INDEX — 509

Preface

An international and multidisciplinary conference on Religion and Law in Independent India was held at the University of Iowa on October 10-13, 1991. This conference was organized by the editor under the sponsorship of the School of Religion of the University of Iowa. A wide range of programs and departments within the University of Iowa, as well as several external institutions contributed significantly to the funding of this project. Without this broad-based cooperation the conference would not have been possible, for we did not believe such a conference would be viable without bringing a reasonable number of distinguished Indian scholars into the discussion. Among those whose contributions made this possible were the School or Religion, College of Law, the Center for International and Comparative Studies, the Center for Asian and Pacific Studies, Office of Academic Affairs, South Asia Studies Program, Department of Geography, Department of History, Global Studies Program, Women in International Development and Kala Mandali.

As for funding our distinguished Indian contributors, The Islamic Council of Iowa made it possible to bring Professor Tahir Mahmood, and the Ford Foundation made it possible for Vasudha Dhagamwar to include the conference as part of her research assignment at Oxford University. Upendra Baxi, Vice-Chancellor of the University of Delhi participated as part of his designation of Ida Beam Distinguished Professor, which included further lectures on his part at the College of Law and Department of Geography. The College of Law supported the cost of bringing Chief Justice P.N. Bhagwati, and the Center for Asian and Pacific Studies sponsored V.S. Rekhi.

This conference was in the planning stage for over two years and from the beginning it was understood by invitees that their papers were to be prepared for a subsequent publication by the same title as the conference. Certain invitees were unable to attend the conference, but their papers nonetheless appear in the volume.

With the appearance of a second edition, I have included several new essays. An essay dealing with the overall structure of religion and law in India was written by the editor. An essay on the legal issues affecting the Sikh community is offered by N. Gerald Barrier, whose work on the Sikhs is well known to those who study South Asia. Michael C. Baltutis, a Ph.D. candidate in Asian religions at the University of Iowa provides a study of public endowments, and Robert J. Stephens, a recent Ph.D. from the University of Iowa analyses issues relating to caste and conversion.

We are pleased to extend our study in this way, the relationship between religion and law in independent India remains a rich field for research, and merits an increased number of workers.

The University of Iowa ROBERT D. BAIRD
Auburn University
September 23, 2004

Contributors

ROBERT D. BAIRD
: Professor Emeritus, History of Religions, University of Iowa.

MICHAEL C. BALTUTIS
: Ph.D. candidate in Asian Religions, University of Iowa.

N. GERALD BARRIER
: Professor Emeritus, South Asian History, University of Missouri.

P.N. BHAGWATI
: Former Chief Justice of The Supreme Court of India.

HAROLD G. COWARD
: Fellow and former Director of the Centre for Studies in Religion and Society, University of Victoria, British Columbia.

VASUDHA DHAGAMWAR
: Executive Director of Multiple Action Research Group, New Delhi.

RICHARD GORDON
: International Tax Program, Harvard Law School.

KAY K. JORDAN
: Associate Professor, Department of Philosophy and Religious Studies, Radford University.

KAVITA R. KHORY
: Associate Professor, Department of Politics, Mount Holyoke College.

GREGORY C. KOZLOWSKI
> Formerly Professor of History, DePaul University.

RICHARD W. LARIVIERE
> Professor of Sanskrit and Dean of the College of Liberal Arts, University of Texas.

GERALD J. LARSON
> Rabindranath Tagore Professor Emeritus, Indiana University, and Professor Emeritus, Religious Studies, University of California, Santa Barbara.

JONATHAN M. LINDSAY
> Associate, Goulston & Storrs, Boston.

TAHIR MAHMOOD
> Professor and Dean of the Law Faculty, University of Delhi.

JOHN H. MANSFIELD
> John H. Watson, Jr. Professor of Law, Harvard University.

ROBERT N. MINOR
> Professor of Religion, University of Kansas.

VASUDHA NARAYANAN
> Professor, Department of Religion, University of Florida.

RONALD W. NEUFELDT
> Professor of Religious Studies, University of Calgary.

V.S. REKHI
> Director, National Law Institute University, Bhopal.

Contributors

BRIAN K. SMITH

    Program in Religious Studies and Department of History, University of California, Riverside.

ROBERT J. STEPHENS

    Recent Ph.D. in Asian religions at the University of Iowa. Instructor, Department of Philosophy and Religion, University of Northern Iowa.

1

Introduction

Robert D. Baird

Although from time to time one hears cries against the method, academics tend to study their data within the context of disciplines. Even scholars whose identification is area studies, and in our case South Asian studies, are identified by the disciplinary badge they wear as historians, sociologists, anthropologists, historians of religions, or legal historians, to name a few. Differing disciplines point to differing methods of investigation. We ask different questions of the same or sometimes different data. And, because of that we inevitably arrive at different conclusions.

Objections to dividing academic inquiry into disciplines have been voiced, frequently because of the insular nature of these disciplines and because of the temptation of seeing one's discipline as a way of explaining the whole.[1] This insular nature of modern academics is manifested in what has been called "tunnel history."[2] Here the discipline of history further divides itself into economic, diplomatic, intellectual, religious, social, and legal history, among others. Modern academic investigations become stuck in their own mire when they carry this insular approach even further and think that only "religious facts" can offer a proper explanation for "religious events," or that only "legal facts" can offer a proper explanation for "legal events." To move outside one's range of self-imposed data and method is to court disaster in reductionism.

Fischer describes what often happens when one insular tunneler bumps into a colleague from a different disciplinary tunnel.

> Unpleasant things are apt to happen when one grimy historical
> tunneler bumps into another, somewhere in the dark, and disputes the

---

[1] See Wilfred Cantwell Smith, "Methodology and the Study of Religion: Some Misgivings," in *Methodological Issues in Religious Studies*, edited by Robert D. Baird (Chico, CA, 1975).

[2] David Hackett Fischer, *Historians' Fallacies: Toward a Logic of Historical Thought* (New York, 1970), pp. 142ff.

right of way with pick and shovel. In these altercations, the fallacy of essence is apt to be the ultimate weapon. Charles Beard, for example, insisted that the United States Constitution was "essentially an economic document." To this, Henry Steele Commager made the absurd reply that it "was, and is, *essentially* a political document." Surely the Constitution was in some respects an economic document and in other respects a political document, and essentially neither, and indeed *essentially* nothing.[3]

To avoid such restrictions, one suggestion is that academics speak more to one another and engage in what has been called *interdisciplinary studies*. But what might such a designation mean? If it is distinct questions and methods of verification that constitute a discipline, what logical sense might it make to suggest that distinct questions and distinct methods of verification could be either mixed or asked simultaneously. For example, to inquire about the relationship of a social reality to a religious belief or ritual is different from asking its philosophical import. The two questions are different, require different forms of analysis, and offer answers on different levels of inquiry. To fail to see these differences is no less detrimental to the search for truth than an insular approach.

However, the point that the appeal to *interdisciplinary studies* seems to be making is that no one discipline exhausts reality, and that reality is sufficiently expansive and complex that even the addition of all of our modern methods is unlikely to exhaust it. If this is true, then seeing reality through an insular tunnel is not seeing reality at all. It is more like the error of the blind men and the elephant, when grasping the tail it is thought that an elephant is like a rope. Part of the elephant is indeed like a rope, but all of it is not.

Another solution to this is *multi*disciplinary studies. This approach does not assume that we can ask different level questions simultaneously, but that we can indeed ask them consecutively. It suggests that our disciplinary questions are all limited but illuminating if we recognize their limitations. And, if those limitations are conceded, even the limited perspective can be true. Approaching data through a multiplicity of disciplines will not result in complete truth either, but it will offer a fuller analysis and a thicker description than an insular disciplinary approach.

This volume contains a series of essays exploring the relationships between religion and law in independent India. It is not often that two areas of study so apparently diverse are seen in such close proximity. Historians of religions have seldom considered the study of law within the parameters of their discipline. And, legal scholars just as seldom deal in an extended way with

---

[3]*Ibid.*, p. 143.

religious issues.[4] To bring such scholars together is an admission that both religion and law can be seen from more than one disciplinary perspective. Law can provide interesting and insightful analyses into the study of religion, and religion might well provide interesting insights into legal matters.

But this volume attempts to go beyond that. For we are conceding that the boundary at which religion and law meet not only has a religious and a legal dimension but other dimensions as well. For we have also joined together with historians, anthropologists, Sanskritists, and political scientists. Moreover, we have sought to include perspectives from both women and men and from Indian scholars who have insights to offer from the inside and others whose distance may offer their own particular perspective.

In spite of the diversity that has been sought, it is woefully clear that our net was not caste broadly enough. Other disciplines might have been included and scholars from other nations might have been invited. The geographical spread was unhappily limited by economic factors. And, in the search for disciplinary diversity our vision was limited to those whose publications had indicated an interest and competence in such matters.

Traditional societies see life homogeneously. That is, religion is not something that is part of life, but that which gives meaning to all of life. Traditional India fits that model. But if that is the case, then simply asking the relationship between religion and law is to ask a question that is the result of secularization. Because of where we stand in history, it is difficult not to ask the question in this way. But we must be quick to admit that the distinction between religion and law, between religion and the secular did not always pertain. And indeed, for many Indian people it does not pertain even today even though that distinction is enshrined in *The Constitution of India*, in legislation, and in court decisions.[5]

While there is no obvious way to organize the essays contained in this volume, there are certain themes that occur and reoccur in various essays. I turn now to several of those themes.

First, there are numerous references to provisions for religion in *The Constitution of India*. Since the constitution is a political, legal, social, religious, and historical document, it is not surprising that it should be scrutinized from a variety of angles. Chief Justice P. N. Bhagwati, in his opening paper discusses

---

[4]It is encouraging in this regard to report on a new journal edited by Tahir Mahmood, *Religion and Law Review*, (Vol. One, No. 1, Summer, 1992) and the *Journal of Law and Religion* (Vol. One, No. 1, Summer, 1983) out of Hamline University in the U.S.

[5]See "Religion and the Secular: Categories for Religious Conflict and Religious Change in Independent India," and "Uniform Civil Code and the Secularization of Law," in Robert D. Baird, *Essays in the History of Religions* (New York, 1991).

the various facets of religious freedom provided in the Constitution as well as the limitations placed upon it by the realm of the secular, thus defining what he sees as the constitutional model of secularism. The discussion is important not only for its content but because it is the mature thought of someone with long experience on the bench, including his final position as Chief Justice of the Supreme Court of India. Harold Coward is interested in the basic philosophical assumptions of the Constitution and in contrasting them with the traditional understanding of human nature found in the *karma* and *guṇa* theory of *Mīmāṃsā* and *Yoga*. Such an analysis provides insights into the basis for potential religious and legal conflict between the two philosophical perspectives. Robert D. Baird seeks to determine what is included within "Hinduism" in the Constitution as well as in later legislation and court decisions. How religious formulations of "Hinduism" effect legal definitions is the point of his analysis.

Second, a distinction must be made between law as determined by the constitution, legislation and the courts, and law "on the ground." There is always a gap between what is legal and what is practiced, between what is legislated and implemented. For example, just because untouchability is abolished in Article 17 of the Constitution is no reason to assume that is has been abolished in the villages. The essays in this collection deal with law on both levels. Of course, any court decision has an "on the ground" effect for the person or institution involved. The Ramakrishna case in which the Calcutta High Court decided that the Ramakrishna Mission was not "Hindu" but a minority religion had a profound effect upon the schools administered by that mission. But, the case has thus far had little if any effect upon other movements. Baird's discussion of "Hinduism," Ronald Neufeldt's discussion of conversion, P. N. Bhagwati's discussion of religion and secularism, Kay Jordan's discussion of devadasi legislation, Robert Minor's discussion of the Auroville case, and Bryan Smith's account of the Ramakrishna case are among those papers which operate on this level.

But Jonathan Lindsay and Richard Gordon's discussion of the implementation of law in a north Indian village demonstrates the existence of a gap between law "in the air" and law "on the ground." Vasudha Dhagamwar deals not only with the theoretical provisions of the Constitution, but how this actually affects women and children "on the ground." Tahir Mahmood's discussion deals not so much with laws that explicitly govern Muslims but with how Muslims are affected by public law. Since both Gregory Kozlowski's essay on political identity of Muslims and Kavita Khory's discussion of the political implications of the Shah Bano case deal with political implications, they also deal with the law where people actually live out their lives. Gerald Larson's distinction between substantive and formal "equality," "caste," "community," "class," and "religion," impinges on this distinction and is theoretically helpful in coming to grips with what he calls "equivocation" in each instance.

Introduction

Third, while many of the papers deal with contemporary issues, there are several which demonstrate that a study of traditional texts can often shed light on such issues. Harold Coward's discussion of Yoga texts, Vasudha Narayanan's discussion of renunciation in Vaishnava tradition, Kay Jordon's discussion of the colonial attitude toward the devadasis, and Richard Lariviere's analysis of parallel realms of law in premodern periods all show that the discussion of contemporary issues cannot fruitfully be cut off from an understanding of history.

Fourth, these papers show that gender is relevant to understanding the relationship between religion and law. Not all issues necessitate raising the gender issue, but some do. One of the most prominent cases affecting women, in this case particularly Muslim women, was the Shah Bano case. It is clear that this important case, ably discussed by Gerald Larson, Gregory Kozlowski, Kavita Khory, and Vasudha Dhagamwar, not only has an important impact upon Muslim women, but upon Muslim men as well. Vasudha Dhagamwar's able essay takes us well beyond Shah Bano, however, and Kay Jordan's essay on devadasi legislation also deals with issues relating to gender.

Fifth, however inadequate may be the categories of majority/minority communities, issues pertaining to these distinctions are dealt with in Gerald Larson's analysis of Mandir/Masjid, John Mansfield's discussion of a Uniform Civil Code, Brian Smith's analysis of the Calcutta High Court's decision making the Ramakrishna Mission a minority, and the essays by Gregory Kozlowski, Tahir Mahmood, Kavita Khory which deal explicitly with laws affecting Muslims.

As the study of religion and law in modern India continues to receive more attention, we can look forward to having these themes, and others as well, analyzed in even more detail. There is little doubt that our understanding of independent India will be enhanced by continued examination of such issues.

2

Religion and Law in India: Adjusting to the Sacred as Secular

Robert D. Baird

The question of the relationship between religion and law in India is a distinctly modern question. In traditional societies such as India, what we term religion is not seen so much as one aspect of society, but rather as basic to all of society. If life can be likened to a pie, religion is not one piece of that pie alongside the pieces labeled politics, economics, social structure, education, and law. Rather, religion is the fruit found in each and every piece of the pie.

Independent India is governed by a predominantly modern human rights oriented constitution brought into being by a Constituent Assembly that was broadly representative and characterized by open debate. Many principles that found their way into *The Constitution of India* were strongly debated, several views often being maintained to the end. *The Constitution of India* is less a consensus document than a document that was forged by an educated elite, strongly influenced by the ideology of the Enlightenment, and guided by influential spokespersons such as B.R. Ambedkar and Jawaharlal Nehru. More traditional voices were heard, but with notable exceptions, it was the voice of the Enlightenment that emerged victorious. This voice sought to protect minority points of view and diverse religious traditions. But inherent in that attempt at protection was the need to compel traditional points of view to give up parts of their traditions in order to provide opportunities for previously disenfranchised people.

In order to understand the place of law and religion in the modern state of India, then, it is necessary to comprehend something of more traditional views that frequently come in conflict with *The Constitution of India* and the laws that are enacted by Parliament intending to implement that Constitution.

In order to do that, we will deal with some basic principles of *Manusmrti*, or *The Laws of Manu*, as it is commonly known.[1] It is unlikely that this text was ever implemented in its entirety. In fact, it contains principles, and then offers alternatives when those principles are violated. That is an acknowledgment that it was not fully implemented. Regarding *Manusmriti*, Brian Smith says "As a text on dharma, it is by definition caught in the universal paradox between 'what should be' and 'what is'—for *dharma* strives to be both descriptive and prescriptive."[2] Furthermore, *Manusmriti* embodies an attempt on the part of the *brahmans* (priests) to capture power from the *kshatriyas* (rulers) for themselves by making them the authority for legal and moral issues.

Wendy Doniger contends that while Hindus always took Manu seriously as principle, other ancient legal texts were more widely used in legal circles. J.D.M. Derrett and Robert Lingat hold that during the British period, *Manusmriti*, in conjunction with the commentaries, was widely used by jurists.[3]

> 'Hindu law', or *dharmashastra*, was applied to nearly 80 per cent of the population of colonial India in matters of marriage and divorce, legitimacy, guardianship, adoption, inheritance, religious endowments, and so on. And in present-day India, Manu remains the basis of the Hindu marriage code, as it defines itself *vis-à-vis* Muslim or secular (governmental) marriage law.[4]

---

[1] All references from *Manusmrti* are from *The Laws of Manu*, translated by Wendy Doniger with Brian Smith (London: Penguin Books, 1991). This translation is in prose and can be readily accessed by the average reader. *The Laws of Man*, translated by G. Buhler for "Sacred Books of the East," Vol. 25, is useful because of its verse pagination and because it leaves technical terms untranslated, thus enabling persons with Sanskrit familiarity to recognize the term behind the translation.

[2] *The Laws of Manu*, translated by Wendy Doniger (London: Penguin Books, 1991), pp. xxxix-xl of the "Introduction."

[3] See the important volume by J.D.M. Derrett, *Religion, Law and the State in India* (London: Faber and Faber, 1968). Also Robert Lingat, *The Classical Law of India*, trans. J.D.M. Derrett (Berkeley: University of California Press, 1973).

[4] *The Laws of Manu*, "Introduction," p. lx.

Religion and Law in Ancient India

Let us proceed, then, by looking into the basic premises of *Manusmrti* and the nature of its legal vision and moral stance.

Divine Sanction

From its earliest attempts to codify what we would now consider laws, the writers of ancient texts claimed a sacred sanction. That is to say, the contents of a text like *Manusmrti*, are of divine origin. They were not arrived at through social experience nor through spirited discussion, but were revealed through spiritual insight. They are part of the created world. They are built into the very nature of things. As such, they are part of a *weltangshauung*, a world-view valid for all humanity. To violate them is to go against the nature of things and thereby come to ruin. Laws, in this view, are not made and unmade according to social needs or human convenience. They are eternally binding upon humankind. In an early passage, *Manusmriti* states that it reveals the origin of religion, of the universe, as well as the origin of the classes and the duties that pertain to each. "The source of religion has thus been proclaimed to you concisely, and the origin of this whole (universe), now learn the duties of the classes."[5] These are the words of the great sage Bhrigu, who received these teachings from Manu, who received them from the Creator of all things. As Brian Smith notes,

> Manu, like virtually all other religious texts, masks its true authorship and indeed must do so in order to posit effectively its own claims to transcendentally based and absolute truth. For religious discourse is always—and necessarily, if disingenuously—represented as anonymous (or as the direct or indirect 'word of God', or the dictates of Manu, the 'first man', either of which comes to the same things.[6]

If the sanction for the religious and legal principles in *Manusmriti* is divine, then it is also the case that religion and law are inextricable bound together,

---

[5] *Ibid.*, 2.25.

[6] *Ibid.*, "Introduction," p. xxii.

and law itself is divinely sanctioned as well. For centuries, Hindus have believed and stated that their law was part and parcel of their religion. In modern times this has been the primary obstacle to forming a Uniform Civil Code as called for in Article 44 of *The Constitution of India*.

Justice

Manusmirti is concerned with justice. Justice is served when every person or group does his or her duty and is treated appropriately in the light of the way the universe inherently is. Manu's universe is not one in which everyone is created with equal abilities or opportunities. Moreover, it is a universe that speaks to *duties* rather than *rights*. Each created group including class, age, and gender, is naturally constituted so as to possess certain duties for the good of the whole. When these duties are realized, justice is achieved.

Inequality

Justice, then, is based on sets of duties that are based not on equal rights but on unequal ability and nature. Just as it is unjust to examine an elementary school child with the same test used to examine a graduating university student, so it is unjust to expect *shudras*, whose very nature is to serve the higher classes, to lead a nation into battle. And it is unjust to expect a *brahmin*, whose nature is spiritual, to do menial tasks no matter how necessary they might be. The four classes (*varnas*) emerge from the body of God, and are therefore part of the creative act and part of the world as it comes from the Creator.

But to protect this whole creation, the lustrous one made separate innate activities for those born of his mouth, arms, thighs and feet. For priests [*brahmans*], he ordained teaching and learning, sacrificing for themselves and sacrificing for others, giving and receiving. Protecting his subjects, giving, having sacrifices performed, studying, and remaining unaddicted to the sensory objects are, in summary for a ruler [*kshatriya*]. Protecting his livestock, giving, having sacrifices performed, studying, trading, lending money, and farming the land are for the commoner [*vaishya*]. The Lord assigned only one activity to a servant [*shudra*]: serving these (other) classes without resentment.[7]

---

7. *Ibid.*, 1.87-91.

Each person's duty is matched with his or her creative nature and, even if occasionally an individual might struggle with the obligation to act according to inherent nature, as the *Bhagavadgita* puts it,

> Better one's own duty, (tho) imperfect,
> Than another's duty well performed;
> Better death in (doing) one's own duty;
> Another's duty brings danger.[8]

Justice, then, is realized when persons, differently constituted, do their assigned tasks. If they fail to do so and if punishment is required, that also is applied unequally. It is based upon the inequality that is built by the divine into the nature of things. If some men are lower than other men, women are lower than men. Women are by nature passionate and not to be trusted alone. They must be subject successively to their fathers, their husbands, and their sons. "In childhood a woman should be under her father's control, in youth under her husband's, and when her husband is dead, under her sons." She should not have independence.[9] Marriage should not be contracted with some kinds of people.[10] Contact with impure people renders those in such close proximity impure as well.[11]

In the implementation of justice, *Manusmriti* emphasizes the importance of honesty in testimony and the trustworthiness of witnesses. Perjury has its penalty, but as in other cases the penalty is determined by where you stand in the class hierarchy. "They say that wise men have proclaimed these fines for false evidence to prevent a miscarriage of justice and to restrain injustice. A just king should fine and banish the (lower) three classes if they give false evidence, but he should merely banish a priest."[12] Usually a distinction is made between the three lower classes and the brahmans. "Manu the son of the Self-existent has proclaimed ten places on which the three (lower) classes may be punished, but the priest should depart uninjured."[13] Distinctions in punishment are also

---

[8] *The Bhagavad Gita*, trans. by Franklin Edgerton (Cambridge: Harvard University Press, 1944), 3.35.

[9] *The Laws of Manu*, 5.148.

[10] *Ibid.*, 3.6-7.

[11] *Ibid.*, 5.85.

[12] *Ibid.*, 8.122-123.

[13] *Ibid.*, 8.124.

made between the three lower classes as well. Fines will differ in magnitude and the severity of the penalty for same offences is determined by the class of the offender. "A ruler [*kshatriya*] who shouts abuse at a priest [*brahman*] should be fined a hundred (pennies); a commoner [*vaishya*] (who does this), a hundred and fifty or two hundred (pennies); a servant [*shudra*] should be given corporal or capital punishment."[14] And, just as the penalty varies in intensity depending upon the class of the offender, so it differs depending upon the class of the one who is offended. "If a man of one birth [*shudra*] hurls cruel words at one of the twice-born [three upper classes], his tongue should be cut out. . . .If he is so proud as to instruct priests about their duty, the king should have hot oil poured into his mouth and ears."[15] Now this is conceived as a scheme of justice in that it indicates how one ought to conduct oneself in the light of the way things are. But life is not limited to the present and the mundane. Assumed in *Manusmriti*'s scheme of justice are the notions of karma and rebirth.

Karma and Rebirth

The doctrines of karma and rebirth permeate the history of Indian religions. It should not be a surprise to find these doctrines connected to legal materials. They do not widely modify law and punishment, but they do supplement such matters by holding that punishments from one life to another augment punishments that kings are expected to impose for crimes committed. In discussing the structure of *Manusmriti*, Wendy Doniger states

> The first chapter (1.26-50) establishes the law of karma and situated within it the creation of the various classes of beings, particularly humans and animals, while the last (12.40-81) reverts to the law of karma to explain how, depending on their past actions, people are reborn as various classes of beings, particularly humans and animals. Midway through the text (6.61-64), the ascetic meditates briefly on the miseries of transmigration.[16]

---

[14] *Ibid.*, 8.267.
[15] *Ibid.*, 8.270-272.
[16] *Ibid.*, "Introduction," p. 1.

Even Brahmans are affected by karma and rebirth. Punishment is often for actions performed not only in the present life, but previous lives. And, one should understand that justice that is unfulfilled will eventually be fulfilled in some future life. So, justice is implemented not merely in this single life, but over the course of multiple lives. "Priests who act like herons or show the distinctive signs of cats fall into the hell called 'Blind Darkness' through the evil effects of past actions."[17] Hells in Indian thought are part of the process of karma and rebirth. They are numerous, as are heavens, but they are not permanent. They are temporary abodes merited by some actions or life styles. While it is legitimate to kill animals for sacrificial purposes, some passages warn against killing for non-religious purposes. "A twice-born person who knows the rules should not eat meat against the rules, even in extremity; for if he eats meat against the rules, after his death he will be helplessly eaten by them (that he ate)."[18] A penalty may be to be reborn as an animal or to suffer reproach in the next life. "A woman who is unfaithful to her husband is an object of reproach in this world, (then) she is reborn in the womb of a jackal and is tormented by the diseases born of her evil."[19] Through religious practices, the results of karma may be mitigated. Nevertheless, persons are counseled to contemplate the results of illicit actions.

> He should think about where men go as a result of the faults of the effects of their past actions and about how they fall into hell and are tortured in the house of Yama; and about how they are separated from the people they like and united with the people they dislike, and are overcome by old age and tormented by diseases; and about how the individual soul goes out of this body and is born again as an embryo, meandering through thousands of millions of wombs: and about the unhappiness that embodied creatures experience as a result of irreligion and the incorruptible happiness that results from achieving the goal of religion.[20]

---

17. *Ibid.*, 8.197.
18. *Ibid.*, 5.33.
19. *Ibid.*, 5.164.
20. *Ibid.*, 6.6164.

Karma and rebirth are not left to bear the whole brunt of justice. Kings have penalties that they are bound to impose. But some evils do take care of themselves, and regardless of the fidelity of the king, no evil act will go unnoticed or unpunished. Truthfulness of witnesses is essential to justice and witnesses should know that

> A witness who speaks the truth in testifying wins magnificent worlds (after death) and unsurpassed renown here on earth; such speech is revered by Brahma. Anyone who tells lies in testifying is helplessly bound fast by Varuna's ropes for a hundred rebirths; therefore one should speak the truth in testifying.[21]

Karma and rebirth are equally applicable to the *shudra*. If the *shudra* serves the other classes according to his duty his next life will be better.

> The servant's duty and supreme good is nothing but obedience to famous priestly householders who know the Veda. If he is unpolluted, obedient to his superiors, gentle in his speech, without a sense of "I", and always dependent on the priests and the other (twice-born classes), he attains a superior birth (in the next life).[22]

Religion and Law in Independent India

In 1947 India became an independent state with the partition of India and Pakistan. Legal developments in independent India can be analysed in terms of *The Constitution of India*, Legislation by Parliament, and the legal decisions of the courts. We will look at religion and law in this order.

The Constitution of India

The Indian Constituent Assembly was broadly representative, and was held to discuss and vote on a constitution for the independent state. In 1949 the Constituent Assembly enacted *The Constitution of India*. The Preamble to that

---

21. *Ibid.*, 8.81-82.
22. *Ibid.*, 9.334-335.

Constitution stated "In our Constitutent Assembly this twenty-sixth day of November, 1949, we do hereby adopt, enact and give to ourselves this constitution." India maintained its intent to be a secular state and Muslims who remained in India were represented in the Assembly. Indian Muslims today constitute the second largest body of Muslims in the world, second only to Indonesia. The Assembly sought to accommodate minorities. When the controversial issue of religious conversion was brought up, there were those Hindus who would have liked to have it outlawed. Such a prohibition was not included in the Constitution after the argument was put forward by Muslims and Christians that to propagate their religion was part of what it meant to be Muslim and Christian.[23]

B.R. Ambedkar, a former untouchable, who was educated at Columbia University (U.S.), chaired the Assembly and exerted considerable influence over it. *The Constitution of India* is, with few exceptions, a modern human rights document. As *Manusmriti*, *The Constitution of India* seeks the implementation of justice. But unlike *Manusmriti*, constitutional this justice is based on the principle of equality. This equality extends to all men irrespective of caste, and to women in the same way as to men. *The Constitution of India* makes special provisions for those who have been the objects of past discrimination in order to seek a level playing field for all Indians. Article 17 abolishes untouchability and Article 16(4) provides for the possible reservation of positions for persons in "backward classes."

The Constitution of India, also in contrast with *Manusmriti*, seeks justice in this life. The doctrines of karma and rebirth are not denied, nor are they affirmed. They are irrelevant. The argument that one is in a lesser position in this life because of acts done in a previous existence does not come to play here. Justice is to be implemented in this life. Moreover, whatever retribution is enacted for those who violate these principles has to be enacted by a duly elected Parliament and is not left to one's karma for punishment.

Furthermore, while *Manusmriti* dealt with *dharma* or duty, the Constitution deals with rights. One member of the Constituent Assembly pointed this out and suggested that in addition to a section on "Fundamental Rights" there be a section on "Fundamental Duties." That was never included. Moreover,

---

[23] For a discussion of the issue of the propagation of religion, see Donald Eugene Smith, *India As a Secular State* (Princeton: Princeton University Press, 1963), Chapter 6.

while *Manusmriti* claims the divine for its authority, *The Constitution of India* does not mention that realm. Elsewhere, I identified the ultimate values whereby Jawaharlal Nehru legitimated his notion of the secular state. Those values were that his view was *rational and scientific, Indian, and modern*.[24] While some Indians might be more traditional in their thinking, they were simply wrong. These principles were basic for Nehru in that they were not in need of justification, but rather were used to justify other decisions. In his speech moving the Objectives Resolution at the Constituent Assembly, he stated:

> ... We adhere to certain fundamental propositions which are laid down in this Declaration. These fundamental propositions, I submit, are not controversial in any real sense of the word. Nobody challenges them in India and *nobody ought to challenge them*, but if anyone should challenge them, well, we shall accept that challenge *and hold our position.* [25]

This modern human rights orientation is asserted in the preamble to the Constitution.

WE, THE PEOPLE OF INDIA, having solemnly resolved to constitute India into a SOVEREIGN DEMOCRATIC REPUBLIC and to secure to all its citizens:

> JUSTICE, social, economic, and political;
> LIBERTY of thought, expression, belief, faith and worship;
> FRATERNITY assuring the dignity of the individual and the unity of the Nation;
> IN OUR CONSTITUENT ASSEMBLY this twenty-sixth day of November, 1949, do HEREBY ADOPT, ENACT AND GIVE TO OURSELVES THIS CONSTITUTION. [26]

---

[24] Robert D. Baird, *Essays in the History of Religions*, Vol. 11, Toronto Studies in Religion (New York: Peter Lang, 1991), p.133.

[25] Jawaharlal Nehru, *Independence and After: A Collection of Speeches, 1946-1949* (New York: The John Day Company, 1950), p. 351 (emphasis added).

[26] S.M. Mehta, *Constitution of India and Amendment Acts* (New Delhi: Deep & Deep, 1990), p. xxiii.

The Constitution of India provides considerable scope for freedom of religious belief and practice. But that freedom is not unlimited. Articles 25 and 26 of the Constitution outline both those freedoms and how they are restricted.

> 25. (1) Subject to public order, morality and health and to the other provisions of this Part, all persons are equally entitled to freedom of conscience and the right freely to profess, practice and propagate religion.
> (2) Nothing in this article shall affect the operation of any existing law or prevent the State from making any law –
> (a) regulating or restricting any economic, financial, political or other secular activity which may be associated with religious practice;
> (b) providing for social welfare and reform or the throwing open of Hindu religious institutions of a public character to all classes and sections of Hindus.
>
> *Explanation I*—The wearing and carrying of *kirpans* shall be deemed to be included in the profession of Sikh religion.
>
> *Explanation II*—In sub-clause (b) of clause (2), the reference to Hindus shall be construed as including a reference to persons professing the Sikh, Jaina, or Buddhist religion, and the reference to Hindu religious institutions shall be construed accordingly.
>
> 26. Subject to public order, morality and health, every religious denomination or any section thereof shall have the right –
> (a) to establish and maintain institutions for religious and charitable purposes;
> (b) to manage its own affairs in matters of religion;
> (c) to own and acquire movable and immovable property; and
> (d) to administer such property in accordance with law.

N.A. Subramaniam has noted that "The importance of Articles 25 and 26 lies not so much in the *grant* of religious liberty but in its *restriction*."[27] Article 25

---

[27] N.A. Subramaniam, "Freedom of Religion," *Journal of the Indian Law Institute*, July-Sept., 1961, p. 350.

is subject to the other provisions of Part III of the Constitution regarding "Fundamental Rights." These include the elimination of untouchability, equality before the law, and provisions for members of backward classes. Furthermore, religious freedom is "subject to public order, morality and health. . ." and cannot stand in the way of social reform.

Now these restrictions on the otherwise free exercise of "religion" constitute an admission that a conflict exists. It suggests that the Constitution may well be in conflict with traditional religious practices. Hence freedom cannot be granted without restriction. Traditional religious systems have the freedom to exist within the provisions of the Constitution. But one cannot justify closing Hindu temples to untouchables on the grounds that it is a religious matter and that their entry will pollute the image enshrined there. In cases where a conflict of this nature arises, religious change becomes a necessity for religious survival. But the survival can only be partial, as the conflicting tradition is modified so as to ease the grounds for conflict.

One of the devices for handling religious conflict is through the categories of "religion" and the "secular." According to the Constitution, life can be divided into these two all-encompassing categories. It is the category of "religion" that is granted freedom. But over against "religion" is the "secular" for which the same degree of freedom is not provided. Sometimes the realms of "religion" and the "secular" are closely related or even overlap, but it is the view of the Constitution that they ought not to be confused. The very use of these categories is strikingly modern, and it is that modernity that necessitates religious change. In *Manusmriti*, for example, the place of women, the nature of marriage, etc., are justified by the same sanction as more traditional "religious" matters. Muslims also hold that personal law and inheritance are as much a matter of Muslim faith and tradition as is prayer. Such religious traditions did not consider "religion" as a segment of existence. Even the Supreme Court recognizes this to have been the case.

> . . . Sometimes practices, religious and secular, are inextricably mixed up. This is more particularly so in regard to Hindu religion because as is well known, under the provisions of ancient Smritis, all human actions from birth to death and most of the individual actions from day to day are regarded as religious in character.[28]

---

[28] *Shri Govindlalji* v. *State of Rajasthan*, *All India Reporter* (hereafter A.I.R.), 1963 SC 1638 at 1661.

Since the Constitution and the more traditional ways of looking at life are ideologies that involve ultimate values, they are both to that extent religious.[29] These categories, then, are not only a means for handling religious conflict and religious change, but are at the same time a part of the religious system whose survival is constitutionally assured. Hence it is determined that religious conflict is handled through categories contained in one of the two conflicting ideologies. The categories of "religion" and the "secular" have become axiomatic, so that neither side of litigation is able to deny or question the categories themselves. The categories are given sanction as part of the ideology of the Constitution. Once the legitimacy of these two categories is no longer questioned, certain activities can be relegated to the "secular," thereby being cut off from the constitutional provisions for "religious" freedom. When this method proves insufficient, other alternatives are taken.

Law for the modern Indian state, then, departs rather significantly from Indian traditional thought. That departure is embodied in the Constitution. While the Constitution has been amended on numerous occasions by Parliament, it is that Constitution as enacted into law and understood by the Supreme Court that is basic to understanding religion and law in independent India.

Legislation by Parliament

During the years 1955-56, Parliament passed a number of laws that are referred to as the "Hindu Code Bill." The scope of this legislative endeavor as well as the discussion that surrounded it demonstrates that the overriding issue was the secularization of law. The religious sanction of personal law which is found in *Manusmriti* continues into the modern period. This results in the claim that personal laws are part of religious traditions, whether one is considering the majority Hindu tradition(s) or the Indian Muslim tradition(s).

Article 44 of the Constitution reads: "The State shall endeavour to secure for the citizens a uniform civil code throughout the territory of India." This article is included in Part IV of the Constitution titled "Directive Principles of State Policy." The articles in this Part are advisory for Parliament, but if not fulfilled, are not judicable. Article 44 is based on the assumption that the Indian

---

[29] For a presentation of a method that enables one to view *The Constitution of India* as a religious document (as well as economic, political and legal), see Robert D. Baird, *Category Formation and the History of Religions* (The Hague: Mouton & Co., 1971).

secular state requires the secularization of law—that civil law should be the same for all Indians in order that nation building can continue and that all persons can be welded together equally into a modern Indian state. This requires that traditional religious expressions become modified so that they are more and more a matter of personal faith, and that the state mold a modern civil code based on justice in terms of equality. L.M. Singhvi states this clearly: "In my view, the evolution and emergence of a uniform civil code is a part of the process of secularization; it is part of our quest for a new and integrated national identity based on the composite culture of India and on enlightened rationalism. This is a vital area for our nation-building and social development."[30] If Articles 25 and 26 secularized social reform, economics and politics, Article 44 necessitates the secularization of law.

At the dawn of independence, Indian law relating to marriage and divorce, inheritance, and joint family property was diverse. Being a Christian, Muslim, Hindu, Jew or Parsi meant that one would be governed by a distinct personal law. Differences were the result of religious differences to be sure, but were also impacted by local traditions and practices. Hindu law was not unified either. The Dayabhaga school was dominant in Bengal and Assam, and the Mitakshara school, along with its four subdivisions, prevailed throughout the rest of India. Likewise, Muslim law operated under irreconcilable diversity.[31] It is against this historical legal setting that Article 44 must be seen. In the state that is envisaged in the Constitution, all citizens are to be equal before the law regardless of religion, caste or gender.

Muslim resistance appeared in the Constituent Assembly when Article 44 (Article 35 of the Draft Constitution) was debated. Five Muslims spoke, and all of them opposed the article, without amending it to preserve personal law (which would have defeated the purpose of the article). The third speaker, Mahboob Ali Baig Sahib Bahadur argued that personal law should not be thought of as part of civil law. For Muslims, laws of succession, inheritance, marriage and divorce "are completely dependent upon their religion."[32] Conceding that

---

[30] Introduction to Tahir Mahmood, *An Indian Civil Code and Islamic Law* (Bombay: Tripathi Private Ltd., 1976), xi.
[31] *Ibid.*, pp. 10-11.
[32] *Constituent Assembly Debates*, 7: 543.

according to Muslim law marriage is a contract rather than a sacrament (*samskara* for "Hindus"), it is nevertheless the way Muslims have handled it. If there is a way other than contract whereby a marriage is authenticated, "we refuse to abide by it because it is not according to our religion."[33] Although it is true that for Muslims marriage is validated by contract, that validation by contract is itself a matter of religious law for the speaker.

Although a couple of the Muslim speakers did grant that at some future time a uniform civil code might be conceivable and acceptable, they uniformly state that personal law relating to marriage, divorce and inheritance are matters of "religion" and that they must be regulated with the consent of the religious groups to which they apply. Hence they stood in opposition to this proposed article and the secularization of law.

K.M. Munshi finally spoke for the article and it was his point of view that carried the day. He reminded Muslim speakers that Articles 25 and 26 already regulated the secular activities associated with religious practice and made room for social welfare and reform. As he saw it, Article 44 merely adds the proposition that the personal law of the country should be united at such a time as Parliament thinks proper. As for the protection of minority rights, he throws back at the Muslim speakers the case of the Khojas and Cutchi Memons. When the Shariat Act (1937) was passed, they followed certain "Hindu" customs. But since they were Muslims, they were forced to abide by Shariat according to the will of the majority of Muslims. Such codes, now as then, have to ask what is in the interest of the whole community, and a small segment cannot reasonably stand in the way of that. Singhvi continues by affirming that the intent of Article 44 is the separation of law from "religion." "We want to divorce religion from personal law, from what may be called social relations or from the rights of parties as regards inheritance or succession."[34] He holds that it is necessary to legislate in matters of personal law without actually interfering with "religion," even if that means a redefinition of "religion." "We are at a stage where we must unify and consolidate the nation by every means without interfering with religious practices. If, however, the religious practices in the past have been so constructed as to cover the whole field of life, we have reached a point where we must put our

---

[33] *Ibid.*

[34] *Ibid.*, p. 574.

foot down and say that these matters are not religion, they are purely matters for secular legislation. This is what is emphasized by this article."[35] Now after over fifty years since independence, Muslim law has not been changed by Parliament. Parliament has been bolder, however, when dealing with "Hindu" law.

On January 2, 1944, the government appointed a Hindu Law Committee under the chairmanship of B.N. Rau "for the purpose of formulating a Code of Hindu law which should be complete as far as possible."[36] The committee of four, including Dr. Dwarkanath Mitter, a former judge of the Calcutta High Court, formulated a Draft Code, and on the basis of this they traveled to the major population centers of India to hear witnesses both for and against the proposed code. To their admitted surprise, most of the witnesses were opposed to the Code on the grounds that it interfered with Hindu religion, i.e. involved the secularization of personal law.

It is the opinion of J.D.M. Derrett that the Hindu Code is a step in the direction of a uniform civil code.[37] His understanding is commonly shared by other scholars as well. Not only is this the view of scholars, but it seems to have been the attitude taken by those involved in the legislative process itself. In answering a proposal that a uniform civil code be enacted, since that is what the Constitution called for (not a partial codification of Hindu law), Jawaharlal Nehru is reported to have responded: "The honorable member is perfectly entitled to his view on the subject. If he or anyone else brings a Civil Code Bill, it will have my extreme sympathy. But I confess I do not think that at the present moment the time is ripe in India for me to try to push it through. I want to prepare the ground for it and this kind of thing is one method of preparing the ground."[38]

The draft Hindu Code Bill was introduced into the old central assembly in 1947 prior to the partition of India, but received such opposition that it was temporarily dropped.[39] The bill was again debated on the floor of the Constituent

---

[35] *Ibid.*

[36] *Report of the Hindu Law Committee* (Government of India Press, 1955), p.1.

[37] J.D.M. Derrett, *Hindu Law Past and Present* (Calcutta: A. Mukherjee, 1957), p.v. See also Smith, *India As a Secular State*, pp. 277ff.

[38] Quoted in P.B. Gajendragadkar, *Secularism and the Constitution of India* (Bombay: Bombay University Press, 1971), p. 124.

[39] Smith, *India as a Secular State*, p. 289.

Assembly (legislative), but again, as a result of intense reaction, was dropped in September 1951. But a new Parliament in 1955 and 1956 passed the substance of the code in the form of four separate bills: Hindu Marriage Bill, Hindu Succession Bill, Hindu Minority and Guardianship Bill, and Hindu Adoptions and Maintenance Bill. The debate that took place on these bills did not center on the secularization of law. By this time those who were opposed to codification because of the secularization of law saw that codification was inevitable, so they attempted to effect what were to them desirable changes. As I argue in more detail elsewhere, most of the issues are issues that revolve around gender.[40] They have to do with divorce, polygamy, the rights of widows to remarry, and the rights of women to inherit property. Throughout, the argument was offered that such changes in Hindu law merely gives to women the same rights that men already have. That argument was a powerful one. The effect on world opinion of the practice of polygamy was also strongly felt. The result is that polygamy is illegal for Hindus in modern India, while it remains legal for Muslims.

The Hindu Code proposed to deal with all Hindus equally apart from caste. The division of society into four *varnas*, is in modern times "totally obsolete" and highly objectionable. This was so obvious that no argument seemed necessary on its behalf. Law must be based on equality.[41] Questions of monogamy, divorce, inheritance are treated as secular matters to be determined by the legislature in keeping with the principles of rationality, science, and social utility. While this is in principle true for Muslim law as well, political issues have forced Parliament to desist. Parliament has indicated it is open to codifying and reforming personal law for minority communities as well if it is asked to do so.

It should come as no surprise to learn that these secular principles are affirmed by P.B. Gajendragadkar, a former chief justice of the Supreme Court of India. According to Gajendragadkar, the secular state aims at the implementation of Article 44, the introduction of a uniform civil code throughout all of India. The Hindu Code was merely a step in that direction, while the government prepared Muslim public opinion for the acceptance of the secularization of Muslim family law as well. "Whether or not polygamy should

---

[40] "Gender Implications for a Uniform Civil Code," *Personal Laws in Modern India*, ed. Gerald Larson (Bloomington: Indiana University Press, in press)

[41] P.B. Gajendragadkar, *The Hindu Code Bill* (Karnataka University, 1951), p. 46.

be allowed, what should be the line of succession, what should be the shares of different heirs, what should be the law of divorce, are matters which should be determined not by scriptural injunctions, but by rational considerations. These are matters 'secular' in character and are outside the legitimate domain of 'religion' as contemplated by Articles 25 and 26 of the Constitution."[42]

In an earlier article, I showed that Nehru legitimated his view of the secular state on the unquestionable ground that is was modern, rational, scientific, and Indian.[43] This is a continuation of the norms that appeared in the work of the Hindu Law Committee. These values are also found in the ground for Gajendragadkar's decisions. The day is gone when one can appeal to ancient texts to settle legal matters. "It would be totally unscientific and unreasonable to go back to these ancient texts to find out how we should regulate our daily life today."[44] Law is part of the secular realm and law changes according to the social and political conditions in which it is found. Hindu law has indeed changed, and it is certainly not of divine origin.[45] Being merely preliminary to a uniform civil code, the Hindu Code Bill must be based on modern principles and not on religious ones. Hence it should not be surprising to hear Gajendragadkar argue that the Hindu Code should not be based on texts, but on principles which are enunciated in the Constitution. "It seems to me that it is the preemptor requirement of the present age that we must have a Hindu Code which is based on absolute equality amongst all Hindus, irrespective of their caste, creed, or sex. If we all agree on this elementary proposition, there must be unanimity amongst us all in bringing about this reform."[46] In the end, then, the Hindu Code Bill was more than a systematic organization of Hindu law for all Hindus. It was also a reconfiguration of Hindu law on the principles of modernity.

The Supreme Court Decides

We will now turn to several important Supreme Court cases to show how the categories of "religion" and the "secular" are used to deal with cases

---

42. Gajendragadkar, *Secularism and the Constitution of India*, pp. 125-126.

43. "Religion and the Legitimation of Nehru's Concept of the Secular State," in *Religion and the Legitimation of Power in South Asia*, ed. by Bardwell L. Smith (Leiden: E.J. Brill, 1978).

44. Gajendragadkar, *The Hindu Code Bill*, p. 47.

45. *Ibid.*, p. 46.

46. *Ibid.*

where traditional religion conflicts with the Constitution. We will also touch on several cases where the Court has had to admit that those categories were not able to resolve the legal issues without the introduction of other principles.

When the Categories of "Religion" and the "Secular" Work. "Religion" is not defined in *The Constitution of India*. Its definition has been left to the courts, particularly the Supreme Court. While the Supreme Court has struggled with the definitional issue, in any given case, if the Court says a certain practice is religious, then it is. Sometimes the "religious" and the "secular" are entwined as in the case of a Mahant who by virtue of being the spiritual leader of a community exercises wide powers of property management. But here the Court did not hesitate to say that the administration of property is not religious but secular and therefore falls under potential government control.

The Supreme Court acknowledged that defining religion would be difficult if not impossible.[47] But it was clear that the definition offered by the American Supreme Court in *Davis* v. *Benson* (13 U.S. 333 at 342) which centered on a Creator and the obligations that Creator imposed on his creation would not help in the Indian arena. To define "religion" in a theistic manner would define Buddhists and Jains out of existence. Moreover, "religion" is more than mere belief.

> A religion may not only lay down a code of ethical rules for its followers to accept, it might prescribe rituals and observances, ceremonies and modes of worship which are regarded as integral parts of religion, and these forms and observances might extend even to matters of food and dress.[48]

In *Commissioner, Hindu Religious Endowments, Madras* v. *Sirur Mutt*, the concept of "essentiality" was introduced. The Court held that what was essential to a religion was to be determined "with reference to the doctrines of that religion itself."[49] At first the Court seemed to say that it was the believers of a religion that would determine what was essential. Later it acknowledged that religions

---

[47] *Commissioner, Hindu Religious Endowments, Madras* v. *Sirur Mutt*, *The Supreme Court Journal* (hereafter S.C.J.), Vol. XXVI, 1954, p. 348.
[48] *Ibid.*, p. 349.
[49] *Ibid.*

are not usually monolithic and that the Court would have to make the determination. In the end the Court was unable to offer a definition of "religion" and contented itself with determining whether specific actions were religious as the circumstances demanded. Although these categories have never been defined by the Courts, they are nevertheless used to resolve conflict. Sometimes a practice is considered unessential to a religion, while on other occasions the Court seems to act on its own advice in *Panachand Gandhi* v. *State of Bombay* that in difficult cases the "court should take a common-sense view and be actuated by considerations of practical necessity."[50]

In *Commissioner, Hindu Religious Endowments, Madras* v. *Sirur Mutt* it was held that the determination of what rituals were necessary in a temple was a "religious" matter, but that the scale of expenses for the rituals was a "secular" matter and could legitimately exist under governmental control. Financial matters, and the acquiring and administering of property are "secular" matters. Hence there is no interference with "religion" if a governmentally appointed Commissioner oversees the daily affairs of the temple, for that is a "secular" matter.[51] When Sikhs contested governmental action legislating the method of representation of the Board which manages their Gurdwaras, it was determined that the manner of representation was "secular" and could be determined by the State.[52]

In *Bira Kishore Deb* v. *State of Orissa*, it was argued that the Shri Jagannath Temple Act of 1954 deprived the Raja of Puri of his personal property.[53] The appellant, using the constitutional categories, distinguished two functions of the Raja. He was the chief servant of the temple (*adya sevak*) and also the sole superintendent in charge of the secular affairs of the temple. The Court affirmed the categories and maintained that the Act in no way limited the Raja in his "religious" functions but only intended to regulate the "secular" affairs of the temple. Section 15(1) of the Act required that an appointed committee provide for the proper maintenance of worship in accord with the Record of Rights. The Court pointed out that there were two aspects to *sevapuja*. The one aspect has to do with the provision of the proper materials for the *puja*

---

[50] *Panachand Gandhi* v. *State of Bombay*, S.C.J., Vol. XVII, 1954, p. 487.

[51] *Digyadarshan R.R. Varu* v. *State of A.P.*, A.I.R. 1970 SC 181.

[52] *Sardar Sarup Singh* v. *State of Punjab*, S.C.J., Vol. XXII, 1959, p. 1123.

[53] *Bira Kishore Deb* v. *State of Orissa*, A.I.R. 1964 SC 1501.

and this is a "secular" matter. After this the servants use the materials according to the dictates of "religion." Section 15(1) of the Act deals with the "secular."

It seems clear that it is the committee that decides what is demanded by the Record of Rights and not the priest or servant. And, it is the duty of the committee to see that the servants carry out the Record of Rights properly. Since this is intended as a guarentee of "religious" integrity, held the Court, it cannot be an interference with "religion." But what the *adya sevak* is left with is the performance of duties mandatory upon him as determined by the committee in the light of the Record of Rights.[54] Hence the determination of duties which are "religious" in accord with the Record of Rights is not itself a "religious" determination. So long as the committee allows (even enforces) the *sevaks* to perform the duties, their "religious" rights have not been touched. So the "secular" management of the temple includes not only the financial matters but also the determination of the "religious" rites demanded by the Record of Rights.

Several petitions representing Vaishnava and Saivite temples in Tamil Nadu contended that the Tamil Nadu Hindu Religious and Charitable Endowments (Amendment) Act (1970) infringed upon their "religious" rights in doing away with the hereditary rights of succession to the office of *archaka* (*pujari*—priest) in their temples.[55] The petitioners held that their rights had been violated under Article 26(b) since "The freedom of hereditary succession to the office of *archaka* is abolished although succession to it is an essential and integral part of the faith of the Saivite and Vaishnavite worshippers."[56]

Examining the *Agamas*, the Court found that only a qualified *archaka* could step inside the *sanctum sanctorum*. The touch of anyone else would defile the image. Moreover, a Saivite cannot serve in a Vaishnava temple, nor can a Vaishnavite serve in a Saivite temple. It was this rule that the principle of hereditary succession was intended to protect. The Court agreed that failure to appoint a person from the appropriate denomination would "interfere with a religious practice the inevitable result of which would be to defile the image."[57] The Court continued by seeking to clarify the concept of essence. It rejected the

---

[54] *Ibid.*, p. 1510.
[55] *Seshammal and Others v. State of Tamil Nadu, Supreme Court Cases,* Vol. II, Part I, 1972, pp. 11ff.
[56] *Ibid.*, p. 18.
[57] *Ibid.*, p. 23.

idea that hereditary succession was essential. What was essential was that the image not be polluted. The Court also conceded that the hereditary principle was common usage and was in practice from antiquity. "The real question, therefore, is whether such a usage should be regarded either as a secular usage or a religious usage."[58] It was the contention of the petitioners that it was indeed a "religious" practice. They held that priests who are to perform "religious" ceremonies may be chosen by the temple on whatever basis the temple decides, and sometimes it is hereditary. The Court agreed that the priest was appointed to a "religious" function, but questioned whether the appointment itself was "religious." Even the priest appointed in a hereditary manner is subject to the disciplinary power of the trustee. Furthermore, any lay founder of a temple can appoint a priest. Appointment is therefore by a "secular" authority, and hence it is a "secular" act. Neither the fact that some temples have followed the principle of heredity, nor the "religious" nature of what the *archaka* does in the temple makes the act of appointment any less "secular."[59] The Court, then, resolved the conflict in favor of the Act by declaring that, although what the *archaka* did in the temple in his function as *pujari* was "religious," the appointment of the *archaka* and the manner in which it was done was a "secular" matter, and legitimately under the jurisdiction of the State.

In *Saifuddin Saheb* v. *State of Bombay*, the religious conflict is built into opposing judgments by members of the Court, but resolved by the majority in terms of the categories of "religion" and the "secular."[60] The issue at stake was whether the Bombay Prevention of Excommunication Act (1949) was in conflict with Articles 25 and 26 of the Constitution. The petitioner in the case was the Dai-ul-Mutlaq who was the head of the Dawoodi Bhora Community of Shia Muslims. Part of the Dai's authority was the power of excommunication. An earlier case had determined that it was within the power of the Dai to excommunicate.[61] The petitioner argued that the practice of excommunication was essential, for without it the purity and continuity of the denomination could not be safeguarded by removing persons unsuitable for membership. It was further contended that the right to worship in a mosque and burial in a graveyard

---

[58] *Ibid.*, p. 24.
[59] *Ibid.*, p. 25.
[60] *Saifuddin Saheb* v. *State of Bombay*, A.I.R. 1962 SC 853.
[61] A.I.R. 1948 PC 66.

dedicated to the community were "religious" rights not to be enjoyed by a person rightly excommunicated.

It was the contention of the State of Bombay that the Dai had the right to regulate religious practices but that excommunication was not an essential part of the "religion" of the Dawoodi Bohra community and hence was a "secular" matter which affected the civil rights of persons. The religious conflict becomes explicit in the contention of the Attorney-General for the State of Bombay when he argued that in abolishing excommunication the Act was "in consonance with modern notions of human dignity and individual liberty of action even in matters of religious opinion and faith and practice."[62]

In his minority judgment, Sinha, C.J., interprets the Act as the culmination of the history of social reform which began with provisions of the Bengal Code which were later incorporated in the Caste Disabilities Act of 1850. In coming to his decision, Sinha, C.J., introduced a slightly different category. Instead of merely speaking of "religion" and the "secular," he referred to excommunication as not being "purely religious" or "wholly religious." It had been recognized that the separation of "religion" from the "secular" was not simple. But when an Act is not "purely religious" this means that there are civil consequences to the activity under consideration.[63] Sinha, C.J., held that he was not called upon to comment upon the "purely religious aspects" of excommunication, nor was he interested in distinguishing what they might be. He was responsible for making a judgment about actions touching on the civil rights of members of the community. Since excommunication treated the excommunicated much as a pariah, and since the Constitution abolished untouchability, the Act is valid. Sinha, C.J. decided in favor of the civil rights while recognizing implications for "religion" which did not concern him.

This is in keeping with the new ideology found in the Constitution. But the Constitution also grants freedom of "religion" and the right of communities to regulate themselves in matters of "religion." It was for this reason that the majority of the Court judged the Act unconstitutional. In arguing for the essentiality of excommunication, Das Gupta, J., appealed to an article in *Encyclopedia of Social Sciences* on "Excommunication" where it was argued that the practice had been a principle means of maintaining discipline and

---

[62] *Saifuddin Saheb* v. *State of Bombay*, A.I.R. 1962 SC 859-860.

[63] *Ibid.*, p. 865.

solidarity in a religious community. Furthermore, it was noted that at the time of initiation the Dawoodi Bohras take an oath of unquestioning faith and loyalty to the Dai. Das Gupta, J., indicated that he was not addressing whether every case of excommunication by the Dai was based on "religious" grounds. But by invalidating excommunication on any ground, the Act made it impossible to maintain the strength and continuity of the "religion." What does Das Gupta, J., do with the attendant "civil rights" which are thereby curtailed? He does exactly what Sinha, C.J., did with the "religious" matters entailed in his "civil decision." They are secondary and not his concern.

In this case the majority argument was in favour of the traditional practice. But it must be noted that although both sides of the Court made their decisions as though the categories were adequate to handle the conflict, both had to ignore one side of it. Both seemed to recognize that excommunication had a "religious" and a "secular" side. Sinha, C.J., acted in the light of the "secular," ignoring the "religious," while the majority judgment passed on "religion" ignoring the "secular." The conflict is resolved by the power of the Court, but not because the categories of "religion" and the "secular" adequately handled it. In other cases the breakdown of the categories is even more apparent.

When the Categories are Inadequate. One device used when the categories are inadequate to handle the conflict without assistance is what might be called *reification*. Reification is the treatment of an historical process characterized by diversity and change as a single objective entity. In the study of religion it is the treatment of "Hinduism," "Buddhism," and the like, as units of thought and practice.[64] Where there exists a conflict between the religious claims of a community and the Constitutional ideology, the Court has used reification in aid of "religion" and the "secular." This method is apparent in *M.H. Quareshi v. State of Bihar*.[65] Contesting the constitutionality of three acts for the prevention of cow slaughter, the petitioners argued that their fundamental rights under Article 25 of the Constitution were abridged, since it was their custom to sacrifice a cow on Bakr Id day. The petitioners claimed that this was enjoined in the Holy Qur'an, but the Court contended that the verses referred to merely stipulated that people should pray and offer sacrifice. Operating under a reified concept

---

[64] Cf. the author's *Category Formation and the History of Religions*, Chapter V.
[65] *M.H. Quareshi v. State of Bihar*, S.C.J., Vol. XXI, 1958, p. 975.

of Islam, the Court made a search for a scriptural statement making the sacrifice of a cow obligatory. A lack of obligatoriness would suggest that the practice was not essential to Muslim faith. Although the petitioners pointed out that it was their custom to sacrifice a cow, and although this was not denied by the Court, their custom was not sufficient. By treating Islam as a reified entity and considering the petitioners as Muslims, their specific contemporary practices could be ignored. When it was found that it was optional for a Muslim (according to Hamilton's translation of Hedaya Book XLIII at page 592) to sacrifice a cow or camel for every seven persons or a goat for each person, it was apparent that for Muslims there was an option. Since the petitioners were Muslims, it must be optional for them as well. Although financial considerations would put that option out of reach for many, that was considered an economic matter and not a "religious" one. Since the sacrifice of a cow was optional for Muslims, it was optional for these Muslims, and since it was optional it was not essential, and since it was not essential it was not protected under Article 26 of the Constitution.

Another concept which takes the court beyond the categories of "religion" and the "secular" is *superstition*. Gagendragadkar, J., used this concept in *Durgah Committee* v. *Hussain Ali*.[66] There he stated that an historical community might sincerely believe that a practice is essential to their religion when it is merely a superstitious accretion. In *Yagnapurushdasji* v. *Muldas*, this concept plays a more decisive role in his decision.[67] The issue was whether the temples of the Swaminarayan Sampradaya sect come under the Bombay Hindu Places of Public Worship Act (1956), sine the appellants contended that they were not Hindus but a separate religion. At the end of a lengthy consideration of the nature of Hinduism and the tenets of the Swaminarayan Sampradaya sect it was concluded that they were Hindus. Of some importance was the fact that the sect had not objected to being so classified in Census reports. This case was decided as a matter of social reform. But Gajendragadkar, J., held that although the contention of the sect began in sincerity, it was founded on superstition.

> It may be conceded that the genesis of the suit is the genuine apprehension entertained by the appellants; but as often happens in these matters, the said apprehension is founded on superstition,

---

[66] *Durgah Committee* v. *Hussain Ali*, A.I.R. 1961 SC 1402.
[67] *Yagnapurushdasji* v. *Muldas*, A.I.R. 1966 SC 1119.

> ignorance and complete misunderstanding of the true teaching of Hindu religion and of the real significance of the tenets and philosophy taught by Swaminarayan himself.[68]

The use of this concept goes hand in hand with reification. First, there was a determination of the essential tenets of Hinduism. Since the appellants contended they were not Hindus, it was also necessary to find out what the Swaminarayan sect ought to believe if it were true to its founder. The result of the Court's research was that, although the appellants were sincere in their contention, they did not properly understand their own faith. And, not to understand one's own faith is to operate with "superstition, ignorance, and complete misunderstanding. . . ."

In *Venkataramana Devaru v. State of Mysore*, the Gowda Saraswat Brahman sect contended that the Madras Temple Entry Authorization Act (1947) which opened their temple dedicated to Sri Venkataramana to all Hindus was a violation of Article 26(b) of the Consititution. They held that who was entitled to participate in temple worship was a matter of "religion." Admitting the precedent that "religion" includes practices as well as beliefs, the Court proceeded to determine whether exclusion of a person from a temple was a matter of "religion" according to "Hindu ceremonial law."[69] The Court observed that along with the growth of temple worship, there also grew up a body of literature called *Agamas* which stipulated how the temple was to be constructed, where the principle deity was to be consecrated, and where the other deities are to be installed. One such text includes degrees of participation.

> In the Nirvachanapaddathi it is said that Sivadwijas should worship in the Garabhagriham, Brahmins from the ante chamber or Sabah Mantabham, Kshatriyas, Vyasias [sic] and Sudras from the Mahamantabham, the dancer and the musician from the Nrithamantabham east of the Mahamantabham, and the castes yet lower in scale should content themselves with the sight of the Gopurum.[70]

---

[68] *Ibid.*, p. 1135.
[69] *Sri Venkataramana Devaru v. State of Mysore*, S.C.J., Vol. XXI, 1958, p. 382.
[70] *Ibid.*, p. 390.

Contenting oneself with the "sight of the gopurum" would mean to view the temple from outside. It is pointed out by the Court that violation of such regulations results in pollution of the shrine and requires purificatory ceremonies. In a 1908 case, *Sankarakinga Nadam* v. *Raja Rajeswara Dorai*, it was agreed by the Privy Council that trustees who agreed to admit persons into the temple whom the *Agamas* did not permit were guilty of breach of trust.[71] The Court agreed that temple entry was a matter of "religion."[72]

But another factor had to be taken into account. Article 25(2)(b) of the Constitution provides that nothing in the Article should prevent the State from making a law "providing for social welfare and reform or the throwing open of Hindu religious institutions of a public character to all classes and sections of Hindus." The Court admitted that "the two Articles appear to be apparently in conflict."[73] The position of the "Hindu social reformers" which culminated in Article 17 of the Constitution abolishing untouchability was then recounted. The reformers objected that "purely on grounds of birth" some Indians were denied access to public roads and institutions which were open to the general Hindu public. This was not defensible on "any sound democratic principle."

The Court held that these were two constitutional principles of equal authority. Appeal was made to the "rule of harmonious construction" whereby two conflicting provisions are interpreted in such a manner as to give effect to both. The Court then agreed to the opening of the temple to all classes of Hindus. The right of the denomination to exclude members of the public from worshipping in the temple, although protected under Article 26(b), must give way to Article 25(2)(b). This does not mean that anyone can go into any part of the temple at any time. Hence the denomination was permitted the right to exclude the general public from certain religious services. The Court felt that it had given effect to both provisions inasmuch as even after the exclusions from certain religious services, "what is left to the public of the right of worship is something substantial and not merely the husk of it."[74]

On the surface this solution seems sensible. But it must be observed that while a portion of the denominational right under Article 26(b) was

---

[71] *Sankarakinga Nadam* v. *Raja Rajeshwara Dorai*, I.L.R. 31 Mad.
[72] S.C.J., Vol. XXI, 1958, p. 390.
[73] *Ibid.*, p. 391.
[74] *Ibid.*, p. 396.

preserved, another portion was taken away. For, while traditional religious practice as described in the *Agamas* did distinguish degrees of participation and involvement in temple worship, it also included the degree of exclusion. Some persons were to "content themselves with the sight of the gopurum." The issue of temple pollution was ignored by the Court. The judgment said, in effect, that traditional practices could not be maintained in their entirety because Article 25(2)(b) denied such practices. Part of the denomination's traditional religious practices are maintained under the "rule of harmonious construction." But, under the same principle another rather significant portion of their religion was eliminated. This case, then, admits the existence of a conflict between tradition and the new ideology, and it implements religious change.

I have called this ideology which distinguishes "religion" and the "secular" a "New Great Tradition."[75] It is enshrined in the Constitution, embodied in legislation passed by Parliament, and enforced in the courts. Since independence there has been occasional opposition to it, none perhaps more threatening than the present opposition from the Hindu right. This segment of India is presently in power politically (2001), and some have called for a revision of the present Constitution. That proposal has itself been the object of considerable discussion. The argument is that under the existing Constitution, minorities have been favored over the majority community and that must change.

Where conflict emerges over the new "Great Tradition," we are witnesses to religious conflict—religious because it is a conflict over the ultimate way one perceives the world. It is a conflict between those who see the world as sacred, who see a sacredness to all life, including the economic, political, social, and legal dimensions, and those who, for whatever reasons, seek to distinguish between "religion," and the "secular" realms of the economy, society, politics and law.

---

[75] "Uniform Civil Code and the Secularization of Law," *Essays in the History of Religions*, p. 172.

3

Religion and Secularism Under the Indian Constitution

P. N. Bhagwati

I deeply appreciate the invitation extended to me by the University of Iowa to participate in the Conference on Religion and Law in Independent India and speak on the subject of religion and secularism under the Indian Constitution. While speaking on this subject, the first question to which I must address myself is: What is secularism? The word "secular" is among the richest of all words in its range of meaning. It is full of subtle shades which involves internal contradictions and of these contradictions the conventional dictionary meaning can hardly give a correct view. But even so, it is instructive to note what the *Concise Oxford Dictionary* and the Encyclopedias state to be the meaning of the word "secular." The *Concise Oxford Dictionary* shows that the adjective "secular" means: "concerned with the affairs of this world, worldly not sacred, not monastic, not ecclesiastical, temporal, profane, lay." The word "secular" according to the *Encyclopedia Brittanica* means: "non-spiritual, having no concern with religion or spiritual matters." This meaning would show that secularism is distinct, opposed to or not connected with religion or ecclesiastical things, temporal as opposed to spiritual or ecclesiastical. *The Encyclopedia of Social Sciences*, after tracing the history of the growth of secularism, ends with the following conclusion:

> The ideal of human and social happiness, as proclaimed by the prophets and leaders of the French Revolution, has continued in the intervening period to mold the temper not only of the French bourgeoisie but also of larger and larger groups in all countries, Protestants as well as Catholic, who are resolved that mankind shall strive by the most enlightened methods at its disposal to establish the maximum of social justice and welfare in this world. The power of this secularized type of idealism derives in large part from its close connection with science; and in this union of social and scientific secularism the movement which since the Middle Ages has been gathering increasing momentum finds its logical climax.

Donald Smith has in a commendable and perceptive study elaborately considered the question as to what is the meaning and content of secularism. "The working definition" of secularism, says Donald Smith "which I would suggest is as follows:"

> The secular state is a state which guarantees individual and corporate freedom of religion, deals with the individual as a citizen irrespective of his religion, is not constitutionally connected to a particular religion nor does it seek either to promote or interfere with religion. Upon closer examination it will be seen that the conception of a secular state involves three distinct but inter-related sets of relationships concerning the state, religion, and the individual. The three sets of relations are:
> 1. religion and the individual (freedom of religion)
> 2. the state and the individual (citizenship)
> 3. the state and religion (separation of state & religion)[1]

Having adopted this definition, Donald Smith proceeds to deal with the problem on the basis that "the basic assumption must be that the secular state will have nothing to do with religious affairs. Any departure from this principle must be justified on reasonable secular grounds."

It may be noticed that the concept of secularism involves several elements. One is that every person must have the same rights as a citizen and must be entitled to the same basic human rights irrespective of the religion which he professes and practises. The other is that there must be complete freedom of conscience, thought and belief and everyone should be entitled to profess and practise the religion of his choice. And lastly, the State should not identify itself with any particular religion nor should it promote or support or discriminate in favor of any particular religion. These three elements are vital to the concept of secularism and I shall presently show they find pride of place in the Indian Constitution.

I may point out at the outset that in *The Constitution of India*, as originally enacted, the word "secular" did not appear in the Preamble to describe the character of the sovereign, democratic Republic of India, nor was the word "secular" used in the relevant provisions of the Constitution which guarantee freedom of religion. The omission to use the word "secular" or "secularism" was not accidental but it was deliberate. The proceedings of the Constituent Assembly show that a member of the Constituent Assembly called Mr. K. T. Shah made two attempts to introduce the concept of secularism by using the word "secular or

---

[1]Donald Eugene Smith, *India As a Secular State* (Princeton, 1963), p. 4.

secularism" in a suitable place. The first of these amendments related to Article 1 of the Draft Constitution which read: "India shall be a union of states" and the amendment sought to insert the words "secular, federal, socialist" after the words "shall be a" in the said Article so that as amended the Article would have read: "India shall be a secular, federal, socialist union of states." The other amendment which Mr. K. T. Shah wanted to introduce was in the form of a new Article and it read thus: "The State in India being secular shall have no concern with any religion, creed or profession or faith...." Both these amendments proposed by Mr. K. T. Shah were opposed by Dr. Ambedkar, the principal draftsman of the Constitution, and were ultimately rejected. Thus it will be seen that the omission of the word "secular" or "secularism" was not accidental but was deliberate. It seems that perhaps the Constitution makers were apprehensive that if the words "secular" or "secularism" were introduced in the Constitution, they might unnecessarily bring in, by implication, the anti-religious overtone associated with the doctrine of secularism as it had developed in Christian countries. The Indian concept of secularism recognises the relevance and validity of religion in life, but seeks to establish a rational synthesis between the legitimate functions of religion and the legitimate and expanding functions of the State and since this concept is clearly brought out in the various provisions of the Indian Constitution, the Constitution makers might perhaps have felt that it was not necessary to use the word "secular" or "secularism," particularly as it might give the impression of establishing a State structure inconsistent with the cultural ethos of the Indian people. This aspect of "secularism," as understood in India, was emphatically asserted by the great philosopher statesman, Dr. Radhakrishnan, when he said: "I want to state authoritatively that secularism does not mean irreligion. It means we respect all faiths and religions. Our State does not identify itself with any particular religion." However, during the Emergency imposed by the government of Mrs. Indira Gandhi, the Preamble of the Indian Constitution was amended by the Constitution (42nd amendment) Act 1976 so as to include the word "secular" before the words "Democratic Republic." This was presumably in order to emphasise the secular character of the Indian Republic which appeared to be developing communal strains. The result is that since 1976 the Preamble to the Indian Constitution proclaims in no uncertain terms that India is a secular Republic. But obviously a mere proclamation that India is a secular State would not make the Indian State secular unless there are adequate provisions in the text of the Constitution which convert rhetoric into reality and give meaning and content to the declaration contained in the Preamble.

Before I proceed to consider how the Constitution of India has in its provisions given shape and meaning to the concept of secularism, it would not be out of place for me to refer to a few basic considerations which must have been present to the mind of the constitution makers when they enacted these provisions. They were aware of the stark reality that India has been traditionally a multi-religious pluralist society. Now a pluralist society implies the inevitable presence of dissensions and disagreements within the community, but it also postulates a community within which there must be agreement and consensus for if a society is to be at all a rational process, some set of principles must motivate the general participation of all religious groups despite their dissensions and differences in the oneness of the community. However, at the same time, this set of common principles must not hinder the maintenance by each group of its own religious and cultural identity. This is a complex problem inherent in a pluralist society. Every pluralist society suffers from certain handicaps and disadvantages which it is required to face and overcome. In the first place, each group has its own history and its own traditions. These discrepant histories affect styles of thought and of interior life. The more deeply they are experienced the more do the differences among citizens appear to be unbridgeable. Secondly, it is not uncommon to find that in a pluralist society there exists a wide measure of conflicting interests, some of them deeply entrenched and powerful—a situation that may sometimes be exploited by fundamentalist elements to imperil the well ordered existence of the society. Having regard to these two handicaps and disadvantages from which a pluralist society is likely to suffer, it is a delicate and difficult process to find a common universe of discourse which must be implicit in every civilised society and which lies at the basis of the concept of a State. The framers of India's Constitution were deeply conscious of these problems which are inherent in a pluralist society and they set about the task of finding a solution to these problems. Many of them were deeply involved in the freedom struggle of the country and they were products of the cultural tradition of India. They realised deeply and intensely the religious psyche of the people of India and their concept of secularism did not see any anti-thesis to religion. Even Jawaharlal Nehru, the Architect of Modern India, who was worried about the impact of organised religion in India which seemed to him to stand for blind belief and action, dogma and bigotry, superstition and exploitation and the preservation of vested interests, said in a moment of introspection:

> And yet I knew well that there was something else in it, something which supplied a deep inner craving of human beings. How else could it have been the tremendous power it has been and brought peace and comfort to innumerable tortured souls? Was that peace merely the shelter of blind belief and absence of questioning, the calm that comes from being safe in harbor, protected from the storms of the open sea, or was it something more? In some cases certainly it was something more.

On another occasion Jawaharlal Nehru complained that "what appears to be wanting in these matters of science and technology is an ethical aspect, some spiritual solution." This perspective of religion and spirituality which Jawaharlal Nehru spoke about can never be intolerant, dogmatic or static. It is engaged in an unceasing enquiry into the spiritual problem of life, the riddle of the universe which still remains and will always remain unsolved. In this context, it is necessary to recognise the profound wisdom of the ancient seers of India that though truth is one it has different facets and the human mind imperfect as it is, perceives only some facets and is unable to see the entire truth. Mahatma Gandhi, the Father of my Nation, expressed this view in his inimitable style in these words:

> Even as a tree has a single trunk, but many branches and leaves, so there is one true and perfect Religion, but it becomes many, as it passes through the human medium. I recognize no God except the God that is to be found in the hearts of the dumb millions. They do not recognize his presence; I do. And I worship the God that is Truth, or Truth which is God, through the services of these Millions.

The Hindu religion which is the religion followed by the large majority of people in India, does not claim monopoly of spiritual wisdom nor does it assert that the path shown by the Hindu religion is the only path that can lead to divinity. It recognises the validity of all religions and believes that each religion leads to the same goal, namely, realisation of divinity within man. It says that there are as many pathways to godhead as there are individual souls. That is why Dr. Radhakrishnan said in words pregnant with meaning: "Hinduism is a movement, not a position, a process, not a result; a growing tradition, not a fixed revelation....We cannot have religious unity and peace so long as we assert that we are in possession of light and all others are groping in darkness. That very assertion is a challenge to a fight." The same spirit of tolerance must characterise all religions in a pluralist society and it is this spirit of tolerance which furnishes the philosophical background to the Indian concept of secularism. Toynbee has referred to the significance of this concept in eloquent and inspiring words. He says:

> The fundamental positive motive for toleration is a recognition of the truth that religious conflict is not just a nuisance but is a sin. It is sinful because it arouses the wild beast in Human Nature. Religious persecution, too, is sinful because no one has a right to try to stand between another human soul and God. Every soul has a right to commune with God in God's and this soul's way; and the particular way concerns none but God and the particular soul in question. No other human being has a right to intervene by the use of any means except non-violent missionary action. And Violence in this field is not only sinful; it is futile; for religions cannot be inculcated by

force. There is no such thing as a belief that is not held voluntarily through a genuinely spontaneous inner conviction. Different people's convictions will differ, because Absolute Reality is a mystery of which no more than a fraction has ever yet been penetrated by—or been revealed to—any human mind. 'The heart of so great a mystery cannot ever be reached by following one road only.' However strong and confident may be my conviction that my own approach to the mystery is a right one, I ought to be aware that my field of spiritual vision is so narrow that I cannot know that there is no virtue in other approaches. In theistic terms this is to say that I cannot know that other people's visions may not also be revelations from God—and these perhaps fuller and more illuminating revelations than the one that I believe that I myself have received from him.

Moreover, the fact that I and my neighbour are following different roads is something that divides us much less than we are drawn together by the other fact that, in following our different roads, we are both trying to approach the same mystery. All human beings who are seeking to approach the mystery in order to direct their lives in accordance with the nature and spirit of Absolute Reality or, in theistic terms, with the will of God—all these fellow seekers are engaged in an identical quest. They should recognize that they are spiritually brethren and should feel towards one another, and treat one another, as such. Toleration does not become perfect until it has been transfigured into love.

The Constitution makers, therefore, placed the individual at the centre of the Constitutional scheme and made his dignity, freedom and well-being its major concern. The Preamble of the Constitution proclaimed as the objective of the Constitutional exercise, freedom and dignity of the individual, social, economic and political justice and equality of status and opportunity for all, regardless of caste, creed or religion. Socio-economic justice as elaborated in the Fundamental Rights and Directive Principles of State Policy was laid down as the beacon-light or the guiding star of the new social order envisaged in the Constitution and the foundations of a Secular State were laid firm and deep.

The framers of India's Constitution were convinced that if there was freedom for everyone to profess and practise the religion of his or her own choice and there was a spirit of tolerance towards those who profess and practise other religions, and religion was confined to affairs strictly religious and was not allowed to intrude into the social, economic and political life of the people which should be guided solely by secular considerations and every individual was regarded as an entity entitled to the same basic rights irrespective of his or her religion, there would be no conflict between religion and secularism. If, as a result of proper education, common men and women understand the true significance and parameters of religious freedom, the path to progress in the material life of the community will not be obstructed or hindered by religion. Religion will, in this process, have to renounce its claim to intervene the material life of the community and will have to confine itself to its legitimate sphere of facing the eternal riddle of the universe. The spirit of inquiry which addresses itself to the problem of eternal verities has always assailed human minds and will always continue to do so. The area of this inquiry is, however, distinct, and different from that of the material life of the community. The endless inquiry into the unknown on which religion is engaged helps to create in the minds of people a sense of ethos or a moral purpose and this sense of ethos or moral purpose would be of help to them even in the pursuit of their material objectives. When societies tend to become secular and modern, theological questions take their proper place in their affairs and an attempt is more passionately made to discover agreement or consensus on practical social and political goals. With this conviction in mind, the framers of India's Constitution envisaged the structure of a society in which every citizen will practise religious tolerance and would maintain communal harmony and not allow religious convictions and beliefs to interfere with the social, economic and political life of the people. This consensus covered a whole constellation of principles that determine the nature and function of the State and the scope and limitations of the government. This was the new secular, social order which the framers of India's Constitution tried to create through the making of India's Constitution.

The framers of India's Constitution shared with the Americans the basic ideology that the State should not interfere with matters which fall essentially within the domain of religion nor should the State promote or support any particular religion or discriminate in favor of or against a particular religion. In the United States the Establishment clause in the First amendment to the Constitution has been graphically described as creating a wall of separation between the Church and the State. In *Everson* vs *Board of Education 330 U.S. 1*, the United States Supreme Court explained the concept of separation of the Church and the State in these words:

> Neither a State nor the Federal Government can set up a church. Neither can pass laws which aid one religion, aid all religions, or prefer one religion over another....No tax in any amount, large or small, can be levied to support any religious activities or institutions, whatever they may be called, or whatever form they adopt to teach or practise religion. Neither a state nor the federal government can, openly or secretly, participate in the affairs of any religious

organizations or groups and vice versa. In the words of Jefferson, the clause against establishment of religion by law was intended to erect a wall of separation between church and State.

Mr. Justice Frankfurter, while affirming the views expressed in the Everson's case observed that the separation of the State and the Church did not merely mean that the State would treat the various religions in its body politic equally. What was really meant was that the spheres of the agencies remained separate and independent. "Separation," he observed "is a requirement to abstain from fusing factions of government and of religious sects, not merely to treat them all equally...separation means separation not something less."

These observations would show that the doctrine of the wall of separation between the State and the Church does not deny the relevance of religion in life, but it insists that the State and the Church function in different spheres and the State should not have anything to do at all with religion. This was emphasised by Mr. Justice Douglas in *Engel* vs *Vitale 370 U.S. 421*, where he said:

> The First Amendment leaves the Government in a position not of hostility to religion but of neutrality. The philosophy is that the atheist or agnostic—the nonbeliever—is entitled to go his own way. The philosophy is that if government interferes in matters spiritual, it will be a divisive force. The First Amendment teaches that a government neutral in the field of religion better serves all religion's interests.

The majority judgment in *School District of Abington Township* vs *Edward Lewis* also observed to the same effect while striking down a rule requiring the reading without comment at the opening each school day of verses from the Bible and the recitation of the Lord's Prayer by the students in unison. It would thus appear that the doctrine of secularism which has evolved in the United States has an underlying assumption of anti-thesis between temporal and spiritual power and provides for the functioning of the State un-fettered by the influence of religion in matters pertaining to the domain of the State, though it does recognise that religion may have a function to discharge in the lives of the citizens and gives liberty to the church to discharge those functions. The Indian Constitution has not wholly accepted the doctrine of a wall of separation between religion and the State. The framers of India's Constitution undoubtedly held the view that the State should neither sponsor nor favour any particular religion and should treat all religions with tolerance and equality, but at the same time they were skeptical of the Establishment clause which would take separation between the church and the State to the extreme where it might border on hostility and begin to operate as a denial of religious freedom itself. Moreover, as men of sound practical wisdom

Religion and Secularism

they could not ignore Indian history or social experience in matters of religion. They knew that, left to itself, religion could permit orthodox men to burn widows alive on the piers of their deceased husbands. It could encourage and in its own subtle ways, even coerce indulgence in social evils like child marriage or even crimes like human sacrifice or it could consign women to the perpetual fate of devadasis or relegate large sections of humanity to the sub-human status of untouchability and inferiority. They were conscious that there were many evils in the social lives of the people alleged love sanctified or supported by religion which needed to be exorcised. They were aware that it was necessary to bring about social reforms with a view to lifting India out of medievalism, obscurantism, blind superstition and anti-social practices. They realised that asking the State to keep its hands off religion would amount to giving constitutional protection to social injustice, exploitation and cruelty in the name of religion. That is why Dr. Ambedkar pointed out in the Constituent Assembly that two prominent religions in India, Hinduism and Islam, occupied almost all aspects of human life and there had not grown up in these two religious groups any tradition of confining religion to spiritual or other-worldly matters. These two religions covered within their fold the entire social behaviour, and if secularism was to become part of the Indian ethos, it could not be possible until some line was drawn between what was religious and what was temporal.

Unlike in the West where such separation between religious and temporal areas of behavior had taken place throughout the process of renaissance and the emergence of secular State had succeeded such separation, the position in India was that the secular State had to perform this historic function of confining religion to its essential sphere and not to allow it to impinge on the temporal area or on the social, economic and political life of the people. Otherwise, it would not be possible to build up a secular state and promote and foster a secular outlook. Naturally, the doctrine of the wall of separation adopted in the United States could not fit the Indian situation. The Indian Constitution had, therefore, to accord to the State power to interfere with freedom of religion to the extent to which it was necessary for maintenance of public order, morality and health or protection of the fundamental rights guaranteed in Part III of the Constitution or providing for social welfare and reform and the throwing open of Hindu temples to all sections of Hindus. The constitution makers did not wish to allow freedom of religion to become an instrument for thwarting the progress of the nation to a new social secular order where each individual will have full liberty and dignity and will be entitled to enjoy equality of status and opportunity irrespective of the religion which he professes or practises.

It is for this reason that Articles 25 and 26 dealing with the freedom of religion were enacted by the constitution makers in the form in which we find them in the constitution. These two Articles constitute the basis of the concept of Indian secularism. It is interesting to note that when the draft of Article 25 was placed for discussion before the Constituent Assembly it did not include the right to propagate one's religion and it also contained a provision that was essential for eliminating communalism from Indian life that "no communal organisation, which by its constitution or by the exercise of its discretionary powers vested in any of its officers or organs admits to or excludes from its membership persons on grounds of religion, race and caste or any of them, should be permitted to engage in any activities other than those essential for the bonafide religious cultural, social, and educational needs of the community." The omission of the right to propagate one's religion was opposed by the Indian Hindu community and ultimately on the insistence of the Indian Christian community, the right to propagate one's religion was included in Article 25. The negative provision in the draft banning communal organisations from engaging in any activities other than those essential for the bonafide religious, cultural, social and educational needs of the community was also omitted when Article 25 was finally enacted. It is an interesting speculation as to whether some of the problems of communalism which are at present threatening to tear apart the social and political fabric of India could have been avoided if communal organisations had not been permitted to engage in political activities. Article 25, as finally enacted, guarantees to every person whether citizen or not, freedom of conscience and the right freely to profess, practise and propagate religion. But this right conferred on every person is subject to public order, morality and health and also to the other fundamental rights guaranteed under Part III of the Constitution. In other words, if there is any conflict between religion on the one hand and public order or morality or health or any other provision of Part III on the other, religion has to yield and that establishes the basic proposition of Indian secularism that considerations of public order, morality and health and considerations relating to fundamental rights enshrined in Part III play a paramount role and religion is not allowed to conflict with them. The concept of secularism to which India is committed does not permit religion to interfere with the functions of the secular state in matters which are secular and this is made amply clear by clause (2) of Article 25 which permits the State, notwithstanding the right to freedom of religion, to make a law regulating or restricting any economic, financial, political or any other secular activity which may be associated with religious practice or providing for social welfare and reform or the throwing open of Hindu religious institutions of a public character to all classes and sections of Hindus. In other words, the effect of clause (2) of Article 25 is that when the State is dealing with economic, financial, political or other secular problems, or is taking legal measures to solve the problems of social welfare and reform, including the problem of throwing open Hindu religious institutions of a public character to all classes and sections of Hindus, freedom of religion cannot be allowed to impede the efforts of the State in that direction and the discussion and the decision of these issues will proceed on secular, social, economic, rational and scientific grounds and religion or any considerations associated with religion will have no relevance in that sphere. Article 25 thus seeks to reconcile the legitimate claims of religion with the equally legitimate claims of the State which is committed to the task of creating a new social order founded on social, economic and political justice.

Article 26 of the Indian Constitution seems to flow from Article 25 as a logical corollary and it deals with freedom to manage religious affairs. It is subject to public order, morality and health. The considerations of public order, morality and health are paramount. Subject to these considerations every religious denomination is given the right to establish and maintain institutions for religious and charitable purposes, to manage its own affairs in matters of religion, and to own and acquire moveable and immovable property. If property is acquired by a religious denomination, it is conferred the right to administer such property, but the administration of the property must be in accordance with law, and law must obviously mean relevant secular law passed by a competent legislature. If any law is validly passed concerning the administration and management of any property, the law will have to be complied with by the religious denomination which owns the property. There is thus deprivation of the State of the power to deal with secular matters relating to religious denominations.

But the question has arisen in India in several important cases as to what exactly religion means and what is the meaning of the expression "matters of religion." Religion has not been defined in the Indian Constitution and naturally, therefore, the content of the concept had to be considered by judicial decisions. The Supreme Court of India in one of the early decisions referred to the meaning of the word "religion" given in *Davis* vs. *Benson 133 U.S. 333* where it was said that "the term religion has reference to one's views of his relation to his creator and to the obligations they impose of reverence for His being and character and of obedience to his will," expressed its view that this definition was neither precise nor adequate. The Supreme Court observed: "Religion is certainly a matter of faith with individuals or communities and it is not necessarily theistic. There are well-known religions in India like Buddhism and Jainism which do not believe in God or in any Intelligent First Cause. A religion undoubtedly has its basis in a system of beliefs or doctrines which are regarded by those who profess that religion is conducive to their well-being, but it would not be correct to say that religion is nothing else but a doctrine or belief. A religion may not only lay down a code of ethical rules for its followers to accept, it might prescribe rituals and observances, ceremonies and modes of worship which are regarded as integral parts of religion." The Supreme Court of India approved of the observation of Latham CS of Australian High Court that "free exercise of religion" guaranteed under S. 116 of the Australian Constitution "goes far beyond protecting liberty of opinion. It protects also acts done in pursuance of religious belief as part of religion."

The question as to which practices can be regarded as part of religion so as to merit protection under Article 26 as matters of religion came to be considered by the Supreme Court of India in several decisions. The view was taken that they must be essential points of religions. If they were not, the State would be entitled to regulate and restrict such practises. The Supreme Court explained which practices can be regarded as constituting the essential part of a religion by stating that the question must be ascertained with reference to the doctrines of that religion itself. The Court would have to determine whether a particular practice or rite is regarded as its essential and integral part of the tenets of a particular religion and in doing so, the Court would have to act with great caution. Otherwise even purely secular practices which are not an essential or integral part of religion are apt to be clothed with a religious form and may make a claim for being treated as religious practices entitled to the protection of Article 26. Similarly, even practices though religious may have sprung from merely superstitious beliefs and may in that sense be extraneous and unessential accretions to religion. Such practices would not be protected under Article 26 as matters of religion. There was a case which came up before the Supreme Court of India in which a religious denomination called Anand Margis claimed it a religious practice to take out a procession in public with their followers wearing round their necks a garland of human skulls. The Supreme Court held that such a practice was not an integral and essential part of religion and that in any event it was abhorrent to morality and it could not claim the protection of Article 26. In another case, the right to manage the property of a temple was held to be secular and not protected by Article 26. On the other hand, the objection of children belonging to the faith of Jehovah's Witnesses against singing of the national anthem was upheld as an integral and essential part of their religion. It will thus be noticed that if the particular practice or rite is found by the Court to be religious in character and an integral and essential part of religion it would be practical and the State would not be entitled to interfere with it, subject to considerations of public order, morality and health; but if it is secular in character, the State can regulate and restrict it. Of course, this task of disengaging the secular from the religious is not an easy one, but under the Indian Constitution, the Courts have to perform this task and achieve a harmonious balance where the freedom of religious convictions genuinely entertained by men comes into conflict with the proper political attitude which is expected from citizens in matters of unity and solidarity of the State organisation. That happened in the Shah Bano case decided by the Supreme Court where secularism triumphed but triumph was short-lived because the Government succumbed to the pressure of obscurantist opinion and enacted legislation setting at naught the decision of the Supreme Court.

One other question which has perplexed the Courts in India has been as to when and by what test can a religious group, following the philosophy or precepts of a religious leader be said to be followers of a new religion distinct and separate from the existing religion or by what test can they be regarded only as a religious denomination within the existing religion. If they fall within the former category, they would have the right under Article 25 and also the right under Article 30 clause 1, but if they fall within the latter category, their only right would be that under Article 26. This question arose in the famous Auroville Case where the Supreme Court by a majority held that the philosophy or teachings of Sri Aurobindo did not constitute a new religion but they were part of Hinduism and the followers constituted merely a religious denomination.[2] The majority of the judges pointed out that Hindu religion was not a mono-credal religion. It comprised a diversity of philosophic concepts, thoughts and ideas which came to be evolved from time to time and they all formed part of Hindu religion. The dissenting judge, however, took the view that whether a new religion had been established or not did not depend upon whether the religious leader intended to found a new faith. What he said, what he preached and his thoughts, ideas and precepts including his dissent or disagreement with the existing religion, might have developed into a new religion over the years. It is the history and perception of the community which is relevant. The dissenting judge accordingly held Aurobindoism to be a religion.

In another decision of the Supreme Court, the followers of Arya Samaj, a reformist movement led by a religious leader called Dayanand Saraswati, were held to be a religious denomination and not the followers of a new religion. The Supreme Court considered Arya Samaj as a reformist movement which rejected manifold absurdities in Smritis and in tradition and attempted to establish a purer and more rational faith within the fold of Hinduism. In another case decided by the Delhi High Court, it was held that Arya Samaj could not be said to be a minority based on religion and was, therefore, not entitled to the right under Article 30 clause 1. This decision has been criticised by jurists. It is pointed out that though Roman Catholics and Protestants comprise the Christian religion, can Roman Catholics who constitute a minority in Ulster as compared to the Protestants who constitute the majority, not be regarded as minority based on religion? Equally in a country like Iran, though Sunnis and Shias both profess Islam, can Sunnis who constitute a minority, not be regarded as a minority based on religion? The question as to what constitutes a minority based on religion may, therefore, ultimately have to be laid at rest in some decision of the Supreme Court.

That the doctrine of the wall of separation between the Church and the State is not wholly accepted in India is also evidenced by Article 27. This Article provides that no person shall be compelled to pay any taxes, the proceeds of

---

[2]See the analysis of the Aurobindo case by Robert Minor (Chapter 14) in which Aurobindoism is seen by the Court as a philosophy rather than a religion at all. [Editor]

which are specifically appropriated in payment of expenses for the promotion or maintenance of any particular religion or religious denomination. Under the First Amendment in U.S. the Congress cannot make appropriations in aid of religious bodies at all, but under Article 27 of the Indian Constitution what is prohibited is payment of taxes for a particular religion and not for the promotion of all religions generally.

Article 28 of the Indian Constitution, however, again emphasises the secular character of the State by providing that no religious instruction shall be provided in any educational institution wholly maintained out of State funds.

No discussion of religion and secularism under the Constitution of India can be complete without reference to Articles 29 and 30 which provide for the cultural rights of minorities, including religious minorities. Article 29 provides for the protection of interests of minorities in respect of their language, script or culture and Article 30 protects the rights of minorities to establish and administer educational institutions. This provision has led to a number of judicial decisions. The question has arisen: how do you determine whether a particular religious or linguistic group is a minority. Do you take the country as a whole or do you reckon with reference to a State or with reference to a district for determining this question. Then what is the meaning and content of this right? Does it entitle a minority to establish and administer an educational institution only for teaching its own religion and culture or does the right extend to establishment and administration of any kind of educational institution including an educational institution which provides general education? When can an educational institution be said to be a minority institution. Is it when a minority is in management and control of the institution or is it when the majority of the students belong to the minority group in question? These and similar other questions have exercised the mind of the Courts and the Courts have consistently taken a liberal view in favour of the minorities with a view to strengthening the protection accorded to them.

These are broadly the constitutional provisions embodying the principal elements of India's national philosophy relating to religion, liberty, equality and tolerance and defining the concept of secularism that is peculiarly the product of India's history and experience and the genius of her profile. Today, due to the forces of fundamentalism which are gaining ground and the obscurantist vocational and divisive tendencies which are developing and the erosion of the spirit of tolerance which is fast taking place, secularism is undergoing severe strains but I have no doubt that with the resilience which the people of India possess and which has helped them to absorb diverse strands of religion and culture coming from outside her frontiers, the Indian Nation will be able to overcome and survive the perils of religious bigotry and fundamentalism and reinvigorate the spirit of secularism which has always been the hall mark of Indian culture and civilisation.

The Indian concept of secularism is no where better described than in the following words of one of the greatest poets of India, Rabindranath Tagore:

Where the mind is without fear and the head is held high,
Where knowledge is free
Where the world has not been broken up into
    fragments by narrow domestic walls;
Where words come out from the depth of truth;
Where tireless striving stretches its arms towards
    perfection;
Where the clear stream of reason has not lost its
    way into the dreary desert sand of habit;
Where the mind is led forward by thee into
    ever-widening thought and action;
Into that heaven of freedom, my Father,
    Let my country awake.

4

India's Constitution and Traditional Presuppositions Regarding Human Nature

Harold G. Coward

A major conflict exists between the Constitution of India and the traditional presuppositions of *karma* and *guṇa* theory. The Constitution, basing itself on British and American models, resolves to secure *equality* for all its citizens as well as granting each religion freedom to practise according to its own beliefs.[1] A clash occurs because traditional Hindu practice presupposes *karma* and *guṇa* theory according to which people are seen to be fundamentally, but not unfairly, *unequal*. Thus by maintaining the freedom of Hinduism to follow its own practise, inequality is seen as justified, while in another place the same Constitution requires equality for all. What the Constitution does not address is whether the provision of equality at birth is true and just while the distinctions of caste and sex made on the basis of *karma* and *guṇa* theory are untrue and unjust. Yet *karma* and *guṇa* are seen by Hindus to be rooted in scriptural revelation. Thus the paradox of a Constitution that sees itself as providing freedom of religion, on the one hand, and yet seeming to remove that freedom on the other when the basic revelations of a religion are found to contravene the Constitution's premise of equality. It is largely left to the courts of India to arbitrate this fundamental clash.

Over twenty-five years ago, Donald Smith recognized that Constitutional provisions which attack the gradations of individuals and groups (the natural result of *karma* and *guṇa* theory) constitute a revolution in the traditional conception of religion in India.[2] But recent scholars seem to have lost sight of this fundamental problem. Krishna Prasad De, for example, in his book *Religious Freedom Under the Indian Constitution*, points out that although the Constitution makes no room for "non-believers"[3] it otherwise embodies the freedom of

---

[1] Durga Das Basu, *Constitutional Law of India* (New Delhi, 1978), articles 14 & 25.

[2] Donald Eugene Smith, *India as a Secular State* (Princeton, 1963), p. 108.

[3] Krishna Prasad De, *Religious Freedom Under the Indian Constitution* (Columbia, Mo., 1977), p. 132.

religion more fully than any other Constitution. He makes the strong claim that "religious freedom under this Constitution is secured in the best way possible under the circumstances peculiar to India and her peoples."[4] J. Duncan M. Derrett, while not as effusive as De, argues that *karma* and *guṇa* rank ordering of traditional Indian society offered a kind of equality of opportunity (in this and future lives) but unfortunately "this could not square with the demands of an industrialized nation, nor with the effects of mobility and earning by both men and women."[5] Consequently, the role of the Constitution and the courts was to take over the balancing act previously the responsibility of the medieval kings; namely, the provision of freedom of religion in a pluralistic context along with a remedial and forward looking claim to equality.

Most of this discussion has focused on the impact of the Constitution on distinctions relating to, castes, untouchables and women. But little attention has been given to the presuppositions underlying these gradations of social groupings, namely, the presuppositions of *karma* and *guṇa* theory. The aim of this paper is to examine these traditional presuppositions, critically compare them to the egalitarian presuppositions of the Constitution, and finally to examine attempts at resolving this fundamental clash.

Traditional Presuppositions of *Karma* and *Guṇa* Theory

In the Hindu tradition individuals are not empirically equal at birth but are seen to be in different states of purity or impurity as a result of their freely chosen behaviour in this and previous lives. All of this is given systematic expression in *karma* and *guṇa* theory. Early in this century Western writers like J. N. Farquhar pictured *karma* and rebirth (*saṁsāra*) as a callous fatalism.[6] While it is possible to find *karma* equated with fate in Indian sources (e.g. in some *Purāṇic* materials), in other instances (e.g. in the *Mahābhārata*) the forces of time and fate appear as non-karmic elements.[7] In the *Upaniṣadic* period *karma* is described as the moral principle of the universe, as the law that regulates the rebirth of *jīvas* or individual embodied souls according to their freely chosen acts in this and previous lives.[8] No birth is an accident. Rather it is a direct result of free choices made in previous lives. Thus the differences between individuals are created by their own different free choices in this and past lives.

---

[4] *Ibid.*, p. 133.

[5] J. Duncan M. Derrett, "Unity in Diversity: The Hindu Experience," *Bharata Manisha Quarterly*, Vol. V, No. 1, April, 1979, pp. 21–36.

[6] J. N. Farquhar, *The Crown of Hinduism* (New Delhi, 1971), p. 142 (Originally published in 1913).

[7] *Karma and Rebirth in Classical Indian Traditions*, ed. by Wendy Doniger O'Flaherty (Berkeley, 1980), p. xxiii.

[8] See, for example, *Chandogya Upaniṣad* 5.10.7.

Traditional Presuppositions 53

The inequality between individuals is self-created through the exercise of freewill. All of this is quite different from modern egalitarian presuppositions: that by nature and birth all people are equal. In the Indian tradition all people equally share in freedom of choice as to whether they engage in good or bad action or thought. The choices freely made determine the differences that exist between individuals, differences that make them empirically unequal. This does not mean that each person is a prisoner of his or her past. Rather, as Cromwell Crawford puts it, "the past, present and the future are all equally grounded in freedom, and, therefore, there is always hope and incentive to moral living. The evil that has been done can be undone, and the good that has been left undone can be done."[9] To assume that in this life everyone is empirically equal would be to ignore the moral responsibility of each individual for previous freely chosen actions and thoughts.

The epic poems, the *Bhagavadgītā* and the *Rāmāyaṇa* continue this theme of individual moral responsibility as constituent of one's human nature. Moral responsibility here involves using one's free choice to make decisions not for oneself and one's own desires but for the good of the whole society by following the revelation of the Vedas and the *smṛtis*. As Cromwell Crawford points out, only as a last resort could the individual follow the guidance of a personal conscience and the dictates of one's own heart.[10] For example, King Rāma, in the *Rāmāyaṇa*, although convinced of Sītā's purity, sent her into exile in the forest because of the people's suspicions that she had not remained pure while she was held captive by Rāvaṇa. Although Rāma seems to have accepted Sītā's purity, he had to act for the good of the whole society, and in so doing he was acting to follow the teaching of the tradition with regard to the duty or *dharma* of a king. Similarly, the *Bhagavadgītā* teaches that the *dharma* resulting from one's free choices in past lives—the role this has given one in the present life—is what must be followed. In this context caste—the karmic status one has in this life—is a direct result of freely chosen deeds in previous lives. Thus, one's present caste is determined by the past and has a moral basis. According to the *Gītā* it is by making good moral choices within the caste situation one finds oneself in during this life that future potentialities can be improved both for oneself and one's society. Consequently the teaching of the *Gītā* that it is better to do one's own *dharma* poorly than to do someone else's *dharma* well. It is by making good choices within the moral basis of one's present life—functionally defined as one's caste or *varṇa*—that one improves one's empirical nature and obtains a higher birth in the next life.[11] It is this same moral principle that lies

---

[9] S. Cromwell Crawford, *The Evolution of Hindu Ethical Ideals* (New Delhi, 1984), p. 49.
[10] *Ibid.*, p. 54.
[11] *Bhagavad-Gītā* 2:31–37; 18:45–48. In order to understand the *Gītā's* view of human nature, it is necessary to see the personality as embracing both *prakṛti* and *puruṣa*. Each of us has, at birth, a psycho-physical nature, *prakṛti*, which is a carry-over from our

behind the *Gītā's* fear of the mixing of castes as resulting in the ruin of both individuals and the whole society.[12]

The *Gītā's* moral explanation of caste as the social consequent of a person's freely chosen karmic actions in previous lives seems to answer the question as to how the system was allowed to prevail without serious protests from the lower castes. Indeed seen from within its own presuppositions traditional Indian society offered equality of opportunity along with carefully designated moral responsibility to all. Each person was confirmed within his or her own society (*varṇa*) which had its essential place within the whole. As Derrett puts it, the *dharmas* or duties of each person and caste, along with the stages of life, must be upheld by the king, subject to his duty to assist in the upward movement of the lower castes and tribes. He also had to protect insti-

---

psychological experience in previous lives. The *Gītā* describes the psycho-spiritual development of one who failed to achieve freedom in a previous life as follows:

> The Blessed Lord said:
> Not in this world nor in the next is such a man destroyed or lost: for no doer of fair works will tread an evil path, my friend, no, none whatever.
> The world of doers of good works he'll win and dwell there countless years: and then will he be born again, this man who failed in spiritual exercise, in the house of holy men by fortune blest.
> Or else he will be born in a family of men well-advanced-in-spiritual exercise, possessed of insight; but such a birth as this on earth is yet harder to obtain.
> There is he united with the soul [*buddhi*] as it had matured in his former body; and once again he strives to win perfection's prize.

> The *Bhagavad-Gītā* trans. by R.C. Zaehner (Oxford, 1969), 6:40-43, p. 240.

The *Gītā's* psychology is realistic. The engaged senses of even a wise person can forcefully seduce the mind (*Gītā* 2:60). As Cromwell Crawford comments, clearly the control of one's past karmic impulses is difficult. But it is not impossible. By virtue of one's higher nature, one can overcome the lower impulses of *prakṛti*. A hierarchical discipline is required so that senses are controlled by the mind (*manas*), mind is controlled by discriminating reason (*buddhi*) and reason is transcended by the Self (*puruṣa*—consciousness) (*Gītā* 3:42). Thus "freedom is correlative to consciousness—the greater the consciousness the greater the freedom. Greatest freedom is achieved when intelligence is informed by the consciousness of the Self." *The Evolution of Hindu Ethical Ideals*, pp. 83–84.

[12] *Ibid.*, 1. 40–42.

tutions such as *aśrams* or monasteries which offered a way of rapid increase in purity to those who sought it. Derrett optimistically summarizes the result of this traditional approach as follows: "The massive chaos of India had a spirit of constructive tolerance, purposeful englobement, all-embracing comprehensive understanding, in which even the most diverse elements had their place, and their hope, in this life, and, if need be, in lives to come."[13] All of this was given legal expression in the *dharmaśāstras*, and systematic theoretical exposition in the teaching of the *Mīmāṃsā* and Yoga *darśanas*.

Both *Mīmāṃsā* and Yoga generally accept the teaching of the *Gītā* but go on to offer their own systematic developments. First, let us examine the *Mīmāṃsā*. Raju summarizes the *Mīmāṃsā* view as follows.[14] Like the *Gītā* *Mīmāṃsā* sees the Self as an eternal, permanent substance that is completely different to the body, the senses, and the mind. Each Self (*ātman* for the *Mīmāṃsā*) survives the death of the body and is reborn with a new body with a character formed from the karmic impulses of previous lives. Consciousness is not the essential nature of the *ātman* but arises in it when it comes into contact with mind (*manas*) as well as some information. But whenever we have consciousness it is always the *ātman* that possesses it, that is, the "I" of the "seeing," "doing" or "knowing." Each *ātman* is trapped in the world by virtue of its body, sense organs and mind. This bondage continues through the beginningless and apparently unending cycle of lives, each of which has been morally caused by the karmic actions of previous lives. Since *karma* is the cause of entrapment in *saṃsāra* or rebirth, release occurs through the removal of *karma*. The purpose of the *Mīmāṃsā Sūtra*, as stated by Jaimini, is the enquiry into *dharma* or duty as a way of removing *karma*.[15]

For *Mīmāṃsā* the doctrine of *karma* or action is closely bound up with the idea of *dharma* or duty. Both are grounded in the ethical action prescribed by the Vedas. Ethical action is further related to *ṛta* the controlling order of the universe. Each person, although free, carries within his or her *ātman saṃskāras* or memory traces of past actions either good or bad. These karmic memory traces do not deprive one of freedom for they are merely impulses or predispositions. Through the use of free choice the effects of evil actions can be countered and cancelled by good actions. Each person's *ātman*, therefore carries from one birth to the next a mixture of the *saṃskāras* from good and evil actions. Sometimes these may cancel one another thus removing *karma* from the *ātman*.

---

[13] Derrett, *Loc.cit.*, p. 28.

[14] P.T. Raju, *Structural Depths of Indian Thought* (Albany, 1985), p. 56. Much of what follows is based on Raju's excellent summary of the *Mīmāṃsā* position, Chapter 2 in his book.

[15] Ganganatha Jha, *Purva Mīmāṃsā in Its Sources* (Varanasi, 1964), p. 8.

The *saṃskāras* or memory traces contain a latent force or disposition (*śakti*) that sticks to the *ātman* until the occasion arises for them to burst into activity. Then they are used up through manifestation. When the last latent *saṃskāras* are exhausted the *ātman* is freed to reveal its *a priori* nature.[16] The way to reach this goal is not by following one's own desires but the Vedic law. In the *Mīmāṃsā* view, this is a path of freely chosen human action chosen says the *Ślokavārttika* in line with the requirements of the Veda.[17] Cromwell Crawford summarizes the *Mīmāṃsā* analysis of karmic actions as being of three kinds: (1) *kāmyakarma*s or optional deeds which gather merit; (2) *pratiṣiddhakarma*s or forbidden deeds which incur demerit; and (3) *nityakarma*s or neutral actions gathering neither merit nor demerit, such as the regular offering of prescribed prayers. When the first two categories of *karma* cancel each other out leaving only *nityakarma*s attached to the *ātman*, then release or freedom from rebirth (*mokṣa*) is realized.[18] In the state of release all would be equal. But before that final realization individuals would vary in nature and character according to the proportion of their good and bad *karmas*.

When we turn to the *Yoga Sūtras* of *Patañjali*,[19] many similarities with the *Mīmāṃsā* view of *karma* are found. *Karma* is described by *Patañjali* as a memory trace (*saṃskāra*) recorded in the unconscious by any action or thought a person has done. The *saṃskāra* remains in the unconscious as predispositions towards doing the same action or thought again in the future. When the appropriate set of circumstances present themselves the karmic memory trace, like a seed that has been watered and given warmth, bursts forth as an impulse toward the same kind of action or thought from which it originated. If one, through the exercise of free choice, chooses to act on the impulse and do the same action or thought again, then that karmic seed is allowed to flower, resulting in a reinforcing of the memory trace within the unconscious. Sufficient repetitions of the same action or thought in this or previous lives produces a strengthened predisposition and establishment of a habit pattern or *vāsanā*.[20] Such a karmic habit pattern or *vāsanā* is the Yoga equivalent for the modern psychological notion of motivation.

As was the case for *Mīmāṃsā* the *saṃskāras* stored up in a previous life carry over into one's rebirth in this life, thus accounting for differences between the character manifested by various individuals. Unlike *Mīmāṃsā*, however, the

---

[16] P. T. Raju, *Loc. cit.*, p. 65.

[17] *Kumārila Bhaṭṭa, Ślokavārttika*, trans. by G. Jha (Calcutta, 1909), *15*, p. 555.

[18] S. Cromwell Crawford, *Loc. cit.*, pp. 102–105.

[19] *Patañjali's Yoga Sūtras*, trans. by Rama Prasad (Delhi, 1978). See also the translation by Bengali Baba, Motilal Banarsidass, 1976.

[20] See *Yoga Sūtras* 2:12–14 & 4:7–9.

saṃskāras do not adhere to the higher self (*puruṣa* in the Yoga system) but rather inhere in the *antaḥkaraṇa* portion of *prakṛti* (which includes *buddhi, ahaṃkāra* and *manas*).[21] It is the *antaḥkaraṇa* aspect of *prakṛti* that is reborn carrying with it the karmic memory traces of previous lives. All *karma* is therefore located in *prakṛti* and obstructs the pure light or consciousness of *puruṣa,* the true Self.[22]

In the *Yoga Sūtras,* however, we also find *Saṃkhya guṇa* theory given full development in relation to *karma. Prakṛti* (our reason, ego, mind, sense organs and body) is conceived in terms of three *guṇas* or substantive qualities: *sattva* (brightness, illumination, intelligence), *rajas* (emotion, movement) and *tamas* (dullness, inertia). Different karmic states are described in terms of different *guṇas.* Bad *karma* involving the injury of another will be dominated by *tamas* with some *rajas* mixed in. Good or dharmic *karma* which acts for the good of others will be dominated by *sattva* with some *rajas* mixed in. Enlightened states in which *jñāna* or discriminating knowledge shines forth are virtually pure *sattva* in nature. Following *guṇa* theory, any mental or physical state, including the condition in which one is born, can be described in terms of the relevant proportions of *sattva, rajas* and *tamas* which are present. And, this proportion is directly attributable to the kinds of freely chosen karmic actions one engaged in during previous lives. Obviously everyone (except those who have reached the final stage of *kaivaliya* or release) will have a different proportion of the three *guṇas.* Therefore, each individual will be different according to the differing proportion of *guṇas* present within his or her *prakṛti* or empirical nature. In *guṇa* terms this difference is described in terms of increasing purity (*sattva*) or impurity (*rajas* and *tamas*). Equality is reached only when one achieves the final state of *kaivaliya* or release in which, through performance of the various *yogaṅgas*[23] (*yamas, niyamas, āsana, prāṇāyāma, pratyāhāra, dhāraṇā, dhyāna* and *samādhi*), one's *prakṛti* has become virtually pure *sattva* revealing the *puruṣa* or true self.[24] It is at the level of revealed *puruṣas* that all individuals may be said to be equal. At the level of *prakṛti,* however, there is only inequality in terms of the varying proportion of *sattva, rajas* and *tamas* present in one's empirical nature. And it is to the *prakṛti* level of life in the empirical world that the provisions of the Constitution apply.

---

[21] Sarasvati Chennakesavan, *Concept of Mind in Indian Philosophy* (Delhi, 1980), p. 30.

[22] The Yoga classification of *karma* is more detailed than that of the *Mīmāṃsā*, having four classes rather than only three. Dasgupta suggests that a colour scheme is employed of white *karma*, black *karma*, white and black *karma*, neither white nor black *karma*. As might be expected white *karma* involves good behaviour and is therefore referred to as *dharma*. Black *karma*, such as harming others is *adharma*. While ordinary life is a mixture of white and black *karma*, a life of complete renunciation leads one to the state of neither black nor white *karma*, the final state before release is realized. See *Yoga Sūtra* 2:12 & 13 and Surendranath Dasgupta, *A Study of* Patañjali (Delhi, 1989), pp. 88–90.

[23] *Yoga Sūtras* 2:29–3:3.

[24] *Yoga Sūtras* 1:51.

In stark contrast to the Constitution's ideal society of this-worldly-equality where all individuals freely rub shoulders with one another, the *Yoga Sūtras* counsel a careful separation in terms of purity versus impurity in aid of the ultimate goal of a higher equality in *kaivaliya*. For example, in *Yoga Sūtra* 2:32, *Patañjali* advises "*śauca* or cleanliness of outer body, internal organs and mental thoughts as a means by which karmic impurities of the nature of *rajas* and *tamas* can be removed and the discriminative awareness of *puruṣa* realized." To be clean or sattvic requires ultimately that one get rid of one's body and impure thoughts. As one progresses toward this goal the stage is reached where disgust is felt toward all manifestations of empirical nature. The practice of purity of body and mind leads the yogi to be disgusted and shrink from contact, not only with the bodies of others, but even from his own body and its excretions. *Vyāsa* in his *Bhāsya* on *Yoga Sūtra* 2:30 says:

> As soon as there is disgust with his own body, he [the yogi] has begun cleanliness. Seeing the offensiveness of the body, he is no longer attached to the body and becomes an ascetic (yati). Moreover there is no intercourse with others. Perceiving the true nature of the body, even after he has washed it with earth and water and other substances, not seeing any purity in the body, could he have intercourse with the bodies of others absolutely unhallowed as they are.[25]

In terms of *guṇa* theory, this means that the body is composed of karmic impurities of the nature of *rajas* and *tamas*. To be clean or sattvic requires ultimately that one get rid of one's body and impure thoughts. Implied in the text is that the further one departs from the relatively pure practice and body of the yogi, the more revolting or tamasic the bodies of others become. There is even the implication that these darker qualities can rub off from the body and mind of another onto oneself. Thus all contact with others is to be avoided, especially with those who are not even trying to be clean: those who eat meat, don't wash properly, indulge in sexual intercourse, and engage in uncouth activity not only in this life but also in previous lives. In Indian society the most likely candidates for this latter group are of course the lower castes and those below the caste structure. One can see how the logic of this *guṇa* system can be extrapolated to the idea and practice of untouchability. At the opposite end of the continuum is the yogi or Brahmin who has used free choice to work hard at purifying body and mind not only in this life but also in previous lives. It is simply not good either for the individual's spiritual progress or the well-being of society to lose such purity by contact with those who, due to their own free choice, are more impure. All of this

---

[25] *Yoga Sūtras* 2:40, *Bhāsya* of Vyāsa, trans. by J.H. Woods, *The Yoga System of Patañjali* (Delhi, 1966), p. 188.

provides a clear and logical basis for distinguishing various levels of *prakṛti* and for the development of a negative attitude toward others of a lower karmic level than oneself. This negative attitude is not based on any dislike for others. In the Yoga view, it is simply a recognition of the empirical fact that all persons are not equally pure due to their own free choices in this and previous lives.

The goal of the yogic practice of cleanliness is to free oneself from the pollution of the *guṇas*. *Vācaspatimiśra* describes it clearly in his "Explanation" on *Yoga Sūtra* 1:16, "The purity of knowledge consists in the steady flow of the quality of essence (*sattva*), due to the removal of active disturbance (*rajas*) and inertia (*tamas*). This brings about recognition of the distinct natures of the *puruṣa* and the 'qualities'."[26] *Vyāsa* makes clear that both the body and the mental states have been purified of *karma* and the dark *guṇas* until the mind has become like a transparent crystal which clearly reflects what is placed before it namely, the *puruṣa*, the true Self.[27]

Unlike the Constitution which aims at producing social equality and full freedom for all in this empirical world, the traditional presuppositions of *karma* and *guṇa* theory are directed towards the attainment of release from this world and the realization of a state of freedom from *karma-saṃsāra* in which all are equal. As is the case with the Constitution, the goals are freedom and equality. Unlike the Constitution, however, the presuppositions of *karma* and *guṇa*, at least as developed in the *Mīmāṃsā* and Yoga *darśanas*, locate these goals beyond everyday worldly life at the end rather than at the beginning.

The Egalitarian Presuppositions of India's Constitution

The Preamble of India's 1949 Constitution resolves to secure to all its citizens justice, liberty, equality and fraternity, assuring the dignity of the individual and the unity of the nation.[28] Robert Baird has noted that this "Preamble," as a statement of the ultimate goals of India, envisages a society in which justice and equality are to be implemented within the present lifespan of its citizens and without reference to *karma* and rebirth. Therefore, it is a this-worldly goal that is presumed.[29] Baird locates the presuppositions of the "this-worldly goal," espoused by Ambedkar, Nehru and Gajendragadkar in their various statements on the formulation of the Hindu Law Code from 1944 to 1956. He states that "the norms by which they found a position 'reasonable' were not

---

[26] *Yoga Sūtras* 1:16, "Explanation" of Vācaspatimiśra trans. by Rama Prasada, p. 31.

[27] *Yoga Sūtra* 1:41 & 1:47–51.

[28] Durga Das Basu, *Constitutional Law of India* (New Delhi, 1978), p. 1.

[29] Robert D. Baird, "Uniform Civil Code and the Secularization of Law" in *Religion in Modern India*, ed. by R.D. Baird (New Delhi, 1981), p. 417.

traditional nor textual, but were based on human rights, equality of the sexes, social utility, and world opinion."[30] The "Preamble" and the statement of "Fundamental Rights" of the Constitution along with the Hindu Code Bill enacted in 1955–56 constitute a manifestation of these presuppositions into what Baird has termed a new "Great Tradition" characterized by secularization.[31] Nehru wanted a complete secularization of Hindu and Muslim law so that there could be a uniform civil code for the country. He also saw the various religions of India as obstacles to the realization of the secular and progressive goals of India.[32] All of this was at the heart of his basic differences with Gandhi, but more of that later. Our present concern is with the views of human nature embodied in the presuppositions of India's new Great Tradition.

Let us begin by working backward from the provisions of the Constitution. It is clear that in the Constitution's view, human nature is such that all persons are equal at least in terms of status and opportunity, for so the "Preamble" declares. Part III, provision 15(1) of the Constitution defines this equality in the following way: "The State shall not discriminate against any citizen on the grounds only of religion, race, caste, sex, place of birth or any of them." Provision 15(2) goes on to elaborate that no citizen shall be subject to any disability, limitation, or restriction in terms of access to public buildings (including Hindu Temples); to the use of wells, tanks, bathing *ghats*, roads, or public resorts; or to be discriminated against in respect of employment. The two main groups in mind here are women and those of low caste. This is made clear by section of provision 15 which allows the state to set up special conditions for the advancement of women and low caste groups without violating the requirement for equality. Provision 17 deals with "Untouchability," which it abolishes. All of these provisions directly attack the gradations of individuals and groups which was the natural result of the classical *karma* and *guṇa* theories, and their view of the body, especially the female body, as being filled with impurities. On the new basis of equality, women are no longer seen as inferior to men by virtue of their greater bodily impurity. Nor are people who eat meat or engage in sex and worldly pleasures to be judged as inferior to the ascetic yogis by virtue of the impurity of their lifestyles. Indeed the very idea of ordering society in terms of the sattvic purity of *guṇa* theory is ruled out by the new Constitution. It is for this reason that D. E. Smith describes the Constitution as introducing a revolution in traditional conceptions that is nothing short of a new standardization of Hindu personal law on the basis of equality rather than on the grounds of karmic

---

[30] *Ibid.*, p. 433.

[31] *Ibid.*, p. 436.

[32] *Jawaharlal Nehru: An Autobiography* (New Delhi, 1984), p. 374 & p. 410.

Traditional Presuppositions

purity.[33] While the Supreme Court of India has broadly defined the freedom of religion guaranteed in article 25(1) in terms of what the religion itself considers to be its essential tenets,[34] it is clear that this does not extend to include the Hindu view of human nature as detailed above in Section I of this paper. Indeed article 25(2) grants to the state broad sweeping powers to interfere in a religion when its tenets, such as those of *karma* and *guṇa* conflict with the Constitution's own presupposition of equality. In fact, the provisions of article 25(2) clearly allow the state to overrule caste practices, reform Hindu personal law regarding marriage, divorce, adoption, succession, and force open the doors of Hindu temples to Harijans on the grounds that these are secular rather than religious matters. Since they are secular issues, it is the Constitution's view of equality rather than the ultimate equality envisaged in *karma* and *guṇa* theory that prevails.

But what exactly are the presuppositions underlying the Constitution's notion of "equality"? We have already noted that the this-worldly norms espoused by Ambedkar, Nehru and Gajendragadkar were that a position such as "equality" should be "reasonable" in terms of human rights, equality of the sexes, social utility and world opinion. Given the appeal to "social utility" in the context of a British education and legal tradition it seems a reasonable surmise that there is some Utilitarian thinking at work in these men. Bentham, the founder of the British Utilitarian movement, wanted somehow to quantify ethical notions such as equality.[35] This resulted in his basic principle of utility which is often glossed as "the greatest good for the greatest number." Underlying this was Bentham's view of human nature which reduced the person to a system of attractions and repulsions in response to pleasures and pains with the ultimate goal of maximizing the good (the pleasures) and minimizing the pains (the evil). In this struggle all persons began equal and deserved equal rights and opportunity under law. All of this, of course, was seen as occurring in a single lifetime, with no notion of rebirth being entertained. Mill, Bentham's disciple, attempted to refine Bentham's view of human nature through the use of associationist psychology and Hume's view of mental functioning. Mill's aim was to show how altruistic behaviour could take place on the part of the person who by nature

---

[33] Donald Eugene Smith, *Loc cit.*, p. 108. For a full discussion of the ethical impact of purity practices see H. Coward, J. Lipner and K. Young, *Hindu Ethics. Purity, Abortion and Euthanasia* (Albany, 1989), pp. 9–40.

[34] *Commissioner, Hindu Religious Endowments* v. *Lakshmindra*, 1954 *Supreme Court Appeals*, pp. 431-432, as reported in *India as a Secular State*, pp. 106–107.

[35] Frederick Copleston S.J., *A History of Philosophy*, vol. 8, *Modern Philosophy: Bentham to Russell*, Part I (New York, 1967), p. 33.

seeks his or her own pleasure.[36] Arising from this view of human nature, Bentham's reforms in England envisaged an equality in citizenship rights and equality before the law. Mill's essay *On Liberty* became a classic statement of the liberal creed (including its argument for freedom of religion) in nineteenth century England.[37] Article 25 of India's constitution which states that all persons have the right freely to profess, practice and propagate religion, along with Nehru's interpretation of the propagation clause in terms of an open "marketplace of ideas" is seen by D. E. Smith as a clear reflection of Mill's liberal tradition.[38] Smith also traces to Bentham the thrust within the Constitution and the Hindu Code Bill to secularize matters such as caste, marriage, divorce, etc., and to remove them from the religious realm.[39] It seems safe to conclude that the Utilitarian principles of Bentham and Mill, along with the egalitarian view of human nature assumed, influenced the drafting of the Constitution and the Hindu Code.

But, British influence appears to be only one-half of the story. Sunder Raman in his book, *Fundamental Rights and the 42nd Constitutional Amendment*, demonstrates that the "Fundamental Rights" section of India's Constitution depends heavily on the Bill of Rights in the United States Constitution.[40] Raman states, "In spite of their long association with the English political system and constitutional law, the members of the Constituent Assembly deliberately departed from the British system and practice and decided to go in for a declaration of fundamental rights in the Constitution on the lines of the American practice."[41] He argues that when a country of such a diversity of peoples as India was being welded together as one state it was essential to guarantee the fundamental rights in order to create a sense of security and safety in the minds of the people regardless of race, religion, caste, or language. Since the Fundamental Rights dealt with in Part III of the Indian Constitution include the rights to equality *and* freedom of religion, the formative influence of American thinking on these articles is crucial to the concern of this paper.

What are the presuppositions regarding human nature that stand behind the tenets of the United States Bill of Rights? The consensus of scholarship on

---

[36] *Ibid.*, p. 37.

[37] *India as a Secular State*, p. 18.

[38] *Ibid.*, p. 176.

[39] *Ibid.*, pp. 275ff. India, it turns out, was the testing ground for some of Bentham's legal reforms before they were adopted in England this under the leadership of Lord Macaulay in the years following 1833.

[40] Sunder Raman, *Fundamental Rights and the 42nd Constitutional Amendment* (Columbia, Mo, 1977), p. 8.

[41] *Ibid.*

Traditional Presuppositions 63

this point suggests that the American Constitution and Bill of Rights assumes a Lockean view of human nature.[42] John Locke's theory of human nature is found in his *Essay Concerning Human Understanding* in which he argues against the possibility of innate ideas and puts forth the proposal that the mind at birth is a *tabula rasa* or blank sheet that acquires content passively through the impact of sensation and the interaction or association of traces left behind by such stimuli.[43] This Lockean view of mental activity being a result of traces upon the "wax tablet" of the mind has a certain similarity to the Yoga theory of *saṃskāras* or memory traces left within the *citta* or mind by previous actions or thoughts. But there is also a key difference which is crucial for our present analysis. Whereas for Locke each newborn child begins life with an empty mind, a *tabula rasa*, and is therefore equal in nature to all others, Yoga theory emphasizes that at birth the mind or *citta* carries with it a storehouse of karmic *vāsanās* or habit patterns built up over a beginningless series of previous lives. Consequently, for Locke everyone is born equal while for Yoga, everyone is born unequal with that inequality being self-created by the *karma* resulting from freely chosen actions in previous lives. Another fundamental difference is the Yoga notion of a *puruṣa* (or the *Mīmāṃsā* counterpart, *ātman*), the idea of an eternal self separate from one's material nature which shines forth as an individual's pure consciousness once all obstructing *karma* has been removed. Such a notion of the self seems totally foreign to modern thought whether of a Utilitarian or Lockean cast, as is the idea that equality is a spiritual goal to be realized at the end of life's *karma-saṃsāra* process rather than a this-world state from which we all begin at birth. The "level playing field" for Locke is the state into which we are born while for Yoga it is the spiritual goal to be attained by all in the end.

The Lockean presuppositions regarding human nature are clearly reflected in the Fundamental Rights of the Indian Constitution. Just as all persons are born equal, therefore, all persons have the right to equality before the law (article 14). While provision is made for some reasonable classifications of individuals and groups, article 14 clearly rests on the presumption that all human beings have a fundamental equality at birth. Classifications of persons into caste groups on the basis of a self-created unequal birth (the traditional presupposition) is rejected on the basis that such classifications have no *objective* basis and are therefore not reasonable.[44] The Lockean view of equality at birth also appears in article 16 which guarantees equality of opportunity in matters of public employment. Not

---

[42] Clinton Rossiter, *The Federalist Papers* (New York, 1961), p. 458.

[43] Frederick Coppleston, S.J., *A History of Philosophy*, Vol. 5, *Modern Philosophy: The British Philosophers* (New York, 1964), Part I, pp. 83ff. See also Gordon Allport's discussion of Locke's viewpoint in his *Becoming* (New Haven, 1955), pp. 7ff.

[44] *Constitutional Law of India*, p. 22.

only is there to be no discrimination on the grounds of caste or sex but the article also makes provision for the principle of equality to be violated for the purpose of favouring backward classes not adequately represented in state services, classes that have been presumably penalized by a society based on the traditional presuppositions of *karma* and *guṇa*. "Untouchability" is likewise forbidden (article 17). And although freedom of religion is given as a fundamental right (article 25), the Lockean view of equality is seen to superceed that right when the religion in question, Hinduism for example in its *karma* and *guṇa* tenants, contravenes the requirement for equality at birth. When such a clash of presuppositions occurs, the constitution ensures the supremacy of the Lockean side by adding in article 25(2) provisions ensuring that the state's definition of equality transcends that of any religion. It is under this provision, for example, that the secularization of the Hindu Law Code has proceeded. The upshot of all of this is that there is freedom "to profess, practise and propagate religion" so long as the presupposition of equality of the religion in question squares with the Lockean presupposition of the equality of all at birth. Clearly this is not the case when the Hindu view of equality according to *karma* and *guṇa* theory is examined. Consequently, in the Hindu case the Constitution is acting to secularize and reform religion by replacing the *karma* and *guṇa* presuppositions with the Lockean view of human nature.

Attempts at Resolving the Clash of Presuppositions

Although not discussed explicitly, the clash between the modern secular assumptions of the Constitution and traditional presuppositions has received some recognition within the Constitution itself. Unlike the secularism of the American Constitution which contains a clear separation between religion and the state, the Indian conception of secularism as manifested in its Constitution is of a different order. S. Radhakrishnan asserts that secularism "does not mean irreligion or atheism, or even stress on material comforts. It proclaims that it lays stress on the universality of spiritual values which may be attained by a variety of ways."[45] The Constitutional scholar P.B. Gajendragadkar comments, "It is necessary to emphasize that Indian secularism...recognizes both the relevance and validity of religion in human life. In the context of the Constitution secularism means that all religions in India are entitled to equal freedom and protection."[46] Indians have widely assumed that secularism is somehow neutral or positive towards religion, thus allowing them to welcome the idea of India as a secular

---

[45] S. Radhakrishnan, "Foreword" to S. Abid Husain, *The National Culture of India* (Bombay, 1961), p. vii.

[46] P.B. Gajendragadkar, "The Concept of Secularism," *Secular Democracy*, Annual Number 1970, p. 71.

Traditional Presuppositions 65

state. This is clearly reflected in the 42nd Amendment Act which inserted the word "secular" into the Preamble of the Constitution. While Constitutional scholars such as Sunder Raman cannot find any real purpose served by the insertion of the word "secular" along with "socialist" into the Preamble,[47] our analysis suggests that the insertion of "secular" brings the Preamble into line with the functioning secular view of human nature adopted in articles 14, 17 and 25, the Hindu Code Bill, and the desire for a universal secular civil code. In another sense, however, the Constitution is not at all secular or neutral towards religion since, as Krishna Prasad De points out, it makes no room for nonbelievers.[48] It follows the traditional approach in assuming that all citizens of India practise religion. If they are not identified as one of the minority religions (Muslim, Sikh, Jaina, Christian, etc.) they are assumed to be Hindus, the majority religion, although the latter is not specifically defined in the Constitution. Thus the traditional view that life within India goes on within a religious context, composed of the majority religion and minority religions but not non-believers, exists side by side with quite opposed Constitutional assumptions which make India a secular state in areas such as that of civil law (marriage, divorce, etc.), where religion no longer controls one's life (Article 25, clause 2(a)). Although the Constitution may be at points internally inconsistent with the Preamble's prescription of a secular India, it may be at the same time a recognition that, as Radhakrishnan put it, secularism for India is not irreligious or neutral but spiritual.[49] Such a religious secularism may also reflect a muddled attempt to incorporate both the traditional *karma-guṇa* view of human nature and the modern Bentham-Locke view of human nature. This suggestion is supported by a social science case study which seeks to show that there is no dichotomy between traditional caste practise (based on *karma-guṇa* theory) and modern secular structures (based on the theories of Bentham, Mill and Locke). Rajni Kothari and Rushikesh Maru in their article "Caste and Secularism in India" demonstrate that it is through the religiously based structures of caste that Indian society is able to participate in modern democratic politics.[50] They go on to note, however, that while caste always had a political aspect to it, this aspect is gaining ground and becoming more important than the religious aspect in modern India. The clash of presuppositions we have been examining is explicitly manifested in the final comment of the study, namely, that participation in secular democratic processes

---

[47] *Fundamental Rights and the 42nd Constitutional Amendment*, p. 13, note 6.

[48] Krishna Prasad De, *Religious Freedom Under the Indian Constitution* (Columbia, Mo, 1977), p. 132.

[49] S. Radhakrishnan, *Loc. cit.*, p. vii.

[50] Rajni Kothari and Rushikesh Maru, "Caste and Secularism in India" in *South and Southeast Asia*, ed. by J.A. Harrison (Tucson, Arizona, 1972), pp. 176–177.

and the spread of egalitarian values is undermining the caste system and the religious culture on which it depends.[51]

On a more theoretical level an attempt at resolving the clash between traditional and modern views of human nature may be found in the political thought of Mahatma Gandhi. In his fine study of Gandhi, Raghavan Iyer observes that all political theory must begin with a coherent view of human nature.[52] Iyer finds that Gandhi's indictment of modern civilization, his view of politics and his conception of ethics are based on his assumptions regarding human nature and human perfectibility. In spite of his criticism of modernity Gandhi's view of human nature was an amalgum of modern Western and traditional Hindu thought. A strong Darwinian element is seen when Gandhi maintains that to become fully human one has to evolve from one's initial condition of being bestial or brutal. This evolutionary presupposition is assumed with the traditional *ahiṃsā* or non-violence teaching of Jaina and Yoga grafted onto it. Humans chose either to evolve upward or to slide downward toward the brute from which all have arisen. It is through *ahiṃsā* that one negates the inherent violence of the brute and moves upwards towards the spiritual realization of one's innate divinity.[53]

In Gandhi's view we recognize many traditional presuppositions. There is a divine essence within each of our natures that is constantly calling us in the upward direction. Free moral choice is the fundamental condition of each person and the means by which one moves in one direction or the other. The choices we make in one life are carried over as *saṃskāras* or memory traces into the next. Thus, as in *karma* and *guṇa* theory there are many lifetimes—as many as are needed until perfection is realized. Perfection is defined by Gandhi as complete mastery of *ahiṃsā* and complete subjugation of the bestial nature within.[54] It is the human privilege and freedom to overcome adverse circumstances. Ghandi's theory opposes "soul-force" and "brute-force." "While brute-force is based on egotism, which creates conflict and misery, soul-force is based on love, trust and humility, which create harmony and true happiness."[55]

Gandhi rejects the view of Bentham and Mill that egotism can lead to altruism. His acceptance of an innate spiritual essence and *karma-saṃsāra* amounts to a solid rejection of the Lockean view of human nature as a *tabula rasa* at birth. Gandhi is perhaps closest to the Buddha in his contention that to

---

[51] *Ibid.*, p. 178.

[52] Raghavan N. Iyer, *The Moral and Political Thought of Mahatma Gandhi* (Oxford, 1978), p. 88.

[53] *Ibid.*, pp. 90–91.

[54] *Ibid.*, pp. 96–101.

[55] *Ibid.*, p. 109.

seek power for oneself is simply to fly against the facts of cosmic and human interdependence and to land one in perpetual frustration. At the sametime he based himself upon the doctrine of unselfish action upheld in the *Gītā* and endeavored to find a new meaning for the heroic ideal of the *Rāmāyaṇa*. For Gandhi all are equal in that all begin in the condition of selfish brutishness and have the possibility of evolving through the exercise of free moral choice for nonviolence, to the spiritual goal of humility and service to all humanity, in which no caste boundaries or degrees of impurity are allowed to become obstacles. Yet Gandhi also maintains the Yogic ascetic ideal of renouncing one's body, but for the service of humankind rather than for one's personal *kaivaliya*. Equality, in Ghandi's view is present both at the beginning and at the end. Rejecting the utilitarian ethic of the greatest good for the greatest number, Gandhi placed his hopes on the perfecting of the whole through the uplifting of individuals. And the perfected whole is not world-denying, not otherworldly, but indeed realized in the political order of this world.

    Nehru and the other drafters of the Constitution and the secularized Hindu Code had little sympathy for Gandhi's resolution of the clash of presuppositions. While Nehru greatly admired the courage with which Gandhi manifested his own synthesis of the traditional and the modern and powerfully embodied it in his own life, Nehru ultimately rejects it as unsuited to the modern secular world.[56] Human nature, Nehru concludes, is egoistically motivated for pleasure and power and therefore needs to be controlled in the ways that the British Utilitarians proposed. Gandhi recognized his fundamental difference with Nehru and argued that the socialism of India must be based, not on the Western belief in the essential selfishness of human nature, but on the Indian view of the perfectibility of the human spirit through non-violence and the harmonious cooperation of all castes, classes and religions.[57] In the end, however, it is the Western presuppositions of Bentham, Mill and Locke, rather than Gandhi's view of the self, that undergird the Indian Constitution and its secularization of traditional religious values.

---

[56] *Jawaharlal Nehru: An Autobiography*, p. 522.

[57] *Ibid.*, p. 535.

5

On Defining "Hinduism" as a Religious and Legal Category

Robert D. Baird

The *Constitution of India*, as presently ammended, defines India as a secular state.[1] Western conceptions of this designation aside, for India this has always involved the state in religious matters. While all persons are guaranteed the right "freely to profess, practise and propogate religion" (Article 25 [1]), this is subject to "public order morality and health." And, it is to be clearly distinguished from "economic, social, political or other secular" activities which might be found in close proximity with religious practices. These "secular" matters can be directly regulated by the state.

Furthermore, the state is obliged to engage in social welfare and reform, and legislation to that end cannot be set aside on the grounds that it interferes with religious freedom. Nor can temple entry laws be set aside because they restrict practices that are admittedly religious (Article 25 [2][b]). Hindu religious institutions of a public nature can legitimately be opened to all classes of Hindus, even to those who were previously excluded because of untouchability. Explanation II of Article 25[2][b] states that "the reference to Hindus shall be construed as including a reference to persons professing the Sikh, Jaina, or Buddhist religion, and the reference to Hindu religious institutions shall be construed accordingly."

Religious and Legal "Hinduism"

Explanation II of Article 25 [2][b] is a constitutional admission of two things. First it admits that there is a difference between the "Hindu religion" and "Hindu" as a legal category. For, the stipulation that "Hindus" in Article 25 [2][b] is to be taken to include persons professing the Sikh, Buddhist, or Jaina *religion* suggests that *as religions* these are distinguishable from "Hinduism" *as a*

---

[1] See Robert D. Baird, "'Secular State' and the Indian Constitution," *Essays in the History of Religions*, Toronto Studies in Religion, Vol. 11 (New York, 1991), chapter VIII.

religion, but that *before the law* they *are* to be included within the category of "Hindu." While Article 25[2][b] deals with temple entry, it also includes matters of social welfare and reform more broadly conceived.

The Bills passed in 1955 and 1956, commonly referred to as the Hindu Code Bill, continue this distinction between Hinduism as a *religious* and *legal* category. The Hindu Succession Act of 1956 applies the Act as follows:

(a) to any person who is a Hindu by religion in any of its forms or developments, including a Virashaiva, a Lingayat, or a follower of the Brahmo, Prarthana or Arya Samaj;
(b) to any person who is a Buddhist, Jain or Sikh by religion; and
(c) to any other person who is not a Muslim, Christian, Parsi or Jew by religion, unless it is proved that any such person would not have been governed by the Hindu law or by any custom or usage as part of that law in respect of any of the matters dealt with herein if this Act had not been passed.

The Hindu Marriage Act (1955), the Hindu Adoptions and Maintenance Act (1956), and the Hindu Minority and Guardianship Act (1956) use almost identical language.[2]

These acts make it clear that the term "Hindu" as a *legal* category includes not only those who are Hindu, Buddhist, Jain or Sikh by *religion* but also anyone who is not a Muslim, Christian, Parsi or Jew. This means that one could be an atheist, reject caste laws, reject the Vedas, indeed go so far as to renounce "Hinduism" as a religion and still be considered a "Hindu" for legal purposes.

Furthermore, since certain groups have made the case that they were not "Hindu" and since the court has declared that they are, the category of Hindu religion is said to include Virashaivas, Lingayats, Brahmo Samaj, Prarthana Samaj and Arya Samaj.

Not only does this cast the *legal* net of "Hinduism" very wide, but it would appear that the burden of proof is upon an individual to show that he or she is not to be considered a "Hindu" legally.

That the legal definition of "Hinduism" goes well beyond any religious meaning that might be attached to it is recognized in most discussions of Hindu Law. Tahir Mahmood makes the point well when he states,

> The expression 'Hindu law,' which may once have been most appropriate is now, surely, a term of convenience, if not a misnomer. At present the law described as 'Hindu Law' is applicable, or may be

---

[2] The former two Acts include the words "domiciled in the territories to which the Act extends." The rest of the language is identical.

applied, to a heterogeneous section of the Hindu citizenry, many groups in which are certainly not 'Hindu' by religion. So, 'Hindu law' is not the 'law of the Hindus.' 'Hindus' are only one of those communities who are governed by this law.[3]

The apparent care with which the legal definition of "Hinduism" is made in the Constitution and the Hindu Code Bills might suggest that there would be little room for confusion as to whom the legal designation "Hindu" applies.[4]

The Ambiguity of Hinduism as a *Religion*

In addition to the fact that applicability of the *legal* designation varies in terms of the context in which it is applied, the *religious* designation "Hindu" is remarkably elastic. In his influential volume, *The Meaning and End of Religion*, Wilfred Cantwell Smith makes his point in characteristic crispness.

> The term "Hinduism" is, in my judgment, a particularly false conceptualization, one that is, conspicuously incompatible with any adequate understanding of the religious outlook of Hindus. Even the term "Hindu" was unknown to the classical Hindus. "Hinduism" as a concept certainly they did not have.[5]

While the modern world of scholarship and public discourse uses the terms "Hindu" and "Hinduism" often with little attention to the diversity and complexity involved, and while many modern Indians have a highly developed Hindu consciousness, Smith would seem to be right about the ancients. Since 1938, Everyman's Library has included a volume titled *Hindu Scriptures*. The 1966 edition, with texts selected and translated by R.C. Zaehner, includes selections from the *Ṛgveda*, *Atharvaveda*, *Upaniṣads*, and the entire *Bhagavadgītā*. Although it did not occur to the editor and translator to question the appropriateness of the title of the volume, nowhere in the texts presented is there any reference to or consciousness of being either "Hindu" or being a part of "Hinduism."

The vast diversity that is apparent in that to which the term "Hinduism" is applied today is the result of the fact that the term was originally of

---

[3] Tahir Mahmood, *Studies in Hindu Law*, second edition, (Allahabad, 1986), p. xlii]. See also J.D.M. Derrett, *Introduction to Modern Hindu Law* (Bombay, 1963), p. 18ff; and Derrett, *Religion, Law and the State in India* (London, 1968).

[4] But, cf. Galanter for the differences here.

[5] *The Meaning and End of Religion* (New York, 1967), p. 63.

geographical significance and an equivalent for India. Hence, Hinduism was the religion of the people who lived in the subcontinent. T.M.P. Mahadevan reinforces Smith's position when he states:

> The name had originally a geographical significance. The Persians who invaded India through the north-western passes of the Himalyas gave the name Sindhu to the region watered by the river Indus; and the word 'Hindu' is only a corrupt form of 'Sindhu.' Hinduism meant the faith of the people of Indus-land.[6]

This same point is made by Sarasvati Chennakesavan, who adds that "such a localisation is only formal, since, as the years passed, the word has come to connote a whole gamut of religious and philosophical beliefs of the people occupying the whole subcontinent."[7]

The attempt to determine what all Hindus have in common is empirically impossible for the geographical category was transformed into a religious category before the full force of historical flux and diversity on the subcontinent had been realized.[8]

> My objection to the term "Hinduism," of course, is not on the grounds that nothing exists. Obviously an enormous quantity of phenomena is to be found that this term covers. My point...is that the mass of religious phenomena that we shelter under the umbrella of that term, is not a unity and does not aspire to be.[9]

As anthropological and fieldwork intensive studies proliferate, the varied diversity of religious belief, values and practice in South Asia has raised anew the question of how to define Hinduism. Members of the panel "Hinduism Reconsidered" at the IXth European Conference of Modern South Asian Studies in Germany in 1986 were asked to reconsider their notions of Hinduism and were

---

[6] T.M.P. Mahadevan, *Outlines of Hinduism*, (Bombay, 1956), p.12.

[7] *A Critical Study of Hinduism* (Delhi, 1980), p.3. It is also part of S. Radhakrishnan's discussion in *The Hindu View of Life* (New York, 1962), p.12, which contains Radhakrishnan's Upton Lectures given at Manchester College, Oxford in 1926.

[8] Robert D. Baird, *Category Formation and the History of Religions* (The Hague, 1971, 1991), p.136.

[9] *The Meaning and End of Religion*, p. 66.

urged to make the reconsideration of what "Hinduism" means a primary topic of their papers and discussion.[10]

Robert E. Frykenberg, in "The Emergence of Modern 'Hinduism' as a Concept and as an Institution: A Reappraisal With Special Reference to South India," traces the use of the term "Hindu" and argues cogently that a variety of mutually exclusive religious beliefs and practices have been considered "Hindu." There is "popular Hinduism," "temple Hinduism," "bhakti Hinduism," "village Hinduism," "tribal Hinduism" in addition to "neo-Hinduism" and the application of the term to the *varnāśramadharma* system.[11] While the term "Hinduism," then, remains "*soft* and *slippery*,"[12] abstract models have been built to define "Hinduism" even though they do not fit with the concrete data of history.

> From Abbe Dubois to Louis Dumont, Cartesian constructions of truly wondrous artistry and symmetry have been built. Like intricate mobiles dangling from the sky, these metaphysical contraptions, with all their intricately moving parts, have bedazzled and fascinated us. Yet when set against the hard details of descriptive data and when applied to historical circumstances on the ground, empirical findings have never quite matched these models.[13]

Such abstract models of "Hinduism" would have to include the neo-advaitin construction of S. Radhakrishnan's *The Hindu View of Life* as well as other modern Hindu constructions of Hinduism. Frykenberg boldly and clearly summarizes the thesis of his paper.

> The central argument of this essay is that, unless by "Hindu" one means nothing more, nor less, than "Indian" (something native to, pertaining to, or found within the continent of India), there has never been any such thing as a single "Hinduism" or any single "Hindu Community" for all of India. Nor, for that matter, can one find any such thing as a single "Hinduism" or "Hindu community" even for any one socio-cultural region of the continent. Furthermore, there has never been any one religion—nor even one system of religions—to which the term "Hindu" can accurately be applied.[14]

---

[10] Gunther D. Sontheimer and Hermann Kulke (editors), *Hinduism Reconsidered* (Delhi, 1989), Introduction by the editors, p.1.

[11] *Ibid.*, p.32.

[12] *Ibid.*, p.33.

[13] *Ibid.*

[14] *Ibid.*, p.29.

W.C. Smith and Robert Frykenberg are not alone in their judgment. Heinrich von Steitencron points out that ever since the term "Hinduism" has been introduced into the study of Indian religions, scholars have sought for an acceptable definition. But the broad religious divergencies in India have stood in the way. Some have centered on vedantic traditions while ignoring folk religion which is not even uniform within itself. Others relied on sociological categories and thereby ignored the religious dimension in attempting to define this "religion." In an attempt to find the essentials of "Hinduism," three ideas were thought to be accepted by all Hindus. They are (1) authority of Vedas, (2) karma and rebirth, (3) and varna and the caste system. von Stietencron goes into some detail to show that none of these are fundamental to all the religious traditions of "Hinduism." His conclusion is that if the term is to be used, it cannot refer to a distinct religion but to a group of distinct Indian religions.[15]

That the term "Hinduism" includes a variety of religious positions and traditions and is less than precise and clear, then, is apparent to an increasing number of scholars in such disciplines as religion, history and anthropology.

I am in agreement with this wide range of modern scholars who hold that the data that has been included within "Hinduism" is exceedingly diverse, that it includes both sophisticated philosophy and folk traditions, beliefs and practices that are dependent upon Vedic traditions and beliefs and practices that ignore them, belief in karma and rebirth and beliefs and lifestyles which ignore such notions, affirmation of the grand world cycles and ignorance of them, monism or tendencies in the direction of monism as well as articulate systems of belief and practice that are diametrically opposed to monism, attempts to affirm the worship of a wide range of deities and positions that limit worship to a specific deity. In the light of this, it would also seem that constructions of "Hinduism" are indeed abstract models which never fit all the actual data of history and frequently appeal to the "Hindu spirit" or some other "reality" that must be found implied within the data or beneath the surface reality and beneath the surface meaning attributed to the data by believers, and are therefore also not empirically verifiable.

Modern discourse has, however, taken the abstract model as historical reality. It is seldom seen, much less conceded, that the basic themes found in all Hinduism, if applied critically, would exclude large numbers of people who have been termed "Hindus." But it is these models of "Hinduism" with which we must work, and given their widespread use, the Constituent Assembly and the Courts have found it necessary to clarify which models are intended when these categories are used.

---

[15] *Ibid.*, p.21.

Religious "Hinduism" as a Basis for Legal Determinations

Since law makes a clear distinction between the religious and legal models or categories of "Hindu" and "Hinduism," the uncertainty of the religious designation might seem to have no bearing on legal matters and court decisions. In fact, there are cases in which the religious meaning of "Hinduism" has no bearing on the outcome of the case. Certain cases which have come before both the High Courts and the Supreme Court deal simply with the extent of legal "Hinduism." Some of them indicate that certain movements fall within *legal* "Hinduism," that is, that "Hindu Law" applies to them. Two cases dealing with the Lingayat sect will illustrate this point. The issue of adoption was raised in a 1960 case which came before the Mysore High Court. The issue was whether a Lingayat could adopt his wife's brother and the question was whether it was valid in law. While the opinion was offered that the Lingayats were "within the fold of Hinduism" and were a reform movement, the issue of the case hinged on the fact that quite apart from notions of religious Hinduism and whether they are *sudras* within the caste system, "the general Hindu law applies to them."[16] The Advocate for the appellant appealed to a prior case before the Privy Council which held that

> The ordinary Hindu law is presumed to apply to Lingayats except in so far as is shown that they have superseded it by their customs and in the absence of proof of any special custom among the Lingayats, there can be no ground for a successful argument in that direction.[17]

This same judgment is expressed clearly in *Tirkangauda Mallangauda* v. *Shivappa Patel*.[18]

> Whether the Lingayats are Hindus or not, we are concerned to see what is the law by which they are governed, and ever since the ruling in *Gopal Narhar Safray* v. *Hanumant Ganesh Safray*, ILR 3 Bom 273 they have been subject to Hindu Law as applied to Shudras.

Based on that statement, the Supreme Court held *in Guramma* v. *Mallappa* that

> In this case it is not necessary to express our opinion on the question whether Lingayats are Sudras or not, for we proceed on the assump-

---

[16] *Sangannagouda* v. *Kalkangouda*, AIR 1960 Mysore 147, at 150.

[17] *Ibid.*, p.149.

[18] AIR 1944 Bom 40.

tion that they are or any rate that the Hindu law applicable to Sudras applies to them.[19]

The case *Shuganchand* v. *Prakash Chand*[20] involved a dispute over adoption and inheritance. Justice Gajendragadkar, writing the judgment, held that although the individual adopting a son was a Jain, and although for Jains adoption is "a purely secular matter,"[21] the legitimacy of adoption is without question because unless a contrary custom is established, Jains are governed by Hindu law. That is, although Jains are distinct from Hindus *religiously*, unless a different practice is established, they are Hindus *legally*.

In *Gogireddy Sambireddy* v. *Gogireddy Jayamma*,[22] a Hindu wife filed a complaint against her husband for marrying a second wife, an offence under sections 11 and 17 of the Hindu Marriage Act (1955). Her husband, the petitioner before the Supreme Court, argued that if he were a Muslim he would not be in violation of any such statute, and therefore the Act discriminated against him as a Hindu. He clearly has religious Hinduism in mind. But the court held that "the body of personal law known as Hindu Law was neither the personal law of all Hindus, nor was it the personal law exclusively of Hindus."[23] As we have shown in The Hindu Marriage Act (1955), legally speaking, Hindus are all those to whom Hindu Law applies. The Court goes to considerable effort to clarify the broad range of those who are legally "Hindus" and that prior to the passage of the Shariat Act, several Muslim communities "such as the Khoojahs, the Cutchi Memons, the Borahs and the Halai Memons were governed by Hindu Law in matters of succession and inheritance."[24] Likewise there were Hindu groups which did not fall under that legal designation. There are not a few cases, then, in which the court determines that a certain person or group falls under the legal designation of "Hindu" without seeking to determine if they are Hindus religiously.

In other cases, both the High Courts and the Supreme Court have considered it necessary to determine whether a given movement was part of *religious* "Hinduism." In *Shyamsunder* v. *Shankar Deo*,[25] the determination was necessitated when the right of an Arya Samaj convert to run for a seat reserved

---

[19] AIR 1964 SC 510 at 520.
[20] AIR 1967 SC 506.
[21] *Ibid.*, p.508.
[22] AIR 1972 Andhra Pradesh 156.
[23] *Ibid.*, p.159.
[24] *Ibid.*
[25] AIR 1960 Mysore 27.

for schedule castes was challenged. It was contended by the Advocate for the appellant that the Arya Samaj organization rejects caste by birth and that when the respondent joined that organization, he not only "professed a different religion from Hinduism," but also, in ceasing to be a Hindu, lost membership in the Samgar caste. The importance of the first question (whether he has ceased to be a religious Hindu) is that Paragraph 2 of the Constitution (Scheduled Castes Order) 1950 stated that "no person who professes a religion different from Hinduism shall be deemed to be a member of a Scheduled Caste." The issue that is raised here is not merely to whom does Hindu Law apply, but who is a Hindu *religiously*. The Court recognizes the status of the question in this way when it states:

> The next question that arises is whether by reason of respondent 1 having become a member of the Arya Samaj, in that way he could be regarded to have professed a religion different from Hinduism.[26]

Although it was noted that the Arya Samaj repudiated caste, and although caste was one of the issues of this case, it was held that Dayanand Saraswati was a Hindu who never repudiated his ancestral religion, but sought to reform it. In the final analysis, what counted for the court was the fact that "the Arya Samaj believes in the supremacy of the Vedas."[27]

In *D.A.V. College, Batinda* v. *State of Punjab*,[28] and again in *A.S.E. Trust* v. *Director, Education*,[29] the Courts reaffirmed that the Arya Samaj was part of the Hindu *religion* and not a separate religion.

No case, however, has been so explicit in seeking to determine the meaning of Hinduism as a religious category than *Yagnapurushdasji* v. *Muldas*.[30] This case had a long history of appeal before it reached the Supreme Court for judgment in 1966.[31]

Seeing that the Bombay Hindu Places of Public Worship (Entry Authorization) Act, 1956 (Act 31 of 1956) and its predecessors which this Act was in-

---

[26] *Ibid.*, p. 30.

[27] *Ibid.*

[28] AIR 1971 SC 1731.

[29] AIR 1976 Delhi 207.

[30] AIR 1966 SC 1119.

[31] This case has been discussed at some length in J.D.M. Derrett, "The Definition of a Hindu," *The Supreme Court Journal*, 1966, pp.67–74; Marc Galanter, *Competing Equalities: Law and the Backward Classes in India* (Delhi, 1984), pp. 305ff; Marc Galanter, *Law and Society in Modern India* (Delhi, 1989), pp.241–248; and V.M. Bachal, *Freedom of Religion and the Indian Judiciary* (Bombay, 1975).

tended to supersede would have required them to open their temples to Harijans, the Swaminarayanan sect sought to sidestep the Act by claiming that they were not a denomination of Hinduism, but rather a distinct and separate religion. The section at issue is section 3 of the Act, described by the Court as follows:

> Section 3 throws open the Hindu temples to all classes and sections of Hindus and it puts an end to any effort to prevent or obstruct or discourage Harijans from entering a place of public worship or from worshipping or offering prayers thereat, or performing any religious service therein, in the like manner and to the like extent as any other Hindu of whatsoever section or class may so enter, worship, pray or perform. The object of the section and its meaning are absolutely clear. In the matter of entering the Hindu temple or worshipping, praying or performing any religious service therein, there shall be no discrimination between any classes or sections of Hindus and others. In other words, no Hindu temple shall obstruct a Harijan from entering the temple or worshipping in the temple or praying in it or performing any religious service therein in the same manner and to the same extent as any other Hindu would be permitted to do.[32]

The appellants, members of the Swaminarayanan sect, known as Satsangis, conceded that they might be considered Hindus for cultural and social purposes, but urged that they were not part of the Hindu religion.[33] Without articulating in detail the abstract model of Hinduism from which they were distinguishing themselves, one can perhaps construct one inferentially from the list of four aspects of their tradition that they felt made them distinct. In the words of the Supreme Court,

> Broadly stated, the case for the appelants was placed before the High Court on four grounds. [1] It was argued that Swaminarayan, the founder of the sect, considered himself as the Supreme God, and as such, the sect that believes in the divinity of Swaminarayanan cannot be assimilated to the followers of the Hindu religion. [2] It was also urged that the temples in suit had been established for the worship of Swaminarayanan himself and not for the worship of the traditional Hindu idols, and that again showed that the Satsangi sect was distinct and separate from the Hindu religion. [3] It was further contended that the sect propogated the ideal that worship of any god other than

---

[32] *Yagnapurushdasji* v. *Muldas*, AIR 1966 SC at 1127.

[33] *Ibid.*, p.1126.

On Defining "Hinduism"

Swaminarayanan would be a betrayal of his faith, and lastly [4] that the Acharyas who had been appointed by Swaminarayanan adopted a procedure of "initiation" (diksha) which showed that on initiation, the devotee became a Satsangi and assumed a distinct and separate character as a follower of the sect.[34]

After dealing at some length with a number of preliminary issues, the Court moved to consider whether or not the Satsangis are Hindus. It was the Court's opinion that "we must inevitably enquire what are the distinctive features of the Hindu religion?"[35] While the court was aware that this might seem inappropriate within the limits of judicial inquiry, and although it was conceeded that it is "very complex to determine,"[36] the issue was judged a "secular" one and the court considered itself "bound to deal with the controversy as best we can."[37]

All attempts whether religious, academic, or judicial, which attempt to construct an abstract model of "Hinduism" begin with the *a priori* that such a thing exists. It is not a matter of it jumping out of the data and asking to be named, but of sorting through the data which apply to "it" and identifying the crucial elements or features.

The Court acknowledges that the data is vast and that the designation was first geographical. It does not rely on judicial precedent in framing its judgment, but as Derrett has pointed out,[38] it relies on authorities who discuss Hindu religion, and it relies on the *Bhagavadgītā*.

All of the authorities to whom appeal is made stress the wide range of Hindu belief and practice. That which had been the obstacle to constructing a model of Hinduism which would fit the concrete data is turned into one of its major characteristics—it is inclusive. The authorities to which the Court appeals also seek to determine what binds this mass of custom and ideas together. Monier Williams used the image of the Ganges, swollen by tributaries and rivulets to show how Hinduism too "is based on the idea of universal receptivity."[39] Radhakrishnan used the image of a tree, likening its branches to the apparently diverse, yet connected beliefs and practices. But beneath it all, for Radhakrishnan, is monism. There is the "non-dual monism" of advaita, the "pure monism" of vishishtadvaita, the "modified monism" of Vallabha, and the "implic-

---

[34] *Ibid.*, p.1126. (Numbers added for analytic clarity).

[35] *Ibid*, p.1127.

[36] *Ibid.*, p.1128.

[37] *Ibid.*

[38] J.D.M. Derrett, "The Definition of a Hindu," *The Supreme Court Journal*, 1966, p.68.

[39] *Yagnapurushdasji* v. *Muldas*, p.1129.

it monism" of Madhva. That even the explicit dualist Madhva is seen as an "implicit monist" indicates how far the data is sometimes stretched in the interest of the abstract model. But these branches are all of the self-same tree. Furthermore, this image is coupled with the notion that truth is many-sided and therefore "this knowledge inevitably bred a spirit of tolerance and willingness to understand and appreciate the opponent's point of view."[40]

Max Muller, in dealing with the six philosophical systems, projects a fund of philosophical knowledge behind the diversity, "a large manasa (lake) of philosophical thought and language far away in the distant North and in the distant past from which each thinker was allowed to draw for his own purposes."[41]

What develops from a less than coherent discussion is a model of "Hinduism" which begins with the Vedas, which holds to karma and rebirth and the world cycles, which is inclusive and tolerant, which has a unified goal of moksha to be pursued by various complementary paths, which includes a variety of gods and scriptures, and which is held together by the "Hindu spirit" or some thread not always visible to the naked eye. This is reinforced with quotations from B.G. Tilak and Arnold Toynbee in addition to the authorities previously cited. Although the Constitution distinguishes between Hinduism, Buddhism, Jainism, and Sikhism as religions, here the Court includes within the model of *religious* Hinduism the Buddha, Mahavira, Guru Nanak, Arya Samaj, Lingayats, and Chaitanya. This model has its highest culmination in the teachings of Ramakrishna and Vivekananda. "...and as the result of the teachings of Ramakrishna and Vivekananda, Hindu religion flowered into its most attractive, progressive and dynamic form."[42] But there is something which holds it all together, for without that, even the abstract model would be impossible.

> If we study the teachings of these saints and religious reformers, we would notice an amount of divergence in their respective views; but underneath that divergence, there is a kind of subtle indescribable unity which keeps them within the sweep of the broad and progressive Hindu religion.[43]

Since the data does not yield a unity on the empirical level, the only solution is to project one and then admit that the unity is "subtle" and "indescribable."

---

[40] *Ibid.*, p.1129.
[41] *Ibid.*, p.1129–1130.
[42] *Ibid.*, p.1130.
[43] *Ibid.*, p.1130.

It is the view of the Court that the Constitution makers held this same view of "Hinduism" when they indicated that for the purpose of temple entry Buddhists, Jains and Sikhs would be considered as Hindus. The Hindu Code Bill was also of like mind. But, as I have pointed out, this is probably not the case since in including these "religions" under the *legal* definition of "Hinduism," they are distinguished from the *religion* "Hinduism." That is, there is the recognition that these do differ as religions, but under law they are treated as one. Hence the Constitution and Parliament both affirm the distinction between the religious and the legal models.

Once having extended the model of religious "Hinduism" as broadly as it did, the Court had little difficulty in determining that the Satsangis were indeed Hindus and that the Act in question did apply to their temples as well as to the temples of other "Hindus."

After a brief survey of the history and beliefs of the Satsangis, the Court held that the contention that they were not part of the Hindu religion was "entirely misconceived."[44] Swaminarayan was a follower of Ramanuja who urged the worship of Krishna and was a Hindu saint who sought to restore the purity of the Hindu religion.

The contentions of the appellants regarding what made them distinct from the Hindu religion were found unconvincing. They contended that no one is a Satsangi by birth but only by initiation, that persons of other religions can receive initiation, that Swaminarayanan is himself treated as a god and is worshipped, that women can receive *diksha*. Special scriptures are honored and special teachers are appointed to worship in the temples.

The Court responded, on the basis of its inclusive model of Hinduism, that frequently in its history a saint or reformer had arisen to restore the tradition to its original purity. And, frequently in the course of time those saints also became the object of worship. Fulfilling its "secular" task, the Court quotes from the *Bhagavadgītā* that whenever religion is in decline and irreligion is in ascendency, God is born to restore the balance and lead the human race to salvation.[45] That members of other faiths undertake *diksha* without ceasing to be members of their own religions simply indicates their desire to absorb the teachings of Swaminarayanan and does not necessitate holding that the sect is not Hindu. The reader is reminded by the Court:

---

[44] *Ibid.*, p.1134.
[45] *Ibid.*

> Didn't the Bhagavad-Gita say: "even those who profess other religions and worship their gods in the manner prescribed by their religion, ultimately worship me and reach me."[46]

The Court concluded that the Satsangis began their suit in 1948 in sincerity,

> but as often happens in these matters, the said apprehension is founded on superstition, ignorance and complete misunderstanding of the true teachings of Hindu religion and of the real significance of the tenets and philosophy taught by Swaminarayanan himself.[47]

Its "secular" task of defining *religious* Hinduism finished, the Court observed that in the light of Article 17 of the Constitution, the issue of the present case is easily decided and the conclusion will be welcomed by the Satsangis themselves. In the light of social reform since the Constitution, the outcome should be obvious to all concerned.

In *Ganpar v. Returning Officer* this inclusive model of religious "Hinduism" is reaffirmed.[48]

> In this connection it is necessary to remember that Hinduism is a very broad based religion. In fact some people take the view that it is not a religion at all on the ground that there is no one founder and no one sacred book for the Hindus. This, of course, is a very narrow view merely based on the comparison between Hinduism on the one side and Islam and Christianity on the other. But one knows that Hinduism through the ages has absorbed or accommodated many different practices, religious as well as secular, and also different faiths. One of the witnesses has described that he considered Buddha as the eleventh Avatar. Indeed there are historians and sociologists who take the view that Buddhism disappeared from India not by any other means but by being absorbed into Hinduism. Therefore if a certain community in a spirit of protest says that they would give up Hinduism and adopt Buddhism it is not likely to make much change either in their beliefs or in their practices. Centuries of habit and custom cannot be wiped out overnight.

---

[46] *Ibid.*, p.1135.

[47] *Ibid.*

[48] AIR 1975 SC 420 at 423–424.

In the 1977 Supreme Court case, *Commissioner for Hindu Religious and Charitable Endowments, Mysore* v. *Ratnavarma Heggade*,[49] the issue turned on whether the Manjunatha temple was a "Hindu" temple and hence to be regulated under the Madras Hindu Religious Endowments Act (2 of 1927). It was the contention of the Board that the temple was a Hindu temple and fell under their jurisdiction. It was determined, however, that it was one of a number of institutions which were part of the "Dharmasthal" which was founded by Heggade who was a Jain. Although the temple in question had a lingam installed in the *garbagriha* and it was worshipped by both Hindus and Jains, finances were handled through the larger complex of institutions called the Dharmasthal. In his supplementary statement which supported the judgment of the court, Justice M.H. Beg articulated an inclusive model for "Hinduism." He pointed out that even today in some quarters the term "Hindu" stands for Indians in general. So, it is not surprising when he seeks to include the Jains within religious Hinduism. "Even as a term used for Indians professing a particular type of beliefs, which are presumed to have an indigenous origin, it is wide enough to include Jains and Sikhs."[50]

But the inclusive model was to play no role in the Court's decision because the Act in question had stated that "for the purpose of this Act, Hindu public religious endowments do not include Jain religious endowments."[51] While Justice Beg was not only arguing that Jains were within the legal definition of Hinduism, but within the religious designation as well, the Act intended to be more restricted.

In 1984, the Supreme Court issued a judgment on a case in which the Ananda Marga cult petitioned that an order prohibiting them from performing the Tandava dance as part of a public procession be set aside. While the order did not prohibit a public procession it restricted the Ananda Margis in that they could not carry human skulls, daggers, swords, tridents, lathis or any other form of weapon in the procession. The court decided that performing the Tandava dance in public was not essential to the profession of Ananda Marga. But in the process of the decision it was necessary to determine if Ananda Marg was a religion in its own right or a denomination within "Hinduism." Quoting from *Yagnapurushdasji* v. *Muldas*, and using an inclusive model for Hinduism it was pointed out that in the development of the Hindu religion, from time to time reformers arose to fight irrational or corrupt practices. But they were absorbed within the Hindu tradition and were not seen as a distinct religion. This was also the case with the Ananda Marga. Although the "essence" was never articulated,

---

[49] AIR 1977 SC 1848.

[50] *Ibid.*, p.1860.

[51] *Ibid.*, p.1852.

the court held that the "writings by Shri Ananda Murti are essentially founded upon the essence of Hindu philosophy."[52] Ananda Marga was seen as falling within the Shaivite order and hence clearly part of Hinduism.[53]

In the light of the inclusive model of *religious* Hinduism articulated by Chief Justice Gajendragadkar and reaffirmed in subsequent cases, one might expect that it would be difficult to argue that one was a minority and not a part of Hinduism. But this issue was pressed again in a case handed down by the Calcutta High Court on October 7, 1985.[54] At issue was the control of appointments by the Ramakrishna Mission of faculty and administrators at Ramakrishna Mission Vivekananda Centenary College, Rahara. By contending that the Ramakrishna Mission was not Hindu, but distinct from religious Hinduism, and a minority religion under Article 30(1) of the Constitution, the Mission sought to maintain control of its appointments and the distinct character of its educational institutions by exempting it from the provisions of the West Bengal College Teachers (Security and Service) Act, 1975 and the West Bengal College Service Commission Act, 1978. If declared a minority religion distinct from Hinduism, they would be placed out of reach of the communist government of Bengal which they believed threatened the distinctive religious nature of their institutions.

In arguing against this claim, the state utilized an inclusive model of "Hinduism" similar to that articulated by the Supreme Court in the Satsangi case. The teachings of Ramakrishna were derived from the *Vedas* and *Upaniṣads*, and were merely an explanation of Hinduism in simple language. Ramakrishna sought to reconcile various Hindu philosophers such as Sankara and Ramanuja. In addition he sought to reconcile not only various Hindu philosophies, but different religious systems such as Hinduism, Christianity and Islam. Ramakrishna was a worshipper and priest of Kali, an important Hindu deity enshrined in the Dakshineswar temple. Swami Vivekananda was an advaitin which is part of the Hindu religion. He went to the World Parliament of Religions in Chicago as a representative of Hinduism and delivered lectures on advaita while there. The monks of the math are Hindu sannyasis, and they continue to observe Hindu rituals and practices. Therefore, it is erroneous to consider the Ramakrishnaites as a minority and as anything other than Hindus.

But the Court saw the issue differently. It began by pointing out that Ramakrishna's teachings could not be considered mere philosophy. They were indeed religion. This distinguished it from the Aurobindo case. Aurobindo's

---

[52] AIR 1984 SC 51 at 55.

[53] *Ibid.*

[54] *Madhab Chandra Bandopadhya and others* v. *State of West Bengal, Calcutta Weekly Notes*, Vol.90, pp.306ff (1985–86).

On Defining "Hinduism"

integral yoga was judged not to constitute a religion. But philosophy is based on "logical reasoning" while the religion of Ramakrishna was based on "a series of religious experiences."[55] That Aurobindo should be distinguished from Ramakrishna on this basis certainly flies in the face of historical data.[56]

But Ramakrishna's religious experience went beyond "Hinduism" to "Religion Universal."[57] The monks of the Ramakrishna order venerate not only Krishna, but also Buddha and Christ, "and, therefore, their performance of Durga Puja does not prove that they are only Hindus and nothing else."[58] In his judgment, Justice Mookerjee refers to the model of "Hinduism" relied upon in the Satsangi case and was bold to quote the statement in the judgment which sees the teachings of Ramakrishna and Vivekananda as the most attractive and dynamic form of Hinduism.

> The development of Hindu religion and philosophy show that from time to time saints and religious reformers attempted to remove from Hindu thought and practice elements of corruption and superstition that led to formation of different sects; Buddha started Buddhism, Mahavir founded Jainism; Basava became the father of Lingayat religion....Guru Nanak inspired Sikhism, Dayanand founded Arya Samaj and Sri Chaitanya began bhakti cult and as a result of the teachings of Sri Ramakrishna and Swami Vivekananda Hindu religion flowered in its most attractive, progressive and dynamic form.[59]

Justice Mookerjee's interpretation of this passage is interesting. He holds that Chief Justice Gajendragadkar did not intend to hold that the faiths mentioned continued as part of the Hindu religion. Yet that seems to be what his language requires. And surely, the language is explicit in saying that Ramakrishna and Vivekananda produced the most attractive and progressive form of the "Hindu religion." The Swaminaryanan sect was surely Hindu since it advocated devotion to Krishna and was based on the vishishtadvaita of Ramanuja.

---

[55] *Ibid.*, p.321.

[56] cf. Robert N. Minor, "Sri Aurobindo and Experience: Yogic and Otherwise," in *Religion in Modern India*, second edition, ed. by Robert D. Baird (Delhi, 1989), pp.393–420. Minor argues convincingly that Aurobindo's system of thought is based on mystical experience and extrapolation from that experience. For Minor's detailed discussion of the Aurobindo case, see chapter 14 of this volume.

[57] *Bandopadhya v. State of West Bengal*, p.321.

[58] *Ibid.*, p.322.

[59] *Ibid.*, p.326.

The Court points out favorably that the trial judge held that the cult and teachings of Ramakrishna were a religious minority distinct from Hinduism on three grounds:

> (i) the religion of Sri Ramakrishna looks upon him as an illustration and embodiment of Religion Eternal which constitutes the core of religious ideals and permits his worship through image.
> (ii) It tolerates all religions and accepts them to be true. It considers all religions to be only different paths leading to the same goal.
> (iii) It believes in the divinity of man and its practice including worship of man.[60]

Also, although certain of the thoughts of Ramakrishna and Vivekananda remain within the limits of vedantic thought, they do not remain strictly within that basis because of the harmony of all religions and the stress on the unity of all religions.[61]

The Court had no difficulty in distinguishing the Ramakrishnaites from the Arya Samaj (cf. *Arya Samaj Education Trust* v. *The Director of Education*). The Ramakrishnaites do not consider themselves a reformist sect within Hinduism, "do not follow Hindu moral code or accept caste system"[62] and "Even non-Hindus could be followers of the faith." Rather, they profess to practice "World Religion." While all religions seek to attain "purity and perfection," it is the methods of attainment that differ from religion to religion and "the method prescribed by Sri Ramakrishna is a distinct one." Because of its emphasis on the ultimate unity of all religions and its appropriation of celebrations from other religions it constitutes a different method and hence a different religion.

The inclusive model of Hinduism utilized in the Satsangi and succeeding cases could have accommodated the followers of Ramakrishna as well. But, in the interests of preserving the religious control of the College, the Calcutta High Court modified that model so that the Ramakrishnaites became distinct. Both the ideas and even language of "world religion," "religious unity," are found in the thought of Sarvepalli Radhakrishnan. But those dimensions of his thought were ignored. Since this case has not yet been considered on the level of the Supreme Court, the decision does not have finality. [As of this date, it has been several years since the case was decided by the High Court]. But, in the light of Supreme Court statements on Hinduism as a religious category, it is difficult to see the Supreme Court affirming this decision.

---

[60] *Ibid.*, pp.327–328.

[61] *Ibid.*, p.330.

[62] *Ibid.*, p.333.

6

Mandal, Mandir, Masjid: The Citizen as Endangered Species in Independent India

Gerald J. Larson

Introduction

Four recent analyses in the political and scholarly literature about contemporary India have provided the intellectual framework and stimulus for what I propose to argue in this paper, and let me begin by citing some relevant passages from these analyses. There is, first, the comment by Dipesh Chakrabarty in his essay, "Invitation to a Dialogue":

> In the India of today one can discern two kinds of political 'languages.' One is the language characteristic of the project of nation-building and involves the rituals of the state, political representation, citizenship, citizen's rights, etc. This is part of our colonial heritage and it is what Indian nationalism owes to the colonial experience. The other language derives its grammar from relationships of power, authority and hierarchy which pre-date the coming of colonialism, but which have been significantly modified by having been made to interact with ideas and institutions supported by British rule...it would be fair to say that historically the first language has been by and large a privilege of the Indian elite classes, while the lives and aspirations of the subaltern classes have been enmeshed on the whole in relationships articulated in the second...the 'codes' of politics in the subaltern domain derive from power-relationships and ideological formations that pre-date colonialism and the importation of the idea of 'citizenship'....To go back to our earlier metaphor, the language of class in India overlaps with the language of citizen-politics only in a minority of instances. For the greater part of our daily experience, class relations express them-

selves in that other language of politics, which is the politics of a nation without 'citizens.'[1]

Second, there is the following comment by the Rudolphs in their work, *In Pursuit of Lakshmi*. Referring to the "centrist ideology" of secularism, they comment:

> The founding myth was constructed between 1885 and 1947 out of the experience of the nationalist era and the trauma of partition. It was sustained for thirty years after independence by Nehru's avoidance of the latent contradictions in the meaning of secularism as the nationalists had defined it. It was challenged after 1980 when mounting distrust and conflict among Sikhs, Hindus, and Muslims made the latent contradictions manifest....The contradiction in India's concept of secularism was its simultaneous commitment to communities and to equal citizenship.[2]

There is, third, Marc Galanter's concluding comment in his work *Competing Equalities*:

> The Indian example is instructive: India has managed to pursue a commitment to substantive justice without allowing that commitment to dissolve competing commitments to formal equality that make law viable in a diverse society with limited consensus. The Indian experience displays a principled eclecticism that avoids suppressing the altruistic fraternal impulse that animates compensatory policies, but that also avoids being enslaved by it. From afar it reflects to us a tempered legalism—one which we find more congenial in practice than in theory.[3]

Finally, there is the recent comment by Khushwant Singh:

> During British rule, the largest proportion of government jobs (40%) was held by Kayasthas. Today their figure has dropped to 7%. Next came the Muslims who were given special privileges by the British. They had 35% of jobs in 1935. In free India their representation has dropped to 3.5%. Christians, likewise favoured by the English, had

---

[1] Dipesh Charkrabarty, "Invitation to a Dialogue," in Ranajit Guha, ed., *Subaltern Studies IV: Writings on South Asian History and Society* (Delhi, 1985), pp. 375-376.

[2] Lloyd I. and Susan H. Rudolph, *In Pursuit of Lakshmi* (Chicago, 1987) pp. 38-39.

[3] Marc Galanter, *Competing Equalities* (Berkeley and Los Angeles 1984), p. 567.

15%; their figure has dropped to 1%. Scheduled castes, tribes and backward classes, who had hardly any government jobs, have achieved a representation of 9%. But the most striking contrast is in the employment of Brahmins. Under the British, they had 3%—fractionally less than the proportion of their 3.5% of the population. Today they hold as much as 70% of government jobs—I presume the figure refers only to gazetted posts. In the senior echelons of the civil service from the rank of deputy secretaries upwards, out of 500, there are 310 Brahmins, i.e., 63%; of the 26 state chief secretaries, 19 are Brahmins; of the 27 Governors and Lt. Governors 13 are Brahmins; of the 16 Supreme Court judges, 9 are Brahmins; of the 330 judges of High Courts, 166 are Brahmins; of 140 ambassadors, 58 are Brahmins; of 98 vice-chancellors 50 are Brahmins; of 438 district magistrates, 250 are Brahmins; of the total of 3,300 IAS officers, 2,376 are Brahmins. They do equally well in electoral posts. Of the 530 Lok Sabha members, 190 are Brahmins. Of 244 in the Rajya Sabha 89 are Brahmins. These statistics clearly prove that this 3.5% of the Brahmin community of India holds between 36% to 63% of all the plum jobs available in the country.[4]

Common to all four analyses is a keen awareness of the dramatic inequities in modern India, a keen awareness of the dilemma or even contradiction between India's commitment to communities versus India's commitment to equal citizenship, a keen awareness that the political balancing act between these competing commitments that worked so well in the first decades of independence is proving impossible to sustain over the long haul, and a keen awareness that issues of caste and religion continue to be remarkably salient features for any adequate understanding of the social reality of independent India.

A Nation Without "Citizens"

The title of my paper, namely, "Mandal, Mandir, Masjid: The Citizen as Endangered Species in Independent India," probably creates the impression that I shall be arguing for the preservation of the endangered species, "citizen," and for the corollary notions of the secular state, a common civil code and the further development of India as a modern, industrial nation-state. But, alas, that is not what I want to argue. I want to argue, rather, the opposite position, namely, that it may well be time to call into question what is meant by such well-known

---

[4] Khushwant Singh, in Sunday: 23-29, December, 1990, p. 19, and cited in Dominic George, "Mandal Commission and the Future of Dalits," *Journal of Dharma*, Vol. XVI, No. 1, Jan.-March 1991, 67.

notions as "citizen," "equality," "caste," "community," "class," and "religion" in modern India. This is not to suggest, let me hasten to add, that I favor a regressive move back to some pre-colonial environment of "a nation without 'citizens'" or that I am in any way opposed or skeptical about the progressive development of India as a modern, industrial nation-state. The former alternative (the regressive move), in any case, is as silly as it is impossible. The latter alternative (the progressive move) is, of course, to be desired, but cannot be attained, I am inclined to think, (a) without a rigorous critique of the discourse of modernity in India, (b) without a fundamental settling of accounts with the indigenous intellectual and spiritual traditions of India that allows those indigenous traditions a meaningful place in independent India, and (c) without some fundamental shifts in the policies and priorities of India as a modern nation-state growing out of the critique of modernity and a more substantive appropriation of the nation's indigenous intellectual and spiritual traditions.

I choose the triad "Mandal, Mandir, Masjid" for my title in order to highlight the three most obvious dimensions of India's social reality involved in the challenge to the discourse of modernity: (1) the so-called "Other Backward Classes" (OBCs) or the "Socially and Educationally Backward Classes" (SEBCs) as analyzed and described in the Report of the Backward Classes Commission, the Chairman of which was B. P. Mandal;[5] (2) the so-called "Hindu majority" (as

---

[5] *Government of India Report of the Backward Classes Commission*, First Part (Volumes I & II) 1980, submitted by B. P. Mandal, Chairman of the Commission, to President Neelam Sanjiva Reddy on December 31, 1980, 130 pp. The need for a Commission "to investigate the conditions of backward classes" is set forth in The Constitution of India, Article 340. A first Commission, under the chairmanship of K. Kalelkar, did its work between January of 1953 through 1955. Its recommendations, however, were not accepted for a variety of reasons, largely because there were inconsistencies in the collection of data coupled with a great deal of dissension among Commission members, including the dissent of the Chairman himself. A second Commission was appointed by Prime Minister Morarji Desai on March 21, 1979 with B. P. Mandal as Chairman of the Commission. Following two extensions the Report was finally submitted in December of 1980 when Indira Gandhi was Prime Minister. The Mandal Report established criteria for identifying OBCs, argued that caste could legitimately be used as one factor in identifying backward classes, clearly separated economic backwardness from social and educational backwardness thereby denying that the problems of the backward classes were only economic rather than social or educational, and made a number of recommendations, including a job reservation quota of 27% for OBCs in central government jobs and schools, special educational facilities for OBCs and a variety of special programs and financial grants and loans for OBCs. Although the Commission determined that the percentage of OBCs is actually some 52% of the population of India, over and above the 22.5% made up of Scheduled Castes and Scheduled Tribes, the Commission recommended only 27% reservations for OBCs so that the combined total of reservations would not exceed 50% of the population, that is to say, 22.5% for SCs and STs and 27% for OBCs for a total of 49.5% reservations overall. The 50% limit was in keeping with previously established guidelines in various Supreme Court

symbolized by the Hindu term for "temple," Mandir); and (3) the so-called "Muslim minority" (as symbolized by the Muslim term for "mosque," Masjid).[6]

decisions. Mrs. Gandhi's government did not implement the Mandal Commission recommendations, although Congress (I) and most other political parties indicated support for the Commission's recommendations. Finally, on August 13, 1990, Prime Minister V.P. Singh issued a Government Order implementing one part of the Mandal recommendations, namely, that portion establishing a job reservation quota of 27% for central government jobs. This triggered a major political explosion in India, including a series of self-immolations by forward caste young people, that eventually played an important role in bringing down the V. P. Singh government. The most recent development is the Government Order of September 25, 1991, under the Prime Ministership of P. V. Narasimha Rao, establishing a reservation quota of 60%, including 22.5% for SCs and STs, 27% for OBCs, and 10% for economically backward forward castes or classes. Also, in the new Government Order, an economic criterion is introduced in order to insure that the economically backward OBCs receive preferential treatment rather than the economically advanced among the OBCs.

[6] If the term "Mandal" symbolizes the social reality of the OBCs or the SEBCs, then the terms "Mandir" and "Masjid" are meant to symbolize the raging conflict between Hindus and Muslims known as the Babri Masjid-Ramjanmabhoomi controversy. I shall assume a general familiarity with this controversy by the reader. By way of a brief summary of the salient events in the controversy, the following: It is claimed by some Hindus that in the year 1528 in the city of Ayodhya in what is now Uttar Pradesh in north India, a certain Mir Baqi, a lieutenant of the first Moghul emperor, Babar, tore down a temple that marked the birthplace of Lord Rama (hence, the expression "Ramjanmabhoomi" or "place of birth of Lord Rama") and built in its place a mosque in honor of the Emperor Babar (hence, the expression "Babri Masjid" or "the mosque of Babar"). There is hardly any evidence to support this claim prior to the nineteenth-century. Very little is known about the city of Ayodhya in ancient times, even whether there was such a place in the conjectured "time" of Lord Rama. Even murkier is the matter of determining the birthdate and place of the divine Lord Rama! Clearly we are in the realm of religious belief for which no historical evidence could possibly count one way or the other. It is the case, nevertheless, that by the nineteenth-century many believed that the location of the Babri Masjid was on the site of the Ramjanmabhoomi. Armed conflict between Hindus and Muslims regarding the site occurred in 1853, again in 1855 and during and after the Mutiny in 1857. Shortly thereafter a compromise was worked out whereby both religious communities could worship at the site, with Hindus using a raised platform (*chatbutara*) for their *puja* in the outer enclosure of the Masjid by the eastern gate or entry to the site, and with Muslims continuing to use the interior of the mosque but only by entering through the northern gate of the site. Tensions continued over the site in the following decades, but it was not until after Independence that a major conflict arose. On the night of December 22–23, 1949 Rama and Sita idols "miraculously" appeared inside the mosque, and the local District Magistrate, in order to avoid further communal conflict, ordered the entire mosque complex locked. He did not, however, demand that the Hindu idols be removed nor did he prohibit Hindu puja at the site. For all intents and purposes, then, the site became a Hindu place of worship, for it obviously could no longer be used by Muslims for worship, locked or not. On October 7, 1949 the Vishva Hindu Parishad (the "World Council of Hindus"), a conservative Hindu organization, began a campaign called "*tala kholo*" or "Break or open the lock!" The campaign was aborted, however, because of the political confusion over

I use the expression "so-called" for each of the three dimensions of social reality, since I am inclined to agree with those who argue that all three designations, namely, OBCs or SEBCs, "Hindu majority," and "Muslim minority" are at best ambiguous designations, at worst serious distortions of contemporary social reality in India. Regarding the designation "OBCs" or "SEBCs," one thinks of the work of the Rudolphs (*In Pursuit of Lakshmi*) who argue that the OBCs represent the "middle peasants" who are rapidly emerging as a "hegemonic agrarian class" (since the early 1970s), making up about 34% of agricultural households but controlling some 51% of the land, especially in the northern Hindi heartland states and Gujarat but also increasingly in the southern and western regions of Karnataka and Maharashtra. The Rudolphs suggest, furthermore, that the OBCs are best understood as the "status aspect" of what they call the "bullock capitalists."[7]

> Bullock capitalists are an economic category grounded in the means and relations of production; the backward classes are defined by the traditional ritual ranking of caste, modified by the British and Indian "official" sociological rankings of India's disadvantaged...the backward castes are the status aspect of bullock capitalists.[8]

---

the assassination of Mrs. Gandhi on October 31, 1984. The campaign was resumed on October 25, 1985 with the additional demand that the Babri Masjid be torn down and a Rama temple be constructed on the site. Finally, on February 1, 1986 a judge of the District Court ordered the locks on the Masjid opened so that Hindus could enter the grounds. At this point the Muslim community became alarmed and formed the BMAC (Babri Masjid Action Committee) in order to stop the Hindu onslaught on the Babri Masjid. Thereafter the VHP started an additional campaign to collect bricks from all over Hindu India in order to construct the proposed Rama temple. Some 200,000 villages sent bricks, and the foundation stone for the proposed temple to Rama was laid on November 9, 1989. In October of 1990 a sacred "chariot journey" (*Rath Yatra*) was begun by L. K. Advani, then president of the conservative Bharatiya Janata Party, from the sacred site of Somnath in Gujarat through Bihar and eventually into Uttar Pradesh and Ayodhya. The journey was never completed, however, for Advani was arrested. In any case, this controversy together with the previously summarized controversy over the Mandal Commission were crucial factors in bringing down the V. P. Singh government. Since then, because of the new elections and the assassination of Rajiv Gandhi, the plan to tear down the Masjid and to construct the temple to Lord Rama has yet to be realized. For a good, albeit overly polemical, discussion of the Hindu side of the controversy, see Koenrad Elst, *Ram Janmabhoomi vs. Babri Masjid: A Case Study in Hindu-Muslim Conflict* (New Delhi, 1990), 173 pp. For a good discussion of the Muslim side, see Asghar Ali Engineer, ed., *Babri-Masjid Ramjanmabhoomi Controversy* (Delhi, 1990), 247 pp. For a balanced, careful and precise scholarly account of the controversy, see Sushil Srivastava, *The Disputed Mosque: A Historical Inquiry* (New Delhi, 1991), 142 pp.

[7] Rudolph and Rudolph, *Loc. cit.*, pp. 52–55.

[8] *Ibid.*, p. 54.

Mandal, Mandir, Masjid 93

Whatever else may be said, we surely can all agree that the designation "Other Backward Classes" is hardly an adequate description and that this important sector of India's social reality requires much more precise treatment. Regarding the designations "Hindu majority" and "Muslim minority," one thinks of the provocative work of Rajni Kothari (*Politics and the People: In Search of a Humane India*) who suggests that it is basically misleading to use the terms "majority" or "minority" in describing the social reality of independent India.

> And yet one must recognize that of late, for the last 15 years at least, there has been a set of problems which has today brought us to a point of crisis in respect of this very relationship between the Hindu 'majority' and the various minorities. By minorities I don't only mean Muslims and Sikhs and Christians but also the great diversity of tribals and large parts of Hindu society itself, *viz.*, its various peripheries such as the Dalits and various other socially depressed and 'backward' castes and communities. They are all minorities. In fact, one way to think about India is as a people and a land made up of a series of minorities. For Hindu society itself is internally highly structured and diverse and pluralistic. There are castes and sub-castes and clans and all manner of groupings and sub-groupings. You go in any region and you will immediately be told that there is this caste and that caste, this grouping and that grouping, this ethnic identity and that ethnic identity—it is all really a set of minorities. It is thus wrong to think of Hindus as a 'majority' except that it is being thought like that of late and that is what is causing the problem.[9]

The last line of Kothari's comment, *mutatis mutandis*, could equally be written with the words "Muslim" and "minority" substituting for "Hindu" and "majority." Thus, the expression "so-called" seems fully justified when referring to the "OBCs" or "SEBCs" (Mandal), the "Hindu majority" (Mandir), and the "Muslim minority" (Masjid). Nevertheless, it is clear enough that the critique of modernity is arising precisely in these sectors of India's social reality however one wishes to quarrel with the designations.

Substantive versus Formal Discourse

But perhaps enough about what I propose to argue and my ruminations about the idioms being employed in my title. Turning instead to my argument

---

[9] Rajni Kothari, *Politics and the People: In Search of a Humane India*, Volume II (Delhi, 1990), p. 485.

itself, what occurs to me as I read the literature regarding Mandal, Mandir, Masjid and the sorts of analyses highlighted in the introduction to this paper (namely, the comments of Chakrabarty, the Rudolphs, Galanter and Khushwant Singh) is not so much the polarity or distinction between "community" and "citizen," or put another way, the purported "contradiction" between independent India's "...simultaneous commitment to communities and to equal citizenship," but, rather, what appear to be remarkable equivocations in the very terms of the distinction, that is to say, equivocations in the notions of "citizen," "community," and so forth, themselves. In other words, the problem is not simply one of sorting out a dual commitment to "community" and "citizen" but a prior duality or multivalence regarding the referents of the constituent terms. These equivocations operate in a variety of ways and on various levels of subtlety. I shall call attention here to only one rather obvious level of equivocation, that between substantive in contrast to formal characterizations of certain fundamental notions, or put another way, empirical, *a posteriori,* actual or real, in contrast to logical, *a priori,* theoretical or ideal. In each instance the equivocation can be related to a current debate in order to highlight how the equivocations complicate various political and theoretical issues in present day India (such as those symbolized by Mandal, Mandir, Masjid).

First, and perhaps most obvious, is the equivocation between the notion of "substantive equality" in contrast to "formal equality." Sometimes this is expressed as the difference between equality of results, on the one hand, and equality of opportunity or equality of treatment, on the other. Andre Beteille, in his recent debate with Louis Dumont characterizes the distinction as one between "distributive equality" and formal equality of opportunity:

> Equality of opportunity can be made into a principle of universality and nothing more by being delinked completely from all considerations of distribution. The crucial question about equality today turns on the way in which we view the relationship between equality of opportunity and distributive equality. There are those who would seek a balance between the two, and there are those who would define the first so as to exclude the second.[10]

---

[10] Andre Beteille, "Individualism and Equality," *Current Anthropology,* Vol. 27, No. 2, April 1986, p. 127. See also the responses to the article by A.S. Ahmed, N.J. Allen, A.T. Carter, T. Ingold, G. Lock, M.N. Srinivas, and H. Varenne together with Beteille's own further response, *Ibid.,* pp. 128-133. See also Louis Dumont's reply to Beteille, entitled "On Individualism and Equality," *Current Anthropology,* Vol. 28, No. 5, December 1987, 669–672; also, Andre Beteille's "Reply," *Ibid.,* 672–676.

This in turn clearly relates to a parallel equivocation between "substantive individuality" in contrast to "formal individuality" or what might be called "substantive citizenship" in contrast to "abstract" or "formal citizenship." I have in mind here, of course, the work of Dumont, Marriott, *et al*, regarding the nature of the "individual" or "citizen" in Indian tradition. Dumont by focusing on hierarchy, holism, and so forth, in South Asian notions of caste has wanted (theoretically) to deny that there is a notion of "individualism" in terms of what I am calling substantive individuality or substantive citizenship. Dumont, rather, reserves "individualism" for the modern, ideological and largely European notion of formal or abstract individualism which correlates with egalitarianism in the sense of equality of opportunity.[11] Similarly McKim Marriott is inclined to deny the notion of substantive individuality preferring instead the notion of "dividuality" because of the "transactional" "fluidity" of caste in South Asia which is dramatically different from the western notion of the isolated or abstract "individual."[12] Andre Beteille in his article "Individualism and Equality" has cogently shown, however, that one need not buy into the Dumontian interpretation of the "individual" and that "individuality" does not necessarily entail "egalitarianism" in the Dumontian sense.[13] The issue here, of course, is that what is usually portrayed as a dual commitment to individuals and communities is, in fact, in an important sense a dual commitment to two kinds of individuals, namely, a substantive individuality or a substantive citizenship, a sort of contextualized notion of "citizen" in which notions of community identity and personal law are paramount, in contrast to a formal individuality, the notion of the abstract individual or "citizen" in which notions of equality before the law, equality of opportunity or equality of treatment apply. When interpreting *The Constitution of India*, therefore, when dealing, for example, with Mandal, Mandir, Masjid, or when dealing with the directive principle of developing a common civil code or when dealing with issues of personal law, it is only partially correct to see the problem as one between a dual commitment to communities and individuals. More to the point is a fundamental equivocation regarding the nature of individuality (and thereby notions of "person" and "citizen") in independent India, and it is by no means obvious that substantive equality or substantive individuality are in any way of less value in all instances than formal equality of opportunity or the notion of equality before the law.

---

[11] Louis Dumont, *Homo Hierarchicus* (Chicago, 1980; second revised edition), pp. 4–8 and passim.

[12] McKim Marriott, "Hindu Transactions: Diversity without Dualism," *Transaction and Meaning*, B. Kapferer, ed. (Philadelphia, 1976), pp. 109–142.

[13] Beteille, "Individualism and Equality," *Loc. cit.*, pp. 121–128.

Second, I would call attention to an equivocation between the notion of "substantive caste" in contrast to formal notions of caste. There is, of course, no more highly contested dimension of Indian studies today than the raging debates over caste and the role of caste in understanding South Asian social reality. Suffice it to mention the names of Dumont, Gould, Marriott, Beteille, Srinivas, Daniel, Appadurai and Inden. Two recent publications in particular have shown all of us who work in South Asian studies that some fundamental rethinking is required concerning caste. I have in mind Arjun Appadurai's provocative review article, "Is homo hierarchicus?" and, of course, Ronald Inden's important book, *Imagining India*.[14] In this context there is no need to enter into these lively debates other than to point out that abstract or formal notions of caste (a la Dumont and other "classic" studies) or diatribes in the modern political literature against "casteism" may seriously mislead the researcher from seeing how caste as a substantive notion is undergoing some interesting shifts in contemporary India. One thinks here of Rajni Kothari's well-known comment that "...those in India who complain of 'casteism' in politics are really looking for a sort of politics which has no basis in society."[15] I also have in mind the intriguing typology of caste set forth in Marc Galanter's "The Religious Aspects of Caste: A Legal View" in which at least three distinct kinds of caste are identified, a "sacral view of caste" (involving ritual-rank ordering), a "sectarian view of caste" (involving isolable caste groups based on sectarian religious orientation but without ritual-rank ordering), and an "associational view of caste" (involving voluntary associations without rank ordering and without any particular religious orientation).[16] The issue here, of course, is that the latter two types of caste, rather than being obstructions in the sense of abstract or formal notions of "casteism," may represent, rather, substantive and promising bases for the development of stable, autonomous voluntary associations in independent India. In other words, it is not at all obvious that substantive notions of caste have no place in the future of independent India. Moreover, if Inden is on the right track, sectarian and associationist views of "substantive caste" in contrast to formal, theoretical ideas of ritual ranking may have been much more prominent in traditional India than we usually realize.

Third, one can point to an equivocation between notions of "substantive community" in contrast to "formal community." Here, of course, one thinks of

---

[14] Arjun Appadurai, "Is homo hierarchicus?," in *American Ethnologist*, 1986, 745-761, and Ronald Inden, *Imagining India* (Oxford, 1990), 299pp.

[15] Rajni Kothari, *Caste in Indian Politics*, cited in *Report of the Backward Classes Commission* (Mandal Report), 1980, *Loc. cit.*, p. 18 and p. 62.

[16] Marc Galanter, "The Religious Aspects of Caste: A Legal View," in D. E. Smith, ed., *South Asian Politics and Religion* (Princeton, 1966), pp. 277–310.

the so-called "centrist ideology" of the secular state in independent India which formally recognizes the existence of a great variety of communities and seeks to maintain a respectful neutrality towards all without favoring any one. This is a purely formal or abstract notion of community almost always linked with the modern notion of "pluralism." In contrast are the substantive communities themselves, for the most part religious, which operate with quite different notions of secularity. Ainslie Embree has expressed the matter well, using a Christian idiom:

> In religion the most famous symbol of the ultimate inability to compromise is the Christian assertion, to outsiders so breathtaking in its intolerance, that outside the church there is no salvation. But, properly understood, in one form or another all religious orthodoxies without exception are driven by inner logic to make such a claim.[17]

T. N. Madan has made a similar point only in a more analytically useful way:

> Tolerance is indeed a value enshrined in all the great religions of mankind, but let me not underplay the historical roots of communal antagonism in South Asia. I am not wholly convinced when our Marxist colleagues argue that communalism is a result of the distortions in the economic base of our societies produced by the colonial mode of production and that the 'communal question was a petty bourgeois question par excellence.' The importance of these distortions may not be minimized, but these analysts should know that South Asia's major religious traditions—Buddhism, Hinduism, Islam and Sikhism—are totalizing in character, claiming all of a follower's life, so that religion is constitutive of society....When I say that South Asia's religious traditions are "totalizing," I am not trying to argue that they do not recognize the distinction between the terms "religious" and "secular." We know that in their distinctive ways all four traditions make this distinction....What needs to be stressed, however, is that these religions have the same view of the relationship between the categories of the "religious" and the "secular."...the search for secular elements, in the cultural traditions of this region is a futile exercise, for it is not these but an ideology of secularism that is absent and is resisted. What is important, there-

---

[17] Ainslie Embree, *Utopias in Conflict* (Berkeley and Los Angeles, 1990), p. 14.

fore, is the relationship between the categories, and this is unmistakably hierarchical, the religious encompassing the secular.[18]

In other words, the substantive religious communities in South Asia are without exception "totalizing" in the sense that they place a higher value on the "religious" than on the "secular." There may, of course, be a broad tolerance, as, for example, in Hindu and Buddhist traditions for the most part, but substantive communities give primary allegiance to particular and concrete values (either in terms of orthodoxy or orthopraxy) that cannot be reduced to abstract or formal notions of pluralism. And, regarding the latter, namely, abstract or formal notions of "pluralism," it is debatable whether abstract or formal community is even a cogent notion, but more about that in the sequel.

Fourth, I would call attention to an equivocation between notions of "substantive class" in contrast to "formal class." Here I am to some extent returning to the introductory comment of Dipesh Chakrabarty when he comments: "...the language of class in India overlaps with the language of citizen-politics only in a minority of instances. For the greater part of our daily experience, class relations express themselves in that other language of politics, which is the politics of a nation without 'citizens.'"[19] Formal notions of "class," whether referring to private capital and the bourgeoisie or to organized labor, have very little substantive meaning in independent India, which is why so much of Marxian analysis in Indian writing has the flavor of speculative idealism. As the Rudolphs have shown in their analysis of India's political economy, only 10% of India's economy is part of the "organized economy" in which the notion of "class" in a substantive sense has any relevance. The remaining 90% of the "unorganized" economy is divided between small-scale cottage industries and trade, representing 23%, and the agricultural sector, representing 67%. This tremendous difference between the class-oriented "organized" economy and the much larger "unorganized" economy leads the Rudolphs to posit what they call a "third actor" in any analysis of the substantive realities in modern India, the "third actor" being the overwhelming presence of the "state," not only by way of controlling the unorganized economy, but more to the point, by way of its controlling the "commanding heights" of fully two-thirds of the organized economy.[20] The issue here, of course, is to suggest that when the Mandal Commission or other documents (including *The Constitution of India*) refer to "Other Backward Classes" or "Socially and Educationally Backward Classes,"

---

[18] T.N. Madan,. "Secularism in its Place," *The Journal of Asian Studies*, Vol. 46, No. 4, November 1987, p. 751 and p. 753.

[19] Note 1, *supra*.

[20] Rudolph and Rudolph, *Loc. cit.*, p. 22.

one cannot avoid the conclusion, as the Mandal Commission rightly recognized, that one is really speaking about the substantive realities of caste and community, unless one wishes to confine one's comments to the 10% of the population to which "class"-discourse has any relevance. Abstract "class"-discourse in independent India is like the snake in the traditional rope-snake metaphor. It cloaks or hides the substantive realities of caste and community. The issue here also is to suggest that the so-called "positive discrimination" or "compensatory policies" of the Government of India have at least as much relevance for the "Hindu majority" as they do for the various "minorities."

Finally, I would call attention to an equivocation between a notion of "substantive religion" in contrast to "formal religion." This brings us back to the discussion above under the third equivocation ("substantive community" in contrast to "formal community"), since the discussion of community in India is inextricable from the discussion of religion. Earlier I quoted T. N. Madan about the "totalizing" nature of India's religious communities, and let me now take Madan's discussion one step further. Referring to the great religious traditions as encompassing or subordinating the "secular" under the "religious," Madan continues:

> Indeed, the world's great religious traditions do seem to speak on this vital issue with one voice. Or they did until the Reformation made a departure in this regard within the Christian tradition.
>
> Scholars from Max Weber and Ernst Troeltsch to Peter Berger and Louis Dumont have in their different ways pointed to the essential linkages among Protestantism, individualism, and secularization.
>
> You all know well Max Weber's poignant statement that "the fate of our times is characterized by rationalisation and intellectualisation and, above all, by the 'disenchantment of the world.'"...Or, to put it in Peter Berger's succinct summing up, "Protestantism cut the umbilical cord between heaven and earth."
>
> This is not the occasion to go into details of the well-grounded idea that secularization is a gift of Christianity to mankind, but it is important for my present concern to note that the privatization of religion, through the assumption by the individual of the responsibility for his or her own salvation without the intervention of the Church, is very much a late Christian idea.[21]

---

[21] Madan, *Loc. cit.*, p. 753.

This "late Christian idea" regarding the "privatization of religion" is, I would suggest, a first crucial step towards what one might call a "formal" notion of religion in contrast to a "substantive" notion of religion. It is the idea of a religion that operates largely in the realm of one's personal ideas and ideals but that has no necessary relation with the larger social reality. One is entitled to believe whatever one wishes so long as it makes no difference! J. D. M. Derrett has nicely (and wryly) characterized this emerging notion of formal "religion":

> In Europe it is accepted, however, that you are not free to do what you believe religion teaches you to do, but only what the State allows you to do. In America and Australia the same formula, *mutatis mutandis*, prevails. You can have what beliefs you choose, provided you do not act upon them in a manner contrary to that determined by the legislators....Europe learnt, painfully, through the century after 1540 or thereabouts that faith could be detached from behaviour, so that liberty of faith could be secured, provided behaviour did not necessarily derive from or rationally reflect it....The unattractive compromise became a fact, and no amount of religion enables an individual to contravene his country's laws, whatever they are. This naturally comforts those who do not think too deeply.....Could it be said that this is what has happened and is about to happen in India?[22]

The point here is that what the Rudolphs have called "persistent centrism" or "the secularism of India's centrist consensus" is in one important sense a legacy of the notion of formal religion growing out of the Protestant Reformation in western religious thought.[23] It is almost a kind of Indic Civil Religion, somewhat on analogy with the American Civil Religion described by Robert Bellah,[24] a peculiar amalgam of Enlightenment rationality and traditional indigenous themes, an ersatz-construct that speaks softly about things religious but carries a big stick, and that "...naturally comforts those who do not think too deeply."

Towards a "Deconstructive" Conclusion

Much more could be said about each of these five equivocations, namely,

---

[22] J. D. M. Derrett, *Religion, Law and the State in India* (New York, 1968), pp. 556–557.

[23] Rudolph and Rudolph, *Loc. cit.*, p. 46.

[24] Robert N. Bellah, "Civil Religion in America," *Daedalus,* Vol. XCVI, 1967, 1–21.

"substantive equality"	vs.	"formal equality"
"substantive caste"	vs.	"formal" notions of caste (Dumont)
"substantive community"	vs.	"formal community" (pluralism)
"substantive class"	vs.	"formal" notions of class (Marxian)
"substantive religion"	vs.	"formal religion" (secular state).

But let me move on quickly to make my concluding comments. Regarding the "substantive" side of the equivocations, that is to say, "substantive" citizenship, caste, community, class and religion, we begin to come very close to Indian notions of *dharma*, contextualized law or what Galanter has called a "principled eclecticism" and a "tempered legalism." Regarding the "formal" side of the equivocations, that is to say, "formal" equality (the modern citizen), caste (contra "casteism"), community (pluralism), class (the "organized economy") and religion ("privatization" and the "secular state"), we come very close to modern notions of the nation-state and modern notions of law. Prima facie the modern conceptions appear to be universal and applicable in any context, until we read an analysis like that of Khushwant Singh that I quoted at the outset and we begin to realize that the so-called formal or universal or abstract conceptualizations have as much of a social base as do the substantive conceptualizations. In other words, we begin to realize the force of what philosophers call the paradox of self-referentiality. The modern, universal conceptualization is only one more substantive conceptualization, even though it passes itself off as universal. It has, in fact, no privileged place. It can only be one more member of the set of substantive, competing conceptualizations. Putting this into the idiom of modern discourse about the secular state, Peter Berger's comment is instructive. Says Berger:

> The secular community would have to abandon its counterpluralistic tendencies and agree to allow all communities of meaning, including the religious ones, to create their own institutions without interference from an ideologically monopolistic state.[25]

Putting this into the idiom of traditional Indian thought, it is to recognize that the notion of *dharma* still has relevance in independent India, that *dharma*, finally, encompasses abstract or formal notions of law. We are back to "principled eclecticism" and "tempered legalism," to be sure, "...more congenial in practice

---

[25] Peter Berger, "From the Crisis of Religion to the Crisis of Secularity," *Daedalus*, 1982, p. 22.

than in theory," but a substantive insight into the human condition that traditional Indian thought has understood and taught us all along.

Perhaps, in other words, Mandal, Mandir, Masjid, ought not to be dismissed as symbols of reaction, fanaticism, fundamentalism and regression. Perhaps they represent, rather, a powerful and important critique of modernity to which independent India should listen and seek to understand, not simply for political reasons, but for the reason as well of coming to grips with its own historic self-identity.

7

Muslim Personal Law and Political Identity in Independent India

Gregory C. Kozlowski

History is culturally ordered, differently so in different societies, according to meaningful schemes of things. The converse is also true: cultural schemes are historically ordered, since to a greater or lesser extent the meanings are revalued as they are practically enacted. The synthesis of these contraries unfolds in the creative action of the historic subjects, the people concerned.[1]

In contemporary terms, the status of Muslims in independent India seems to be symbolized by an elderly lady and an ancient mosque. Each of these has generated debate, discord and violence on a scale almost unknown since Partition.[2] How have those two sets of events: one originally an interfamily squabble, the other apparently a purely local fracas, come to such prominence in the public life of a nation nearly one billion strong? Scholars as well as journalists seem agreed that the turmoil is the result of communalism:[3] that is to say that pre-existing, religious communities have created clashes over the Shah Bano case and the Babri Masjid. The accounts given by any one commentator are, of course, richer than a brief description conveys. Some tend to assign more blame to fundamentalist Muslims, while others place the onus on militant Hindus. A few fault the character of India's political and legal systems. They chide the former for trying to turn communal discord into a momentary electoral advantage[4] and the latter for succumbing to pressure from politicians. Even so, every

---

[1] Marshall Sahlins, *Islands of History* (Chicago, 1985), vii.

[2] Ainslee Embree, *Utopias in Conflict* (Berkeley, 1990), p. 75ff.

[3] Embree, *Ibid.*; also, A. Engineer, editor, *Babri Masjid Ramjanambhoomi Controversy* (Delhi, 1990); this volume contains over thirty articles on the subject, representing opinion in many Indian newspapers.

[4] V. Mehta, "Letter from New Delhi," *The New Yorker*, August 19, 1991, pp. 66–77.

critic seems agreed that the communities were there before the events.[5] Arguments over the rights and wrongs of a divorced Muslim woman or whether a particular piece of ground in Ayodhya should be occupied by a mosque or a mandir are but occasions for the reaffirmations of ancient, conflicting, religious solidarities.

Certain components of both Hindu and Muslim communal consciousness do have their roots in the distant as well as the nearer past. Among Hindus, a renewed awareness of religious identity, together with an assertive pride in their faith, can be dated to the various reform and revival movements of the nineteenth and twentieth centuries.[6] Among Muslims, reformism appeared as early as Ahmad Sirhindi and Shah Walliullah in the seventeenth and eighteenth centuries. An expanding number of preachers, together with events in the Muslim world outside of India, have given reformists more influence in this century.[7]

Apart from the dynamics of religious revivalism, several other social and political forces have contributed to the current situation. One of those is human fertility. At present, more Muslims, Hindus, and others, living in the subcontinent are engaged in making history. Connected with that is an expansion of print, radio and televison media. A Doordarshani and All-India Radio culture has made hundreds of millions of Indians aware of events in their nation as well as in the world outside of South Asia. Nevertheless, scholarly accounts of modern

---

[5] In terms of European history, the seminal works on communities and collective acts, especially violent ones, are N. Davis, "The Rites of Violence: Religious Riot in Sixteen Century France," in her collection of essays, *Society and Culture in Early Modern France* (Stanford, 1975), pp. 152–87 and E. Thompson, "The Moral Economy of the English Crowd in the Eighteenth Century," *Past and Present*, 50 (1971), pp. 76–136; for a critique of their perspective, S. Desan, "Crowds, Community and Ritual in the Work of E. P. Thompson and Natalie Davis," in *The New Cultural History*, L. Hunt, editor, (Berkeley, 1989), pp. 47–71; historians of South Asia have begun to apply this approach, the most notable example being, S. Freitag, *Collective Action and Community: Public Arenas and the Emergence of Communalism in North India* (Berkeley, 1989).

[6] K. Jones, *Socio-religious Reform Movements in British India* (Cambridge, 1989).

[7] D. Vajpeyi, "Muslim Fundamentalism in India: A Crisis of Identity in a Secular State," in *Religious and Minoritu Politics in South Asia*, D. Vajpeyi and Y. Malik, editors, (New Delhi, 1989), pp. 51–70; A. Ahmad, "The Naqshbandi Reaction," and "The Wali-Ullahi Movement," in *Studies in Islamic Culture in the Indian Environment* (Oxford, 1964), pp. 182–90, 218–38; B. Metcalf, *Islamic Revival in British India: Deoband, 1860–1900* (Princeton, 1982); however, most seem to assume that the reformists have carried the day which is perhaps a premature declaration of victory, see, G. Kozlowski, *Muslim Endowments and Society in British India* (Cambridge, 1985), pp. 73–78.

Indian history stress ideological and political structures rather than the impact of such important, but elusive forces.

The emergence of a hierarchically organized national state, with its origins in the British raj, counts as a significant development.[8] Over the past century, government has affected everyday social life in a way unprecedented in premodern polities. For example, the modern state has given Muslims a Personal Law with rules clearer and more rigorously enforced than in any previous epoch.[9] Since a centralized state's courts have undertaken the enforcement of that law, Muslim Personal Law has become, of necessity, an aspect of public life qualitatively different from the legal practice of premodern Muslim kingdoms, where the Islamic Guide to Conscience (*shariah*) was often out of the purview of the rulers or in conflict with their aims.[10] The courts of India, on the other hand, have supplied two fundamental propositions concerning Muslims and their law which have become part of political life. The first is that all Muslims constitute a community. The second is that all Muslims adhere strictly to a single body of law. Though both ideas concur with those of Muslim reformers,[11] consistent application of those principles by the courts has given those propositions greater reality in the past century than they had in "traditional" Muslim states.

Strictly legal investigations seem to neglect the importance of that development. Academic studies of law tend to follow one of three approaches: formalist, realist and critical.[12] Formalists concentrate on the development of legal doctrine. Realists look at law as part of a more general policy-making enterprise. Proponents of the critical method try to connect law to society at large. With regard to the history of law in India, the formalist and realist perspectives have, with a few prominent exceptions,[13] dominated discussion of the subject. Thus, many histories of law in India are records of statutes and precedents reaching back into the British period. The political aims of the raj's

---

[8] H. Blomkvist, "The Soft State: Making Policy in a Different Context," *Studies in Comparative Politics*, D. Ashford, editor (Pittsburg, forthcoming).

[9] G. Koslowski, "When the 'Way' Becomes the 'Law'," in *Studies in Islamic and Judaic Traditions, II*, W. Briner and S. Ricks, editors, (Decatur, Ga, 1989), pp. 97–112.

[10] M. Hodgson, *The Venture of Islam, I*. (Chicago, 1974), pp. 238, 318, 351.

[11] F. Sheikh, *Community and Consensus in Islam: Muslim Representation in Colonial India, 1860–1947* (Cambridge, 1989); see also reviews of the book by G. Minault, *Journal of Asian Studies*, Vol. 49, no. 4 (November, 1990), pp. 980–82 and G. Kozlowski, *American Historical Review*, Vol. 96, no. 1 (February, 1991), pp. 244–45.

[12] R. Gordon, "Critical Legal Histories," *Stanford Law Review*, 36 (1984), pp. 57–124.

[13] M. Galantar, *Law and Society in Modern India* (Delhi, 1989).

administrators or those of independent India do not weigh heavily in such explanations of the current legal system.

Taken on its own terms, the Constitution of India employs a realist perspective. Law is clearly a matter of government policy. Article forty-four under the heading of "Directive Principles of State Policy," envisions a "uniform code" applicable to all citizens. A commentary on the intent of Article forty-four makes the point plainly enough: "The object of this article is to introduce a uniform personal law, for the purpose of national consolidation. It proceeds on the assumption that there is no necessary connection between religion and law in a civilized country."[14]

This essay follows a critical legal analysis in that it assumes that neither formalist nor realist perspectives adequately explain the complex interactions surrounding the Shah Bano case or the Babri Masjid controversies. It argues that India's many social, legal and political contradictions create communities only in a highly abstract sense. They constitute the fragments of communitarian life, but not communities.[15] Muslims in independent India experience community as a sometime thing. Events such as the Shah Bano or Babri Masjid controversies constitute part of a process in which Muslims are still creating a legal and political identity. The historical present is part of a reevaluation of the past that is something more and less than a restatement of it. Both past and present are being transformed by that interaction, but a persistent Muslim political identity has yet to appear.

As an illustration of that theme, the following essay considers the relationship between Muslim Personal Law, a hybrid artifact of British colonialism, and the practice of *fiqh*: the application of the standards of the Islamic Guide to Conscience (*shariah*) to daily life in general terms. It then turns to a discussion of Shah Bano and the Babri Masjid in the context of that relationship, showing that such specific conflicts become the foci of Muslim political life without really contributing to the foundation of a coherent and abiding political program.

---

[14] D. Basu, *Commentary on the Constitution of India, vol. 2*, Fourth edition (Calcutta, 1962), p. 315.

[15] D. Lelyveld, "Who Gets to Talk, Who Gets to Listen? Oratory and Printing in British India," unpublished paper delivered at the annual meeting of the *Association for Asian Studies*, Chicago, April 7, 1990; for an illuminating consideration of the notion of community, see, J. Ladd, "The Concept of Community: A Logical Analysis," in *Community*, C. Friedrich, editor, *Nomos II, Yearbook of the American Society of Political and Legal Philosophy*. (New York, 1959), pp. 269–93.

Creating Muslim Personal Law

British imperial institutions: courts, law schools and administration, were the agencies which came close to codifying Muslim Personal Law, or as people during the raj called it, "Muhammadan Law." Contemporary Muslim thinkers as different as A.A.A. Fyzee, a secularist, and Mawlana Abul Ala Mawdudi, a leading proponent of Islamic revival, agree on that point. They differ about whether or not that influence is beneficial.[16]

Not all of the Islamic law was taken into account when the British began to codify it in the nineteenth century. Criminal law was largely ignored almost from the start. The last vestiges of it disappeared in 1862 with the passage of the Indian Penal Code and the Code of Criminal Procedure. In 1872, the Law of Evidence eliminated any Muslim influence on that legal matter. Later on, legislation changed the age of majority from puberty to eighteen years of age. Since independence, the government of India has made similar adjustments such as raising the legal age of marriage.[17] Such alterations do not appear to have elicited much comment or opposition from Muslims in India.

By 1947, the only elements of *shariah* recognized by the courts involved questions of marriage and inheritance. In that, the practice of the British and their successors may have resembled that of Muslim states where the *shariah* tended to be restricted to issues of personal status.[18] A more significant development concerned the modern state's restriction of the number of rules applied to Muslims and the hierarchical authority of the courts which enforced them.

As a Guide to Conscience, *shariah* always had as its most important task finding the religiously sanctioned course of action in particular circumstances. Certain accepted principles did underlie that process, but over the centuries differences of opinion emerged among the various recognized masters of *fiqh*: the application of religious tests to individuals. For example, within the Hanafi tradition, texts recorded many disagreements between the eponym of the school, Abu Hanifa, and his closest disciples, Imams Abu Yusuf and Muhammad.[19] In Indian history, the range of practice was further extended by the variety of local customs. In some matters, such as the rights of women to property, South Asian

---

[16] A. Fyzee, "The Reform of Muslim Personal Law in India," *Humanist Review*, 2 (1967), pp. 369–405; also, "The Muhammadan Law in India," *Comparative Studies in Society and History*, 5 (1963), pp.401–15; A. Maududi, *The Islamic Law and Constitution*, K. Ahmad, trans. (Lahore, 1960), pp. 39ff.

[17] A. Fyzee, *Outlines of Muhammadan Law, 4th edition* (Delhi, 1974), pp. 48–50, 55ff.

[18] Hodgson, *Loc. cit.*, pp. 341–48.

[19] Burhan al-din al-Marghinani, *Al-Hidaya*, C. Hamilton, trans., (*Hedaya*), reprint edition (Lahore, 1975), pp. 231–40.

Muslims tended to restrict the opportunities which females had to exercise their Quranic prerogatives, especially in claiming ownership of real estate.[20] Differences went far beyond the distinction between *shiʿas* and *sunnis*. Social status and region largely defined the range of acceptable behavior.

Gradually, as the power of the British increased, their administration and their courts tended to limit the number of rules they would enforce. In general, the courts came to favor a bookish approach to *shariah*. If the Holy Quran demanded that estates be divided in specific portions to specified heirs, then the courts insisted that Muslims obey their own scripture.[21] In several instances, the use of endowments (*waqf*) for instance, the courts of British India created an Islamic law where none had existed before.[22] By contemporary moral standards, such judge made law may have worked to enhance the status of groups, especially women, but the process created a situation in which jurists applied rules which were increasingly distant from the actual practices of Muslims. That point is highly relevant to understanding the Shah Bano controversy discussed below.

While studies of the history of *shariah* during the Mughal period do exist, they tend to explicate the ideal, rather than the actual practice of *fiqh*.[23] The Mughals did not, even at the height of their power, attempt to enforce a single code of Muslim law among all of their subjects. Indeed the apparatus by which they enforced it was very loose. *Qadhi*, the term often translated with the word "judge," in practice referred to a hereditary notable whose most important task was mentioning a ruler's name during the Friday sermon.[24] *Kotwals*, the local imperial officials responsible for maintaining order in a district, apparently meted out justice according to administrative standards which did not necessarily mirror the dictates of *shariah*. Likewise revenue officers dealt with questions on the inheritance of imperial grants which should have been the preserve of *shariah*. They did not always follow strictly its prescriptions.[25]

---

[20] G. Kozlowski, "Muslim Women and the Control of Property in North India," *The Economic and Social History Review I,* Vol. 24, no. 2 (1987), pp. 163–81.

[21] *Ibid.*

[22] Kozlowski, *Muslim Endowments*, pp. 96–155.

[23] M. Akbar, *The Administration of Justice by the Mughals* (Lahore, 1948).

[24] "Life of Guru Nanak," in *Shri Guru Adi Granth*, E. Trump, trans. (London, 1877), pp. 20–30.

[25] B. Cohn, "The Initial British Impact on India: A Case Study of the Benares Region," *Journal of Asian Studies*, vol. XIX, no. 4 (1961), pp. 418–31; S. Rashid, "*Madad-i Ma ʿash* Grants under the Mughals," *Journal of the Pakistan Historical Society*, 9 (1961), pp. 98–108.

If the content of Muslim law was not uniform, was there unanimity among the *ulama*, the guardians of *shariah*? In South Asian history, no single institution enjoyed the kind of authority in matters of *shariah* which, for example, Al-Azhar had in Egypt. Traditions of learning were associated with a number of different families or towns: the Firangi Mahalis of Lucknow, the Abbasis of Ciryacot and the many descendents of Shah Walliullah. The reformist movements of the nineteenth century brought several new trends. Like the Deobandis, reformers tended to anchor themselves in theological schools (*madrasahs*). While that did not obviate the association of sacred knowledge with a comparatively few "learned and holy men," it did shift the focus from individuals to networks of institutions. Even so, almost every prominent Muslim scholar of the past century and a half counted himself, or was regarded by his followers, as a major reformer. Antipathies between various Muslim scholars did not disappear. In contemporary terms, Deobandis, "Barelwis," Ahl-i Hadisis and other associations of religious scholars continue to engage in mutual criticism and condemnation.[26]

Just as the practice of the British courts narrowed the number of precepts accepted as Muslim or Muhammadan law, their own hierarchical organization gave a kind of finality to *shariah* which it could not attain when authority was localized and distributed among many *madrasahs* as well as individuals. Especially after the reorganization of the courts following the Revolt of 1857, a single system of appeal linked a town munsif or subordinate district judge to a series of high courts and the Privy Council in London. Since 1947, the system has changed only slightly; the hierarchical lines now lead to the Supreme Court in New Delhi.

During the raj most of the judges charged with the application of Muslim law were not Muslims. The few who were Muslims were trained in the same law schools as their Hindu and British colleagues. None of the prominent Muslim jurists of the imperial age came from families which maintained a tradition of learning in *shariah*.[27] When independence came in 1947, the court system was taken over from the raj almost unchanged. Today, comparatively fewer Muslims sit on the bench in India—a reflection, perhaps, of the "brain

---

[26] Metcalf, *Islamic Revival, Loc. cit.*; U. Sanyal, *In the Path of God: Maulana Ahmad Riza Khan Barelwi and the Ahl-e Sunnat wa Jama ʿat Movement in British India, c. 1870–1921* (Delhi, forthcoming), based on her Columbia University dissertation of the same title; D. Lelyveld, *Aligarh's First Generation: Muslim Solidarity in British India* (Princeton, 1978); K. Muhammad, *Tazkirat al ʿulamaʾ, A Memoir of the Learned Men of Jaunpur*, M. Sanaullah, trans. (Calcutta, 1934).

[27] *Indian Judges* (Madras, 1932).

drain" to Pakistan, but those who do seem to come exclusively from the ranks of the "modern-trained" rather than the *madrasah* educated.

Since the installation of that judicial system, a number of controversies have occurred concerning the courts' interpretation of Muslim Personal Law. On these occasions, a very few Muslims have objected to non-Muslims applying Muslim law. But most only argue with interpretations provided by a system they accept. Some reform-minded Muslims did call upon believers to eschew the secular courts and solve their disputes by seeking an informed opinion (*fatwa*) from a religious scholar. The results of such appeals have been mixed. The seminary at Deoband issues thousands of those opinions (*fatāwā*) every year. Many of them, however, deal with matters of ritual purity or the etiquette of the pilgrimage. Disputes concerning property, such as Shah Bano's case, tend to find their way into the state courts since they have the means of enforcing the judgments they provide.

Shariah and *Fiqh* Outside The Government Courts

In contemporary India, some of the faithful still submit their disagreements to the arbitration of religious scholars. They may have many reasons for taking that course. Personal piety may move them. Loyalty to a particular, locally prominent, group of scholars and the tendency they represent also influences them. Since *fatāwā* can be used as evidence in the secular courts, some individuals may be seeking confirmation of their side of the argument. Perhaps they come because the cost of obtaining a scholar's opinion is miniscule when compared to the expense of a law suit in the government courts. The following account of the work of one such individual: the *mufti* of a *madrasah* located in Hyderabad, Andhra Pradesh, provides a contrast to the style of governmentally sponsored courts and illustrates this essay's argument that the Muslim Personal Law which those official bodies administer does not fully comprehend the day to day life of Muslims in South Asia.[29]

The *mufti* of the Jamia Nizamiyyah Madrasah usually interviewed clients on his own and issued *fatāwā* on his own authority. The final written version of any opinion, however, bore not only his own signature, but the letterhead of the institution he represented, together with the signatures of the school's chief and a board composed of three or four members of the faculty. On difficult questions, he consulted the other scholars of that council. Such

---

[29] The following account is based on, G. Kozlowski, "Loyalty, Locality and Authority in Several Opinions (*fatwa*). Delivered by the *Mufti* of the Jamiah Nizamiyyah Madrasah, Hyderabad, India," *Social Science Research Council* seminar: "The Making of a *Fatwa*," Granada, Spain, January, 1991.

Muslim Personal Law

instances, he affirmed, were rare, but the procedure of issuing a written opinion made it plain that the *mufti*'s authority derived from the *madrasah* as well as from his own knowledge.

Guidebooks for the conduct of hearings, taking of evidence, and delivering of a *fatwa* recommend what might be called a semi-public approach. Such texts seem most concerned to avoid any appearance of collusion between the scholar and the interested parties.[30] They do not envision an audience much larger than that. Indeed, a certain delicacy in dealing with private matters seems to call for an avoidance of extensive outside involvement. The *mufti* referred to here met with individuals in his study at the Mamia Nizamiyya. About five or six requests for *fatāwā* come in everyday; some in writing, many made by people who simply show up at the school. No previous appointment was necessary, but people generally arrived between the hours of ten and three. If the *mufti* was holding class or otherwise engaged, most individuals waited in an adjoining class room. If, however, the person seeking an opinion was a notable of the local community, the scholar sometimes dismissed a class to confer with him.

When asked to describe the most frequent kinds of issues raised before him, this *mufti* answered, "marital relations and inheritance." How did he go about adjudicating such matters? In response to that question, he pointed to the many volumes lying on tables about him and said, "they tell me what to do." Other skills were certainly crucial to his task. For example, the *mufti* was invariably polite and soft spoken. These things seemed to put his petitioners, most of whom were shopkeepers and farmers, at their ease. Unlike some of the *ulama* who suffer from a "big turban" complex,[31] this man, as well as the *madrasah* he represented displayed a humble demeanor. As one of his colleagues put it, "Learning should not be a barrier between scholars and the pious but ignorant." The *mufti* also exhibited a talent for the penetrating, but non-threatening question. While he conceded that experience aided him in that regard, he attributed even these people skills to what he found "in the books."

The texts he referred to purport to be absolute guidelines. They are also inaccessible to most of the faithful, not only because they are written in Arabic, but because their format, featuring a text surrounded by commentaries, commentaries on commentaries, and all manner of scholia obviously require special training to read. Yet, in practice, the *mufti* managed to negotiate between the absolute authority of the books and the requirements of the individuals engaged in a dispute. For example, he cited a case which concerned a woman's divorce of her husband. According to a literal interpretation of the texts to which the *mufti*

---

[30] al-Maghinani, *Loc. cit.*, pp. 337–38.

[31] Brinkley Messick, "Kissing Hands and Knees: Hegemony and Hierarchy in *Shari ʾa* Discourse," *Law and Society Review*, Vol. 22, no. 4 (1988), pp. 637–59.

pointed, women have few opportunities to divorce their husbands.[32] Yet, in this instance, a woman who had left her husband, taking their children with her, wrote a letter to the man in which she said, "If you come near me again, you will be giving me a divorce (*talaq*)." When her husband, more or less by accident, wandered into the courtyard of the place where she was staying, she insisted that he had thereby divorced her. The *mufti* and the full council of the *madrasah* granted her a divorce. Explaining their decision, the *mufti* said, "What could we do? After all, she did not want to live with him."

Bendings and stretchings of *shariah* texts in this way may fit the day to day needs of particular Muslims. They do not create public, political controversies. They may satisfy or dissatisfy individuals seeking some confirmation of the rightness of their own position and the wrongness of their opponents, but those who feel themselves the losers must chose between allowing the conflict to slide gradually into obscurity or of taking the matter into a much more public venue. Those who lack the financial resources to fight a suit in the state supported courts are more likely to consign their grievances to familial and local memory. Those possessing the wealth and time may chose to take the matter to a court which is, quite literally, higher.

The *mufti* of the *madrasah* just described meets with his petitioners in his own, book-strewn, study. He sits on a folded quilt only inches higher than his clients who sit on a floor covered by mats. His room also serves as a classroom and a dining room, when he hosts his colleagues for lunch. By contrast the courtrooms originally built during the raj, and which remain unchanged in form in independent India, more closely resemble Protestant churches. Benches set beyond a rail serve as seats for anyone who wishes to witness the proceedings. The rail itself separates those directly interested from that larger audience. The judge's desk is like a pulpit, raised far above participants and onlookers who wait to hear the word. If it is not exactly the word of God, the entire structure of the room seems to indicate that it is the next best thing: the law.

While the *mufti*'s authority rests on his knowledge of Arabic texts and the reputation which his *madrasah* has in its immediate locale, that of the courts rests on their status as governmental institutions. The *mufti* in the divorce case noted above was able to provide a flexible reading of the texts, but the government courts have seldom been so adept at fitting their judgements to individual circumstances. Indeed, the proccedure of the courts works to diminish the influence of the personal and particular. Judiciable points of law are their primary consideration. Because of that almost every dispute among Muslims becomes a

---

[32] Aaron Layish, "*Qadis* and *Shariʾa* in Israel," *Asian and African Studies*, 7 (1971), pp. 237–72, 241–48; L. Carroll, "The Muslim Family Laws Ordinance, 1961," *Contribution to Indian Sociology*, (NS), Vol. 13, no. i (1986), pp. 20–30.

question of Muslim Personal Law. At such times, arguments in court seem to lose any subtlety and become contests in which that law is either excoriated for its supposed inadequacies or defended as the absolute legal norm for all Muslims in the subcontinent.

Shah Bano's Case

A number of nineteenth century law suits which became famous as controversies over Muslim Personal Law began as interfamily disputes.[33] Shah Bano's case began as such a wrangle. It also illustrated the way in which the character of conflict changed when it reached the state courts.

In the early 1930s, Shah Bano married her first cousin Mohammad Ahmed Khan. Such cross-cousin marriages were common enough among some Muslims in South Asia. Mohammad Ahmed some years later demonstrated that by contracting a second marriage with yet another first cousin, Halima Begum.[34]

Marriage between close relatives seemed to be part of an attempt to preserve the social status of families which already possessed some degree of prominence.[35] It appeared to answer the fear that if women married "strangers," they would claim their inheritance rights and call for a partitioning of an extended family's estate. Such fragmentation of economic resources would lead to a decline in social and economic standing. As the Shah Bano case demonstrated, cross-cousin marriage was not entirely successful in forestalling interfamily disputes. The very closeness of the parties involved, both in terms of kinship and residence, often made the conflicts sharper. Something of that sort happened within the extended family to which both Mohammad Ahmed and Shah Bano belonged.

The dispute, which concerned a piece of land in which the entire family had an interest, had been going on for two generations before Shah Bano and her husband took it up. Their arguments became more and more bitter. Shouting matches in the courtyard of their dwelling alternated with long periods when the parties avoided each other and did not speak at all. Since the *haveli* in which they lived had belonged to Mohammad Ahmed's parents and he had his law offices there, when the conflict became too trying, Shah Bano had little choice but to leave. She claimed to have been driven out, while her husband contended that she had left of her own accord.

---

[33] Kozlowski, *Muslim Endowments*, pp. 144ff.

[34] The following is based on S. Naqvi, "The Shah Bano Case: the Real Truth," in A. Engineer, *Loc. cit.*, pp. 66–70.

[35] On cross-cousin marriage in the Middle East, see, D. Eickelman, *The Middle East: An Anthropological Approach* (Englewood Cliffs, NJ, 1981), p. 123ff.

In 1975, when she departed the family home, Shah Bano had three grown sons, all of whom were gainfully employed. She also had a claim to some of the family property. Her sons and daughters, however, were disturbed at their mother's leaving Mohammad Ahmed's dwelling. They feared, apparently, that they would be at a disadvantage to their half-siblings when it came time to divide up Mohammad Ahmed's sizeable estate. They encouraged their mother to take the matter to court. Hoping to head off a full fledged legal battle, Mohammad Ahmed divorced Shah Bano.

Shah Bano made several pleas to the court. Most of them concerned her claims to the disputed piece of family property which caused the trouble between the spouses in the first place. One of her plaints, however, was for maintenance. The First Class Magistrate's court of Indore did award her support by invoking article 125 of the Code of Criminal Procedure, an act adopted almost verbatim from the British original promulgated in 1874. The article's intent was to prevent female vagrancy by forcing husbands to support legally married women whom they had forced out of the marital domicile.

Indian courts had invoked article 125 of the Code on many other occasions, including cases involving Muslim women.[36] Mohammad Ahmed, Shah Bano's attorney husband, was acting as counsel for several women who were making the same plea as Shah Bano. Yet, those suits did not become the pivot points of a national controversy. What was special about that one? Both Shah Bano and her husband displayed a certain skill in managing the media and so the case began to receive considerable public notice. Shah Bano's advanced age, illiteracy and seeming indigence made her not only a good story, but an icon for all of those who have found Muslim Personal Law biased against women. By contrast, Mohammad Ahmed's wealth and assurance that he stood for Islamic principle made him a perfect foil.[37] The familial grievances which prompted the entire matter began to fade into insignificance as the Muslim Personal Law became the focus of the controversy.

When the case reached India's Supreme Court, Justice Chandrachud wrote the opinion. Reviewing his judgment, one finds some token verses from the Holy Qur'an cited, followed, somewhat incongruously, by a passage from *The Laws of Manu*, and a brief quotation on Muslim life in Egypt from the nineteenth century orientalist Edward Lane. On balance, decisions in previous court cases,

---

[36] For example, *Ahmedalli Mohammad Hanif Makandar* v. *Rabiya*, 1977 *Bombay Law Reporter* 238.

[37] N. Mody, "The Press in India: The Shah Bano Judgment and Its Aftermath," *Asian Survey*, Vol. XXVII, no. 8 (August, 1987), pp. 935–53.

many of them given during the raj, were the crucial sources informing Chandrachud's opinion.[38]

Initially, the Congress government backed the Supreme Court's verdict. They put forward as a spokesman Arif Khan of the Ministry of Home Affairs. The Prime Minister even congratulated him after he defended the decision in Parliament.[39] Soon after, the Congress reversed its stance and began to support a piece of legislation known as *The Muslim Women's (Protection of Rights on Divorce) Bill*.[40] By excluding Muslims from the force of article 125 of the Criminal Code, the act made it impossible for other women to follow Shah Bano's example.

Eventually, a group of religious scholars persuaded Shah Bano that the verdict in her favor was contrary to the will of the community. As she is reported to have said, "If the majority of the community thinks it is wrong, how can one individual be correct?" As to the character of that solid community, a footnote to the incident is illustrative. The scholars who argued Shah Bano into renouncing the judgment in her favor were outsiders to Indore and they were associated with the Deobandi school. The imam of Shah Bano's local mosque, who identified himself as a Barelvi, was most upset by this development. He approved of her decision, but deeply regretted that outsiders and Deobandis had got her to make it.[41] When last heard from, Shah Bano was engaged in another law suit attempting to obtain the repayment of her bridal gift (*mehr*) not at its 1932 value of Rs. 3,000, but at its 1980s worth of Rs. 120,000.[42]

Had the original argument over property involved sons and fathers or brothers and brothers it would not likely have become a national dispute, even if some infringement of Muslim Personal Law had been part of it. In almost every society the status of women, especially with regard to property rights, is highly ambiguous. At nearly the same time as the Shah Bano case, some Indian Christians were agitated when the state courts overturned long-standing custom and gave a woman a share in her parents' estate.[43] In other times and places women and domestic politics have become crucial in the conduct of politics.[44]

---

[38] *Mohammed Ahmed Khan v. Shah Bano Begum*, AIR 1986 S.C. 945.

[39] Embree, *Loc. cit.*, pp. 98–99.

[40] For a text of the bill, *Asian Recorder*, Vol. XXXII, no. 24 (June 11–17, 1986), pp. 18927–29.

[41] Naqvi, *Loc. cit.*

[42] Embree, *Loc. cit.*, p. 98.

[43] Embree, *Ibid.*, p. 92.

[44] S. Maza, "Domestic Melodrama as Political Ideology," *American Historical Review*, Vol. 94, no. 5 (1989), pp. 1249–64.

The passion generated in domestic melodramas can become the basis for a challenge to the political status quo. In Shah Bano's case, both critics of the Muslim Personal Law and defenders of it managed to draw opposite conclusions from the same material. While supporters could praise Muslim Law's extension of women's rights, their antagonists could rail against its inadequacies.[45] Among Muslims themselves, individuals divided on the issues. In the end, no single communal view prevailed. The public controversy temporally gave an appearance of community, but as the heat of controversy cooled, the semblance of unity evaporated. The status of Muslim women remains as ambiguous today as it was a century ago.[46]

Mosque, Mandir and Politics

The origins of the controversy over a piece of land in Ayodhya are murkier than those which gave rise to the Shah Bano troubles. Some commentators believe that the Babri Masjid would not have come into the spotlight, if it had not followed so closely the passage of the Muslim Women's Bill. A backlash to the seeming favoritism shown Muslims prompted Hindu demands for access to the mosque and for its conversion into a temple. To them, a certain amount of political cynicism by Rajiv Gandhi and the Congress leadership made it possible for the situation to get out of hand.[47] For others, the violence stemmed from the failure of the government to punish Hindus for their attacks on Sikhs in November of 1984. This gave Hindus the impression that any action on their part would be overlooked by the police. Another sort of backlash, this one by Hindus to Sikh violence in Panjab or the troubles of Kashmir, also appears crucial in some commentaries.[48]

While the root of the national turmoil seems uncertain, the history of the site is as doubtful. The so-called "Hindu fundamentalists" claim that it was the site of the birth of Lord Ram and that a temple from the Gupta era (at least) occupied it until it was demolished by the Mughal emperor Babar sometime around 1527. He ordered a lieutenant to build a mosque from the rubble of the temple.

Archeologists and historians have waded into the struggle with claims of their own. According to them, the mound on which the mosque sits was actually a Buddhist stupa. As for the mosque itself, it was probably built by the Sharqi

---

[45] Kozlowski, "Shah Bano's Case."

[46] A. Thanawi, *Perfecting Women*, a partial translation of his *Bihisti Zewar* by B. Metcalf (Berkeley, 1990), see especially Metcalf's introductions to chapters.

[47] A. G. Noorani, "The Babri Masjic-Ram Janambhoomi Question," *Ibid.*, pp. 56–82.

[48] "Babri Dispute Not a Major Issue," *Ibid.*, pp. 125–28.

sultans of Janpur in the fifteenth century.[49] The inscription linking it to Babar may have been added in the last century after the first affrays over the building. They also point to many disagreements among Hindus themselves concerning the birthplace of Ram, several locations in and around the town having that distinction. Yet, none of these appeals to fact seems to alter the minds of those who say it is the spot and hold that a temple once stood there.

Having a mosque occupied by Hindus is not something unprecedented in the history of India. Especially after 1947, many mosques ceased to serve their usual functions. They have been converted into barns, dwellings and temples. Attempts by Muslims to reclaim them have met with little support from the courts.[50] Therefore, the mere occupation of a mosque might not by itself be a sufficient provocation for reaction.

One source of the trouble lies in the history of the Faizabad-Ayodhya area itself. It has been the scene of mayhem and riot since the middle years of the previous century. Many of the events apparently did not involve the mosque per se. Cow slaughter, for example, caused some of the bloodiest disturbances.[51] Though a distinct minority in the area, Muslims were a highly visible presence, since Faizabad was the capital of the Mughal province of Avadh and, for a time, capital of the Lucknow Nawabs. A certain amount of resentment by the majority may have contributed to attempts to claim the Babri mosque once the British raj removed the Nawabs as potential guardians for a minority which might have seemed overbearing.

As a legal issue, the Babri Masjid does not directly concern the Muslim Personal Law. Rather it concerns the status of Muslims in independent India. In the first law suits of the 1880s, local Hindu holymen contended that they were the owners of the land on which the Babri mosque was located. British district judges held that the mosque could stay, but left a certain amount of uncertainty over the issue by allowing that the Hindu claims might be true, but after several centuries the matter could no longer be decided.

The next stage of the dispute began after independence. Perhaps, local Hindus took the establishment of government in which coreligionists were the majority to redress an injury dating from the British raj. In late December of 1949, two small idols appeared in the mosque. A few pious Hindus asserted that this was a miraculous advent. Muslims and cynics charge that Hindus surreptiously brought them to the mosque. As crowds appeared and local officials began to fear a riot, the magistrate padlocked the mosque. Though Prime Minister Nehru and other leaders ordered the idols removed, local officials

---

[49] S. Shrivastava, *The Disputed Mosque: A Historical Inquiry* (New Delhi, 1991).

[50] S. K. Rashid, *Wakf Administration in India* (New Delhi, 1978).

[51] S. Frietag, *Loc. cit.*, pp. 206–07.

managed to obfuscate the command by repeating their conviction that excessive bloodshed would result.[52] Guards placed in the mosque were not always attentive to their duty. A few priests and devotees were allowed to hold devotions in a semi-private fashion from time to time. This practice gave those who petitioned the courts to give them the permanent right to worship the deities in the mosque a precedent of sorts.

On February 1 of 1986, the district judge of Faizabad issued a writ demanding that the padlocks be broken and Hindus allowed to conduct puja in the mosque. Riots broke out in many other towns of India, but Ayodhya remained fairly calm. Why had the resolution of an old argument failed to move local Muslims to violence, but sparked it in places as far away as Tamilnad?[53] Communalism was identified as the cause. Many blamed Hindu fundamentalists with a political axe to grind, but Muslims also came in for criticism of a similar type. Just as earlier violent incidents in Ayodhya-Faizabad were part of a local tradition of conflict, riots in other towns and cities of India may have also been part of some purely internal pattern activated by events in Uttar Pradesh.

If nothing else, the reaction to the opening of the Babri mosque demonstrated the close connection between law, politics and religion. Religiously inspired violence suddenly seemed to constitute a serious threat to that hoary conjunction between law and order. If such a hazard did exist, almost four years later it no longer looms quite so dangerously on the horizon. Some other sequence of local confrontations may raise the warning again, but will that represent an advance in Muslim political life?

Conclusion

All the debate generated by the Shah Bano and Babri Masjid controversies confirmed that Muslim legal and political identity is significant in modern India. Any assertions about the character of that community seem marked by a conventional array of counterfactual statements appearing in the media as well as in scholarly analysis. Muslims either are backward and barbaric in their treatment of women, or they were forward looking and liberal when it came to female rights. The Islamic law is either a quaint relic of the dark ages or God's luminous path to a better world. In political terms, Muslims are either communalists who skillfully use the threat of violence to get their way in the political arena or dupes for vote-hungry politicians and "media mullahs." In historical terms, none of those categorizations has much to recommend it as a method of analysis.

---

[52] S. Tripathi, "One Hundred Years of Litigation," *Babri-Masjid*, *Loc. cit.*, pp. 16–27.

[53] D. Goyal, "At Peace with Themselves," *Ibid.*, pp. 125–28.

As noted earlier in this essay, Muslims in South Asia for the most part live in local communities. They are acutely aware of distinctions between region, ethnicity, class, and religious tendency. In the seventeenth and eighteenth centuries, reformers called upon Muslims to give up their local religious customs, especially those tainted by long association with the unbelievers. In part because reformers seem to have adjusted themselves to localism and in part because their efforts have created new distinctions, the ideal of religious uniformity has not yet been met.[54] Toward the end of the nineteenth century, political leaders, many of them almost self-appointed, have tried to mold the community into a solid bloc with a unified agenda. Their efforts have likewise not been successful. Even the demand for a separate Muslim state failed to attract unanimity. Some of the subcontinent's most respected *ulama* were among the opponents of the demand for Pakistan.[55] At the same time, a modern government which aimed at centralization beckoned, even used a certain amount of force, to make Muslims fit into a national state. A fair number of Muslim intellectuals heeded that call, but most believers remained content in the smaller worlds they knew best. Events together with the institutions of the state were able to draw them into the larger world only on an occasional basis.

The law and the courts were two of the state's most important tools in accomplishing the aim of creating a modern, secular nation. Both of these shared in certain ways the perspectives of reformist Muslims. They held the view, sometimes against the hard facts of localism, that Muslims were a single community governed by a single law.

Muslims in South Asia are not the first people to experience this kind of shift in the focus of their social, religious and political life from the purely local to the national. In France, for example, government courts did much to turn "Peasants into Frenchmen." Official efforts met with a certain amount of resistance. The invocation used in peasant litanies as late as the first decade of the twentieth century: "From justice, Oh Lord, deliver us!" was but one indication that local communities even in so-called advanced nations resented and resisted incorporation into cosmopolitan systems.[56] In contemporary India, the people who seek redress in the government courts are generally those with wealth and

---

[54] U. Sanyal, *Loc. cit.*; A. Ahmed, *Discovering Islam: Making Sense of Muslim History and Society* (London, 1988), sees one of the forcing driving Muslim history as the tension between the ideal and the practical. This would also include the tension between the "Great" tradition: that is to say, in C. Geertz's—see, *Islam Observed* (New Haven, 1968), terminology, a "scripturalist" emphasis, and the "Little" traditions: the various local expressions of belief.

[55] Z. Faruqi, *The Deoband School and the Demand for Pakistan* (New York, 1963).

[56] E. Weber, *Peasants into Frenchmen* (Stanford, 1976), pp. 50–66.

education. The rest seem bent on avoiding state justice if at all possible. Nevertheless, the courts have been more effective than the politicians or the preachers left to their own devices. Events such as Shah Bano's case or forced opening of the Babri Masjid have had a nation-wide impact, but they are tied to the passions of the moment. They do not engender communities which outlive hurt and anger.

Muslims and their leaders have acquired a stereotyped character in both scholarly and popular accounts of the current situation in India. Few accounts present them as complex creatures. Symbolization has only a slight connection to the people symbolized. Familial and local disputes can be more acrimonious because participants know each other so well. There are other ties of affection or the simple necessity of getting on with daily life which bring about an end to hostilities. In modern India's national life, all the passion of domestic discord has been preserved, but without the possibilities for reconciliation. State organizations have enhanced distinctions between right and wrong without providing any way to conciliate opposing views. In that process, a fragmented Muslim political identity is likewise preserved and the shape of some future Muslim community remains blurry.

8

Interaction of Islam and Public Law in Independent India

Tahir Mahmood

Introduction

According to the Islamic juristic classification of nations a particular country can be *dar al-Islam* (one which owes allegience to Islam), *dar al-harb* (one hostile to Islam) or *dar al-amn*, one at peace with Islam. How does modern India fit in this grouping? Constitutionally, India does not and cannot owe allegience to any religion, but is at the same time not hostile to either religion in general or any particular religious faith. As is well known, *The Indian Constitution* envisages secularism as the basic philosophy of the state. There being no definition anywhere in the Constitution of the express "secularism" or of any of its derivatives, its implications are traced in related statutory provisions. For this purpose are generally invoked those articles of the Constitution which prohibit religion-based discrimination between persons, assure freedom of religion to individuals and sections of citizens and give the minorities, including religious minorities, certain special rights relating to education, culture and language.[1] Reference is also made in this connection, rightly, to those provisions of the statute which clarify that the right to religious freedom does not debar the State from enacting social-welfare legislation and from regulating non-religious activities associated with religion.[2] Equally indicative of the possible place of religion vis a vis the state are those provisions of the Constitution which seek to protect certain religious beliefs or practices of chosen communities. That the Sikhs can carry swords by way of a fundamental right and the State must stop by law slaughter of the sacred cow are very meaningful provisions of the statute.[3] They clearly indicate that the State may in its wisdom honour established tradition of all religions prevailing on the Indian soil as long as they do not

---

[1] *The Constitution of India*, Arts. 14, 15, 16, 25, 26, 29, 30, 27.

[2] Arts. 25(2), 15(4).

[3] Arts. 25, expn.I, 48.

openly clash with the mandatory provisions of the statute. Going by the philosophy of the Indian Constitution, India is, thus, neither *dar al-Islam* nor *dar al-harb*; it is a *dar al-amn* where the state is at peace with, and not hostile to Islam; where followers of Islam equally share with the other Indians all constitutional and legal rights, freedoms, obligations and limitations. Let us see how in this *dar al-amn*, India, public law responds to the tenets and dictates of Islam. As is well known, Islam is not a mere religion and has to offer a lot more than rules of God-man relationship and rites and rituals. This fifteen-hundred year old religion has, in the course of time, established a complete way of life, a socio-moral ideology and a system of public and private laws. Seen as a whole, Islam is a code of life containing do's and don'ts of various degrees—*fatz* or *wajib* (mandatory), *mandub* or *sunna* (recommended), *hasam* (prohibited), *makruh* (reprehensible) and *mubah* (permitted). We will examine how the public law of India responds to and deals with Islam's purely religious tenets on one hand and its extra-religious principles on the other.

Islamic Beliefs and Practices: Response of Indian Public Law

The five basic precepts in Islam—called *arkan-i-khamsa*—are: (i) *shahada* (affirmation of faith), (ii) *salat* (prayers), (iii) *zakat* (Islamic tax), (iv) *siyam* (fasting) and (v) *hajj* (pilgrimage in Mecca). Books of Islamic theology mention these as the fundamentals of religion—*iman* and ʿ*amal*, faith and action—which every born and convert Muslim man and woman must accept and adhere to. Seen through the principles of the Indian Constitution in relation to religious freedom, while the first of these falls in the realm of beliefs, the remaining four represent practice of religion. Belief in and practice of religion both being guaranteed by the Constitution, the legal entitlement of Indian Muslims to their *arkan-i-Khamsa* remains, in principle, protected by the statute, subject, of course, to the general constitutional limitations on freedom of religion. We will analyse here one by one the position of each of the Islamic *arkan-i-Khamsa* in the context of the public law of India.

At the outset it may be noted that the India law cannot compel any one who claims to be a Muslim to subscribe to the beliefs and practices of Islam. In a Madras case it was held:

> If a person is born into a particular religion...the mere fact he is of an unorthodox type or has no belief personally in the tenets of that religion would not take him out of the category of persons professing that religion.[4]

---

[4] *G. Michael* v. *S. Venkateswaran* AIR 1952 Madras 474.

Islam and Public Law

Reflecting the policy of Indian public law this principle equally applies to Muslims. Much less can the state in India force a Muslim to practice his religion. Any compulsion by the state is in this regard out of question. What is to be seen is whether the law in India freely allows belief in and practice of Islamic religion on a voluntary basis.

Shahada: the Basic Faith

Shahada the basic article of faith, affirms two fundamental beliefs—(A) that there is no god but One Supreme and Unseen God, and (B) that Hazrat Muhammad was the Prophet of God. While there is no statute in India stating this to be the essential doctrine of Islam, it has been so registered by the courts.[5] In a recent Kerala High Court judgment it was observed, "Belief in oneness of God is indubitably the first fundamental belief an unquestioning embrace of which makes one of Muslim...nothing is more obnoxious to Islam than non-acceptance of unity of God."[6]

No statutory law or administrative regulation anywhere in the country directly or indirectly denies to any Muslim the right to affirm the *shahada*. In day to day life, however, situations do arise where a Muslim has to think whether what he is required to do deprives him of his belief in a profession of the first principle in the tenet of *shahada*, viz. *wahdania*—belief in oneness of God.

Soon after the advent of independence some Muslim theologians debated whether the newly adopted national anthem of the country, expected to be recited by Muslim children in the schools and by others elsewhere, on national occasions, clashed with the Islamic belief in One Supreme God. On a deeper analysis Rabindranath Tagore's Bengali-language song adopted as the national anthem was, however, found to be in complete accord with Muslim monotheistic philosophy.

Another patriotic song, in Sanskrit, opening with the words *vande matram*—I bow to the Motherland—is, however, still rejected by some Muslims in view of its apparent repugnance to the basic Islamic tenet of *wahdania*. While anti-Muslim forces in the country publicly demand: Those who must live in India must sing *vande matram* "agar Bharat mein rahna hoga to bande matrim' kahna hoga," no law makes it compulsory for anybody to sing either *vande matram* or even the national anthem. The Constitution and law only demand

---

[5] *Narantakath Avullah* v. *Parakkal Mammu and others* AIR 1923 Madras 171.

[6] *Shihabuddin* v. *K.P. Ahammed* AIR 1971 Kerala 206.

respect for the latter,[7] and the judiciary holds a view that one cannot be compelled to sing even the national anthem.[8]

In many public and private schools daily prayers to be joined by all children contain hymns of the polytheistic faiths of India. School textbooks too are replete with mythological beliefs and stories of those faiths. This is so mainly since Hindi, adopted as the medium of instruction, is yet to be developed as a secular language free from Hindu religions beliefs.

Stories of Hindu gods and goddesses, and their supernational and divine powers and actions often form part of textbooks not only of language and literature but also in history, sociology and even natural sciences, both in Hindi and English. The result is that a blatant violation of the constitutional provisions against compulsory religious preaching in the schools[9] has in practice become an established reality in many parts of the country.

Observance of Hindu religious rites at government and public ceremonial functions is a frequent occurence. Never are Muslim or Christian rites performed at such functions. Of course the Qur'an and the Bible are recited along with Hindu scriptures during national mournings; but happy occasions seem to have no place for non-Hindu rituals. Thus, while the Constitution's promise of secularism and equality of religions is often ignored in practice, the Muslims have willingly or unwillingly to violate their oath of allegience to strict monotheism by participating in polytheistic observances.

Coming to the second party of the *shahada*—belief that Syedina Muhammad was God's prophet—the Indian law recognizes it to be one of the fundamental dogmas of Islam. Judicial rulings agree that one who denies his prophethood cannot be a Muslim.[10] But how about the belief that he was the *Khatam-un-Habiyin*—"seal" and, therefore, the last of the prophets? Well known is the fact that it is India that gave birth to the Ahmadiya sect which proclaimed and recognized its founder Mirza Ghulam Ahmad Qadiyani as a prophet. Now living in all countries of the subcontinent, are the Ahmadis Muslim, despite their belief that they claim to have had another prophet hundreds of years after Hazrat Muhammad.

Undoubtedly under the Constitution of India the Ahmadis are entitled to their peculiar beliefs. But can they insist on being treated as Muslims by the Indian law? The answer of the courts is "yes." In 1923 an eminent lawman of the subcontinent Sir Zafrullah Kahn, himself an Ahmadi, had forcefully argued in

---

[7] Art 51A. (a)

[8] *Bijore Emmanuel* v. *State of Kerala* (1986) 3 SCC 615.

[9] Art. 28 (1).

[10] Supra note 5.

the court and convinced it that his community was Muslim.[11] In a leading Kerala case of recent years,[12] V. Khalid (later himself judge of the state High Court and then of the Supreme Court) strongly refuted Sir Zafarullah's views and argued that one who denied that Hazrat Muhammad was the last prophet of God could not remain a Muslim at the same time. Delivering the judgment, Krishna Iyer J. found no merit in the argument. He admitted that, "In major religions monopoly of spiritual finality is not infrequently claimed by each for the Truth as revealed or illumined through its Prophet or founder, and acceptance of this Truth constitutes the faith."

However, on examining at some length salient features of the Ahmadiya creed including the distinction it makes between "full prophets" and "sub-prophets" he laid stress on the community's faith in Hazrat Muhammad as the last "full prophet," and declared: "Looking at the issue devoid of sentiment and passion and in the cold light of the law, I...hold that Ahmadiya sect is of Islam and not alien."

The assertion that the heretic belief of the Ahmadis regarding the finality of Hazrat Muhammad's prophetic mission took them out of the fold of Islam was rejected by him with these words, "Every departure from orthodoxy is not apostasy, although witch-hunt is not the monopoly of any particular religion when polemics appear and libertarian trends assert themselves." Justice Iyer had an erroneous presumption that there was no consensus in the Muslim world regarding the Ahmadiya being heretics. "Islam is an international religion" he stated and added, "Therefore the question of consensus in the community, if it is to be the touchstone, must transcend national frontiers...consensus in the context must mean a broad unanimity in the Islamic world." The judge wondered if Sir Zufarullah Khan could represent the Islamic Republic of Pakistan at international forums how could the Ahmadis be regarded as non-Muslim. He could not have known then that Pakistan would in the near future enact a constitutional provision to declare that the Ahmadis were to be regarded as a non-Muslim minority in that country.[13]

Namaz: The Islamic Prayer

Namaz is a particular form of prayer to be offered in a series of fixed postures including standing still, kneeling down, sitting and prostrating—there being prescribed prayer—wordings in Arabic to be uttered in each of these postures. There are five obligatory daily prayers to be offered at dawn, noon,

---

[11] *Narantakath Avullah* v. *Parakkal Mammu and others* AIR 1923 Madras 171.

[12] Supra note 6.

[13] Pakistan: *Constitution*, art. 260(3) (b) as amended in 1974 and 1988.

afternoon, evening and late evening called *Fajr, Zuhr, Asr, Maghrib* and *Isha* respectively; and all these must be said by all adult men and women regularly and punctually. Though these may be said individually, men should offer each *namaz* preferably in a group either at a mosque or elsewhere.

On each Friday the noon-prayer's, *Zuhr*, is replaced with the congregational *Juma* prayer, arranged in bigger mosques. By tradition it is considered more important than daily prayers. Besides, on the two *Id* days obligatory congregational prayers are held in the mosques and Idgahs. A recent Kerala judgment takes note of names and approximate timings of the five daily prayers.[14] Many other court rulings refer to *Juma* prayer.

In the Indian constitutional terminology *namaz* is a practice of religion to pursue which Muslims have a fundamental right within the limits set by the statute. Eminent constitutionalist H. M. Seervai explains:

> An individual Muslim has the right to profess his religion. He may do so by offering prayers at home or in a public place. But he has equally a right to offer prayers in a mosque. (p. 936)...Religion has both a personal and institutional side. No doubt men can pray in their homes...but throughout the ages men have worshipped in temples, churches, mosques and the like. In practice the personal right is inseparable from the institutional right.[15]

Individual *namaz* offered in the privacy of homes or even in a public place raises no complications. Group-prayers are offered even at railway stations and airports and in government buildings on occasions when practicing Muslims assemble in these places. No legal or administrative agency interferes with this practice. Certain matters relating to offering *namaz* in mosques have, however, been regulated by the public law of India, sometimes to the annoyance of certain sections of the community.

The five daily prayers are announced in the mosques by the call of the *muazzin*. Called *azan*, it is considered sacred; whether it is answered or not, those who hear the call should respect it by stopping for a while all worldly business. Now all major mosques in India are equipped with public address systems and *azan* is called on amplifiers. This is often objected to by those who feel disturbed by it. In numerous cases entertaining such objections civil authorities or the police have imposed restrictions on the use of amplifiers in the

---

[14] *Pathanamthitta Majilissae Islamia* v. *Nagoor Meeran Sheik Muhammad* AIR 1963 Kerala 49.

[15] H. M. Seervai, *Constitutional Law of India*, 3rd edition (Bombay, 1983), p. 929.

mosques; and in judicial opinion such restrictions have the sanction of public law. In a Calcutta case, Sinha J. observed:

> Congregational prayers are a beautiful feature of the Muslim religion; and one remembers with pleasure the romantic sound of an early morning mu'azzin from the turrets of an upcountry mosque on a misty morning. But to transform this in a noisy fanfare is neither artistic nor necessary. I find nowhere that the religion of the Muslims enjoins it.[16]

Bitterly criticising how on Hindu festivals loudspeakers "doll out cheap jazz or cinema music" the judge said he was "surprised to hear that the cancer has now spread into the precincts of Muslim religious institutions." Explaining his viewpoint he added:

> May be that what is sought to be propagated in this instance is not profane music but a call to the faithful for offering daily prayers, but the objection remains...what is distasteful and abhorrent in the house of man is singularly inappropriate and even irreverent when used in the house of God. Prayer is intended when used in the house of God. Prayer is intended to be a silent communion with the creator. It does not call for a tumultuous preclude or a noisy accompaniment.

Another practice relating to congregational *namaz* that has attracted judicial scrutiny is spilling over of the congregation, on the roads around the mosques. In a Bombay case where civil administration had directed a local mosque that the Friday congregation of *namazis* must not spill over the road on a specified side and the directive was challenged in the court, it was held:

> Every community undoubtedly has a right to pray and worship in accordance with its own religious practices. No one can or should have any objection to such prayers being offered....But this cannot be done in violation of law....Encroachment of a public street or footpath for religious purposes, whether it is for offering prayers or for constructing a temple, is equally contrary to the provisions of law and must be prevented.

I am amazed and amused at the judicial naiveté that failed to distinguish between brief announcements of prayer time at a mosque and playing profane

---

[16] *Masud Alam and others* v. *Commissioner of Police and others* AIR 1956 Calcutta 9.

music for long hours in the Bombay case, and between building a permanent place of worship on a road and using it for half an hour once a week. I think in both the cases the judges drew parallels only in their anxiety to dispel any impression of being unduly against religion-based practices of the Muslims only. I feel that in a country where in busy residential localities and commercial places we often find our roads blocked by private marriage processions, and where our ears are pierced by deafening music and songs, there can be no justification for putting a blanket ban on such practices for *azan* and *namaz* only. In a stray case where the ban is inevitable to protect communal harmony or public order it may, of course, be upheld.

Particular mosques in India have faced other serious problems and since the mosque is undoubtedly a pivotal institution in Islam, these problems have been seen as those of the Muslim religion itself in this country. We will revert to them later.

Roza: the Islamic Fast

Siyam—daytime fasting during the holy month of Ramadhan (9th month of Muslim calendar)—is the second *farida*, or obligatory practice, in Islam. During this whole month, between sunrise and sunset adult Muslim men and women must fully abstain from food, water and sex. Popularly called *roza*, the fast is prefixed and suffixed by ceremonial eating known as *sahri* and *iftar* respectively. Practice of Ramadhan-fasting is not even remotely affected by the Indian public law. Of course, unlike many Muslim countries eating in houses remain open in India all day also during Ramadham. Amplifiers are used in the mosques throughout the month to announce the time of *sahri* and *iftar*. This too is often objected to by non-Muslims. In this case since loud-speaker announcements are made from the mosques in the last hours of the night, the objection has been even more severe. In many cases the practice has been banned. Such cases are, however, much less in number than those in which unfettered use of amplifiers has been enjoyed.

Custodians of state authority, including the President, prime minister, cabinet ministers and presiding officers of legislatures arrange in Delhi and state capitals lavish *iftar* parties attended by eminent citizens and diplomats. As public exchequer partly meets expenses of these parties, their constitutional propriety is often whispered about.

Zakat: Charity Tax

Every Muslim adult male or female, owning wealth in excess of the prescribed limits must pay a tax of 2 1/2% of the excess, to be used for the benefit of the indigent in the society. This is *zakat*, the fourth among the *arkan-i-khamsa* of Islam. Usually paid during the month of Ramazan, well-defined principles of accountability to and rates of *zakat* and its collection by state agencies are found in the books of *Sharīʿa* law. *Zakat* can be given individually to the poor or to institutions catering to the poor. When the state collects it, the benefit of the general public will be among its lawful uses. Many modern Muslim countries have codified *zakat* law in the form of statutes. There *zakat* is collected by the state. In some other countries, while *zakat* remains a private religious affair, the state imposes also regular income tax called *dariba*. In India *zakat* is generally paid by Muslims, voluntarily and individually, to the mosques or religious seminaries.

Opinion in the Muslim world is divided on whether *zakat* is a general tax on individual's resources or only a religious levy. In India many Muslim taxpayers are of the view that payment of direct taxes to the state absolves them of the liability to pay an additional amount in the name of *zakat*. General public opinion, however, regards *zakat* as a religious levy, for which reason neither the secular state can deal with it, nor payment of taxes to the State would absolve one of liability to *zakat*.

Nothing in the Indian law in any way interferes with voluntary payment of *zakat*. Of course, the Indian taxation laws give no relief, rebate or exemption on amounts paid by a Muslim tax-payer as *zakat*—although certain other specified charities and donations are eligible for such relief. Numerous Muslims here are thus subject to double taxation, paying both *zakat* under the dictates of religion and state taxes under the law of the land. Under the *zakat* rules, of course, amounts paid as state taxes can be deducted from the income of a person liable to *zakat*.

As regards collection of *zakat* under state authority, since the beginning of the British rule there never has been any law providing for it. A few years ago the government of the South-Indian state of Karnataka proposed to enact a law for this purpose (at the behest of one of its Muslim ministers). The move was opposed, among others, by the Muslim Personal Law Board, which ruled that State interference in a religious matter (which in its opinion *zakat* was) was uncalled for. There never has been any such move in other parts of India.

On the festive day of *Id-ul-Fitr* which follows Ramazan and marks the successful completion of the month-long fasting, those accountable to *zakat* have to pay for the benefit of the poor, a fixed charity called the *fitra*. Like *zakat, fitra* too does not entitle the payer to any relief under the tax laws of India.

In a recent Supreme Court decision,[17] where relief was sought for exemption from the taxable income of a Muslim assessee a big amount advanced

---

[17] *Wealth-tax Comm., Bhopal* v. *Abhdul Hussain Mulla Muhammad Ali* AIR 1988 S.C. 1417.

by him to a friend as *qarze-e-hasana*, the court expressed its inability to help. It was not sure what *qarze-e-hasana* meant. This Islamic charity which takes the form of a loan repayment which depends on the debtor's goodwill and cannot be sought legally, thus failed to get tax relief under the state laws due to the claimant's failure to explain its true nature and rationale.

I sometimes wonder why the taxation laws of India, which do recognize the religion based Hindu Undivided Family (HUF) and make special provisions for it, cannot also recognize for the same purpose some of the Islamic religio-economic concepts—at least the mandatory *zakat* and *fitra* if not voluntary transactions like *qarze-e-hasana*. *Zakat*, surely, is an absolutely essential religious practice in Islam—obligatory in the first degree. In view of this, at least the amount paid as *zakat* by a Muslim assessee may on proof of payment, be allowed to be deducted from his taxable income.

Haj and Id al-Adha

The fourth obligatory religious observance of Islam—the Haj—is a three-day ritual commemorating the four-thousand year old story of patriarch Abraham's divinely inspired actions of sacrifice and prayers. It takes place every year in the 12th month of the Muslim calendar in and around the city of Mecca in Hijaz (now the Kingdom of Saudi Arabia). To join it at least once in life is a mandatory religious obligation of all those male and female Muslims whose health and financial resources permit it.

In all periods of post-Islamic history India has sent a large contingent of pilgrims to Mecca. Until 1932 Haj traffic from India was in the hands of private travel agencies. Exploiting religious sentiments, dishonest elements did a roaring business. In 1896 Protection of Mohammedan Pilgrims Acts were enacted locally by the Bombay and Calcutta provincial legislatures in order to provide a system of licensing pilgrim-brokers and regulating their activities with a view to protecting the hajis from exploitation at their hands. In 1932 the Central legislature came out with the Port Haj Committee Act setting up surveillance committees in all three port cities from which Haj pilgrims sailed (Bombay, Calcutta, Karachi). After the advent of Freedom, while all Haj traffic got centralized in Bombay, under the Constitution "pilgrimage to places outside India" was declared a Union-List subject which could be regulated by parliamentary legislation.[18] Acting under this provision, in 1959 Parliament passed the Haj Committee Act to organize the Haj, and to institute a Haj Fund. Today the Haj pilgrimage from India both by sea and air is managed and regulated in all its aspects by a statutory machinery and its subordinate agencies. Every year on

---

[18] Seventh Schedule, List-I, Entry 20.

the occasion of Haj the government sends to Saudi Arabia goodwill and medical missions at its own expense. Constitutional propriety of this practice and of State-management of Haj in general has been disputed by some critics. Nevertheless, the State remains closely associated, legally and administratively, with Haj which it keeps under its own management and control. At its venue, Hijaz, Haj management has now been fully taken over by the government of Saudi Arabia. Nearly a hundred pilgrim-inns privately built by former rulers of princely Indian states in Mecca and Madina have now gone out of the owner's hands. Known as *rubats*, these have been either acquired by the Saudi government or illegally occupied for commercial purposes by their local supervisors. The government of India is now inventing rules of international law and using diplomatic channels to seek compensation for these lost properties.

While those who have been able to perform Haj complete their rituals in Mecca, the rest of the Muslims all over the world celebrate the occasion in the form of the festival of *Id-al-Adha*. The hajis in Mecca and all other well-to-do Muslims elsewhere must offer on this occasion the *qurbani*—ceremonial slaughter of an animal to feed the poor and entertain relatives and friends. This is *wajib*—obligatory. In India the festivity of *Id-al-Adha*—locally called *Baqrid*—has given rise to the religious problem of cow-slaughter.

Among the animals used all over the world for *Id-al-Adha-qurbani* has been the cow which as per a religious belief of dominant sections of Hindus is an object of worship. During the Mughal rule in India, taking cognizance of this local religious belief the Muslim emperors and kings beginning with Babar down to Sultan Hyder Ali of Mysore had magnanimously prohibited by law slaughter of cows for all purposes including the Baqrid-sacrifice. During the British days, pursuing the divide and rule policy, the ban was lifted. Despite demands, while Macaulay's Penal Code of 1860 did not include sanctions against cow-slaughter, its substitute in the Muslim dominated Kashmir—the Rambir Penal Code—did. In British India the subject remained a major cause of Hindu-Muslim tension. With the advent of freedom the scene changed. It is no secret that Article 48 of the Constitution directed the state to take steps for prohibiting slaughter of cows in recognition of the Hindu religious belief about the sanctity of the cow. Local legislation and administrative regulations have answered the call of Article 48 in many parts of the country.

In the State of Bihar the local anti cow-slaughter legislation was challenged in the court, arguing that the ban deprived the Muslims of a religious practice. Those who threw the challenge, however, failed to produce any reference from the Qur'an or Hadith enjoining compulsory killing of a cow by way of *qurbani*. Noting this, in the celebrated *Hanif Qureshi* decision,[19] the

---

[19] *M. H. Quareshi* v. *State of Bihar* AIR 1958 S.C. 731.

Supreme Court emphasized that the general Hindu "reverence" for the cow had to be considered in deciding the case. It upheld the law, holding that a cow was only one of the animals permitted in Islam for the ritual of *qurbani*. Though unlike a goat which discharged the *qurbani*-liability of a single person, a cow (as also other permissible larger animals) could discharge the same religious liability of as many as seven persons, this provision in the court's finding had an economic and not a religious basis.

It is undoubtedly true that for discharging the *qurbani*-liability on the Baqrid day, killing a cow is not *farz, wajib* or even *mandub*. On the contrary, though the Prophet did not prohibit eating of the cow, he did warn his people of beef-borne diseases, in view of which eating the cow should be regarded as *makruh*. By no logic of interpretation can, in my opinion, killing a cow be regarded as an essential religious practice of the Muslims. On the contrary, abstaining from it conforms to the Islamic teaching that Muslims must respect religious sentiments of others if this does not deprive them of their *faraiz* and *wajibat* (obligatory religious practices).

Qur'an: The Islamic Scripture

Wherefrom do the fundamental *shahada* tenet and the four mandatory Islamic *arkan*—*namaz, roza, zakat and Haj*—whose position at the Indian public law we have discussed, derive their authority and binding nature? Certainly from the Holy Qur'an, the only revealed book of the Muslim religion.

Containing nearly 6000 verses arranged in 114 chapters under 30 parts—all in Arabic prose—the Qur'an is believed to contain God's words received by Hazrat Muhammad from God through Gabriel. Collected in writing during the Prophet's own life time, its authentic text standardized fifteen years after his death under the orders of Caliph Othman, is till now read and recited by the Muslims throughout the world with utmost reverence. Belief in the divinity of the Qur'an is an inseparable part of Islamic religion.

In India while there is no statute referring to Qur'an as the supreme scriptural authority of Islam, the courts dealing with Muslim religious matters have often referred to it as the paramount source of Islamic teachings and the Shari'a law.

Unfortunately, on more than one occasion attempts have been made in this country to drag the holy book into ugly controversies and to denigrate it, much to the annoyance of the Muslims. It was one such major incident of the twenties of this century in the wake of which eminent Muslim nationalist leader of the time Maulana Mohammad Ali Jauhar had succeeded in getting new section—295A—inserted into the 1860 Indian Penal Code. The new provision provided penalties for the offence of insulting the religion of any section of citizens "with deliberate and malicious intention of outraging religious feelings of

Islam and Public Law

that class." Nothing can be more ridiculous than the same provision of the Code now being invoked by miscreants to demand legal proscription of the Qur'an itself. In the Calcutta case of *Chandmal Chopra*,[20] the petitioner mischievously selected certain Qur'anic verses—all disjointed, torn out of context and distorted in translation—to claim that the Holy Book "incited violence," "disturbed public tranquility," "promoted feelings of enmity, hatred and ill will on the ground of religion" and had ignited the political turbulence in West Asia. On the basis of these foolish claims he prayed for a declaration that the Qur'an both in original Arabic and in translation in various languages stood "forfeited to government" under section 95 of the Penal Code. The Muslims all over the world were stunned to see that Padma Khastgir, J. not only allowed initial admission of the atrocious petition but in a rare demonstration of judicial impropriety also rushed to the press with its details. Their reaction jolted the central and state governments whose counsel vehemently opposed the petition in the court. Dismissing the petition *in limine*, Bimal Chandra Basak, J. (to whose court the petition was later transferred) observed that taking the action against the Qur'an as desired by the petitioner "would go against the preamble of the Constitution," "violate provisions of Article 25," "take away the secularity of India" and "deprive a section of the people of their right to thought, expression, belief, faith and worship"—rather "a class of persons of their human rights." The judge also declared that sections 153-A and 296 could not be applied to religious scriptures. On the contrary, in his opinion, it was one who mischievously tried to so misread and mistreat the Qur'an who would be guilty of the offences under those sections.

Passing strictures against Padma Khastgri, J., Justice Basak said:

> The court should be circumspect in such kind of matters and be very cautious about the same. Otherwise, though it may attract cheap publicity but may cause untold misery and disruption of religious harmony. The High Court should have been spared of the embarrassment caused. The petition should have been rejected forth with and in limine as unworthy of its consideration as soon as it was moved.

While Islam's supreme Scriptural authority was thoughtfully saved against a mischievous affront, during the course of his judgment Justice Basak also made, incidentally, a brilliant exposition of the nature of the Qur'an and the Muslim belief about its divinity. Worth quoting are the following words:

---

[20] *Chandanwal Chopra* v. *State of West Bengal* AIR 1986 Calcutta 104.

> For Muslims the Qur'an is *ipsissima verba* (the very words) of God Himself. It is God speaking to man, not merely in 7th century Arabia to Arabs but eternally to every man throughout the world....It is eternal, breaking through into time, the transcendent entering history and remaining here, [available to mortals to handle and to appropriate the Divine becomes apparent]....The Qur'an is *al-Furqan*, i.e., showing truth from falsehood and right from wrong....Muslim religion cannot exist without Qur'an.

Denigration of the Divine Revelation that the Qur'an is supposed to contain and the personality and character of its recipient Prophet Muhammad have occasionally been subject of unwarranted vituperation also in Indian and imported books. Censorship laws of the state, including certain provisions of the Indian Penal Code 1860 and the Customs Act 1962 (sec. 11) have been liberally used by successive governments since independence to ban such offending works. Among the books so proscribed in India have been Thomas and Thomas on the Prophet, Kurt Frishler on his wife Syeda Aisah, Desmond Steward and Ram Swarup on Islamic religion and Salman Rushdie's *Satanic Verses* (banned in 1956, 1963, 1975, 1983 and 1988, respectively). The "freedom of speech" clause in the Constitution was fondly invoked by the critics of the ban in each case, especially in respect of the last mentioned work. Similar criticism was heard when Nikos Kazantzakis's *Christ Crucified* was banned, but not when on popular demand the government banned Aubrey Menen's *Ramayan* (1957), Stanley Walpert's *Nine Hours to Rama* (1962) and, recently, the imported Urdu play "Bakra Qiston Par" for its alleged denigration of the sacred cow. I have a convinced opinion that the basic philosophy of the Indian Constitution includes respect for religion, and the statutory right to freedom of speech has to be viewed in the light of this philosophy. The public law in our country can imitate neither the West in general in allowing attack on religion under the subterfuge of freedom of speech, nor a particular western country to limit its blasphemy laws to a chosen religion only.

Sectarian Beliefs and Practices

Existence of various sects and ideological groups among the Muslims is well known. They differ from one another in respect of subsidiary religious beliefs and practices and on that basis regard each other as theologically wrong or even guilty of blasphemy or *kufr*. In India, public law would not sit on judgment regarding the authenticity of the conflicting beliefs. The state claims to be unconcerned with theological refinements and does not want to play the role of a mentor or religious reformer. A dominant majority of Indian Muslims are Sunni; the Shi'as are a small minority. Legislative enactments and judicial precedent do

Islam and Public Law 135

recognize the separate existence of these two sects. (The Sunni Muslims often regard the Shiᶜas as Kafir and vice versa.) After the rise of Imam Khomaini in Iran, alarmed with his global popularity among the orthodox Muslims some leading Sunni Ulama of India declared the Imam and all Shiᶜites to be non-Muslim, "exposing" in their writings their un-Islamic beliefs and practices. The state could hardly take notice of all this. In many past cases the courts have recognized the Shiᶜas as a Muslim sect,[21] and the public law of modern Indian sticks to this opinion. The tendency among the various sects of Muslims "to charge others with unbelief and treat them as heretics" has been noted by an Indian court with disapproval.[22]

About certain practices of Indian Muslims and their Islamic basis or validity there are serious differences among various groups and factions of the Muslims. A particular practice followed by one of these may be regarded by another as *bidᶜat* (unauthorized innovation), *gunah* (a sinful act) or even *kufr* (blasphemy or irreligion). Undoubtedly there is such a deep influence of local religious, mythological and ritualistic practices of India on its Muslim citizens that in the course of time has come into existence some indigenous brands of Islam in this country. The Indian Constitution in effect protects all these Indian versions of Islam and does not discriminate between them. Believers in puritanic Islam—called *wahhabis*—are, no doubt, perfect Muslims in Indian judicial opinion.[23] But so are those following local innovations, called the *bidᶜatis*. Their innovative religious practices, even if prima facie un-Islamic, have constitutional protection in this country.

Besides the sects and ideological groups, there are among the Muslims various *madahib*—schools of law, which differ from one another on important theological and legal points. Four among these—the Hanafi, the Shafiᶜi, the Jafari and the Ismaᶜili—are found in India; the first two among the Sunnis and the other two among the Shiᶜas. The Shiᶜa Ismailiya are in fact more than a mere school of law. In India there are followers of both the internal divisions of this sect—the Nizaris and the Mustᶜalis, locally called *Khojas* and *Bohras*—and the latter are further divided into the Daʾuidi and the Sulamiani groups. Indian law recognizes all of them and does not discriminate between them in any matter. Some old judicial decisions contain their detailed historical account describing them as Muslim sects and subsects.[24]

While the Hanafi/Shafiᶜi Sunnis and the Ithna Asharis of India have no organized church, Khojas and Daʾudi Bohras do have their respective head-

---

[21] *Jiwan Khan and others* v. *Habib and others* AIR 1933 Lahore 759.

[22] *Naran Avullah* v. *Parakkal Mammu and others* AIR 1923 Madras 171.

[23] *Bechi* v. *Ahsan-ullah Khan* ILR (1890) 7 Allahabad 461, 494.

[24] *Agha Khan*, (1866) 12 BHCR 323; *Burhanpur*, (1974) 75 9A1.

priests—the *Imam-e-Hazir* for the former and the *Dai-e-mutlaq* for the latter. Imam-e-Hazir Price Aga Khan's *Dastur-iul-Amal*—the binding code of conduct for the Khoja community—has not yet been tested for its validity under the Indian public law, but the *Mithaq* of the Da'udi Bohras has been in trouble for some time, due to revolt against it by a dissentient group within that sect. In 1948 the Privy Council had recognized *Dai-e-Mutlaq's* power to excommunicate members of the sect on religious grounds, subjecting it to certain procedural requirements. The disappointed group them sought intervention of the then doyen of Bombay politics Morarji Desai, on whose swift action the local legislature passed the Excommunication Act 1949 putting a blanket ban on the impugned practice. After the commencement of the Constitution, the Act was challenged on behalf of the *Dai-e-Mutlaq* for its alleged illegal interference with a religious matter. Three judges of a four-member bench of the Supreme Court declared it to be unconstitutional, holding that laws providing for social welfare and reform could not "reform a religion out of existence." In their opinion the impugned Act "struck at the very life of the community," depriving it of the power "to protect itself against dissidents and schismatics." The right under article 26 of the Constitution was not subject to preservation of civil rights—it was pointed out. The fourth judge, Chief Sinha, thought otherwise and viewed the Act as an anti-untouchability law protected by art. 17 of the Constitution.[25] Seventeen years later during Morarji Bhai's prime ministership, the Bohra dissident group secured appointment of a public committee chaired by Judge N. Nathwani to probe into the *Dai-e-Mutlaq's* allegedly arbitrary powers. In its strongly-worded report bitterly criticizing Bohora religious practices, the committee described the Bombay Excommunication Act as a "step in the right direction" and recommended Parliamentary legislation on the same lines.

The international Islamic community on the whole recognizes no *Dai-e-Mutlaq* or other similar authority; and excommunication is quite alien to it. There is in fact no church and no clergy in Islam proper. Outlawing excommunication, therefore, could not have reformed Islam out of existence; it could put an end only to a limited sectarian custom. However, as I said earlier, the Indian public law protects every brand of Islam—Indian or foreign— and not necessarily what the dominant Muslim majority across the globe regards as Islam. Talking of profession and practice of religion, it safeguards not only broad religious communities, but also every sect or subsect within a community. How the parent community in general views the beliefs and practices of a minuscule sect among it, has no relevance for the Indian law as interpreted by the courts.

Practices not conforming to Islam proper, or which the majority of Muslims view as un-Islamic, are of course followed not only by the Da'udi

---

[25] *Saifuddin Saheb* v. *State of Bombay* AIR 1962 S.C. 853.

Bhoras. Numerous individuals and groups among the Indian Muslims often adhere to such practices. Under the Constitution of India, citizens have a fundamental duty "to develop scientific temper, humanism and spirit of inquiry and reform."[26] In the discharge of this duty citizens must be helped by the state through action taken by it under the social-reform clause of Article 25. But can, in light of those provisions of the Constitution, the State restrict a blatantly un-Islamic practice? The answer of the courts seems to be an emphatic "no." The policy of the State has so far been of a total non-interference, allowing all kinds of superstitious practices to pass for Islam.

The same voice of Justice Gajendragadkar (in *Dargah* case AIR 1961 S.C. 1402) trying to differentiate, in the context of Islam, between true religion and "accretions that sprang from superstition" has been shouted down by dissenting views that would accept as Islam things which are actually *kufr* or *shuris* and therefore *harain*.

Worship and veneration of graves, for instance, is a common practice in this country. It makes *wahdaniya* the affirmation of exclusive faith in One Supreme God meaningless. The Prophet of Islam is on record to have warned his followers against veneration of even his own grave. But, in India, thousands of big and small pirs and faqirs lying in their graves are worshipped in gross violation of the true Islamic faith. None of the numerous waqf laws enacted by the central and state legislatures empowers the state to put any restrictions on the practice of prostration and other forms of worship pursued at the tombs and shrines. On several occasions state authorities and courts have been approached by right-thinking Muslims in search of officially enforceable curbs on worship of graves, but never has there been a positive response. Familiar with and used to idol worship, Indian judges perhaps find nothing wrong in worshipping graves. In their eyes, both are sacred—equally protected by the country's public law.

In recent years, the famous Dashipura graveyard case of Varanasi brought to limelight the practice of veneration of family graves. This led to friction between the Sunni and Shiʿa Muslims across the country and, while the Supreme Court ordered shifting of the graves, a debate followed on whether religion allowed a grave to be shifted from its original place.

In its repeated decisions, the Supreme Court enumerated at length the rituals and ceremonies, observed by the Shiʿas around the said graves and, regarding them in effect as constitutionally protected religious practices of a section of the Muslims, directed the Sunnis to move the graves to a specified distance.[27] As precedents for permissible shifting of graves the court cited the

---

[26] Article 51 A(h).

[27] *Abdul Jabiy* v. *State of U. P.*, AIR 1984 S.C. 882; *N.I.I. Ltd.* v. *N.I.N.I.H. Ltd* AIR 1981 S.C. 1298.

historical cases of double burial for Emperor Jahangir and Queen Mumtaz Mahal—first at the place of their death and later in the mausoleums built for them. While none questioned the judicial recognition of the un-Islamic Shi'a practices, the Sunnis refused to move the graves on the plea that their religion did not allow it. No serious effort was made either by the court or by any enforcement agency to get the judicial directive executed.

The belief that Islam prohibits shifting of graves has also been responsible for keeping away from home the moral remains of a national hero of the past. There have been demands in Independent India to reclaim and bring back to the country things which form part of the nation's historical heritage but are at present found in foreign lands. Among these is the Rangoon-based grave of Bahardur Shah Zafar the Mughal Emperor in whose name the 1857 war of Independence was fought with the British. Muslim theologians' verdict is that unless there is evidence that the Emperor was buried in Rangoon by way of *amana* (temporary deposit), Islam would not permit transfer of the grave to another place. Accepting the verdict the government was refrained from moving in the matter. National sentiments have, thus, been kept subservient to religious susceptibilities—notwithstanding that the poet-emperor on the eve of his demise, had lamented of being denied the chance of being buried in his homeland.

Superstition about graves has resulted in the creation of a spiritual aura for the Muslim cemeteries. Qabristans are treated as religious places. In quite a few cases Muslim cemeteries have been acquired for public purposes by the State under the land-acquisition laws, and the community has objected to it on religious grounds. That the law on religion under the Constitution is subservient to the law on acquisition of property in the statute is, however, fully established. The Allahabad High Court once said that acquisition of a graveyard could not be held to take away the right of any "living person" to profess religion and declared: "The freedom enunciated in Art. 25 is a personal freedom....It is not a freedom guaranteeing preservation of graves where bodies of some others lie."[28]

Shrines and Mosques

The cult of worshipping graves has resulted in the establishment of a large number of tombs and mausoleums scattered all over the country. The most well known among them is Ajmer—the shrine of Sufi saint Moinuddin Chisti which, since 1955 has had a state-controlled establishment governed by Parliamentary legislation (the Dargah Khwajah Saheb Act 1955), and which the Supreme Court in a recent case (AIR 1987 S.C. 2213, *Saulat Husain*) chose to describe as a "venerable shrine of universal recognition." Thousands of other so-

---

[28] *Mohammad Ali Khan* v. *Zucknow Municipality* AIR 1978 Allahabad 280.

called Muslim shrines are covered by central and state laws relating to waqf administration. Many of these, including the Dargah of Shaikh Saleem Chisti at Fatehpur Sikri are now "protected monuments" as declared by competent authorities under the Ancient Monuments and Archeological Sites and Remains Act 1958 or one of its local substitutes. Ban on public prayers in about 250 mosques—many of them situated on the premises of such monuments—has been disapproved and, in certain cases, defied by concerned Muslims.

That Articles 25 and 26 of the Constitution were overridden by Article 31 (now repealed), and still are by Article 31A, so as to validate acquisition of religious places by the State is now an established judicial opinion. In the *Khajamiam Waqf* case,[29] the Supreme Court had specifically extended it to Muslim shrines. The Allahabad High Court once emphatically upheld the constitutional validity of acquisition of mosques, on the basis of a recorded interview of an eminent Egyptian jurist al-Marghinani that the mosque was not an "institution" in the legal meaning of that term.[30]

In the so-called Muslim shrines one can witness all sorts of wholly un-Islamic practices. Seldom would, however, the state interfere with any of these. There is a solitary instance of state legislation for this purpose. In the dargahs of the undivided Punhab, dance festivals were arranged on special occasions. Outraged, some Muslim theologians demanded a legislative ban on the practice to meet which the local legislature enacted the Music in Muslim Shrines Act 1942. Now in force in the states of Punjab and Haryana, it is a penal law which provides punishment for dancing in the Muslim shrines. Prostration at and virtual worship of the graves, which are surely more un-Islamic than dance, have never been stopped in any Muslim shrine either by law or under a court order.

Ignoring the true Islamic principles, the Indian law hardly makes any distinction between the so-called shrines, which indeed have no religious sanctity in Islam, and the mosque which undoubtedly has a pivotal place in the Islamic religious system. Basically, a house of prayer like a church, the mosque is also used for other solemn purposes and as a seminary. There are in India millions of big and small mosques, including *jama masjids* and *idgahs* built mainly for congregational prayers on Fridays and the two *Id* days respectively.

The Constitution of India empowers the State to make laws for "throwing open Hindu religious institutions of a public character to all classes and sections of Hindus."[31] In omitting a similar provision for mosques, the statute takes note of the Islamic theory which does not allow restricting a mosque to any particular sect, group or school of law, but ignores the reality that in this

---

[29] *Asbestos Cement Ltd.* v. *Sawarkar* AIR 1971 S.C. 101.

[30] *Mohammad Ali Khan* v. *Zucknow Municipality* AIR 1978 Allahabad 280.

[31] Art. 25.

country Shiʿas, Sunnis, Ahle Qurʾan, Ahle Hadith and Ahmadis, etc., do often quarrel on the right of offering namaz in particular mosques. Of course the courts have, in many cases, clarified the Islamic legal theory which does not allow sectarian reservation of any mosque.[32]

Two very recent developments relating to mosques in India are worth mentioning. The first of these relates to the *imams* of mosques. The *imam* is a religious functionary who leads the groups and congregations of prayers in mosques and is paid for this service by the mosque administration. Now pending before the Supreme Court is a petition, known as *Jamil Ilyasi* case, in which a group of *imams* have demanded application and enforcement of the Minimum Wages Act of 1950 so that they get suitable remuneration enabling them to earn a reasonable livelihood. Surprisingly, there has been no slogan of undue interference with religion in this case; though a recent move by the U.P. government to enforce the said Act to the Muslim seminaries in the state had to be dropped due to the objection of the Muslim leaders.

The second notable development having a bearing on the mosques is the enactment of the Places of Worship (Special Provisions) Act 1991 which declares that religious character of places of worship existing at the time of Independence shall not be disturbed, and makes it an offense to change religious character of any place of worship which shall be punishable with imprisonment, fine and loss of right of participating in elections. Section 3 of the new measure speaks of place of worship of "any section" of a religious denomination and prohibits its "conversion" into a "place of worship of a different section of the same religious denomination." This indirectly offers statutory recognition to the un-Islamic trend of associating mosques with particular "sects" among the Indian Muslims.

The new measure expectedly and understandably excludes the Ayodhya mosque where forced conversion into a temple is *fait accompli*. Not long ago, in *Tejraj's* case, enforcing relevant constitutional provisions a F. B. of the Madhya Pradesh High Court had ordered immediate removal of a Hindu object of worship installed by force in a Jain temple[33] —holding that "Any suggestion that for certain reasons it may be difficult and even impossible for the [government] to carry out orders of the court can only be viewed with dismay and cannot but impel us to say that it would be end of the Rule of Law" (p. 119). There is no explanation why similar orders could never be passed by any Indian Court in the case of the Ayodhya mosque. On the contrary, the Supreme Court in its wisdom refused to interfere with the volatile *Shilapujan* processions moving to Ayodhya from all parts of the country with the avowed object of converting the mosque

---

[32] *Mohd. Wasi and others* v. *Bachchan Sahib and others* AIR 1955 Allahabad 68; *Haji Mohammad Sayeed and others* v. *Abdul Ghafoor and others* AIR 1955 Allahabad 688.

[33] *Tejraj* v. *State of Madhya Bharat* AIR 1958 Madhya Pradesh 115.

Islam and Public Law

into a temple, holding that this was a constitutionally-protected practice of Hindu religion.[34] Undoubtedly the *fait accompli* at Ayodhya owes itself, in part, to executive and judicial helplessness in strictly enforcing clear constitutional principles. The new legislative measure of 1991—eminently answering the call of the Constitution—is an attempt to pre-empt similar happenings elsewhere. While openly communal organizations are opposing it with all their might, advocates of secularism have kept mum.

Freedom of Private Life Style

Does the Indian public law allow the Muslims to live their lives freely in accordance with what they believe to be the Islamic style? Seeking answer to this question in the Indian administrative law, we come across different situations differently handled.

In a recent Kerala case[35] where a Muslim police constable, denied permission to grow a beard, challenged the administrative ban under Article 25 of the Constitution, the High Court ruled that the statute did not protect "non-essential" religious practices. A few *hadith* of the Prophet asking people to grow beards were brushed aside by the Court, saying: "These statements made by the Prophet made apparently in different contexts are only *Sunnah* (optional) and are not understood as obligatory for every Mussalman to follow." Nothing with apparent approval state counsel's argument that the then President of the Islamic Republic of Pakistan late General Zia-ul-Haq did not wear a beard, the court refused to view wearing a beard as a religious obligation for the Muslims. While in a later case the Madras High Court followed suit,[36] I wonder if the administrative compulsion to shave off the beard, upheld by the courts, does not amount to violation of the humanitarian—if not the religious—law.

Major public-service rules in India—those relating to bureaucracy, police and civil administration, etc., restrict the right of a married person to marry again, even where the personal law applicable allows it.[37] Does this administrative restriction take away a religious freedom and is hence violative of the

---

[34] 1989 (2) SCALE 937.

[35] *Mohd. Fasi* v. *Superintendent of Police, Alleppy and others* 1985 KLT 185.

[36] *B. Mokhtar Pasha* v. *The General Manager, Personnel and Administration, Bharat Heavy Electricals, Ltd.* 1986 MLJR 221.

[37] All India Service (conduct) Rules 1968, Rule 19; Central Civil Services (conduct) Rules 1964, Rule 21; U.P. State Government Servants (conduct) Rules, Rule 27; M.P. Municipal Service (Executive) Rules 1973, Rule 10 (1).

Constitution? No, say the Indian courts[38] —rightly, in my opinion. The conditional permission for polygamy rather reluctantly given by the Qurʾan for exceptional cases can surely be regulated by the state. Such regulation cannot be tantamount to banning practice of religion.

The practice of *purdah*—the veil—among the Muslim women of India came under judicial scrutiny in two recent cases in the context of requirement of election laws regarding voters' photographs to be compulsorily affixed on their identity cards. In Bengal administrative orders issued for this purpose under Representation of the People (Preparation of Electoral Rolls) Rules 1956 were challenged for their constitutional validity on behalf of two women—one Hindu and the other a Muslim—contending that forcing those purdanashin ladies to get photographed was a violation of their right to practice religion. D. N. Sinha, J. of the Calcutta High Court separately dealt with the position of the two petitioners.[39] The plea that *purdah* was also a Hindu religious practice was contemptuously dismissed by the judge in these clearly acrimonious words:

> Students of history will find that the system of *purdah* is alien to our soil, and never existed during the period of Hindu civilization. During the most illustrious periods of our history women were as free as men....In our epics also we do not find prevalence of the system of *purdah*. Purdah actually came into existence during and after the Muslim invasion of India and was the result of expedience and not religion.

On behalf of the Muslim plaintiff, lawyers cited in the court Ahmadi commentator Mohammad Ali Lahori's translation of the Qurʾan and an Urdu version of the *Mishkat al-Masabih*. Reacting to the two references the judge observed:

> There is no express injunction (in the Qurʾan) about keeping *purdah*. Moderation of social intercourse of the two sexes is advocated and it has been laid down that women should cast down their looks and not display their ornament in public. The annotators hold that there is no absolute injunction against covering of the face or the hands....What have been laid down are questions of prudence and general deportment. The matter, therefore, rests not on religion but on social practice. Such a practice would have infinite variations. The extremely orthodox may give it a texture which to the less orthodox

---

[38] *V.M. Taharullah*, AIR 1986 (2) CAT 526 (Madras); *Khizer Basha* v. *Indian Airlines Corporates* AIR 1984 Madras 379.

[39] *N.K. Sikdar* v. *Chief Election Officer* AIR 1961 Calcutta 289.

would seem repellant. It would be impossible to administer the law by treating as subject to these infinite variations in social practice.

The objection to being photographed was brushed aside by the judge in these words:

> It seems to be firmly established that there is an absolute injunction against any picture or representation of the Prophet, of which we must take judicial notice. But there does not seem to be any equally cogent religious injunction or immutable social practice with regard to others.

Reference was made in the judgement, approvingly, to the government counsel's argument that frequent appearance of the pictures of the then Iranian Queen Farah Diba in the world press went against the plea that *purdah* was incumbent on all Muslim women. Surely neither the counsel nor the judge had any idea of what shock Iran had in store for them: that only a few years later Khumaini's revolution made things in that country wholly different is common knowledge.

In 1988, a Muslim judge of Andhra Pradesh High Court came out with an altogether different ruling on the issue of *purdah*.[40] Here at issue was the constitutional validity of the requirement of a photograph for exercising franchise under the Rules concerning the local Municipalities Act 1965, which a number of Muslim voters had challenged. Their lawyers cited Abdul Latif's translation of the Qur'an, the Urdu version if *Durr-ul-Mukhtar*. Abdul Ala Maududi's book on *Purdah* and a *fatwah* issued by the Madarsa Baqiat-us-Salihat at Vellore—all saying that getting photographed was prohibited, or even *haram*, in Islam. Refusing to re-interpret the classical texts, the judge held:

> A citizen professing Islam cannot be put to election either to act contrary to the religious injunction to be entitled to exercise his franchise or to observe the religious practice and forgo the right to vote.

This, the judge firmly believed, would be a violation of Article 25(1) of the Constitution. He granted a general relief that female voters could neither be compelled to appear before men to establish identity nor be disqualified from exercising right to franchise on declining to be photographed.

---

[40] *M. Peeran Saheb* v. *Special Officer, Punganur Municipality* AIR 1988 Andhra Pradesh 377.

I am inclined to agree with the Calcutta High Court's reading of the Islamic texts on *purdah*, since not only has *purdah* of the Indian fashion never been a universal practice of the Muslim world but eminent Muslim scholars have even denied that it is so enjoined by the Qur'an and Hadith. Personally, I don't believe in the Islamic basis of *purdah*. Yet I feel that denying right of franchise to women in purdah is not the proper way of changing popular beliefs in this regard. Of course, it will be utterly unconstitutional to force any Muslim woman to observe purdah against her wish; but it will be equally unconstitutional, I think, to drag one out of it against her wish, by imposing loss of civil rights. It should be left to every woman's free choice. Surely only a minuscule group would opt for *purdah*; and if they say this is their religion, let them take pride in it. Time can and will take care of them; legal compulsion cannot.

Mandatory Do nots in Islam

Leaving the do's of the Islamic code of conduct when we look into the dont's of Islam we find that the things believed to be absolutely prohibited by this religion are *lahm-ul-khinzir, khaamr* and *maisir*—pork, intoxicants and gambling, respectively. While pork is declared *haram* by the Qur'an in a mandatory language, consuming intoxicants and gambling are under the Holy Book sinful since "their bad points exceed their good points" (II:219). The Indian public law, which has in its fabric nothing having a bearing on pork-eating, agrees with Islamic teachings in looking with disfavor at consumption of intoxicants and gambling. The Directive Principle of art. 47 in the Constitution asking the State to bring about prohibition had enthusiastic Muslim support during its formation in view of its accord with the Qur'anic law on the subject. Constitutional validity of the Bombay Prohibition Act 1949 and its parallel in Madras (1937) have been upheld by the enforce the Shari'a law on *khamr*. So do the laws and regulations on intoxicating drugs.

The Public Gambling Act 1867 and its parallels in local legislation, on the other hand, agree with Islamic injunctions against *maisir*. So does sec. 294 IPC which prohibits lotteries as a private business. Muslim juristic opinion regards lottery as gambling. Opinion of the Supreme Court that "gambling could not be regarded as trade or business" under art. 1(1)(g) of the Constitution (AIR 1957 S.C. 669) impliedly enforces the philosophy of Islamic law.

The antigambling principle of the Qur'an is extended by an influential section of Muslim theologians to all speculatory transactions including insurance of life and property, which they regard as equally un-Islamic. The insurance laws of India have, however, never made any exceptional provisions for the Muslims. Of late, requirement of compulsory life insurance under service conditions for government and public-sector employment has often been referred by Muslim employees to the *muftis* with queries regarding its validity in Islam, and the replies of the *muftis* have not been uniform. Notably, at a grand seminar recently held at Hyderabad the Islamic Fiqh Academy of India decided to legalize insurance of life and property on the part of the Muslims "in view of the exceptionally grave conditions prevailing in India in which both life and property of individual Muslims are often exposed to unforeseen and unexpected risks." This decision desperately taken by those who have always been convinced of the applicability of the anti-gambling verses of the Qurʾan to the modern concept of insurance—tenability of their conviction apart—indeed speaks volumes about the acute feelings of insecurity which Muslims in certain parts of the country have, of late, developed.

Riba, or usury, is clearly prohibited by the Qurʾan. In the Muslim world there is a controversy if this prohibition applies only to private transactions or covers also interest on bank deposits, provident fund and other securities. Opinion that the latter falls within the net of the Qurʾanic negation of *riba* has led to the establishment of what are known as "interest-free banks" in many countries. In India, while all the banking laws fully apply to the Muslims, dominant sections of the Muslims in the contrary are not even convinced that bank-interest is usury. Some Muslim Philanthropists have in different parts of the country tried Islamic interest-free banking under the euphemism of "non-banking financial cooperation," having permits duly issued by the RBI. An international seminar on Islamic economies held at Delhi in January 1989 resolved to make efforts for "relaxation of banking laws of India to accord legal status to interest-free Islamic financial institutions in the country" (Resolution 6).

There are Muslims in India who regard birth control as un-Islamic, the view having been formed on the basis of an extended meaning of the Qurʾanic verse prohibiting (*mauʾuda*) infanticide and the Prophet's saying that a child whom God wanted to take birth would be born even if its parents practiced *azl* (birth control). They have demanded exemption from the laws and regulations relating to birth control, including the Medical Termination of Pregnancy Act 1971. There are, however, eminent *ulema* who have publicly upheld Islamic validity of family planning, for which reason perhaps the state laws, policies and programmes in this regard have not so far been challenged in a court. I have a convinced opinion that there is nothing in Islamic teachings prohibiting planned parenthood and that the Indian public law on the subject does not in any sense compel or encourage a Muslim to do what his religion prohibits. As regards organ transplant, the consensus in the Muslim world is that applying the principle of *hadi* (gratuitous transfer) a living Muslim can donate his eyes, etc., either as a gift *inter vivos* or as a testamentary donation. While another group regards all forms of organ transplant as disfigurement of the human body prohibited by religion, all agree on the sale of an organ being *haram* in Islam. Whatever organ-transplant laws are in force in India—of course, there are few—do not exempt the Muslims from their scope.

A much talked about salient feature of Islam is its egalitarianism. "There are no different castes in Islam—all Muslims are equal in the sight of God" is an oft-quoted emphatic declaration of the Prophet. The consistency with which the Muslims of India have claimed adherence to this principle in theory but disregarded it in practice over long periods of history is indeed amazing. The Indian schedule-caste law, which in effect says that no Muslim group can be included among such castes though it may be awfully backward economically, conforms to the theoretical egalitarianism of Islam, but ignores the realities of the Muslim situation in this country. Social stratification into caste is less un-Islamic than the practice of worshipping graves. If the Indian public law must not bother about the latter's repugnance to true Islam, there is no reason why it cannot take notice of the Muslim castes which are established features of Indian Islam—especially when in view of their social and economic backwardness they fall within the purview of constitutional provisions sanctioning special measures for weaker sections of the society.

Conclusion

The story of interaction if Islam and public law in independent India is indeed fascinating. There has been mutual give and take, recommendation and adjustment. Basic Islamic values agree with the basic philosophy of the Indian public law. The humanitarian law of Islam, remarkably, finds its parallels in the Constitution of India, and the two do not clash. The Qur'anic declaration *lakum dinukum wa liya din* (for you your religion, for me mine), for instance, echoes in the "freedom of conscience" clause of Article 25 of the Constitution. The provisions of Art. 145 relating to equality before law and equal protection of laws agree with the Prophet's well-know Last Sermon declaring: "No one is superior to another, neither the rich to the poor, nor an Arab to a non-Arab, nor the white man to black—all are equal in the sight of God." Similarly, many of the Fundamental Duties now enshrined in Art. 51A of the constitution are also religious obligations of the Muslims. Parts of the Indian Constitution relating to Fundamental Rights and Duties, on a careful analysis, are found to be not only protective of Islam as a religion but also reflective of the basic social philosophy of Islam. The same is also true of the chapter on "Offences against Religion" in the Indian Penal Code. The strict Qur'anic warning that followers of any religion should not use abusive language against any other religion or its followers is, for instance, echoed in sections 153A and 295A of the Indian Penal Code.

Islam thus shares a lot with the Indian public law. And, in turn the Indian public law protects Islam and Islamic institutions. There are no special statutes dealing with administration of Islam, like those in force in Malaysia, Brunei and Singapore—not even in the Muslim-dominated Kashmir and Lakshdweep. Yet Islam has an establishment owned and sponsored by the State

Islam and Public Law

and regulated by public law. The Wakf Council and the Haj Committee, both established under central statutes, wakf sections in ministries at the Centre and in state capitals; exercise of qazis' judicial powers by secular courts, the Kazis Act 1880 empowering government to appoint quazis for non-judicial functions, state recognition of settlement of disputes by the Sharīʿa courts in certain parts of the country, and above all the established practice of the government in respect of Islamic institutions, all indicate the existence of an official establishment. In any case between Islam and the State in India there is no U.S.-type "wall of separation."

There is, indeed, ample place for Islam in and under the public law of India if Islam is to be seen as one of the many religious faiths prevailing in this country. Islam's claim of all-embrassiveness, like that of Hinduism, cannot, however, be fully accommodated by the public law of India. In the context of Hinduism and Islam the public law of a secular country believing in equality of all religious faiths has to separate the religious from the extra-religious teachings. And it eminently conforms to Islam itself, which classifies its precepts into two distinct groups—(a) *ʿibadat* and (b) *muʿamalat*—spiritual and temporal. In a modern secular state which does not and cannot adopt Islam as its political creed, only the *ʿibadat* can expect statutory protection; *muʿamala*t can possibly be protected only in a professedly Islamic state. And as far as the Islamic *ʿibadat*—fundamental beliefs and mandatory practices—are concerned, the protection accorded by the theory of Indian public law is indeed remarkable. As regards the judicial interpretation of that law, talking of "essential" and "non-essential" practice of religion, the courts seem to be speaking language of Islamic jurisprudence which distinguishes *farq* or *wajib* from *mustahab* or *sunna*. But there seems to be no reason why the latter two may not be allowed if they do not contravene an express provision of the country's public law or are not clearly repugnant to the fundamentals of Islam itself.

Leaving the theory and coming to the actual practice, we find that those who are charged with the job of interpreting and applying the public law on religion do sometimes go wrong. That there are in India, unfortunately, deep prejudices against Islam and its followers is a bitter reality. Those who do silently share such prejudices cannot be expected suddenly to get rid of these on becoming part of government, bureaucracy, public administration or judiciary. Continued anti-Islam prejudices and misconceptions among them sometimes create situations in which clearly liberal provisions of public law find themselves actually applied in a less liberal way. When after retirement judges and public servants join political parties openly hostile to Muslims and publicly speak against Islam, it is hard to believe that during their official tenure they have buried their anti-Islam prejudice. And, then, there may be many others whose prejudices remain hidden. When authentic history is denied by holding that Islam preached degradation of women, or that the grand alma mater at Aligarh was not created by the Muslims or that Tipu Sultan's patriotism and religious tolerance was folklore, then existence of prejudiced brains among the executors and appliers of law gets confirmed beyond doubt. When least regard for basic Islamic values and slightest resistance to character assassination of Hazrat Muhammed are contemptuously called fundamentalism, words indiscriminately used and actions thoughtlessly taken by prejudiced or misinformed individuals exercising public authority have often changed the course of Indo-Islamic legal history—sometimes to the detriment of Muslims themselves. In any case, not all interpreters, executors and appliers of our public laws can be expected to be infallible or even as magnanimous as the noble makers of these laws were. The problem of Islam in my country is neither public law nor the public in general; it is the attitude of a few amongst us whose prejudices, pre-conceived notions and sometimes obstinacy, often does not allow them to properly use their authority when deciding on a problem confronting Islam or its followers. The solution lies in inculcating a sense of justice, fair play, large-heartedness, open-mindedness and magnanimity. These are the characteristics of law-enforcing individuals which Islam in India needs and the Constitution of the country sanctions and promotes.

I would conclude by asserting that Ram Raj must indeed be as alien to the Indian public law as Nizam—Mustafa—if both these concepts mean theocracy. But if Ram Raj's concern for the Hindu religio-moral values and the Vedic standards of justice and fair play can have any relevance to public law, equally relevant to it must be the religio-moral values of Islam and the Qur'anic standards of a just society. And in the ultimate analysis both will in fact be found identical, sharing similar concern for the welfare of mankind. They together constitute our national heritage. Both have molded the history and culture of India—and both will continue to have a place of honor under the public law of secular India.

9

The Shah Bano Case: Some Political Implications

Kavita R. Khory

Introduction

In April 1985, the Supreme Court of India ruled that under Section 125 of the Criminal Code, Ahmed Khan, a Muslim from Indore in Madhya Pradesh, was required to pay maintenance to his former wife, Shah Bano. This seemingly innocuous event generated tremendous controversy and hostility amongst the Muslims in India and raised fundamental questions about the nature of Indian politics. Almost immediately, the Congress party government as well as other political parties and a wide range of social and political organizations in India were embroiled in the ensuing debate on key issues encompassing religion, law and politics.

This paper examines the linkage between religion and politics in India as exemplified by the Shah Bano case. It should be noted at the outset that the Shah Bano case is by no means a unique example of the nexus between religion and politics in South Asia. Historically, religion has played a central role in the politics of the region. While the partition of India and the creation of Pakistan on the basis of Islam in 1947 is the most critical example of this phenomenon, the significance of religion in the political arena did not end with the division of the subcontinent. In fact, it raised a new set of questions regarding the role of religion in Pakistan and India's political systems. While Pakistan continues to debate the role of Islam in defining its social, economic, legal, and political structures, it appears that the Indian state is also far from resolving the apparent conflict between aspirations of religious communities and the secular notion of the Indian polity. Although there are obvious and significant differences between India and Pakistan's religious concerns and their management, it is clear that religion remains a contentious issue in the politics of both countries.

Issues of caste and religion are at the forefront of contemporary Indian politics. While one cannot deny the continued salience of religious issues and symbolism after 1947, India in the 1990s seems to be confronting a renewed, more powerful politicization of religion. The more conspicuous examples of religious and caste conflict in recent times include the Babri Masjid-Ram Janmabhoomi dispute in Ayodhya, the controversy over the Mandal Commission report that played a large part in bringing down V. P Singh's government in November 1990, and the so-called Hindu militancy or revivalism in some parts of India.

While important in its own right, the Shah Bano case provides us with an excellent vehicle for examining the broader trends in Indian politics that are signified by these events. First, it forces us to reevaluate the continued salience of religious identity in the political arena. Second, it raises a series of questions regarding the rights of minority groups, whether ethnic, linguistic, or religious, within a democratic system. Third, and perhaps most importantly, the Shah Bano case has revived the debate over defining secularism in the Indian context, particularly in the way it guides state policy towards the demands of religious communities. Lastly, the case has brought to the forefront lingering antagonisms, common misperceptions and a pervasive sense of insecurity shared by both the Muslims and the Hindus in India. The Shah Bano case is particularly useful for examining relations between the two communities, as well as the related and much discussed, but vaguely defined phenomenon, described variously as Hindu "fundamentalism," "militancy," and even Hindu "nationalism."

My discussion of the Shah Bano case is divided into two parts. First, a brief summary of the case is followed by an examination of the diverse responses to the judgment from within and outside of the Muslim community. As we shall see, the judgment generated varied and often conflicting reactions amongst the Muslims, members of the government, the Congress party, and other political parties and organizations. I intend to explain why many Muslims vehemently opposed the Supreme Court's decision, as well as the government's initial decision to support it. Because the Shah Bano case led to renewed debate over replacing Muslim Personal Law with a common civil code, we will examine the controversy regarding the continued use of Muslim Personal Law based on the *Shariat*. We are concerned mainly with the political dimensions of the issue rather than its legal ramifications.

The second part of the paper focuses on the Congress government's attempts to contain the negative electoral implications rising from the Muslim community's opposition to the judgment. By implementing the Muslim Women's Bill, which, in effect, overturned the Supreme Court's earlier decision, the government hoped to stem some of the Muslim hostility. In doing so, however, the Congress generated considerable opposition amongst its own party members, moderate Muslims and women's groups, and the Hindu community at large, which had welcomed the judgment. What motivated Rajiv Gandhi's government to undertake such an action despite its initial support of the Supreme Court's decision? To answer this question, we will focus in particular on the

The Shah Bano Case

Muslim community's relationship with the Congress and the extent of its electoral influence. We need to consider whether the government was simply reacting to the immediate circumstances of the Shah Bano case, or was it guided by more complex and perhaps less obvious reasons.

Finally, we will briefly explore the varied notions of secularism in India with reference to government policy on religious issues in general, and the Shah Bano case in particular. To what extent has the Indian state succeeded in managing, if not resolving, the conflict between the prerogatives of religious identity and the demands of an ostensibly secular polity?

Ahmed Khan, Shah Bano and the Supreme Court

Although the Shah Bano case first assumed prominence in the Indian media in 1985, it originated in 1978 when Ahmed Khan of Indore in Madhya Pradesh divorced Shah Bano, to whom he had been married for forty-four years. Ahmed Khan returned Rs. 3,000 (about $300) which had been her *mehr* or marriage settlement from her family, as required by Islamic law. Rather than accept the settlement based on Islamic tenets, Shah Bano sued her former husband for maintenance under the Criminal Procedure Code of India. As a result of this appeal she was awarded Rs. 180 per month for maintenance purposes.[1] The Shah Bano case gained national attention when Ahmed Khan appealed this judgment to the Supreme Court of India on the basis that as a Muslim he had to obey the *Shariat*, which required only that he pay her maintenance or iddat, for three months. The Supreme Court upheld the Madhya Pradesh High Court's decision granting Shah Bano continued maintenance from Ahmed Khan. The Supreme Court ruled that under Section 125 of the Criminal Code a husband was required to pay maintenance to a wife without means of support.[2]

While the Supreme Court decision in itself challenged the more conventional interpretations of Islamic law, Chief Justice Chandrachud's disparaging comments regarding the practice of Islamic law and the status of Muslim women further intensified Muslim opposition to the judgment. The Supreme Court gave not only its own interpretation of the *Shariat* but it also exhorted the government to implement a uniform civil code which would replace Muslim Personal Law. In his conclusion Justice Chandrachud stated that

---

[1] Ainslie T. Embree, "Religion and Politics," in Marshall M. Bouton, ed., *India Briefing, 1987* (Boulder, Colorado, 1987), p. 58.

[2] For a copy of the Supreme Court decision refer to C. J. Chandrachud, "The Judgement," in Asghar Ali Engineer, ed., *The Shah Bano Controversy* (Bombay 1987), pp. 23–34.

> It is also a matter of regret that Article 44 of our Constitution has remained a dead letter. It provides that "The State shall endeavour to secure for the citizens a uniform civil code throughout the territory of India."...A common civil code will help the cause of national integration by removing disparate loyalties to laws which have conflicting ideologies....It is the state which is charged with the duty of securing a uniform civil code for the citizens of the country and, unquestionably, it has the legislative competence to do so.[3]

The Supreme Court's decision was significant for the Muslim community in two respects. First, in formulating its judgment, the court made several disparate references to Islamic law and indicated that its decision to grant maintenance to Shah Bano was in accordance with the *Shariat*.[4] In doing so, the court was essentially interpreting Islamic law, which drew considerable ire from the Muslim community, particularly members of the clergy, who argued that it was not only inappropriate for a secular court to interpret religious law but that it set a disturbing precedent whereby the *Ulema's* interpretations could be overruled by secular jurists.[5] Second, Justice Chandrachud's appeal to introduce a uniform civil law in the country was viewed by the Muslims as a challenge to their continued practice of Islamic law in India as it pertains to issues of succession, inheritance, marriage, and divorce.

It was difficult for the Congress government to remain aloof from this controversial and much publicized decision, particularly in view of Justice Chandrachud's reference to Article 44 of the constitution and the call for implementing a uniform civil code in India. What seemed to be a relatively trivial issue concerning the maintenance of a divorced Muslim woman became a national issue that polarized individuals, groups, political parties, and the government.

Muslim Reactions to the Judgment

We need to stress at the outset that the Muslim community was by no means completely united in its opposition to the Supreme Court judgment. While it appears that most Muslims responded in varying degrees against the Shah Bano decision, it would be incorrect to assume that all Muslims reacted similarly. Given that Muslims in India are deeply divided by linguistic, cultural, social, and regional differences, it is not improbable that they would react differently to the

---

[3] *Ibid.*, p. 33.

[4] *Ibid.*, pp. 28–29.

[5] Nawaz B. Mody, "The Press in India: The Shah Bano Judgment and Its Aftermath," *Asian Survey*, Vol. XXVII, No. 8, August 1987, pp. 940–941.

The Shah Bano Case 153

Shah Bano case as well. Therefore, we will also look at the responses of those Muslims, who were perhaps not as vocal, but nonetheless significant, in their support of the Supreme Court's decision.

Muslim reactions against the Supreme Court verdict ranged from numerous meetings and conferences organized by several Muslim groups, such as the Jamiate-Ulema-e-Hind, the Jamia Millia Islamia, and the All India Muslim Personal Law Board to mass protests in various regions of India, including Uttar Pradesh and Bihar, which have a significant Muslim population. The large scale demonstrations against the judgment led to the common perception that most Muslims opposed the decision as well as any discussion of formulating a common civil code. The strongest attacks against the decision were voiced by the Muslim clergy, who believed that the Supreme Court's attempt at interpreting Muslim law directly challenged their authority.[6] The clergy's prominence in leading the attack against the judgment was not entirely welcome by the more moderate segments of the community. For example, Shahid Siddiqui, editor of the leading Urdu weekly *Nai Dunya*, claimed that

> Every small-town maulana has become a leader now with narrow objectives and narrow interest. If the controversy is not resolved quickly, these people will take the community behind by two or three decades.[7]

Regardless of how the more moderate elements amongst the Muslims viewed the clergy, it is clear that the Ulema's stance against the judgment was shared by a large number of Muslims.[8] The Shah Bano case brought together disparate segments of the community, who could agree on little other than the claim that the Supreme Court's decision was a direct intervention in the fundamental religious rights of the Muslims in India.

Those Muslims who opposed the judgment argued that the Supreme Court's decision and its statement on the need to create a uniform civil code threatened their religious autonomy and their Islamic identity. Syed Shahbuddin, an aspirant for national leadership of the Muslim community and a Janata member of the Lok Sabha expressed this widely shared sentiment. "Ours is not a

---

[6] Engineer, *Loc. cit.*, p. 13.

[7] Shekhar Gupta, "The Quran: The Last Word," *India Today*, January 31, 1986, p. 55.

[8] Because of the lack of systematic surveys, as well as some reticence on the part of those who supported the judgment, it is difficult to verify precisely the extent of opposition to the Supreme Court's decision. However, based on a selection of primary and secondary sources, one can assert with some certainty that a relatively large number of Muslims were against the judgment.

communal fight. It only amounts to resisting the inexorable process of assimilation. We want to keep our religious identity at all costs."[9]

While the judgment itself was sufficient to rouse the Muslims, several other events heightened the community's sense of insecurity. Some of the more notable examples in this regard include the national Hindu reaction in 1981 to the local conversion of a few untouchables to Islam; the killing in Assam of more than a thousand Muslims during the 1983 state elections; the terms of Rajiv Gandhi's settlement in 1985 of the Assam regional agitation, which deprived some Muslim immigrants of their citizenship and others of the right to vote for ten years; and lastly the reopening, by an order of the local court, of the Ram Janmabhoomi temple at Ayodhya in Uttar Pradesh, regarded by Hindus as the birthplace of Rama but claimed by local Muslims to be the Babri Masjid, a mosque reputedly built by the Mughal Emperor Babar.[10] Taken in conjunction with the Sikh-Hindu confrontations in North India, many Muslims viewed these events as part of a larger pattern of Hindu revivalism and nationalism. Under these circumstances, the Muslim community's strong reaction against the judgment was not surprising.

Whereas religious and/or political challenges may evoke the strongest response amongst Indian Muslims, we cannot ignore the impact of economic concerns on the community's sense of well-being and security. It is argued that a large number of India's 80 million Muslims remain at a disadvantage in terms of literacy, education, and job and business opportunities.[11] Although these problems are not restricted to the Muslims, they have heightened the perception that the community is isolated from the mainstream of national life.[12] While economics does not entirely explain the politicization of religious identity, it is one of the more commonly used rallying points for mobilizing groups on the basis of religion, ethnicity, language, or regional affiliation in India and elsewhere. For the Muslims in India, the Shah Bano case reinforced the perception that their lack of economic development as a community inevitably weakened them in the national political arena. The implicit threat to the practice of Muslim law as manifested in the Supreme Court's decision was seen as an attempt to assimilate Muslims within the larger "Hindu" culture and to deprive them of the autonomy to manage the personal affairs of the community members.

---

[9] Gupta, *Loc. cit.*, p. 55.

[10] Lloyd I. Rudolph and Susanne Hoeber Rudolph, *In Pursuit of Lakshmi: The Political Economy of the Indian State* (Chicago, 1987), p. 44.

[11] Gupta, *Loc. cit.*, p. 54.

[12] Ainslie T. Embree, *Utopia's in Conflict: Religion and Nationalism in Modern India* (Berkeley, 1990), p. 50.

The Shah Bano Case

Although the more conservative elements amongst the Muslims seemed to dominate the community's response to the judgment, there were several individuals and groups, mainly members of women's organizations within the community, who supported the decision. For them the ruling was a significant step in their struggle against those who abused and misused Quranic laws to justify the exploitation of women. For example, Zoya Hassan, an active campaigner for reform and codification of Muslim Personal Law, argues that the varied and often conflicting interpretations of the *Shariat* provided by the Muslim clergy creates more confusion and leads to discrimination against women.[13] While disagreeing with the common belief that the majority of Muslims, particularly women, are with the *Ulema* on the issue of maintenance, she claims that most of the Muslim women, particularly in the villages, are reluctant to speak out in favor of the decision. What is apparent, however, is that there is considerable ambivalence regarding the decision even amongst the educated, urban Muslim women.[14] Although many women as well as liberal men in the community feel the need for formalizing Islamic Personal Law, they are not all in favor of establishing a common civil code.

The Government's Response

The government initially supported the Supreme Court's verdict in the Shah Bano case. Arif Khan, a Muslim and a Minister of State expressed the government's position when he claimed that the Supreme Court had made a "progressive and correct interpretation of our religious law."[15] Rajiv Gandhi's support of the decision seemed to fit his image of a moderate and progressive politician, who was particularly concerned with the rights of women in India.[16] Although the government formally agreed with the decision, there was considerable dissension even within the Congress party. For example, Maulana Ziaur Rehman Ansari, the Union minister of state for the environment conducted a three-hour long tirade in parliament against the judgment. Similarly, Maulana Asad Madani, president of Jamiat-ul-Ulema-e-Hind and the Congress (I)'s key Muslim campaigner wrote a strong letter to the prime minister indicating how upset the Muslims were with the party.[17] As Muslim protests against the judgment gained momentum, Rajiv Gandhi found it increasingly difficult to maintain

---

[13] Gupta, *Loc. cit.*, p. 57.

[14] Mody, *Loc. cit.*, p. 46.

[15] Gupta, *Loc. cit.*, p. 54.

[16] Embree, in Bouton, *Loc. cit.*, p. 59.

[17] Gupta, *Loc. cit.*, p. 56.

his support of the decision and his minister Arif Khan, who had acted as the government's spokesman on the issue.

Other Views of the Judgment

For the most part, the Hindus responded favorably to the Supreme Court's judgment in the Shah Bano case. Again, while one should be cautious about assuming that all Hindus in India responded uniformly to the decision, it appears that most of them were particularly satisfied with the Supreme Court's emphasis on the need to create a uniform civil code. Many Hindus had not forgotten the bitter battle waged in the 1950s when the Hindu Code Bill was enacted, which reformed the Hindu law on marriage and inheritance and simplified divorce. The Hindus have repeatedly argued that if their laws could be reformed by state policy, why should not Muslim laws undergo similar codification and reform.

The Hindu reaction may be explained in part by what Shekhar Gupta terms "the paradox of a majority's minority complex."[18] He argues that the Hindu community which constitutes more than 80 percent of the population regards itself as a minority in India. For instance, Hindu organizations claim that

> The Hindus are being discriminated against—being denied their share of power by minorities voting as blocs, witnessing a dilution of their religious values by a liberalization that has spared other religious faiths, and being ill-treated in those parts of the country where they are themselves a minority or close to becoming one.[19]

While it is beyond the scope of this paper to delve into the perceived grievances of some Hindu groups and organizations, it is, however, a significant factor in understanding the way in which the Hindus reacted to the Supreme Court ruling. Moreover, Muslims regard the more militant manifestation of Hindu grievances as a threat to their religious identity and autonomy.[20] For many Muslims, the Shah Bano judgment was in some respects an indication of Hindu efforts to assimilate other religions within the fold of Hinduism. The Hindus, on the other hand, viewed the decision as a way of bringing about a more

---

[18] Gupta, "The Gathering Storm," in Marshall M. Bouton and Philip Oldenberg, eds., *India Briefing, 1990* (Boulder, Colorado, 1990), p. 31.

[19] *Ibid.*, p. 31.

[20] For a discussion of contemporary "Hindu fundamentalism" refer to Yogendra K. Malik and Dhirendra K. Vajpeyi, "The Rise of Hindu Militancy: India's Secular Democracy at Risk," *Asian Survey*, Vol. XXIX, No. 3, March 1989, 308–325.

uniform approach to the diverse religious groups and practices in India, particularly in the realm of personal law.

Apart from the Bharatiya Janata Party and the Marxists, who openly supported the judgment, the other political parties, such as the Janata Dal refrained from opting for one side or the other. The Janata Dal was particularly optimistic about receiving some of the Muslim vote, alienated from the Congress. To some extent, the Janata Dal's calculations paid off when its candidate Syed Shahbuddin won a by-election in north Bihar in December 1985. A year earlier, Rajiv Gandhi's Congress (I) had won the Kishangaj constituency, which spreads along the India-Bangladesh border and has a large number of Bengali-speaking Muslim peasants. The constituents rejected the Congress candidate by a large margin although he was the general secretary of Jamiat-ul-Ulema-e-Hind, a religious organization. While it is difficult to establish whether there were other reasons for the Congress candidate's defeat, it seems that the government's support of the Supreme Court decision contributed to its loss of Muslim votes in this by-election. The Congress' election defeat in north Bihar was important for two reasons: one, it indicated that the party's Muslim constituency was dissatisfied with its stand on the Shah Bano case; and two, it contributed to Congress' decision to reevaluate its earlier support of the judgment.

The Government Reconsiders Its Stand

Within a year of the Supreme Court's judgment the government was reconsidering its earlier support of it. The Congress government modified its stance in response to several important factors. First, it was clear that Muslim protests against the decision were growing rapidly and showed few signs of abating unless the government altered its position on the issue. Second, and perhaps most importantly, the Congress party suffered electoral setbacks in a number of constituencies throughout the country. In regions with significant numbers of Muslims, opposition parties successfully exploited the Shah Bano case and the perceived threat to Muslim identity in India. For example, in Assam, the newly constituted United Minorities Front (UMF) won 18 assembly seats. Almost all of these constituencies has a Muslim majority. The UMF campaigners focused on two key issues: one, the threat to immigrant Muslims from the Assam accord; and two, the threat to Muslim identity all over the country from the Shah Bano judgment.[21] Similar instances of the Muslim votes going to other parties were reported from Bijnore, parts of Orissa, and West Bengal. Although it is not easy to gauge exactly how the Muslims voted, it seems that sufficient numbers of

---

[21] Gupta, *Loc. cit.*, p. 55.

Muslims voted against the Congress as a result of its support of the Shah Bano judgment.

It was clear to the Congress party that the Muslims' electoral support had diminished considerably following the judgment. Although in the Lok Sabah the Muslim vote can by itself win no more than fifty seats, it can affect electoral outcomes decisively in about a hundred other constituencies. Moreover, in Bihar, Uttar Pradesh, West Bengal, and Assam, no national party can assume office without a reasonable share of the Muslim vote.

Since before independence the Congress party has had the political support of the orthodox and conservative elements amongst the Muslims, particularly from the Jamiyat-ul-Ulema, an organization of Muslim clerics associated with the famous Islamic university at Deoband. The Jamiyat's cooperation with the Congress is based on a tacit agreement under which the *Ulema* would give their support provided that the Muslim Personal Law is maintained, as would endowments, mosques, and other institutions and aspects of Muslim culture.[22] The Congress' liberal and secular approach under Nehru and later Mrs. Gandhi also drew the secular, liberal and even Marxist Muslim politicians to the Congress party. In most general elections since 1947, Muslims have predominantly voted for the Congress party.[23] It is evident that in siding with the Supreme Court's ruling the Congress alienated a large segment of its traditional Muslim electoral support. Given the strong electoral compulsions, it was inevitable that Rajiv Gandhi would eventually modify his party's stand on the Shah Bano case.

In order to ensure the continued support of Muslim voters and to prevent further outbreaks of violence, Rajiv Gandhi's government introduced a bill in Parliament that effectively abrogated the precedent set by the Supreme Court's award of maintenance to Shah Bano. According to the bill, Section 125 of the Criminal Procedure Code which requires husbands to support their divorced wives, was not applicable to Muslim marriages. In the proposed legislation, known as the Muslim Women (Protection of Rights on Divorce) Bill, maintenance to a Muslim divorced woman is to be provided by her former husband only during the *iddat* period, and the *mahr* (marriage portion) or other properties given at the time of marriage to be paid at the time of divorce. After the *iddat* period, it is the responsibility of the woman's family to provide for her. If relatives do not have the means to pay such maintenance, the woman could appeal to the *waqf*, the charitable trusts maintained for pious purposes.[24] The bill was in accordance

---

[22] Paul R. Brass, *The New Cambridge History of India: The Politics of India Since Independence* (New York, 1990), p. 191.

[23] For a summary of Muslim voting patterns in India refer to Brass, *Ibid.*, pp. 197–99.

[24] Mody, *Loc. cit.*, p. 949.

The Shah Bano Case

with the *ulema's* interpretation of the *Shariat*, which held that when the marriage contract is terminated by divorce, the husband's financial responsibilities cease. The bill was passed by both Houses of Parliament in May, 1986. Arif Khan, who had eloquently defended the judgment, resigned from the government in protest.

The prime minister defended the bill, claiming that it would further secularism in India by ensuring religious communities of fundamental rights.[25] There was no indication in his speech that at the time of independence the Congress had strongly favored the creation of common laws to enhance the secular nature of Indian society. While the bill may have appeased Muslim religious leaders, it was criticized by many liberals, both Muslims and Hindus. Whereas Muslim and Hindu critics of the bill agreed that it severely undermined the rights of Muslim women, they differed on key implications of the bill. First, and most importantly, they seemed at odds over what the bill meant for the rights of religious communities in India. For example, most Hindus believed that the bill weakened Indian unity by catering to Muslim separatism and allowing them to place membership in their religious community over their national allegiance.[26] Needless to say, this kind of response alienated even moderate Muslims from the Hindus. Regardless of their support for or opposition to the bill, most Muslims were concerned about their status and rights as a religious minority in India.

Second, when Hindus, such as the journalist Arun Shourie, faulted the bill for its injustice to Muslim women, many Muslims, both liberal and conservative, believed that it was a thinly disguised attempt on the part of Hindus to express contempt for the Muslims and their religious practices. Muslims who opposed the bill were often hesitant to voice their views for fear of seeming to agree with Hindu intolerance.[27]

Those Muslims who were against the bill argued that it perpetuated social injustice and undermined the rights of Muslim women. Zoya Hasan's comments are representative of this view.

> The bill was not at all necessary at the moment. It is against women. It undermines the rights of Muslim women. It exonerates the main culprits—the husbands who divorce their wives. It seeks to pass on the responsibility to maintain the divorced Muslim woman to her natural family....It is not the question of the personal law of a community, but that of the abandoned getting social justice.[28]

---

[25] Embree, in Bouton, *Loc. cit.*, p. 65.

[26] *Ibid.*, p. 65.

[27] Embree, *Utopias in Conflict*, p. 109.

[28] Engineer, *Loc. cit.*, p. 158.

Madhu Kishwar, editor of *Manushi*, a feminist journal in India, highlights the complex and controversial nature of the bill. While recognizing the broader implications of the bill, she maintains that it has intensified hostility and violence against the Muslims. In questioning the Hindu community's belief that the Muslims were in fact more powerful and influential than their numbers or economic and political status in society suggests, she forces her readers to confront widely held but unsubstantiated perceptions.

> Most Hindus are being led to believe that this bill demonstrates the sinister designs of those Muslims who want to 'break up the country.' For instance, a prominent Hindu politician is supposed to have remarked that this bill is proof that the mullahs and the Muslim League are running the country. This is indeed a bizarre distortion of reality. The Muslim community may occasionally be given some token concession because they represent an important vote bank. However, in reality, they are in no position even to protect themselves from continued pogroms and riots. They are continually losing even the precarious foothold they once had in the country's political economy.[29]

It has been suggested that Rajiv Gandhi responded to electoral pressures by attempting to appease both Hindus and Muslims. As the Rudolphs' and Francine Frankel point out, the introduction of the Muslim Women's Bill in parliament almost coincided with the opening of the Babri Masjid-Ram Janmabhoomi site in Ayodhya in February 1986.[30] As noted before, the site was disputed by both Hindus and Muslims. In the past, the local court had restricted both Muslims and Hindus from entering the area in order to prevent any outbreak of violence. In January 1986, Rajiv Gandhi directed the chief minister of Uttar Pradesh to ensure that this time the restrictions would not be implemented. On February 1, 1986, the district judge ordered the gates opened. Further, the magistrate's statements appeared to endorse the claims of the Hindus to the site.[31] It appeared that Rajiv Gandhi was trying to keep both communities satisfied. On one hand, Muslim protests against the Shah Bano judgment resulted in the

---

[29] Ibid., pp. 236–237.

[30] For a discussion of Rajiv Gandhi's approach to the Muslim Women's Bill and the Babri Mosque-Ram Janmabhoomi issue refer to Lloyd and Susanne Rudolph, *Loc. cit.*, pp. 44–45, and Francine R. Frankel, "India's Democracy in Transition: the Search for a New Consensus," *World Policy Journal*, Summer 1990, pp. 534–536.

[31] Frankel, *Loc. cit.*, p. 535.

introduction of the Muslim Women's Bill, on the other hand, sensing Hindu opposition to the bill, the prime minister attempted to appease them by reopening the disputed site.

Rajiv Gandhi's actions in this regard exemplified the way in which religion and politics are linked in India, whether in specific communities or at the national level. His policies were not unique; his mother and predecessor, Indira Gandhi, had certainly pandered to religious sentiment during the latter part of her tenure in office. Her approach to the Sikh conflict in Punjab, and her attempts to mollify the Hindus in Haryana for electoral purposes, brought religious issues to the forefront of national politics. To an extent, her actions contributed towards further politicizing religion and almost guaranteed the continued significance of religious issues in the national arena. Rajiv Gandhi's election campaign in 1984 also emphasized religious themes and symbols drawn primarily from Hinduism. This is by no means a new trend in Indian society. Much has been written, for example, about Mahatma Gandhi's liberal use of religious symbols for political purposes.

Secularism in India

The Shah Bano case has revived the debate over what secularism means in the Indian context. Many Indians, as well as Western academics, have written extensively about how secularism may be translated and applied in India. From Donald E. Smith's *India as a Secular State*[32] to the contemporary writings of Baird, Embree, and the Rudolphs, scholars have sought to define the concept of secularism and to understand its practical and policy implications for Indian society. More importantly, recent scholarship has cautioned us against relying on Western notions of secularism in order to explain or criticize Indian attempts at creating a secular polity. While it is beyond the scope of this paper to present an extensive discussion of secularism in India, a few brief remarks in this regard are necessary.

First, we need to understand the concept of secularism and its evolution in India in order to explain the current discourse that is taking place. This is important because our perception of this and other key social and political concepts inevitably influences our response to contemporary issues and conflicts. In this sense, not only secularism but also words such as communalism, fundamentalism, and nationalism have multiple, often negative connotations. For example, one frequently hears of Islamic or even Hindu fundamentalism, but few attempts are made to explain these concepts in relation to the broader political discourse.

---

[32] Donald Eugene Smith, *India as a Secular State* (Princeton, 1963).

Jawaharlal Nehru, while acknowledging the "comfort" and "stabilization" religion could bring to a society, was critical of the restrictive nature of organized religion. He argued that

> organized religion, allying itself more to theology and often more concerned with its vested interests than with things of the spirit, encourages a temper which is the very opposite to that of science. It produces narrowness and intolerance, credulity and superstition, emotionalism and irrationalism.[33]

Considering that the subcontinent was partitioned on the basis of religion in 1947, it was impossible for Nehru to avoid religious issues and conflicts despite his seeming dislike of organized religion. He and many of the postindependence generation of Indian leaders believed that only secularism would ensure against further religious divisions in India. The question, however, was whether secularism in India would follow a Western tradition of separating church and state, or if it would reflect a modified Indian version for managing religious differences.

The version of secularism that evolved in India was similar to the Western notion in some respects but differed in others. Secularism in India meant that the state would not patronize any religion and would allow for complete freedom of practice for all religious groups.[34] Although this notion of secularism was enthusiastically espoused by Indian leaders, implementing it was a more challenging task.

The Indian state confronted two key issues which seemed to question the very essence of its professed secularism. First, it was forced to choose between its avowed neutrality on religious issues and the pressure to reform some religious practices in India. In the 1950s Jawaharlal Nehru's government opted to reform and codify Hindu laws pertaining to marriage, succession and adoption. In codifying Hindu laws, the government had essentially signalled its willingness to involve itself in religious issues if and when necessary. Second, in response to this policy the Hindus demanded that a similar codification should be undertaken for Muslim personal laws. The Indian government's response at this time was that such an action would undermine Indian secularism and alienate the Muslims. For the Muslims, secularism meant the freedom to follow their religion and all its tenets without any interference from the state. For many other Indians, including some Muslims, secularism required uniforms laws applicable to all citizens.

---

[33] Jawaharlal Nehru, *Discovery of India* (New York, 1946).

[34] Myron Weiner, *The Indian Paradox: Essays in Indian Politics* (New Delhi, 1989), p. 31.

The Shah Bano Case 163

While the Congress Party under Nehru expressed its intent to implement uniform civil laws in the future, it did not resolve this fundamental issue, which is once again plaguing Indian leadership.

The Congress government's responses to the Shah Bano case in the mid-eighties suggests that the struggle to define and implement secularism in India is far from over. As Francine Frankel observes, the Muslim Women's Bill reflected a notion of secularism which "required the government to give equal recognition to all religions and ensure that no community was deprived of anything basic to it."[35] While electoral compulsions may partly explain Rajiv Gandhi's later rejection of the Supreme Court verdict, his government faced a more important question reminiscent of the 1950s: how does the state reconcile group interests with the demands of common citizenship. Although the Muslim Women's Bill may have appeased conservative Muslims, it has not resolved this outstanding question. Its significance is not restricted to the Muslims but also concerns other religious communities like the Sikhs, the Christians and the Parsis, as well as ethnic groups in India.

Conclusion

The Shah Bano case is indicative of three key trends in contemporary Indian politics. First, it is an important example of the inextricable link between religious and political issues in India. For the Muslims, Islam provides comprehensive guidelines for conducting oneself in the so-called secular or political realm. Therefore, any efforts to extract forcibly the religious element from the political sphere is resisted. Muslims in India are not the only ones to oppose state intervention in what they believe are their fundamental rights as citizens of secular India. Christians and Parsis have expressed similar reservations regarding the implementation of a uniform civil code. While this is not a new or significantly different trend in Indian politics, it is certainly reinforced by the controversy surrounding the Shah Bano case and the Muslim Women's Bill.

Second, the Shah Bano case amongst others demonstrates the weakening "secularism of India's centrist consensus."[36] Whereas secularism may not have been defined more precisely under Nehru and his peers, there was a certain degree of consensus amongst them regarding secularism as an ideology and a constitutional arrangement. The most important goals were the creation of a common national identity and economic development. As recent events indicate, these goals may be more elusive than anticipated originally. In many ways, the consensus of the first 25 years after independence has been replaced by strong,

---

[35] Frankel, *Loc. cit.*, p. 534.

[36] Rudolf and Rudolph, *Loc. cit.*, p. 46.

often violent disagreements over the fundamental principles of the Indian polity. Although the banner of secularism is raised frequently to justify pluralist practices, it is also used to condemn minority demands as a threat to national integrity.[37] Such criticisms are leveled against those Muslims who wish to abide by the *Shariah's* tenets in matters of personal law. Sikh demands for recognition of Sikhism as a religion distinct from Hinduism evoked similar responses.

Third, and perhaps most importantly, the Shah Bano case is representative of the way in which group divisions within Indian society are increasingly manipulated for political reasons. As noted before, Rajiv Gandhi and his mother before him did not hesitate to use religious sentiments for garnering electoral support. For example, Mrs. Gandhi frequently stressed that Muslim safety against Hindu fundamentalists could be preserved only by the Congress party.[38] Moreover, with the recent prominence of the BJP and its "Hindu-oriented" message in Indian politics, it is unlikely that we will see a significant change in this particular mode of politicking.

Despite the prominence accorded to religious identity in this paper, it is only one amongst several variables in South Asia's political culture. Regional, linguistic, ethnic, identities and class affiliations are equally important. While these identities are dynamic and their significance may vary according to the context, they are vital for our understanding of South Asian politics. Identities are formed, modified, and exercised in the political realm in response to several key factors: these include urbanization, mass communication, the spread of education, and growing social mobility. Moreover, they may be reinforced by the way in which policymakers respond to group demands. For instance, government policies in the form of preferential treatment or quota systems encourage groups to organize on the basis of a particular identity in order to derive maximum benefits from such programs.[39] Lastly, group identities are strengthened when challenged by others. These challenges may come from other groups in society in the form of migration and/or economic and political competition, or they may result from government efforts to impose a common national identity on diverse groups. The recent rise in ethnic nationalism in South Asia and in other parts of the world may be attributed in part to such processes.

Meanwhile, India continues in its struggle to define secularism and, more importantly, to resolve what role the state should play in issues and disputes concerning religious groups in India. Although the debate over formulating a common civil code continues, it seems that the efforts of individual religious groups to reform their own laws may be more acceptable and effective in the long

---

[37] Brass, *Loc. cit.*, p. 202.

[38] *Ibid.*, p. 202.

[39] Weiner, *Loc. cit.*, p. 30.

run rather than relying on state initiatives. The important point, however, is not whether we can separate religion and politics but how to structure their relationship in the Indian context.

10

Sikhs and the Law: A Century of Conflict over Identity and Authority

N. Gerald Barrier

While most of the essays in this volume focus primarily on aspects of religion and law in post-1947 India, each contributor is acutely aware that recent developments in the constitution and courts tend to mirror cultural and political factors that are embedded in Indian culture and history. This is particularly true of the Sikh experience. During the last century, Sikhs have struggled with issues arising from conflict over identity and the persistent challenges associated with their minority status. These inevitably involved legislation and the courts, first in a colonial setting and then in the often turbulent events after independence. Laws and court decisions have helped frame Sikh politics and debate over the nature of Sikhism, establishing identity markers as well as the boundaries and procedures that continue to influence Sikh public life. The interaction of religion, politics and law persists in the Punjab as well as among Sikhs dispersed throughout the world.

This evaluation of how the courts and the law interact with modern Sikhism will address three related questions. First, what role did the courts and legislation play in Sikh attempts to reinforce boundaries, identity, and sources of authority during the pre-1947 colonial period? Other scholarly work has explored the broader issues and conflicts underlying such matters, and therefore after a brief review of Sikh ideology and institutions, attention will be paid to specific laws and their long-term ramifications. Secondly, how have the Indian constitution and the courts affected Sikh politics and identity? This necessarily involves discussion of the relationship between the interaction of religion and politics in the Punjab, and the central role of legal norms and procedures in the resulting public discourse. Thirdly, since Sikhs now are a global community, what are the implications of the interaction between Sikhs within the diaspora and local laws and courts? The concluding section therefore highlights how legal issues and procedures affect Sikhs abroad, with particular attention to the adaptation and change of Sikhism in a North American context. What happened to Sikhs reflects continuity of struggle over identity and authority as well as new patterns that have implications not only for those in the diaspora but also Sikhs in the homeland.

Sikh Identity, Politics and the Law in Colonial Punjab

British policies and the transfer of western institutions into the Punjab transformed the political culture and created new challenges that mobilized Sikhs and other Punjabis. As in [the] rest of India, the western rulers adapted to local circumstance and put into effect fresh procedures and approaches to governance. Building support among perceived "natural leaders" such as aristocrats and families controlling religious sites became a priority. Former land grants generally were continued, and the prestige of prominent landed families was enhanced through special education, recruitment to key government posts, and other means of patronage. After a brief period of close association with Christian missionary activities, the foreign civil service avoided interference in religious institutions, social practices, and local custom. The Punjab legal code reflected elements adapted from other parts of India as well as particular attention to "customary law," especially as it pertained to rural activities involving marriage, inheritance, and caste/tribal measures. Keenly aware of the competition and conflict among the three major religious groups in the Punjab (approximately 50% Muslim, 35% Hindu, and approximately 13% Sikh), the British attempted to balance interests and at times manipulated different communities for their own purposes. When "self-government" institutions were created largely due to imperial pressure, local bureaucrats continued their patriarchal dominance through careful appointments and minimizing direct elections.[1]

Policies and laws affecting Sikhs received particular attention because of the community's assistance in the mutiny, the prominence of Sikh recruits in

---

[1] Background in N.G. Barrier, "The Punjab Government and Communal Politics," *Journal of Asian Studies*, Vol. 27 (1968), pp. 523-539. Also, overview in Ian Talbot, *Punjab and the Raj, 1849-1947* (Delhi, 1988).

the post-1857 army, and the centrality of Sikhs (especially Jats) in the rural fabric of central Punjab. The first British officials decided to make permanent grants to shrines by Sikh rulers and simultaneously extend ownership to the families associated with each institution. The decision at the time was intended to placate the local population but which within fifty years created problems when the managers and "owners" of the institutions increasingly came to be seen as marginal or even "non-Sikh" by Sikh activists. Moreover, the British tailored revenue policy and colonization of new canal lands to maximize the prosperity and hence the loyalty of Sikh landed farmers. Recruitment of Sikhs into the army became a priority, and funds were provided to preserve rare Sikh documents and to translate their holy scripture, the *Adi Granth*.[2]

At the same time, Sikhs were seen as potentially dangerous, an element in Punjab society that had to be controlled carefully. Officials moved quickly to put down a potentially dangerous uprising of radical Sikhs, the Kukas, in the late 1860s, and shortly thereafter prevented the son of Ranjit Singh, Maharajah Duleep Singh, from returning to the Punjab and possibly rallying Sikh support. Instead of non-intervention in Sikh affairs, the government pursued deliberate policies to dominate central institutions such as the Golden Temple, and later the Khalsa College. As one key bureaucrat noted, the government could not "stand aloof" and let troublemakers use traditional resources for their own ends. The "high-spirited and excitable Khalsa" had to be contained at virtually any cost.[3] Consequently British authorities used regulations and informal means to insure that friendly and pliable Sikhs headed the centers of religion and education.

This balance of coercion and conciliation in turn helped perpetuate Sikh ambivalence toward the government and western culture in general. Until the 1947 partition, and afterward, Sikhs keenly worried about their minority

---

[2] Discussed in Tony Ballantyne, "Resisting the 'Boa Constrictor' of Hinduism: The Khalsa and the Raj," *International Journal of Punjab Studies*, 6:2 (1999), pp. 195-216; Ian Kerr, "British Actions Towards the Sikhs and the Golden Temple in the Last Half of the 19th Century," in Parm Bakshish Singh, et al., eds. *Golden Temple* (Patiala, 1999), pp. 87-99. Also, Barrier, "Sikh Politics in British Punjab Prior to the Gurdwara Reform Movement," in Joseph O'Connell, ed. *Sikh History and Religion in the 20th Century* (Toronto, 1988), pp. 159-190.

[3] C.L. Tupper note in "The Golden Temple or Darbar Sahib at Amritsar," Punjab Government Home Confidential File A, Printed Notes, March 14, 1890.

status and threats from the outside, either missionaries or the Arya Samaj. Within a loosely organized group of associations and publicity networks that came to be seen as the "Singh Sabha movement," competing publicists and their followers attempted to reform and revive Sikh institutions, and at the same time fought innumerable internal battles over who had the legitimate right to speak for the community on basic issues relating to Sikh identity. Some Sikhs accepted a multiplicity of traditions and local customs, even claiming at times that Sikhism was a Hindu sect. Other Sikhs, known as the "Tat Khalsa," claimed that Sikhs were totally separate and should be led by *amritdharis* and *kesdharis* (initiated Sikhs and uninitiated Sikhs maintaining key symbols including uncut hair). *Sahajdharis* (Sikhs who followed the teachings of Guru Nanak but were uninitiated and rejected the necessity of wearing the 5 Ks) should be marginalized in all Sikh institutions. This increasingly dominant Tat Khalsa tried to eliminate popular cults and strengthen Sikh cultural boundaries. [4]

Sikh political struggles over legitimacy and control of resources increasingly involved engagement with the British over specific policies and laws. Support from the rulers, either in terms of patronage or legislation, was seen as vital to the future of Sikhs and their faith. A new organization formed in 1902, the Chief Khalsa Diwan, attempted to be a spokesman for Sikhs in public arenas and to serve community needs by unifying factions, expanding resources and institutions such as schools and social service agencies, and working closely with the British.

Between 1902 and 1918, the Punjab government and Sikhs led by the CKD jockeyed back and forth over procedures and laws seen as vital both to strengthening the community politically as well as defending the key proposition of the "Tat Khalsa", "Hum Hindu Nahin" (We are Not Hindu). Both British and Sikh leaders had to compromise on many occasions. The government feared giving too much to the aggressive elements of Sikh society at the cost of alienating some Sikhs and many Hindus. The CKD also had to compromise to maintain a semblance of unity within the minority Sikh community, as well as insuring that its claims would be met without permanently undermining British cooperation. In some areas, agreement was possible. Several regulations and

---

[4] Background in Harjot Singh Oberoi, *The Construction of Religious Boundaries* (Delhi, 1994); Barrier, "The Singh Sabhas and the Evolution of Modern Sikhism, 1875-1925," in Robert Baird, ed. *Religion in Modern India*, 3rd rev. ed. (Delhi, 1995), pp.192-223.

laws addressed the legitimization of Punjabi as an important language in the postal system, exams, and in specific educational networks. Similarly, the British and the CKD met halfway on claims about holidays, with some birthdays of Gurus being given special preference in the official calendar. In terms of Sikh symbols, the British liberalized regulations about the size and wearing of kirpans, along with new rules on dietary requirements and turbans.[5]

The most dramatic legislation, involving the legitimization of a distinctly Sikh marriage ceremony (*anand*), reflected the difficulties encountered by the Tat Khalsa and the British in trying to meet the demands of various constituencies. Competing marriage ceremonies, some with Brahmins, Vedic mantras, and sacred fire, were common among Sikhs, creating conflict and potential legal problems. In late 1907, the CKD thus pushed a dramatic new bill that would in essence create a "Sikh" ceremony recognized by the courts. The Singh Sabhas mobilized hundreds of meetings and petitions supporting the effort, but opposing groups among Sikhs and most definitely from the Hindu side also marshaled resources. The British felt legislation was necessary but refused to give in completely. The resulting Anand Marriage Act of 1908 consequently was a compromise, establishing that marriage ceremonies associated with Sikh tradition would be legitimate but only for those Sikhs who preferred the ritual. The Act was permissive and not the legally binding requirement for all Sikhs that Tat Khalsa advocates had championed.[6]

The controversy over marriage symbolized the CKD's difficulties in winning British approval as well as resolving issues that tended to divide Sikhs. For example, efforts to develop acceptance of adjustments to the traditional Sikh calendar based on the Hindu system foundered, as did efforts to improve treatment of women and low caste Sikhs. Adopting a general guide to Sikh life, a "rahit maryada," that deals with ritual and addressed Sikh identity, also aroused controversy and had to be shelved because of the marked divergence in public opinion on the matter.[7]

---

[5] On the CKD, "Competing Visions of Sikh Religion and Politics: the Chief Khalsa Diwan and the Panch Khalsa Diwan, 1902-1928," *South Asia*, Vol. 23 (2000), pp. 33-62.

[6] On the debate and the Act, Barrier, "Competing Visions," pp. 43-45. Especially useful are reports in *Khalsa Samachar*, September-October 1909, and a letter by Sewa Ram Singh, *Khalsa Advocate*, September 5, 1909.

[7] The Panch Khalsa Diwan challenge reviewed in Barrier, "Competing Visions," pp. 48-56. Details on these and related issues in Lal Singh, *Itihas Panch Khalsa Diwan* (Bhasaur, 1967).

The inability of the CKD to consolidate Sikh opinion amid persistent attacks from its opponents (both radical Tat Khalsa and pro-Hindu Sikhs) weakened the effort to move forward in two especially controversial legal and political areas, reform of gurdwaras and increased representation of Sikhs in the legislatures to be created by constitutional reforms after the First World War. The Singh Sabha movement had given priority to removing allegedly Hindu mahants and idols from key Sikh gurdwaras. Initially these campaigns met with limited success through compromise with local officers and scattered court cases, but in general, such efforts took too long and aroused a backlash from the British who feared turning over the centers of wealth and power to an increasingly aggressive section of Sikhs. The negotiations reached an impasse in 1917, the very time when the government rejected special considerations for Sikhs in the new reforms, and offered them instead less than 20 per cent of reserved seats in the Punjab legislature.[8]

As the province descended into the chaos surrounding the 1919 disturbances, Sikh efforts to gain control of the gurdwaras and an enhanced role in the political system moved from the bargaining table to the streets. Sikhs lost the battle for broader representation, but five years of sustained non-violent campaigns against the British won the war over gurdwara administration. The resulting compromise legislation, the 1925 Punjab Gurdwaras Act, established the political and religious institutions that were to remain central to Sikh public life on a permanent basis.

The 1925 enactment actually was the second gurdwara legislation passed in the Punjab. In 1920, a new organization, the Shiromani Gurdwara Parbandhak Committee, had begun a campaign to control major Sikh shrines and to remove Hindu influence and pro-British supporters. The SGPC had a democratic constitution with a requirement that all Sikh voters and representatives must adhere to the requirement of the 5 Ks. The activist ally of the new Tat Khalsa organization, the Akali Dal, spearheaded a series of marches and confrontations. To head off the mounting Sikh campaign, the British worked with Punjab legislators to pass the Sikh Gurdwaras and Shrines Act (VI of 1922) which gave

---

[8] On the CKD and the British, Petrie, "Memorandum on Recent Developments in Sikh Politics, 1911), reprinted in *Panjab Past and Present*, Vol. 4 (1970), pp. 300-79. Also, detailed assessment of Sikh political successes and failures in Rajiv Kapur, *Sikh Separatism* (London, 1986), pp. 47-104.

Sikhs a larger role in supervision of gurdwaras but maintained some of the claims of the families traditionally associated with the shrines. Sikhs generally rejected the legislation, and tensions mounted. When Malcolm Hailey became Lieutenant Governor in 1924, he took positive steps to rebuild relations with the Akali Dal and the SGPC, and a year later, the new act replaced the 1922 version.[9]

The heated legislative procedures that produced the 1925 Act highlighted existing divisions among Sikhs and also the concerns of the Hindu community. While most Sikhs including the Akali Dal and the SGPC welcomed the underlying principle that Sikhs would control gurdwara administration through a central body, some distrusted details concerning the centralization of authority and specific language. Hindus portrayed the bill as a British betrayal. Many of the final passages thus emerged from compromise and negotiation. For example, Tat Khalsa demands that only *amritdhari* Sikhs could vote and be elected was replaced by a deliberately vague definition of who was a Sikh. Anyone "who professes the Sikh religion" is a Sikh under the Act, and if challenged, can legitimize the claim by declaring "I solemnly affirm that I believe in the *Guru Granth Sahib*, that I believe in the Ten Gurus, and that I have no other religion." The only requirements for voting was that Sikhs must [be] over 21 years of age, be enrolled on electoral lists, and not be *patit* ("fallen Sikh", an initiated Sikh who cuts hair or commits other grievous offences). To avoid controversy, terms such as *sahajdhari*, *amritdhari*, and *kesdhari* were not mentioned in the Act.

The details for activating Sikh control and subsequent procedures were quite explicit. Specific gurdwaras would be notified and added to a schedule appended to the Act, or added later by an agreed upon process. Two committees were established to facilitate administration of the Act. First, a Sikh Gurdwara Tribunal consisting of three lawyers or judges (not necessarily Sikh and appointed by the government) had the responsibility of determining whether a

---

[9] In addition to the Kapur monograph, a contemporary account by Teja Singh, *Gurdwara Reform Movement and Sikh Awakening* (Jullundur, 1922); Mohinder Singh, *The Akali Movement* (Delhi, 1978). Documents in M.L. Ahluwalia, *A History of Sikh Politics and Gurdwara Reforms* (New Delhi, 1990). The key study of the legislation and its implementation is Kashmir Singh, *Law of Religious Institutions-Sikh Gurdwaras* (Amritsar, 1989). Also, see Surjit Singh Gandhi, *Perspectives on Sikh Gurdwaras Legislation* (Delhi, 1993).

place of worship was a gurdwara, addressing controversies over property and compensation, and related matters. Courts were excluded from intervening in gurdwara matters in which the Tribunal exercised jurisdiction, but appeals from its decisions could be appealed to a bench of the High Court. In addition, a Judicial Commission, consisting three of Sikh lawyers and judges, would hear petitions and deal with matters concerning gurdwara administration. The Punjab Government would fill all vacancies, with one member being "official" and the other two selected from a list prepared by the Central Board. Decisions from this special judicial body were considered final although in specific circumstances, appeals could be made to the High Court. The actual governance of gurdwaras involved creation of a committee of management for each notified gurdwara and overall supervision by a Central Board, with 120 elected members, representatives from the four takhts (traditional religious centers) and the Darbar Sahib, Amritsar, 12 members from the Sikh states, and 14 members resident elsewhere in India, co-opted by the Board. Other details about meeting procedures and the role of an Executive committee set the framework for the operation of the central body.

The Gurdwaras Act had immediate and longer terms consequences for Sikhs and Sikhism. First, the legislation brought to power two inter-related Tat Khalsa groups already active in Punjab politics, the SGPC and the Akali Dal. Although not named in the Act, the SGPC became the central board and has remained so since 1925. The SGPC had its own constitution, requiring members to maintain the 5 Ks, and while the Act does not specify such a requirement for the board, for all practical purposes *amritdharis* and *kesdharis* assumed control of the SGPC. Similarly, the Akali Dal, which headed the gurdwara reform movement and was an important Sikh party in the Punjab legislature, successfully contested the first elections within the SGPC. The Act thus legitimized the central role of the SGPC and the Akali Dal in Sikh public life and established a close relationship between the statutory body and the broader political system. Initially the SGPC played primarily a supervisory role over local committees, only directly administering the Akal Takht Sahib and the Takht Kesgarh Sahib. Expenditure of funds and decisions tended to be handled by local committees. However, the legal structure was established for the SGPC to expand its authority and centrality in Sikh affairs.[10]

---

[10] On Akali politics, K.L. Tuteja, *Sikh Politics* (Kurukshetra, 1984); essays in Paul Wallace, Surendra Chopra, ed. *Political Dynamics and Crisis in Punjab* (Amritsar, 1998).

The legislation also had the unintended consequence of merging the legal power of an elected body, the SGPC, with the traditional respect Sikhs afforded to the institution that combined Sikh religion and politics, the Akal Takht in the Golden Temple complex. In the British period, the managers and granthis of the Akal Takht had played a minimal role in Sikh affairs, often reaching decisions or circulating messages without the power of enforcement. For example, in the 1880s, it issued an edict "excommunicating" Gurmukh Singh, a leader of the Tat Khalsa movement, and in 1919, gave an award (a siropa or ceremonial shawl) to the British General Dyer who had caused the Amritsar massacre. In 1921, the SGPC took over the Golden Temple and named the first *jathedar* (literally, leader of a jatha or group) to head the Akal Takht. From that point onward, the *jathedar* tended to coordinate decisions and policies with the SGPC and the Akalis. Under the 1925 Act, the SGPC appointed all *jathedars* to takhts in the Punjab, including the Akal Takht. Thus while Sikhs historically respected the Akal Takht as a central institution, now the fiscal and administrative power of the SGPC, combined with Akali muscle, reinforced its edicts and enhanced its importance.[11]

The rise of the Akalis brought to an end an era of introspection and intellectual activity among Sikhs. Earlier the CKD had emphasized education, discussion of ideology and identity, and in general, attempted to create an atmosphere of cooperation and compromise among Sikhs that would maximize the overall strength of the community while playing down conflict. The Diwan continued to play that role in politics and education, especially through its annual Sikh Educational Conference, but clearly the Akalis and the SGPC had assumed the mantle of representing Sikhs and Sikhism.

Only infrequently did these new leaders seriously engage central issues affecting identity and boundaries. In 1928, for example, the SGPC and the four takhts "separated" or excommunicated a major Tat Khalsa activist, Teja Singh Bhasaur, for publishing the Adi Granth without one section, the *ragmala*. In fact, Teja Singh had pursued a campaign of demanding *amritdhari* control and a rejection of any "non-Sikh" elements such as the *ragmala* (allegedly written by a Muslim) for over two decades with minimal repercussions. Teja Singh and his Tat Khalsa network had opposed the Gurdwaras Act as a sell-out to the

---

[11] On the history of the Akal Takht, Harjinder Singh Dilgeer, *The Akal Takht* (Jullundur, 1980).

British and Hindu interests. When he openly defied the SGPC, the Akalis, and the Akal Takht as mere political pawns, pursuing *manmat* goals (false motives based on greed and power rather than following *gurmat* or teachings of the Gurus), they finally had the power and the will to take action against their opponent.[12]

The incident did not result from the leadership's over-arching concern with clarifying doctrine and ideology. To the contrary, the Akalis and the SGPC were concerned primarily with politics and were willing to compromise on doctrine when necessary. In 1920, for example, the Akalis issued a flier that said for "political" and not religious reasons, a broad definition of "Sikh" should include *sahajdharis*.[13] Numbers counted, not symbols and initiation. This approach also was reflected in the preparation of a Sikh code of conduct, the Sikh Rahit Maryada. Although the details of decision-making underlying the final editing of the *maryada* remain unclear, the matter received attention from 1931 onward, and finally, the SGPC issued a published version in 1950.[14]

The Rahit Maryada systematized most of the existing Sikh practices concerning rites of passage, worship, and boundaries involving daily life. While a distinctly Tat Khalsa work grounded on an understanding of Sikhism as totally separate from Hinduism and with values that transcended Punjabi culture, the document again was a compromise and avoided dealing with earlier controversies such as calendar, rules affecting women, and topical matters such as administration of institutions. Specific non-Sikh acts and penance (*tankhah*) were outlined, with resolution of major issues to be decided by large representative bodies. Nothing was mentioned about excommunication, either procedures or

---

[12] Issues reviewed in Barrier, "Competing Visions," pp. 59-61. The *hukamnama* (edict) reproduced in Dilgeer, *Akal Takht*, pp. 71-72. Also, *Shiromani Gurdwara Parbandhak Committee Ailan 82* (1928).

[13] *Sikh Kaun Hai?* (Amritsar, 1920). This also is clear from the negotiations and rhetoric leading to the 1925 Act. Background in Kapur, documents in Ahluwalia.

[14] On the evolution of the document in D.S. Chahal, "Who is a Sikh?", *The Sikh Review*, Vol. 42 (1994), pp. 21-33. Also extensive documents in Chahal's website on the Rahit Maryada. On broader issues concerning rahit, works by W.H. McLeod including *Who is a Sikh?*(Oxford, 1989), and particularly his forthcoming volume on the Khalsa tradition and rahit, to be published by Oxford in 2002. Various editions of the Sikh Rahit Maryada circulate. One is *Sikh Reht Maryada: the Code of Sikh Conduct and Conventions* (Amritsar, 1994).

the decision-making process. The only reference to authority besides the supremacy of the *Guru Granth Sahib* was a concluding reference to the Akal Takht which permitted appeals from local congregations.

The central definition of "who is a Sikh" incorporated the earlier broad approach of the CKD and in the Gurdwara Act: "any man or woman who has faith in One God, the Ten Guru Sahibs (from Sri Guru Nanak Dev Ji to Sri Guru Gobind Singh Sahib), *Sri Guru Granth Sahib* and the Bani and Teachings of the Ten Guru Sahibs; has faith in the Amrit of the Tenth King; and does not believe in any other religion, is a Sikh." The definition does not draw sharp boundaries and leaves open interpretations as to the dominant role of *amritdhari* or initiated Sikhs. The choice of the phrase *nisacha rakhda* (to believe in) can be interpreted as requiring initiation or simply affirming the value of such an action. Other ambiguities include details about Anand marriage requirements and funerals. The attempt to establish a quasi-legal framework for Sikh identity and daily life thus contains many vague references and expectations that could and would become the center of fierce controversy years later.

From the beginning, the SGPC served not only as an administrative body but an active player in Punjab politics and in the ongoing struggle over the nature of Sikhism. The courts further complicated its role. The Gurdwaras Act had resulted from hastily developed accommodation among various interest groups. Some of the ambiguities in the original legislation had to be addressed immediately, such as the ambivalent language regarding intent, history, and Sikh belief. The courts, for example, found that the reference to "Sikh" referred to a living person who professes the Sikh religion, but left open questions about the religious intent of deceased individuals associated with shrines but who had not openly called themselves Sikhs as operable under the Act. Also some shrines were linked to Sikhs who died before the time of Guru Gobind Singh, thereby raising the obvious issue of how Sikhs in earlier periods could have believed in the Ten Gurus. Details over the authority of Tribunals set up to investigate and reach decisions about whether or not a shrine fell under the provisions of the Act also came under attack as Sikhs and Hindus sparred regularly in the judicial system. A 1930 Amendment Act therefore addressed these and related issues, generally clarifying the principles underlying the early Act.

The second set of problems to be resolved involved the administrative and fiscal relationship between the SGPC and specific shrines and gurdwaras. The original Act had unclear language and left the central body without adequate supervisory powers or financing. Many gurdwaras did not pay their anticipated contributions to the SGPC and in essence continued to operate parochially. In addition, various factions fighting for control of the SGPC involved the Judicial Commission in a series of cases centering on budgets. In 1943, virtually all the Sikh members of the Punjab legislature therefore supported an amending act that changed the original legislation in several important ways. In the area of finances, the bill provided more flexibility and a broader mission for the SGPC, including additional funds for social uplift and missionary work. Along those lines, the Sikhs proposed reserving 12 seats for scheduled castes. The SGPC and delegated committees also were empowered to play a larger role in the administration of gurdwaras. Passed after lengthy and often rancorous debate, the 1944 Amendment Act therefore consolidated the power of the SGPC and made it without question the center of gurdwara administration and at the same time a valuable political prize.[15]

The Act also introduced terminology and an interpretation of Sikh identity that went beyond the generalities of the original legislation. The terms *amritdhari* and *patit* were defined, with statutory requirements that potentially had legal implications and could be actionable in courts. An *amritdhari* meant individuals who were initiated according to Sikh rites, and *patit* referred to a person who being a *kesdhari* Sikh (with unshorn hair but not initiated) trims or shaves his beard, or an *amritdhari* who commits any one or more of the four forbidden *kurahits* (cutting hair, smoking, eating Halal meat, adultery). Individuals were not eligible for election as members of the SGPC or a local gurdwara committee if they were *kesdhari* without being initiated, drank alcohol, and could not read and write Gurmukhi. This left open the question as to whether *sahajdhari* Sikhs could be members. In fact, except in one instance, all members of the SGPC henceforth were *amritdhari*, but some Sikhs with cut hair served in gurdwara committees and also special posts and committee associated with the SGPC.

The nature of the Gurdwaras Act and the consequences of its implementation in terms of fiscal resources, administrative details, political activity, and ideology meant that while the Act established the framework for regularizing gurdwara administration, it created new arenas of competition and controversy. The relationship between the SGPC and the Akali Dal, the role of the Akal Takht and the other takhts (with their appointed *jathedar*), ambivalent

---

[15] Discussion of amendments in Gandhi, *Perspectives*, pp. 145-216.

definitions and procedures, how and when courts and the provincial/state government could intervene in Sikh affairs, and the legality of edicts and documents such as the Sikh Rahit Maryada—all were to become pivotal as Sikhs attempted to regroup and move forward after partition and in the new nation of India. The Gurdwaras Act and provisions growing out of the new Constitution of India meant that law, politics, and religion were to remain inseparable in everyday Sikh life.

Sikhs and the Law in Independent India

The events associated with two dates, 1947 and 1984, have shaped the nature of Sikh politics, public discourse, and virtually every other aspect of Sikh life and culture. The partition of India uprooted Sikh society and economic well-being in West Punjab, but ironically, the substantial forced migration of large numbers and the division of the province laid the groundwork for an eventual transition from minority to majority status in the reorganized state after 1966. That in turn forced an ongoing reassessment of Sikh-Hindu relations and coalition politics, both of which involved issues of identity and legitimization of leadership. Partition had the immediate effect of arousing old fears of external threats and danger to the community, as well as heightened insistence upon the need for protection and additional resources. The talk of a separate Sikh homeland, emerging in the 1940s during the heated events leading to partition, gave way to an insistence that since Sikhs now were part of India, they should be treated with respect and aided in every way possible. This emerged most clearly in the protracted negotiations over the future constitution of India, and in parallel discussions over language and treatment of minorities including the depressed or untouchable castes. The resulting laws and procedures created bad feeling among many Sikhs, exacerbated before, during, and after the events of 1984. The attack on militants in the Golden Temple, Operation Bluestar, shocked Sikhs throughout the world and fostered a groundswell of anger and self-examination, soon to be followed by the anti-Sikh riots that fanned the already smoldering antagonism toward Hindus and an apparent Hindu raj at the center. Earlier laws, both central as well as the Gurdwaras Act, came under intense scrutiny after 1984, and became a major focus of community debate as Sikhs tried to figure out what had happened, why, and the implications for the future.

Sikh politicians had an opportunity to play only a minor role in the debates over the constitution for independent India. Few Sikh delegates initially joined the Constituent Assembly, and the subsequent addition of another handful came at the price of compromise and extended negotiations. All the delegates were painfully aware of trying to balance secular laws with the need for protection of minorities including whether or not to continue reserved seats for untouchables and others. The debates went on for days with little Sikh participation. The most effective presentations probably came from Giani Gurmukh Singh Musafir, Bhupinder Singh Mann, Hukam Singh and Harnam Singh. They weighed in on issues judged vital to the Sikhs—language, reserved seats, division of administrative units along linguistic lines, and a variety of safeguards for Sikhs. The major arguments mirrored those heard before the 1919 and the 1935 reforms, an insistence that Sikhs should be given influence beyond their actual share of the population. This was based on Sikh patriotism, loyalty to Congress aims in 1947, the large number of Sikhs in the military, and the particular needs created by the loss of life and fortune, especially in Lahore and the canal colonies.[16]

Sikh representatives lost on almost every vote, either in subcommittee or in the general assembly. Attempts to have four Sikh castes receive reservation status by inclusion on critical schedules failed, and only those in Uttar Pradesh who registered themselves as Hindu untouchables reaped any protection. Despite strong Sikh opposition, Hindi in the Devanagari script was adopted as a national language. The teaching and utilization of Punjabi written in Gurmukhi resulted from parallel negotiations in the Punjab which created Hindi and Punjabi zones, not through a states reorganization program as championed by Sikhs. Approximately 35 per cent of the Hindu-dominated Punjab, Sikhs led by Akali Dal called for separate representation to defend community rights against the "communal mentality" of Hindus. No concessions were made since it was argued that Sikh wealth and education would insure that the community played a major role in Punjab politics and administration. Several Sikh delegates refused to sign the finished constitutional document, and the Akalis subsequently denounced the Indian Constitution as giving too much power to the center, undermining personal freedom, and in general not doing enough to protect Sikh interests.[17]

---

[16] Based on the debates in *Constituent Assembly of India* (1947-1949). I am indebted to Robert Baird for loan of the multi-volume set.

[17] Background in J.S. Grewal, *Sikhs of the Punjab* (Cambridge, 1990), pp. 182-194; Sangat Singh, *The Sikhs in History* (New Delhi, 2001), pp. 250-284.

Sikhs revisited the need for reservation, linguistic states, and special assistance to Sikh areas of the Punjab on a regular basis, both in negotiations with the Congress and in election campaigns. One of the potentially most controversial parts of the constitution, Article 25, went virtually unnoticed at the time. The Article guarantees the freedom of religion, but then proceeds to indicate that other state obligations in areas of social welfare and reform cannot be set aside on the grounds of interference with religious rights. With regard to the issue of temple entry laws, these cannot be challenged on religious grounds (Part 2b). The explanation of this limitation creates the problem for Sikhs. "The reference to Hindus shall be construed as including a reference to persons professing the Sikh, Jain or Buddhist religion, and the reference to Hindu religious institutions shall be construed accordingly." As numerous scholars have noted, the explanation explicitly refers to Sikhism as a separate religion, and is included only for administrative or legal purposes. The wording actually mirrored the existing legal status of Sikhs. With the exception of Anand marriage, Sikhs had been unnamed in most earlier laws, unlike Parsis, Christians, and Muslims. The courts have upheld such an interpretation, and in fact, Anand marriage and the right to wear a kirpan as a religious symbol have been recognized as distinct aspects of Sikh religion. Discussions in the constituent assembly suggests that legislators were attempting to separate religious and secular issues, and had no intention of eroding Sikh identity.[18] The subsequent Hindu Marriage Act (1955), the Hindu Succession Act, the Hindu Minority and Guardianship Act, and the Hindu Adoption and Maintenance Act contains the same references. Each is not based on traditional Hindu law but rather secular approaches resting on universal concepts and models of English law. A leading Sikh legal specialist, Professor Kashmir Singh of Guru Nanak Dev University, has emphasized that the progressive nature of such laws are not only unobjectionable to Sikhs but in fact, tend to mirror the stated values of Sikhism in terms of the equality of men and women. He does argue, however, that the nomenclature is unfortunate and should be changed to leave no doubt about a separate Sikh identity.[19]

---

[18] Robert Baird, "On Defining 'Hinduism' as a Religious and Legal Category," in Baird, ed., *Religion and Law in Independent India* (Delhi, 2004), pp. 69-81; also, Kashmir Singh, "Sikhs and Personal Law," in Kharak Singh, ed., *On Sikh Personal Law* (Chandigarh, 1998), pp. 59-71.

[19] Kashmir Singh, "Sikhs," p. 70. A different perspective is in Harbinder Pal Singh, "Sikh Personal Law and the Constitution," *The Sikh Review* (May 1997), pp. 738-744.

Sikh opposition to article 25 and subsequent acts designated with the "Hindu" reference became strident and more central to public discourse by the early 1980s. Frustration with Indian government policies and the rise of fresh calls for a separate Sikh state, Khalistan, along with accelerating communal violence, led politicians to make an amendment of the offensive articles and laws a fundamental goal. The Akali leader Parkash Singh Badal went so far as to publicly burn a copy of Article 25 in New Delhi. Both Sikh and Hindu politicians used the constitutional wording for their own purposes in ensuing confrontation.

Prior to 1984, debate over the nature of the Sikh Gurdwaras Act and its possible revision also evoked strong feelings. The SGPC was a key element in the struggle to control the Punjab political system. It had legitimacy and also appreciable communication and financial networks despite losing control over 170 gurdwaras in Pakistan following partition. Initially the SGPC and the Akali Dal aligned with the Congress, but then responding to Hindu Mahasabha and Arya Samaj claims against the Sikhs, Akali leaders called for a separate Punjabi Suba. From that point onward, the SGPC moved further from being an institution involved with gurdwaras and social programs, and instead became a battleground for Akali and Congress activists. The Congress took over control of the SGPC for a short period 1953-54, and passed several amendments to the Gurdwaras Act that bolstered its position including expanding the power of government to remove members of the Judicial Commission and expanding SGPC links with Sikhs in a newly formed state (Patiala and East Punjab States Union, PEPSU). The Akalis then won an SGPC election, but in 1958, the Congress took over again. Holding the reins of the SGPC and the state government, the Congress passed another set of amendments. These extended SGPC direct control over additional gurdwaras and widened the scope of expenditures to include any reasonable religious or charitable purpose. A special Religious Fund for the purpose of promoting Sikh religion was established. These changes were designed to strengthen the Congress position, but as happened earlier, the move backfired. The Akali Dal took control of the SGPC, and from that point onward, the Congress withdrew from active politics within the organization and instead tried to shape its policies and limit its power from the outside.[20]

---

[20] Background in Gandhi, *Perspectives*, pp. 220-234. Also a useful, connected political history of the 1950-84 period is found in Sangat Singh, *Sikhs*, pp. 284-365.

During this period, the SGPC had attempted to expand its influence in the Punjab and beyond by proposing a new Gurdwaras Act that would bring all Indian gurdwaras under one administration, including the princely states. In 1953, it asked the Law Commission to consider a revised Act for presentation to the Lok Sabha. This was done in 1958, but created such opposition from Sikhs and others that the matter died without action. At issue were who would pay for the much larger expenses and the requirements that all voters had to know scripture by heart and demonstrate an ability to read and write Punjabi in Gurmukhi. Some Sikhs also feared greater interference from central authorities.

When events reached an impasse in 1959, the Akali leader Master Tara Singh and Prime Minister Nehru met and agreed on principles to guide future legislative and policy decisions. A new committee with nominees from the Center and the Akali Dal would implement a policy of non-interference in Sikh religious affairs and gurdwara management. In addition, future amendments to the Act would be made only with SGPC concurrence. Fresh elections would be held, and Nehru committed himself to help resolve any outstanding issues. In fact, nothing happened until 1966, when as a result of the reorganization of the Punjab, the SGPC became an inter-state statutory body, subject to the control of the Center, which could initiate future amendments. Since Haryana had been carved out of the Punjab, both the Haryana and Punjab High Courts had jurisdiction over appeals from the Judicial Commission. The Center also had the right and responsibility to set election dates and named the Gurdwara Election Commission to supervise preparation of rolls and the actual vote.[21]

Another complication arose in 1971 when Delhi Sikhs asserted their independence from the SGPC, which until that time had indirect but no statutory influence over non-Punjab gurdwaras. Following violence and incessant bickering, the President of India appointed a five-member review committee, and over SGPC objections, the Delhi Sikh Gurdwaras Act (Act 82 of 1971) was passed. Gurdwaras would be supervised by a committee of 46 members including the ex-officio jathedars of takhts, and some nominees. Besides reinforcing SGPC concern over losing control of important gurdwaras and their income, the 1971 Act became a political and ideological milestone. Only *amritdhari* Sikhs were eligible for elected positions, and only Sikhs with uncut hair could vote. The legislation thus cut across earlier compromises and stood as a Tat Khalsa

---

[21] Kashmir Singh, *Law*, pp. 284-288; also overview of legislation and politics in Kashmir Singh, *Sikh Gurdwaras Legislation* (Amritsar, 1991), pp. 26-28.

model for who was a Sikh and who should dominate Sikh public life.[22]

The Gurdwaras Acts, the Indian Constitution and Sikh personal law, and related issues about authority such as the role of the SGPC and the Akal Takht again came to the forefront after 1984. Operation Blue Star, the assassination of Indira Gandhi, and the anti-Sikh riots in Delhi and elsewhere accelerated the popularity of militant Sikhs and brought immediate reprisals from the Indian government and its agents. For approximately a decade, nothing was normal in the Punjab. Competing forces fought for control of the Golden Temple, the SGPC and the Akal Takht, moderate politicians were killed and driven underground, and an atmosphere of oppression and intolerance prevailed. Western and Sikh scholars who pursued research allegedly contradicting traditional views of religion, politics, and history came under attack. Neo-Hindu politicians were seen behind all alleged anti-Sikh policies, and in general, Sikhs viewed themselves as a persecuted minority and Sikhism in mortal danger.[23]

Sikhs responded to the crisis by re-asserting what were judged basic elements of Sikh identity. Old legal and cultural issues now aroused high passion tinged with a sense of threat and the need for aggressive action. The mobilization of Sikhs across the world was pervasive and in many instances divisive. Editorials, meetings, tracts, and marches echoed a common theme—Sikhism is a distinct world religion under attack and must be defended at every turn. In such an atmosphere, Sikhs challenged the underlying assumptions of the Indian Constitution, arguing that the secular clauses really were disguise for a Hindu agenda aimed against all minorities and especially Sikhs. Sikhs must have their separate state and a legal basis for their separate identity.[24]

Almost every Sikh political manifesto and resolution demanded that any reference to Sikhs as Hindus be eliminated, and that in addition, Sikh personal law should be written into legislation and enforced. One common ap-

---

[22] The best study of Delhi Sikh politics and the Act is Jitinder Kaur, *The Politics of Sikhs: A Study of Delhi Sikh Gurdwara Management Committee* (Delhi, 1986).

[23] One of the most useful surveys of the politics is Grewal, *Sikhs*; also Grewal and Indu Banga, eds., *Punjab in Prosperity and Violence* (Chandigarh, 1998); Harish Puri, et al, eds., *Terrorism in Punjab* (Delhi, 1999). On the intellectual issues, J.S. Grewal, *Contesting Interpretations of the Sikh Tradition* (Delhi, 1998).

[24] Major themes almost every month in the Chandigarh journal, *The Spokesman*, and *The World Sikh News*. Also the Calcutta journal, *The Sikh Review*, frequently carried articles on various Sikh approaches to legal issues, the Sikh Rahit Maryada, and the Akal Takht.

proach has been to see the Sikh Rahit Maryada, prepared and publicized by the SGPC, as the basis for Sikh law. That document, plus the precepts in the Adi Granth, decisions from the Akal Takht, and current usage, could be codified and written into legislation. Perhaps a highly qualified committee or group of intellectuals could prepare a draft, which after consultation, would become the basis for a constitutional amendment. Such suggestions have come from seminars and articles, and also occasionally references to Sikh law and practice in statements and edicts from the SGPC. Another strategy emphasized rewriting sections of the Indian Constitution to highlight specific laws and procedures for each religious community.

The arguments face two seemingly insurmountable problems. First, Sikhs cannot demonstrate specific ways that the Constitution and court opinion have damaged their community. Leaving law and order regulations aside, serious challenges to Sikh social and cultural practices have been minimal. In the area of religious symbols, for example, the kirpan is specifically designated as a religious symbol for Sikhs, although at times officials backed by the courts have placed limits on the size of swords, or having more than one in possession. Such instances often relate to particular security needs in key government buildings or on airlines. Changes in procedure and negotiation would seem to be a more effective means of dealing with these problems rather than trying to address them into an amended constitution.

More importantly, Sikhs could never agree on a uniform Sikh code. As in the case of the Singh Sabha period, Sikhs are much more unified in demonstrating what they are not, Hindu, than defining the boundaries, rituals, customs, and social practices that constitute a Sikh way of life. One only has to look at the ongoing controversies among supposed leaders of the community, in the SGPC and the takhts, to realize the difficulties in developing a distinct code. Kashmir Singh has summarized this quite aptly: "In case the demand for a separate Sikh Personal Law is conceded, it will amount to opening a Pandora's box. Every Sikh political power and youth organization who claim finality in each of their assertions, will unnecessarily be bothered to make suggestions leading to useless controversies."[25] He goes on to note that as a universal religion with followers across the world, any prescribed new body of law may not be adopted

---

[25] Kashmir Singh, "Sikhs," p.70. One of the most interesting and critical essays, on Sikh "Identity Crisis" by Jagtar Singh is in the *Indian Express*, November 1, 1998 (on-line edition).

or recognized by them or by the law of their new residence. The point is well taken. One only has to look at the varying perspectives in contemporary Sikh chatrooms and list-serves, or to track the controversies reviewed regularly in *The Sikh Review* or other journals, to realize the difficulties of moving from theoretical constructs to specific laws. Legislating on dowry, women's rights, legitimate Sikh names, and so forth indeed would indeed be counter-productive. If an "intellectual body" were named to prepare the outlines of Sikh legal requirements, that group immediately would become highly politicized as factions and power-brokers attempt to dominate the agenda.

Sikh determination to assert a separate identity as well as demonstrating the importance of Sikhism as a world religion invariably fostered fresh discussions of gurdwara administration after the early 1980s. In the prior decade, Sikhs and the central government agreed on the need for amendments, and a small committee prepared a draft. The SGPC and Indian officials went back and forth for years without resolution and much enthusiasm. A revised draft prepared by a special committee (the Dalam Committee) circulated another draft, but again, no decision was made. Yet another version has surfaced recently with the same result.[26]

If Sikhs seem to agree that gurdwara administration needs broadening and that apparent defects in the current system should be addressed, what has prevented creation of a new act? First, any amendments would involve immediate political consequences, either strengthening the hands of those in power, or diffusing authority to an all-India based body. The SGPC wants to maintain control, and the Indian government does not want to relinquish any powers arising from the intra-state nature of the existing and future legislation. Because of close links between leaders of the Akalis and the SGPC and the central government headed by the BJP, both tend to pursue common policies that will not disturb existing arrangements. In fact, the SGPC has been able to strengthen its power through notifications from the Indian government, such as in April

---

[26] Background in Kashmir Singh, *Sikh Gurdwaras Legislation* (Amritsar, 1991). I appreciate Kashmir Singh's great assistance in providing documents, notifications, and a copy of the 1999 draft for this paper, along with comments on the issues and an earlier draft. He helped me avoid several serious errors, but the final interpretations are mine alone. Discussion of the 1999 bill in the *Tribune*, March 29, 2001, and other editorials, reports and letters in that period. On the *sahajdhari* exclusion, petition from the Sahajdhari Sikh Federation, *Tribune*, September 20, 2001.

1998 when 37 gurdwaras with an income of 7.40 crore annually were transferred to the SGPC (*Indian Express*, April 30, 1998). The SGPC also has been successful in securing official support to clarify murky issues such as the status of the fifth takht, Damdama Sahib. Although generally recognized as a major takht by Sikhs for at least half a century, the legal position of its jathedar was uncertain and only finally made legitimate by an April 23, 1999 notification issued by the Indian government.

Other internal Sikh matters also hinder general acceptance of any new legislation. Many gurdwaras now beyond the supervision of the SGPC have some reluctance in sharing funds and also experiencing interference in local practice. The politics of the Gurdwaras Act are even more complex because vested interests within the community have their own agendas. At the time of SGPC, state, or Lok Sabha elections, competing parties lambast the other and blame opponents for inaction.

Competing interests suggest an even more basic problem. Drafts and revisions highlight fundamental issues about authority and Sikh identity that have tended to be avoided in existing legislation. Reflecting the sentiment of the Delhi Act, the 1986 Dalam proposals have a broad definition of "Sikh" at the outset (a person who believes in one God and follows the teaching of *Sri Guru Granth Sahib* and the ten Gurus and does not profess any other religion), but then allows only Sikhs with unshorn hair to vote, and a much narrower base of *amritdharis* to be members of Boards. *Sahajdharis*, many of whom are prominent Sikhs especially outside the Punjab, thus would be relegated to a secondary role. In addition, the draft incorporates the observance of the Sikh Rahit Maryada as a requirement for all voters and officials. In terms of administration, the Act would constitute a Central Board, State Boards, and Regional Boards, with various membership arrangements. At the Central level, provision is made for co-opting *sahajdhari* Sikhs (two-three) including one from a group of well known saints, up to twenty-four scholars, lawyers, and other prominent Sikhs, five from the scheduled castes, the Head Granthi of the Darbar Sahib and the jathedars of the takhts. All the nominated members could attend and participate but not vote. Other requirements for board members at every level include no drinking, no smoking, and an ability read and write in Gurmukhi. Provisions are made for ten elected members of scheduled castes from the Punjab. Subsequent versions either continue the practice of reserved seats for women (a notification in 1996 added provisions for 30 women including five from the scheduled castes) or they eliminate that provision.

The proposed 1999 bill refined earlier drafts and made some changes, often controversial. All references to *kesdhari* and *sahajdhari* have been eliminated, also *kurehat* (defined earlier as an *amritdhari* cutting hair, using tobacco, eating Kutha meat, and committing adultery). *Patit*, earlier referring to *kesdharis* cutting hair and *amritdharis* committing any of the *kurehats*, is changed to any Sikh who commits a *kurehat*. The general definition of Sikh in the Dalam version is amended to include a requirement in "Khande-ka-Amrit bequeathed by the Tenth Guru," keeping unshorn hair, and not using tobacco in any form. All electors must be "Sikh" but only *amritdharis* can hold office. The 1999 proposals continue a mix of elected members and co-opted members for the Central Board, but non-elected members would have limited voting rights.

Besides establishing a complex network of requirements, boards, and administrative detail, the Dalal bill and its successors attempt three major innovations that have ideological and political consequences. First, while women, scheduled castes, and *sahajdharis* are incorporated in various ways, the decision-making function rest upon a balance between a large *kesdhari* constituency and a smaller elite group of initiated Sikhs. Criticism on this principle has been sharp, especially among Sikhs who fear that marginalizing specific groups may weaken the resources and appeal of Sikhism. Secondly, the newest versions respond to growing conflict over religious and social authority among Sikhs by trying to establish an acceptable system for reaching decisions that affect Sikhs everywhere. The Dalam draft establishes a "Central Religious Body" composed of a variety of *amritdhari* Sikhs (former and existing jathedars, respected religious leaders) who will deal with "controversial matters of Panthic importance." Headed by the Jathedar of the Akal Takht, the committee would consult and then make a "decision for the guidance of the Sikh panth." The 1999 version strengthens the role of the Jathedar of the Akal Takht, meeting in conjunction with the other jathedars and the Head Granthi, and makes decisions on "panthic matters...final and binding on the whole Sikh Panth." The next section Act focuses on the role of the jathedars of the takhts and the granthis of the Darbar Sahib, their qualifications, hiring, and dismissal. The provisions are very general, with loopholes and ambiguities that mirror Sikh uncertainty as to relationship between the SGPC and the jathedars, and who has ultimate authority in Sikhism. Finally, the proposed revision addresses increasingly complex judicial processes that frame administration and the operation of the SGPC. The Judicial Commission and the Tribunal are combined in one body, a Sikh Gurdwaras Tribunal, with a broad mandate to adjudicate disputes. Members are to be chosen by the central government from a list provided by the SGPC. More importantly, appeals are taken out of the regular court system and now would be heard by a new Sikh Gurdwaras Appellate Judicial Authority.

These legal innovations are responses to the most pressing problems confronting Sikhs. First, the new act would clarify the position of the SGPC and remove wherever possible, any ambiguities about its authority and role. The influence and power of the SGPC would be strengthened and in essence complete its transition from the administrative body to one that would have even more influence as a spokesman for Sikh culture, social values, and religious doctrine. The SGPC would lead in ensuring that the "Sikh *maryada*" and Sikh principles be followed in every gurdwara. It would be able to take over any religious or charitable institutions or endowment or school under certain circumstances, set up new trusts for education and to improve the morals of the community, and have sole right to print, publish and distribute the *Guru Granth Sahib*. Furthermore, a Trust linked to the SGPC would initiate and publish books on history, religion, and culture, and could pursue prosecution of individuals and organizations not complying with SGPC supervision.

The potential expansion of financial support and networks across India, however, also means that the SGPC elections and decision-making would be a more impressive prize than earlier. As it stands now, SGPC members, staff, and a broad system of patronage influence much of what transpires in local religious and political institutions. Corruption and misuse of power are common knowledge, and factions use every means possible to control the institution. The recent struggle between the head of the Akalis and the Punjab government, Parkash Singh Badal, and the long-time President of the SGPC, Gurcharan Singh Tohra, led to Badal's takeover of the SGPC, creating new fault lines among Sikhs and in the eyes of many observers, at least temporarily damaging the legitimacy of the institution as a "Sikh Parliament."[27]

---

[27] For example, the critical articles in *The Sikh Review* and *The Sikh Bulletin* (Roseville, California). *The Spokesman* has been a persistent voice questioning SGPC, Akali, and Jathedar politics. On the SGPC decisions concerning supervision of publishing the *Guru Granth Sahib*, morality, historical writing, and "Dharm Parchark" ("preaching of religion" or missionary activities), reports in the following *Tribune* issues are useful: October 3, 2000; January 7, 2001; April 1, 2001; May 5, 2001. On the charge of blasphemy for those publishing selections from the *Guru Granth Sahib* or pictures of the Gurus on marriage cards and calendars, *Tribune*, September 1, 2001.

Secondly, besides broadening the functions of the SGPC through the creation of a new "Central Religious Body," the new advisory board would help the Executive Committee deal directly with contentious issues of "panthic importance." Sikhs increasingly have expected the SGPC to reach authoritative decisions, in close conjunction with the jathedars and especially the Jathedar of the Akal Takht. Since the 1970s, the Jathedar has been very involved in political and religious matters, issuing edicts, issuing *hukamnamas* or orders on general or specific problems, and using excommunication as an ultimate threat and weapon. At one point in the late 1990s, one Jathedar of the Akal Takht, Ranjit Singh, began excommunicating individuals for alleged misconduct and tried to prevent his own expulsion by excommunicating leaders of the SGPC. The resulting chaos and threats to the legitimacy of not only the SGPC but the Jathedar as premier Sikh religious leaders have led the drafters of the new legislation to suggest minimal requirements for future appointees to the key jathedar and Granth posts, the terms of their employment, duties, and guidelines for removal. The jathedars could take up any matter, as a group, but before reaching a decision, they would have to refer the matter to the Central Religious Body and possibly a large convened "*Sarbat Khalsa*" meeting which would give opinions. Although written in general terms, the underlying purpose of these innovations is quite clear. The SGPC wants an elaborate process of reaching decisions on controversial issues, with appropriate supervision and checks and balances so as to prevent some of the individual pronouncements that have created turmoil and bad feeling. The new law would balance the call for the Jathedar of the Akal Takht to be totally independent of all restraints with the perceived need to insure that the position arise from a democratic process and not be autocratic.[28]

Finally, the SGPC and those supporting the new legislation are trying to modify the role existing procedures and court decisions play in SGPC and Akali politics. Recently, for example, the independent Judicial Commission has heard many cases involving maladministration and illegal actions by members of the central body. While steering clear of deciding "who is a real Sikh" under

---

[28] Seminar proceedings and articles in Jasbir Singh Ahluwalia, H.S. Dilgir, eds., *Sri Akal Takht* (Chandigarh, 1994). On the excommunications, and *hukamnamas*, background and editorial comments in the *Tribune*, February 19, 2000; March 14, 2000; and especially, "Hukamnamas: A Record of Sorts in Three Years," October 26, 2000. On manipulation of "maryada," *The Spokesman* (January 2001), pp.7-8, and (December 2000), pp. 29-32.

existing definitions of the Act and the Sikh Rahit Maryada, which for some has been the basis for legal appeals and public charges, the Commission has been drawn into the mire of factional fighting. It has heard cases on whether specific individuals are "*patit*" or "fallen Sikhs" who because of their actions cannot hold office, claims about qualifications, requirements about membership including whether family members of SGPC officials must be initiated, and related matters. Wading through a thicket of contempt charges and petitions, the Commission also had to evaluate the circumstances and legality of the firing of individuals, including the Jathedar of the Akal Takht, Ranjit Singh. Similarly, the High Courts have been involved in a range of appeals. Another active body associated with the current Act, the Election Commission, has been drawn into the question of who can vote. Primarily a central government body, the Commission has insisted that the definition of Sikh in the original Act serve as the basis for registration despite some SGPC and Akali efforts to limit rolls only to those meeting the same type of Tat Khalsa criteria governing Delhi elections.[29] One piece of legislation designed initially to resolve who could control Sikh gurdwaras thus remains a persistent feature of Sikh public life, creating boundaries and arenas within which Sikhs fight each other and external opponents, and providing a catalyst for ongoing debate over Sikh identity.

Sikhs, Legal Issues and the Courts, and Identity in the Diaspora

Disputes over the SGPC, the Akal Takht as a legal and traditional authority in Sikhism, the applicability of the Sikh Rahit Maryada, and legal decisions and legislation affecting Sikh identity, all have implications for Sikhs living outside India. By the 1970s, Sikh had major centers in North America, England, and other parts of the world. Most institutions and issues tended to be local and reflected immediate concerns. Disputes occurred over gurdwaras, but constitutions and bylaws required by law set boundaries on

---

[29] A detailed record of the various court proceedings and decisions by the Gurdwaras Act tribunals is found in a chronological guide to Punjab political and religious news issued annually: Mohinder Singh, *Punjab 1998* (New Delhi, 1999); *Punjab 1999* (New Delhi, 2000); *Punjab 2000* (New Delhi, 2001). The massive reference includes summaries of articles from major newspapers, including the *Tribune* and the *Indian Express*. Particularly useful are High Court discussions, *Tribune*, September 20, 2001; Harbans Lal, interview, *Tribune*, February 27, 2001.

disputes and became involved in the courts only in extreme cases. Local customs blended with rituals and some aspects of daily life mirrored in the Sikh Rahit Maryada. The SGPC and even Punjab politics did not appear to be an important concern in the life of the diaspora community.[30]

This changed dramatically in the late 1970s and afterward. The calls of "Sikhism in danger" and the instantaneous mobilization of Sikhs everywhere after the traumatic events of 1984 set the stage for major developments among Sikhs. A fresh insistence upon cultural boundaries and Sikh identity intensified sensitivity to legal restrictions and led to a series of court challenges aimed at protecting Sikh symbols, especially the turban and the kirpan. In addition, this new focus on boundaries and identity, combined with the successful efforts of pro-Khalistan or militant Sikhs to control gurdwaras, fostered conflict and inevitable court cases. While the processes and events created somewhat similar patterns throughout the diaspora, developments in the U.K., Canada, and America especially illustrate how the Sikh encounter with a variety of western courts and laws have helped influence Sikhism beyond Punjab.

The legal issues confronting Sikhs in England have their roots in a broader pattern of racism evoked by the inability of segments of the British population to deal with the influx of immigrants after the Second World War. Cultural insensitivity and insistence on maintaining English laws led to numerous incidents over housing, social mores, and eventually, clothing and symbols such as the turban. One case in 1959 focussed on whether a Sikh could wear his turban as conductor. Initially the Transport Committee disavowed any exception to uniform requirements, but after years of pressure from local Sikhs, the decision was reversed in 1966. Another incident led to protest marches and a threat of immolation. Eventually the Indian Ambassador intervened, and after negotiations, the dress code was waived so that Sikhs could wear turbans. Similarly, Sikhs had to fight for exemptions from wearing safety helmets, leading finally to a decision by the House of Lords in favor of Sikhs. The House already had heard

---

[30] Much of the literature of this period is surveyed in Darshan Singh Tatla, *Sikhs in North America: An Annotated Bibliography* (Westport, Ct., 1991). Useful case studies include Bruce La Brack, *The Sikhs of Northern California* (New York, 1988); Tara Singh Bains, Hugh Johnston, *the Four Quarters of the Night: The Life Journey of an Emigrant Sikh* (Montreal, 1995); Hugh Johnston, "Development of the Punjabi Community in Vancouver Since 1961," *Dravidian Ethnic Studies*, Vol. 20, no. 2 (1988), pp. 1-17; Bhagat Singh, *Canadian Sikhs Through a Century, 1897-1997* (Delhi, 2001).

a major case involving hair and turban in 1983. A headmaster of a private school refused to admit a Sikh unless he cut his hair and removed his turban. The case came under the Race Relations Act 1976, and involved complicated legal issues about race and ethnicity. On March 24, 1983, a panel of five judges recognized Sikhs as "a group of persons forming a community recognizable by ethnic origins... which qualifies as a racial group" and thereby found in favor of the Sikhs. Although the British government has been reluctant to insist on acceptance of Sikh religious identity with the European Community, such as in reference to European helmet laws, today U.K. officials generally recognize the validity of unshorn hair and the turban as vital elements for initiated and *kesdhari* Sikhs.[31]

The evolution of large Sikh communities in British Columbia and in major urban areas across the country has forced Canadians toward a greater tolerance of diversity. Multiculturalism eventually has become an accepted feature of cultural and social policy, and the Sikhs have played a role in changing Canadian attitudes and law. The cases involving Sikh identity, especially the turban and kirpan, usually fall under the Canadian Human Rights Act, which prohibits discrimination on race, national or ethnic origin, color, religion, age, sex, sexual orientation, and other considerations. Each province had its own Human Rights Code, which with some variation offers specific protections. Under the Act and Code, a Human Rights Panel hears cases, and decisions can be appealed in the regular court system.

Two turban cases were noteworthy before 1984. The first involved Ishar Singh, a devout Sikh who applied for a position at Security Investigation Limited. The company had a policy of hiring only clean-shaven candidates, along with a uniform code demanding a hat. Ishar Singh's son, T. Sher Singh (awarded the Order of Canada in 2002), handled the case, which argued discrimination was blatant and undercut religious belief. The lead Commissioner

---

[31] The Sikh Coalition website has background and documents on these cases. The debate and issues raised during at the Motor-cycle Crash Helmets (Religious Exemption) Act 1976 is reproduced in Sydney Bidwell, ed., *The Turban Victory* (Southall, U.K., 1987). Similarly, the kirpan generally has been recognized as a legitimate religious symbol, and when appropriate measures are taken to insure its non-viability as a weapon (such as short length and dull blade), the courts, school officials, and the police have worked out public display with a minimum of disturbance. As in North America and elsewhere, the wearing of a kirpan is far more contentious in public transport, particularly air travel.

decided that Ishar Singh was deeply religious, and that his grievances had broader implications for other Sikhs. He also ruled that the company could not argue the policy on the basis of public prejudice, but rather hard facts demonstrating the necessity of policy. Ishar Singh therefore could wear a turban at work.[32]

The second case became a legal landmark, with not only a negative ruling on the right to wear a turban but also demonstrating the difficulty of interpreting provisions of the Human Rights Act. Karnail Singh Bhinder was a trained electrician who lodged a complaint in 1978 against an order to wear a hard hat. The Human Rights Board ruled discrimination, but the Appellate Division overturned its decision. The judges divided 2 to 1 against Bhinder, and when final decision was rendered in 1983, six Supreme Court judges favoured the company and four, Bhinder. The minority argued that a turban would not imperil safety, and that the right to practice religion was central. The majority argued that the Tribunal had found the requirement sound for non-Sikhs, and that since the issue pertained to only one individual, the only remedy was legislative change. Noting English courts had changed the law, they said that until Canadians did the same, the effect of discrimination was permissible.

Only seven years later, the Supreme Court in essence over-turned the legal grounds for the Bhinder decision. Only two of the original judges from the earlier case were on that court, including Chief Justice Dickson who had argued for Bhinder. The Dairy Pool Case involved a member of the World Wide Church of God, Jim Christie, who would not work on a specific day because of religious obligations. Relying on the Bhinder decision, the various courts had ruled against Christie. The Supreme Court took into account a passage from a "Special Report to Parliament on the Effects of the Bhinder Decision," which argued that since 1983, the Human Rights Commission felt limited in addressing direct discrimination involving a wide range of issues. The Court agreed, and set up a test as to whether rules were rationally linked to job permanence, and if employees could be accommodated. Individual rights had to be taken into consideration.[33]

---

[32] Major rulings and critical analysis in Satwinder Singh Gosal's essay, "Quest for Justice: Enforcing the Rights to Wear the 5 Ks," in document section, Sikh Coalition website.

[33] Bhinder and the Canadian National Railway company, Federal Court of Appeal Decision, April 13, 1983; Supreme Court of Canada Decision, December 17, 1985. Decisions and commentary, Sikh Coalition website. Also, discussion in Gosal, "Quest." On the Dairy Pool decision, decision by the Alberta Human Rights commission and upholding of the principles by the Supreme Court. Documents, Sikh Coalition website.

Subsequent turban cases reflect judicial balance between religious faith and job requirements. The most controversial involved whether Sikh Mounties could wear turbans rather than a traditional hat. After years of negotiation, the government and the RCMP permitted Sikhs to wear turbans, but then an interest group challenged the decision. In 1994, a Human Rights Tribunal upheld the decision, accepting the argument that the turban was central to Sikh identity. In 1999, the courts decided the turbans could be accomodated without serious threat when Sikhs operated motor-cycles. A year later, in a case on whether workers for the gas company had to be clean-shaven so that they could wear a gas mask, the appeals court supported the B.C. Human Rights Tribunal which argued that public safety had precedence over religious belief.[34]

The public display of the kirpan has aroused even more public interest. Especially after 1984, Sikhs have insisted on wearing the ceremonial dagger. A pivotal case involved school safety. Officials argued that kirpans were weapons and must not be carried by students. The Peel Board of Education, Ontario, apparently had offered a compromise that allowed Sikhs to carry small symbolic replicas, or kirpans stitched into sheaths, but the Sikh community had found the position unacceptable. The Human Rights Tribunal decided that several schools had permitted Sikhs to wear kirpans limited to six inches, and no violence occurred. The Ontario Provisional Court agreed that the religious symbols, reasonably sized and worn under clothing, should be permitted.[35]

Air safety was another matter. Several airlines had developed arrangements allowing small kirpans on planes. In a highly publicized case, however, one airline had a rigid security plan that prevented a prominent Sikh from travelling with his kirpan. After days of testimony that supported the kirpan as a vital religious symbol and suggested that it probably would not be used as a weapon, the panel decided against the defendant on the grounds that the airline

---

[34] Documents, Sikh coalition website, and discussion by Gosal, "Quest." Also background on the cases in Bhagat Singh, *Canadian Sikhs*, pp. 204-221. On the gas mask issue, *Grant v. Canada*, 1995, T-499-91, documents in www.canlii.org/ca/cas/fc/1994fc61.

[35] Peel cas reviewed in Bhagat Singh, *Canadian Sikhs*, pp. 221-2. *Ontario Human Rights Commission and Harbhajan Singh Pandori v. Peel Board of Education*, April 2, 1991; appeal and final judgements, Court File A49/91 OJ No. 3200, Ontario Court of Appeals. Sikh Coalition website. Kirpan cases frequently derive from transport cases and local decisions, such as the refusal of the Brampton Transit to permit kirpans, finally resolved with an apology to Sikhs, discussed in *World Sikh News*, June 23, 1989.

had a right to set up guidelines in lieu of all-Canada agreements or statutes. The panel did recognize the importance of the kirpan for Sikhs, however, and recommended either legislative relief or that Canadian airlines develop a comprehensive policy.[36]

Unlike Canada and the England, where statutes relating to human rights and race relations establish the procedures and rules for jurisdiction on aspects of Sikh identity, American courts approach such matters in terms of freedom of religion. The First Amendment guarantees have been reinforced by the Religious Freedom Restoration Act of 1994, which says that government cannot impose a law that burdens the free exercise of religion unless it can prove a "compelling" interest. The Act was a response to a 1990 Supreme Court decision that allegedly broadened the power of intervention into religious observances and possibly headgear such as turbans for Sikhs (immediately after the decision, the Occupational Safety and Health Administration had canceled an earlier exemption permitting Sikhs to wear turbans instead of hard hats). Sikhs joined with numerous religious organizations and the ACLU to support the new legislation. Also in support was Justice Sandra Day O'Connor, who argued that First Amendment had been enacted to "protect the rights of those whose religious practices are not shared by the majority and may be viewed with hostility."[37]

Before the 1990 decision and subsequent Act, Sikh symbols had been protected in several jurisdictions. In New York, for example, a 1986 case involved possession of a kirpan on a subway platform. The lawyers for the defendant, Partap Singh, argued that the granthi was required to wear the 5Ks, including the kirpan. While supporting the general rule against exhibiting knives with exposed or unexposed blades, the court took into consideration the religious issues involved and decided that the continuance of the prosecution would not be in the furtherance of justice. Similarly, Sikhs and local school systems, such as in Yuba City, had worked out compromises about wearing

---

[36] Ontario Tribunal, Canadian Human Rights Act Decision, July 9, 1999. Court documents including the decision supplied by Professor W.H. McLeod, a witness supporting the kirpan as an essential religious symbol for initiated Sikhs. I am indebted to Professor McLeod for the large packet of material. On the more general issues, an interesting section on the kirpan in *Benchers Bulletin, Law Society of B.C.* (March-April 1995), Sikh Coalition website.

[37] Background on passage of the Act and O'Connor's quote in *India Abroad*, May 28, 1993, p. 14.

Sikhs and the Law: A Century of Conflict over Identity and Authority

kirpans with short, dulled blades and sewn into a sheath. In fact, turbans frequently were permitted under local, state and federal law. A subsequent attempt to work out a similar compromise in a dispute near Los Angeles, involving limits of size and access, failed because of an impasse between school officials and the Sikh family involved.[38]

The major exception to the overall acceptance of Sikh symbols has been a shift in military policy towards turbans. Between 1958 and 1974, the Army exempted conscripted Sikhs from regulations requiring soldiers to cut their hair, shave, and wear on specified types of jewelry and headgear. In 1974, the exemption for unshorn hair and iron bracelets was expanded to cover enlisted Sikhs. A few years later, faced with growing requests for similar exemptions for others, the military reviewed the problem and concluded that discipline would be weakened by exemptions. Also, concern with chemical attacks and gas masks seem to make beards untenable. A 1981 regulation therefore removed blanket exemptions for new recruits, but continued them for Sikhs already in the military. A year later a Sikh, Guru Sant Singh Khalsa attempted to enlist, and when denied admission, he sued. The Appeals Court for the Ninth Circuit in 1985 gave precedence to military requirements and said that as long as an appellant does not enlist, regulations do not interfere with free exercise of his religion. A strong dissent by one judge argued that the court have trivialized the basic principles of the Sikh religion, and denied Sikhs the right to serve in the military which in India had been a part of their traditions.[39]

Since 1994, the courts have tended to support the turban and kirpan as religious symbols. Sikhs have managed to mobilize successfully and gather both legal and legislative support for their position. When owners of the Grove Lounge in New Jersey issued a "no hats" policy, for example, a young Sikh teenager was denied entrance. The owner settled out of court when confronted by evidence and potentially large compensation. The same family successfully

---

[38] On New York, *New York* v. *Partap Singh*, 135 Mis.2d701; 516 NYS2d412, May 13, 1987; Gurdev Singh Cheema case, 67F3d883(9th Cir 1995). Sikh Coalition website. Background on the kirpan issue, Vinay Lal, "Sikh *Kirpan* in California," in Mohinder Singh, ed., *Sikh Forms and Symbols* (Delhi, 2000), pp. 107-141.

[39] 779 F2d 1393(9th Cir 1985), 84-5880. May 7, 1985. Sikh Coalition website. Recent decisions include July 1999 regulations that restrict the kirpan as a religious symbol in the Army Reserve.

had fought an earlier battle against a soccer referee who barred another son from a game because he would not take off his *patka*. In 1997, a computer science professor at Princeton, Jaswinder Pal Singh, was denied entry into a Manhattan Mexican restaurant for refusing to take off his turban. That eventually led to a revised policy and a $10,000 payment. Domino Pizza also got into trouble when a Sikh refused to shave his beard to train as a manager. The Maryland Human Relations Commission charged religious discrimination, and after almost eight years of legal review, Domino had to revise its no-beard policy, provide back pay, and offer Prabhjot Kohli a job.[40]

Kirpans naturally create a more difficult problem, especially in parts of the country with few Sikh residents. In rural Ohio, for example, a Sikh veterinarian underwent trial for carrying a concealed weapon, a very small, dulled kirpan sewn inside his clothing. The judge and prosecution denied that the kirpan has any religious symbolism, and the jury found Harjinder Singh guilty. The Appeals Court went ballistic. After reviewing other kirpan cases and noting that none of the state witnesses knew anything about Sikhism, the Court reprimanded the judge and the prosecution. Lecturing the lower court and the public on free expression of religion, the court noted that had the prosecution been successful, Sikhs would have been banished from Ohio, and why? "That a veterinarian would be punished for having a dulled blade of two-and-one half inches sewn inside his clothing as required by his religion."[41] Despite that ruling, in 1999 Ohio police stopped a granthi and charged him with carrying a six inch dangerous weapon. This time many Sikh institutions, the SGPC, Congressmen, the Governor Richard Celeste, and Interfaith organizations got involved, and the Court summarily dismissed the case: "To be a Sikh is to wear a kirpan—it is that simple. It is a religious symbol and in no way a weapon."[42]

---

[40] *Domino's Pizza* v. *Praabhjot S. Kohli*, Court of appeals of Maryland 347 Md 258, 701.A.2d.91, October 9, 1997. Reports on other stories, *India West*, March 5, 1999; *India Abroad*, August 3, 2001.

[41] Quote from J. Painter judgement, appeal C950777, Court of Appeals of Ohio, First Appellate District Hamilton County. Harjinder Singh case, December 31, 1996. Sikh Coalition website. I appreciate Ranbir Singh Sandhu for supplying documents on these Ohio kirpan cases.

[42] Quote and background in *India Abroad*, December 17, 1999. Further comments and background in *India Today*, December 20, 1999. A similar case in Oakland, *Contra Costa Times*, June 12, 1998, from Steward.com.Human Rights Cases.

The renewed interest in Sikh identity and defense of religious traditions involved in these interactions between Sikhism and the courts also fostered a decade of confrontation and conflict within important Sikh institutions in the diaspora. From 1984 onward, many Sikhs quit cutting their hair, joined mass protests for the first time, and became involved in militant organizations that blossomed outside the Punjab. In North America, new youth and radical networks moved to dominate the print culture with journals, tracts, and printed circulars. To be a good Sikh became virtually synonymous with support for the Punjab freedom struggle, or Khalistan. The focus of many such activities became control of the center of Sikh public life, the gurdwaras. Controversies over "who is a Sikh" and who will lead became common. The resulting battles between groups disrupted relationships, split congregations, and led to continual competition and virtual warfare.[43]

As in the case of the SGPC and Sikh institutions in the Punjab, the courts became central to this new fusion of religion and politics. Unlike the Punjab, where politicians often managed to influence judicial decisions or the composition of tribunals, the courts in North America attempted to stay neutral and reach balanced decisions that would resolve conflict. Every gurdwara battle eventually had legal consequences, often criminal cases when assault or threats occurred, and in civil hearings because of election campaigns and takeovers. The cases involved procedure, bylaws, finances, and sometimes libel. Even after a faction won or lost, the courts had to deal with the legal aftershock, deciding on the legitimacy of votes and who had rights. Generally judges did not get involved with arguments about Sikh tradition and ideology that kept popping up in the proceedings. One persistent claim, for example, was that the Sikh *sangat* or congregation could reject any bylaw or procedure in an open meeting. Courts rejected the argument consistently and held participants to a strict accountability based on legal evidence. Constitutional matters and procedures were judged central, disputes over the Sikh way of life were not. With regards to *sahajdhari/amritdhari/kesdhari* relations, decisions were based primarily on the Constitution, not who really represented Sikhism. When lawyers used any argument to build a case, references to the Sikh Rahit Maryada, the Akal Takht,

---

[43] The recent radicalization of Sikh society and politics in the U.K. and North America extensively reviewed in Darshan Singh Tatla, *The Sikh Diaspora: The Search for Statehood* (Seattle, 1999).

the SGPC and its rules, and non-binding attempts at conflict resolution by independent Sikhs assembled as a *panj piare* appeared occasionally. Again, such efforts mirrored the model of the mixture of raw politics and religious maneuvering so often found in the SGPC and various Akali factions.[44]

Three pivotal cases illustrate how Sikhs tried to balance legal requirements with appeal to "higher" or external sources of authority, often with unexpected results and rulings from the courts. The most dramatic for Sikhs throughout the world, the *langar* case in British Columbia, is well known. There militants tried to control several key gurdwaras and use the appreciable resources for their own ends. When court proceedings seemed to be going against them on judicial grounds, they involved the jathedar of the Akal Takht, Ranjit Singh, who excommunicated several prominent leaders including a controversial journalist soon assassinated. The basis for the excommunication was that those in control were permitting the use of chairs in the dining hall rather than having everyone sit on the ground. In fact, the practice had been quite common in numerous gurdwaras, and in those now targeted, even under earlier extremist leadership. Ranjit Singh nevertheless focussed on a handful of Sikhs who had disobeyed an edict from the Akal Takht and removed them from the panth. The militants hoped that public pressure and the aura of the Akal Takht would force the moderates to withdraw. To the surprise of many Sikhs, the moderates then challenged the intervention, and finally, under court supervision, won control of the gurdwaras. Interestingly, at one point, the militants tried to argue that since several leaders had been excommunicated, they no longer were Sikhs and automatically their positions fell vacant. The courts rejected the claims about Sikh tradition and authority, and eventually supervised new elections.[45]

Before and after the Vancouver events, two proceedings involving American gurdwaras highlight the process whereby religion, law, authority and

---

[44] Gurdwara administration and politics evaluated in N.G. Barrier, "Gurdwaras in the US: Governance, Authority, and Legal Issues," *Understanding Sikhism*, Vol. 4, no.1 (January-June 2002), pp. 31-40. Also, Barrier, "Controversy among North American Sikhs," *International Journal of Punjab Studies*, Vol. 6 (1999), pp. 217-240.

[45] See Hugh Johnston, "Sikhism and Secular Authority," in Van Die Marguerite, ed., *Religion and Public Life in Canada* (Toronto, 2001), pp. 346-362. Supreme Court ruling, Docket 982044, Society Act, Khalsa Diwan, September 1998. Also, background in Bhagat Singh, *Canadian Sikhs*, pp. 280-316, 406-409.

governance became intermeshed in legal proceedings. The first, in Fairfax, Virginia, involved a prolonged fight not only over control of a gurdwara but the nature of the Sikh religion itself. The more recent in Michigan shows how politics and local feuds end up in the courts and produce a costly legal procedure that again evokes different views on the nature of Sikhism and Sikh institutions.

In Fairfax, the Sikh Foundation of Virginia has operated a gurdwara since 1979 under a constitution and bylaws. Around 1990, newly arrived Sikhs aligned with some of the congregation in an effort to control the SFV. Differences involving personality and budget were part of the problem, but particular emphasis was placed on a political agenda that included support for Khalistan. When a former Jathedar of the Akal Takht, Darshan Singh Ragi, participated in religious services, for example, the more radical Sikhs physically attacked him as a traitor to Sikhism. On March 28, 1993, the militants brought in many new members, broke up a meeting, and took over the gurdwara. Under court order, the groups met, and the leaders of SKV were attacked, leading to convictions of several of the radicals. The court set up a fact-finding procedure that undoubtedly would have led to the return of the gurdwara and the SFV back to the original officers, but to prevent this, the militants claimed the courts had no jurisdiction since Sikhism was hierarchical/connectional like the Catholic Church and hence fell outside Virgina law. When the counter-claim was made that Sikhism is always congregational, the commissioner held hearings not on facts but on the nature of Sikh tradition and practice.[46]

The hearings included many affidavits and four days of hearings on Sikh concepts of authority and the nature of the local *sangat*. Those defending the take over made three arguments. First, according to Sikh tradition, maryada, Sikhism always is egalitarian, and thus a majority decides an issue (through a resolution or *gurmata*) and can over-ride legal constraints. Another was that a group of five *amritdhari* Sikhs who constituted a *panj piare* had the authority to resolve conflict. The visitors, basically hand-picked by the radicals, decided those contributions as one requirement for eligibility for election was against

---

[46] Background in Barrier, "The Fairfax Virginia Gurdwara Case and Sikh Identity," in Pashaura Singh and Barrier, eds., *Sikh Identity* (Delhi: 1999), pp. 365-378. Major discussions, editorials, letters, in *World Sikh News*, 1993-94. Especially useful documents in *World Sikh News*, April 19, May 27, 1994. Final ruling, Fourth Report of Commissioner in Chancery, Circuit Court of Fairfax County, July 16, 1996.

rahit, as were dues and other elements of the constitution. The trustees rejected the report that totally supported the radicals, but the *panj piare* recommendations that mediation not the courts was an appropriate Sikh approach and that only *kesdharis* and *amritdharis* could lead the congregation focussed attentions on the Sikh Rahit Maryada and expanded the discussion. Finally, probably for the first time in recent history, the Akal Takht became involved. After an exchange of documents, the Jathedar Manjit Singh ordered that the case must be withdrawn from the courts and settled according to "panthic principles." He then asserted *amritdhari* dominance and that he alone would approve any management arrangements in the future. Rather than accepting the Jathedar's position, the SFV trustees thanked him and then said he had no authority to intervene in local matters, especially when constituted under specific statutes. Warning of dire consequences and the significance of the intervention as a precedent, they called on the Jathedar to reconsider. From that point on, Manjit Singh withdrew from the conflict, and decisions on very basic issues of Sikh religion and governance were left to the local courts and Sikh opinion throughout the world.

The hearings in the summer of 1994 brought to a head the divergent opinions within modern Sikhism. One group argued that the Sikh religion was similar to the Catholic Church, with the Pope (Jathedar) at the top, all property belonging to the panth, and a common creed, the Sikh Rahit Maryada. The trustees, most scholars, and a former Jathedar Darshan Singh said that Sikhism always had been congregational with no set rules or a single source of authority except the *Guru Granth Sahib*. They also disputed the claim that the SGPC had recognized authority over Sikhs everywhere, and that any advice (*adesh*, the word used by Manjit Singh) or an edict automatically required Sikh submission. Sikhs throughout the diaspora joined in the debate, with letters, fiery editorials and articles, and representations. Western legal procedures and the autonomy of local gurdwaras thus became engaged with proponents of a radical view of Sikhism quite different in practice and in ideology from that found in the diaspora or even in Punjab.

The court ultimately rejected the radical claims, ruling that gurdwaras were congregational and that legal authority rested with those following gurdwara bylaws and a constitution. The trustees resumed control. Some who lost the decision set up a new organization and wrote a constitution based on the Sikh Rahit Maryada, Akal Takht authority, and *amritdhari* control. The Akal Takht Jathedar then declared the actions a model for "real" Sikh organizations, one that would prevent future legal hassles and resolve all conflicts in a panthic fashion according to maryada.[47]

A subsequent conflict among Sikhs in Michigan also grew out of financial, personal, and political differences and threatened to repeat the Fairfax arguments in yet another U.S. court. Competition between groups in the Sikh Society of Michigan emerged in the 1980s, and came to a head in 1996.[48] One prominent family helped finance many of the gurdwara's activities but had not been deeply involved in management, while others controlled the daily operations. Some of the latter faction had been active in Khalistan activities and criticized the major contributors for not boycotting Indian officials. In early 1996, a leading contributor, Gurmale Singh, agreed to head up a fund-raising campaign for a new facility on the condition that the new Sikh Center of Michigan would have bylaws placing its leadership in the hands of major donors. Obviously designed to insure an affluent and committed leadership, the level of support for patrons was an initial $50,000 or 10 per cent or annual income, with initial contributions of $25,000 or more for individuals eligible as Directors. The new bylaws also had provisions for plaques and other honors for significant contributions, and a rule that no funds could be used for political purposes. Membership would be open to any Sikh who believed in God, the ten Gurus, and the *Guru Granth Sahib*, and the voting requirement was an annual contribution of $500 or 2 per cent, whichever was less.

The Sikh Society Working Committee and the congregation adopted the new constitution in April, transferring power for the new Center to the Sikhs involved in planning and insuring success in fund-raising and construction. As often happens in gurdwara politics, disruptions then occurred, with voiced concerns over issues such as lack of reference to the Akal Takht. A compromise was reached with the addition of possible Akal Takht influence in religious but not temporal matters. Other issues emerged, and in a series of heated encounters

---

[47] Ranjit Singh to Surinder Singh Hansra, August 20, 1998, deposition exhibit in the Michigan Gurdwara case.

[48] Based on depositions and final rulings in the *Sikh Society of Michigan, Inc.* v. *Sikh Center of Michigan*, Inc. Et Al, Oakland County Circuit Court Case 96-535016-CZ. I served as an expert witness during the proceedings, and have personal copies of all major documents in the case.

and public meetings, heated charges and even violence were directed at the leaders of the new Center. Their opponents then broke up meetings, took over, the congregation split, and the courts intervened.

In the next year, the inevitable legal and rhetorical battles began in earnest. A series of letters charged the Grewals with theft and "unpanthic" activities. Levels of membership came under attack as elitist and against Sikh egalitarianism, as did the mention of honoring contributors.

Grewal was portrayed as a "permanent dictator" opposing the sangat and wanting to be a *mahant* (a term associated with those in legal control of Punjab gurdwaras prior to the reforms). The Sikh Center built a convincing case with supportive documents, and then its opponents countered with the use of religious doctrine, tradition and Sikh authority to neutralize bylaws. Depositions and documents contain frequent discussion of the Akal Takht and Sikh Rahit Maryada, and had proceedings gone to trial, the Fairfax issues would have been re-argued. Fortunately, the judge pressed for a settlement in light of the Center's willingness to compromise and thereby avoid more expense than the estimated half million dollars already committed. When the judge showed signs of reaching a summary judgment probably favoring the new Center, all concerned agreed to end the personal attacks and divide the resources. The Sikh Center has grown to become a major center for Sikhs in the area, and soon will build an elaborate gurdwara.

These and similar gurdwara disputes in North America illustrate the Sikh struggle over the relevance of religion and tradition in governance and legal structures. While militancy and the cry for Khalistan have subsided, the embarrassing encounters have led to discussion and modernization of constitutions with clarified membership requirements and a closing of loopholes. Reference to the Sikh Rahit Maryada and Akal Takht can be found in some revisions, but virtually no congregation wants to place its local resources and decision-making in the hands of external forces. A few also have moved away from elections and tried to find more peaceful and acceptable means of selecting leaders. Building bylaws and criteria for leadership around a thoughtful understanding of "who is a Sikh?" is a predominant theme, especially since many influential Sikhs are not *kesdhari*. While the majority of Sikh opinion probably tends to favor leadership by *kesdharis* and *amritdharis*, Sikhs are practical and want to avoid division and wasting resources. Similarly, reluctance to have external forces over ride the legal system takes into account local needs and the danger of outsiders intervening for ideological or other purposes. As editorials and the Punjab experience suggests, creating binding arbitration procedures or leaving matters to the decisions of special committees may eliminate court jurisdiction but at the same time, create new arenas for conflict.[49]

The ongoing adaptation of diaspora Sikhs to new social and legal challenges suggests that they will play a major role in focusing issues and agendas in the future. In the Punjab, the perennial concerns with the courts and identity continue, but the discussion and patterns seem repetitive and do not point toward significant change. The Gurdwaras Act and central legislation remain political targets, especially during elections, but changes in details concerning personal law, women, dalits, and defining "who is a Sikh" would have unforeseen results and possibly weaken those in power. However, the situation is far from static. Courts continue to rule in cases that have implications for Sikh identity and politics. For example, the Indian Supreme Court recently designated the *Guru Granth Sahib* as a "juristic person" for purposes of legal cases relating to control of gurdwaras and their resources. The implications of such rulings remain unclear, but each generates fresh debate on the nature of Sikhism and its relationship to other Indian religions.[50]

The SGPC and the various takhts still claim to represent Sikhs throughout the world, but mounting evidence from chat rooms and public demonstrations outside the Punjab suggests that diaspora Sikhs are increasingly self-assured and independent in their thinking. Led by increasingly sophisticated and educated professionals, Sikh organizations are responding creatively to ongoing legal proceedings about beards, turbans, and kirpans and at the same time helping educate the public to minimize cross-cultural misunderstanding. Most recently, this dynamism was evidenced in the concerted Sikh response to the racial profiling and attacks after the September 11th terrorist attacks. Within days, new websites and information systems were created, teams of legal specialists helped individuals and prepared guidelines for conduct in airports

---

[49] *The Sikh Review* regularly contains articles on these and related topics. For example, "Adopt or Adapt," February 2001, pp. 49-56; "Sikhs March into the Third Millennium," January 2001, pp. 23-34; "Moral Ethos of Khalsa Panth," April 2001, pp. 49-54. Also the seminar proceedings, " Gurdwara: Past, Present and Future," a special edition of *Understanding Sikhism*, Vol. 4, no. 1 (January-June 2002).

[50] Discussed briefly by Kashmir Singh, "Aad Guru Granth Sahib a Juristic Person," *Understanding Sikhism*, Vol. 3, no. 2 (July-December 2001), pp. 24-28.

and Sikh rights, and mass meetings combined themes of loyalty and Sikh pride. Sikh activists worked with Congressional and local politicians to pass legislation identifying and protecting Sikhs, and they lobbied federal agencies effectively.[51] The mobilization was reminiscent of the massive response to the gurdwara reform movement. Just as the morchas and sacrifices in the early 1920s helped create new Sikh institutions and laws, so the maturity and pride reflected in recent Sikh initiatives will have ramifications not only within global Sikhism but in the Punjab homeland itself.

---

[51] The following websites and list-serves contain innumerable documents and debate over the implications of the September events for Sikhs, as well as reports on political maneuvers, policies, and travel up-dates: Sikh_Dispora@yahoogroups.com; Sikh Coalition.com; Sikh Media Watch and Resource Task Force.com; Sikh_Agenda @yahoogroups.com; Sikh Communications.com; Sikh Media Watch.com. An initial review of major themes and developments in N.G. Barrier, "Kala September: Crisis and Response among American Sikhs," *Understanding Sikhism*, Vol. 4, no. 1 (January-June, 2002), pp. 6-9.

11

The Personal Laws or a Uniform Civil Code?

John H. Mansfield

The Present Situation

The idea that there should be a uniform law for India on the subjects traditionally governed by the personal laws of the different religious and ethnic communities—marriage, divorce, maintenance, adoption, guardianship, succession, and so forth—is of relatively recent origin. If early British administrators toyed with the idea, it was later discarded as utopian and unwise.[1] The notion of separately codifying the different personal laws lingered longer,[2] to be replaced by the more modest goal of changing aspects of these laws that conflicted with values the British held fundamental or when change was requested by important elements in the affected community.[3]

The idea of a uniform civil code covering the traditional subjects of the personal laws does not seem to have been put forward until after Independence. The Congress Party's pronouncements before that time did not advocate such a step, but some, on the contrary, took the position that there ought to be constitutional protection of the personal laws. So far as is known, the idea of a uniform civil code was first proposed during debate in the Constituent Assembly and its committees.[4] But once the notion of a uniform civil code was put forward, it rapidly came to be accepted as an important part of the effort to

---

[1] See Tahir Mahmood, *Muslim Personal Law, Role of the State in the Indian Subcontinent* (Nagpur, 2d ed., 1983), p. 5 (referring to attitude of some of Warren Hastings' colleagues); M. P. Jain, *Outlines of Indian Legal History* (Bombay, 4th ed., 1981), p. 370.

[2] See Jain, *Outlines*, pp. 405, 427–29, 439; Mahmood, *Muslim Personal Law*, p. 14.

[3] E.g., Sati Regulation, 1829; Hindu Widow's Re-Marriage Act, 1856.

[4] See K. C. Markandan, *Directive Principles in the Indian Constitution* (Bombay, 1966), pp. 104–10, 190–97; Mahmood, *Muslim Personal Law*, pp. 77–78.

construct an Indian national identity, over against the separate identities of caste, religion and ethnicity.[5]

Article 44 of the Directive Principles of State Policy in the Indian Constitution gives expression to the goal of a uniform civil code. It proclaims: "the state shall endeavor to secure for the citizens a uniform civil code throughout the territory of India." Like the other Directive Principles, this one "shall not be enforceable by any court, but...[is] nevertheless fundamental in the governance of the country and it shall be the duty of the State to apply...[it] in making laws."[6] As will be discussed below, the Constitution did not abolish the system of personal laws and require that there be a uniform civil code; it only held forth a uniform civil code as an ideal towards which the state should strive.

Repeatedly during the years since the Constitution was adopted, voices have been raised demanding to know why action has not been taken to bring about the fulfillment of the constitutional ideal. A famous example of such an utterance is the one made by the Supreme Court in its *Shah Bano* judgment.[7] The intensity of the Muslim reaction to the Supreme Court's judgment in that case was partly explained by the inclusion of this utterance and the suggestion that what the government had failed to do, the Court itself might undertake. Criticism of the sort expressed by the Supreme Court may not be entirely justified. If one examines the debates in the Constituent Assembly on the subject of a uniform civil code, they include assurance that there was no intention to force a uniform civil code upon any community that was strongly opposed to it.[8] The hope was, rather, that change would take place within communities, particularly within the Muslim community, that would bring the members to feel that their own interests would best be served by a uniform civil code. Perhaps it can be said that Article 44 imposed upon the state a duty to encourage such a change of attitude,[9] and that successive governments, for reasons to which the Constitution gives no recognition, have shirked this duty. On the other hand, it equally can be argued that what has occurred—the absence of any significant movement towards a uniform civil code—is a situation that it was contemplated by the framers of the Constitution might occur.[10] If Hindu, Parsi and Christian attitudes towards a

---

[5] See Mahmood, *Muslim Personal Law*, p. 80, quoting Ambedkar in the Constituent Assembly to the effect that "uniformity in fundamental laws, civil and criminal" would be a means to help maintain the unity of the country.

[6] Constitution of India, Art. 37.

[7] *Mohd. Ahmed Khan* v. *Shah Bano Begum*, A.I.R. 1985 S.C. 945, 954.

[8] See Markandan, *Directive Principles*, p. 109; Mahmood, *Muslim Personal Law*, pp. 83–84.

[9] See Mahmood, *Muslim Personal Law*, p. 95.

[10] See Mahmood, *Muslim Personal Law*, p. 96.

Personal Law v. Uniform Civil Code

uniform civil code may have changed to a degree, Muslim resistance has only stiffened as the years have passed. Consequently, it can be argued, in view of the legislative history of Article 44, it should not be the subject of severe criticism that the project for a uniform civil code has not gone forward.

Debate over the question of a uniform civil code has varied in intensity during the years since the Constitution was adopted. In the early 1970s there was a surge of activity: conferences, publications, reports.[11] The last six or seven years have seen a similar rise in activity, due in part to the *Shah Bano* judgment and the debate over legislation to reverse it.[12] Discussions about a uniform civil code have been indirectly affected by other matters: the Ram Janmabhoomi-Babri Masjid controversy;[13] the 1986 sati incident in Deorala, Rajasthan and the anti-sati legislation that resulted from it;[14] the conflicts in the Punjab and Kashmir; and the increase in communal violence in many parts of India.

Beginning in the mid-1980s an "anti-secularist" critique of nationalist orthodoxy has emerged. The reasons for this phenomenon are complex, but some suggestions can be made. During the early years of independence, it was seen as important by leaders of the new nation that India should become a political entity as strong and unified as any. In the British period there had been those who had said that there was no such thing as "India," and that what passed under that name was simply a congeries of castes, sects and other religious and ethnic groups. The leaders of the new India felt it important to refute this proposition. The idea that India should be a nation-state in the same sense and to the same extent as the strongest nations of the West, sprang certainly from a genuine concern for the welfare of the people of India, but it also had roots in a need for status and prestige. One characteristic of a true nation-state, it was thought, was that it had a unified substantive law, not different laws for different religious and ethnic communities.[15] The existence of different laws, whose applicability depended upon religion or ethnicity, was seen as a badge of inferiority; it suggested a

---

[11]See Mahmood, *Muslim Personal Law*, pp. 117–32; Ramala M. Baxamusa, *A Historic Perspective on Muslim Personal Law in India* (Trivandrum, Second National Conference on Women's Studies, April 9–12, 1984), pp. 20–21 (lists activities).

[12]E.g., N.R. Madhava Menon, ed., *National Convention on Uniform Civil Code for All Indians* (New Delhi, 1986); Vasudha Dhagamwar, *Towards the Uniform Civil Code* (New Delhi, Indian Law Institute, 1989).

[13]See *The Hindu* (Intern'l ed.), Feb. 7, 1987, p. 1, col. 1 (reporting that the Rajiv Gandhi government had decided to go slow on its plan for a voluntary uniform civil code because of, among other things, reports that Muslim "protest against the Code had merged with the agitation over the Babri Masjid issue").

[14]The Commission of Sati Prevention Act, 1988.

[15]See remarks to this effect during the debates in the Constituent Assembly, cited in Markandan, *Directive Principles*, pp. 191–92, 195.

political entity prone to disintegration, one that would have little influence in the world.

It is not necessary to take sides on the question of whether it was desirable for India to embrace the western idea of a nation-state. Gandhi certainly had stood against it. It is enough to note that in recent years there has been increasing controversy on the subject. A factor contributing to this change may have been the growing support around the world for the rights of religious and ethnic minorities within territorial states. This movement stresses the interest of these groups in preserving their distinctive cultures and in being protected against pressure to conform to the majority culture. The spectacle of large political entities in different parts of the world collapsing and giving place to smaller entities based on ethnicity, religion or language or combinations of these factors, rather than strengthening the idea that a powerfully centralized, culturally homogeneous nation is essential for order and prosperity, may have confirmed for some the view that the pressing task for India is not to increase central power and cultural homogeneity, but to find an alternative to the "nation-state" model, an alternative that will sustain unity through some form of "pluralism."

The "anti-secularist" critique of nationalist orthodoxy has been led by an group of eminent political scientists, sociologists and historians. Among these may be mentioned Ashis Nandy,[16] T. N. Madan[17] and T. K. Oommen.[18] It is possible that in some cases at least, the anti-secularists are converts from nationalist orthodoxy. Although the anti-secularists have not to any significant extent addressed the issue of a uniform civil code, their general criticism of orthodox nationalist ideology may have implications for this issue.

In his book published in 1990,[19] Oommen summed up the major points made by the anti-secularists. The goal of a single secular national culture, Oommen thinks, was a mistake. Such a culture is not required for the unity that is needed to maintain order and achieve prosperity. Indeed, the aim of achieving it may have worked against these objectives. Oommen accepts the idea that there can be many "nations" within India. These nations may be based on culture and language. Nations based on religion, on the other hand, involve an unacceptable

---

[16] Ashis Nandy, "An Anti-Secularist Manifesto," in *Seminar* (No. 314, 1985), pp. 14–24; Ashis Nandy, "The Politics of Secularism and the Recovery of Religious Tolerance," in Veena Das, ed., *Mirrors of Violence. Communities, Riots and Survivors in South Asia* (Delhi, 1990), pp. 69–73.

[17] T. N. Madan, "Secularism in Its Place," J. Asian Studies, vol. 46, pp. 747–59 (1987); T. N. Madan, "Coping with Ethnic Diversity: A South Asian Perspective," in Stuart Plattner, ed., *Prospects for Plural Societies* (Washington, D.C., American Ethnological Soc., 1984), pp. 136–45.

[18] T.K. Oommen, *State and Society in India, Studies in Nation-Building* (New Delhi, 1990).

[19] *Ibid.*

risk of secession. In this latter opinion, Oommen is influenced, no doubt, by Partition and the present troubles in the Punjab and Kashmir. He is supportive of religious "pluralism" so long as it does not have a territorial basis. It may be that Oommen's belief that India does not need a single national culture neglects to some extent the necessity of some shared values if India is to exist at all. He seems to place his own faith in some rather vague humanistic values.[20]

Oommen appears to approve the existing system of personal laws and to be opposed to a uniform civil code: "[C]ultural pluralism in India necessitates the recognition and operation of legal pluralism."[21] The "timidity in evolving a uniform civil code" points to the fact that Indian "secularism meant not only non-interference in the affairs of other communities but also developing a positive appreciation of their distinct style of life."[22] Opposition to a uniform civil code on the part of the anti-secularists, if that is their position, could derive in part from an anti-western strain in their thinking, a tendency to reject what they see as an undesirable aping of the West and to embrace that which is indigenous and authentically Indian. Although there are those who suggest that a uniform civil code could embody the best of Indian ideas,[23] the fact of the matter is that the content of a uniform civil code would almost certainly be inspired by modern western values, just as were most of the legislative enactments during the British period—for instance, the Contract Act[24] and the Transfer of Property Act[25]— that touched upon subjects dealt with by the personal laws. Furthermore, the very idea of a single law applicable to all, regardless of community, on such topics as marriage and succession, is inescapably an import from the West.[26]

---

[20] *Ibid.*, pp. 129, 206.

[21] *Ibid.*, p. 41.

[22] *Ibid.*, p. 105. See Veena Das and Ralph W. Nicholas, "Family and 'Household.' Difference and Division in South Asian Life," in *Personnel in the Family Courts* (Delhi, Legal Literacy Project, Dep't of Adult, Continuing Education & Extension, University of Delhi, 1989), pp. 1–28, describing the complex ideas underlying the "household," relations between men and women, and insiders and outsiders, and asking why one would want to create a single set of rules governing everyone, including Hindus and Muslims, in these matters.

[23] See N.R. Madhava Menon, ed., *National Convention on Uniform Civil Code for All Indians* (New Delhi, 1986), p. xi, citing as an objective of Convention, among others, to present a draft code that would reflect "the cumulative wisdom of the great cultural traditions of India...."

[24] 1872.

[25] 1882.

[26] See Werner F. Menski, "The Reform of Islamic Family Law and a Uniform Civil Code for India," in Chibli Mallat and Jane Conners, eds., *Islamic Family Law* (London, 1990),

Oommen considers it the function of the state to "reform" the different religions in India and to remove from them "obscurantist practices," practices, that is, that are "in violation of the principles of freedom, equality and justice."[27] He does not seem to appreciate the possibility of a conflict between the goal of "reform" and the objective of maintaining "cultural pluralism." What is his position, for example, on Muslim polygamy, on the absence of a duty of a Muslim man to maintain his former wife, on unequal rights of inheritance for sons and daughters? Are these "obscurantist practices" that stand in need of "reform" or are they expressions of a healthy "pluralism"?

With the attitude of the anti-secularists towards a uniform civil code, it would be interesting to compare the positions of various groups that are presently active in furthering the cause of Hinduism as they understand it. I have in mind such groups as the Arya Samaj, the RSS, the VHP and the BJP. The VHP, to speak of only one of these groups, seeks to create a Hinduism that will have strong links with tradition, but at the same time be able to compete successfully in the modern world with other religions and with secular ideologies. It seeks to unite a wide variety of castes and sects and to appeal to that increasingly numerous class of persons who wish to be both modern and Hindu. The Hinduism the VHP promotes is intended to have a certain dominance in India and to be recognized as more truly Indian than other religions. What would be the stance of the VHP on the subject of a uniform civil code? In view of its objectives, it might have a more ambivalent attitude on this issue than on certain others, such as special constitutional protection for minority educational institutions, the constitutional status of Kashmir and the removal of mosques allegedly built on sites sacred to Hindus.

If we assume that a uniform civil code would be entirely secular in its values, it might represent for the VHP too complete a break from tradition. Furthermore, a uniform civil code, applicable to all residents of India, would undermine the notion of the Hindus as a distinct community. It seems improbable that the VHP would favor a return to the *dharmaśāstras* or to the Anglo-Hindu case law interpreting them. Such a return would involve giving up practices that provide bridges between orthodox Hinduism and modernity and which have become acceptable to many Hindus. In fact it may be the case that the present Hindu Code, adopted by Parliament in 1955–56,[28] is a fairly good approximation of what the VHP would like for Hindus. Although the code's values are predominantly secular, it retains a few traditional elements that may be

---

pp. 254, 289, suggesting that there is a growing realization in India that uniformity is a western concept that may be unsuitable for complex third world legal systems.

[27] Oommen, *State and Society*, pp. 27, 206, 212, 214.

[28] The laws covered marriage, divorce, custody, adoption, maintenance, guardianship and succession.

Personal Law v. Uniform Civil Code

of symbolic importance. Religious ceremonies, for instance, are still effective to bring about valid marriages[29] and conversion to a religion other than Hinduism is ground for divorce.[30] More important, the present code preserves the notion of the Hindus as a community. It seems improbable the VHP would wish to see this code made applicable to all residents of India. More likely, in line with ancient attitudes, it would prefer to hierarchize the different groups in India in accordance with their ways of life.[31]

The Personal Laws and the Constitution

The British Period

The story of the British decision to apply the laws of the different religious communities on specified topics, rather than to replace them with English law or with a body of law representing general western ideas prevailing in the late eighteenth century is well known. Warren Hastings' Plan of 1772 required that in regard to the topics of "inheritance, marriage, cast, and other religious usages, or institutions, the laws of the Koran with respect to the Mahometans, and those of the Shaster with respect to the Gentoos, shall be invariably adhered to...."[32] This commitment was subsequently extended to other groups.[33] The list of topics varied somewhat for the mofussil and the presidency towns, but the essential elements of the commitment were clear. Furthermore, the decision taken in 1772 was consistently adhered to in successive enactments of Parliament and the Indian legislatures, and in royal charters estab-

---

[29] Hindu Marriage Act, 1955, §7.

[30] *Ibid.*, §13(1)(ii).

[31] Mahmood, *Muslim Personal Law*, p. 128, states that RSS leaders Golwalker and Swami Tatriji were opposed to a uniform civil code. See also Tahir Mahmood, *An Indian Civil Code and Islamic Law* (Bombay, 1976), p. 5. The BJP, on the other hand, has issued statements favoring a uniform civil code. See statement by Advani, reported in *New York Times* (Intern'l Ed.), Dec. 1, 1989, p. A6. For a description of changes in the BJP position on the relation between Hindu culture and Indian national identity, see Kameshwar Chondary, "BJP's Changing View of Hindu-Muslim Relations," *Econ. and Polit. Weekly* (Aug. 17, 1991), pp. 1901–04. See also Gyanendra Pandey, "Hindus and Others: The Militant Hindu Construction," *Econ. and Polit. Weekly* (Dec. 28, 1991), pp. 2997–3009. For the suggestion that groups like the VHP would not favor a return to the *śāstras*, see Rajeev Dhavan, "The Dharmasastra and Modern Indian Society: A Very Preliminary Exploration" (1990) (unpublished), p. 41.

[32] 3 Digest of Regulations and Laws Enacted by the Governor General in Council for the Civil Government of the Territories Under the Presidency of Bengal 1–13 (J.E. Colebrook, ed., 1807).

[33] See Jain, *Outlines*, pp. 369, 393–94, 414; Mahmood, *Muslim Personal Law*, p. 3.

lishing courts in India.[34] It received additional support from Queen Victoria's proclamation following the Mutiny, which contained a command that those in authority "abstain from all interference with Religious Belief or Worship" and that "generally, in framing and administering the Law, due regard be paid to the ancient Rights, Usages and Customs of India."[35]

How the list of topics in the Plan of 1772 was arrived at has been a matter of speculation. Professor Derrett suggested that the British had been influenced in drawing up the list by their familiarity with the division of jurisdiction between the secular and ecclesiastical courts in England.[36] They might have been influenced as well by general ideas prevailing in Europe at the time regarding the nature of religion and its relation to the secular. From a theoretical point of view, there is no reason to think of marriage and succession to property, for example, as having any more to do with religion than commercial transactions or taxation, if by religion is meant the relation between this world and a realm of absolute value. Whether Indians of various religions at the end of the eighteenth century would have agreed with the British in finding significance in the list drawn up by Hastings is a difficult question.[37] There had been lengthy experience in India of different religious and ethnic groups living side by side, and this surely compelled the development of ideas about what in religion it is more or less important that the state should recognize. From an Indian point of view, the line drawn by the list of 1772 may not have represented a sharp departure from earlier practice.[38] Furthermore, even if there was some change, as time went on and Indians had experience of the distinctions made by the British, this could have influenced their own attitudes about what in religion it was particularly important the state should recognize. That which pertains to the family and its property and the other listed topics could have come to seem the very core of religion.

In the administration of law on the listed topics, initially the British were impressed primarily by the religious textual law. The Plan of 1772 specifically

---

[34] See Jain, *Outlines*, p. 465; Tahir Mahmood, *Personal Laws in Crisis* (New Delhi, 1986), pp. 7–9.

[35] Panchanandas Mukherji, *Indian Constitutional Documents* (Calcutta, 1915), pp. 355–58.

[36] J. Duncan M. Derrett, *Religion, Law and the State in India* (New York, 1968), p. 233.

[37] See Rajkumari Agrawala, "Uniform Civil Code: A Formula Not a Solution," in Tahir Mahmood, ed., *Family Law and Social Change* (Bombay, 1975), p. 116, suggesting that family has always been considered by Hindus and Muslims to be a special preserve of religion.

[38] But see Jain, *Outlines*, pp. 372–73, suggesting that Hastings' Plan gave a degree of state support to Hindu law that it did not enjoy in the Mogul period.

referred to the śāstras and the Koran. In time, however, they became aware of the importance that many groups in India attached to customs not based upon textual sources.[39] Today the term "personal laws" generally refers to the religious textual laws, but on other occasions it seems to be used to embrace all laws that are applicable to a person because of his religious or ethnic identity.[40] Although demanding standards of proof were developed regarding custom, on the listed topics the British courts came to defer to it as much as to the textual law.[41] Indeed, if a custom was properly proved, it would prevail over the textual law.

Personal law might be applied in the case of unlisted topics as well. This result was reached by means of the direction, which first appeared in the Bengal Regulations of 1781, to look to "justice, equity and good conscience" as a source of law when no other source of law was required.[42] If the personal law conformed closely to the expectations of the parties, "justice, equity and good conscience" might dictate that the court apply the personal law even though the subject was not a listed one.[43] During the second half of the nineteenth century, codification increasingly narrowed the zone within which the personal laws would be allowed to apply on unlisted topics.

The personal law on listed topics would not be set aside simply because it conflicted with "justice, equity and good conscience."[44] Professor Derrett has called attention to a Privy Council decision in which a court in India was severely reprimanded for employing the standard of justice, equity and good conscience to override a Muslim husband's right under Islamic law to have his wife returned to

---

[39] See Jain, *Outlines*, pp. 384, 474, 479–82.

[40] In *State of Bombay* v. *Narasu Appa Mali*, A.I.R. 1952 Bom. 84, the judgments restricted the term "personal laws" to religious textual laws. See also Mahmood, *Muslim Personal Law*, pp. 3–4, describing the "religious civil laws" as the "personal laws" and distinguishing them from "custom." But see Mahmood, *Personal Laws in Crisis*, p. 43, referring to "custom-based diversities in the sphere of personal-laws."

[41] See Jain, *Outlines*, pp. 479–82.

[42] See J. D. M. Derrett, "Justice, Equity and Good Conscience," in J. N. D. Anderson, ed., *Changing Law in Developing Countries* (London, 1963), p. 133.

[43] See J. Duncan M. Derrett, *Essays in Classical and Modern Hindu Law* (Leiden, 1978), vol 4, pp. 18, 20; J. D. M. Derrett, "Justice, Equity and Good Conscience," in J. N. D. Anderson, ed., *Changing Law in Developing Countries* (London, 1963), p. 140; Jain, *Outlines*, pp. 382–84.

[44] J. Duncan M. Derrett, *Essays in Classical and Modern Hindu Law* (Leiden, 1978), vol. 4, p. 9; J. D. M. Derrett, "Justice, Equity and Good Conscience," in J.N.D. Anderson, ed., *Changing Law in Developing Countries* (London, 1963), pp. 140, 147–48.

him.[45] The Privy Council did indicate, however, that the personal law would not be enforced, even on a listed topic, if it was "in plain conflict with...the achievements of a more advanced and civilized society...."[46] For example, a Muslim husband would not be entitled to have the assistance of the courts in having his wife returned if she would be exposed to a danger of serious harm.[47] "Justice, equity and good conscience" might provide the rule of decision on a listed topic if the personal law gave no clear answer, or if the parties were of different religions and there was a conflict of personal laws.[48]

The Present Basis for the Application of the Personal Laws

How are the personal laws part of the law of India today? As already indicated, during the British period they were made the rules of decision by a series of regulations, statutes and charters extending from 1772 right down to Independence. What happened to the personal laws as a result of the adoption of the Constitution in 1950?

Art. 372(1) of the Constitution provides: "[A]ll the law in force in the territory of India immediately before the commencement of this Constitution shall continue in force therein unless altered or repealed or amended by a competent Legislature or other competent authority." This would seem to settle the matter, for surely "law in force" can reasonably be interpreted to include the personal laws, which, as already noted, had been recognized and enforced by the state for one hundred and seventy-eight years. Article 372(3) provides: "The expression 'law in force' in this article shall include a law passed or made by a Legislature or other competent authority in the territory of India before the commencement of this Constitution and not previously repealed, notwithstanding that it or parts of it may not be then in operation either at all or in particular areas." This provision would not seem to weaken the proposition that 372(1) preserves the personal laws, for it does not narrow the definition of "law in force," but simply makes it clear that laws which for one reason or another were not "in operation" at the time the Constitution was adopted are included in the term "law in force."

---

[45]*Moonshee Buzloor Ruheem* v. *Shumsoonnissa Begum*, (1867) 11 M.I.A. 551, 614, discussed in J. Duncan M. Derrett, "Justice, Equity and Good Conscience in India," *Essays in Classical and Modern Hindu Law* (Leiden, 1978), vol. 4, pp. 10–11.

[46]11 M.I.A. at 614–15.

[47]11 M.I.A. at 615.

[48]See J. D. M. Derrett, "Justice, Equity and Good Conscience," in J. N. D. Anderson, ed., *Changing Law in Developing Countries* (London, 1963), pp. 139, 144.

The same term, "laws in force,"[49] accompanied by the same explanation regarding laws that happen not to be "in operation," appears in Article 13, in that part of the Constitution devoted to the Fundamental Rights. Article 13(1) provides: "All laws in force in the territory of India immediately before the commencement of this Constitution, in so far as they are inconsistent with the provisions of this Part [the Fundamental Rights], shall, to the extent of such inconsistency, be void." In a High Court decision in 1952, *State of Bombay* v. *Narasu Appa Mali*,[50] it was held that the term "laws in force" in Article 13(1) does not include the personal laws. This decision seems to have acquired a special authority, perhaps because of the eminence of the judges, Chief Justice Chagla and Justice Gajendragadkar, who rendered it.[51] They were assisted to their conclusion that "laws in force" in Article 13(1) did not include the personal laws by reference to the term "law in force" in Article 372. They noted that in Article 372(2) it was provided that in regard to "law in force," the President of India was authorized to make such adaptions and modifications as were necessary to bring the law into accord with the Constitution. They could not believe it was intended to give the President such a power over the personal laws. As a consequence, they read "law in force" in Article 372, and "laws in force" in Article 13(1), not to include the personal laws. The court's reading of Article 372(1) perhaps need not be taken as the last word on the subject, but it gives reason to search for other possible bases for the continued existence of the personal laws.[52]

The Seventh Schedule to the Constitution lists the subjects over which the Center and the States have legislative jurisdiction. Item 5 of List III, the Concurrent List, has been pointed to as supporting the continued existence of the personal laws.[53] It lists, as within the jurisdiction of both the Center and the States: "Marriage and divorce; infants and minors; adoption; wills, intestacy and succession; joint family and partition, all matters in respect of which parties in judicial proceedings were immediately before the commencement of this Constitution subject to their personal law." But this provision is not directed to

---

[49] The use of the plural seems without significance.

[50] A.I.R. 1952 Bom. 84.

[51] See Mahmood, *Personal Laws in Crisis*, p. 14, referring to *Narasu Appa Mali* as a "celebrated case" and to the Justices who decided it as the "best of law-brains in the country."

[52] In Mahmood, *Personal Laws in Crisis*, p. 9–10, the view is taken that Article 372 retains the personal laws in effect. Judicial decisions are cited, but *Narasu Appa Mali* is not mentioned in this connection.

[53] See *Narasu Appa Mali*, A.I.R. 1952 Bom. at 89; *Gogireddy Sambireddy* v. *Gogireddy Jayamma*, A.I.R. 1972 A.P. 156, 160–61.

the question of the continued existence of the personal laws: it simply provides authority to make law on the topics specified, topics to which, until 1950 at least, the personal laws were applicable.

Article 44 of the Directive Principles of State Policy is another constitutional provision that has been invoked to support the personal laws. Article 44, as noted earlier, calls upon "the State to endeavour to secure for the citizens a uniform civil code." What need would there be, it is asked, to exhort the state to take steps to secure a uniform civil code to replace the personal laws if, by force of the Constitution itself, those personal laws were rendered no longer in effect?[54] Of course, if the personal laws had not been preserved by the Constitution, there would have been no law in force at all on the listed topics, and there would have been an imperative need for legislative action to fill the void. There is some awkwardness in using a Directive Principle of State Policy, which is not "enforceable in any court," although "fundamental in the governance of the country,"[55] as the basis for an inference that the personal laws were preserved. Familiar enough is the controversy over the relation between the Directive Principles and other parts of the Constitution.

But a solution to the question of the continued existence of the personal laws perhaps can be found by combining Article 44 with an implication drawn from legislative history. The issue of the personal laws received some attention in the Constituent Assembly. Muslim members sought to keep Article 44 out of the Constitution and even to have the personal laws protected by express constitutional provision. They failed in this effort, but, as already noted, assurance was given that a personal law would not be overridden unless the affected community was ready for change. There is no indication that anyone in the Constituent Assembly thought that the Constitution, as adopted, abolished the personal laws. If such a possibility had occurred to anyone, there certainly would have been vigorous objection, especially by Muslims. There would have been a demand that the continuance of the personal laws be expressly stated, even if they were not to receive immunity from future legislative action. The personal laws had been applied for a long time, and it seems most unlikely that, in the absence of explicit discussion of the question, the framers of the Constitution intended their immediate abolition. Indeed, the intention seems reasonably clear, simply to encourage the legislature to move cautiously towards a uniform civil code, with full awareness of the delicate nature of the subject.

---

[54]See *Narasu Appa Mali*, A.I.R. 1952 Bom. at 87, 89, 91, relying on Article 44 for the continuance in force of the personal laws.

[55]Constitution of India, Art. 37.

Personal Law v. Uniform Civil Code

The Personal Laws and the Fundamental Rights

Assuming that the personal laws were preserved in force by Article 372(1), or by Article 44 combined with an implication from legislative history, are these laws void, nevertheless, in whole or in part, because of conflict with the Fundamental Rights?

The text of Article 13(1) has already been noted. It provides that all "laws in force" insofar as they are inconsistent with the Fundamental Rights shall be void. This clause deals with laws that existed at the time the Constitution was adopted. The following clause, Article 13(2), focuses on laws that will come into existence subsequent to the adoption of the Constitution. It provides: "the State shall not make any law which takes away or abridges the rights conferred by this Part [the Fundamental Rights] and any law made in contravention of this clause shall, to the extent of the contravention, be void." In Article 13(3)(a) it is then stated that "'law' includes any Ordinance, order, bye-law, rule, regulation, notification, custom or usage having in the territory of India the force of law...."[56]

In *Narasu Appa Mali*, already referred to, Chief Justice Chagla, in his judgment, concluded that "laws in force" in Article 13(1) did not include the personal laws. He was assisted to this conclusion by the fact that the definition of "law" in 13(3)(a) did not include the personal laws. From this same definition in 13(3)(a) he concluded that "customs and usages" were within "laws in force" in 13(1). In his view, what distinguishes the "personal laws" from "customs and usages" is that the former are based upon religious texts. Thus the Chief Justice seemed to hold that a personal law, as he understood the term, which existed at the time the Constitution was adopted, would not be void even if it conflicted with the Fundamental Rights, but that a custom or usage that conflicted with the Fundamental Rights would be void. In regard to statutory laws existing at the time the Constitution was adopted, addressed to the topics traditionally covered by the personal laws, Chief Justice Chagla seemed to think that these, like custom and usage, fall within the term "laws in force" in 13(1) and would be void if in conflict with the Fundamental Rights.

As far as 13(2) is concerned, the provision addressed to actions taken by the state subsequent to the adoption of the Constitution, the Chief Justice gave no clear answer. It may be he thought that here too the personal laws would not be ruled by the Fundamental Rights. The prohibition of 13(2) is against the state

---

[56] 13(3)(b) contains the provision, already noted, that "'laws in force' includes laws passed or made by the Legislature or other competent authority in the territory of India before the commencement of this Constitution and not previously repealed, notwithstanding that any such law or any part thereof may not be then in operation either at all or in particular areas."

'making" any law. How could the state make the personal laws? They are drawn from the religious texts. Some of the language in Chief Justice Chagla's judgment suggests that he also thought that custom and usage were exempt from 13(2). He expressed the view that the definition of "law" in 13(3)(a), which included custom and usage, could not apply to 13(2), because how could the state "make" a custom? But this reading of his judgment would produce the strange result that customs are exempt from 13(2) even though they are not exempt from 13(1). Chief Justice Chagla made no statement regarding the position of statutes under 13(2), but it is perhaps fair to infer that he thought they came under 13(2), just as he thought they came under 13(1). But this result may be difficult to reconcile with a statement in his opinion that the Constitution leaves it to the legislature to modify and improve the personal laws.[57]

Justice Gajendragadkar agreed with Chief Justice Chagla that the personal laws are not within the term "laws in force" in 13(1). However, in dictum, he seemed to suggest that "customs or usages having the force of law" also are exempt from 13(1). Statutes, he appeared to believe were not exempt. As to 13(2), Justice Gajendragadkar took the position that no custom or usage having the force of law could validly be made the basis of any law if the custom or usage offended the Fundamental Rights. This would seem strange if custom and usage, as he suggested, are exempt from 13(1).

As indicated, both opinions in *Narasu Appa Mali* suggest a distinction under Article 13 between statutes and other forms of law. It is difficult to understand what would warrant such a distinction. Suppose a statute were enacted in a bona fide and reasonable effort to state the law of a particular community. If judicial interpretation of a community's personal law is exempt from the test of the Fundamental Rights, why should not legislative interpretation be as well? If the legislature had no interest in stating the law of a particular community and was simply adopting a rule it thought desirable, that would be a different matter.[58] It is also not clear, so far as Article 13 is concerned, why custom and usage should have a different status than personal laws based on texts, especially if the custom or usage relates to one of the traditionally listed topics and is based on religious belief.

Assuming that the personal laws are subject to the Fundamental Rights, do they violate them in whole or in part? It is in regard to Articles 14 and 15, the

---

[57]A.I.R. 1952 Bom. at 89.

[58]Mahmood, *Personal Laws in Crisis*, pp. 21–23, takes the position: "All these laws [statutes]—both old and new [those enacted before and after the adoption of the Constitution]—being an outcome of direct state action, should be within the ambit of Article 13 of the Constitution." Id. at p. 21. But then he seems to qualify this statement by directing criticism particularly to actions taken by the parliament "on the soil of an independent and secular India." Id. at 23. I.e., statutes enacted since 1947 or 1950.

first prohibiting the state from denying to any person the equal protection of the laws and the second prohibiting the state from discriminating "on grounds only of religion, race, caste, sex, place of birth or any of them," that questions principally arise. One question is whether it is constitutionally permissible to have different laws for different groups, defined according to religion, caste or ethnicity. Such distinctions are, of course, the very foundation of the personal law system in India. Another question is whether it is permissible for the personal law of a group to treat members differently according to whether they possess certain characteristics. Is it permissible, for instance, for a personal law to have different rules for men and women? Under Muslim law it is easier for a man to secure divorce than a woman. Under several of the personal laws, rights of succession differ for sons and daughters. If constitutional justification is to be found for state recognition of these distinctions, it must lie in a claimed value, to be discussed shortly, of maintaining the different cultures of religious and ethnic groups in India. If the state, either through legislation or judicial interpretation, is engaged in a bona fide and reasonable effort to uphold this value, it can be argued that, under Articles 14 and 15, there is justification for both the system of personal laws generally and particular features of these laws, such as different treatment of men and women. If the state is not engaged in any such attempt, but is simply enforcing what it believes to be a desirable rule, which would be the case with a uniform civil code, this value of protecting cultural identities that exist independently of the state cannot be invoked.

We are discussing the constitutional permissibility of the system of personal laws and particular features of these laws, not what is constitutionally required. But even when it is only a question of constitutional permissibility, some significance perhaps can be found in Articles 25 and 26 of the Constitution, which guarantee religious liberty, although in a highly qualified manner, and Article 29, which recognizes the right to maintain distinct cultures. Perhaps personal laws based upon religion are on a different constitutional footing than personal laws based on secular values, assuming it is proper to use the term "personal laws" in a secular connection. In regard to religion, the constitutional provisions cut both ways: whereas Article 15 prohibits the state from discriminating on the ground of religion, Articles 25 and 26 single out religion for special protection.

As noted earlier, Article 13 has separate provisions dealing with laws in force at the time the Constitution was adopted and laws that come into existence subsequently. This suggested the possibility that laws in one of these categories might be subject to the Fundamental Rights, but not laws in the other category. But if, as we are now assuming, the personal laws are subject to the Fundamental Rights, surely they are subject to them in the same way and to the same extent no matter when they came into existence.

Another of the distinctions touched upon in *Narasu Appa Mali* may reappear here: Does a law that rests upon a text have a different constitutional status than a custom or usage, so that whereas a text-based law may survive attack under Articles 14 and 15, a mere custom or usage might not? There seems no justification for different treatment in these situations, at least if we assume that the custom is no less religious than the text. Indeed, in the British period it came to be established that a custom properly proved could oust the textual law.[59]

Finally, there is the distinction between listed and unlisted topics. It is uncertain, as we have seen, what the original reasons were for the list. But in any case, as already noted, as time has gone by, many Indians have come to see the listed topics as especially closely connected with religion. On these topics, the British would not set aside the personal law even if it conflicted with "justice, equity and good conscience." For unlisted topics, on the other hand, the personal law would be set aside if it conflicted with this standard.[60] This history could lead to the conclusion that an especially strong commitment on the listed topics found its way into the Constitution, with the consequence that even if a law that discriminates on one of the bases forbidden by Articles 14 and 15 might on an unlisted topic be unconstitutional, a similar law on a listed topic would not be. For example, a law treating Muslims and Hindus, or men and women, differently in regard to divorce might be valid, but not a law treating them differently in regard to, say, the right of preemption.[61] But, of course, even in regard to a listed topic, a provision in a personal law that conflicts with a value fundamental to the Constitution probably is not valid, any more than a law would have been valid in the British period if it conflicted with what the British held to be fundamental.

Constitutional attacks on the system of personal laws and particular features of the personal laws in fact have been rejected on the rationale that even if the personal laws are subject to the Fundamental Rights, they do not violate them.

In *Gurdial Kaur* v. *Manghal Singh*,[62] for instance, it was held that a custom of a particular caste that excluded a mother, who was a widow, from the succession to the estate of her deceased son if she had remarried, but not the father under the same circumstances, did not violate Article 15. The court rejected both the argument that the enforcement of this custom discriminated

---

[59] See Jain, *Outlines*, pp. 479–82.

[60] *Ibid.*, pp. 382–84.

[61] *Ibid.*, p. 384; Paras Diwan, *Muslim Law in Modern India* (Allahabad, 4th ed., 1987), p. 235 (British courts not required to enforce right of preemption of real property as part of Muslim personal law, but as matter of "justice, equity and good conscience").

[62] A.I.R. 1968 Pun. 396.

Personal Law v. Uniform Civil Code

among castes and the argument that it discriminated against women. The court made the unhelpful observations that if the mother's arguments were accepted, "it would be impossible to have different personal laws in this country, and the Court will have to go to the length of holding that only one uniform Code of laws relating to all matters covering all castes, creeds and communities can be constitutional," and that "it is too much to suggest that all heirs belonging to any sex must have the same rights of inheritance."[63]

In *Sudha* v. *Sankappa Rai*,[64] Madras had passed an act relating to marriage and divorce for the Aliyasanthana community. The act provided that if a petition for divorce had been filed and a specified amount of time had elapsed, the court should grant a divorce without inquiring into the grounds a party might have, an approach that was in accord with the custom of the community. Thus divorce in this community was easier than in certain others. An attack on the act on the ground that it denied equal protection of the laws as guaranteed by Article 14 was rejected by the court. This was not a case of "discrimination," the court said, but of "classification":

> Each of these laws has a history of its own. No section of the community is shown to have been subjected to hostile discrimination, to adversely affect the rights of a section of the people or an individual, but classification is to advance the cause of a section of the people without harming the interests of the others. The Legislature must be presumed to have acted in the interests of the community at large as well as all sections thereof.[65]

In *Narasu Appa Mali*, an alternative holding of the court subjected the personal laws to the Fundamental Rights, but found that the legislation there involved, the Bombay Prevention of Hindu Bigamous Marriages Act, 1946, did not violate the Fundamental Rights. Under the act, taken with provisions in the Penal Code relating to bigamy and the different personal laws, Hindus who committed bigamy were punished severely, Christians and Parsis moderately, Muslims not at all. The court held that these differences in treatment were capable of justification in that whereas Christians and Parsis had always been monogamous and could be kept so by a mild punishment, and Muslims were so accustomed to polygamy and generally backward that there was no present hope of changing them, Hindus, being subject to currents of opinion within their own

---

[63] *Ibid.*, at 398–99.

[64] A.I.R. 1963 Mys. 245.

[65] *Ibid.*, at 247.

communities against polygamy, might be made monogamous by stern measures.[66]

That the system of personal laws may be retained without violating the Fundamental Rights does not mean that it constitutionally must be retained. An argument that it must be retained would rely on Articles 25 and 26, guaranteeing religious liberty, and Article 29, affirming the right to maintain a distinct culture. But the implication of Article 44, which requires the state to attempt to secure a uniform civil code, surely stands against any such suggestion, as does the authorization in item 5 of the Concurrent List in the Seventh Schedule, to legislate on the topics to which the personal laws traditionally have been applied. But may there perhaps be exceptional circumstances in which the personal laws constitutionally must be respected? Perhaps not all of the topics to which the personal laws traditionally have been applied are on an equal constitutional footing. The weight of the state's interest may be different. There are situations in which Article 25 or 26 appear to require special treatment of religion.[67] May these situations possibly include some of those to which the personal laws are usually applied? For instance, suppose a uniform civil code requires a person to perform a certain action before a state official in order for a marriage to be valid. Might a person who has a religious objection to the requirement be constitutionally entitled to exemption? But it would be one thing to hold that Articles 25, 26 and 29 sometimes require exemption from a state rule of general applicability and another to hold that they require the state to involve itself in finding and applying the law of a religious or ethnic community. And yet there can be no doubt that in regard to certain topics at least, the state is constitutionally required to uphold private ordering. It is certainly required to give effect in some way to contracts, the laws of voluntary associations and dispositions of private

---

[66]See A.I.R. 1952 Bom. 87-88, 93–94. See also *Srinivasa Aiyar* v. *Saraswathi Ammal*, A.I.R. 1952 Mad. 193, 195–96 (prosecution of Hindus for bigamy; different treatment of Hindus and others not based solely on ground of religion); *Gogireddy Sambireddy* v. *Gogireddy Jayamma*, A.I.R. 1972 A.P. 156.

Mahmood in *Personal Laws in Crisis*, p. 14, states that no court has said that continued application of separate personal laws is in violation of the Fundamental Rights and that the Supreme Court has expressed the opinion that application of different religious endowment-administration laws to different communities is not unconstitutional.

[67]E.g., *Sardar Syedna Taher Saifuddin Saheb* v. *State of Bombay*, A.I.R. 1962 S.C. 853 (statute prohibiting excommunication violated Article 26); *M. Peeran Saheb* v. *Special Officer*, A.I.R. 1988 A.P. 377 (disqualification of Muslim females from voting because of refusal to be photographed violated Article 25).

property. But does this obligation extend to upholding the private ordering of ascriptive groups based on religion or ethnicity?[68]

The Advantages and Disadvantages of the System of Personal Laws

General Considerations

Assuming that the Constitution neither requires that the system of personal laws be abolished nor that it be retained, the question of its desirability from a nonconstitutional point of view must be confronted. In addressing this question, the teachings of the personal laws themselves of course cannot be dispositive. It may well be that one or more of the religions in India require the state to enforce a particular body of rules upon the members of a community, or for that matter upon all the inhabitants of India, but this cannot be determinative for the Indian state. For the state, decision must be based upon its own ideology.

Strengthening national unity frequently has been cited as a reason for having a uniform civil code.[69] Increased unity will mean less communal conflict and indirectly affect economic prosperity and national security. There is not likely to be any quarrel with the values stated. The difficulty lies in the proof.[70] The comparative effect on national unity of different personal laws and a uniform civil code probably needs to be considered topic by topic, rather than generally. For example, what is the effect on national unity and communal conflict of the existence of different laws on polygamy? Do Hindus resent the fact that Muslims have a special privilege, or do they feel, rather, that the state's "reform" of Hinduism has been a benefit conferred upon it?[71] Do different laws of succession create hostility among religious communities? If there had been since Independence a uniform code on the traditional topics of the personal laws, would there have been less communal violence than there has been? Some have noted

---

[68] See Mahmood, *Personal Laws in Crisis*, pp. 19–20, discussing the applicability of Arts. 25, 26 and 29 to the personal laws.

[69] See Markandan, *Directive Principles*, p. 192, citing debates in the Constituent Assembly. The Supreme Court in its *Shah Bano* judgment stated: "A Common Civil Code will help the cause of national integration by removing disparate loyalties to laws which have conflicting ideologies." A.I.R. 1985 S.C. at 954.

[70] For expressions of scepticism regarding the effect of a uniform code on national unity, see Rajkumari Agrawala, "Uniform Civil Code: A Formula Not a Solution," in Tahir Mahmood, ed., *Family Law and Social Change* (Bombay, 1975), pp. 121–22.

[71] See the suggestion of the latter attitude by Acharya Kripalani during the discussions on the Hindu Code in 1955, quoted in Donald E. Smith, *India as a Secular State* (Princeton, New Jersey, 1963), p. 288.

that there have been uniform laws on a large number of subjects—for example, the criminal law and the law of contracts—for many years, and yet communal conflict has continued and indeed increased.[72] If a uniform civil code were adopted today, what would be its effect on communal conflict in the next few decades? Its effect in the future might be different than what it would have been during the period since Independence. Some believe that a uniform civil code would only increase communal tension. Certainly predominant Muslim reaction to the statement about a uniform code in the Supreme Court's *Shah Bano* judgment lends support to this view. A more effective way to assure national unity, it can be argued, is to reassure religious and ethnic groups that their personal laws will be respected. The empirical question of the effect on national unity and communal harmony of adopting or not adopting a uniform code should not be confused with the matter mentioned earlier, the notion that some national leaders had, and perhaps still have, that there is a sort of logical contradiction between the idea of a nation-state and a system of different personal laws.

Probably the most interesting and important point to be considered in regard to the desirability or undesirability of a system of personal laws is the argument that such a system helps to affirm the distinct identities of ethnic and religious groups, and that this is a positive advantage. It is an advantage, it is suggested, because in affirming the identities of these groups, the state contributes to the well-being of the individuals who compose them. In particular, it contributes to their sense of existing and of having meaning in their lives.[73] This sense of existing and having meaning, it is argued, is something that citizenship in a nation-state alone cannot confer. Although the anti-secularists, earlier referred to, who have come to the defense of cultural "pluralism," have not given a significant amount of attention to the question of the system of personal laws, the idea that such a system performs a useful function in confirming people's sense of existing and having meaning may be consistent with their general ideas.

Against the suggested argument in favor of the personal laws stands, of course, the opposite view that the individual is not enhanced but diminished by membership in most of the ethnic and religious groups that exist in India, and that the help he needs from the state is not reinforcement of these identities, but liberation from them. In supporting the system of personal laws, the state helps to keep these imprisoning identities alive. Quite apart from the question of the effect on national unity, the liberation of the human spirit, it is suggested, requires

---

[72] E.g., Rajkumari Agrawala, "Uniform Civil Code: A Formula Not a Solution," in Tahir Mahmood, ed., *Family Law and Social Change* (Bombay, 1975), p. 121.

[73] For an excellent discussion of disruption of identities and psychological disorientation in India today, and the steps people take to deal with these problems, see T. G. Vaidyanathan, "Authority and Identity in India," *Daedalus*, Fall, 1989, pp. 147–69 (Proc. Amer. Acad. Arts and Sci., vol. 118, No. 4).

Personal Law v. Uniform Civil Code

the elimination of the system of personal laws and the adoption of a uniform civil code.

Defenders of the system of personal laws cite in support of their position the example of different territorial laws.[74] If territorial legal pluralism is desirable—and no one doubts that it is to some extent—why not nonterritorial ethnic and religious legal pluralism? All recognize that it would be an injustice for the conqueror of a territory to sweep away all the laws of the inhabitants and replace them with his own. To do so would be to deprive the inhabitants of an important constituent of their identity, to commit a kind of cultural genocide. So also in the case of the laws of nonterritorial groups, it is argued. There is some force in the analogy. In the territorial case, although territory is an important aspect of identity, it is not the only one. Other factors, such as language, race, culture, religion, shared history and law play a part. Why by removing the territorial factor should the whole force of the argument in favor of preserving identity through law be destroyed?

It is important to distinguish between affirming the law of an ethnic or religious group in the sense just referred to and upholding contracts and the laws of voluntary associations, a subject touched upon earlier. What is affirmed in the latter situation is private ordering through individual choice. The enforcement of the law of a voluntary association finds justification in the choice made by each individual member to accept the law of the association. In the case of ethnic and religious groups in India, however, the application of their laws can seldom be justified on any such voluntaristic basis. Although some consideration of individual choice may occasionally appear—here we touch upon the complex subject of conversion—for the most part ascriptive elements are predominant. The fundamental question for the state, therefore, as already noted, is whether, given its own ideology, there is value in maintaining the identities of ethnic and religious groups through the enforcement of their laws, even though these groups are predominantly ascriptive. Of course all identities that are received, or even imposed, rather than individually chosen, are not for that reason automatically to be condemned. The identity that comes from being a member of a family, or for that matter a citizen of a territorial state, are examples. Furthermore, the borderline between ascription and choice is often indistinct: if a young person elects to be initiated into a religious sect to which his family has long belonged,

---

[74]See Rajkumari Agrawala, "Uniform Civil Code: A Formula Not a Solution," in Tahir Mahmood, ed., *Family Law and Social Change* (Bombay, 1975), p. 122; Master-Moos, "The Personal Law of the Parsees," in Narmada Khodie, ed., *Readings in Uniform Civil Code* (Bombay, 1975), p. 116 (adopting a single family law for India would be like forcing all Europe under a single family law); Markandan, *Directive Principles*, p. 107 (quoting Hussain Imam in the Constituent Assembly).

does he freely choose as an individual to be initiated into the sect, or is the reality more complicated than that?

State policy may exclude from all private ordering a particular subject. For example, the minimum age for marriage.[75] In this situation both individual choice and the laws of ascriptive groups are ousted. On other topics, state policy may exclude, not private ordering as such, but only private ordering through the law of ascriptive groups. The state's readiness to enforce the consequences of individual choice may stand unimpaired. For example, an individual's decision to be governed by a particular law of intestate succession might be respected even though that same law would not be applied by reason of his membership in an ascriptive group.

A reason sometimes put forward for protecting the identities of religious and ethnic groups, which could include through the recognition of their personal laws, is that when there are different cultures within a nation, improving dialogue is possible.[76] If one group learns of the ways of another, it may become aware of its own deficiencies and decide to eliminate them, perhaps by borrowing from the second group. Sometimes the suggestion is that the dominant culture, which is prone to the self-satisfaction that comes with power, will be humbled by what it learns from minority cultures. But the argument also can be directed against minority cultures: they must take into account the values of the dominant culture and consider whether their own ways stand in need of improvement. The emphasis on "dialogue" can lead to an outcome quite contrary to respect for distinct cultural identities. It may be that the identity of a particular group consists precisely in keeping uncontaminated by the world the revelation it believes it has received, which may include specific rules regarding such subjects as marriage, divorce and succession. Is this identity not to be respected because the group will not engage in give-and-take with the dominant culture, in other words will not submit to the view, probably the product of the dominant culture itself, that there can be progress in ideas about how to live?

The suggestion that the personal laws of ethnic and religious groups should be upheld because of the value of maintaining cultural identities could be argued to be especially applicable in the case of minorities.[77] Minorities, defined

---

[75] The Child Marriage Restraint (Amendment) Act, 1978, sets the minimum age for marriage of females at 18 and males at 21.

[76] See Adeno Addis, "Individualism, Communitarianism, and the Rights of Ethnic Minorities," 66 *Notre Dame L. Rev.* 1219, 1224 (1991).

[77] See Mahmood, *Muslim Personal Law*, p. 123, including among the reasons why most Indian Muslims are opposed to a uniform civil code that "Muslim personal law is regarded by a majority of Muslims as a symbol of their identity in Hindu dominated India. The fact that they are in a minority, to whose religion Hindu masses generally are hostile, makes the attitude of Muslims extremely rigid."

either numerically or from the point of view of power, stand in special need, it may be thought, of having their cultures affirmed by the state. Their sense of worth may be fragile and, understandably, they may be sceptical of the ordinary political process. Furthermore, the argument that "pluralism" is the best antidote to alienation and secessionist tendencies may be especially persuasive in the case of minorities. Article 30 of the Constitution, which gives special protection to minority educational institutions, reflects this view. On the other hand, it is a notable feature of the present Indian scene that it is not the minorities alone that feel insecure and anxious about the future. Many Hindus share this anxiety and either attempt to reaffirm tradition or, like the VHP, to develop new forms that bind together past and future. Special protection of minorities is strongly opposed by such groups.

If the personal laws of the minorities were recognized, it is perhaps not quite correct to say that the personal law of the majority necessarily also would be recognized. It is true that if the minorities were exempted from the general law, what would be left would be the law applicable to the majority. But this law would not be the majority's personal law in the sense in which we have been using that term. The law applicable to the majority would as likely be imposed upon it as created by it. Even though there is a "democratic" political process, an important distinction still would be likely to remain between the state and the majority, especially in India, so that the law applicable to the majority would reflect the values of governing groups rather than those of the majority community or the congeries of communities that make up Hinduism. Everyone would agree that this is an accurate description of the circumstances attending the adoption of the Hindu Code of 1955–56. Even if Hinduism is seen to have a large capacity for development, it is not likely to be contended that in adopting laws for the Hindus in 1955–56, Parliament was simply striving to reflect a change that had already taken place among the mass of Hindus. Rather, it was seeking to draw Hindus onto a new path, one alien to their traditions. Still, because Hindus are in the great majority in India, and obviously have more influence with the state than the minorities, the adoption of the Hindu Code in 1955-56 may not have significantly undermined their sense of worth or alienated them from the state. But the matter is not free from doubt. As pointed out earlier, the attitude of Hindu organizations such as the VHP towards the existing Hindu Code is unclear.[78]

---

[78]See M. N. Srinivas, "On Living in a Revolution," in James R. Roach, ed., *India 2000: The Next Fifteen Years* (Riverdale, Maryland, 1986), pp. 4, 23, stating that many Hindus have a grievance against the government for radically altering their laws in 1955–56, and that many think the government's sensitivity to, and respect for, the culture and institutions of minorities contrasts sharply with its attitude towards Hindu culture and institutions.

Is the Identity Value in Fact Upheld by Present Indian Law?

General Considerations

If the value of affirming the identities of ethnic and religious groups is the principal reason for the system of personal laws, it is worthwhile to consider the extent to which that value is in fact being supported. As has recently been observed, assertions concerning ethnic and national identity must be viewed with caution, for the processes of identity formation are not well understood.[79] To the extent that the state is not simply recognizing an independently existing identity, but creating and shaping one, it cannot invoke in justification of its activity the identity value that we have been considering. If the identity value is not well supported by the law, changes perhaps can be made so that it will be better supported. On the other hand, if the identity value is not well supported and the reason for this is that importance is not really attached to it, the considerations claimed to outweigh this value should be brought into the open and submitted to careful examination.

Threshold Questions

In protecting the identity of cultural and religious groups through recognition of their personal laws, certain threshold ideas generated by the state's own ideology seem inescapably involved. For example, it is necessary for the state to decide what qualifies as a group for the purpose of receiving recognition through the enforcement of personal law: certain types of relationships may be judged not to qualify.[80] Also it would seem unavoidable that the state have its own criteria regarding what constitutes membership in a group for the purpose of imposition of group law on an individual, although these criteria may make some reference to the attitudes held by the individual and the group. In addition, the state must have its own notion of what is meant by "law" for the purpose of determining what is the law of a group. Although reference to sacred texts and

---

[79]M.R. Anderson, "Islamic Law and the Colonial Encounter in British India," in Chibli Mallat and Jane Connors, eds., *Islamic Family Law* (London 1990), pp. 205, 219. On the complexity of contemporary caste identification, see Steve Barnett, "Identity Choice and Caste Ideology in Contemporary South India," in Kenneth David, ed., *The New Wind. Changing Identities in South Asia* (The Hague, 1977), pp. 393–414.

[80]A religious or ethnic group could be very small and still have an elaborately developed law. A particular family might have its own law or custom. We have been speaking of groups, but it is not nonsensical to speak of an individual having his law. This could refer to a commitment inferred from his general way of life, which might be different from his actions or expressed choice on a particular occasion.

seers long dead may be required, it seems doubtful that acceptance by the living will be left wholly out of account. At the same time, the state's notion of the "law" of a group may point not simply to what a majority of the living members believe at a particular time, but to more enduring commitments. To the extent that the answers to these threshold questions flow from the state's own ideology rather than from ideologies that exist independently of the state, to that extent the state's system of personal laws will uphold the identity value in a way that is less than perfect.

Who Decides

What strikes many observers of the Indian legal system is not only that there are different laws for different religious and ethnic communities on certain topics, but that all these different laws are determined and administered by a single judicial system. That it is the courts of the state that perform this function undoubtedly affects the content of the laws that are administered.

It is common knowledge that however conscientiously the judges of the early British period tried to enter into the spirit of the classical Hindu law and the Islamic law, a consequence of their activity was, to some extent at least, to bring into existence something significantly different from those laws. The fact that the judges were British and carried in their heads ideas very different from those of the Hindu pundits and Muslim kazis who advised them, more or less foreordained this outcome. Also, as later became well understood, the very institutions and procedures that the British created to administer the laws were so different from those of the Hindu and Islamic legal traditions that the substance was bound to be affected. Stare decisis alone was a powerful engine for transformation, because it gave to the decisions of the state's courts a status that they had never enjoyed under either Hindu or Muslim rulers. The tendencies of the British effort to find and apply the Hindu and Islamic laws, which had the effect of changing them, probably were only accentuated by the decision in 1864[81] to eliminate the court pundits and kazis and have the judges decide the legal questions unaided.

If the circumstances just mentioned are taken into account, the question naturally is presented to what extent the Anglo-Hindu case law, insofar as it is still applied by the Indian courts, and not replaced by the Hindu Code of 1955–56, and the Anglo-Muslim case law,[82] which is still fully administered, can be

---

[81] See J. D. M. Derrett, "British Administration of Hindu Law," *Compar. Studies in Soc. and Hist.* (1961), vol. 4, pp. 10, 32.

[82] Professor Tahir Mahmood has sharply criticized the Anglo-Muslim case law (and its further development by the courts of independent India) for its departures from Islamic law. His main point is that the courts have relied on texts he considers unauthoritative. Mahmood, *Personal Laws in Crisis*, pp. 49–63.

defended on the ground that they uphold identities that exist independently of the state. In order fully to uphold the identity of an ethnic or religious group through the enforcement of its laws, it would seem necessary to give effect to the institutions and processes created by the group to determine and apply its law, for these are as much part of the law as the substantive rules.

In India, not only are the laws of religious and ethnic groups determined by the courts of the state, but the judges of these courts frequently do not belong to the religion the law of which they are to find. The suggestion that the judges assigned to hear a case should be selected on the basis of religion would be strongly resisted: selection on the basis of religion would be seen as seriously compromising the secular character of the state. The five-judge bench in the *Shah Bano* case, which determined among other issues the Muslim law of maintenance, was composed entirely of Hindu judges. If judges were assigned on the basis of religion, difficult questions of classification would arise. In a particular case it might not be enough that a judge was a Muslim: he might have to be of a particular school of Islamic law. And if customary law were involved, it might be necessary to find judges who belonged to the group whose custom was to be determined. Although it may be possible for a judge who is not of a particular religion to go a long way in entering into its spirit and presuppositions, to the extent that he is not able fully to achieve this, the identity value will not be perfectly upheld.

The Kazis Act of 1880 was the result of an effort by some Muslims to have the determination of questions of Islamic law placed in the hands of Muslims. But the effort failed and the British refused to confer judicial powers on the kazis.[83] Instead, what was enacted was a strange exercise of state power. Among some Muslims it was thought that kazis could not function—and they were believed necessary for certain purposes—unless they were appointed by the state.[84] This idea may have been based upon religious beliefs and influenced by experiences under the Mughal and early British regimes. The Kazis Act accommodated this sentiment by providing for state appointment of kazis when there were any considerable number of Muslims in an area who desired it. There was also to be consultation with the principal Muslim residents. But the act carefully refrained from specifying what the duties of kazis might be,[85] denied that they had any judicial powers, and specified that the act should not be

---

[83] See Mahmood, *Muslim Personal Law*, pp. 54, 57–58. The British also rejected a demand of the ulema that judges determining questions of Muslim law be Muslims. See *Ibid.*, pp. 47, 49.

[84] See Statement of Objects and Reasons appended to the Kazis Act.

[85] A Maharashtra amendment to the act, adopted in 1978, confers upon the kazis in that state the duty to keep records of marriages.

Personal Law v. Uniform Civil Code

construed to prohibit anyone from acting as a kazi even if not appointed by the state. Thus the act kept the authoritative decision of questions of Islamic law firmly in the hands of the state's judges, who might be of any religion or none at all, while at the same time authorizing the state to make appointments of kazis, implying some sort of link between the state and the kazis, a suggestion that could, perhaps, have a modest effect on the religion.

Conferring judicial powers on kazis needs to be distinguished from upholding their decisions as arbitrators selected by the parties to settle a dispute.[86] In the latter situation there is state support for private ordering through individual choice, as distinguished from private ordering through the law of ascriptive ethnic or religious groups.

The debate over the Dissolution of Muslim Marriages Act, 1939, reproduced the controversy over the kazis. Quite apart from the issue of whether Islamic law permitted women to obtain divorce, and if so on what grounds, many of the ulema opposed the act because it allowed judges who were not Muslims to decide issues of Islamic law. But the effort to secure Muslim control of the administration of the law of divorce was unsuccessful.

The Parsi Marriage and Divorce Act, 1936,[87] adopted, it is said, at the behest of the Parsi community,[88] provides for special tribunals called Parsi Matrimonial Courts. The judges of these courts are High Court judges or District Court judges, but the courts also include "delegates," who must be Parsis. The delegates are chosen by the state government "after giving the local Parsis an opportunity of expressing their opinion in such manner as the respective Governments may think fit."[89] The judge is to determine questions of law, the delegates questions of fact.[90] Possibly the fact that the delegates are Parsis will give to their fact-finding a distinctive character: they may have background factual information that non-Parsis do not have. It is hard to avoid the belief, however, that such trouble would not have been taken to require that the delegates be Parsis unless it was thought that by this means Parsi views on matters of value would have some chance of having an influence on the case. Thus the Parsi Marriage and Divorce Act may present an instance in Indian law in which the state has made it possible for the adherents of a particular religion to play a role in the determination and application of their own law. But will the Parsis who serve as delegates be authoritative spokesmen for Parsi law or,

---

[86] See Mahmood, *Muslim Personal Law*, p. 58.

[87] As amended by the Parsi Marriage and Divorce (Amendment) Act, 1988.

[88] See Statement of Objects and Reasons appended to the Act.

[89] Section 24.

[90] Section 46.

because of the method of their selection, will they be primarily spokesmen for state values? As noted above, provision is made in the Parsi Act for consultation with local Parsis on delegate selection, but what assurance is there that those consulted themselves will be authentic spokesmen for Parsi values?

The recently authorized Family Courts,[91] so far actually instituted in only a few large cities, may also throw into relief the question of who decides what the law is. Under the act authorizing the creation of these courts, it is provided: "[I]f the Family Court considers it necessary in the interest of justice, it may seek the assistance of a legal expert as *amicus curiae*."[92] Under this provision may experts on the various personal laws be introduced into the functioning of the courts? It seems correct to assume that the personal laws will continue to be applied by the Family Courts, and that Parliament did not intend by the creation of these new institutions to effect a change in the substantive laws.[93] Might the old court pundits and kazis make a reappearance in the Family Courts of modern India? There are those who believe that if this is not possible under the Family Courts Act as it stands, efforts should be made to amend the act to assure that cases under the personal laws are decided by persons who are "experts in those laws and can appreciate their letter and spirit."[94]

Particular Situations

The Shariat Act of 1937[95] provides an example of how difficult it can be in regard to the personal laws to determine whether the state is affirming the independently existing identity of an ethnic or religious group or asserting its own values. In that act, which was a response to lobbying by certain Muslim groups,[96] the state imposed the Shariat on all Muslims for most of the topics on

---

[91] Family Courts Act, 1984.

[92] Family Courts Act, 1984, §13. See also §§5 and 12, permitting the state government and the courts to provide for association with the court of persons whose association would enable the court to exercise its jurisdiction more effectively, in accordance with the purposes of the act.

[93] Although a strained argument might be made that from the statement in the act that in choosing judges an endeavor should be made to select "persons committed to the need to protect and preserve the institution of marriage," §4(4)(a), a legislative intention in regard to the substantive law can be inferred.

[94] See Mahmood, *Personal Laws in Crisis*, p. 136.

[95] Muslim Personal Law (Shariat) Application Act, 1937.

[96] See Statement of Objects and Reasons appended to the act; Mahmood, *Muslim Personal Law*, pp. 17, 24–26.

the list to which the personal laws traditionally have been applied.[97] The Muslims affected by the act[98] included a number of groups that had theretofore followed the Hindu law on certain topics, such as succession. Those who had successfully campaigned for the act believed it wrong to mix Islam with elements of Hindu or customary law. It is not certain what their view would have been if the groups in question had not only observed the Hindu law of succession, but had repudiated Islam entirely. Perhaps they would have thought that the members of these groups were no longer Muslims, and so there was no reason to bring them under the Shariat.

Did the application of the Shariat to the groups that had theretofore observed the Hindu law of succession uphold the identity value that we have been discussing? As noted earlier, in the application of the personal laws certain threshold questions unavoidably are presented that require resort to the ideology of the state. The issue of whether the groups that observed the Hindu law of succession should have been considered part of a larger group, "Muslims," for the purpose of applying a particular law, would seem to be such a question. The answer to the question might involve difficult issues of history and interpretation, and not be provided simply by the fact that the groups considered themselves Muslims. Furthermore, were those who demanded that the Shariat be imposed upon these nonobservant groups authentic spokesmen for Islam? To the extent that the answers to these questions are uncertain, to that extent it is not clear that the Shariat Act upheld the identity value. Possibly the British decided for purely pragmatic and political reasons to appease powerful Muslim interests by subordinating one group to another. It is interesting to note that although the Shariat Act suppressed the Hindu law to the extent that it had been observed by certain groups, it did not attempt to unify the various schools of Islamic law, all of which continued to be recognized as acceptable versions of the Shariat.

The Dissolution of Muslim Marriages Act, 1939, already referred to, which allowed Muslim women to obtain divorce under certain circumstances, also presents the question whether the value of maintaining group identity is being supported by the state or some other value. There is a principle of Islamic law, recognized by one school at least, that under certain circumstances it is permissible to look to all of the schools of Islamic law to see if divorce is permitted under any of them.[99] However, Professor Tahir Mahmood states that

---

[97] The act imposed the Shariat in regard to intestate succession, special property of females, marriage, dissolution of marriage, maintenance, dower, guardianship, gifts, trusts and some wakfs.

[98] The act applied the Shariat to "Muslims" but did not provide a definition of "Muslims". See Mahmood, *Muslim Personal Law*, p. 27; Paras Diwan, *Muslim Law in Modern India* (Allahabad, 4th ed., 1987), p. 1 (on who is a "Muslim").

[99] See the Statement of Objects and Reasons appended to the act.

he Dissolution of Muslim Marriages Act contained some changes in the original proposals that had no support in any of the traditional schools of Islamic law.[100] Thus, even though the legislature purported to rely on the views of the ulema and "the Muslim community,"[101] possibly the act represents not simply, as sometimes stated, a consolidation and clarification of Muslim law,[102] but a "reform" of that law in accordance with modern ideas about divorce and the equality of men and women.

The recent Shah Bano Act,[103] which deals with the rights of divorced Muslim women to obtain maintenance, may represent a good faith effort on the part of the legislature to support the identity of a religious community by upholding its personal law. The purpose of Parliament in adopting the act was to reverse the Supreme Court's decision in the *Shah Bano* case, which some believed involved a departure from Islamic law. Professor Mahmood thinks that in the Shah Bano Act, Parliament made some mistakes about Islamic law.[104] To the extent that this is true, it cannot be said that the act fully supports the identity value, even though the mistakes may have been inadvertent.

As already mentioned, the Hindu Code of 1955–56 is a difficult case in which to contend that the state has affirmed a group identity that exists independently of the state. The Code introduced a large number of rules—for example regarding divorce and adoption—that find no warrant either in the *dharmaśāstras* or in the Anglo-Hindu case law. No doubt Parliament thought it had a responsibility in respect to the Hindus, but the responsibility was, as already suggested, to separate them from their past and to provide them with a new identity. Thus many of the rules in the Hindu Code can only be justified from some point of view other than the identity value.

Options

Introducing an optional feature into the personal law system has the effect of undermining the identity value without appearing to do so. At least this is true if the personal law in question, fairly interpreted, does not permit the option. In 1972, an adoption bill without any religious limitations was introduced into Parliament. Some Muslims demanded that Muslims be excluded from the operation of the bill, since Islamic law does not permit adoption. There was Parsi

---

[100] Mahmood, *Muslim Personal Law*, p. 45.

[101] See Statement of Objects and Reasons appended to the act.

[102] *Muhammad Baksh* v. *The Crown*, A.I.R. 1950 Lah. 133, 134.

[103] Muslim Women (Protection of Rights on Divorce) Act, 1986.

[104] Tahir Mahmood, "Islamic Family Law, Latest Developments in India," in Chibli Mallat and Jane Connors, eds., *Islamic Family Law* (London, 1990), pp. 300–04.

opposition as well.[105] Ultimately the combined opposition led to the defeat of the bill. Professor Mahmood, commenting on this incident, could not understand how reasonable persons, including Muslims, could be opposed to the bill or demand that any particular group be exempted. After all, he said, if adoption is a sin for Muslims, the bill did not require them to sin; it only permitted them to do so. How can it be justified, he asked, to seek the help of the state to prevent Muslims from sinning if they choose to do so?[106] But the Adoption Bill without the exemption of Muslims could have undermined the identity value. If some of those who might wish to adopt would be properly classified as Muslims, and if under Islamic law adoption by Muslims is not permitted, if the state permits these people to adopt, it undermines the group and its identity. If the state supports individual choice in the matter, it elevates individual choice above the group's decisions. In fact, it supports an alternative Muslim identity that conflicts with the identity embodied in the law of the group, an alternative identity that combines aspects of Islamic law with the practice of adoption.

There is an optional feature in the Shariat Act. Although, as already stated, in regard to most topics the act imposed the Shariat on all Muslims, including groups that had theretofore followed the Hindu law in certain matters, in regard to a few topics—adoptions, wills and legacies—individuals were to be governed by the Shariat only if they made an election in its favor. The existence of this option did not please many of the ulema, who wanted full enforcement of the Shariat on all Muslims. At the same time the option tended to undermine the identity of the groups that had not observed the Shariat on these topics. This was so because the act empowered individual members of these groups to opt out of the group's laws and accept the Shariat. Within these groups in fact there had been controversy about whether observance of the Shariat was consistent with their true identity. Ironically, the Shariat Act provided that if an individual elected to be governed by the Shariat on the optional topics, this decision bound his descendants as well. In other words, the very provision that exalted individual choice for one generation rejected it for the generations to come.

The Shah Bano Act also has an optional feature. It permits a Muslim couple, when marrying, to submit themselves to the maintenance provisions of the Criminal Procedure Code, rather than to the Islamic law as expressed in the

---

[105] See Mahmood, *Muslim Personal Law*, p. 114; J. Hinnells, "Parsi Attitudes to Religious Pluralism," in Howard G. Coward, ed., *Modern Indian Responses to Religious Pluralism* (Albany, New York, 1987), pp. 199, 212 (referring to Parsi opposition to an adoption bill in 1980).

[106] See Mahmood, *Muslim Personal Law*, p. 112; Tahir Mahmood, *An Indian Civil Code and Islamic Law* (Bombay, 1976), p. 101.

Shah Bano Act.[107] The couple is thus provided with an opportunity to adopt secular ideas regarding maintenance following divorce, while continuing, in the eyes of the state at least, to be Muslims.

The Special Marriage Act, 1872, was pioneer legislation in the matter of options to escape from the law of the group. If two persons married under that act, they were no longer governed by their personal law. In regard to succession, they became subject to the India Succession Act.[108] In order to marry under the Special Marriage Act, the couple had to renounce their religion. For some communities, providing for this complete break from the group might not be inconsistent with the maintenance of the group's identity: the individuals do not threaten group identity because they are simply out of the group. Under the present Special Marriage Act, adopted in 1954, however, renunciation of religion is no longer required. Furthermore, in the case of two Hindus marrying under the act, under a 1976 amendment they continue to be governed by the Hindu law of succession.[109] In other words, the state gives recognition to an alternative Hindu identity.

Professor Derrett suggested some years ago that all the personal laws might be made optional. That is, there would be a uniform civil code, which generally would be applicable, but individuals could opt out of it and into one or another of the personal laws.[110] In 1987 Rajiv Gandhi's government, some thought in response to criticism of the Shah Bano Act, announced it was considering introducing a bill for a "voluntary civil code," but it then decided not to go ahead with the project.[111] Of course these options would give supremacy to

---

[107] Muslim Women (Protection of Rights on Divorce) Act, 1986, §5. See Tahir Mahmood, "Islamic Family Law, Latest Developments in India," in Chibli Mallat and Jane Connors, eds., *Islamic Family Law* (London, 1990), p. 304.

[108] Indian Succession Act, 1925.

[109] Special Marriage (Amendment) Act, 1976, §21A. In the well-known case of *Maneka Gandhi v. Indira Gandhi*, A.I.R. 1984 Delhi 428, appeal dismissed, A.I.R. 1985 Delhi 114, it was held that although Sanjay and Maneka Gandhi had married under the Special Marriage Act, since they were both Hindus (notwithstanding that Sanjay's father had been, at least at one time, a Parsi), Sanjay's estate was governed by the Hindu Succession Act rather than the Indian Succession Act, with the result that Indira Gandhi, his mother, was entitled to a share.

[110] J. D. M. Derrett, "The Indian Civil Code or Code of Family Law: Practical Propositions," in Narmada Khodie, ed., *Readings in Uniform Civil Code* (Bombay, 1975), p. 29. See also Derrett's *Religion, Law and the State in India* (New York, 1968), pp. 550–51, suggesting that a "civil code" be applied in matters of succession unless a Muslim had made an election to have the Shariat apply.

[111] See *The Hindu* (Intern'l ed.), Feb. 7, 1987, p. 1, col. 1.

Personal Law v. Uniform Civil Code 239

individual choice and turn the system of personal laws into a system of voluntary associations.

Professor Mahmood once suggested that there might be a referendum of each community and the majority could choose whether to continue with the personal law or accept a uniform civil code.[112] This suggestion supports neither the group identity value, nor individual choice, but a regime of majority rule within each group. But majority rule may have nothing to do with the identity of a group from a religious and historical point of view. Under the law of the group, there may be no authority in the majority to determine the true way of life.

Questions in the Margins

The Personal Laws after the Adoption of a Uniform Civil Code

If the adoption of the Hindu Code in 1955-56 did not entirely eliminate the pre-existing Hindu personal law—for instance, it did not touch endowments, and although it affected the Hindu Undivided Family did not abolish it—likewise the adoption of a uniform civil code might not entirely eliminate the personal laws. Indeed the question of the ways in which the personal laws might survive presents subtle and interesting points.

Consider *Biju Uthup* v. *Fr. George Manjunkal*,[113] a recent lower court case from Kerala. In that case the plaintiff sought recognition of his right to be married in a parish church of the Kottayam Diocese. The Kottayam Diocese had been created by the Pope in the early twentieth century for members of the Knanaya community who were Catholics. Another section of the community, although Christians, did not recognize the Pope. The plaintiff's father concededly had been a member of the Knanaya Catholic community and of the parish in question, but he had married a woman who, although a Catholic, was not a member of the Knanaya community. The plaintiff was the off-spring of this union. The bishop of the Kottayam diocese ruled that because plaintiff's father had married someone not of the community, the father had ceased to be a member of the community and his children by this marriage were not members either. Since the plaintiff was not a member of the community, the bishop ruled, he had no right to be married in the parish church.

The Kerala court disagreed. It held that under the law of the Knanaya Catholic community, the fact that the plaintiff's father had married outside the

---

[112] See Tahir Mahmood, "Common Civil Code, Personal Laws and Religious Minorities," in Mohammed Imam, ed., *Minorities and the Law*, (Bombay, 1972), pp. 460, 476; V. Dhagamwar, *Towards the Uniform Civil Code* (Bombay, 1989), p. 47.

[113] Additional Magistrate's Court, Kottayam, Kerala (Nov. 24, 1990).

community did not prevent the plaintiff from being a member. Plaintiff had become a member, the court held, as a result of long attendance at the parish church and acceptance by the local church group. Since the plaintiff was a member of the Knanaya Catholic community, the court held, he was entitled to be married in the parish church.

What is first to be noticed about this case is that the court attached no importance to what the bishop had decided was the law of the community. It apparently felt entitled to decide for itself what the law of the community was in regard to membership and the right to be married in the parish church. Actually, the court found that the law of the community favored decision by the local church group on these questions. Plaintiff had wished to be a member of the community and the local group had accepted him into its fellowship.

It is unclear whether the court in *Biju Uthup* considered the Knanaya Catholic community an ascriptive group or a voluntary assocation. Perhaps it considered it an ascriptive group in the sense that although acceptance of plaintiff by the local group was a condition of membership, it was not a sufficient condition: if plaintiff had not been a descendant of someone who had been a member, he could not be a member.[114] If this is correct, it may be proper to see the case as involving an application of the "personal law." If it is simply a case of interpreting and enforcing the provisions of a contract, the law of a voluntary association or the terms upon which property was given, it might seem misleading to speak of the case as one involving the personal law.[115]

---

[114] See also *Joshua* v. *Geevarghese Mar Diocorus*, 1985(1) I.L.R. (Kerala Series) 1. In that case the court found that a bishop, in issuing an excommunication order against plaintiff, had exceeded his jurisdiction under church law. The court enjoined the bishop and other officials from implementing the excommunication order and from interferring with priests who were willing to give plaintiff communion and other benedictions. The court noted the seriousness of excommunication to the plaintiff because he was of this church "by nurture and by nature." *Ibid.*, 21.

[115] *Biju Uthup* is distinguishable from the well-known Supreme Court decision regarding excommunication. *Sardar Syedna Taher Saifuddin Saheb* v. *State of Bombay*, A.I.R. 1962 S.C. 853. That case did not involve a dispute regarding the proper interpretation of the law of a group and whether that law authorized excommunication. The Bombay legislature had passed an act flatly prohibiting excommunication from any community, regardless of the grounds. The Court held that this prohibition violated Article 26 of the Fundamental Rights of the Constitution. (One judge also found a violation of Article 25.) The Court recognized a right in a religious community to maintain its identity through excommunication of members who do not adhere to orthodox beliefs, even though this may have serious consequences for them. The particular community involved in the case was the Dahwoodi Bohras. It is mentioned in one of the judgments that the Dahwoodi Bohras have an initiation ceremony, *Ibid.*, 869, but it is not made clear whether because of this fact the community should be considered a voluntary association or whether there is an ascriptive element present.

Personal Law v. Uniform Civil Code 241

What would become of a case like *Biju Uthup* if a uniform civil code were adopted? It is to be noted in the first place that the subject involved in *Biju Uthup* is not one of those that would be expected to be addressed in a uniform civil code. It concerns, for instance, not the validity of a marriage in view of the ceremonies performed, the age of the parties or the relationship between them, but the right to be married in a particular church. Still, if the claimed right is founded on contract or on the law of a voluntary association, it might be expected that the terms of the contract or the law of the voluntary association would be enforced regardless of whether or not a uniform civil code had been adopted. Indeed there might be a constitutional right to have them enforced.[116] But what if the claimed right is founded on the law of an ascriptive group? Would it be enforced in view of the adoption of a uniform civil code? It might be argued that it should be enforced, because the adoption of a code that covers some topics and establishes rules applicable to all on these topics, provides no reason to cease to enforce the personal laws of ascriptive groups on other topics. The counter argument would be that the adoption of a uniform code covering some topics traditionally governed by the personal laws implicitly repudiated any involvement by the state in the enforcement of any part of the laws of ascriptive groups. Its adoption, in other words, implied a general rejection of the idea that the state should lend its support to maintain the identities of these groups through the enforcement of their personal laws.

The Relation Between the Personal Law and Other Bodies of Law

A question is sometimes presented regarding the relation between the personal laws and some other body of law. Legislative and judicial decisions addressed to this question need to be examined to determine whether they uphold or undermine the personal laws and the identity value that these laws serve. An example is the relation between the law of the Hindu Undivided Family, a law that, as already mentioned, survived the adoption of the Hindu Code in 1955-56, and the tax laws. In one case it was the gift tax law that was involved.[117] The karta of the family had thrown his individual property into the family hotch-pot. Under the law of the Hindu Undivided Family, the karta's individual property, which is entirely at his disposition, can be converted into family property simply by an act on the part of the karta that clearly evidences his intention to bring about this result. There need be no knowledge of his act on the part of the other

---

[116] Although in some other jurisdictions there would be a constitutional difficulty in courts' answering religious questions in the course of interpreting provisions in contracts and the laws of private associations. E.g., *Presbyterian Church in the United States* v. *Mary Elizabeth Blue Hull Memorial Presbyterian Church*, 393 U.S. 440 (1969).

[117] *Goli Eswariah* v. *Commissioner of Gift Tax*, 1970 I.T.R. (S.C.) 675.

members of the family, nor acceptance of the property by them. In the case in question, the court held that under these circumstances, there was no "transaction" under the tax law such as was required to create liability for a gift tax. Subsequently the legislature amended the statute to reverse this result.[118]

If after the karta had thrown his individual property into the family hotch-pot, he had continued to treat it as his own and the state had provided no remedy to the other coparceners, it could not be denied that the Hindu law of the Undivided Family had been repudiated. The state would no longer recognize that law's concept of how change in ownership can be effected from individual property to family property. Instead, it would recognize only transactions based on concepts drawn from some other body of law relating to gifts. On the other hand, if the other coparceners did have a remedy against the karta for continuing to deal with the property as his own, it is not clear that the Hindu law of the Undivided Family would be contradicted by imposing a gift tax. The Hindu law does not speak directly to the question of taxation. Perhaps a state policy in favor of imposing a tax under the circumstances, when gifts as ordinarily understood are taxed, can be enforced without undermining the law of the Hindu Undivided Family and the Hindu identity it serves.

In other cases the courts held that if the karta threw his individual property into the family hotch-pot, the income from the property was no longer his for income tax purposes, but family income,[119] and also that in computing the karta's wealth tax, there should be attributed to him only his proportional share of the property as a member of the family, not the entire property.[120] These results also were reversed by legislation.[121] It may be harder to reconcile imposition of taxes in these situations with continued recognition of the personal law. Imposition of the taxes seems to rest upon the idea that the property is still entirely the karta's property. If there is a repudiation of the personal law, and so of the identity value it serves, this should be admitted and the competing value claimed to justify the repudiation openly appraised.[122]

---

[118] See S. R. Karabanda and Prem Nath, *H.U.F. Tax Planning and Assessment* (Delhi, 4th ed., 1992), p. 52.

[119] *M. K. Stremann v. Commissioner of Income Tax*, 41 I.T.R. 297 (1960), affirmed (1965), 56 I.T.R. (S.C.) 67. Under a provision of the income tax law, if there was a "transfer" to minor children, income from the property would be deemed still the income of the karta, but the courts concluded that because of the special doctrine of the Hindu Undivided Family regarding the throwing of individual property into the family hotch pot, there was no "transfer."

[120] See S. R. Karabanda and Prem Nath, *H.U.F. Tax Planning*, p. 52.

[121] See *Ibid.*, p. 52.

[122] *Commissioner of Wealth Tax v. Abdul H.M.M. Ali* (1988) S.C.C. 562, was another wealth tax case. A Muslim taxpayer had transferred funds to his partner. He contended

Conclusion

The foregoing discussion has sought to identify the various considerations relevant to a choice between the present system of personal laws and a uniform civil code. Among those that have been mentioned, particular attention has been given to what I have called the identity value, the value, that is, of an ethnic or religious group within a territorial state being able to maintain its distinctive identity and through this its members' sense of existing and having meaning. But giving weight to this value, it can be argued, is improper, because Article 44 of the Directive Principles embodies an adverse judgment against it. If there is legislative discretion under Article 44, it must be confined to prudential considerations, such as how much resistance there would be to a uniform code and what injurious consequences might flow from this resistance. However, what seems a permissible reading of Article 44 leaves open for consideration the weight and persuasiveness of the identity value, as it is presented in the Indian context. The Framers of the Indian Constitution understood the complexity of the Indian social and religious situation and realized that an unforeseeable future might provide new insights into the problem of the personal laws, including the advantages and disadvantages of giving weight to the identity value.

But of course if the identity value is not well served by the existing system, unless there is some practical proposal how the system might be changed to serve that value better, it cannot be invoked in justification of present arrangements. Features of the system that do indeed cast doubt on whether the identity value is well served have been pointed out. It has been noted, for

---

that under a doctrine of Islamic law there was only a moral obligation to repay and that the existence of this obligation should not be considered part of his wealth. The tax authorities determined otherwise. This finding was affirmed by the court on the ground that the taxpayer had offered no proof of the alleged Islamic legal doctrine and, furthermore, that at some point in the proceedings the taxpayer himself had characterized the transaction as a debt. Suppose under the general law of debt, in the circumstances given, which circumstances would include the beliefs of the parties concerning the enforceability of the obligation, there was a legally enforceable obligation to repay, but under Islamic law, in these very circumstances, there was not. Obviously, if the state is to uphold the Islamic law, it must not enforce repayment. It also would seem that a wealth tax should not be imposed, for to impose a wealth tax would be to ignore the Islamic law notion that the obligation is not legally enforceable.

For another situation involving the relation between the personal law and another body of law, see *State of Bihar* v. *Zuberi*, A.I.R. 1986 Pat. 166, which involved the Bihar Land Ceiling Law. The court interpreted the law to require that religious differences be ignored in determining entitlement to units of land, with the consequence that an aspect of the Hindu Mitakshara law that would have given a Hindu family an advantage over a Muslim family was ignored.

example, that in the application of the personal laws, certain threshold questions necessarily are presented and are answered, not from the point of view of the personal laws, but from the point of view of the state's own ideology. The state approves certain processes of group identity formation and not others. It has also been noted that the tribunals of the state, applying the personal laws from the outside so to speak, inevitably have difficulty entering into the spirit and presuppositions of the personal laws, so that their decisions are bound to reflect to some degree their own values. Instances have been pointed out where the identity value has certainly been undermined, although in a covert manner. For a final judgment on this question of the undermining of the identity value, a more thorough study of the personal law system than has been attempted here would be necessary. But enough has been done, perhaps, to suggest a possible conclusion that although compromises and limitations are to be found, the state administration of the system of personal laws does give substantial support to the identity value, so that the system should not be abandoned simply on the ground that it fails to achieve what it sets out to do.

More important, the foregoing discussion would seem to make clear that to put the choice as one between the personal law system and a uniform civil code is to pose the issue too sharply. In this connection the Supreme Court indeed may have done a disservice in its *Shah Bano* judgment in suggesting that a case concerning a Muslim woman's right to maintenance from her former husband involved the question of a uniform civil code. Even those who are clear that there should be such a code readily agree that certain groups, tribal groups for instance, should be exempt. This is a concession to the identity value. Furthermore, when pressed, they are likely also to concede that a reasonable case can be made out for excluding certain topics from a uniform civil code. Herein lay the value of considering the *Biju Uthup* case. That case involved a subject—the right to be married in a church—not usually thought of in connection with a uniform civil code. The case presents the question whether all aspects of the personal laws of ascriptive groups should be abolished if a uniform code is adopted. But even within the familiar list of personal law topics, it may be sensible to make distinctions. For instance, from the point of view of the identity value, the rules relating to marriage may be more important than the rules relating to succession. Likewise, from the point of view of state interests that compete with the identity value, a different importance may attach to different subjects on the familiar list. Such a particularizing approach, of course, has something in common with what has been going on since 1772. But the weight to be ascribed to the identity value, as well as that to be ascribed to other state interests, may be significantly different than in the past. With the benefit of intervening experience of a complex and ever-changing Indian society, an open-minded approach seems called for, one unconstrained either by the hesitancy of a foreign ruler to interfere in the laws and customs of subject peoples, or by a purely theoretical notion that a nation-state cannot exist without a uniform substantive law on all subjects. The nation-state that India needs is one that is adapted to its special circumstances.

12

Religion, Politics and Law in Contemporary India: Judicial Doctrine in Critical Perspective

V. S. Rekhi

India is passing through a particularly depressing period in which previously accepted ideas of secularism and avoidance of use of religion in legislative elections are undergoing revision.[1] The last general elections to the Parliament and some of the State legislative assemblies were overt with religious issues. "Never before," says Kuldip Nayar, "has the Indian electorate had to face such intense communal and casteist slogans."[2] The electoral contest was redolent of communal riots afflicting pre-partition days. Intense communal hatred and religious bigotry marked the election campaign. Tempers ran high, for the elections had come after a particularly gory phase of communal strife.

In the decade of the eighties some 4500 communal riots have occurred causing 7000 deaths.[3] The Delhi riots following the assassination of Indira Gandhi cost 3870 lives.[4] In the last two years the situation further deteriorated contributing to about 500 deaths, not including the 6289 deaths caused in Punjab, and destruction of property worth over 20 million dollars.[5] Prior to elections in May this year some 169 people were killed within a fortnight in the State of Uttar Pradesh.[6]

The colossal loss of life, the senseless destruction of property and the total abandonment of remorse raise poignantly the question why after four

---

[1] Zafar Agha, "Ram and Mandal: An Existential Dilemma," *India Today*, 15 May 1991, pp. 22–23.

[2] *Ibid.*, p. 22. Kuldip Nayar is among the foremost journalists of modern India and has been India's ambassador to the United Kingdom.

[3] *India Today*, 15 January 1990.

[4] *India Today*, 15 February 1990. The estimate is based on the report of the Citizens Justice Committee though the Federal Government has only conceded 2733 casualties.

[5] *India Today*, 31 December 1990.

[6] *India Today*, 15 May 1991.

decades of commitment to a secular polity and abnegation of use of religion in electioneering has India come to be so seriously afflicted with communal strife.[7] A crucial query like this is likely to elicit different responses.

A quick survey of literature reveals at least five different theories which seek to explain large-scale communal violence in India. The traditionalists explain communal violence as a hangover of the bitter history of Hindu-Muslim strife fomented by the British as part of their policy of "divide et impera."[8] Sociologists prefer to explain communalism in terms of either historical circumstances of particular riots[9] or class disparities and conflict.[10] Modern historians using a dependency perspective have argued that communal riots represent collective action resulting from the imperatives of the social situation of submerged groups that inclines them to action aimed at re-establishing their self-image.[11] Theorists building upon the relative autonomy of the religious sphere from the political sphere prefer instead to argue that religion is being "abused" for secular purposes[12] or that the power elites coopt religion to subserve their own interests.[13] Finally, theorists of ethnicity argue that the denial of the identity of ethnic communities based on religion, language or caste, particularly as a concomitant to the claim that Hindu ethos represents the Indian

---

[7] This is not to say that communal riots in India has been a new phenomenon. Ghurye traces them to early settlements of Muslims in India. *See*, G.S. Ghurye, *Social Tensions in India* (1965), pp. 304–51.

[8] For analysis of religion based strife during the British era, *see* R.P. Dutt, *India Today* (London, 1940); K.B. Krishna, *The Problem of Minorities* (1939); and W.C. Smith, *Modern Islam in India* (London, 1946).

[9] Ghuyre, *Ibid.* Engineer has carried forward this tradition in presenting detailed analysis of post-independence riots. See A.A. Engineer, *Communal Violence in Post-Independent India* (1984).

[10] A.R. Desai, *Social Background of Indian Nationalism* (Bombay, 1948).

[11] Pandey, "In Defence of the Fragment: Writing about Hindu-Muslim Riots in India Today," 26 *Economic & Political Weekly* 559 (1991); Chakraborty, "Communal Riots and Labour: Bengal Jute Millhands in the 1890," H. Alavi & J. Harris, editors, *South Asia* (1989), p.186; Ghosh, "Communalism and Colonial Labour: Experience of Calcutta Jute Mill Workers 1880–1930," 25 *Economic & Political Weekly PE 61* (1991); Bandhopadyay, "Community Formation and Communal Conflict: Namasudrs Muslim Riot in Jessore-Khulna," 25 *Economic & Political Weekly* 2563 (1990).

[12] D'Souza, "Roots of Present Communal Crisis," *Economic & Political Weekly* 1333 (1991).

[13] Engineer, "Muslims in a Multi-Religious Society," 25 *Economic & Political Weekly* 2420 (1990).

nation, tends to break out in violent outbursts.[14] Among the variables paraded, however, law is systematically overlooked. The reason for the omission is not far to seek.

The inbuilt premise of much sociological thinking about law in both its consensus and conflict models is that legal doctrine is a dependent variable and is therefore of little consequence.[15] On the other hand those who subscribe to a formalist model of law have another reason. They feel that the law in a secular state per se seeks to uphold secularism and can have little to do with the use of religion in distorting the democratic process. This paper questions the assumptions implicit in both the formalist and sociological paradigms. It seeks to challenge the belief that law does not significantly affect social practice. It argues that policy choices made by the courts in India in dealing with election matters have significantly affected the use of religion in elections. It is the contention of this paper that the highest Court in India has been singularly unresponsive to the rising threat of religious interference with the democratic process. Judicial conceptualization of religion and its role in communitarian life in India has to do a great deal with the increasing use of religion in elections since judicial doctrine is at least a significant variable in determining what would count as impermissible use invalidating elections. The conceptions and distinctions adumbrated by the Court have conditioned thought and social action in significant ways.

The legal doctrine relating to the use of religion in elections has conceptualized religion as something very individual and related to supramundane and other-worldly matters and hence necessarily distinct from sheer superstition on the one hand and from ethical values of right conduct on the other. Three distinctions have been considered by the courts to have crucial importance: sacred–profane, religion–ethics, and religious–communitarian. The binary distinctions delineate the zone of the permissible and the prohibited. The appeal

---

[14] Puri, "Politics of Ethnic Communal Identities," 25 *Economic & Political Weekly* 703 (1990); Puri, "Communalism and Regionalism," 22 *Economic & Political Weekly* 1132 (1987); Alavi, "Politics of Ethnicity in India and Pakistan," *South Asia, Loc. cit.*, p. 222; Washbrook, "Ethnicity in Contemporary Indian Politics," *South Asia, Loc. cit.* p. 174. Both Alavi and Washbrook tend to mix ethnicity with class conflict as explanatory variables. Alavi refers to interests of the "salariat" and Washbrook believes in the efficacy of particularizing interests in mobilizing support to break class interests.

[15] In a perceptive review, Parson has argued that sociologists tend to either (downgrade) the importance of legal systems or, (present) a "slanted" interpretation of their nature and significance, because of "an absolutist stress on the overwhelming centrality of one functional aspect of the societal system." Parsons, "Law as an Intellectual Stepchild," H.M. Johnson, editor *Social Systems and Legal Processes* (1978), pp.11, 31.

to the sacred or religious is outlawed, but the appeal to profane, ethical or communitarian has been considered permissible. The distinctions follow little logic, nor are they congruent with each other. This turns the legal doctrine into an enigma. We contend that the dichotomies are premised on the distinction between the private and public domain of human life. The sacred or the religious is believed to belong to the private domain and hence irrelevant to elections. The Court has missed the contradiction inherent in the private/public[16] dichotomy and the resulting doctrine often leads to contrarieties and inconsistencies.

In the first part of the paper we begin by outlining the development of the doctrine at the level of the apex Court. In the second part alternative explanations for the policy choice of the Court are considered. The explanations range over a large area as different theoretical traditions are brought to bear upon the doctrine. In the third part the paper focusses upon the community-building potential of religion which has been persistently ignored by the Court and which requires a different kind of judicial articulation.

Development of Doctrine

The Representation of Peoples Act, 1952, enacts the polity-religion differentiation. It declares appeals to voters in the name of religion to be "corrupt practice," use of which vitiates electoral mandate.[17] The Court has therefore

---

[16] On the recent critique of Public/Private distribution, *see* generally, Klare, "The Public/Private Distribution in Labor Law," 130 *Univ. Penn. L. Rev.* 1358; M. Kelman, *A Guide to Critical Legal Studies* (Cambridge, 1987); Hutchinson and Monahan, "Law, Politics, and the Critical Legal Scholars: The Unfolding Drama of American Legal Thought," 36 *Stanford L. Rev.* 199 (1984); Tushnet, "Critical Legal Studies: A Political History," 100 *Yale L. J.* 1514 (1991).

[17] S. 127(3) of the Representation of Peoples Act, 1952, as enacted, defined "corrupt practice" *inter alia* as under:

"The systematic appeal by a candidate or his agent or by any other person, to vote or refrain from voting on grounds of...religion or the use of, or appeal to, religious symbols...for the furtherance of the prospects of that candidates election."

In 1961, it was amended to read as follows:

"The appeal by a candidate or his agent or by any other person with the consent of a candidate or his election agent to vote or refrain from voting for any person on the ground of his religion...or the use or appeal to religious symbols...for the furtherance of the prospects of election of that candidate or for prejudicially affecting the election of any candidate."

been required to determine whether a particular practice pursued by a candidate in his electoral strategy amounts to a "corrupt practice" because it involves appeal to religion. An analysis of the cases involving challenges to elections for use of religion as a "corrupt practice" shows that the Court has distilled into law albeit unconsciously, the traditions of colonial administrators turned anthropologists to whom all religion was but superstition having doubtful ontic existence. The distinction made by such colonials between religious (superstitious) and profane (rational) matters has been unquestioningly adopted by the Court.

The all or nothing approach implicit in the water-tight distinction between the religious and the profane has a troublesome fallout effect as well because in early anthropology the distinction was brought out along with another distinction between the ethical and the religious, the former being identified with the great Hindu tradition in India and the later being representative of the religion of the laity.[18] The Court has conceptually delimited the two spheres of the ethical and the religious in such a manner that appeal in the name of "great tradition" has been legitimated for being ethical in content but the religious preference of the powerless, the have-nots, the poor and the immiserated have been systematically excluded perhaps for reasons of having been closely associated with the here-and now worldly interests of such groups and therefore rejected as superstitions. The this worldly-other worldly distinction involved in the surreptitious preferences for forms of religion standing higher in the much debated evolutionary scale of religion itself attests to the elitist preferences of the apex Court.

Finally, the positivist distinction between the religious and the profane has also been translated by the Court into a further distinction between the personal and the communitarian, the former relating to the realm of religion and the later to the realm of the profane. Thus appeal to religion in the form of personal preference for any form of the supramundane came to be delegitimated but appeal to solidarity building characteristics of such preference became permissible. The distinction reinforced the communal divide in India as it allowed free use of religion based ethnic identities in elections. Added to the other distinction made between the ethical and the religious it meant that the Court manifested a preference for a highly differentiated form of religiosity

---

Two crucial differences were mady be the amendment: (i) even a single appeal to religion became culpable; and (ii) not only positive appeals but also negative designed to harm other candidates were also made culpable.

[18]On the "Great Tradition" in India, see M.B. Singer, *When A Great Tradition Modernizes: An Anthropological Approach to Indian Civilization* (London, 1972).

sublimating the pursuit of worldly goods, in other words the religion of the *literati* and not the *laity*.

Preferring the Literati over the Laity

In *Shubh Nath* v. *Ram Narain*,[19] the electoral scene was set in the Adivasi dominated area of Bihar. The appellant was a member of the Hos tribe. He had been allotted the election symbol of a rooster. His party distributed leaflets in verse where an appeal was made by the rooster for votes. The rooster is not a religious symbol among the Adivasis but is used as a sacrificial bird particularly for curing diseases. Therefore, the question was whether the use of appeal from a sacrificial bird amounted to appeal to religion. Among the things which had been allegedly said on behalf of the rooster was the statement in verse- "give me *chara* (food) in the shape of vote I am victorious. Do not forget me, otherwise I tell ye the sons of man will suffer eternal miseries." The Court by a majority opinion held that the appeal was symbolic. It meant that voting for the rooster would please the deities and failure to vote would displease them. Invoking the deities amounted to appeal in the name of religion.

Justice Subbarao, in his dissent drew a distinction between canvassing on the ground of religion and using myths to allegorize the cause of the candidate. He said that the candidate could very well and lawfully say that he would act like Christ in the cause of voters and would sacrifice himself for the cause of voters like a goat before the *Kali*. The versified appeal was of like nature and could not be considered as an appeal in the name of religion. Thus Subbarao did not dissent from the major premise of the Court distinguishing between the sacred and profane spheres of life but he significantly modulated it through the distinction between myth and religion. And, it was his opinion that has been followed by later courts.

The opinion of the majority was that a sacrificial object denotes tribal solidarity. The rooster was therefore, a religious symbol. Left to itself it may have meant that the appeal to any symbol which reinforces the particularistic loyalties of a collectivity in the name of religion is outlawed. But Subbarao, in his dissent, drew a distinction between religious symbol and myth, even though the difference between appeal to mythology and appeal to religious symbols wears thin if it is remembered that the myth is also used to reinforce solidarity. Levi Strauss has brought out the solidarity potential of mythical stories.[20]

---

[19] AIR 1960 S.C. 148.

[20] *See*, E. R.Leach, Claude *Levi-Strauss* (New York, 1970). For an alternative view, *see*, B.R. Malinowski, *Myth In Primitive Psychology* (New York, 1926); R.W. Firth, *History and Traditions of Tikopia* (1961).

Religious objects and mythical stories both perform the function of reinforcing solidarity of the candidate with the voter. The distinction between myth and sacrificial object is one without difference particularly in the context of elections.

The essence of government by consent through election lies in the assumption that the election process secures at least a highly generalized albeit nebulous assent of the voter to the broad policy preferences represented by the candidate and his political party. In spite of the tremendous criticism which has been systematically raised against the ballot box as an indicator of public preferences this assumption still holds.[21] One basic feature of such assumption is that the political system is not based on any ethnic or primordial loyalties but is assumed to be legitimated by consent elicited by the programme of the political party through periodic elections on the basis of universal adult franchise. Subbarao could be harking back to this principle when he stated that the appeal to ethnic solidarity was in principle incongruous with the democratic ethos and its use amounted to a corrupt practice. The rooster symbolized ethnic solidarity and hence arose the need to interpret the appeal as a myth. But that created another doubt. Was Subbarao denigrating ethnic religion with the reference to myths drawn from mainstream Hindu religion? There is good reason to believe that it was so as he was willing to permit mythical references but not religious appeals though both performed sociologically the same function of building identities. The majority opinion was comparatively on more secure grounds as it did not seek to defend the appeal as a myth, but it was the opinion of Subbarao that was taken as the rule of the Court in subsequent cases. And, that opinion had another pernicious possibility also.

The ethnic solidarity/democratic polity dichotomy can be read as a judicial restatement of the state-society and profane-secular axis of post-Enlightenment debate. It shares the same image of man as the ultimate datum. Subbarao was therefore, in *Shubh Nath* reenacting eighteenth century west European debates in the Indian context without realizing that in India the divorce between society and state and its corollary divorce between religion and state do not necessarily contribute to the freedom of the individual. It may instead contribute to the continued exploitation of the havenots because often the only way open to such groups is to organize themselves around their traditional loyalties for they are yet to learn the art of organizing themselves in terms of their perceived worldly interests. And, the traditional interests are necessarily perceived in terms of the religious idiom which emphasizes the collectivity over the individual. In this discourse of the collectivity symbolism dominates, for it stands for group solidarity and common interest of the under-privileged. To

---

[21] For a penetrating critique of the Indian political system see, R. Kothari, *Democratic Polity and Social Change in India: Crisis and Opportunities* (Bombay, 1976).

refuse the Adivasi the right to appeal to his collectivity but allow others to appeal in the name of religious myth is consciously to choose to mystify the experience of the under-privileged and deny him his identity in the name of secularism. But, that is what the Court did in the case below.

The question of religious symbolism gets treated in dramatically different ways when it is raised by a member of the twice-born caste. In *Raman Bhai* v. *Dabhi*[22], the question was whether the symbol of a star allotted to the candidate's party was misused as a religious symbol when an appeal was made on behalf of the candidate through some pamphlets drawing upon the imagery of the polar star—Dhruva that is a symbol of eternity and permanence in the Hindu great tradition. The pamphlet in question set out five meanings of Dhruva which were perhaps meant to indicate the qualities of the candidate if not of the party which sponsored him. These qualities were mentioned as follows—

> Dhruva means eternal.
> Dhruva means firm.
> Dhruva means guide.
> Dhruva means determined.
> Dhruva means one devoted to religion.

Here was an upper-caste candidate sponsored by the right-reactionary Swatantra party which had been floated by the Ex-Maharajahs and non-socialist leaders of the undivided Congress Party who had left that party in the aftermath of the rise of Indira Gandhi. The pamphlet clearly implied that the candidate, if not the party, was devoted to religion. The religiosity of the candidate/party was certainly put forward as a positive feature which may appeal to the religious among the voters. Nevertheless Justice Mudholkar chose to ignore the religious potential of the appeal by trying to convert Dhruva into a myth so as to conform to the distinction made by Subbarao in Shubh Nath.

Mudholkar denied Dhruva any divinity. He made a distinction between reverence and worship on the one hand and between worship and religion on the other hand. Dhruva was revered but not worshipped as godhead. Mudholkar held that Dhruva was promised his exalted position because he had been steadfast in his devotion and had completely surrendered to God. But Dhruva was never considered a godhead. Mudholkar stressed the fact that Dhruva "was not raised to the status of divinity i.e. to say, he did not join the company of the 33 crore deities which are said to comprise the Hindu pantheon." At least the rooster had a better fate in *Subh Nath* than Dhruva in *Raman Bhai*. But that was not all.

---

[22]AIR 1965 S.C. 669.

Another distinction was drawn by the Court between qualities associated with Dhruva and qualities peculiar to Hindu religion. Mudholkar went on to say that the qualities associated with Dhruva were no different from the qualities which were given to good "persons professing other religions or systems of belief as well." Dhruva was thus shifted from the sphere of religion to ethics by virtue of his universal qualities. But in its zeal to distinguish ethics from religion the Court went further to deny even some of the basic traditions of Hindu religion—the *bhakti* tradition.

In an obvious aside about the contemporary Indian scene, Mudholkar bewailed about the sycophantic qualities of people little realizing that one great tradition of religion in India is the *bhakti* tradition in which much sycophancy is glamorized as devotion. Denying the religious nature of such devotion Mudholkar observed—

> Worship of mortals is so common, at least in our country, that no one can seriously attach religious significance to it. Such worship has no connection whatsoever with religion and is often motivated by fear of authority or by hope of reward.[23]

Mudholkar distinguishes between matters secular and matters religious. Anything that related to the mundane world or was motivated by fear or avarice was not religious. In order to be so it had to relate to matters spiritual or other worldly. The lack of historicity of such a concept of religion need not be emphasized. One has only to recall his Weber.[24]

It is now sociological common place that religion is motivated by worldly concerns even though it may express them in an other-worldly manner. The Court completely ignored the relation between religion and society stressing the autonomy of the religious spheres from the social spheres, inter alia, denuding religion of all potential of either reinforcing social solidarity or revolutionizing existing social relationships. This is ahistorical.

It is well known that in India the needs of laity to have a theodicy of suffering led to the emergence of the *Bhakti* version of religion. The eminence of the Guru emerged as the medium of solace and salvation. In his sardonic comment on worship of mortals Mudholkar implicitly denied the religiosity of the *Guru* tradition. The distinction, however, meant that while elite practices of

---

[23]*Ibid.*

[24]"The most elementary forms of behavior motiviate by religious or magical factors are oriented to this world....Furthermore religious or magically motivated behavior is relatively rational behavior....It follows rules of experience." M. Weber, *Economy and Society*, G. Roth and C. Wittisch, editors (New York, 1968), pp. 399–400.

ethical virtue received the imprimatur of the Supreme Court, the religious preferences of the common man were denied. In this sense the Court in *Raman Bhai* itself reinforced the great tradition of brahmannical religion and at the same time left the religion of the laity within the scope of prohibition on the use of religion in elections. The avenues for use of beliefs of the common man to influence political judgment were closed. The Court not only indirectly subverted the purpose of the legislative prohibition but also used it to bear heavily on the *laity* as opposed to the *literati*.

The distinction between the religion of the *laity* and *literati* was made earlier by the Supreme Court in *Jagdev Sidhanti* v. *Pratap Singh*[25], where the site of the conflict was Haryana. The elected candidate had used a flag on which the word *Om* was printed. It was obviously a symbol used by the members of the Arya Samaj. It had been argued that the Arya Samaj had organized the political movement which had the real object of promoting feelings of enmity and hatred between the Sikh and Hindu communities. The Election Tribunal held that *Om* was not a religious symbol, but the High Court had come to the contrary conclusion. On appeal to the Supreme Court, Justice Shah distinguished between symbols of spiritual significance and symbols of religious significance.

Shah admitted that *Om* had high spiritual efficacy but he denied that it had any religious significance. He argued that a symbol stood for or represented "something material or abstract." In order to be a religious symbol there must be a visible representation of a thing or concept which is religious. *Om* was not a religious symbol because it did not represent a thing or concept which was religious. As if afraid of his own temerity the judge took recourse to the doctrine of burden of proof claiming that it was for the petitioner to prove that the candidate or his agents had used the symbol of *Om* which burden they had failed to discharge. But if that was so Shah should have avoided expressing an opinion about the religious nature of the *Om* symbol. The gratuitous dicta came in handy to the parties and the Court in attempting a distinction between the undistinguishable and creating a hiatus between religion and culture in *Kultar*.

In *Kultar Singh* v. *Mukhtiar Singh*[26] the Court considered the communitarian aspect of religious beliefs, and in keeping with its wont limited the statutory ban to only matters of conscience. It refused to extend the ban to cultural bonds built by congruence on matters of conscience.

---

[25] AIR 1965 S.C. 183.
[26] AIR 1965 S.C. 141.

Dissociating the Personal from the Cultural

In *Kultar* the bone of contention was a pamphlet from the Sikh community residing in other countries. In it an appeal was made to the Sikhs resident in India in the following words—

> This is not the time to criticize the weaknesses of the leaders of the Panth; the need is that in the coming General Elections you should defeat the opponents of the Panth the same way as you did in the last Gurdwara Elections. Every Sikh vote should go to the representatives of the Akali Dal, and we hope that this prayer of ours from far off will be accepted by you and you will once again preserve the honour of the Panth. Victory of the panth will maintain the honour of the Panth.[27]

Coming two months after *Sidhanti* the principal question in this case was whether Panth referred to Sikh religion or to some secular matter. Gajendragadkar, conceded that etymologically the word "Panth" could indicate Sikh religion but he held that in the context of the pamphlet it did not mean Sikh religion. It only denoted Sikh politics.

Chief Justice Gajendragadkar relied upon the reference to the election of the Gurdwara Prabandhak Committee in the pamphlet. He said that the reference to those elections really meant that the word "Panth" stood for the Akali Dal Party among other Sikh parties. The distinction drawn by Gajendragadkar itself begged the question.

The gravamen of the complaint in *Kultar* was that the Akali Dal Party candidate was representing himself as the candidate of Sikh religion. The use of Panth to refer to the elections to a religious management body definitely reinforced the relationship of Panth with Sikh religion. It did not distinguish Sikh religion from Sikh politics. Yet, the Chief Justice was willing to relate Panth to politics and separate the domain of politics from the domain of religion. This separation reinforced the divide which became a part of the ideological baggage of independent India. The Court simply ignored realities. Time has shown that the identity of the Sikh religion and the Akali Dal involved an overlapping of religion and politics which is now being asserted in the terms of claims for a Sikh homeland.

The inadequacy of *Kultar* to meet the complex issues raised by group identities built on religious foundations came forth clearly in *Ambika*.[28] The

---

[27] *Ibid.*, p. 144.

[28] *Ambika Sharan Singh* v. *Mahant Mahadevanand Giri*, 3 SCC 192 (1969).

election of *Ambika Singh* was challenged on grounds of his having made an appeal on the basis of his Rajput caste. The Court in an obiter observed—

> A command by a religious head to his followers that it was their primary duty to support a particular candidate was held sufficient to vitiate the election and it was not considered necessary to have the names of the persons to whom the command was addressed.[29]

This obiter was the first indicator of changing attitude.

A decade later in *Abdul Husain* v. *Shamsul Huda*[30] Krishna Iyer employed a different reading of the opinion in *Kultar* seeking perhaps to prove that *Kultar* was more restrictive than it was considered. According to Krishna Iyer *Kultar* showed that religious appeal could conceivably be made even in a situation where the opposing candidates belonged to the same religion. But from this he drew the strange inference that *Kultar* outlawed such appeals. In *Abdul Husain* a candidate who professed Islam sought to placate the Hindu voters by stating that his mother was a Hindu. The question was whether this amounted to an appeal in the name of religion. Krishna Iyer in his trenchant style observed—

> It is a matter for profound regret that political communalism far from being rooted out is foliating and flourishing largely because parties and politicians have not the will, professions apart, to give up the chase for power through politicising communal awareness and religio-cultural identity. The Ram-Rahim ideal and the secular ideology are often the Indian politician's election haberdashery, not his soul-stuff. Micro-and mini-communal fires are stoked by some candidates and leaders whose overpowering love for seats in the Legislature is stronger than sincere loyalty to secular electoral processes. Law can efficiently regulate and control if wider social legitimation is forthcoming and this key factor is absent, so much so wrong methodology becomes rampant.[31]

This judicial observation can be read both as an expression of sheer disgust with the things as they are in politics and/or a reluctant recognition of the ground realities of political life where discourse of the under-privileged at least is still imbued with religion. In fact a little earlier Krishna Iyer had observed—

---

[29]*Ibid.*, p. 497.
[30]AIR 1975 S.C. 1612.
[31]*Ibid.*, p. 1622.

Within the fold, variables operate and blurred areas exist. A fanatic may seek votes castigating his co-religionist rival with reforming zeal as a de facto apostate. But to delve meticulously into these dark mines of divergent opinions and clashing practices and hold that 'religious appeal' has been invoked is to overdo legality and hamper social advance.[32]

The Krishna Iyer reaction is typical of the elite group in India, because he axiomatically assumes that "to declare oneself an offspring of a religious renegade is not to appeal to religion. It is unlikely because it does not socially pay." That this is not the feeling of the masses is more than obvious from the very well known fact that Brahmans supported Indira Gandhi even though she had married a Parsi. An election agent for the Congress (I) Party, who was also later the Joint Secretary of the party, told this writer that in a pre-election meeting of the Brahmans somebody objected that Mrs. Gandhi had married a Parsi and therefore, was a renegade who ought not to be favored. The caste leaders said, so what, "she had still Brahman blood in her veins." Krishna Iyer seems to forget this ground reality. The appeal of *Abdul Husain* lay not in the fact that his mother was a Hindu, but in the fact that in claiming descent from a *Hindu* mother he was appealing to the solidarity which Hindu religion symbolized. Even tenuous links pay. In one of the keenly contested elections where the Congress(I) had put up a Muslim candidate one of his opponents harangued that the candidate ate beef and had been a *razakar* agitator in the pre-partition days. An election agent for this candidate could subdue the feeling by simply pointing out that even if the candidate was a Muslim he would "only touch the feet of Indra Gandhi—a brahman." It was unrealistic for Krishna Iyer to assume without any kind of evidence that the appeal to Hindu ancestry would not pay.

The distinction between religion and communitarian values made in *Kultar* troubled Justice Beg in *Z.B. Bukhari* v. *Brij Mohan Mehra*[33] Bukhari's election was challenged on the ground that he had alleged that another Muslim candidate was not a true Muslim because he was a member of the Congress(I), a political party that supported legislative change in *shariat* (Muslim Personal Law). He had canvassed that he was opposed to any interference with the *shariat* and should, therefore, be considered a better Muslim who deserved to be preferred by the Muslims. It had been argued on behalf of Bukhari that the matter of personal law related to this world and was not a religious matter. The argument itself had a wry humor for a candidate who canvassed for votes on a "Islam in danger" platform.

---

[32]*Ibid.*, p. 1617.

[33]AIR 1975 S.C. 1788.

Justice Beg denied the validity of the argument. He said that if all human activity in this world could be labelled secular on the ground that it appertained to this world as against the other world, all religious thoughts and activity could be described as secular. Therefore, religious matters need to be conceptualized differently. As a matter of propriety and comity if Beg wanted to overrule what his brethren had persistently held earlier he should have referred the matter to a larger bench. But these perhaps were small matters for tormented souls, particularly because the argument implied that preservation of personal laws was not a religious issue. It may be recalled that even in the Constituent Assembly the question whether personal law formed part of religion had proved very vexing causing serious differences between the Sub-Committee on Fundamental Rights and the Committee on Minorities. The differences could not be resolved but were only subdued for the time being by a compromise hammered out in the Advisory Committee which retained the guarantee to *practice* religion so as to include personal law within the protection of Art. 25 of the Constitution but subjected the whole guarantee to the possibility of interference in the form of future legislation bringing about social reform.[34] Beg may have been unwilling to endorse an argument which cut so deep into matters close to the heart of minorities. Therefore, without referring to the sacred-mundane distinction that the Court had adopted earlier, Beg came up with his own concept of secularism that was considerably broader. He said that anything which was done in this world without seeking the intervention or favor or without claiming a divine power or being was secular. In fact, he went on to say that secularism was a system of utilitarian ethics. Beg quoted Maitland to the effect that a secular state had to ensure "that the existence or exercise of a political or civil right or the right or capacity to occupy any office or position under it or to perform in any duty" did not depend upon the profession or practice of any particular religion.[35] He said that the state had to be neutral in extending its benefits to citizens of all mold and therefore, a candidate at an election to a legislature could not "be allowed to tell electors that their rivals are unfit...on grounds of their religious profession or practices." Beg believed that to allow such canvassing would amount to an assault on "the basic structure of our democratic state."

This opinion came just at the eve of the declaration of emergency in 1975 when the proposal to amend the Constitution and incorporate the expression "secular" in the preamble to the Constitution was being widely canvassed. The opinion does not show any realization of the realities of political life in which

---

[34] A. Rekhi, *Law, Society and Oppression of Women*, Unpublished SJD Dissertation, Harvard Law School (1992).

[35] *Ibid.*, p. 297.

religious discourse plays a great part. Krishna Iyer had taken judicial notice of that but Beg ignored it perhaps wishing it to disappear. The escapism was expressed through the ideological form of separation of church and state expressed in the preference for Utilitarianism. Beg's indulgence in a jurisprudence of conceptions was in a way functional to creation of a mystique of law-religion dichotomy which belied social reality.

An example of the kinds of linkages that religion formed with the electoral process at the existential level in India emerged in *Hari Singh* v. *Popatlal*[36] There the successful candidate, who had been sponsored by the Congress(I), had promised to a caste leader an amount of Rs. 10,000/- and also pledged to build a hostel for the residence of the students of his caste group. It was not proved that the voters knew of this promise and therefore, the Court held that an offer which had not been communicated to the voters did not amount to influencing the voters.

The bargain model implicit in the line of reasoning completely ignored the location of a caste leader in the social configuration in India. The essence of leadership of a caste lies in the ability of the leader to get things done for the caste. He speaks for the collectivity and if he so speaks he could so listen too. The offer of an advantage redounding to his caste group would necessarily affect the feeling of the voters of that caste if the leader was somebody who counted.

The proper question for the Court in *Hari Singh* was to ask whether the person to whom the offer was made was a caste leader. Once that was answered in the affirmative the Court could have taken judicial notice of the fact that a caste leader would share with his followers the offer which had been made to him. Evidence had established in the instant case that the person in question went to great extent to preserve his leadership potential. He had in the first public meeting, where Indira Gandhi was present, thrown to the winds a bundle of currency notes allegedly representing the ten thousand rupees which Congress(I) had given him to change his party allegiance. This was just a stunt as he changed his party affiliation a little later, but it performed a profound social function legitimating his leadership showing that he was willing to sacrifice personal gain for the welfare of his caste fellows. It could be inferred from these circumstances that the person was a caste leader. If an offer was made to him it was as good as an offer made to the whole caste. The Court however persisted in ignoring the harsh realities of political life by utilizing juridical conceptions drawn from the law of contract.

The dimensions that the combination of money-power with religion had acquired in elections emerges from a subsequent case where the Court again acted in the manner of an ostrich refusing to face the real world. In *Laxmi Raman*

---

[36] AIR 1976 S.C. 271.

v. *Chandan Singh*[37] the candidate had promised to build a Muslim school at a village in his constituency where the majority of residents were Muslims. The candidate allegedly went at midnight to the village where he learnt that the Muslims would vote for anybody who would construct a school for their children. He offered to pay the money for such construction and actually paid that amount to one of his own agents. The Court considered the story to be "ridiculous." Those who know electioneering in India perhaps would have come to a different conclusion. The Court even disbelieved another story of a contribution of Rs. 3,000/– for building a mosque though in both cases the recipients had been identified and had admitted receipts.

Harsh reality again confronted the Court in *Ebrahim Sulaiman Sait* v. *M.C. Mohammad*[38] There it was alleged that Mr. Sait had said in an election speech that the Jan Sangh, a political party leaning towards Hindus, had caused the killing of Muslims and burning of mosques in North India. He had also described the Muslim League (Opposition) Party of Kerala as anti-religious. The question was whether the speeches appealed to religion. The Court held that even though the speech had a communal tone, it did not make an appeal in the name of religion. "Communal parties were allowed to function in politics" in India. An appeal made to voters on communal basis should not,therefore, be viewed as "corrupt practice." It cited *Kultar* as an authority for the proposition. The Court held that an appeal to communitarian feelings was only an *indirect* way of appealing to religious considerations. This is misreading *Kultar*.

It may be recalled that in *Kultar* an appeal was made in the name of Panth and the basis for the decision of the Court was that Panth did not stand for Sikh religion but for Akali Dal as a political party. In no way could it be said that the Court in *Kultar* was making a distinction between direct appeal to religion and indirect appeal to religion.

Again, the Court in Sait was trying to accommodate black letter law to political practice as it had evolved in Independent India by propounding an absolutely new distinction between direct and indirect appeals. Apart from the fact that in Indian constitutional jurisprudence the court has shown greater fascination for, contrary canon of construction—what cannot be done directly cannot be done indirectly,[39]—the direct-indirect dichotomy has been presumably given a decent burial in Cooper.[40] Resurrecting it without even as much as the

---

[37] AIR 1977 S.C. 587.

[38] AIR 1980 S.C. 354.

[39] Singh, "What Can't be Done Directly Cannot be Done Indirectly," 5 J. Indian L. Inst. 173 (1963).

[40] *R.C. Cooper* v. *Union of India*, AIR 1970 S.C. 564.

benefit of consideration by a larger bench attests further to the fragmented functioning of the Court.

Sait also attests to the feelings that the Court has not been contending with reality. The call for recognition of reality is understood by the Court as a call for accommodation to the use of religion in elections. The Court in *Sait* virtually permitted communal appeals to be made by candidates in elections subverting totally the constitutional vision. The situation was too much at tangent with the constitutional commitment and therefore the problem resurfaced again in *Harcharan*.[41] There the Akali Dal candidate was elected. It was argued that *Hukumnamas* or orders were issued by the Akal Takht on its official pad and under its official seal seeking support for the candidate. The *Hukumnamas* did not direct overtly that the vote be cast for candidates sponsored by the Dal but they also left little to the imagination.[42] Evidence was also on record that Akali Dal leaders delivered public speeches and wrote articles with similar content.[43]

Faced with this situation the Court resurrected parts of the Beg opinion in Bukhari. It appealed to secularism, and without benefit of reconsideration, rejected the dichotomy built in *Sait* between the direct and indirect use of religion. The Court held that it would disregard the form and would like to proceed on a broader basis. And yet, the Court, speaking through Justice Mukharji, reiterated the dichotomy that Subbarao had asserted in *Shubnath*, for the judge observed:

> It would not be an appeal to religion if a candidate is put up by saying 'vote for him' because he is a good Sikh or he is a good Christian or he is a good Muslim, but it would be an appeal to religion if it is publicised that not to vote for him would be against Sikh religion or against Christian religion or against Hindu religion - or to vote for other candidate would be an act against a particular religion. It is the total effect of such an appeal that has to be borne in

---

[41] *S. Harcharan Singh* v. *S. Sajjan Singh*, AIR 1985 S.C. 236.

[42] An article appearing in *Akali Times inter alia* stated "It becomes a religious commitment for every sikh to treat his vote a property of the Akali Dal and should stick to it by all means. To be a sikh is to adhere to the Guru. To follow the sihism is not a small thing it is a gift bestwoed by the Almighty Vaheguru. Those who are admitted into the Sikh fold, they protect this faith even at the cost of their lives." *Ibid.*, p. 242.

[43] One of the pamphlets *inter alia* stated "The sikhs living in Punjab and out of it should think seriously that their political and religious life can then only be saved if the akali dal rules in Punjab. In the coming elections the support of Indira Congress by any sikh will be a stab in the back of sikh interests," *Ibid.*, p. 243.

mind in deciding whether there was a appeal to religion as such or not.[44]

These observations too do not disclose any realization of the identity building function of religion even though they travel beyond the formal distinction between religion and community. The link between religion and community has become the bone of contention in recent past. The identity and community building function of religion became the crux of the problem when the BJP and its allies like Shiv Sena unleashed their election propaganda appealing to the element of *hindutva*. Their principal argument has been that under the Congress rule a particular variety of pseudo-secularism consisting of unabashed appeasement of minority groups had been practiced at the cost of the national identity of India. There are various shades of meaning of this national identity some more troublesome than others. As these appeals were widely used in the last parliamentary election and state assembly election, petitions challenging these elections are making preliminary rounds in the courts. None of these have yet been finally heard but the Bombay High Court in its opinion on a preliminary issue has made certain observations in *Damodar Tatyaba* v. *Vamanrao Mahadik*.[45]

The observations in Damodar are, of course, obiter because the preliminary question in this case was whether election speeches made by persons, who are not themselves candidates or election agents can form the basis of a challenge on ground of "corrupt practice" and if so was it necessary for the petitioner to indicate the particular sentences or phrases in the speech which tend to make an appeal in the name of religion. The High Court held that both these objections had no foundation. In respect of the speeches it held further that the question whether a certain speech amounted to "corrupt practice" depended on the over-all effect and impression and the emphasis on word and mannerism of the speakers. The Court observed the following:

> To take a very simple example. The sentence, *"Garva se kaho hum Hindu hain"* (say with pride we are Hindus) by itself would be innocent. I would, in fact, say that it is a sentence, the sentiments of which are highly laudable and shared by all right minded citizens of India. There can be no doubt that the race and religion of Hindus has within it great virtues. One of the greatest being its tolerance, love and acceptance of all other races and religion. However, even a sentence as innocent and laudable as above can be converted into a

---

[44]*Loc. cit.*, p. 247.

[45]AIR 1991 Bombay 373.

corrupt practice. If such a sentence is made at an Election time with the intention of furthering the prospect of election of a candidate or prejudicially affecting the prospect of another on the ground of religion, race, caste and/or community it would become a corrupt practice. This would necessarily depend on the context in which it is made, the context of the speech itself and to a certain extent the manner in which it is said and emphasized. For example at election time, the speaker talks about the superiority of Hindus. This may be in context of Hindus as a race, religion, caste or community. Persons other than Hindus may be termed inferior and/or 2nd class citizens. Depending on the context and emphasis this may again be on grounds of race, religion, caste or community. The speaker may call for the creation of a "Hindu Rashtra" and talk about either decimating or exporting all people of other races, religion, caste or community who refuse to accept such a "Hindu Rashtra." By the speech "Hindu" may be called upon to vote for a "Hindu" candidate or refrain from voting for a non-Hindu candidate. This again may be on grounds of race and/or religion and/or caste and/or community. By the speech it is made out, that for the protection of Hindus as a race and/or religion and/or caste and/or community it is absolutely necessary that people vote only for Hindus. In a speech such as this, even the laudable sentence "say with pride we are Hindus" could be made to completely change its context, depending on the manner in which and time at which it is said and emphasized.

A perusal of this observation shows that the Court was still enamored of the distinction between the religious and the profane. Translation of the distinction into community groups is difficult to make. The court was not prepared to do so unless the speeches seek to denigrate particular castes or communities or unless an appeal was made specifically in the name of religion. This is in essence a continuation of the *Sait* doctrine which was itself overruled in *Harcharan*. Perhaps for that reason the Court does not use the expression direct and indirect and instead talks of effect of the speech on the pattern of voting. The real question is thus not permitted to surface. That question is: given the identity building and reinforcing functions of religion can the use of religion to build communitarian support in favor of a candidate amounts to a corrupt practice. Section 123(3) of the Representation of Peoples Act, 1952, does not in terms differentiate between the communitarian and the personal aspect of religion. That distinction has been built by the Court itself assuming that Section 123(3) enacted the utilitarian dichotomy. The question therefore, is not whether an appeal to communitarian values is barred by Section 123(3). It is whether an appeal to religion includes an appeal to the identity building structure of religion. One school of thought which is now emerging around the problem of ethnicity argues that ethnic identities based on language and religion can not be ignored and should ethnic loyalties be permitted to influence elections even when they involve appeals made in the name of religion.[46]

Understanding the Failure

The failure of the Court to rise to the need of making an operational success of the prohibition on use of religion in elections is not a simple matter. Its complexity can be appreciated at different levels. At the doctrinal level it can be argued that the Court has relied on the distinction between the "religious" and the "profane" without realizing that the utilitarian wisdom is not the last word on the role of religion in society. Secondly, the argument may be extended to say that the distinction, made by the Court, is inadequate for a post-colonial society. Thirdly, it may be argued that the Court has preferred to stress the individual liberty dimension of religion in view of the constitutional commitment to the freedom of the individual in matters of conscience guaranteed by Art. 25 of the Constitution of India. The preference for individual liberty has contributed to the neglect of communitarian values serviced by religion.

Inadequate Conceptualization of Religion

The principal characteristics of the concept of religion adumbrated by the Court is the distinction between the religious and the profane spheres of life. The water tight distinction between the two spheres resulted from a mixture of utilitarian metaphysics and early anthropological beliefs. The distinction was first made by scholars whose imagination had been influenced by the way in which Indian culture was perceived by the British[47] as "steeped in magic and superstition."[48] Early anthropologists had emphasized the irrational nature of religious beliefs. Frazer defined religion as "propitiation or conciliation of powers superior to man which are believed to direct and control the course of nature and of human life"[49] And, Taylor taught that primitive man arrived at

---

[46]I.I. Rudolph & S.H. Rudolph, *In Pursuit of Lakshmi* (Chicago, 1987); Larson, "Mandal, Mandir, Masjid," in this collection.

[47]C. Alvarez, *Decolonizing History*, 2nd edition (1991), p. 18ff. Also see generally, M. Cole, G.L. Grlick &D.W.Sharp, *The Cultural Context of Learning and Thinking* (New York, 1971).

[48]L.D. Wurgaft, *The Imperial Imagination* (Middletown, Conn., 1983), p. 55.

[49]J.G. Frazer, *The Golden Bough* (New York, 1922), p.4.

religious belief by faulty reasoning from effect to cause.[50] Malinowski substituted the argument with functional under-pinnings.

Malinowski claimed that there were two spheres of action : one based on scientific knowledge and the other on non-rational beliefs. Religious or magical beliefs could not be explained in a scientific manner because religion became relevant only in the sphere that was beyond rational understanding and human control. The strong emotional interest in such situations combined with its inherent uncertainties produces tensions and exposes the actor to frustration. Religion manages such tensions.[51] Thus, at the hands of early anthropologists religion acquired a supra mundane nature and a social function. The inadequacy of such a concept is brought out by Durkheim as its failure to account for the element of reverence that religion arouses, but of it later.

In limiting itself to the utilitarian distinction between the religious and the profane spheres, the Court preferred to follow the early anthropologist. The preference may be an echo of India's colonial past.

In the eighteenth and the nineteenth century sociology of religion was basically done in India by European travellers. Their work can be divided in two major groups—one group took up the task of recording popular religions. The other group was mainly interested in textual analysis of religious symbols and philosophical concepts of which Max Muller can be cited as an example. The theoretical interests in this period were limited to the contrast between tribal religions and philosophical traditions of Hinduism. The principal problem was framed in terms of continuities between the folk and the philosophical traditions. Risley's definition of Hinduism as "magic transformed by metaphysics"[52] summarizes the approach of these scholars. These scholars subscribed to the evolutionary bias considering tribal variants of religion as representatives of earlier evolutionary stage on some unilinear scale of religious evolution.

During the later colonial period some of the Indian scholars took up what may be called acculturation studies or fusion studies which aim at tracing the course of adaptation of one religious tradition to another religious tradition[53] thereby reinforcing the approach of early anthropologists.

Only in the post-independence period did sociological studies of religion build on the Durkheimian hypothesis searching for religious correlates of social

---

[50] Generally see, E.B. Tylor, *Primitive Culture* (London, 1871).

[51] B. Malinowski, *Crime and Custom in Savage Society* (London, 1951), p. 14.

[52] H.H. Risley, *The People of India* 2nd ed. (Delhi, 1969), p. 233.

[53] See, S.C. Roy, *Oraon Religion and Customs* (Delhi, 1985, first published: 1928).

structure. Srinivas related the Coorgi cults to social structure.[54] But that development is ignored by the Court.

Overlooking the Function of Religion in Colonial Society

No opinion of the Court shows an awareness of the relation of religion to social structure either in general or in particular relation to elections. The gross neglect could be premised on the gut feeling that religion was really irrelevant to polity. But, there is another possibility too. The colonial power too considered indigenous religion irrelevant to its purpose and the neglect of the Court is a pointer to the possibility that the Court was cast in the same mold.

In a colonial situation the separation of state from society is a fundamental datum. The state represents the colonial power. The predominant bulk of society represents the colonized who are subservient to the interest of the colonizing power. The purpose of the state is to extract as much as it could from the colony and to plough back as little as possible to keep the colony going for the while. There is, thus, an inherent contradiction built into the situation. The concept of the modern state arose in western Europe principally for the purpose of transforming the power-base from the feudal lords to the bourgeoisie but in a colonial situation the state represents the metropolitan power for which the masses have to work. It is, thus, a reversal of the classical situation of western Europe. Man is replaced by the metropolitan power as the center of polity. Extraction of surplus value constitutes the ethos of the state. Thus, while secularism is related to freedom of the individual in western political experience it gets transmuted into relations of dependency[55] in the colonial society.

---

[54] See M.N. Srinivas, *Religion and Society Among the Coorgs of South India* (1952).

[55] Dos Santos has defined *dependency* as "a conditioning situation in which the economies of one group of countries are conditioned by the development and expansion of others." Dos Santos, "The Crisis of Development Theory and the Problem of Dependence in Latin America," H. Bernestein, editor *Under Development and Development: The Third World Today* (1973), p. 76. The *dependency* scholars differ among themselves about the mechanism of under-development. Some focus on external trade, while others consider articulation of traditional model of production resulting in the creation of a vast class of immiserated people suffering super-exploitation, as the cause of under-development. For typical examples of dependency perspective see generally, P. Baran, *The Political Economy of Growth* (1957); A.G. Frank, *Capitalism and Underdeveopment in Latin America* (New York, 1967); J.G. Taylor, *From Modernization to Modes of Production* (1979); J. Petras, *Critical Perspectives on Imperialism and Social Class in the Third World* (New York, 1978); P.T. Bauer, *Reality and Rhetoric: Studies in the Economics of Development* (Cambridge, 1984).

Religion, Politics and Law

Dependency gives new meaning to secularization. On the one hand, the divorce of religion from the state leaves the colonial power devoid of any moral restraints on its exploitative potential. On the other hand the threat to traditional values add to religion a super sanctity in the eyes of exploited masses. They come to perceive religion as the space for escape, sanctuary or protest. The colonial experience in India shows active use of religion as a form of protest against the colonial power.[56]

This use of religion as the medium of protest, reinforces the antagonism of law and religion. Law goes with the colonial power as its principal instrument of authority. The situation is epitomized in the observations of Alexander Dow, that the sword and not the *Firman* of a weak emperor forms the basis of British power in India.[57] Colonial history in India brings out forcefully the conflict between law and religion as an arena of protest against the colonial power. Much of this is presented as costs of "modernization" since in the jargon of the neo-literati pre-British India was a cesspool of superstition and traditionalism.

It is rather unfortunate that the legal history of British-India has assumed with even less than a superficial examination that the British followed a policy of non-interference with personal laws leaving not only the belief structures but also the institutional structures of religions intact. The functionality of religious institutional structures in maintenance of the traditional modes of production insured their continuance for on them depended the revenues of the colonial power.[58] It therefore, was keenly interested in keeping such structures intact. Whenever it really interfered with such structures it went out of its way to ensure that the change did not in any way interfere or seriously jeopardize the real interests of the colonial government. Just to take one example, when Bentinck was considering the question of abolition of Sati, he was willing to go ahead only when he realized that the landed elite class of Hindu society in Bengal which itself had been a creature of the colonial power, would really go with the measure.[59] It is also well known that as Indian opinion gradually became more vociferous and assertive under the leadership of people like Tilak, the colonial power developed cold feet not because of any fear of native resistance but because of fear of jeopardizing the economy of the colonial government. This fear was however, expressed in terms of great respect for tradition envisaged by the colonial power. Maxwell, the Home Member of the Central Legislative

---

[56] A.R. Desai, *Peasant Struggles in India* (Bombay, 1979).

[57] Alexander Dow, quoted in M.P. Jain, *Legal History of India* (1965).

[58] Washbrook, "Law, State, and Agrarian Society in Colonial India," 15 *Modern Asian Studies* 3 (1981).

[59] 1 C.H. Phillips, *The Correspondence of Lord William Cavendish Bentinck* (Oxford, 1977), p. 342.

Council, told the Council on the occasion of discussion on the proposed Deshmukh Bill for Rights of Hindu Women in property that "the attitude of the government to measures of social legislation (is that) in the first place before supporting such measures they must be satisfied that they have the overwhelming support of the community or communities which they affect."[60]

The colonial professions of non-intervention camouflaged reality. Not only did the colonial power reinforce traditional structures of dominance but it also used the secularization thesis to underline the process of exploitative extraction. Brahmannical or dominant caste religion helped the indigenous feudal lords. No wonder that in the subaltern psyche the remedy lay in the search for a new messiah or a new religion. Secularism had exploitative connotations in colonial India for it reinforced the axis relations of the dominant classes with the ruling power. Little realization of this seems to inform the treatment accorded to religious liberty, in Independent India.

Inadequacy of the Constitutional Vision

Arts. 25[61] and 26[62] of the Constitution of India form the core of the constitutional vision but the Court has approached these articles with certain pre-

---

[60]1 *Legislative Assembly Debates* (1940), p. 1971.

[61]*Freedom of Conscience and Free Profession, Practice and Propagation of Religion*:

(1) Subject to public order, morality and health and to other provisions of this Part, all persons are equally entitled to freedom of conscience and the right freely to profess, practice and propagate religion.

(2) Nothing in this article shall affect the operation of any existing law or prevent the state from making any law:

>(a) regulating or restricting any economic, financial, political or other secular activity which may be associated with religious practice;

>(b) providing for social welfare and reform or the throwing open of Hindu Religious instituions of a public character to all classes and section of Hindus.

Explanation I- The wearing and carrying of *kirpans* shall be deemed to be included the profession of Sikh religion.

Explanation II- In sub-calause (b) of clause (2), the reference to Hindus shall be construed as including a reference to persons professing the Sikh, Jain or Buddhist religion and the reference to Hindu religious institutions shall be construed accordingly.

[62]Art 26 reads: *Freedom to Manage Religious Affairs*:

conceived notions about the nature of the right and the hegemony of highly evolved form of religion.

The Nature of the Right to Religion

The Court has read the constitutional guarantees in respect of religion with the assumption that they crystallize the Enlightenment philosophy of toleration,[63] laying the Indian provisions alongside those made by the U.S. and Australian constitutions. It has used with great relish the precedents emanating from the superior courts in those two countries only lightly peppered with the realization that the ground realities in India may deserve variation bringing about accommodation with such realities.

The Court thus accepted the definition of religion as elaborated by the US Supreme Court in the early case of *Davis*[64] with the caveat that the theism implicit in that definition be dropped in its application to India because many heretical religions in India denied the existence of God.[65] The definition of religion was also expanded to include practice besides profession of belief. Reliance for this was placed on Australian precedents.[66]

These accomplishments stood for identifying religion with beliefs rousing reverence in the sacred and the ritual necessarily accompanying such belief. The collectivity building potential of religion was for the moment eclipsed. As such orientation of religion necessarily impinged on the attention of

---

Subject to public order, morality and health, every religious denomination or any section thereof shall have the right-

    (a) to establish and maintain instituion for religious and charitable purposes;

    (b) to manage its own affairs in matters of religion;

    (c) to own and acquire movable and immovable property; and

    (d) to administer such property in accordance with law.

[63] For a brief history of the policy of toleration in England and United States, see Swicher, "The Politics of Toleration: The Establishment Clause and the Act of Toleration Examined," 66 *Ind. L. Journal* 772 (1991).

[64] *Davis* v. *Beason* 133 U.S. 342 (1899).

[65] *Comm. H.R.E.* v. *L.T. Swamiar*, AIR 1954 S.C. 282. Perhaps the Court took a leaf out of the later expansion of the *Davis* definition by the U.S. Supreme Court itself so as to cover transcendentalism in *Fowler* v. *Rhode Island*, 69 L. Ed. 828 (1953).

[66] *Adelaide Company* v. *Commonwealth*, 67 C.L.R. 116, 127. Here the High Court had observed that religious liberty went "far beyond protecting the liberty of opinion" to include protection "for acts done in pursuance of religious belief as part of religion."

the Court in cases involving sects having distinct beliefs and practices academics took no little pleasure in court-baiting. Tripathi blamed the Court for its failure to realize that the denominational rights guaranteed by Art. 26 were only ancillary to the individual freedom of conscience guaranteed by Art. 25 and had no life of their own[67]; and Alexandrowicz felt that the policy underlying the approach of the Court reflected the same tendencies "which in the last century eliminated the Church in Europe from its wider field of activities."[68] Reading constitutional provisions relating to freedom of religion with an emphasis on the individual nature of the guarantee is to foster the State-Society distinction that forms part of the Enlightenment tradition. Along which this also went a surreptitious preference for high-brow religiosity.

Hegemony of the Literati Doctrine

Initially having entertained the claim of religious practice to be included into the ambit of the protection, the Court began in the sixties a surreptitious operation of limiting the protection of the constitutional provisions to only highly evolved form of religion. This was accomplished by introducing an exception in *Durgah Khwaja Sahib*.[69] Justice Gajendragadkar referred to the parity between secular practices that were not an essential part of religion and "practices though religious...(that) sprung from merely superstitious beliefs." The later class of practices may too be considered "extraneous and unessential accretions to religion itself" and may be deprived of constitutional protection. He reiterated the same in *Tilkayat Govindlalji*.[70] Ever since then, the distinction between "mere superstition" and "religion" became an integral part of Indian constitutional doctrine. Groves was tempted to observe that this development introduced "an additional element of hostility to religious freedom" and "infused in the Constitution a principle" not apparent from the text of the Constitution.[71]

The philosophy underlying the distinction was revealed by Justice Subbarao, in an extra-judicial writing:

---

[67]Tripathi, "Secularism: Constitutional Provision and Judicial Review," *Secularism: Its Implications for Law and Life in India*, ed. by G.S. Sharma (Bombay, 1966), p. 186.

[68]Alexandrowicz, "The Secular State in India and in the United States," 2 *Journal of the Indian L. Inst.* 287 (1960).

[69]*Durgah Committee, Ajmer* v. *Syed Husain Ali*, AIR 1961 S.C. 1402.

[70]*Tilkayat Govinlalji* v. *Rajasthan*, AIR 1963 S.C. 1638.

[71]Groves, "Religious Freedom," 4 *Journal of the Indian L. Inst.* 191 (1962).

In India, particularly in villages, people belonging to various religions were living together amicably. Most of the ancestors of various religions were at one time Hindu....The disparity between the...sub-castes was so enormous; that it had become the main source of conversion to other religions and a fertile field for thorny dissensions for political objectives.[72]

Subbarao apparently construed Hindu religion in catholic terms as the primeval religion out of which all other religions emerged. Gajendragadkar added another dimension to the hegemonic concept of Hindu religion in *Satsangi*.[73] There the question was whether the *swaminarayan satsanghi* denomination, which also had Muslim and Parsi members, could be considered a Hindu denomination so that its temples could be thrown open to persons belonging to the scheduled castes. The Court cited the *Gītā* as an authority for the proposition that worship of any godhead was worship of God and diversity in the means of attaining salvation was a characteristic feature of Hindu religion. Any group that believed in the efficacy of *jñāna* could be treated as Hindu even though it differed upon the value of *karma*. The Court thus consciously not only preferred the literati doctrine of *jñāna* over the *bhakti* that formed the kernel of mass religiosity among Hindus, but also legitimized the claims of elite Hindu religiosity to represent national ethos in India. The parallel development was reflected in *Shubhnath* and *Raman*.

The moral hegemony accorded to the Hindu literati doctrine effectively screened the community-forming functions of religion. In its romance with utilitarian foundations of the nineteenth century policies of toleration, the Court has completely overlooked the communitarian aspects of religion, a much needed corrective provided by contemporary sociological theory.

Perspectives from Contemporary Sociological Theory

The judicial doctrine is expressive of the compartmentalization of life between the spheres of the secular and the sacred which in the words of Baird, marks a new great tradition.[74] Baird also realizes that the new great tradition occasions religious conflict "because it is a conflict over the ultimate way one perceives the world. It is a conflict between those who see the world as sacred, who see a sacredness to all of life, including the economic, political, social and

---

[72]Subh Rao, "Caste and Creed under the Constitution," 7 *The White Star* 4.

[73]*Shastri Yagnpurushdasji* v. *Muldas Bhudardas Vaishya*, II SCJ 502 (1966).

[74]Robert D. Baird, "Uniform Civil Code and the Secularization of Law," R.D. Baird, editor, *Religion in Modern India*, first edition (New Delhi, 1981), p. 417.

legal dimensions, and those who for whatever reasons seek to distinguish between religion and the secular realms of the economy, society, politics and law."[75] The distinction is premised on the positivist differentiation between the spheres of the noumenal from the phenomenal which marked the post-enlightenment era.

The separation of the sacred from the secular spheres of life leaves the Hobbesian problem of order unattended. If society is composed of self regarding individuals it becomes difficult to explain how it hangs together. Classical sociologists like Marx, Weber and Durkheim addressed themselves to the problem and as part of their endeavour, rejected the distinction between the sacred and the secular spheres. Marx met the problem by reducing the sacred to the secular treating all religions as super-structural reflections of the gross economic interest of the dominant class. Weber and Durkheim did not subscribe to such reductionism and instead tried to account for the relation between the two spheres, theorizing implicitly that inter-connections between the two militate against any water tight demarcation. Common to these three is the belief that ideas are necessarily related in someway to the existential sphere of life.

The anti-positivism of Weber consisted in his conception of social science as one engaged "in analyzing society as a structure of meaning-endowing actions centered on the human subject."[76] Society, therefore, denoted the behavior of a plurality of actors in so far as in its meaningful content the action of each takes account of that of others and is oriented in those terms. Weber recognised that religion was a major institution providing meaningful content to social action. The meaning could both be subjective and objective. At the subjective level religion answered for the actor the cognitive question who she was and also the theodical question how she could make sense of the circumstances in which he found himself. At the objective level religion was conceived by Weber in terms of the tradition of *Religionssoziologie*,[77] as a phenomenon manifested collectively in a society. The phenomenon consists in a relatively autonomous set of ideas that are consciously produced, sustained and modified by religion specialists who strive for rational-ethical consistency. Weber's thesis of the relation between the protestant ethic and the rise of

---

[75]*Ibid.*, p. 418.

[76]A. Swingewodd, *A Short History of Sociological Thought* (London, 1984), p. 143.

[77]*Religionssoziologie* is typified by an aprioristic functional approach like that of Simmel. see, G. Simmel, *The Sociology of Religion* (C. Rosenthal, tran. 1959). This stands in contrast to *Religionwissenschaft* tradition which treats religion as an individually experienced *sui generis* phenomenon. See J. Wach, *The Comparative Study of Religions*, ed. by Joseph M. Kitigawa (New York, 1958).

capitalism was a demonstration of the broad cultural implications of religious ideas on the formation of capitalism as a system.[78]

Weber conceived religion as a mode of progressive adaptation. He was of the view that specialists of religion progressively contribute to an increasing rationalization of religion and such rationalization in turn contributes to greater relative autonomy of the religious and other spheres of life ultimately culminating in a society where "the intellect has created an aristocracy based on the possession of rational culture and independent of all personal ethical qualities of man."[79] The religious ideas are, thus, recognised by Weber to have transformative capacity. The greater the rationalization the more the autonomy of the various spheres of life.

Weber took it for granted that the process of religious rationalization is leading towards secularization where the central features of the modern world that had emerged from a religious matrix attain autonomy in the sense that they acquire their own logic of change. He argued that secularization simply means that the objective unity of life characterizing primitive society is functionally substituted by social institutions operating in distinctive and specialized sectors as functional equivalents of the same sacred character that initially held life in primitive societies together. The role of religion in any society for Weber, therefore, defines the charter of possibilities available to individual actors in conformity with the imperative of collectivity and where this function is taken up by specialized institutions religion recedes to the background.

Durkheim followed a different track as he considered religion to be a *sui generis* phenomenon. His concept of religion matured only slowly over time. He began with an instrumental version of religion conceiving its role as that of "of assuring the equilibrium of society and adapting it to external conditions,"[80] but later he veered over to conceiving religion as a social phenomenon, the primitive social phenomenon from which others subsequently emerged by a process of

---

[78] See, M. Weber, *The Protestant Ethic and the Spirit of Capitalism* (London, 1985, first pub. 1930).

[79] Weber, "Religious Rejections of the World and Their Directions," H.H. Gerth and C.W. Mills, editors, *From Max Weber: Essays in Sociology* (New York, 1958), p. 355.

[80] Durkheim, "Les Etudes de Science Sociale" 12 *Review Philophique* 61 (1886) referred to in S. Lukes, *Emile Durkheim* (1973), p. 238.

differentiation.[81] The change from naive instrumentalism to an essentialist[82] concept of religion is perceivable in Durkheim's definition of religion as "an integrated system of beliefs and practices relative to sacred things, that is separate and taboo, which unite in one moral community called a church all those who adhere to it."[83]

The definition has two integrated dimensions. First, it premises religion on an absolute opposition between the sacred and the profane. Only the sacred can elicit reverence since it is not governed by positivist causality and is as such unexplainable in terms of rational cognition. The failure to account for it in an empirical manner is the key to the feeling of reverence that religion elicits from human beings.[84] For this reason anything that could pertain to the world perceivable by the senses could not be sacred. Its profanity consisted in its empirical existence.

Secondly, Durkheim attests to the community-constitutive properties of religion which was a distinct advance over the utilitarian distinction that denied all relevance to religion. He asserted that in the beginning "all is religion." Religious symbols make possible the kind of inter-subjectivity which generates the consensus that informs social solidarity. Durkheim had originally believed that collective consciousness denoted the representations shared by all members of the society but in his analysis of rites he shifted to the position that the collective conscience owes its existence not to be content of such representations but to the structure of the group identity that is established and continuously renewed through identification in common with the sacred by means of such

---

[81] Scholars have traced the change to the influence of Robertson Smith, the British Historian of Religion, see Lukes, *Ibid.*, p. 235. Durkheim acknowledged the influence in defending himself against the charge of Germanism.

[82] The notion of essence denotes "a fixed possibility whose character may be delimited apart from our acquaintance with the existence which embodies it." MacIntyre, "Essence and Existence," P. Edwards, editor *Encyclopedia of Philosphy*, vol. 3 (New York, 1967), pp. 59, 61.

[83] E. Durkheim, *The Elementary Forms of Religious Life* (New York, 1965), p. 65.

[84] Explaining the nature of religion Durkheim had observed: "Since social pressure operates in mental ways, it could not fail to give men the idea that outside themselves there exist one or several powers, both moral and, at the same time, efficacious, upon which they depend. They must think of these powers, at least in part, as outside themselves, for these address them in a tone of command and sometimes even order them to do violence to their most natural inclinations. It is undoubtedly true that if they were able to see that these influences which they feel emanate from society, then the mythological system of interpretations would never be born." Durkheim, quoted in R. Robertson, *Meaning and Change* (New York, 1978), p. 68.

collective representations. To begin with the identity of the person is only a mirror image of collective identity and is, therefore, the expression of a mechanical form of social solidarity. Later with the differentiation of social structure individuals free themselves from a collective consciousness coextensive with their whole personality structure and at the same time they also distance themselves from the basic religious consensus. The processes is represented by three parallel developments—rationalization of world views, the generalization of moral and legal norms, and individuation of individuals. The upshot of the development is summed up by Durkheim in the following words:

> The dissociation of nature and the divine is so complete that it degenerates into antagonism. At the same time, the concept of divinity becomes more general and more abstract, for it is formed, not of sensations, as originally, but of ideals....The idea of man replaces in law, morality and religions that of (particular individuals)....(The rules of law and morality) linked at first to local circumstances, to particularities, ethnic, climatic, etc., free themselves little by little, and with the same stroke become more general. What makes this increase of generality obvious is the uninterrupted decline of formalism.[85]

There is a functional need for religion because something is needed to explain deprivation,[86] otherwise such deprivations would affect the solidarity needed to uphold the collectivity. Durkheim, therefore, gave religion a function consisting in building of the solidary characters of the society.

Following Durkheim it is common place in contemporary anthropology[87] and sociology[88] to treat religion as an institution having important community building functions. It is impossible to think of religion only as an

---

[85] E. Durkheim, *The Division of Labor in Society* (1933), p. 131.

[86] "What is needed if social order is to reign is that the mass of men be content with their lot. but what is needed form them to be content, is not that they have more or less but they be convinced they have no right to more. And for this, it is absolutely essential that there be an authority whose superiority they acknowledge and which tells them what is right." E. Durkheim, *Saint-Simon and Socialism* (1958), p. 200.

[87] "The sacred symbols function to synthesize a people's ethos—the tone, character and quality of their life, its moral and aesthetic style and moode—and their world-vie—the picture thay have of the way things in sheer actuality are, their most comprehensive ideas of order." Geertz, "Religion as a Cultural System," *Anthropological Approaches to the Study of Religion,* ed. by M. Banton (London, 1966), pp. 1,3.

[88] P.L. Berger, *The Sacred Canopy* (Garden City, N.Y., 1967).

exclusively private, personal matter having no relation to formation of group or community identities. A realistic reappraisal is, therefore, needed of the group solidarities that religion builds and the dialectical relationship in which such solidarities stand with the social identity. On the one hand human beings are members of collectivities which share the same life world and by virtue of such sharing such collectivity forms a solidarity. On the other hand the very same individuals are parts of a society that claims loyalty. The resulting tensions are manifested in ethnic upsurge all around us. No all or nothing solution can hope to cater to the complexity of the situation. The dichotomy of sacred an profane or private and public is an all or nothing solution and is as such counter-productive. It is better to comprehend the phenomenon on a sliding scale. At end of the scale in a modern society the marks of ethnic identity are "empty symbols" because of the "desocialization" of ethnic groupings in such society.[89] The other end is represented by intensification of groupism under conditions of "rapid social change and certain tendencies to anomic social disorganization and alienation."[90] It is difficult to argue that religion in India is an empty symbol or may be treated as an empty symbol in respect of the political process as the process of desocialization of ethnic groupings is yet to take place.

If religion cannot be treated as an "empty symbol," its true role must be realized if it is not to warp the political process and turn the hopes of building a societal community in India into nought. Sociologists have considered this problem more under the rubric of secularization.

Parsons has argued that secularization involves a recognition by adherents of different religious that "they can belong to the same moral community—which may be a predominantly secular, politically organized society."[91] He also suggests that this process is strengthened by the identification and intensification of common elements in different religious traditions.

Parsons has built upon a theme that begins with Durkheim as he attempted to trace the normative validity of institutions back to a normative agreement tied to religious symbols. But Weber too contributed the cognitive aspect to it.

> That much of what men in a society take for granted even in their most routine behavior actually involves basic beliefs and

---

[89]D. Schneider, *American Kinship* (Englewood Cliffs, N. J., 1968).

[90]Parsons, "Some Theoretical Considerations on the Nature and Trends of Change of Ethnicity," *Ethnicity: Theory and Experience*, ed. by N. Glazer & D.P. Moynihan (Cambridge, 1975), pp. 53, 68.

[91]Parsons, "Belief, Unbelief and Disbelieve," *Action Theory and the Human Condition* (New York, 1978), p. 240.

assumptions without which they cannot function. In his sociology of religion he set himself the task of formulating clearly these underlying principles and assumptions.[92]

The core difficulty with Weber's work lay in the relationship between "his analytic insistence upon meaningfulness as the centerpiece of sociological study (action as the basic unit of analysis) and his interest in the meaningfulness of the world (particularly the modern industrial world)."[93] Parsons sought to meet this problem by arguing that religious ideas are rationalized interpretations of the subjective meaning of the world. Such ideas are defined as ultimate ends or values that influence action. Parsons argued that there was a correspondence between the positions of Weber and Durkheim in respect of the distinction between the moral and non-moral motives of action in relation to norms and the distinction between the quality of norms as such and the broader element of which these are manifestations. Finally, he argued that both of them were in agreement on the conclusion that a society can only be subject to a legitimate order only in so far as there are common value attitudes are widely held in society.[94]

Contemporary sociologists build upon the identities in the work of Weber and Durkheim. Constraints of space prevent us from entering into any detailed analysis of such sociologists but by way of example we may refer to three of them—Berger, Douglas and Habermas. These three nurtured in different traditions come to very close approximations in their concept of religion.

Berger[95] builds upon phenomenological theories tempering them with Weber. Berger argues that men are congenitally compelled to impose a meaningful order upon reality. All culture is a humanly constructed world of subjectively and inter-subjectively experienced "meanings." Order in society is provided by a coherent, over-arching organization of symbols which provide a meaningful world for individuals to live in. Each individual needs a personal sense of order which sense hinges on an appropriation of an identity that is reckoned with the larger social world. This culture arises from the three simultaneous moments of externalization, objectivization and internalization and is manifested in religion.

Religion is a symbolic universe whose importance lies in its capacity to help maintain a stable and plausible reality of everyday life. The plurality of roles and competing priorities of everyday life are organized through religion into

---

[92]R. Bendix, *Max Weber: An Intellectual Portrait* (Berkeley, 1977), p. 273.

[93]R.Robertson, *Ibid.*, p. 88.

[94]T. Parsons, *The Structure of Social Action* (1949), pp. 669-71.

[95]*See*, P. Berger, *supra* n. 88 and P. Berger & T. Luckmann, *The Social Construction of Reality* (Garden City, N. Y., 1966).

a meaningful whole at the individual level. Religion, therefore, provides effective legitimation as it interprets the order of society in terms of an all embracing order. Marginal experiences of life and anomic episodes are legitimated in terms of the symbolic universe that religion builds.

Mary Douglas built on Durkheim but again tempered it with Weber. In her attempt to grasp the working of the social system she makes a distinction between social *group* and *grid*. A *group* means the outside boundary that people have erected between themselves and the outside world while a *grid* means all the other social distinctions and delegations of authority that they use to limit how people behave to one another.[96] She argues that the combination of *group* and *grid* create four possibilities: strong *grid* strong *group*, strong *grid* weak *group*, weak *group* weak *grid*, weak *grid* strong *group*. Where the *grid* is strong moral and normative prohibition are strong; where the *grid* is weak the individuals have more scope to deal with one another as they wish. She argues that cultural categories are "the cognitive constrainers" in which social interests are defined and classified, argued, negotiated, and fought out. "There is no way in which culture and society can part company, nor any way in which one can be said to dominate the other."[97] In a collectivity where there is a weak *group* and weak *grid* the boundaries of social arrangements are vague and the ties among the members are also weak. The cosmology of such a *group* is least ritualistic. Where there is a strong *grid* but a weak *group* the collectivity exists as the link between constituents sub-groups or individuals. In such a collectivity man trusts in the power of the rule. Where the there is a strong *group* but weak *grid* the society is well bounded by highly corporate organization. The power of the state is supreme. Douglas does not think that we have yet a collectivity in which there is a strong *group* and a strong *grid*.

Modernity for Douglas changes the shape of society but it does not mean that social relations and rituals for the renewal of such social relations are not needed. Therefore, religion continues with the difference that new social forms of cosmology may come into being including secular cosmology. Questions of the nature of *group* and *grid* will dictate the cosmology whether the society is new or old.

Habermas similarly builds on an amalgamation of Weber with Durkheim in his search for an explanation of the nature of religion in modern society but tempers both with the social psychology of Mead. Of course, Habermas is too complex an author to be presented in any brief form. He has not yet developed a systematic treatment of religion but he views religion as an evolutionary process.

---

[96] M. Douglas, *In the Active Voice* (London, 1982), p. 138.

[97] Douglas, "The Effect of Modernization on Religious Change," *Daedalus* (1982), pp. 1, 12.

He assumes that individuals need some kind of personal integration which depends on unifying cultural norms thus, linking self development to unified world views provided by society.[98] In a later work Habermas says—

> Individuals owe their identities as persons exclusively to their identification with, or internalization of, features of collective identity, personal identity is a mirror image of collective identity. So it is not at all true that we are more personal as we are more individualized. The only principle of individuation is the spatiotemporal location of the body and the desiring and feeling nature that is presented with the organism for the process of socialization—or, as Durkheim says, alluding to the classical tradition, "the persons." If one considers how strongly subjective experiences are shaped by culture, this thesis is implausible.[99]

Questions of meaning arise because of anomic or marginal experiences which bring forth doubts about the rationality of the world. Religion helps by purporting to order the world according to meaningful universalistic principles. The actual manner in which religion performs this function varies with the kind of society in which it operates. Habermas identifies four kinds of societies— neolithic, archaic, developed and modern. In a neolithic society there is little need of a rationalized world view as the world of nature blends indiscriminately with the world of myth so that the individual does not develop a need for the meaning of the self and its integration. Only with a more rationalized world view the need for a coherent sense of personal integration arises, therefore, in archaic and developed civilizations religious world views become important as a source of personal integration and unified understanding of group like. In modern society as technology advances and the control over nature increases the functions of religious world views change. The knowledge about the nature of the world becomes a distinct sphere and religious world views become limited to problems of personal meaning and to problems of social integration.

The recent advances in theorizing about religion strongly bring home the message that religion can not be divorced from the structure of society and the place of individual in it. Religion is inevitably involved in the meaning given by a human being his existence and his place in the collectivity. The thesis of two domains ignores the social functions of religion and therefore, the judicial doctrine built upon it necessarily reflects the strains of discrepancy with reality. The

---

[98] J. Habermas, *Legitimation Crisis* (Boston, 1975), p. 117.

[99] J. Habermas, *The Theory of Communicative Action* (Boston, 1987), p. 58.

need is to develop judicial concepts more responsive to the social functions that religion does not.

Conclusion

The principal difficulty lies in the commitment of judicial doctrine to the Cartesian distinction between the spheres of the sacred and the secular. The preference for the dominant ideology of the bourgeoisie state in the nineteenth century incapacitates the Court from realizing the role of religion in the contemporary Indian society and its meaning to the individual in such society. The Court does not realize the operational impact of its ideological commitment claiming all the time that it is doing little beyond translating the commitment of the founding fathers of the Constitution of India. The truth, however, is that the Court has translated its own ideology and perhaps has also been blissfully unaware of its consequences.

The ideological preference of the Court can also be understood as a product of its colonial heritage with a built in bias for public—private dichotomy as it is expressed in a hierarchical society. The effort of the Court to distinguish religion from ethics in India is not a mere reiteration of the civil religion problematique[100] since it is not limited to the delineation of common values of Indian society. It is, on the contrary, an attempt to distill the essence of hierarchy by treating the religious preferences of the elite class as the embodiment of national if not universal ethics.

The dichotomies generated by the Court threaten the individual and the group identities that are built around the cognitive and theodical complexes of meaning and the organizing functions premised on religion. The call for secularism often appears to ethnic minorities based on religion as an invitation for denudation of their distinctiveness and nameless submergence through a generalizing nationalizing juggernaut.

The ideological commitment of the Court is therefore a symbol of loss of meaning and identity at the individual level and is objectively constitutive of the proverbial melting pot. As the centrifugal pull of ethnicity becomes stronger the doctrinal myth gets under great strain as is being currently felt in cases involving the use of religion in the last parliamentary election in India. The time has come for demystifying judicial conceptions so as to reveal their ideological commitment to the ethos of the ruling elite and begin in earnest the search for alternatives which may accommodate the community building functions of religion in the organization of a democratic polity.

---

[100]See, Bellah, "Civil Religion in America," *Beyond Belief*, ed. by R.N. Bellah, (New York, 1970); ed. by R.E. Richey, *American Civil Religion* (1974).

13

Women, Children and the Constitution: Hostages to Religion, Outcaste by Law

Vasudha Dhagamwar

Part I

WE, THE PEOPLE OF INDIA, having solemnly resolved to constitute India into a DEMOCRATIC REPUBLIC[1] and to secure to all its citizens:
JUSTICE, social, economic and political;
LIBERTY of thought, expression belief, faith and worship;
EQUALITY of status and of opportunity;
FRATERNITY assuring the dignity of the individual and the[2] unity of the Nation;
IN OUR CONSTITUENT ASSEMBLY this twenty sixth day of November 1949, do HEREBY ADOPT, ENACT AND GIVE TO OURSELVES THIS CONSTITUTION.

With these words of the preamble did the Constituent Assembly promise a brave new world to the people of India. These promises were further embodied in parts III and IV of the Constitution, viz, the parts dealing with Fundamental Rights (Arts. 19–35) and Directive Principles of State Policy (Arts. 36–51), respectively.

Equality was guaranteed by as many as five articles, nos.14-18. Liberty of thought was guaranteed by articles 19–22, four in number. Arts. 25–28 guaranteed the right to freedom of religion, including the right to establish and administer educational institutions.

Art. 13 made it quite clear that any laws in force that were inconsistent with fundamental rights would be void to the extent of their inconsistency and

---

[1] Substituted by Constitution (Forty second amendment) Act 1976, S.2 With "Sovereign Socialist Secular Democratic Republic"

[2] Substituted by *Ibid.* with "unity and integrity of the nation."

also provided by clause (2) that "the State shall not make any law which takes away or abridges the rights conferred by this part and law made in contravention of this clause shall, to the extent of the contravention, be void."

The Directive Principles of State Policy, as the title of Part IV implies, were only directions, and as such, they were, unlike Fundamental Rights, nonjusticiable. But they aimed at guiding state policy towards realising JUSTICE, social, economic and political, for the people of India. This included, *inter-alia*, directives for introducing a uniform civil code (Art. 44) and providing free and compulsory education for all children up to the age of fourteen (Art. 45).

In keeping with this concern for justice, the Right to Equality was modified to permit special concessions for scheduled castes, scheduled tribes, women and children. This reverse protective discrimination was not permitted on grounds of religion or sect.[3]

What sort of society did the Constitution, or rather the framers of it, envisage for India? There seem to be two kinds of promises made to the citizens by the Constitution in the preamble, as well as Parts III and IV.

The declaration in the preamble regarding Justice and Equality, the Fundamental Rights which guaranteed equality and almost all Directive Principles of State Policy, promised equal rights, equal opportunities, equal treatment in equal circumstances, to sum up, equality before the law and equality of status as a citizen. This is one cluster of rights under the Constitution, one kind of perception of the individual who dwelt in the sovereign territory of India.

There is a second cluster. This consists of that part of the preamble which held out the promise of liberty, of not only thought and expression, but of faith and worship; and those Fundamental Rights which guaranteed more specifically, and in some detail, Freedom of Religion. No less than four articles are devoted to the Freedom of Religion.

The first of them, Art. 25, begins with the conditions subject to which it guarantees freedom of conscience and free profession, practice and propagation of religion. It begins "subject to public order, morality and health and to other provisions of this Part, all persons are equally entitled to freedom of conscience and the right freely to profess, practice and propagate religion."[4]

It also goes on to say "(2) Nothing in this article shall affect the operation of any existing law or prevent the State from making any law

---

[3] Religion, however, was crucial to the definition of scheduled castes. For sometime scheduled caste converts to Buddhism were denied this status and the consequent reservation in education and in service. Some Muslim 'castes' are acknowledged as scheduled castes. Christians are currently asking for this status to be extended to them. Scheduled tribes, on the other hand, may be Christian or animist or Buddhist.

[4] Art. 25 Clause (1)

(a) regulating or restricting any economic, financial, political or other *secular* activity which may be associated with religious practice;

(b) providing for social welfare and reform or *the throwing open of Hindu religious institutions of a public character to all classes and sections of Hindus*"[5] (*emphasis added*).

Art. 26 dealt with freedom to manage religious affairs, again subject to public order, morality and health. Art. 27 guaranteed freedom from payment of taxes for the promotion of any particular religion. Art. 28 guaranteed freedom from compulsory attendance at religious instruction in educational institutions wholly maintained out of State funds.

Arts. 29 and 30 guaranteed protection of the interests of minorities. Between them they guaranteed the rights of any section of citizens to conserve their distinct script and language and culture and the rights of minorities to establish their own educational institutions. Art. 29 however also lays down that in no institutions funded wholly or partly by the State could anyone be denied admission on grounds of religion, race, caste, language or any of them.

Thus the second cluster acknowledged, though with many more reservations and provisos, that citizens, though equal, may have distinct identities, because of their differing languages, religions and cultures.

The denial to the Kurdish minority in Turkey and the Armenians in the Kurdish occupied areas of Iran of the right to speak their mother tongues *even in their homes*, points to the need to protect what would otherwise seem an obvious and natural right of every human being. It also confirms the wisdom of the founding fathers of the Constitution, if such a confirmation was at all needed.

The two clusters, or the two perceptions of the citizen who dwelt under the Constitution are distinct, but they need not be contradictory. Nothing in them warrants that. Rather, they contribute to a rounded perception of the many needs of a human being, and the many roles he or she plays. They were clearly seen as complementary by the framers of the Constitution.

Yet, the two clusters have not harmonised. The vision of the founding fathers has turned out to have been in certain respects, severely astigmatic.

That all was not well with this vision was already indicated during the debates of the Constituent Assembly on both Parts III and IV. The Directive Principles of State Policy were debated first, and Art. 35 (later to be renumbered Art. 44) aroused a great deal of debate. This article was a direction to the State to endeavour to secure for the citizens a uniform civil code throughout the territory of India. It is unnecessary to be reminded that Directive Principles are not

---

[5] Art. 25 Clause (2)

justiciable. They only lay down the direction in which the State should move. They enjoin certain actions upon the State but no citizen can compel the State to act upon them. They are purely recommendatory in character.

Three members of the Constituent Assembly had objected strongly to this situation. They were Mr. Minoo Masani, Rajkumari Amrit Kaur and Mrs. Hansa Mehta. All three of them had been members of the sub committee on Fundamental Rights which had recommended that the application of the uniform civil code, though highly desirable, should be made voluntary. Recording their minute of dissent these three members said "One of the factors that has kept India back from advancing to nationhood has been the existence of the Personal Laws based on religion which keep the nation divided into watertight compartments in many aspects of life. We are of the view that a Uniform Civil Code should be guaranteed to the Indian people within a period of five to ten years in the same manner as the right to free and compulsory primary education has been guaranteed...within ten years. We, therefore, suggest that the Advisory Committee might transfer the clause regarding a uniform civil code from Part II to Part I[6] after making suitable modifications in it."[7]

The dissenters were of course somewhat mistaken about the nature of article 36, a directive principle on free and compulsory education for all children. It was not a fundamental right and 40 years after the Constitution was enacted it is still awaiting action. The state was not so keen or zealous in safeguarding the rights of children as these three members had hoped. Moreover, if the uniform civil code had been promised with a time limit set on it, it would still have been a directive principle, and despite their recommendations could not have been transferred to Fundamental Rights. The comparison made between these two rights—education and civil code—was unfortunate, but prophetic. Neither has yet seen the light of day.

When the Directive Principles came up for the final round of debate, several Muslim members of the Constituent Assembly opposed Art. 35[8] as it

---

[6]In the Constitution as it was finally adopted, draft Part II became Part IV, Directive Principles of State Policy; draft Part I became Part III, Fundamental Rights.

[7]Shiva Rao "Framing of India's Constitution" Vol. II, *Select Documents* (Bombay, 1969) p. 177.

[8]The numbers of the articles were different in the draft and the Constitution as finally adopted. Draft Art. 35 became Art. 44. Draft Art. 36 became Art. 45. Art. 13 became Art. 19, Arts. 19–24 became Articles 25 to 30 in the final form. In the debates as quoted, the draft numbers have been retained as used by the spekers. Everywhere else articles have been given the number they have in the Constitution as adopted. As far as possible both sets have been mentioned, to avoid confusion, or else the contents of the articles have been briefly mentioned.

stood, and wanted a proviso to be added to it. Worded variously, it sought to exempt the personal laws of any community from state interference.[9] This would appear to be another way of deleting Art. 35 from the Directive Principles altogether. The advocates of this proviso were Messrs. Mohammed Ismail Sahib, Naziruddin Ahmed, Mahboob Ali Baig Bahadur, B. Pocker Sahib Bahadur and Hussain Iman. They argued that the diversity of cultures that prevailed in India could not be contained in a uniform civil code; that the British in 150 years of their rule and the Muslims in 500 years of theirs had not imposed such a code; that civil code should refer to civil laws other than personal laws. Even geographical diversity was pulled in to be of service—there were 400 inches of rain in a year in Assam, and none in Rajastan. How could such a country have a uniform civil code? It was also claimed that the article was antagonist to Art. 19 which guaranteed freedom of religion. Notably no one said that they spoke on behalf of the Muslims, though all of them represented Muslims of their individual states. The speakers claimed that they represented the views of all minorities and indeed of many Hindus, who, they said, were opposed to a uniform civil code. On the other hand, if the majority community were unanimous in their support of a uniform civil code, then its imposition by the majority on the minorities was to be condemned as tyrannous, and anti-democratic. As Pocker Sahib Bahadur put it "It is the duty of the majority to secure the sacred rights of every minority."[10]

Mr. Alladi Krishnaswami Ayyar, Mr. L Krishnaswamy Bharathi, Mr. K. M. Munshi and others tried to counter these arguments against the uniform civil code with others of their own. Thus it was pointed out that most certainly the British had interfered with personal laws, including the Muslim personal law, for they had passed the Shariat Act in 1937. By this act several Muslim communities who followed Hindu law of inheritance—the Khojas and Cutchi Memons of Gujarat, the Muslims of North West Frontier province, and the Malsan Muslims who followed the matriarchal law of inheritance—were all brought under the Shariat to the grave displeasure of the Khojas and the Cutchi Memons. It was also pointed out that uniform family laws and uniform civil codes prevailed all the world over, that Muslim countries like Egypt or Turkey did not allow minorities to have their own personal laws.[11]

Mr. K.M Munshi, who was an eminent lawyer, gave a further clarification. Referring to the charge that the directive principle regarding the uniform civil code was against the fundamental right to freedom of religion, Mr. Munshi pointed out

---

[9]*Constituent Assemby Debates* (*CAD*) VII, pp. 540–552.

[10]*CAD* VII, p. 545.

[11]*Ibid.*, p. 546–550.

As regards article 19 the House accepted it and made it quite clear that 'Nothing in this article shall affect the operation of any existing law or preclude the state from making any law (a) regulating or restricting...' (I am omitting the unnecessary words) or other secular activity which may be associated with religious practices; (b) for social welfare and reforms. Therefore the House has already accepted the principle that if a religious practice followed so far covers a secular activity or falls within the field of social reform or social welfare, it would be open to Parliament to make laws about it without infringing this Fundamental Right of a minority.[12]

Mr. Munshi went on: "It must also be remembered that if this clause is not put in it does not mean that the Parliament in future would have no right to enact a civil code." Art. 19 permitted the Parliament to do so. When Dr. Ambedkar rose to make the concluding remarks in this debate, like Messrs. Ayyar and Munshi he also pointed out that Muslim personal law in India was neither immutable nor uniform. He said

> It is no use making a categorical statement that Muslim law has been an immutable law which they have been following from ancient times. That law as such was not applicable in certain parts and it has been made applicable ten years ago. Therefore if it was found necessary that for the purpose of evolving a single civil code applicable to all citizens irrespective of their religion, certain portions of the Hindu law, not because they were contained in Hindu law but because they were found to be most suitable, were incorporated into the new code projected by article 35, I am quite certain that it would not be open to any Muslim to say that the framers of the civil code had done great violence to the sentiments of the Muslim community.[13]

Dr. Ambedkar's summing-up was clear in its perceptions, and bold in its formulation. With his next sentence however he seems to have abandoned both these qualities for short term gains.

> My second observation is to give them an assurance. I quite realise their feelings in the matter, but I think that they have read rather too much into article 35, which merely proposes that the State should

---

[12] *Ibid.*, p. 547.
[13] *Ibid.*, p. 551.

endeavour to secure a civil code for the citizens of the country. It does not say that...the State shall enforce it upon all citizens merely because they are citizens. It is perfectly possible that the future parliament may make a provision by way of making a beginning that the code shall apply only to those who make a declaration that they are prepared to be bound by it...."[14]

Dr. Ambedkar recalled that this was the method followed when the Shariat Act was enacted in 1937. He then continued, "It would be perfectly possible for the parliament to introduce a provision of that sort; *so that the fear which mv friends have expressed here will be altoaether nullified*" (emphasis added).[15] Dr. Ambedkar said that he therefore opposed the amendments. Art. 35 was then put to the vote and adopted by a voice vote. It was later renumbered as Article 44. It reads: "the State shall endeavour to secure for the citizens a uniform civil code throughout the territory of India." This is how it stands enshrined in the Constitution.

Anyone reading the concluding reply of Dr. Ambedkar to the debate cannot fail to be amazed, as well as disappointed. The draughtsman and the jurist in him could see that if the uniform civil code was enacted, it could not be faulted, either because it was *ultra vires* the Constitution—the strong ground—or because of the alleged historical special circumstances of the Muslim law—a weak ground. The statesman and the politician in him, however, evidently thought it expedient to give back all that the jurist had just taken away from the defenders of personal law. Had anyone else in any other forum interpreted this article to mean that the State need only pass the universal civil code, it need not enforce it, there can be hardly any doubt that Dr. Ambedkar would have criticised him in no uncertain terms. Yet the need to mollify the opposition led him virtually to throw away the uniform civil code. Not only this: the words used by him "...it does not say that...the State shall enforce it upon all citizens merely because they are citizens" reduced citizenship to a second place, with religious identity taking the pride of place.

Sadly, one has to concede that when faced with the moment of truth Dr. Ambedkar gave way. It would have been better to have had a blunt, bitter and resolute debate on the uniform civil code, put it to division, rather than blur the issues for the sake of a quick passage for the article.

The Achilles heel of the majority community proved to be Art. 39 (later renumbered Art. 48) which sought to ban cow-slaughter, combining it with a directive to organize agriculture and animal husbandry.

---

[14]*Ibid.*, p, 551.

[15]*Ibid.*, p. 552.

The Muslim members of the House were unanimous in their support, on the grounds that they respected the religious sentiments of their Hindu brethren. But still the majority stuck to the position that theirs was an economic measure. Finally Mr. Saadullah (Assam: Muslim) said that "(T)hose who put it on economic front...do create a suspicion that the ingrained Hindu feeling against cow-slaughter is being satisfied by the backdoor"[16]—as indeed it was! He also warned that the economic arguments could be proved to be wrong. But still the government persisted in the stand they had taken. Since they were in the majority they got away with it and the article could be adopted.

Fundamental Rights were debated next.[17] Art. 13 (as it then was, before being renumbered Art. 19) was most comprehensive and far-ranging. It may well be described as the most definitive article of them all, guaranteeing in clause (1), subclauses (a) to (g) the seven freedoms of speech and expression; of peaceable assembly; of forming associations and unions; of movement; of residence and settlement in any part of India; to own property;[18] and to practice any profession, occupation or trade.

Clauses (2) to (6) generally protected the right of the State to legislate in those very matters in the interest of sovereignty and integrity of India, of the general public and of the Scheduled Tribes in particular and also in the interests of public order. The State also reserved the right to lay down professional qualification and to exclude citizens from any business, industry or service which would be undertaken exclusively by the State.

During the debate on Art. 35 i.e. on the uniform civil code as one of the directive principles, Mohammed Ismail Sahib had already said that personal law was amongst the fundamental rights and he "along with other friends" had given amendments which he would move "at the proper time."[19] He did so now. He moved two new sub clauses to Art.13 (I). subcl.(h) to follow the personal law of the group or community to which he belongs or professes to belong and (i) to personal liberty and to be tried by a competent court of law in case such liberty is to be curtailed.[20] Ismail Sahib proceeded to argue for sub clause (i) at some length. He said:

---

[16]*Ibid.*, p. 578.

[17]The debate on the Directive Principles of State Policy took place during 19–25 November, 1948. Article 35 was debated on 23rd November. The Fundamental Rights were debated during 25 November–8 December, 1948.

[18]sub clause (f) i.e. the right to property was omitted by Constitution (Forty-fourth Amendment) Act 1978, S. 2 w.e.f. 20.6.1979.

[19]*CAD, Loc. cit.*, p. 540.

[20]*Ibid.*, p. 721.

> Personal law is part of the religion of the community or section of people which profess this law. Anything which interferes with personal law will be taken by that community and also by the general public who will judge this question by some common sense, as a matter of interference with religion. Mr. Munshi...said that this had nothing to do with religion. He as an illustrious and eminent lawyer should know that this question of personal law is entirely based on religion. It is nothing if it is not religion. But if he says that a religion should not deal with such things, then that is another matter.

This might seem as though Ismail Sahib was about to concede the point. But no. He continued:

> It is a question of difference of opinion as to what religion should do or should not. People differ and people holding different views on this matter must tolerate the other view. There are religions which omit altogether to deal with the question of personal law and there are other religions *like Hinduism and Islam* (emphasis added) which deal with personal law. Therefore I say that people ought to be given liberty of following their personal law.[21]

Mr. Ismail Saheb admitted that Dr. Ambedkar was right in saying that there were sections of Muslims who did not follow the Shariat. But he said

> (i) it is not reasonable to say that simply because a section of people do not want to follow a certain law of a certain religion or a certain part of that religion that other people...should be compelled not to follow that part of religion....That is not really reasonable, sir, and it is really immutable to the people who follow this law and this religion, because people, as they understand it have not got the right to change their religion as they please.[22]

The question about how could Khojas, Cutchi Memons North West Frontier Province and North Malabar Muslims be compelled to give up their personal law and come under the Shariat was neatly sidestepped. The mutated law was still immutable. Even Hindus were declared to have religion that dealt inseparably with personal law. Less logic and more desperate determination were on display.

---

[21]*Ibid.*, p. 722.
[22]*Ibid.*

Mr. Ismail Sahib insisted that under its treaty obligations, Turkey had agreed to allow minorities to have their family law and personal law. As to Egypt—"whatever the minorities wanted...in fact more than what they wanted has been granted to them. And if the personal law had also been a matter in which they wanted certain privileges, that would also have been granted."[23]

In other words, Egypt did not have a separate personal law for its minorities. The rest was a matter of conjecture.

It may be noted that both in the debate on uniform civil code and on Fundamental Rights, Muslim members claimed to speak on behalf of other minorities who were present in the House, but elected from general constituencies—and of Hindus. None of them supported the Muslim speakers, nor even the Sikhs who had separate representation. If anything, there was opposition from the rest of the House. Amongst them was Mr. Tajamul Husain (Bihar: Muslim) who was most vocal in his support of secularisation of the State and separation of the State from religion. It may well be remembered that the three members who wanted a uniform civil code to be a fundamental right were Mr. Minoo Masani, a Parsi, Rajkumari Amrit Kaur, a Christian convert from the Royal House of Patiala, and Mrs. Hansa Mehta, a Hindu. It has to also be admitted that no one put up a vigorous opposition to these and similar views and demands, as should have been done. Perhaps, confident that they could direct the vote with their sheer numerical strength, the Congress Party as well as others who were opposed to encroachment by religion on areas secular did not consider it necessary to take the debate to its conclusion. Had they seen the shape of things to come, they might well have done so. But no one could be expected to look ahead to times 30 or 40 years away!

This conjecture of the possible reason for silence from the Congress benches is not a figment of this author's imagination. Time and again members of other parties were driven to complain of what can at best be described as highhanded or autocratic behaviour of the Congress members. Two instances of it are given in Appendix I.

Ismail Sahib also moved a new clause (7) which read—"Nothing in clauses (2) to (6) of this article shall affect the right guaranteed subclause (h) of clause (1) of this article."[24]

Of clause (7) Mr. Ismail Sahib said,

> This is consequential. The personal law is presumed to be guaranteed by the previous amendment, that is the new subclause (h) to

---

[23]*Ibid.*, p. 723.
[24]*Ibid.*

clause (1) of article 13 and this clause (7) seeks to preclude law as a result of clauses (2) to (6).[25]

Mr. Ismail Sahib did not elaborate on the proposed clause (7). He shifted back to subclause (i) of which he said,

> This had nothing to do with the minority or the majority. It concerns itself with the right of every citizen. Personal liberty is the core of the whole freedom....But here, Sir, in this bulky Constitution this question of personal liberty is left almost as an orphan. Only one mention is made of personal liberty, i.e. in article 15, and it is left there, it is left to be taken care of by "procedure established by law." I do not here enter into the controversy whether it should be by "due process of law" or by "procedure established by law." But what I want to say is that only a mention has been made in the Constitution with regard to personal liberty.[26]

As Mr. C. Subrananiam was quick to point out, questions of personal liberty come under article 15 (later renumbered 21). The intention however seems to have been to link personal law with personal liberty and in the unexceptional company of the former to get the latter into article 13. Clauses (8) and (9) which were then moved by Ismail Saheb confirm this feeling. Clause (8) is identical with clause (7) except that it refers to subclause (i). Clause (9) lays down that no existing law which affects adversely the right guaranteed by subclause (i) to clause (1) of article 13 shall operate and no new law which does the same shall be passed by the Parliament after the Constitution comes into effect. Mr. Ismail said that they were consequential amendments.[27]

It must be mentioned that Professor K.T. Shah moved a similar amendment to protect life and liberty of the individual and to guarantee that no person should be deprived of either except with due process, nor be denied equality before the law or equal protection of the laws.[28]

Given that draft article 8 (which became article 14) guarantees equality before the law as well as equal protection of the laws, the second half of the proposed amendment was redundant. And, as had already been pointed out, article 15 (later 21) dealt with the first part of it. However, Professor Shah placed

---

[25] *Ibid.*

[26] *Ibid.*, p. 723.

[27] *Ibid.*, p. 725.

[28] *Ibid.*, p. 726.

his amendment in a prominent place at the very beginning of article 13 and in a separate clause.

Reverting to the amendments to article 13 to protect personal laws, we find Mr. Karimuddin taking a more strident attitude. He said,

> The people outside and the Members of the Constituent Assembly must realise that there is not a single Muslim in this country—at least I have not seen one—who wants a change in the mandatory provisions of religious rights and personal laws, and if there is one who wants a change in the mandatory principles or religion as a matter of personal law, then he cannot be a Muslim.[29]

He therefore defined his terms and got the answers he wanted! This kind of thinking or argument, as one discovers on successive occasions, right up to the debate on the Muslim Women (Protection of Rights on Divorce) Act, was not peculiar to Mr. Karimuddin. He then continued,

> If you really want to protect the minorities because this is a secular State it does not mean that people should have no religion—if this is the view of the minority Muslims or any other minority that they want to abide by their personal law, those laws have to be protected.[30]

When Maulana Hasrat Mohani, a very senior member of the House was recognised soon thereafter, he was greeted with loud cheers. The Vice President remarked graciously that he was "glad the House recognises the excellent services rendered by Maulana Hasrat Mohani to this country. He was the first to stand for total independence of our Motherland."[31]

The loud cheers however soon turned to something else and the Chair had to restore order in the House. Speaking on Mr. Ismail Sahib's amendment to protect personal law under article 13, the old gentleman said,

> I would like to say that any party, political or communal, has no right to interfere in the personal law of any group. More particularly I say this regarding Muslims. There are three fundamentals in their personal law, namely religion, language and culture which have not been ordained by any human agency. Their personal law regarding

---

[29]*Ibid.*, p. 756.
[30]*Ibid.*, p. 757.
[31]*Ibid.*, p. 758.

divorce, marriage and inheritance has been derived from the Koran and its interpretation has been recorded therein. If there is anyone who thinks that he can interfere in the personal law of the Muslims, then I would say to him that the result will be very harmful. (Vice President: Order, order!) He should remain convinced—and I declare in the House—that Mussulmans will never submit to any interference in their personal law and they will have to face an iron wall of Muslim determination to oppose them in every way.[32]

Order was again restored by requesting members to resume their seats. Mr. Mohani was not given any reprimand for literally threatening the House. In the speeches of all three distinguished members one certainly senses an iron-clad determination to keep their personal law untouched. This determination or will is not, however, expressed in ways that are rational or supported by facts. Thus Mr. Ismail Sahib while admitting that Muslim law has not been observed by all Muslims even in India, insists that it is immutable for those who follow it—and therefore immutable for all is implicit in the conclusion, how else could he justify putting it under Art. 13?

Mr. Karimuddin states that he does not know one Muslim in the whole of India who is willing to accept a change in his personal law. He follows up this statement by asserting that should there be one such, then he is not a Muslim!

Mr. Mohani's statements fall even shorter of logic and even facts. He begins by saying that the three fundamentals of personal law are religion, language and culture. It is a little difficult to follow what he means by "fundamentals of." Grammatically it would imply that religion, language and culture are subsumed under personal law. But on their own showing this cannot be; other Muslim speakers have been claiming protection for personal law because it is part of religion. Personal law is subsumed under the general heading of religion, and not the other way round. The argument for culture and language as fundamentals of religion is even weaker. With any religion that is practiced worldwide as indeed both Islam and Christianity are, the language and cultures of their adherents vary enormously. Even in India this was the case.* The birth of Bangladesh was triggered by attempts to force the Bengali speaking East Pakistanis to accept Urdu as the national language.

Admittedly, the irrational or the emotional argument cannot be always countered conclusively. The solution perhaps lies in making general statements regarding policies to be followed and the over-all directions to be adopted by the polity. This was not done. Every opportunity to clarify what sort of State was envisaged by the framers of the Constitution was allowed to slip by. The

---

[32]*Ibid.*, p. 759.

Congress Party relied heavily on its majority to steer the Constitution their way, leaving confusion and misunderstanding in their wake. The easy way thus eventually proved to be the hard way.

As may be expected, there was a great deal of debate on Art. 19 which guaranteed Freedom of Religion. On the one hand there were many proponents of secularism. On the other was Mr. Ismail Sahib who made one more effort to secure total immunity from interference by the State for his personal law. In between was Mr. Loknath Misra, who was unhappy because he felt that Hinduism was getting a bad deal in its own land.[33]

For quite different reasons both Mr. Tajamul Husain and Mr. Misra wanted the right to propagate one's religion to be deleted. Mr. Misra felt that it had led up to partition of India and had been similarly misused by the Christians for political ends. He said, let people propagate their religion but do not make it a fundamental right.[34]

Mr. Tajamul Husain's reasons were quite opposite. He wanted the above words to be replaced with "and practice religion privately." He explained "I submit sir, that this is a secular State and a secular State should not have anything to do with religion. So I would request you to leave me alone to practice and profess my own religion privately."[35]

Because their reasons were different the two members disagreed in their amendments to expl. (I) of Art. 19. Mr. Misra wanted the permission given to Sikhs to wear the Kirpan to be extended to all others who had visible signs of religion.[36] Mr. Husain wanted it to be deleted and replaced with a new provision forbidding even dress and names which disclosed the religion of that person.[37] None of these amendments were adopted.

Thinking on very different lines, Mr. Ismail Sahib moved that a new clause (3) be inserted after Art. 19 (2) which would read "(3) nothing in the clause (2) of Article 19 of this article should affect the right of any citizen to follow the personal law of the group or the community to which he belongs or professes to belong."[38]

Earlier, he had explained his reasons for moving his amendment: Art. 19 (2) (a) allowed the State to regulate or restrict secular activities associated with religious practice.

---

[33] *Ibid.*, p. 823.

[34] *Ibid.*, p. 824.

[35] *Ibid.*, p. 818.

[36] *Ibid.*, p. 822.

[37] *Ibid.*, p. 818.

[38] *Ibid.*, p. 830.

> this practice of personal law may, by a stretch of imagination be brought under the secular activities associated with religion. Therefore I propose to make it clear that so far as personal law is concerned, this article shall not affect the observance thereof by the people concerned.[39]

This amendment was also negatived, again without any debate.

Art. 19 (later renumbered Art. 25) is of peculiar interest to us as it is for the first time that the Constitution used the word "secular." Art. 25 clause (2) (a) contains the first mention of this word. It reads:

> (2) nothing in this article shall affect the operation of any existing law or prevent the State from making any law.
> (a) regulating or restricting any economic, financial, political or *other secular activity* which may be associated with religious practice. (*emphasis added*)

It is thus evident that the framers of the Constitution did not consider all activities connected with a religious practice to be religious, and therefore protected by the freedom of religion guaranteed by Art. 25. Instead, they distinguished between religious practice and secular activities associated with it, but not an integral part of it.

Subclause (b) of Art. 25 clause (2) puts this proviso to good use immediately; read with clause (2) it declares

> (2) nothing in this article shall affect the operation of any existing law or prevent the State from making any law
> (b) providing for social welfare or reform or the *throwing open of Hindu religious places of a public character to all classes and sections of Hindus*. (*emphasis added*)

Social welfare and reform are general concepts open to wide range of interpretations and applicable to all religions. The throwing open of Hindu religious places of public character to all Hindus is a specific reform. Instead of leaving it to the Parliament the Constitution made it almost binding on the latter to enact this reform.

It is also to be noted that Art. 17 which abolished untouchability in no uncertain terms comes before the cluster of articles on Freedom of Religion. It is

---

[39]*Ibid.*, p. 829.

part of the Right to Equality guaranteed by the Constitution. Its abolition was clearly not seen as interference with the right to profess or practice any religion. No one, least of all this author, would dispute the absolute and urgent necessity to abolish the practice of untouchability. Its abolition was necessary for the health of Hinduism, and also for the polity which has benefitted demonstrably from the contribution of those who had been hitherto denied access to every opportunity. Indeed Dr. Ambedkar, that able jurist and draftsman, is a distinguished and poignant example of men and women who had been stamped with the searing brand of untouchability. Nevertheless, it would require a bold person to say that untouchability was not a Hindu religious practice. Fortunately Dr. Ambedkar and his colleagues on the drafting committee as well as in the Constituent Assembly did possess that boldness.

Thus, even while guaranteeing Freedom of Religion, the framers of the Constitution took care to put one of those practices under the Right to Equality (as being counter to it) and therefore abolished it. Secondly, they made it quite clear that there was no indiscriminate or uncritical permission to practice one's religion regardless of social needs, and that there was a distinction between religious practice and secular activities associated with it. The latter were not exempt from State intervention in the name of freedom of religion. How far members such as Mr. Ismail Sahib and others who thought like him accepted this perception is a different matter.

Keen debate also took place over provisions regarding freedom of attendance at religious instruction or worship at certain educational institutions (article 22) and the cultural and educational rights of the minorities (articles 23–24).

Mr. Ismail Sahib was opposed to this ban on religious education in State schools. He proposed another article 22 to substitute for it. It said,

> No person attending an educational institution maintained, aided or recognised by the State shall be required to take part in any religious instruction in such institution without the consent of such person if he or she is major or without the consent of the respective parent or guardian if he or she is a minor.[40]

Mr. Ismail Sahib explained his amendment:
> It will not be necessary for a secular State to ban religious education in State institutions. Sir, it will not be in contravention of the neutrality or the secular nature of the State to impart religious instruction. It will be going against the spirit of the secular State if

---

[40]*Ibid.*, p. 866.

> the State compels the students or pupils to study a religion to which they do not belong. But, if the pupils or their parents want that religious instruction should be given in institutions of their own religion, then it is not going against the secular nature of the State.[41]

The word secular appears three times in this short paragraph.

Mr. Shibban Lal Saxena was on the same line of thinking as Mr. Ismail Sahib, as the amendment he proposed indicated. Mr. Saxena moved a new article 22 to read:

> The State shall not compel anyone to have religious instruction in a religion not his own in schools against his wishes, but the State shall endeavour to develop religious tolerance and morality amongst its citizens by providing suitable courses in various religions in schools.[42]

Mr. Saxena explained that he was concerned that article 22 would deprive the majority community of its right to impart religious instruction to its children in school. He was keen that this right should also be extended to children of the minority community, where they were present in large enough numbers. While protecting the minorities from compulsion of attending religious instruction of the majority, he felt that religious instruction should not be banned per se.[43] To be fair to him, he did not utter the word secular in explaining his amendment.

Mr. Tajamul Husain wanted no religious instruction to be given in any school. He introduced an amendment which would cause article 22 (I) to read: "No religious instruction shall be provided in any educational institution."[44] Mr. Husain could also support his amendment, diametrically opposed though it was to Mr. Ismail Sahib's, by a reference to the secular nature of the Indian State. "What is the use of calling India a secular State," he asked, "if you allow religious instruction to be imparted to young boys and girls? By this article you do not prevent if parents want to give religious instruction to their children. But they are at liberty to do so at home and nobody will object to it."[45]

---

[41]*Ibid.*, p. 860.
[42]*Ibid.*, p. 867.
[43]*Ibid.*
[44]*Ibid.*, p. 871.
[45]*Ibid.*, p. 871.

Professor K. T. Shah's amendment was that the words "wholly" should be followed by "partly" so that religious instruction should not be given in schools maintained wholly or partly out of State funds.[46] The words "by the State" were deleted[47] at the instance of Dr. Ambedkar, who moved the amendment.[48]

Article 22 (1) thus read: "No religious instruction shall be provided in any educational institution wholly maintained out of State funds." This is how it stands in the constitution, renumbered Art. 28. (1) Art. 22 had a clause (3) which said:

> Nothing in this article shall prevent any community or denomination from providing religious instructions for pupils of that community or denomination in an educational institution outside its working hours.[49]

Mr. Ismail Sahib wanted an amendment to this clause to insert the words "or in" after "outside" thus permitting religious instruction to be given both during as well as after school hours, on the grounds of practicability, and also what looks like the secular nature of the State.

> Sir, only if religious instruction is allowed to be given in public State owned institutions where people will compete with each other to show the best of their religions to the world and thereby (sic) undesirable rivalries, competitions, bickering and heart-burnings will really be eliminated.[50]

He continued

> Once again I want to stress the fact that it is in the interest of the State to give a grounding to children in religion. What is wanted for the stability of society as well as the State is moral grounding, moral background, and the only way to give this moral background is through religion.[51]

---

[46]*Ibid.*, p. 868.
[47]*Ibid.*, p. 887.
[48]*Ibid.*, p. 871.
[49]*Ibid.*, p. 875.
[50]*Ibid.*, p. 876.
[51]*Ibid.*

Mr. H. V. Kamath had a third point of view. He argued that recognition of minority institutions should not be withdrawn if they made attendance at religious instruction compulsory as would be the consequence of clause (2) of Article 22. Mr. Kamath was quick to point out that clause (2) laid down that no person attending an institution recognized by the State or receiving aid out of State funds shall be required to take part in religious instruction. At the same time, Arts. 23–24 allowed the minorities to establish and maintain their own educational institutions. Was it intended that they should not be allowed to give religious instruction? Mr. Kamath felt that while aid may be made conditional, recognition should not be. If recognition was denied the schools would not flourish. He argued that, under Arts. 23 and 24, minority institutions had the right to make religious instruction compulsory.[52] This was yet another interpretation of the obligation of the secular State.

Mr. Jaspat Roy Kapoor pointed out that clause 3 of Art. 22 was not in consonance with clause (1) of the same article, and should be deleted.[53] This amendment was adopted. A fresh clause (3) was introduced, which came close to Mr. Ismail Sahib's substitute for article 22. It stands as Art. 28(3) in the constitution. It reads:

> 28(3) No person attending any educational institution recognised by the State or receiving aid out of State funds shall be required to take part in any religious instruction that may be imparted in such institution or to attend any religious worship that may be conducted in such institution or in any premises attached thereto unless such person, or if such person is a minor, his guardian has given his consent thereto.

The debate on all these articles should make one fact evident. There was no clear understanding, no agreement, on how the words secular or secular State were to be used in the context of the Indian Constitution. This most basic and vitally important concept had received too little attention from the jurists and constitutional experts who had drafted the Constitution. The thought that India would be a secular State was clearly implicit in the constitutional proceedings and debates and indeed outside the House. But it was not spelt out in detail.

One notable exception was Professor K. T. Shah who moved an amendment to Article 1 of the Constitution. He proposed that it should read "India shall be a secular federal socialist union of states." He expounded his reasons for this amendment at some length. On the proposed insertion of the word secular he said

---

[52] *Ibid.*, p. 873.
[53] *Ibid.*, p. 874.

...as regards the secular character of the State, we have been told time and again from every platform that ours is a secular State. If that is true,...I do not see why the term could not be added or inserted in the Constitution itself...to guard against any possibility of misunderstanding or misapprehension. The term 'secular' I agree, does not find place necessarily in Constitutions on which ours seems to have been modelled. But every constitution is framed in the background of the people concerned....

The secularity of the State must be stressed in view not only of the unhappy experiences we had last year and in the years before and the excesses to which in the name of religion, communalism or sectarianism can go, but I intend also to emphasise by this description the character and nature of the State which we are constituting today, which would ensure to all its people, in all its dealings between man and man and dealings between citizens and government the consideration that will actuate will be the objective realities of the situation...no extraneous consideration or authority will be allowed to interfere, so that the relations between man and man, the relation of the citizen to the State...may not be influenced by those other considerations which will result in injury or inequality between several citizens.[54]

Undoubtedly the speech leaves much to be desired, but it was a beginning. Its suggestion was not debated. Dr. Ambedkar discussed one other amendment suggested by Prof. Shah, viz. insertion of the word socialist and at the end he rejected the entire amendment. The congress Party followed his direction. An opportunity to debate the basic concept of secularism was lost.

The American model of secularism which demanded strict separation of State and religion was obviously not going to serve India.[55] But what did the Indian model signify? What did equal treatment or respect for all religions imply in concrete situations? The Constitution was silent on this vital point. Thus, when the time came to act upon the promises made in the Constitution, that document itself could provide no clear answers or even guidelines.

Part II

As we have seen in the first half of the paper, the relationship between religion and law and the place that the former could occupy in a secular state was

---

[54]*Ibid.*, p. 400.

[55]V.P. Luthera, *The Concept of the Secular State and India*, (Bombay, 1964), Chapter 12.

not clarified. Indeed, secular state or secularism were not concepts that were made clear during the very crucial Constituent Assembly Debates. The problems left unsolved, the statements that went unchallenged, made themselves felt barely a year after India celebrated her first Republic Day on 26th January, 1950 under the new Constitution of India.

In 1951 the Congress Government introduced the Hindu Code Bill. The Union Law Minister was Dr. B. R. Ambedkar and under his able guidance this Bill sought to make radical changes in the Hindu personal law, to wit, marriage, succession, adoption, guardianship and maintenance. The Hindu Code Bill met with bitter opposition from all quarters, including the Congress Party.[56] The debate on the Hindu Marriage Bill was opened by Mr. Naziruddin Ahmed, who had also represented the Muslims of West Bengal in the Constituent Assembly, and participated in the debates that centred round religion and personal law. Mr. Ahmed raised the objection that this Bill was violative of the Constitution and that it offended Art. 15 which said: "Art. 15(l) The State shall not discriminate against any citizen on grounds only of religion, race, caste, sex, place of birth or any of them."

Yet this law was being made for one community, thus discriminating between different religions.[57] However, Mr. Ahmed refuted the suggestion that instead of the Hindu Code Bill there should be a uniform or Common Civil Code.[58] He said that a law that was bad for Hindus could not be made good by being applied to all.[59] The reason it was bad for Hindus, apparently, was that it interfered with their personal law.[60]

The thrust of the debate, however, was evidently not so much that the Hindu Code Bill violated Art. 15(1) or even Art. 25(1), but that it went against Art. 44, which said that "The State shall endeavour to secure for all its citizens a uniform civil code throughout the territory of India."

The chief demand was that the Code should be made applicable to all Indian citizens. Members of the Hindu Maha Sabha did not further their cause by pleading that all citizens of Hindustan or India were Hindus.[61] But otherwise

---

[56]*Lok Sabha Debates*, Part 2, Vol. 8. 1951. Columns 2357–2555. Debate on the Hindu Marriage Bill as part of the Hindu Code Bill. All references till further mention are from this volume.

[57]Col. 2357.

[58]from several members. Cols. 2365, 2368, 2373, 2376, 2381, 2396, 2400. Some of them wanted an optional but comman code.

[59]Col. 2408.

[60]Cols. 2374, 2410.

[61]Col. 2373.

this demand was put forward with considerable force and a great deal of logic. It was pointed out that if polygamy was unjust to Hindu women, so was it to Muslim women. If it was to be abolished for the Hindus, the same should be done for Muslims.[62] If the Hindu law of inheritance and succession was to be changed to give property rights to women because of the claims of fair play, justice and equity, then, the new law "should be made applicable not only to Hindus but to all citizens who happen to be within our jurisdiction and for whom we can legislate."[63]

It was pointed out that the Hindu Code would not further Art. 44 "(b) because this is not only not endeavouring to secure for the citizens a uniform civil code but trying to enact a different code for a section of the people."[64]

It was also pointed out that a law for Hindus alone could be challenged in courts as violative of Art. 15(1). The Bombay Hindu Bigamous Marriages Act had in fact been declared *ultra vires* because it interfered with the personal law of the Hindus.[65]

If a uniform code could not be enacted, asked some, because it would interfere with the religion of the Muslims, then how was this Code not an interference with the religion of the Hindus? Shyamanandan Sahaya put the situation into words with clarity and economy. Either the reform was a social reform, and in that case the Law Minister could not talk of the religious susceptibilities of the minorities or it was a religious reform, and in a secular state it had no place.[66]

Some members tried to reach a compromise by suggesting that the Hindu Code should be optional in its application. Every citizen who was a major (or on attaining majority) should be allowed to choose to be governed by the Code. Otherwise he would remain under his personal law. The suggestion thus was for a uniform but voluntary code, to run along side of all the personal laws, with the option of choosing to be governed by the Code. If no choice was made the person would remain under his or her personal law.

Another suggestion was that state governments in their legislatures should have discretionary powers to decide to which class of persons the code would be extended and when it should come into force.[67] But this proviso would

---

[62]Col. 2386.

[63]Col. 2375.

[64]Col. 2400.

[65]*Narsu Appa Mali*. This judgment of the District Court was reversed by the High Court in ILR (1951) Bom 775.

[66]Cols. 2384, 2386, 2489–90.

[67]Col. 2367.

still restrict the Act to Hindus, as the main feature of the Code would remain a law for Hindus.

When Dr. Ambedkar replied to some of these suggestions he claimed to be surprised that those who had been against the Hindu Code should have started asking for a uniform code. He did not believe that the leopard was changing its spots. If they wanted a civil code, he asked, did they think that it would take very long to have it? His surmise was that this was exactly what they thought—it had taken five years for the Hindu Code to be drafted, so it would take ten years for the uniform civil code. "I would like to tell them that the common code is there. If they want it, it can be placed before the House in half an hour."[68]

Needless to say, this bluster convinced no-one. Despite repeated invitations or challenges from those who opposed the Code to produce his common code, Dr. Ambedkar did not do so. Although he said that the Special Marriage Act and the Indian Succession Act were the embryonic Civil Code needing minor alterations, the Law Minister did not fulfil his promise or his threat. Instead, he accused those who asked for it of being ignorant, and foolish, not realising the sentiments of different communities.[69] Here Dr. Ambedkar went back to the concept of secular state.

> It is all very good to say that we have proposed in our Constitution a secular State. I have no idea whether the Members, when they use the word secular State really mean what the Constitution is intended to mean. It does not mean that we can abolish religion; it does not mean that we shall not take into account the religious sentiments of the people. All that a secular State means is that this Parliament shall not be competent to impose any particular religion upon the rest of the people.... We are not here to flout the sentiments of the people.[70]

As one member interjected, he was doing it—to the Hindus. Mr. Ananthashayanam Ayyangar charged Dr. Ambedkar with forcing Hindus to change their religion overnight. The Special Marriage Act already permitted Hindus to opt out of the ancient law. "What more is necessary? Now you want to convert these people who follow the ancient law at the point of bayonet to your way of thinking. Why do you want me to change my religion?"[71] Another member

---

[68]Col. 2465.
[69]Col. 2466.
[70]Col. 2466.
[71]Col. 2519.

congratulated Dr. Ambedkar with unconcealed sarcasm for inventing a new religion.[72]

Dr. Ambedkar was assured by several members that if they were opposed to the Code it was because it was only for Hindus. If it were made a common code many of the objections would be withdrawn.[73] Mr. Shyamanandan Sahaya was even more blunt in admonishing the Law Minister.

> There is no use saying that such of our friends here who advocate the passing of a civil code do not really want it. Pardon me for saying so, but let me assure the Hon. Law Minister that it is not so. The feeling is that if you want to put the whole country on a certain basis even if it meant some sacrifice, do so, and we will gladly accept it. But you pick and choose and single out one community who perhaps would not be prepared to fight with you on that issue. If you pick out that community and do what you like with it, and the rest say "Don't touch our religious susceptibilities" then that is where the real difficulty arises.[74]

The Law Minister came under heavy criticism for his unwillingness to seek a mandate from the people for his Code; the General Elections were due next year. Several members accused him of rushing the Code through because he knew that the people were not in favour of it.[75] Dr. Ambedkar had drawn this accusation on his head by dismissing this time the entire electorate as ignorant![76] Nor was Dr. Ambedkar prepared to make the Code optional. He thundered,

> I want to make this statement that I should never agree to exempt any province from the operation of this law. Let there be no doubt about it at all that the Hindu Code shall be a uniform code throughout India. Either I will have that Bill in that form or not at all.[77]

---

[72]Col. 2491.
[73]Col. 2510.
[74]Col. 2496.
[75]Cols. 2501, 2511.
[76]Col. 2467.
[77]Col. 2472.

Women, Children and the Constitution

These were prophetic words. Dr. Ambedkar had to settle for the second option because he could not carry his own party with him.

With hindsight, it is quite clear that the code could not have been voluntary. It would not only have meant enormous paper work and administration; in an illiterate country it would have been a dead letter, serving only to confuse. The Government failed, not in their perception of what social justice demanded, but in restricting it to one community, and most important, in not taking the House into their confidence. This they could certainly have done over the need to enact a compulsory code. There was, however, no way they could explain why the Code was to be for Hindus only.

The Hindu code made its reappearance in December 1952, in the Rajya Sabha, when the first parliament met. So did all the arguments that had been raised against it and all the replies that the Government had mustered against the objections.[78] The Law Minister Mr. H. V. Pataskar did not shed any better light on the subject than his equally distinguished predecessor had done.

In 1955, when Mr. Pataskar opened the second reading of the Hindu Marriage Bill with a brief history of this legislation, he was stopped in his tracks by a single question by Acharya Kriplani, a veteran Congress member and freedom fighter, who could not be dismissed as being communal. Kriplani asked, whom did the Law Minister represent? Did he represent the Hindus or did he represent the people of India?[79] Mr. Pataskar was too shrewd not to know where this was leading. His reply clearly indicated this, though it could not save him. The Law Minister said,

> I represent the people of India. I do not claim to represent here the Hindus. On the contrary, I was trying to make out that there was nothing like a Hindu 200 years ago in this land. It is only when the British administration was introduced that this term came in. I might for the information of the members say this. The Indian Succession Act was passed. If it was Indian, to whom it was made applicable; to all Indians or at any rate majority of the Indian people. But they, that is, the British did not want to make it applicable to the majority of the people who were either Hindus or Muslims. It is called the Indian Succession Act; it only applied to Christians because the

---

[78]*Lok Sabha Debates*, Part 2 Vol. 4, 1955. 2nd and 3rd readings. 26 and 29 April, 1955 and 2, 3, 4, 5, May, 1955. The HMA was passed by the Lok Sabha on 5 May, 1955, having already been passed by the Rajya Sabha before the second reading commenced in the lower house. All references below are to this volume, unless specifically mentioned to be otherwise.

[79]Col. 6483.

> Government was Christian. That is a different matter. Except the Hindus and the Muslims all the rest were Indians in the eyes of the British. In regard to Hindus and Muslims they did not want to interfere so far as marriage, succession etc. were concerned. Therefore I say that I represent the Indians and what I am trying to do is in the interest of Indians.[80]

An extraordinary speech in which no two sentences formed a logical sequence, with an even more extraordinary conclusion for anyone, least of all the Law Minister for the Government of India. It naturally provoked the logical retort from two members. Why a *Hindu* Marriage Act—why not an *Indian* Marriage Act?

But this retort proved to be a life line for the Law Minister, who had been floundering in a morass of his own making. For at least one of the objectors was a member of the Hindu Maha Sabha. With dignity, though still without any logic, the Law Minister replied, "I am aware that they raise these objections not from the point of view of doing something for Indians; but they are trying to persist in the separation of Hindus and Muslims from others which was the result of foreign administration."[81]

The opponents of the Hindu Marriage Act made several unacceptable points—for example they feared it would lead to immorality by permitting divorce. The advocates of it made several good points—for example Mr. Pataskar pointed out that the eighty percent of the Hindu population had permitted divorce, so it was not that much against Hindu law. But the fact remained that the Government could not justify making a separate code for Hindus. It was also clear that they intended to do so on the strength of their majority. Acharya Kriplani said as much at the conclusion of the debate. He remarked that both sides had quoted the scriptures, so had the Law Minister.

> We call our State a secular State. A secular State goes neither by scripture nor by custom. It must work on sociological and political grounds. If we are a democratic state, I submit we must make laws not for one community alone. Today the Hindu community is not as much prepared for divorce as the Muslim community is for monogamy....Will our Government introduce a Bill for monogamy for the Muslim community? Will my dear Law Minister apply the part about monogamy to every community in India?...I tell you this is the democratic way. It is not the Mahasabhaites alone who are

---

[80]Col. 6483.

[81]Col. 6483.

communal; it is the Government also that is communal, whatever it may say. It is passing a communal measure. You shall be known by your acts not by your profession. You have deluded the world so often with words. I charge you with communalism because you are bringing forward a law about monogamy only for the Hindu community. You must bring it also for the Muslim community...the Muslim community is prepared to have it but you are not brave enough to do it.[82]

But the Government had made up its mind long ago. Both in 1951 and 1955 objections were raised to the various bills which made up the Hindu code, which were seen as interference with Hindu religion and Hindu personal law which regarded marriage as a sacrament and an indissoluble union. In 1951 one member had even asserted that "the very basis of the Hindu religion is the caste system and secondly the particular way in which marriage is held. It is held to be sacramental and therefore it is held to be indissoluble....But one by one these fundamentals are being removed."[83] Another objection to the imposition of monogamy and introduction of divorce in the Hindu law was that Hindu society was not ready for it.[84]

The Government made no effort to refute these objections. It simply went ahead. These objections were important because they were to surface yet again when various legislations which came under the Uniform Civil code were debated in the future. Modern Indian legal history is full of such instances of deja vu. And even more interesting is the fact that the Government response to them was to be markedly different from what it had been to the Hindu Code Bills, because this time the objections came from non-Hindus.

One cannot close this subject without referring to the constant insinuations by the Government that all those who objected to the Hindu Code were reactionaries. The Anti Untouchability Act was also passed in 1955, even as the Hindu Marriage Bill was being debated furiously. There was not *one* voice in support of untouchability,[85] not even from those who had claimed a fundamental status for the caste system in Hindu religion. Perhaps the insinuations were not entirely correct; perhaps they were a handy instrument for a government who did not know how else to defend their irrational policy. As Kriplani said—the Government was being just as communal as anyone else.

---

[82] Col. 7375.

[83] *Lock Sabha Debates*, Part II Vol. 8. 1951. Col. 2374.

[84] *Ibid.*, Part II Vol. 8. 1951. Cols. 2491–6, 2518. *Ibid.*, Part II Vol. 4. 1955. Cols. 6483, 6513, 6854.

[85] *Ibid.*, Part II Vol. 4. 1955. debated and adopted on 28 April, 1955.

Whether it was that, or the lack of courage, or any other reason, over the Hindu code legislations the Government surely ignored the Constitution they themselves had virtually drafted. For the first time, the Constitution was a hostage to religion and ignored by the law-makers. It was not to be the last time.

In 1946, even before independence, the Bombay State Government had enacted Bombay Hindu Bigamous Marriages Act. In 1951, *Narsu Appa Mali* came up before the division bench of Chagla C.J. and Gajendragadkar J.[86] The petitioner had married bigamously, and had been taken to court.

Narsu Appa challenged the validity of the Bombay Act [BHBMA] on the ground that it was *ultra vires* Art. 25(l). For Hindus it was a religious necessity to have a son, a sacred duty for spiritual benefit. Polygamy was based on this requirement. He argued that the Act was also *ultra vires* Arts. 14 and 15(l) of the Constitution, to wit, the right to equality and the right to protection against discrimination on grounds of religion. Narsu Appa Mali had been successful in the district court, where the BHBMA had been declared *ultra vires* the Constitution.

In his judgment, Chagla C. J. reversed the lower courts decision. He rightly drew "a sharp distinction between...religious faith and belief and religious practices."[87] The State protected the former. Where the latter went against public order, morality or health or "a policy of social reform upon which the State had embarked then the religious practice must give way."[88] Thus the BHBMA did not contravene Art. 25(1). It was protected by Art. 25(2)(b), as a measure of social reform.

But what of Arts. 14 and 15(1)? Here the court were clearly not easy in their minds. Chagla C. J. conceded that Muslims had been left out, though they also permitted and practised polygamy. But the learned judge said that there was a reasonable basis for it. It was a historical fact that Muslims and Hindus had separate religious laws based on their religious texts. "Article 44 itself recognises separate and distinctive personal laws because it lays down as a directive to be achieved that within a measurable time India should enjoy a Uniform Civil Code."[89] Thus Art. 44 was made to do duty to justify the enactment of a law for one particular community, which is surely the exact opposite of its intention.

One can quite see that court was not inclined to throw out a legislation that was very much in keeping with social justice. Until the Hindu Marriage Act became law in 1955 this author remembers women from areas adjacent to Bombay State, envying the Hindu women who resided in that state because of the

---

[86] *Narsu Appa Mali* v. *the State of Bombay*, ILR [1951] Bom. 775.

[87] *Ibid.*, 778.

[88] *Ibid.*

[89] *Ibid.*, 781.

special protection they had against polygamy, and the right to divorce that they could exercise. But by validating the BHBMA the learned judges perhaps did a greater and graver wrong. The subordinate courts judgment had been cited during the debates on the Hindu Code in 1951. Had the Bombay High Court upheld it, the threat of having a whole Code declared *ultra vires* the Constitution might have compelled the Government to consider the Uniform Civil Code seriously. In 1949 Bombay State had passed another act, called the Bombay Excommunication Act, by which it became illegal to excommunicate anyone. The Syedna or High Priest of the Dawoodi Bohra community had excommunicated two followers of this sect, one in 1934, the other in 1948. They challenged the excommunication as being in contravention of the Bombay Excommunication Act [BEA]. This case was heard first by a single judge and then by a division bench of the Bombay High Court, presided over by Chagla C. J. sitting with Bhagwati J.

In this case, *Syedna Taher Saifuddin* vs *Tyabbhai Mousaji* and another[90] Chagla C. J. discussed the meaning of excommunication. It did not mean throwing a person out of his community to which the person continued to belong.

> What the act of expulsion or excommunication does was to deprive him of certain rights and privileges, and the legislature felt that in the spirit of changing times it was not proper that any member of any community should be deprived of his rights and privileges— excommunication does not merely refer to the point of time when the person is expelled from the community but it refers to a continuing state during which (the person) is deprived of his rights and privileges.[91]

Under this interpretation excommunication was invalid under the Act of 1949, because its consequences continued after that date, when the Act came into force.

The Court also held that the BEA was protected under Art. 25(2) (a) which permitted the state to undertake social reform. In arriving at this conclusion Chagla C.J. referred to other judgments of his court, *Narsu Appa*, and *Emperor* v *Kalidas Amtharam*.[92] In the latter the Harijan Act of Bombay State which outlawed untouchability had been challenged. In all three cases the object of legislation was held to be social reform and if the removal of social disabilities required the creation of a new offence, then the legislature was legally empowered to do so.

---

[90] AIR 1953 Bom 183.

[91] *Ibid.*, para 10.

[92] AIR 1949 Bom 168.

Art. 26(b) which gives freedom to every religious denomination "to manage its own affairs in the matters of religion" was also invoked by the petitioner. The Court found that this Article had not been infringed or violated by BEA. It held: "when a religious denomination seeks to deprive a member of his legal rights and privileges, it is doing much more than managing its own affairs."[93] The learned judge went even further.

> Religion has nothing whatever to do with the right of excommunication or expulsion. As we have said earlier while referring to Art. 25, it is more a question of religious practice than a matter of religious faith or belief.[94]

Full nine years later the Syedna's appeal was heard by the Supreme Court, sitting in a full bench. In one of the most unfortunate judgments ever to be given by that Court four judges out of five found in favour of the Petitioner and his right to excommunicate members of his sect.

Another bizarre aspect of *Saifuddin Saheb* v *the State of Bombay*[95] was the fact that this case was argued for the petitioner by Mr. K.M. Munshi, who had been such a staunch champion in the Constituent Assembly of the article on uniform civil code. Writing for the majority of the judges[96] Das Gupta J. said

> The excommunication of a member of a community will affect many of his civil rights as is undoubtedly true.... The right given under Art. 26(b) has not however been made subject to the preservation of civil rights. The express limitation in Art. 26 itself is that this right....will exist subject to public order, morality and health.[97]

The learned judge concluded,

> ...the fact that the civil rights of a person is affected by the exercise of this fundamental right under Art. 26(b) is therefore of no con-

---

[93] AIR 1953 Bom 183 at para 18.

[94] *Ibid.*, para 18.

[95] AIR 1962 SC 853.

[96] Justice Das Gupta wrote the judgment on behalf of himself and two brother judges. Ayyangar J. wrote a separate but concurring judgment. Sinha J. dissented.

[97] AIR 1962 SC 853 para 41.

sequence. Nor is it possible to say that excommunication was prejudicial to public order, morality and health.[98]

Das Gupta J. went on to say,

> The mere fact that certain civil rights which might be lost by members of the Dawoodi Bohra community as a result of excommunication even though made on religious grounds and that the Act prevents such loss does not offer sufficient basis for a conclusion that it is a law providing for social welfare and reform.[99]

Ayyangar J. who wrote a separate but concurring judgment said that "by the phrase laws providing for 'social welfare and reform' it was not intended to reform a religion out of existence or identity."[100]

That the Supreme Court of India would or indeed could put civil rights of a citizen second to his obligations as a member of a religion was a situation that would have been unimaginable until this judgment in Saifuddin Saheb. This is how far the Constitution had been brought from the priority it had given to the Right to Equality and the Right to protection against discrimination, to Justice, Liberty, Equality, Fraternity.

In 1972 the Government introduced the Indian Adoption Bill in the Rajya Sabha. Presenting the Bill the Union Minister for Law said that it was the first step towards the Uniform Civil Code. After it was passed there would be only one law of adoption throughout India for all citizens. Those sections of the Hindu Adoption and Maintenance Act which dealt with adoption would be repealed by the Indian Adoption Act.

This Bill was sent to a Joint Committee of both Houses. The Committee also interviewed a large number of distinguished citizens to elicit their views. Objections to the Bill were raised by Muslims and by members of scheduled tribes. The latter did not want property to go outside the tribe, so they wanted adoption to be from within the tribe. Nor did they want the child's name to be changed. They also found the compulsory requirement about registering the child's adoption to be onerous.

When it was put to them, however, that a universally applicable bill could not cope with so many variations or exceptions, the tribal spokesmen said

---

[98] *Ibid.*, para 42.
[99] *Ibid.*, para 44.
[100] *Ibid.*, para 64.

"In that case, let that be done which is best for the country."[101] The Muslim spokesmen objected on somewhat different grounds. They said that the Act, if passed, would allow Muslims to disobey the Quranic injunction against adoption. The practical difficulties were about inheritance and the number of persons one would not be able to marry. It was pointed out that no Muslim need ever adopt as the act was only an enabling legislation; the answer was that even "bad" Muslims should not be allowed to adopt, which the proposed legislation would permit. The Joint Committee asked some Muslim leaders why they had not objected to the Special Marriage Act when it was passed in 1954.[102] This time the reply was that they would have done so but no-one asked them for their views. The Joint Committee did not make the point that secular states are not required to compel anyone to follow his or her religion.

In August 1976 the Joint Committee made its report to the parliament, suggesting certain amendments. The most important one was to grant exemption to scheduled tribes from the application of the Act, unless notified in the state gazette for specified tribes.

The three Muslim members of the Joint Committee wrote a minute of dissent. They had recommended, they said, that Muslims should be omitted from the purview of the Act, but the Committee had rejected their amendment on four counts.

1. The Bill was in greater interests of children, and their welfare transcended religious barriers.
2. It did not compel Muslims to adopt.
3. It was not against the Quranic injunctions.
4. It was the first step towards the Uniform Civil Code.

The dissenting members felt that any change in the Muslim Personal Law would impair the secular character of the Constitution. One of them went even further. He declared:

> Muslims as a community should not have the option to get into or run away from the applicability of any of the provisions of the Muslim Personal Law, rather in our frame of society, there should be

---

[101]For detailed discussion see Vasudha Dhagamwar, *Towards the Uniform Civil Code* (Bombay, 1989), Chapter 2, pp. 7–18 passim.

[102]The Special Marriage Act 1872 was revised and re-enacted in 1954. One major change was that people marrying under it did not have to renounce their religion any more, as they had to do under the old Act, even when both of them belonged to the same religion. Both Acts allowed inter-religious marriage without conversion.

> no such law to give any community including the Muslims, a liberty of abandoning their personal law.

This dissenting note came from parliamentarians and Members of the Committee. It is painful to note that even they had failed to understand that a secular state cannot compel observance of religion.

An amusing consequence of the state following these guidelines for legislation would be to take away the right Christians had laboured hard to get, to wit, the right to propagate their religion. For the one who converts surely "runs away from" his or her religion!

The Adoption Bill died a quiet death when the Parliament was dissolved in March 1977. It may be recalled that June 1975-March 1977 were the years of Emergency for India. Even so the Adoption Bill was shelved.

A fresh Bill was introduced in the Lok Sabha on 16.12.1980. It was substantially different from the first one on the following points:

> It gave no exemption to Scheduled Tribes.
> It exempted the Muslims.
> It allowed the Hindu Adoption and Maintenance Act 1956 and other customs of adoption to coexist.

This bill was undoubtedly a step away from the Uniform Civil Code. It would have allowed two Acts and an indeterminate number of customs to prevail simultaneously. Litigation and uncertainty would have been the result. And all in the name of the Uniform Civil Code.

This time the Bill was sent to the Minorities Commission, who examined the objections—this time—of the Parsi-Zoroastrians. The Parsis who were against the law were opposed to non-Parsi children being adopted by the Parsis, both because property would pass into non-Parsi hands and because their entry would pollute the Fire Temple. It was argued that if Muslims could be exempted, so could be the Parsi-Zoroastrians. Other members of the community, however, informed the Commission that if Parsis were excluded, they would challenge the exemption as *ultra vires* the Constitution, regardless of what the provision was for Muslims.

The Minorities Commission said in its report that no one could be excluded from the operation of the law in the name of religious freedom. "The majorities as well as the minorities within a religious minority have the freedom to believe, profess and practise their own version of their religion"[103] said the

---

[103] *Fourth Annual Report the Minorties Commission* 1.1.81 to 31.1.82 GOI (1982). Also see Vasudha Dhagamwar, *Loc. cit.*, appendix 5.

Commission. The fate of the Minority Commission's Report is not known. Like its predecessor, this Bill lapsed when the Parliament was dissolved in 1984. Given the problems the Bill would have created, it is perhaps just as well. But the history of the Adoption Bills does point out the extent, the manner and the rapidity with which the concepts of secularism were being eroded, priority being given to religious sentiments.

It hardly needs saying that in all the objections to the adoption act children were nowhere in sight. Nor was any attention spared for the Constitution with its sweeping promises, or even for Art 44. The concentration, the spot-light, was on religion. One also notices that those who objected to the Act were aggressive while those who supported Adoption were hesitant, and on the defensive. Once again the Constitution, and this time the children as well, were held in a locked grip by the champions of religious identity.

In 1976, while the first Adoption Bill was in the Joint Committee, the Government secured an amendment to the Special Marriage Act [SMA], which went virtually unnoticed. A new S.21A was inserted in the SMA whereby two Hindus marrying under it would no longer be governed by the *Indian* Succession Act [ISA]. Instead they would be governed by the *Hindu* Succession Act. Non-Hindu couples, or couples of whom one partner was a non-Hindu, continued to be governed by the ISA. It may be remembered the SMA allowed couples married already under their personal laws to claim its benefits by registering their marriage under the SMA however many years later the registration may follow. These benefits were monogamy, rights of divorce for both partners and more favourable succession rights—more favourable than either Hindu or Muslim laws conferred on the women. Of these the Hindu Marriage Act had already conferred the first two in 1955. Successive amendments had made the grounds for divorce under both Acts almost identical. The only difference was in the rights of succession. This had been the very reason given by Dr. Ambedkar for exempting Hindus married under the SMA from the operation of the Hindu Succession Act. The Law Minister had told the Lok Sabha:

> Anyone who is aware of the provisions contained in the (Indian) Succession Act with regard to inheritance and the provisions contained in this bill will have no doubt that so far as women are concerned, the provisions of the Succession Act are far more liberal than the provisions contained in the present Code. It does not therefore seem right that people who have...become entitled to the more liberal provisions contained in the Succession Act should be dragged down and brought under the present Code.[104]

---

[104]*Lok Sabha Debates*, Part II Vol. 8 1951. Cols. 2463–64.

And yet this is precisely what was done in 1976.

There is one distinction between the two situations. There never was an Indian Adoption Act. The right of a child to a home regardless of its religion had never been acknowledged. On the other hand the rights of women under the SMA had existed since 1872. These were quietly taken away more than a century later. In some ways this was worse, and indeed was not to remain the only instance of its kind.

So far the debate had been about changes in personal law. In 1973 it shifted to criminal law. Until then, since the adaptation of the English common law system to India—since 1860, in fact, it had been axiomatic that one criminal law would govern all Indians. S.488 of the Criminal Procedure Code 1898 (Cr. P.C.) was a provision by which a wife could claim maintenance from her husband, regardless of their religion or their personal law. Women of all faiths did use this provision to secure maintenance from their husbands.

After independence the Cr. P.C. was radically overhauled, and emerged as Criminal Procedure Code 1973. Many of its provisions were the same. New S.125 embodied old S.488, with one difference. The Joint Committee on the Criminal Procedure Code had recommended that the definition of wife should include divorced wife.[105] Their recommendation was based on the fact that Muslim men could divorce their wives at will and thus avoid paying them maintenance. After the enactment of the Hindu Marriage Act Hindu divorced wives were also in financial straits.

However, the intentions of the Joint Committee were frustrated. Pressure was generated by Muslims in the Parliament to secure a major change in the law on maintenance. It must be conceded that the Government chose not to resist the pressure. S.127 empowers the magistrate to vary or cancel the order for maintenance under certain circumstances. Sub clause (3) (b) was now inserted in it. It read

> S.127 (3) Where any order has been made under S.125 in favour of a woman who has been divorced by, or had obtained a divorce from the husband, the Magistrate shall, if he is satisfied that the woman has been divorced by the husband and that she has received, whether before or after the date of the said order, the whole of the sum which, under any customary or personal law applicable to the parties, was payable on such divorce, cancel such order—

This sub section was clearly intended to get an exemption to the Muslim husband indirectly, with the payment on divorce referring to *Mehr* and *iddat*.

---

[105] Joint Committee Report on the Cr. P.C. Bill 1970 GOI (1972).

However, in a series of judgments the Supreme Court made it clear that this was not their interpretation of S.127 (3) (b). In *Bai Tahira*[106] where the petitioner had been divorced in 1962, the Supreme Court declined to apply S.127 (3) (b) retrospectively, when they heard the appeal in 1979. Secondly Iyer J. speaking on behalf of a unanimous bench said this provision had a social purpose preventing moral and material dereliction. This section would therefore only operate where the husband had adequately provided for the divorcee under his customary law. Interest on the R.5000/—Bai Tahira had received in mehr was not enough to keep her body and soul together for a day!

In *Fazlunbi*[107] Justice Iyer once again wrote the judgment on behalf of the Full Bench saying that *mehr* was not a "payable on divorce" as it could be demanded at other times. In *Zohara Khatoon*[108] Justice Fazal Ali, speaking on behalf of the full bench, said Explanation (b) to S.125 which defined wife to include divorced wife, overruled the personal law of the parties.

In none of these cases were the provisions or injunctions of the personal law discussed. In *Mohd Anmed Khan* v *Shah Bano*[109] this is exactly what happened. This case was first heard by a division bench of Justice Fazal Ali and Justice S. Varadarajan. In it Md. Ahmed Khan, a successful barrister, had appealed against the award of maintenance of R.179.80p per month to his wife, on the grounds that it was against his rights under the Muslim Personal Law. The counsel for the petitioner said that *Bai Tahira* and *Fazlunbi* had been wrongly decided. "The decision also appears to us to be against the fundamental concept of divorce under the Mahommedan law which has been expressly protected by S.2 of the Muslim Personal Law (Shariat) Application Act 1937."[110]

This case was referred by the division bench to a full bench. It was heard by five judges, including Chief Justice Chandrachud who wrote the judgment for a unanimous court. The arguments in this case from both sides relied upon the Muslim personal law and the Qur'an. The secular argument that SS. 125–127 Cr. P.C. were meant to prevent destitution and as such applied to all women, was not used. Art. 25 2(b) was nowhere in sight. The Court did hold that S.125 overrode personal law but it also said that the "Qur'an imposed an obligation on the Muslim law to make provision for the divorced wife."[111] The

---

[106]*Bai Tahira* v. *Ali Fissali* AIR 1979 SC 362.

[107]*Fuzlunbi* v. *Khader Vali* AIR 1980 SC 1730.

[108]*Zohara Khatoon* v. *Mohammad Ibrahim* AIR 1981 SC 1243.

[109]AIR 1985 SC 945.

[110]*Ibid.*, p. 947.

[111]*Ibid.*, p. 952.

Court dismissed the case. Shah Bano remained entitled to her maintenance of R.179.80p per month. But not for long.

The aftermath of the *Shah Bano* judgment as the case is called has been well documented. It was totally unprecedented, though in the light of all that had been said on earlier occasions, one feels that it should not have come as a surprise. Through it all the primacy of the Muslim personal law was asserted as a reason for undoing the Supreme Court judgment. A private members bill was even introduced for the purpose by a Muslim league member of Parliament, one Mr. Banatwala. The Government appeared committed to the existing law. But, the spokesman from the Treasury benches Mr. Arif Md Khan justified the *Shah Bano* judgment by saying that it was entirely within the Qur'an, so the parameters of the debate remained within personal law. It's scope and relevance to secular legislation was not challenged. The Constitution does not seem to have come into the discussion at all.

The private member's bill would have invariably been defeated. The Government persuaded him to withdraw it by promising one of its own and introduced it in record quick time. It was called ironically the Muslim Women's (Protection of Rights on Divorce) Bill 1986, and it took away the Muslim woman's right, if she was a divorcee, to claim maintenance from her husband under S.125. For the first time in over a century criminal justice was going to depend upon the religion of the parties. The Government had to issue a three line whip to get the Bill passed, but pass it, it did.

The Muslim Women's Bill was only the culmination of a process that began in 1973. Had S.127 been amended to provide that any money settled on the divorcee in any other context by her husband would be offset against her claims under S.125 that would have been a sensible, practical and non-religious provision. What was sown in 1973 was reaped in 1986. The Constitution and the women were once again brushed aside because religion came first.

One of the main reasons why the liberal intellectuals, most of whom are technically Hindus, have not bestirred themselves over the intrusions of personal law into secular domains has been that the encroachments came from a minority whose needs had to be respected. Incidentally, this perception is in itself somewhat dubious for it identifies an individual or a class, not in terms of citizenship but in terms of their religion. Secondly being a minority they are not expected to affect the nature of the state, which would remain secular, for the majority community was not expected to go their way.

All these assumptions were suddenly shattered when Roop Kanwar was burnt along with her Rajput husband's body in 1987. The first reaction of some women activists was to demand a fresh legislation to punish the offence of Sati. The Rajputs naturally claimed that if a new law was needed then their act had not been illegal at the time it was committed. They also claimed minority status— which any caste in India can do—and the protection that went with it. With the exception of the communists, members of all political parties paid obeisances to the Sati. None were expelled, and one, Mr. Kalyan Singh Kelvi, later became a Minister in the Union Government. In the 1989 elections even the Muslim candidate for the Congress from Roop Kanwar's constituency spoke respectfully about Sati. Those of us who were in favour of a clarificatory legislation to declare that Sati was an aggravated form of murder were in a minority and were not heard. Instead the cry for a separate legislation was taken up and Commission of Sati (Prevention) Act 1987 was rushed through the Parliament, thus creating a separate offence, with religious overtones.

This was, however, not the most frightening aspect of the legislation. That lay in the preamble, which repeated almost verbatim the first section of the anti suttee regulation passed by Lord William Bentinck's government in 1827. It begins: "Whereas Sati or the burning or burying alive of widows or women is revolting to the feelings of human nature and nowhere enjoined by any of the religions of India as an imperative duty." If the scriptures could be used to prove, (as the Qur'an had been used in the Muslim Women's Bill debates), that Sati was so enjoined, where would that lead the Government? Were the compulsions of a democratically elected government identical with those of a colonial predecessor? Are we back to a period where laws must be passed with an eye to religion, howsoever it may be interpreted?

Conclusion

In 1976, Parliament amended the Constitution for the forty-second time in forty-six years. By this amendment the Preamble to the Constitution declared India to be a sovereign *socialist secular* democratic republic, instead of merely a sovereign democratic republic. Soon thereafter the Special Marriage Act was amended. In the next eleven years the Indian Adoption Bill died a second time; the Muslim Women's Act and the Sati Act were put on the statute book.

Intellectuals who had remained silent and aloof during the Shah Bano-Muslim Women's Bill agitations found it difficult to intervene on Sati, because the average person was beginning to tire of the one way harangues and sermons directed only at Hindus. One even heard the defensive argument, "How can one oppose something if so many believe in it?" when the question was of stopping worship and glorification of the spot on which Roop Kanwar had been burnt. Certainly if the Muslim Women's Bill had to be passed on the grounds that so many Muslims supposedly wanted it, then by the same token, glorification of Sati, if so many Hindus (equally supposedly) wanted it, could also not be opposed. This argument could be extended to cover Sati itself. The criminal law of the land had already washed its hands of the Muslim divorcee. It had also accorded separate—and dare one say it—an exalted status to Sati. There is no reason why the above logic could not be extended to any social reform, be it anti-untouchability, anti-child marriage, anti-dowry, or for greater property rights for women. All of the above mentioned examples qualify as interference with religion.

The doors of the Babri Masjid, closed since 1948, were opened in 1986, supposedly as a trade-off to the Hindus, for the Muslim Women's Bill—a classic example of two wrongs making a colossal blunder. The subsequent events and the belligerent policies adopted by the Bharatiya Janata Party, the Vishwa Hindu Parishad and the behaviour of their followers, as though they were battling to serve their religion, no longer drew the kind of criticism one used to expect from the liberal intelligentsia, for an excellent reason. Over the years, the intelligentsia, by putting minorityism above secular values and the Constitution, had lost the moral authority to do so. Instead, some of them talked about the tolerant, all embracing nature of Hinduism. They criticised the BJP for semitising Hinduism, i.e. for making it intolerant and monotheistic. Altogether a line that seeks to placate by flattery, and more to the point, seeks to do so by telling Hindus what is fundamental Hinduism. Thus, in the most unexpected way, secular liberals were found adopting a fundamentalist line. One may also add that as most of these thinkers had in the past been sweepingly critical of all that is Hindu, they were not taken seriously. Their argument was brushed aside as less than honest. The net result, which may be tragic for India, is that the serious champions of secularism have lost their credibility.

From the very beginning, during the Constituent Assembly Debates, in the Parliament, in other public fora, much had been said about the nature of Indian secularism—or is it the Indian nature of secularism. From all kinds of platforms senior statesmen declared that for India, secularism was not a denial of religion, but its affirmation. India was not anti-religious. It respected all religions equally. Unlike the United States of America, India could give grants to denominational schools—but to all of them. It could intervene in the affairs of religious places, regardless of which religion they professed. The Indian model was one of pluralism, a pluralism of tolerance.

Over the years, and beginning even as freedom of religion and the uniform civil code were being debated, the Indian model has undergone a sea-change. Alternately, its limitations and therefore true potential have been revealed. It now seems to be moving in the direction of pluralism of fundamentalism.[112]

It would not be an exaggeration to describe articles 14, 15, 19 and 21 as the bedrock on which Fundamental Rights are built. The first two concern us here. Article 14 guarantees the right to equality before the law in unconditional terms. Article 15 contains a prohibition against discrimination against any citizen

---

[112] I am indebted to Jairus Banaji of St. John's College, Oxford for this expressive phrase.

on grounds of religion, race, caste, sex, place of birth; this prohibition is subject only to what is termed as reverse discrimination. The two together contain the logic that informs all the Fundamental Rights and also many of the Directive Principles of State Policy. Article 17, which abolishes untouchability and article 25 which entitles all persons equally to freedom of religion arise from articles 14 and 15. It is because all citizens are free from discrimination that their freedom of religion can be a fundamental right. Yet, the Constitution qualifies this freedom in several ways in the article that recognises it. This is how article 25 reads:

> 25 Freedom of conscience and free profession, practice and propagation of religion—(1) subject to public order, morality and health and to the other provisions of this Part, all persons are equally entitled to freedom of conscience and the right freely to profess, practise and propagate religion.
> (2)   Nothing in this article shall affect the operation of any existing law or prevent the State from making any law
> (a)   regulating or restricting any economic, financial, political or other secular activity which may be associated with religious practice;
> (b)   providing for social welfare and reform or the throwing open of Hindu religious places of a public character to all classes and sections of Hindus.

It should be very clear to anyone that freedom of conscience and religion is bounded on all sides, and subject to severe and large restrictions. It was never intended to overshadow other rights in the Constitution or to overwhelm its secular character. Yet this is precisely what has been happening. Article 25 is now virtually interpreted to mean that subject to religious constraints the state may introduce, or even retain laws which regulate secular activity as described by subclause (2) (a) or provide for social reform. The Constitutional validity of a law is to be adjudged, it appears, in terms of the offence it might give to the religious sentiments of a community, or rather the leaders of that community, rather than in terms of subclauses (a) and (b).

Articles 14 and 15 are therefore also made subordinate to article 25 as it is being interpreted—one almost said "wielded"—now. The secular, egalitarian, non-sectarian character of the Constitution is thus very much at risk. The people who dwell under the Indian tricolour are also in danger of ceasing to perceive themselves as one people, and identifying themselves more and more as followers of a particular religion, with a resultant impact on loyalties. This has even happened with the army after the Blue Star operation, and with the police in the occupation of the Babri Masjid.

Women and children have always had identities rooted in their families. Their first obligations are seen to be to the family, and their rights are circumscribed by this actor. So much so that attempts to ban child labour or to introduce

Women, Children and the Constitution

free and universal compulsory education have been killed even by well meaning activists, on the plea that parents need the child's wages or unpaid labour. Ironically, under S.125 of the Cr. P.C. a minor child can claim maintenance from its parents only if they are able to provide it. But the needs of the family must be met by the child unconditionally. During the controversy which raged over the Muslim Women's Bill, supporters of the judgment and S.125, Cr. P.C. were accused by those who were for the Bill for taking an undue interest in their neighbours' wives. Those so attacked defended themselves by saying that Muslim women were their sisters. Neither side mentioned the salient fact that they were citizens of India, entitled to equal protection of their rights, just as they were entitled to vote.

It is not by accident that personal law is also known as family law. If the pluralistically fundamentalist model of secularism gains ground, family and family law will make stronger claims on the polity. Women and children will stand to lose much more. Those promises of the Constitution which were to create a more just, more egalitarian society for all would not be implemented to the extent to which they are countermanded by various religions or personal laws. Women, children and the Constitution will become, more than ever, hostages to religion, denied by the law of their own land.

Appendix I

After the debate on Part I of the constitution had ended, the vice President Mr. H. K. Mukherjee, proposed that the House move on to Part IV, immediately, without a pause. This led to general protest from the non-Congress members. Mr. Kazi Syed Karimuddin was the first. They had been taken unawares, he said. They had come prepared with amendments to Parts II and III and they had not been informed that the Assembly would "leap" from Part I to IV. Mr. Amiyo Kumar Ghosh added that they had been taken aback.

Mr. Ananthashayanam Ayyangar, from the treasury benches found Mr. Karimuddin's compliant "strange." He said every member was generally ready with his amendments. Mr. Pocker Sahib then expostulated that this expectation was very unfair, it was impossible for members to be ready with amendments to 300 or 400 articles of the Constitution. He requested the Chair to proceed in sequential order or to adjourn the House for some time.

Loknath Misra's remarks sound despairing, if not desperate. "Sir, so much is happening behind the scenes that we are not only puzzled, we cannot even run the race....If such things are to happen, and thing go on behind us, kindly ask us to get out and then let things go on as they like." He too requested the Chair to give the House time to prepare their amendments.

Mr. Mahavir Tyagi's comments clarified the procedures adopted outside the House. "Sir, may I request the party leaders and whips of the majority party to be considerate and take a charitable view? It is rather unfortunate and unfair that for the failure of the Congress Party to decide issues amongst themselves, they should force the whole House to accommodate them in this manner." He also requested the Chair either to take up business the members were prepared to discuss, or to adjourn the House. The House was adjourned till the next day when Part IV could be taken up.[113]

A similar situation arose later in the year when rules and conditions for the candidates standing for the office of the President of India were being discussed. Prof. K. T Shah from Bihar moved an amendment that any minister wishing to contest the presidential election should resign his post. In this he was supported by Mr. Loknath Misra from Orissa and by Mr. Shyamanandan Sahaya from U.P who said that in their states candidates for office of president of state or even district Congress Committee had to resign from the Cabinet. In Orissa they had to resign even from the legislative assembly. All three speakers were repeatedly heckled from the Congress benches. Finally, Mr. Tajamul Husain from Bihar made a very strong protest heavily laced with sarcasm.

> Mr. Vice-President, I am and in fact the whole House is, very grateful to you and also particularly, I would say to the Hon'able Dr. Ambedkar for allowing us to speak. We know your powers. You can stop us at any time you like, but I would always request you to allow us even at this stage to speak as we are for the first time and last time drawing up the Constitution for the whole of India. You will pardon me for using the word "gagging" officially, but do not gag us. Let us speak. The Constitution is not going to be framed within a year as the Government of India are expecting. They are mistaken. It does not matter if it finishes in two or three years, but give us time to speak.[114]

---

[113]*CAD*, VII (1), pp. 469–472.
[114]*Ibid.*, pp. 1028–1034.

14

Devadasi Reform: Driving the Priestesses or the Prostitutes Out of Hindu Temples?

Kay K. Jordan

The devadasis of India have been characterized by some as Hindu priestesses and by others as prostitutes. The characteristic common to all devadasis is that they were women dedicated by their parents or by themselves to serve a deity. These dedications often came about as expressions of gratitude to a deity for the conception or safe delivery of a child or the recovery of a family member from serious illness. The dedication ceremony of a devadasi included a symbolic marriage to the god whom she would serve. All women given in marriage to gods were called *nityasumangali* or ever-auspicious women, because they could never be widowed. As omens of good luck they were asked to dance in marriage processions and to string some of their own beads into the bridal tali which was tied around the bride's neck at the climactic moment of a south Indian wedding. Although forbidden to marry and dwell with mortals, these auspicious women were not expected to remain chaste. The Hindu *Śāstras* did not regard the devadasis as prostitutes.[1]

Although the devadasis were perceived as positive symbols during the reign of the Hindu kings, changes in both the perception and activities of these women occurred in the nineteenth and twentieth centuries. Criticism by foreign missionaries and journalists of the association of religion and sexual promiscuity embarrassed the Indian westernized elite. The loss of both royal patronage and the decline of the patronage of wealthy zamindars, the redistribution of wealth away from the temples, urbanization and industrialization also caused changes in the activities of the devadasis and attitudes toward them.

Originally, the word "devadasi," which literally translated means "maidservant of the god," referred to rigorously trained South Indian temple dancing women who served in prestigious temples. These devadasis were actually an occupational group rather than a caste. Acceptance as a devadasi was contingent not upon birth but rather upon initiation through the dedication cere-

---

[1] K.K. Pillay, *The Sucindram Temple* (Adyar, 1953), p. 287.

mony and proficiency as a dancer or singer.[2] Social and legal reformers have chosen to broaden the usage of the term "devadasi" by applying it to any woman dedicated to a deity. The names and duties of women dedicated to serve deities in other parts of India and other sectors of society varied widely. They were known as *bhavins, naikins, jogtins, basavis, kasbis, maharis, bogam sani khudikar,* and *aradhini*. Most of the women being dedicated as devadasis today come from the lower castes and have little or no official temple duties.

The purpose of this essay is to discuss the paradoxical impact of reform legislation on the religious and social status of the devadasis. My thesis is that reform legislation prohibiting devadasi dedication in some cases significantly deprived women of religious status while in other cases such legislation has served to alleviate the exploitation of women. This legislation, which is the result of the secularization of Indian society, restricts the expression of certain Hindu religious beliefs such as the idea that one may gain religious merit by dedicating a daughter to serve a deity or that an individual gains religious merit through such service.

Both before and after independence, the government of India has worked to eliminate devadasi dedication and service as an expression of Hindu piety. The provincial legislatures of Madras and Bombay passed laws aimed at gradually phasing out the devadasis from the Indian religious scene in 1929 and 1934 respectively. Immediately after independence in 1947, the Madras Legislature passed a law banning devadasi dedication. The legislatures of Karnataka and Andhra Pradesh enacted new legislation in 1982 and 1987 respectively because the earlier laws were only partially effective.

Scholars differ in their assessment of whether the prevention of dedication legislation represented a significant denial of religious freedom. J. D. M. Derrett, noting that "the lives of these women did not disturb the Hindu conscience for more centuries than can be counted...until missionary-inspired education made Hindus self-conscious about it,"[3] criticized this legislation. To the contrary, Donald Eugene Smith, defending the secularization of the Indian state, argued that while the practices of *sati* and *devadasi* "may have some basis in Hindu religion,...the state still has constitutional power to ban them"[4] for the sake of public order, morality and health.

The changes in the legal and religous status of the devadasis reflect the secularization of Indian society. "Secularization" refers to a process by which practices and institutions previously viewed as religious cease to be so regarded and to "a process of differentiation which results in the various aspects of society

---

[2] Amrit Srinivasan, "Reform and Revival: The Devadasi and Her Dance," *Economic and Political Weekly* 20/44 (November 2, 1985), p. 1869.

[3] J. Duncan M. Derrett, *Religion, Law and the State in India* (London, 1968), p. 452.

[4] Donald Eugene Smith, *India As a Secular State* (Princeton, N.J., 1963), p. 4.

economic, political, legal and moral, becoming increasingly *discrete* in relation to each other."[5] Increasingly over the past one hundred years, Indian ideas and institutions have been critiqued or validated by their rationality and benefit to individuals in the temporal world without regard for their connection to the sacred or any concept of the afterlife. Secularization has denied the divine origin of Hindu law and shifted the power of defining social and religious norms and values from brahmins and kings, whose power was divinely mandated, to the governing elite of India who derive their power from the people. Hence, secularization has affected the issue of devadasi dedication by devaluing the connection of the devadasi to the sacred and by giving a secular government the power to regulate religious expression.

Devadasis In Colonial India

Our discussion of devadasi reform will be divided into two sections. First, we will look at changes in the religious and legal status of the devadasis under British colonial rule. Second, we will discuss the status of the devadasis today and recent devadasi reform legislation. The changes in the legal, social and religious status of the devadasis during colonial rule can be divided into three stages: (1) recognition of devadasi customary law by colonial courts; (2) central government efforts to ban and prosecute prostitution without singling out the devadasis and (3) colonial provincial government passage of legislation aimed at eliminating the devadasis.[6]

Court Recognition of Devadasi Customs

Efforts to reform or eliminate devadasi dedication and service as a religious expression are of recent origin. The High Courts established by the British Crown following the 1857 Mutiny administered an uncodified civil law based on either Hindu or Muslim religious texts. These courts recognized the devadasis as a distinct and identifiable group within Indian society possessing a customary law which included: (1) absolute ownership of property by women; (2) the right to adopt one, and sometimes more than one, daughter; (3) inheritance from mother to daughters; (4) preference of daughters over sons in inheritance; and (5) preference of devadasi relatives over non-devadasi relatives in inheritance. These customs differed significantly from those followed by the majority of Hindus.

---

[5] M. N. Srinivas, *Social Change in Modern India* (Berkeley, 1966), p. 119.

[6] A complete discussion of devadasi reform in colonial India is contained in my dissertation: "From Sacred Servant to Profane Prostitute: A History of the Changing Legal Status of the *Devadasis*, 1857–1947" (Unpublished Ph.D. diss., Univ. of Iowa, 1989).

Even though the civil courts accepted and affirmed devadasi customary law, the legal status of these women became ambiguous when provisions of the 1861 Indian Penal Code outlawing the prostitution of minors were applied to them. In some cases, the validity of adoptions was denied. In other cases, persons were actually prosecuted for dedicating girls to temple service or giving them in adoption to devadasis. This ambiguity arose, in part, because Indian civil law at this time was based on sacred sources, that is, religious texts and customs, while the criminal code was based on secular sources, that is, modern political thought and values. Only legislation specifically recognizing or rejecting devadasi customs could eliminate the ambiguity embodied in the Indian legal system.

The Central Government and Devadasi Reform

In 1858, the British crown assumed direct rule of India immediately following a mutiny caused, in part, by the colonial government's ban on religiously mandated widow burning and insensitivity to the feelings of both Hindu and Muslim soldiers that biting a cartridge greased with pig fat violated their religious beliefs. At that time, Queen Victoria made the following statement outlining a policy of government noninterference in matters of religion:

> Firmly relying ourselves on the truth of Christianity, and acknowledging with gratitude the solace of religion, we disclaim alike the right and the desire to impose our convictions on any of our subjects. We declare it to be our royal will and pleasure that none be in anywise favoured, none molested or disquieted, by reason of their religious faith or observances but that all shall alike enjoy the equal and impartial protection of the law; and we do strictly charge and enjoin all those who may be in authority under us that they abstain from all interference with the religious belief or worship of any of our subjects on pain of our highest displeasure.[7]

While the central government of India was theoretically bound by this policy of noninterference, in actual practice, the government assumed that religious expression would be limited in conformity with certain utilitarian standards of

---

[7] "Queen Victoria's Proclamation, 1 November 1858," in *The Evolution of India and Pakistan 1858 to 1947: Select Documents*, edited by S. H. Philips, H. L. Singh, and B. N. Pandey (London, 1962), p. 11.

individual safety and common standards of law and morality held throughout the world.[8]

In the late nineteenth century, a significant number of Hindus strongly believed that devadasis were an integral and necessary expresssion of Hinduism. When the government considered strengthening the child protection provisions of the 1861 Penal code in 1872 and 1903, the governments of Bombay and Madras advised that the Hindu population might rebel if such measures were applied to the devadasis.[9] The government was hesitant to pass child protection legislation which specifically exempted the devadasis district because distinguishing ordinary unacceptable prostitution from acceptable "religious" prostitution would evoke criticism from English religious organizations for recognizing and preserving such prostitution.[10]

While the British officials of the colonial central government were reluctant to enact devadasi reform legislation, the Indian elite actively supported it. The proposal of devadasi reform bills by Indian social reformers reflected their recognition of the absence of an organizational framework for effecting religious change within Hinduism and also of the power of government to regulate religious expression. In 1912, two members of the Indian westernized elite, legislators Maneckji Byramjee Dadabhoy,[11] a Parsi, and R. N. Mudholkar,[12] a Hindu brahmin, proposed bills banning adoptions by devadasis and making the dedication of a girl under sixteen as a devadasi a criminal offence.[13] According to custom, girls were supposed to be dedicated as devadasis before puberty. The colonial government delayed enactment of these bills by drafting a generic child protection bill which it circulated along with the devadasi reform bills for the consideration of local governments. In the long run, neither legislation banning devadasi dedication nor the more general child protection bill was enacted. The child protection bill was rejected in 1913 by Hindu legislators, who feared that

---

[8] This formulation of the standard for the limitation of religious expression was recommended by Lord Landsdowne in the debates over the 1891 Age of Consent bill quoted in Charles Heimsath, *Indian Nationalism and Hindu Social Reform* (Princeton, N. J., 1964), p. 172.

[9] Govt. of India, Home Dept. (Judicial), *Proceedings*, July 1873, Nos.151–205, quoted in No. 205.

[10] *Ibid.*

[11] Government of India. Home Department (Judicial) *Proceedings*, April 1912, No. 27.

[12] Govt. of India, Legislative Dept., *Proceedings*, May 1914, Nos. 100–07, No. 100.

[13] Introduction of bills touching on any area of religious reform required the sanction of the Governor General prior to introduction in the legislature. This sanction was given to Dadabhoy's bill, however, permission to introduce such a bill did not constitute Government endorsement of its content.

girls removed from "immoral" environments might be placed in rescue homes run by Christian missionaries.[14] The colonial government was unwilling to commit funds for the establishment of rescue homes. Recent legislation in Karnataka commits significant sums for the rehabilitation of devadasis.

After World War I, devadasi reform was again discussed in 1922 when India, as a member of the League of Nations, was asked to ratify the League's International Convention for the Suppression of Traffic in Women and Girls.[15] Discussion of this convention led to the passage of a recommendation that the Governor-General-in-Council "enact a law prohibiting the wholesale traffic in minor girls...ostensibly intended as *Devadasis* but in reality used for indiscriminate immoral purposes."[16] This law was proposed by a Hindu attorney, Hari Singh Gour who believed the devadasis were prostitutes and that their existence was inconsistent with the Hindu religion. Gour expressed one of the perennial criticisms of devadasi dedication, when he complained that the irreversible marriage of young girls to temple gods by their parents permanently deprived those girls of the freedom to marry or choose some other "moral" lifestyle. Once more, the British Indian government side-stepped the issue of devadasi reform and amended the Indian Penal Code to protect all girls under eighteen (previously girls under sixteen were protected) and by making it a crime to dispose of a minor knowing that she would probably be used as a prostitute after she came of age.[17]

In 1927, V. Ramadas Pantulu, a Hindu legislator from Madras, proposed a resolution recommending that the government enact legislation prohibiting the dedication of unmarried minor girls as devadasis.[18] Pantulu suggested phasing out the devadasis by eliminating the financial incentive for dedicating daughters to temple service. The colonial government denied the need for any new legislation, and suggested that concerned citizens form vigilance associations to

---

[14] *Ibid.*

[15] Govt. of India, *Proceedings of the Legislative Assembly*, Vol. II, 1922, p. 2224. Sir William Vincent of the Home Department recommended that this convention be ratified with the provision that sixteen rather than eighteen be defined as the age of majority for Indian girls.

[16] Govt. of India. *Proceedings of the Legislative Assembly*, Vol. II, 1922, p. 2599. The reason that Gour recommended the government draft as law was that bills sponsored by individuals rarely passed in the legislature. Government sponsored bills were better drafted and cleared many administrative hurdles before introduction in the legislature.

[17] The legislation was formally called "'A Bill further to amend the Indian Penal Code and the Code of Criminal Procedure, 1898, for the purpose of affording greater protection to persons under the age of eighteen years.'" The discussion of the bill was quoted in 1922 Judicial Home, 820 from *Legislative Assembly Debates*, Vol IV. No. 9, p. 13.

[18] "Extract from the *Council of State Debates*, Vol. II, No. 31," p. 1 contained in *Ibid.*, p.2.

support the enforcement of existing laws. In response, Pantulu withdrew his bill from consideration.

The central British Indian colonial government avoided passing any law which targeted the devadasis. Government documents show no particular concern for Hindu religious freedom as an abstract value, but rather show pragmatic concern to prevent riot or rebellion.

Local Legislatures and Devadasi Reform

When it became clear that the central government would never pass legislation specifically penalizing devadasi customs or revoking devadasi privileges, the Indian westernized elite shifted their efforts to enact reform legislation to provincial legislatures where they had gained power through post-World War I political reforms.

Dr. S. Muthulakshmi Reddy, a well-known medical doctor and India's first female legislator proposed several resolutions and laws related to abolishing the devadasi system.[19] In 1927, she piloted a resolution through the Madras Legislative Council recommending that the government legislate a ban on devadasi dedication.[20] In 1929, she successfully sponsored an amendment to the Madras Hindu Religious Endowments Act eliminating the financial incentive which perpetuated the devadasi system.[21] Devadasis either had the right to live on certain lands or the right to a share of the produce of land on condition that they perform temple service. Aging devadasis counted on their daughters to continue the family tradition of temple service and thereby guarantee continued possession or income from land. Reddy believed that government enfranchisement of such lands and sale or gift of that land to the devadasis would eliminate the need for those aging devadasis to dedicate a daughter to temple service. While neither temple service nor devadasi dedication were outlawed, the bill set the stage for the gradual abandonment of devadasi dedication and consequentially the absorption of this unique community into the larger patriarchal society. The younger generation of devadasis married men and their special customs faded into history.

---

[19] A more detailed discussion of the role of S. Muthulakshmi Reddy as an advocate for devadasi reform appears in my paper "Feminist Scholarship and the Problematic Case of Devadasi Reform in India," presented at the Annual Meeting of the American Academy of Religion, New Orleans, LA, November 17–20, 1990.

[20] Govt. of Madras, *Proceedings of the Madras Legislative Council*, Vol. XXXVIII, 1927, p. 415.

[21] Govt. of Madras, *Proceedings of the Madras Legislative Council*, Vol. XLIII, 1928, p. 272.

Like other Indian reformers before her, Reddy assumed that the legislature was an appropriate place to argue that devadasi dedication and service were inappropriate expressions of Hinduism. Reddy believed that the devadasis practiced prostitution. Contending that chastity was the supreme virtue for Hindu women, she concluded that devadasi dedication and service were inconsistent with Hinduism. She claimed that this system was the product of superstitious beliefs such as the god's need for female attendants or the god's wrath if denied such attendants.[22] Her other arguments in favor of devadasi reform reflect the impact of modern political theories which emphasized the value of the individual. Reddy complained that some devadasis were dedicated by their parents at a tender age and denied the opportunity to choose another lifestyle. Even if the legal age for dedication was eighteen, she believed that girls raised in a devadasi household were corrupted by their immoral environment and were therefore unable to understand or choose a moral lifestyle. Such girls, she believed, were committed not only to a life of vice but also condemned in many cases to suffer from venereal disease. Reddy was unable to persuade the legislature to enact an immediate ban on devadasi dedication and service.[23]

When Reddy's bills were being considered by the legislature, the devadasis wasted no time in complaining that such legislation limited their free expression of religion and potentially deprived them of their livelihood. They sent memorials to the legislature declaring that their true purpose was religion and service and citing texts on the proper worship of Vishnu and Shiva to support their religious status. Claiming that their order was originally composed of chaste temple servants, the devadasis asked for support in reforming and educating their community.[24] Instead of abolishing their order, they suggested that the government simply punish those individuals who practiced prostitution. They claimed that the only support within the devadasi community for a ban on dedication came from self-interested males.

---

[22] Govt. of Madras, *Proceedings of the Madras Legislative Council*, Vol XXXVII, 1927, p. 415–17, 513.

[23] Govt. of Madras, *Proceedings of the Madras Legislative Council*, Vol. XLVI, 1929, p. 621.

[24] Government of Madras, Law Dept. (General), *Proceedings*, Dec. 20, 1927, G. O. 4079. Contemporary scholars question the apologetic myth that devadasis were originally chaste. Instead, both Frederique Marglin and Amrit Srinivasan suggest that in the past Indian society did not object to the concubinage and sexual freedom associated with these women. In fact, as stated earlier, the devadasis were regarded as symbols of feminine auspiciousness and vitality. Frederique Marglin, *Wives of the God–King: The Rituals of the Devadasis of Puri* (Delhi, 1985), p. 9; Srinivasan, "Reform and Revival," pp. 1869, 1875.

In August of 1934, a devadasi reform bill was passed by the Bombay Legislative Council.[25] This bill made devadasi dedication a crime and included a plan whereby the government would enfranchise the temple lands currently used to support devadasis and then deed those lands to the devadasis for nominal fees. It also legalized marriages of former devadasis to men.[26] A bill banning devadasi dedication was passed by the Madras Legislature in 1947. The bill, which was identical with one reported out of committee in 1939, was passed after Independence but before the Indian Constitution came into effect. By 1947, India had changed so dramatically that there was little protest against this bill which not only banned devadasi dedication but made it a crime for women to dance in temples and marriage processions. One legislator, Mrs. M. N. Clubwalla, praised the bill and summarized the viewpoint of the Indian westernized elite saying that the Government had earned the gratitude of "hundreds of women who though not due to any fault of their own, have been smarting under the yoke of the worst humiliation and social ignominy." She praised Dr. Reddy for awakening the consciences of women and men "to the existence of the evil of a separate class of women whose honour and character were exploited by the interested men,...."[27]

Devadasis In Independant India

Before discussing recent devadasi reform legislation we should assess the impact of the 1934 Bombay Prohibition of Devadasi Dedication Act and the 1947 Madras Prohibition of Devadasi Dedication Act and of less direct attacks on the devadasis, such as the withdrawal of government patronage. It appears that devadasi reform legislation effectively ended the dedication and service of temple dancing girls in many prestigious temples, but that such legislation was ineffective in preventing the dedication of low caste women to village temples. Recent literature suggests that devadasi reform has, in some cases, deprived women of religious status and income, but in others has rescued them from exploitation.

Contemporary scholarship presents us with two contrasting portraits of the devadasi. The writings of Marglin, Srinivasan, and Kersenboom-Story describe the devadasis as skilled dancers and ritual specialists who were once revered by society. The publications of the Joint Women's Programme, Shankar's study, and that of Rozario, Rasool, and Kesari present them as low caste and untouchable women exploited by higher castes who lure them into prostitution sanctioned by superstitious religious beliefs. These contrasting

---

[25] Govt. of Bombay, *Bombay Legislative Council Debates*, Vol. XL, 1934, p. 430.
[26] Govt. of Bombay, *Bombay Legislative Council Debates*, Vol. XXXVIII, 1933, p. 475.
[27] *Ibid.*, p. 97.

portraits complicate the assessment of whether or not devadasi reform legislation unnecessarily restricted religious freedom.

Devadasis Deprived of Religious Status by Reform Legislation

Let us review the literature which portrays the devadasi as a skilled and dignified ritual specialist who lost status and income because of the passage of devadasi reform legislation. Marglin's study of the devadasis at the Jagganatha temple at Puri asserts that only girls from the castes permitted to give water to brahmins were allowed to become devadasis. In other words, only members of the upper three castes could become devadasis and both *śudras* and untouchables were categorically excluded from such service.[28] These devadasis were not required to remain chaste. Ideally, either the king or brahmin priests might become their paramours. Actually they were permitted to have sexual relations with any member of the water-giving castes of Puri.[29] These devadasis were not considered prostitutes (women who earn their living through the sale of sexual favors), instead they were supported by the patronage of the king. Even when their lovers brought them significant gifts, these gifts were not considered payment for sexual favors.[30] Marglin denied that "temple prostitution" or "ritual intercourse" was practiced by these devadasis, who would never have considered polluting the temple by having intercourse within it.[31]

No laws restricting devadasi dedication have been passed in Puri, but the withdrawal of government patronage has almost completely eliminated devadasi temple service. One devadasi, who desires to carry on the tradition can barely scrape together the money for the flowers and food required by her part in the festival drama of the birth of Krishna.[32] According to Marglin, these devadasis experienced an immediate decline in status when royal patronage ended with the death of Ramcandra Dev in 1958. At about this time, the state took over management of the temple and the pilgrims ceased to pay attention to the devadasis.[33] Although these devadasis were the legitimate heirs to ritual status and the repository of an artistic tradition, representatives of the National Academy of Music and Dance from Delhi visiting Puri snubbed them.[34] The devadasis interviewed

---

[28] Marglin, *Loc. cit.*, p. 68.

[29] *Ibid.*, p. 90.

[30] *Ibid.*

[31] *Ibid.*, p. 90.

[32] *Ibid.*, p. 39.

[33] *Ibid.*, p. 87.

[34] *Ibid.*, p. 34.

Devadasi Reform

by Marglin were seeking husbands for their daughters instead of dedicating them to temple service, because of the lack of support for preserving and maintaining the devadasi tradition.

The dignity of the devadasis of Tamil Nadu described by Amrit Srinivasan is equal to that of the devadasis of the Jagganatha Temple at Puri. These devadasis were not prostitutes in the ordinary sense of the word. Their mothers and grandmothers exercised considerable power in the selection of their lovers, who were generally brahmins or members of the landed and commercial elite. Liaisons with Muslims, Christians or lower caste men were forbidden. Patrons drew status from their association with the devadasis because these women were married to divine husbands. These devadasis functioned as ritual specialists who attracted patronage to the temple through their skill and beauty. Srinivasan's field research did not uncover any evidence of ritual intercourse or tantric practices.[35]

The impetus for devadasi reform, according to Srinivasan, came from two sources: (1) devadasi males who were involved in the anti-Brahmin movement and (2) from Indian nationalists and upper caste women. The men of the devadasi community felt emasculated by matriarchal control of family resources and overshadowed by the prestige of their sisters.[36] During the centuries when the sexual freedom of the devadasis was culturally and religiously acceptable, high caste married women never studied dance for fear that it would damage their reputations. Nationalists, largely composed of upper caste Hindus, supported devadasi reform so they could promote *Bharata Natyam* as an Indian art form free of its association with sexual promiscuity.[37] Hence, Srinivasan asserted that devadasi reform legislation served the needs of the devadasi males and those of the revivalists, but displaced the only female ritual specialists in the Hindu tradition. The high social status of the devadasis, their high degree of artistic talent, and their social acceptance is evidenced by the ease with which many of them married into high caste familes.[38]

Saskia Kersenboom-Story emphasized the cultural and religious importance of the devadasi as a *nityasumangali*, or ever-auspicious woman. The function of a devadasi *nityasumangali* was to protect people from danger and to radiate an energy which helped them to gain wealth, preserve good health, obtain

---

[35] Srinivasan, *Loc. cit.*, 1869–70.

[36] *Ibid.* p. 1873.

[37] *Ibid.*, pp. 1874–75.

[38] Amrit Srinivasan, "Temple 'Prostitution' and Community Reform: An Examination of the Ethnographic, Historical and Textual Content of the Devadasis of Tamil Nadu, South India" (Unpublished Ph.D. diss., Cambridge University, 1984), pp. 2, 16.

children, and secure marital happiness.[39] According to Kersenboom-Story, confusion regarding the character and activities of the devadasis was rooted in misuse of the term "devadasi." Denying that all women married to deities, who might be *nityasumangalis* could rightfully be called devadasis, she asserted that only women members of the *melakkaran* caste dedicated to deities could properly be called devadasis. Some of the devadasis she interviewed were either formally married to brahmins or "wives on the basis of affection" of brahmins.[40]

Like Marglin and Srinivasan, Kersenboom-Story thought that the decline of royal patronage contributed substantially to the demise of the devadasi tradition. Her assessment of the reform movements is that while "they succeeded in desstroying [sic] the most prominent and refined class of *nityasumangalis*," they did not destroy the cultural need for a female symbol of auspiciousness. Hence, the cruder forms of the *nityasumangali* such as the low caste *basivis* (*basavis*) and *Ellamadasis* (*Yellamadasis*) continue to exist and the highly skilled artists who represent the devadasi tradition have been deprived of the temple as the platform and context for expressing their artistry.[41]

In the writings of Marglin, Srinivasan, and Kersenboom-Story, we see a portrait of the devadasis as highly skilled and culturally valued female ritual specialists. We wistfully view their departure from Hindu temples, brought about by devadasi reform legislation and the end of royal patronage.

Other "Devadasis" and the New Reform Legislation

Other recent studies of the "devadasis" suggest that in spite of laws banning devadasi dedication, many girls and women from untouchable castes are dedicated to deities and exploited as prostitutes. One such study was prepared by the Joint Women's Programme, a group which played a significant role in establishing the need for new and effective devadasi reform legislation in Karnataka and Andhra Pradesh. This organization compiled informative reports, met with government officials and held press conferences in support of such legislation.[42] Recent studies by Jogan Shankar and Sister Rita Rozario along with Javeed Rasool and Pradeep Kesari also support the image of the contemporary devadasi

---

[39] *Ibid.*, p. 205.

[40] Kersenboom-Story, *Loc. cit.*, p. 56, note 3.

[41] *Ibid.*, p. 207.

[42] Joint Women's Programme (JWP), "The Devadasi Problem," *Banhi* (1981/2) and JWP, "Prostitution with Religious Sanction," *Banhi* (1989).

as a low caste female dedicated to serve a deity who will probably earn her living as a prostitute.[43]

The government of Andhra Pradesh estimates that there are about 16,000 devadasis in that state.[44] In the Satara District of Maharashtra, as many as 5,000 women may have been dedicated to Krishna by the Mahanubhav sect. The total number of girls in the Maharashtra-Karnataka border area dedicated to Yellamma, Hanuman and Khandoba temples may be as high as 250,000.[45] As many as 5,000 girls are dedicated annually to the goddess Yellamma and later sent to brothels in Bombay and Pune. In the town of Nipani in Belgaum District 200 out of the town's 800 prostitutes are devadasis. The harijan community of Athani (total population 30,000), consists of 5,000 persons divided into 500 families out of which 98% of the families practice religiously sanctioned prostitution.[46] In Yellampura village in Belgaum District (total population 5,700) there were 85 devadasis all from groups identified by the government as scheduled castes. Thirty-nine of these devadasis practiced prostitution.[47] Only a portion of the girls and women dedicated to village deities wind up in urban areas, many of them continue to live in small cities and rural areas where they also practice prostitution. No estimate of the total number of devadasis in India is available. However, it is noteworthy that according to the study completed by Rozario, Rasool, and Kesari which sampled 1100 randomly selected persons who lived in red light districts, public and private rescue homes, areas where girls are often dedicated to deities and later become prostitutes and locations where prostitutes are often recruited, 22.7% of the sample practiced prostitution with some sort of religious sanction.[48]

Some of the low caste women dedicated to deities are called "*basavis.*" A *basavi* is generally the child of parents who dedicated their daughter to serve a god because they had no son. According to customary law, a daughter dedicated as a *basavi* and her children are the legitimate heirs to her father's property. A *basavi*, who is permitted to take a regular lover, is forbidden to marry and her children are regarded as belonging to her father's family rather than that of their biological father. Under normal circumstances, the property of a man lacking a

---

[43] Sr. M. Rita Rozario, Javed Rasool, and Pradeep Kesari, *Trafficking in Women and Children in India: Sexual Exploitation and Sale* (New Delhi, 1988), pp. 53–54. Jogan Shankar, *Devadasi Cult: A Sociological Analysis* (New Delhi, 1990).

[44] Shankar, *Loc. cit.*, p. 49.

[45] *Ibid.*, pp. 16–17, 18.

[46] Rozario, Rasool, and Kesari, *Loc. cit.*, pp. 53–54.

[47] Shankar, *Loc. cit.*, pp. 98–99, 106.

[48] *Ibid.*, p. 47.

son reverts to his male relatives. The term *"basavi"* originally referred to a bull who runs free and may be rooted in the old village custom whereby Hindus sometimes dedicated a breeding bull for village use after the death of a family member.[49] The term "basavi" now refers to a woman who is sexually available.[50]

The girls and women dedicated to Yellamma are categorized as either being devadasis, who cater to men's sexual needs, or as *jogtis*, who serve the goddess without catering to men.[51] The goddess Yellamma, whose full name is Yellamma-Renuka, is popular among low caste people because she is supposedly comprised of a high caste and a low caste woman. One version of the Yellama-Renuka story is that Renuka used to fetch water for the rituals performed by her husband, the sage Jamadagni, in a pitcher of sand balanced upon a snake which served as a head-rest for the pitcher. One day when Renuka went to fetch water she was distracted by handsome Gandharvas frolicking in the water. For an instant, she thought about how she might have married a Gandharva and lived in luxury. Immediately the pitcher of sand, which had been held together by her virtue, crumbled in her hand. Her husband grasped what had happened and ordered his sons to behead Renuka. The two elder sons refused but the youngest, twelve-year-old Parushurama, obeyed. After the deed was done, Jamadagni offered three boons to Parashurama, who immediately asked for the restoration of his mother to life. Jamadagni told the boy to fetch the head of a Matangi woman (a particular untouchable caste) and place it upon the trunk of his mother's body. At once, she came to life and thereafter has been worshipped as Yellamma-Renuka. Since that day, members of the Matangi clan and other untouchable castes have offered their daughters to her for use by her son Parashurama.[52]

The reasons people continue to practice devadasi dedication can be divided into the following four categories: caste exploitation, religious beliefs, economics, and lack of education. Let us look at each category in turn.

---

[49] Fred Fawcett, "On Basivis: Women Who Through Dedication to a Deity Assume Masculine Privileges," *Journal of the Anthropological Society of Bombay*, vol. II, 1892, p. 322.

[50] For further discussion of *basavis*, see Rozario, Rasool, and Kesari, *Loc. cit.*, p. 81 and JWP, "Venkatasani," and "The Basavi Cult," in "Prostitution with Religious Sanction," *Banhi* (1988), pp. 49–61, pp. 1–20.

[51] JWP, "The Devadasi Problem,"*Loc. cit.*, p. 7.

[52] Rozario, Rasool, and Kesari, *Loc. cit.*, p. 52.

Caste Exploitation

Devadasi dedication gives upper castes access to lower caste women and even provides religious sanction for it. The cost of the devadasi dedication ceremony is usually born by a wealthy patron who has the right to spend the first night with the newly dedicated devadasi. According to the Joint Women's Programme, the prevalence of devadasi dedication among low caste groups destroys the self-esteem of their women because this practice is contrary to the usual Hindu emphasis on chastity in women.[53]

Religious Beliefs

Impoverished low caste parents, who wish to offer the best they have to the goddess, dedicate their daughters out of sincere religious commitment.[54] The devadasis themselves believe they are serving the goddess. The dedication ceremony makes it possible for them to practice prostitution without being socially ostracized by other castes and also for society to regard their children as legitimate. Although their religious duties are generally negligible, their acceptance as auspicious women in high caste homes on particular ritual occasions gives them a sense of importance and self-worth.[55] Other religious beliefs which perpetuate devadasi dedication include fear that the goddess will be angry if at least one daughter is not dedicated, belief in the sanctity of religious vows, belief that the goddess specifically chooses some women by causing a jat or knot to grow in their hair. An aging devadasi may influence parents to dedicate a daughter by soothsaying and oracles which are sometimes motivated by a bribe from a patron or by that devadasi's need to adopt a daughter to care for her in her old age. Shankar blames the oppressive patriarchal ideology of Hinduism for the persistence of devadasi dedication.[56]

Economics

Acute poverty, landlessness, pauperization due to famine and dependency on dominant groups contribute to the continuation of devadasi dedication.[57] One cause of the extreme poverty in the Maharashtra-Karnataka

---

[53] JWP, "The Devadasi Problem," *Loc. cit.*, pp. 12, 31.
[54] Shanker, *Loc. cit.*, p. 125.
[55] *Ibid.*, p. 124.
[56] *Ibid.*, p. 163.
[57] *Ibid.*, p. 163.

border area, where large numbers of devadasis are dedicated, is the failure of successive governments to fund water projects in that area.[58] In this impoverished region it is not uncommon to hear low caste persons say, "'A beautiful girl is equivalent to three acres of land.'"[59] Promises of easy money by agents of brothels and local girls who became rich also contribute to continued devadasi dedication.

Lack of Education

The lower castes who dedicate daughters are generally illiterate, ignorant and subject to manipulation by persons of higher caste and class. The Joint Women's Programme described the literacy rate among the devadasis as "practically zero." Although not all the persons in the study done by Rozario, Rasool, and Kesari were devadasis, 88% of their 1100 respondents were illiterate.[60]

The picture of contemporary devadasis painted by the Joint Women's Programme, Shankar, and the study directed by Rozario is far less romantic than the one painted by Marglin, Srinivasan, and Kersenboom-Story. A significant number of low caste girls and women are dedicated to deities and doomed to live as prostitutes subject to venereal disease and premature aging. These devadasis are exploited by their parents, their patrons, and society with religious sanction. It is not surprising that the governments of Karnataka and Andhra Pradesh have recently sponsored devadasi reform legislation and developed social programs to alleviate the causes of devadasi dedication.

Recent Devadasi Reform Legislation

Karnataka

Although the 1934 Bombay Devadasi Protection Act and the 1947 Madras (Prevention of Dedication) Act theoretically were in force in portions of Karnataka, these laws had little or no effect on the practice of devadasi dedication in rural areas. Therefore, the Karnataka Devadasis (Prohibition of Dedication) Bill, 1982 was enacted. This bill, the first one ever to be presented in the Kannara language, nullified the dedication of any woman to a deity, either before or after the passage of the act, with or without her consent. It legalized the

---

[58] JWP, "The Devadasi Problem," *Loc. cit.*, p. 31.

[59] Shankar, *Loc. cit.*, p. 115.

[60] JWP,"The Devadasi Problem," *Loc. cit.* p. 32; Rozario, Rasool, and Kesari, *Loc. cit.*, pp. 68, 124; Cf. Shankar, *Loc. cit.*, p. 163.

marriage of any woman previously dedicated to a deity and declared the children of such marriages to be legitimate. The bill made performing, permitting, taking part in or abetting the performance of a devadasi dedication a crime punishable by up to three years of imprisonment and a fine of up to two thousand rupees. A stiffer penalty, of up to five years imprisonnment and a fine of up to Rs 5000 was prescribed for parents and guardians found guilty of dedicating a girl in their care to a deity. The bill empowered the government to make rules, subject to legislative approval, for the enforcement of the act and for the care, protection and rehabilitation of devadasis.[61] In contrast to earlier devadasi reform legislation which could only be prosecuted if someone filed a complaint, the new bill made dedication a crime against the state.[62]

Y. Ramakrishna, Minister for Law and Legislative Affairs introduced the bill by quoting a proverb from the *Arya Vakya*, "Where women are honored, God is pleased."[63] Citation of this Sanskrit text, implied that Hinduism properly observed honored and protected women.

Denying that the reform legislation interfered with religious freedom, K. H. Srinivas affirmed the right of the state to discriminate between appropriate and inappropriate religious expressions. If the government did not reject the dogmatic superstitions that were often intertwined with religion, he believed it could not protect the downtrodden from exploitation.[64] He assumed that true religion supported the dignity and equality of all humans. Agreeing with Srinivas that devadasi dedication was rooted in dogma and supersititon, G. K. Kale, asserted that reform legislation without education and job training would be futile.[65]

No one seriously opposed passage of this bill; instead, the discussion centered on its implementation. The bill provided for loans to enable the devadasis to purchase sewing machines and promised Rs. 5000 to men who married devadasis. Ideally, the government believed that the fines collected from persons convicted for violating this law would generate significant income for the government which could then be used to to offset the expense of providing social programs to train and rehabilitate the devadasis.[66]

---

[61] My source for the bill's provisions is an English translation of the bill published in JWP, "The Devadasi Problem," *Loc. cit.*, p. 46.

[62] Govt. of Karnataka, *Legislative Assembly Debates*, Vol. CXXXXII, 1982, p. 233. The Assembly's discussion of the devadasi reform bill was translated for me by Arun Kumar.

[63] *Ibid.*, p. 234.

[64] *Ibid.*, p. 212.

[65] *Ibid.*, p. 230.

[66] *Ibid.*, p. 233–34.

The Members of the Karnataka Legislative Council welcomed the devadasi reform bill. No serious questions regarding the appropriateness of the bill were raised. Some legislators suggested that social workers instead of police should be involved in enforcing it, while others suggested that the government should allocate more money for the implementation of the bill.[67] The Government of Karnataka's commitment to fund the rehabilitation of the devadasis differed markedly from the policies of the British colonial government which was unwilling to commit the Empire's resources, which were largely derived from the exploitation of India, for social work among the poor of India.

Andhra Pradesh

In 1987, the Andhra Pradesh Legislature passed a law similar to the one passed by the Karnataka legislature prohibiting devadasi dedication. This statute nullified devadasi dedication either before or after passage of the law, whether performed with or without without the consent of the individual dedicated. It legalized the marriage of devadasis and declared the children of such marriages to be legitimate. It provided that any person found guilty of performing, promoting, taking part in or abetting the performance of devadasi dedication might be sentenced to a term of imprisonment of up to three years and fined up to Rs. 3000 but not less than Rs. 2000. If the person convicted of such a crime was related to the girl or woman dedicated, that person might be imprisoned for five years and fined up to Rs. 5000.[68] The government of Andhra Pradesh, like that of Karnataka, plans to provide rehabilitation programs for devadasis, allocate house sites and construct houses for them, and to educate their children.[69]

Devadasi Reform and Religious Freedom

Does devadasi reform legislation violate the provisions of the Indian Constitution which guarantee freedom of religious expression to both individuals and groups? Devadasi reform legislation definitely prevents women from voluntarily dedicating themselves to serve a deity and also restricts the freedom of religious expression of parents who sincerely believe that dedicating a daughter to

---

[67] Govt. of Karnataka. *Karnataka Legislative Council Debates*, Vol. CXXXXII, 1982, pp. 220–230. My interpretation of these debates is based on a translation provided by V. Srinivasan.

[68] *Andhra Law Times* (Supplement) 1988, pp. 38–40. The law came into effect as the "Andhra Pradesh Devadasis (Prohibition of Dedication) Act 1988. At the time, this chapter was written, the legislative debates of this bill were unavailable in the United States.

[69] Shankar, *Loc. cit.*, p. 154.

Devadasi Reform

serve a deity protects them from divine wrath, brings about blessings in this life, or contributes to their salvation.

Article 25 of the Indian Constitution guarantees all citizens freedom of religious belief and expression with certain limitations. It states:

Art. 25 (1) Subject to public order, morality and health and to the other provisions of this Part, all persons are entitled to freedom of conscience and the right freely to profess, practice and propagate religion.

(2) Nothing in this article shall affect the operation of any existing law or prevent the state from making any law—

(a) regulating or restricting any economic, financial, political or other secular activity which may be associated with religious practice;

(b) providing for social welfare and reform or the throwing open of Hindu religious institutions of a public character to all classes and sections of Hindus.[70]

While devadasi reform legislation restricts the free expression of religion, such legislation is in accord with the Indian Constitution which specifies that religious freedom is guaranteed subject to "public order, morality and health." From the viewpoint of the government, the prostitution of the devadasis was a violation of commonly accepted norms of morality. Another limitation on the free expression of religion is that the state shall not be precluded from "providing for social welfare and reform." The government could easily justify banning devadasi dedication as a means of reducing the incidence of prostitution in India and thereby reforming and benefitting society.

The Preamble of the Indian Constitution affirms the dignity of every individual; guarantees social, economic and political justice; equality of status and opportunity; as well as liberty of thought, expression, belief, faith and worship.[71] The practice of devadasi dedication limits the freedom of individuals and also diminishes the the dignity of women. In most instances, devadasis are dedicated by their parents and are thereby prevented from later choosing to marry or lead a life more attuned to the generally accepted moral norms of society. The prostitution which so often follows devadasi dedication makes sex a commodity

---

[70] Quoted in Smith, *Loc. cit.*, p. 135.

[71] G. C. Venkata Subbarao, *Computerised Constitution of India* (Hyderabad, 1985), p. 1.

to be purchased rather than the expression of a relationship between two persons and diminishes the dignity of the woman who sells herself or is sold by others.

The ban on devadasi dedication is also in accord with Article 46 of the "Directive Principles of State Policy," which states that "the State shall promote with special care the educational and economic interests of the weaker sections of the people, and in particular, of the Scheduled Castes and the Scheduled Tribes, and shall protect them from social injustice and all forms of exploitation."[72] The term "scheduled castes" refers to those groups who have traditionally experienced social discrimination. Most of the girls and women dedicated as devadasis today belong to scheduled castes. The poverty and ignorance prevalent in these castes cause parents to dedicate daughters to serve deities. Legislation banning such dedication reduces the exploitation of these castes who are giving up their women to lives of prostitution in which they will be exploited by procurers and customers. Hence, again we see that restricting the practice of devadasi dedication is in accord with the Indian Constitution.

Conclusion

Society's perception of the devadasis and, in fact, the identity, character and activities of the devadasis have changed significantly over the past century. In the late nineteenth century, the British colonial court system acknowledged them as a distinct and identifiable group of women possessing their own customary law of adoption and inheritance. British colonial officials refused to pass reform legislation specifically directed at the devadasi community because a significant number of Hindus regarded them as an essential part of their religious tradition. The Indian westernized elite pressed for devadasi reform because they believed they had the right to distinguish between appropriate and inappropriate expressions of the Hindu tradition.

The reform legislation passed by provincial legislatures along with the decline of royal patronage drove the devadasis who might be considered to be Hindu "priestesses," from prestigious temples. There can be no doubt that these women lost religious status and that the Hindu tradition lost a powerful symbol of feminine auspiciousness.

The goal of recent devadasi reform legislation is to eliminate religiously sanctioned prostitution which involves the exploitation of the impoverished and illiterate lower castes by educated and economically secure persons belonging to higher castes. While this legislation restricts the religious freedom of parents who wish to dedicate daughters to a deity and that of women who feel called to dedicate themselves to a deity, such limitations are in accord with the Indian

---

[72] Quoted in Shankar, *Loc. cit.*, p. 89.

Constitution. The secularization of Indian society has caused the government to assume the authority to distinguish appropriate expressions of religion from inappropriate expressions. The government of India, like other modern nations, is more concerned with the temporal well-being of its citizens than their spiritual well-being. While prohibiting devadasi dedication which frequently leads to prostitution, premature aging, and death from sexually transmitted diseases may limit the free expression of religion, it certainly contributes to the temporal well-being of potential victims of this custom. With proper enforcement, the new legislation may succeed in driving religiously sanctioned prostitution from Hindu temples.

Devadasi reform legislation has indeed had a paradoxical impact on the role of women in the Hindu tradition. On the one hand, it is sad that there are no female ritual specialists in Hindu temples and that the devadasi is fast fading as a symbol of feminine auspiciousness. On the other hand, it is good that low caste girls and women will no longer be dedicated for the purpose of satisfying the lust of upper caste men.

15

Renunciation and Law in India

Vasudha Narayanan

Ramanuja, the eleventh century teacher venerated by the Śrivaiṣṇava tradition of south India, had a wife who according to all biographical accounts, was somewhat conservative and quarrelsome. When her husband invited his teacher's family home for dinner, she fed them, but proceeded to cleanse and ritually purify the house after they left, because they were of a lower caste. On another occasion, she refused to give food to hungry devotees, by lying that there was no food in the house. Later, she picked a quarrel with another teacher's wife. Annoyed, and not believing in any half-measures, Ramanuja cried: "You have made explicit the statement that women are the abode of all sins; you are guilty of offending the devotees of the lord." He packed her off to her paternal home, and then renounced his life as a householder:

> He thought: "I shall, as the scriptures say, adopt either a mendicant or the lord as my preceptor and enter the next stage of life; I shall become a sannyasin (renunciant)."...Considering the lord to be his preceptor, he begged, "give me the *tridanda* (three staffs that are tied together), saffron robes etc...[emblems of a renunicant/monk]." The lord gave Ramanuja all that he requested through a priest, and asked Tirukacchi Nampi to escort Ramanuja to the monastery.[1]

Several points are interesting in this narrative and we shall unpack some of these issues, and relate them to the broader context of the Hindu tradition(s) and modern law in this paper. One of the initial questions is, whatever happened to Ramanuja's wife? If it had happened today (and certainly men do become renunciants or *sannyāsis*, although it is infrequent), what would her legal rights have been? Can she also become a renunciant? Is she entitled to divorce? What does she inherit? Second, we can ruminate on the notion of caste; Ramanuja had considered a person of supposedly lower caste to be his guru, much to the

---

[1] Pinapalakiya Perumal Jiyar, *Guruparamparāprabhāvam, āṟayirappaṭi*, ed. by S. Krishnasvami Ayyankar (Triucci, 1975), pp. 173-174.

discomfiture of his wife. Other narratives tell us that Ramanuja's entourage consisted of lower-caste renunciants, and this is not something that is generally approved by first and second century texts that deal with *dharma*. Are lower caste men allowed to renounce life and their families and become *sannyāsis*? Third, we see that Ramanuja decided to have the "lord as his preceptor" and be initiated by the lord. Is this valid now, legally, and what are the parameters recognized by the law in India to judge if indeed the renunciation has been total and complete? Finally, what are the issues dealing with religious leadership, law, and renunciation in the Śrivaiṣṇava tradition? This paper will deal with these issues, and while I will refer to cases from other parts of India, in order to be more cogent and work with some internal logic, I shall focus on the Śrivaiṣṇava community of south India and work with their concerns.

The Śrivaiṣṇava tradition of south India became organized around the time of its fifth, and most important teacher (*acarya*), Ramanuja (circa 1017 –1137 C.E.). The word "Śrivaiṣṇava" occurs in the Tiruvenkatam (Tirupati) temple inscriptions as early as 966 C.E., and it is probable that a community bearing that name existed even from the ninth century. The Śrivaiṣṇava community emphasizes exclusive devotion to the lord Viṣṇu and his consort Śrī. Like many of the other Hindu traditions, it accepts the Sanskrit Vedas, the epics *Rāmāyaṇa* and *Mahābhārata*, and the *Purāṇas* as scripture, but in addition to these, also claims that the poems of twelve Tamil poet-saints known as the āḻvārs are "revealed." The āḻvārs lived between the seventh and ninth centuries C.E. The word *āḻvārs* is traditionally derived from the Tamil root *al* ("deep"), and the title was given to eleven men and one woman who are said to have been immersed deep in the love of Viṣṇu. The acceptance of the āḻvārs as paradigmatic devotees is a significant stance taken by the community in the tenth and eleventh centuries C.E., because they came from all castes and one of them was a woman. The only woman āḻvār, Antal, refused to get married to a human being, insisted that her bridegroom was the lord himself and composed poems expressing her passion for the lord. What we have here, is a community that has had a heritage of being "liberal" in the eleventh century C.E.; a community that venerated a woman who refused to get married, and in a sense, defied social norms; a community that revered the works of poets like Tiruppan āḻvār who was an "untouchable" as revelation. The Śrivaiṣṇava community, therefore, is not as misogynistic as you may have thought it to be, by hearing the first story. Ramanuja's entourage had included women, and many of them were his direct disciples.

Ramanuja's renunciation of the world was extremely significant to his followers; over and over again, they call him as the "king or emperor of ascetics/renouncers" (*yatiraja, yatindra, yatisarvabhauma, yati bhupati, yatic*

Renunciation and Law

cakravarti etc.).² Before his death, Ramanuja apparently appointed seventy-four men as the teachers of his tradition. Many of them were householders; but after the fifteenth century, some of the religious leadership in the Śrivaiṣṇava tradition passed on through renunicants who were heads of *mathas* ("cloister;" "monastery").

Basic to our discussion is the cognizance of the normative four stages of life described by classical Hindu texts. Beginning around the second century B.C.E. these texts identify four stages of life (student, householder, forest-dweller and renunciant) that male members of the upper three classes of society may undergo. Women did not *generally* have this choice, though there have been many exceptions; it has been observed that in the Hindu tradition, "a woman's religion is her family life."³

Women and Renunciation

We shall start by making a distinction between renunciation and asceticism; this is just to keep terms clear in this paper. The distinction is useful and has profitably been used by social anthropologists. The word "renunciant" will be used for the Indian word "*sannyāsi*," to refer to those people who have renounced the world formally, and with ritual ceremonies performed their own funeral rites to mark the social and civil death of their earlier identities. This ceremony releases them from the commitments and obligations of their earlier personalities and they enter a new and final stage of life described in the Hindu texts of law. The word "ascetic" will be used in a more general fashion, to include, but not be limited to renunciants. Many women, especially widows and abandoned wives accept ascetic practices (mode of dress, celibacy, fasting etc.) and their life style may be similar to that of the renunciant. However, they are not initiated into a separate stage of life; that of the *sannyāsi*-renunciant who has *rejected* the duties incumbent on a person in worldly life; rather the ascetic widow or abandoned wife is *fulfilling* the duties that she perceives to be imposed on her by society. The renunciant's style of life that a widow adopts is still in conformity with the duty (*dharma*) of a woman; formal "renunciation" (*sannyāsa*) denotes a rejection of such *dharma*. While the practices of the widow and the female renunciant may be similar, it must be recognized that the *intent* behind them puts them in very different categories in the Hindu tradition; the

---

² On the details and occurences of these titles, see my paper "Renunciation in Saffron and White Robes," *Monastic Life in the Christian and Hindu Traditions*. edited by Austin Creel and Vasudha Narayanan (Lewiston, 1990), p. 170–172.

³Leslie, Julia, *The Religious Role of Women in Ancient India: A Discussion of the Strīdharmapaddhati of Tryambakayajvan*, Ph.D. Thesis, Oriental Studies Faculty, University of Oxford, 1983.

ascetic life style of a widow indicates that she is *accepting* a traditional role that has been considered normative by society and by male authored texts; being a renunciant shows her *rejection* of that role and her traditional duties as a woman (*strīdharma*) and all that is associated with this life.

The status of a woman whose husband has become a renunciant is ambiguous at best. On the one hand, she is still socially considered to be a *sumangali*, an "auspicious woman" whose husband is alive. She still continues to dress as a *sumangali*; those of us familiar with Indian society know that in many conservative homes, the dress code of an elderly woman may change somewhat dramatically after her husband's death. Although the wife, or ex-wife of a man who has become a *sannyāsi* is still considered to be a *sumangali*, because of his "civil death," she inherits his property like a *widow*, and legally, because of his non-performance of conjugal duties, she has the right to sue for *divorce*.

There are many reasons based on which a person may sue for divorce under the Hindu law: if the spouse has virulent and incurable leprosy; if the spouse has communicable venereal disease; if the spouse has been missing for seven years and has not been heard of; if the spouse renounces the world by entering a religious order, or any number of other reasons. It is important to note that there are two parts to the sentence on renunciation: rejection of the world *and* the entrance into another order. There must be a total, complete abandonment of the world *and* an entering a religious order. Merely saying that one has renounced the world is not sufficient (*Kondal Rao* v. *Iswara Sanyasi*, 33 M.L.J. 63 at 65). The renunciation must be absolute; he must also renounce the desire for worldly things (*Sital Das* v. *Sant Ram*, AIR 1954 S.C. 606). The husband must also prove that he has undergone a positive act or ceremony by which he has entered an order; without the performance of the necessary rights, the renunciation will not be complete (*Baldeo Prasad* v. *Arya Priti Nidhi Sabah*, 1930, All. 643 at 644). There must be an initiation by a guru into the order of sannyasis by the appropriate mantra (*Satyanarayana Avadhani* v. *Religious Endowments Board*, 1957 A.P. 824 at 826); in some orthodox orders it must be proved that there has been a necesary ceremony like "Biraja Homa," "Pinda Dana" or "Prajagathi Yesthi." In *Krishna Singh* v. *Mathura Ahir*, the supreme court held that the question of whether a person has become a sannyasi has to be determined not according to the orthodox view, but according to the usage or custom of the particular sector or fraternity; that a religious denomination or fraternity enjoys complete autonomy in the matter of laying down the rites and ceremonies which are essential. It also specified that the recitation of the *presha mantram* or the renunciation formula is considered to be essential. Thus, in a sense, Ramanuja getting his initiation directly from God, without a guru, would only be acceptable today, if it could be proved that this was the custom in his religious *sampradāya* or tradition.

Renunciation and Law

In any case, once a person formally becomes a renunciant, his wife has the right to sue for divorce. According to religious law, a renunciant is considered as one who has "given up all pleasures and properties and whose sole duty is to...wait for the call for departure from this world. Such a person cannot be expected to fulfil the obligations of matrimony, chief of which is marital cohabitation, a thing which is forbidden for one who has entered the Sanyasi order."[4] This notion is seen in spirit in the story of Govinda Perumal (Empar), Ramanuja's cousin in the eleventh century. Govinda Perumal's marriage had not been consumated and his mother sought the intervention of Ramanuja, believing that her son would listen to him. Ramanuja asked Govinda Perumal to spend the night with his wife:

> The next morning, Ramanuja asked with a faint smile: "what did you do all night?" Govinda Perumal replied: "I felt the glow of the lord's presence everywhere, and could not be alone with my wife." Ramanuja said, "Do you know that according to the sacred texts, 'a twice born man cannot exist even for one day without being in one of the four stages of life?'" Govinda Perumal asked of Ramanuja, "Graciously initiate me, your servant, into the *sannyasa* stage of life."[5]

Performance of conjugal duties was seen as essential to the householder stage of life; according to Ramanuja's interpretation, by not performing his duties, Govinda Perumal was not a householder in the true sense of the word. Since scripture dictated that one could not be "in-between" stages, and he clearly rejected the householder stage and longed to be a renunciant, he was initiated as a renunciant immediately.

However, in the history of the Hindu tradition, there have been men who wore saffron robes (the customary apparel of a renunciant) and who still cohabited with their wives. Court rulings in this century have confirmed that such people cannot be considered as *sannyāsis* if they are still with their wives (*Sri Raghava Dass* v. *Sarjupayamma*, A.I.R. 1942 Mad. 43).

Despite the importance given to Ramanuja's renunciation, the Śrīvaiṣṇava tradition does not believe that becoming a *sannyāsi* is important or even necessary to gain liberation. According to their theology, they are saved because of their spiritual connection with their teachers, and not because of their own efforts. Many of the prominent teachers like Vedanta Desika in the

---

[4] Venkataraman S., *N. R. Raghavachariar's Hindu Law: Principles and Precedents*. 8th edition. (Madras, 1987).

[5] *The Splendor*, Loc. cit., pp. 219–220.

thirteenth century were householders. There is also no practice of jumping stages and going directly from the stage of a celibate student to a celibate *sannyāsi*, as is seen in the case of other traditions. Ramanuja and Govinda Perumal were both married, but renouncing their wives, they entered the fourth stage. Similarly, the pontiffs of the various mathas (monasteries) are *sannyāsis* today, but only after having been householders for many years. The third stage of life (forest dweller) was never considered important; in initation rituals today, sometimes, the person spends one night in the third stage before he is initiated as a *sannyāsi*.

Nor is there any great urge to become a *sannyāsi*, even among the very learned people. In one of the subsects of Śrivaiṣṇavism, the munitraya vatakalai sect, a pontiff who passed away in 1989 apparently nominated six different people to succeed him. All of them were married and had families; and all of them respectfully declined the honor. Generally, in these cases, if a man is willing to become the next leader of the community, he will be initiated as a *sannyāsi* and ascend to his seat either just before or soon after the former pontiff dies. It is not necessary for a pontiff to nominate a *sannyāsi* for the position; he may well nominate a married man. It is sufficient if he becomes *sannyāsi* after he is nominated and theoretically accepts the request. When a person so accepts the nomination, in many cases, the married disciples and other followers either set up monetary trusts or otherwise help the pontiff's ex-wife and family, who have so suddenly been left alone.[6]

Women do not become *sannyasinis* within the Srivaiṣṇava movement today, but they could do so in the past. K. V. Raman, professor of archeology, writes that that Ramanuja had some women renunciants (*korri*) as his disciples. I have not encountered it in any biographical information, but it must be noted that a lot of this hagiographic literature is androcentric. However, we do know that there were Śrivaiṣṇava women renunciants in Kanchipuram around thirteenth century. An inscription in the Kanchipuram temple states that a woman ascetic called Perarulalan korri ordered that her jewels be sold after her death and the monies were to be used for buying land for the temple.[7] Another renunciant called Tiruvattiyur-korri donated cattle so that a lamp could be lit in the temple.[8] The fact that women in the medieval ages made so many donations in their own names is itself striking; still more striking is that some of these women had

---

[6] I heard this from conversations with friends of the pontiff's families, but they were reluctant to be quoted or mentioned by name. They said that they looked after the family's welfare and even mentioned prominent contributors to the cause, but did not want the details to be used. This was *kainkarya*, loving service, done privately, and they did not want any publicity from these actions.

[7] K. V. Raman, *Sri Varadarajaswami Temple—Kanchi: A Study of Its History, Art and Architecture* (New Delhi, 1975), p. 135.

[8] 388 of 1919; quoted by K. V. Raman *Op. cit.*

renounced life and made their new name (the word "korri" or renunciant was added to their names) last for centuries by inscribing them on stone. Unfortunately, the tradition of female renunciation, like their names, has become, literally, *petrified* over the centuries.

We know that in the larger Hindu tradition, that women *do* and in the past, *have*, become renunciants, even though the classical texts have only allowed this stage for "regenerate" or twice born men. Women and *Śudras* have been left out of this grouping, but, as the British discovered over many years, while Hindu tradition has used hyperbole in declaring the religious-legal texts (*dharma śāstras*) to be an exposition of the Vedas, it didn't mean that they had to be *followed*. Even Manu, who lived around the beginning of the Christian era, and who wrote a major work on religious law, refers to female renunciants in passing, but the commentators are quick to point out that he probably refered to Buddhist or Jain nuns. Some commentators attribute a passage to Baudhayana, according to which even some orthodox women were allowed to become renunciants, but that passage is, interestingly enough, not found in many texts.[9] Catherine Ojha has writen about women ascetics (*sannyasinis*) in Hindu history and has done an anthropological study of some women renunciants in Benares. Lynn Teskey Denton has worked with some groups of women renunciants, again in Benares. Some of these women even undergo the *atma śraddha* rites (death of the self). Some celibate women lead organizations like the Siddha Yoga movement; in many of these orders, the leader is called "Ma" or "Mata" (mother). One such example is the "Mother Guru" discussed by Charles White.[10] Most of these women renunciants are seen in northern India; very few come from the south of India. The many socio-cultural reasons for this remain outside the scope of this discussion, but it is possible that harsher attitudes towards widows in some communities and in some parts of India lead them initially to adopt the lifestyle of an ascetic, and later on, as a full fledged renunciant.

One of the reasons why Śrivaiṣṇava women—and men—do not enter the fourth stage of life is because of a different interpretation that they give for the word "*sannyāsa*." Vedanta Desika (1268–1368) quotes a verse from a text called *Laksmi Tantra*, according to which the words *sannyāsa, prappati* ("surrender"), *saranagati* ("going for refuge") and *tyaga* ("abandonment; renunciation") are all considered to be synonyms. *Prapatti* or *Saranagati* is surrender to God, seeking him and his consort, the Goddess Laksmi as one's refuge. The lord's grace saves the human being and one only needs to surrender oneself to

---

[9] *Manu Smṛti* VIII 363, and the notes for 363 by G. Buhler.

[10] Charles S. J. White, "Mother Guru: Jnanananda of Madras, India," *Unspoken Worlds: Women's Religious Lives in Non-Western Cultures*, Nancy A. Falk and Rita M. Gross, eds. (San Francisco, 1980), pp. 22–37.

him. This fusion of detachment and domesticity certainly does not highlight the importance or necessity of abandoning the world and renouncing one's family. Men and women of all castes could, and according to the tradition, *should*, surrender themselves to Visnu in order to be saved; this became one of the distinctive characterestics of the Śrivaiṣnava community. What this meant in theological terms was that *even* women and *Śudras* were given access to salvific rituals.

Renunciation and Issues of Caste

Not withstanding the lukewarm status of *sannyāsa* in the Śrivaiṣnava tradition, we may still ask the question: can a member of the fourth class, i.e., a *Śudra* become a renunciant? According to the classical legal texts, only men of the upper three classes could go through all the four stages of life. *Śudras* and women are usually lumped together in one low category even for trivial issues: for instance, according to Manu, men of the upper classes will sip water three times to purify themselves, but women and *Śudras* should sip water only once (*Manu*, V–139). Therefore, according to some brahmin-based normative texts, *Śudras* were barred from the four stages of life and could not become renunciants.

Śudra ascetics are seen in the tradition of Ramanuja and in many Śaiva orders in south India.[11] However, it had widely been held that under Sastraic law, that a *Śudra* could not enter a religious order by renouncing his worldly connections in a manner that would be tantamount to civil death.[12] But in *Krishna Singh* v. *Mathura Ahir*,[13] a landmark case that is quoted over and over again, the Supreme Court made it clear that though the orthodox view does not allow *Śudras* to become *sannyāsis*, the existing practice in India is contrary to such a view and that at the present time, a Hindu of any caste can adopt the life a *sannyāsi*. It was further declared that where according to custom or usage, a *Śudra* can enter into a religous order, such usage will be recognized and the ban on *Śudras* becoming *sannyāsis* stands abrogated by virtue of the mandates embodied in Part III of *The Constitution of India*.

---

[11] Robert Lester, "Bhuvanagiri Swami and the Ekāṅgi Tradition." Paper presented at the conference on *Asceticism in the Hindu Tradition*, University of Florida, February, 1987.

[12]*Krishnaji* v. *Hannmaraddi*, 58 B 536: 36 Bom. L.r. 814: 194 B 385; *Dharamapuram Pandarasannadhi* v. *Virapandian* 22 M 302; etc.

[13] AIR 1980 SC 707.

Renunciation and Law

Questions of Authority

In *Krishna Singh* v. *Mathura Ahir*, the Supreme court observed, "In applying Personal Laws of the parties [the judge] could not introduce his concept of modern times, but should have enforced the law as derived from recognized authority sources of Hindu Law, i.e., *Smṛtis* and commentaries refered to and interpreted in various judgments of the High Courts except where such law is altered by usage or custom as modified or abrogated by statue." This leads us to ask what "custom" means and there have been several definitions. A typical description can be seen in the judicial committee's observation on the notion of custom in *Subhani* v. *Nawab*:

> It is undoubted that a custom observed in a particular district derives its force from the fact that it has from long usage obtained in that district the force of law. It must be ancient, but it is not of the essence of this rule that its antiquity must be carried back to a period beyond the memory of man—still less that it is ancient in the English technical sense. It will depend upon the circumstances of each case, what antiquity must be established before the custom can be accepted. What is necessary to be proved is that the usage has been acted upon in practice for such a long period and with such invariability as to show that it has by common consent, been submitted to as the established governing rule of the particular district.[14]

This notion of *custom* is integral in the understanding application of law in India. Because of custom, divorced women among the Manipuris are entitled to a right of residence in their parents home[15]; Dudekelas, a group of Muslims in Andhra Pradesh, are governed by Hindu law for succession and inheritance[16]; if a Kamma woman dies without children, and without making her will, all the presents given to her husband by her parents should be returned to them.[17] And so too, custom permits a *Śudra* to become a *sannyāsi*, if it can be established that the community has had this practice for a long time. This landmark decision was made in *Krishna Singh* v. *Mathura Ahir*[18] where the question of inheritance of

---

[14] ILR 1941 Lah 154: AIR 1941 PC 21.

[15] *Ningol Angothi* v. *Nangmaijing Sharma*, 1953, Manipur 8.

[16] *Rosanna* v. *Subanna* ILR 1979 AP 100.

[17] *Venkata Subbiah* v. *Bhujangayya* 1960 AP 412.

[18] 1980 SC 707; 1980 All LJ 299.

some property arose. It was alleged that a Śudra cannot become a renunciant, and so the property of the Śudra sannyāsi in question should devolve to the natural relatives, and not to the spiritual community. The supreme court asserted that indeed a Śudra could become a sannyāsi, and therefore, the natural relatives could not be the heirs.

Ascetics and Renunciants

We had observed earlier that one can adopt an ascetic life style, but that does not mean that one is a renunciant or a *sannyāsi*. To be an renunicant, a person will have to show a complete abandonment of all secular property and a final withdrawal from worldly affairs. After his civil death, he is excluded from inherting anything from his natural relatives[19]; neither he nor his natural relatives can succeed to each other's properties.[20] Merely calling oneself an ascetic (*bairagi*) or religious mendicant does not indicate he is formally a *sannyāsi*, and he may still succeed to property.[21] In the last case mentioned, it was also ruled that if a son becomes a Bairagi (i.e., an ascetic without formally being initiated as a renunciant), the father *cannot* adopt another son, because the Bairagi's capacity to confer spiritual benefit still continues. (It was widely assumed that one of the main reasons for adopting a boy is because of his capacity to fulfill scriptural obligations and do the correct rituals for his father's salvation).

Even if he a person becomes a renunciant and does undergo civil death, he still may acquire and hold private property, but that will devolve, not on his natural relations but according to special rules of inheritance.[22] The property of a *sannyāsi* devolves to his disciples; in the classical texts of Mitakshara (II. viii) and Viramitrodaya (III. viii. 2) these articles are generally described as being his clothes, books and a few necessary articles. However, a renunciant may hold extensive properties as the head of a *matha* or as the manager of some religous or charitable endowment, and succession to such property is regulated by the special custom of the foundation. If a *sannyāsi's* renunciation is less than complete (and we have seen the various acts that are considered to make his renunciation acceptable to the law), his natural heirs may inherit his personal property.

---

[19]*Gouri* v. *Niader*, 18 C.W.N. 59: 23 I.C. 287; *Parshottam* v. *Bessaibhai*, 34 Bom L.R. 852: 1932 B 549.

[20]*Pandit Parma Nand* v. *Nihal Chand* 1938 65 IA 252: ILR 1938 Lah 453.

[21]*Teeluck Chunder* v. *Shyamachurn* 164 I WR 209.

[22]1938 65 IA 252: ILR (1938) Lah 453.

A Question of Succession

Most pontiffs select or nominate a disciple to succeed them to the role of leader of a community. We have already observed that there is no great rush on part of householders to compete for this position; yet in many Hindu communities there have been legal cases on this issue of succession. The Śrivaiṣṇava community witnessed several in the nineteenth century. In *Rangachariar* v. *Yegna Dikshatur*,[23] the issues of "incomplete nomination" and partial abandonment of the world were at question. The plaintiff (Dikshatur) sued for declaration of his right as the leader, the "jeer" of a *matha* and said that he had been nominated by the previous pontiff. It was revealed in the course of the trial that while there was nomination, the other disciples opposed the selection. The dying pontiff initiated Dikshatur, and asked him to undergo the rituals to make him a renunciant soon. The pontiff died before the plaintiff was fully initiated. During the trial it came out that the plaintiff had not uttered the *presha mantram* that was vital to the initiation process, and in any case, after the death of the pontiff, he did not become *sannyāsi*. In the initial ruling, the court gave a period of four months for the plaintiff to become a renunciant and assume leadership; both plaintiff and the defendants appealed against this judgement. The plaintiff said that if he was not to be made the head of the community, he saw no point in becoming a renunciant, and so pleaded for more time. In the appeals, the judges expressed his opinion that the plaintiff was probably not initiated fully, his right to assume the position of leadership eased on his omission to become a *sannyāsi*, there was no similar case of succession in the tradition and dismissed the case. He also referred to the the unscrupulous behavior of the defendants and dismissed their appeal too.

Because of the sizeable wealth accumulated by many of the organizations and monasteries that hold together various renunciants, questions of succession and leadership are increasingly referred to the legal system. One such case, *Krishna Singh* v. *Mathura Ahir* initially entered the judicial system in 1951 and it was 1980 before the Supreme court finally gave its verdict. It is curious to note the authorities cited by the justices in their judgement included several outdated treatises and works by Indian and western authors: Hastings' *Encyclopedia of Religion and Ethics* (circa 1928); H. H. Wilson's (1786–1860) works, J. N. Bhattacharjee's *Hindu Castes and Sects* (1896) and Mukherjea's *The Hindu Law of Religious and Charitable Trusts* (Tagore law lectures, 1936). Thus, Sherring's *Hindu Tribes and Castes* (1871) is quoted to describe the initiation of a Dasanami *Sannyāsin*, rather than a more recent work by a Dasanami *Sannyāsin*, Hastings' information on why only Brahmins and the

---

[23] 13 Mad 524; Appelate civil, 1890.

"twice-born" should become renunciants, and and Wilson's works are profusely quoted to interpret Hindu law. In judgments pertaining to the issues of renunciation—and in other fields as well—the judges sometimes act like "panditas" or traditional interpreters, but an obvious handicap is the lack of training that the justices have in the History of religion.

It is because of the recognition that there are *many* Hindu traditions and castes, many sources of religious and social authority, that we have the highlighting of notions of custom, practice, and usage in the interpretation and the application of the law. Renunciation, like the Hindu tradition, is not generic; it always comes with a brand name. While some of the core rituals bear similarity, the details are determined by the specific code dictated by the group, community, order, or spiritual brotherhood into which the renunciant is entering. Who can become a renunciant, and how he or she does it, is not so much dictated by the ancient codes of law, the *dharmaśāstras*, as by a twentieth century community that may or may not touch base with scripture. Usually, of course, a pious member of any Hindu tradition, believes that what s/he practices is in tune with the *dharmaśāstras*, and there is a conitinuity of tradition and custom.

Professor Lariviere, in his excellent article, "Justices and *Panditas*: Some Ironies in Contemporary Readings of the Hindu Legal Past" observes that "even though the office of *pandita* (traditional expert) has long been abolished from the courts and the very training of modern *panditas* has become rare, the texts of the *dharmaśāstra* tradition continue to be used in a very 'panditic' fashion by the courts of modern India." He writes that the justices function as *panditas*, and the "texts they cite are mere window dressing for the interpretations of Hindu law they seek to promulgate." The British did try to eliminate the perceived inconsistencies of the traditional legal system which was based on the interpretations of the *dharmaśāstras* and replace them with the precedents of the judge. The British had assumed that the *dharmaśāstra* was internally consistent and that it applied to all Hindus, and did not realize how flexible and elastic the texts were at the hands of skilled commentators and interpreters. In modern India we are confornted with an irony in respect to the use of *dharmaśāstra* in contemporary decisions:

> The courts very often use these texts to legitimize the law that had evolved through the case law: they interpret classical texts in ways that support current practice, received ideas, current social norms, and so forth in much the same way as the *pandita* of pre-British days.[24]

---

[24] Richard W. Lariviere, "Justices and *Panditas*: Some Ironies in Contemporary Readings of the Hindu Legal Past," *The Journal of Asian Studies*, Vol. 48, No. 4, November, 1989.

Renunciation and Law

The *dharmasāstras* may be used as rough pointers; they are not edicts carved in stone. The commentarial role still goes on in the skillful process of uniting notions of legal precedents with the importance of custom and usage. For Hindu law, there is a dual heritage to be reckoned with; a dual set of scripture and interpretation at work: the dharma texts and localized interpretive judgments on the one hand, and the British system of legal precedents and uniformity on the other. Judgments in cases like *Krishna Singh* v. *Mathura Ahir* makes it clear that the innovative and dynamic process of adapting the *śāstras* to fit the modern age is more important than just using legal precedents.

Hindu literature is filled with hermeneutical essays and commentarial traditions. When one reads the judments rendered in cases like *Krishna Singh* v. *Mathura Ahir* in their entirety, one may perceive that the commentarial process is not limited to literature or theology. The learned justices in India interpret, and as Ong described the process, they "bring out what is concealed in a given manifestation,...make evident what in the manifestation is not evident to the milieu in which the interpreter's audience lives." It is the traditional function of hermeneutics when

> something foreign, strange, separated in time, space or experience is made familiar, present, comprehensible; something requiring representation, explanation, or translation is somehow "brought to understanding"—is interpreted.[25]

In the rulings of the judges, "the hermes process" is at work, the *pandita* is still going strong. If Ramanuja's wife were to have her day in court today, Ramanuja would have to prove that his entrance into the *sannyāsi* order was in line with custom and tradition, even though there were no "human" witnesses to the actual sacrament. Ramanuja's wife would have inherited his belongings, because, with he had undergone a "civil death;" but she would be treated like an auspicious woman, a *sumangali*, because her husband was alive, and would have been eligible for divorce, if she so chose, because of his abandonment of home and non performance of the duties of a householder. And for every one of these rights, there would be a modern legal precedent to support the case.

---

[25] *Ibid.*, p. 757.

16

Auroville and the Courts of India: Religion and Secular

Robert N. Minor

On November 8, 1982, the Supreme Court of India ruled in the case of S. P. Mittal, the Sri Aurobindo Society and others versus the Union of India, that the Auroville (Emergency Provisions) Act of 1980 did not violate constitutional provisions for freedom of religion. The Act provided for the temporary control of the township of Auroville by the government of India in order to restore order and promote the purposes of the township's Charter as set down by the second guru of the Aurobindo movement, the Mother (Mirra Alfassa Richard, 1878–1973), on June 19, 1967.

This decision was another in a line of judgments the Supreme Court was called to set down on the issue of religious freedom in India. Articles 25 and 26 of the Indian Constitution provide for "freedom of conscience and the right freely to profess, practise and propagate religion," but subject these rights to "public order, morality and health," and insure the government's right to regulate and restrict "any economic, financial, political or other secular activity which may be associated with religious practice."[1]

---

[1] The full text of Articles 25 and 26 of the Constitution is:

    25. (1) Subject to public order, morality and health and to the other provisions of this Part, all persons are equally entitiled to freedom of conscience and the right freely to profess, practise and propagate religion.

    (2) Nothing in this article shall affect the operation of any existing law or prevent the State from making any law—

        (a) regulating or restricting any economic, financial, political or other secular activity which may be associated with religious practise;

        (b) providing for social welfare and reform or the throwing open of Hindu religious institutions of a public character to all classes and sections of Hindus.

    Explanation I.—The wearing and carrying of *kirpans* shall be deemed to be included in the professions of Sikh religion.

    Explanation II.—In sub-clause (b) of clause (2), the reference to Hindus shall be construed as including reference to persons professing the Sikh, Jaina or

These Constitutional restrictions on religion, as Baird points out, "make it clear that the traditional religious expressions cannot exist if they are in conflict with the Constitutional religious model."[2] Crucial to the constitutional model, but lacking in most traditional religions, is the assumption that there is a distinction between two realms of life which are designated "religion" and "secular." In spite of the fact that these terms are ambiguous, the categories they designate were left undefined in the Constitution[3] and, thus, the Courts were left to define them. The Courts were required to come up with a legal definition of religion and of the secular which would embody what they believed the Constitutional model to be. That this has been difficult and that even the categories "religion" and "secular" themselves have proven to be inadequate, Baird has already argued.[4] In the context of his analysis, the following is a study of the resolution of one case in 1982 which included some reanalysis of the categories "religion" and "secular." Its sphere was somewhat different than previous cases because the Court was called on to decide if a community were a religion, not merely whether a ritual, practice or other institution belonging to an accepted religious community was "religious." Though the Court declared that it would rely upon past definitions, the majority opinion did not clearly argue from this definition and the minority opinion found it useless. The decision, however, continued the pattern which increased the realm of the "secular," that is, the realm of government regulation.

Buddhist religion, and the reference to Hindu religious institutions shall be construed accordingly.

26. Subject to public order, morality and health, every religious denomination or any section thereof shall have the right—

    (a) to establish and maintain institutions for religious and charitable purposes;

    (b) to manage its own affairs in matters of religion;

    (c) to own and acquire movable and immovable property; and

    (d) to administer such property in accordance with law.

[2]Robert D. Baird, "Religion and the Secular: Categories for Religious Conflict and Religious Change in Independent India," in *Religion and Social Conflict in South Asia*, ed. by Bardwell L. Smith (Leiden, 1976), p. 50.

[3]Though the members of the Constituent Assembly agreed that India should be "secular," and though the term itself would be added to the Constitution by the Constitution Amendment Bill of 1976, there was considerable disagreement about the actual meaning of the term so that it could even be used on both sides of a debate. See Robert D. Baird, "'Secular State' and the Indian Constitution," in *Religion in Modern India*, ed. by Robert D. Baird, 1st ed. (Delhi, 1981), pp. 389–416.

[4]*Ibid.*, pp. 47–63.

Auroville and the Courts

The Auroville Conflict

On February 28, 1968, the Mother founded the township of Auroville, "the city of Dawn," five miles northeast of Pondicherry. Her goal was to develop a place where on the basis of the *Weltanschauung* of her predecessor, Sri Aurobindo (1872–1950), people could put into practice his "Integral Yoga." The Mother and Aurobindo's followers were convinced that this *Weltanschauung* and Integral Yoga were revealed to Aurobindo as a result of his yogic experiences. These "supramental experiences" convinced him that the universe was an evolution of the Divine, which is characterized as both eternal Becoming and eternal Being. This evolution of consciousness is to proceed beyond the current level of human knowledge, Mind, to levels in which the limitations of logic will be transcended. Integral Yoga is the promotion of this further evolution by pushing beyond Mind and by reaching down to pull lower levels on the evolutionary scale, animal, vegetable and mineral, to higher levels.[5]

Though it may have much in common with the activities of those who do not accept Aurobindo and the Mother's *Weltanschauung*, such as promoting the conservation of natural resources, their position clearly became another of the alternative views of reality available among the religions and philosophies of the world. But Aurobindo and the Mother did not see it so. According to the definition of "religion" they accepted, their own viewpoint was not a "religion" but the true position behind all the "religions." They thus defined these other positions as "religions" and treated them in the same manner that some of these "religions" do other "religions." They relativized the positions which they called "religions" in terms of their own position, and confidently believed that the believers in these other positions would eventually evolve to accept the position of Aurobindo.[6]

The township meant to embody their position grew slowly. Its population was made up mostly of foreign nationals who evolved a town meeting form of government. Grants were accepted from private individuals and organizations in India, Europe and the Americas. The Indian central government and some of its state governments provided grants for specific projects in Auroville. The central government brought the Auroville project before UNESCO, which responded with much moral and some financial support and recommended the project to its member nations as "an international cultural township."

---

[5] For a full discussion of Aurobindo's viewpoint and its development see Robert M. Minor, *Sri Aurobindo: the Perfect and the Good* (Columbia, MO, 1978).

[6] On their view of other religions see Robert N. Minor, "The Response of Sri Aurobindo and the Mother," in *Modern Indian Responses to Religious Pluralism*, ed. by Harold Coward (Albany, 1987), pp. 85–104.

With the Mother's death in 1973, and the absence of her leadership, two groups began to vie for the support of their own visions of the nature of Auroville and, thus, for leadership. The Sri Aurobindo Society, founded by the Mother in 1960, moved to consolidate its control. It had been the official recipient of funds for Auroville as well as its legal representative to the government. The foreign "pioneers" living in Auroville resisted the moves of the Society, believing that they more correctly understood the Mother's intentions for Auroville's government. Legal and physical clashes took place as the conflict between the two groups escalated. On December 21, 1976, the Ministry of Home Affairs set up a committee to investigate the matter. It confirmed irregularities, mismanagement and misuse of funds.

Not until 1980, was an examination of the Sri Aurobindo Society's books by the Central Bureau of Investigation ordered by the Government. The President of India proclaimed "The Auroville (Emergency Provisions) Ordinance" on November 10. The Sri Aurobindo Society responded by obtaining an anticipatory injunction from the Calcutta High Court, but the Central government appealed and the injunction was vacated.

On December 2, 1980 the Lok Sabha, and, on December 9, the Rajya Sabha, passed "The Auroville (Emergency Provisions) Act" "to take over, for a limited period, the management" of Auroville. It became effective with the President's assent on December 17, 1980. Auroville was now officially under government control.[7]

The Sri Aurobindo Society again responded by filing a civil suit in the Calcutta High Court contending that the Parliament had passed an act in conflict with the West Bengal Societies Registration Act and that it was interfering in a religious institution and, thus, violating Articles 25 and 26 of the Constitution. This and other petitions were transferred to the Supreme Court of India which issued a partial injunction but ordered that the International Advisory Council provided for in the Act be constituted by the government. In December, 1980 over 90% of the Aurovillians represented by K. Tewari filed a petition in support of the Government. The Court accepted the petition on December 19 and the Aurovillians were accepted as a party to the case. The Court agreed to hear the case in January, 1981, but the hearing was postponed a number of times.

---

[7] The Act was extended through "Amendment Acts" in 1985 and 1987. What appears to be a final resolution was passed in September 1988: the "Auroville Foundation Act, 1988" makes the Central Government the owner of all property and assets related to Auroville and sets up a permanent foundation with a "Governing Board" appointed by the government as the main authority within the foundation. For a more complete analysis of the conflict see Robert N. Minor, "Nonroutinized Charisma: The Case of Aurobindo and Auroville," in *Religion in South Asia: Essays in Honor of Robert Eric Frykenberg*, ed. by John Paul and Keith E. Yandell (Delhi, forthcoming).

Auroville and the Courts

In May, 1981, the Court issued several orders regarding the case. On May 8, it ordered the Government-appointed administrator, L. P. Nigam, a retired judge of the Allahabad High Court, to value the 37,000 shares in Geo Industries and Insecticides, India, Ltd. belonging to the Society; ordered the Executive Committee of the Society to report the assets of the Society which relate to Auroville; directed that the Executive Committee of the Society "will not interfere in any manner with the construction of the Matrimandir, the charge of which has been given to the Aurovillians"; and ordered the residents of Auroville to "submit to the Administrator a detailed list of the respective day to day activities which are conducted on the property called Auroville...." One result of this order was that the Society could no longer block cement permits and funds for the Matrimandir, the large structure in the center of Auroville which was being built as a symbol of the Mother and the Spirit behind the evolution of the universe.

On May 13 the Supreme Court ordered that "none should attempt to create fixed assets in Auroville property without prior permission in writing of the Administrator." All property that is created will be under "the collective ownership of the community residing in Auroville." On July 9, the local Tindivanam court magistrate ordered that proceedings regarding ownership of Auroville cashew plantations be dropped. The Society had claimed ownership of the plantations. On August 7, the Supreme Court turned down two applications from a group of paid village workers and German visitors led by Shyamsunder, a leader in the Society, which sought to add their names "as party-respondents in the writ petitions." The rejected petition had called for their inclusion under the term "Aurovillians," for the rejection of the government takeover of Auroville, and for a revival of the old committees of the Society to manage Auroville. Finally a group of Europeans working to raise support for Auroville in Europe added a petition to the Court endorsing the standpoints of the Government of India.

The Arguments

The Court eventually heard arguments and on November 8, 1982, set down its decision. In doing so it was deciding "religious/secular" issues in a new realm. In past cases the Court was dealing with what it agreed was a religion or religious community for which it was required to decide whether a practice or other component was "secular," and thus capable of regulations, or "religious," and thus protected by Articles 25 and 26 of the Constitution.

In those cases the Court was required to answer questions such as : Was a religion's right to manage the properties of a temple secular or religious? Was the Swaminarayan religious sect Hindu? Is it a secular matter to decide what rituals and ceremonies of a religion are essential? Is the appointment of a priest a religious or secular matter? In all those cases a community which the Court had presupposed was a part of a religion or was religious was attempting to define which of its activities are "religious."[8] In the Auroville case, however, the Court was asked to determine whether or not a whole community, a thought system, and the resulting institutions, actually constitute a religion and its components.

The petitioners in the Auroville case had argued that the followers of Sri Aurobindo accept his beliefs and, thus form a religious denomination in the same manner that the followers of Ramanuja, Madhva and other religious teachers do. Since in a 1954 case, *Commissioner, Hindu Religious Endowments, Madras* v. *Sirur Mutt*, the followers of Ramanuja and Madhva were viewed as religious denominations by the Court, the followers of the religious teacher Aurobindo also constitute a religious denomination. They share a common faith and organization and have a distinctive name.

Quoting Sri Aurobindo and the Mother and the opinions of others, the petitioners argued that though Sri Aurobindo and the Mother rejected "religion," "religiosity," and "religionism," they were not averse to "True Religion." The petitioners also submitted their own definition of "religion" and "religious denomination":

> the ingredients of religion are:
> (1) A spiritual ideal;
> (2) A set of concepts or precepts on God-Man relationship underlying the ideal;
> (3) A methodology given or evolved by the founder or followers of the religion to achieve the ideal; and
> (4) A definite following of persons having common faith in the precepts and concepts;
> and in order to constitute a 'religious denomination' two further ingredients are needed;
> (5) The followers should have a common orginisation;
> (6) They should be designated and designable by a distinct name—This may usually be the name of the founder himself.[9]

---

[8]See for example, the following cases: *Commissioner, Hindu Religious Endowments, Madras* v. *Sirur Mutt*, SCJ XVII 1954 335–361;*Panachand Gandhi* v. *State of Bombay*, SCJ XVII 1954 480–493; *Shri Govindlaiji* v. *State of Rajasthan*, AIR, Supreme Court, 1963 876–1667.; *Yagnapurushdasji* v. *Muldas*, AIR, Supreme Court, 1966 1119–1135; *Seshammal and Others* v. *State of Tamil Nadu*, SCC, II, Part I (1972). These and others are carefully analyzed in Robert D. Baird, "Religion and the Secular...." pp. 47–63.

[9]*S. P. Mittal* v. *Union of India*, AIR 1983 SC 25–26.

The petitioners then pointed out that in the case of Sri Aurobindo and his followers, one can identify an ideal, concepts, a methodology, a definite following with organizations such as Ashrams, as well as practices such as the chanting of the mantras and the offering of flowers, the use of symbols for identification, and the existence of places of pilgrimage such as the Samadhi of Sri Aurobindo and the Mother in Pondicherry. Thus, according to the petitioners' definition, Aurobindo had set up a religion.

The contention of the respondents and the Solicitor-General of India was that the teachings of Sri Aurobindo do not constitute a religion and that neither the Society nor Auroville are religious denominations. They submitted that membership in the Society requires only that one must subscribe to its aims and objects. In face, rule nine of the "Rules and Regulations of the Sri Aurobindo Society" states that: "The membership is open to people everywhere without any distinction of nationality, religion, caste, creed or sex." Since by the Society's self-definition membership is universal, they argued, the Society cannot be a religious denomination. One must lose one's previous religion to join another and that is not required here. Under this definition of "religion," then, a religious denomination cannot encompass others in an inclusivistic manner; it must require the abandonment of other religions for one to join it.

Further, they argued, a religious denomination must be new and distinctive. But, though Aurobindo may have introduced some innovations, his view is substantially "a part of the Hindu philosophy." Whereas others might have argued thus to claim that Aurobindo's views are a part of the religion of "Hinduism," the petitioners argue that this identification with "Hindu philosophy" makes it non-religious.

Finally, they argued that since Aurobindo claimed insights from meditation, his teachings cannot be religious. Because scientific experiments have been able to study meditation's effects on the body, meditation is a science, they said. Even the Court declared meditation secular in *Hiralal Mallick* v. *State of Bihar* in 1977, referring to claims made in the West in studies of Transcendental Meditation: "Modern scientific studies have validated ancient vedic insights bequeathing to mankind new meditational, yogic and other therapeutics, at once secular, empirically tested and trans-religious."[10] Similarly in a 1977 criminal case the Court recognized the use of meditation as appropriate when discussing a "spiritual dimension" of the Indian Constitution which may be projected into penology: "Indian courts may draw inspiration from Patanjali sutra even as they derive punitive patterns from the Penal Code (most of Indian

---

[10]*Ibid.*, p. 26. See *Hiralal Mallick* v. *State of Bihar*, AIR 1977 SC at 2243.

meditational therapy is based on the sutras of Patanjali."[11] Therefore, the respondents argued that Aurobindo's Integral Yoga is a science not a religion.

The Decision

The Court was unanimous in its rejection of the writ petitions. The Auroville Act, the justices said did not violate either the West Bengal Societies Registration Act or Articles 25 and 26 of the Constitution. For our purposes it is the Justices' discussion of the definitions of the categories "religion" and "secular" in the Auroville case that interest us. On this discussion the majority view was written by Justice R. B. Misra and the minority view by Justice Chinnappa Reddy.

Both opinions agreed that historically Aurobindo, the Mother, and the Society had claimed that the Sri Aurobindo Ashram, the Society, and Auroville were non-religious institutions. In bringing the Auroville project to the government and then to UNESCO, the project was proposed as a "cultural township" which was in "full consonance and conformity with India's higher ideals and aspirations."[12] The reason the Government of India took the project to UNESCO was "for the development of Auroville as an international cultural township," not a religious institution. Likewise the Memorandum of Association of the Society speaks of it as a "scientific research orginisation," as does the application for exemption under the Income Tax Act. In the majority opinion, the Society cannot first say that it is secular and that Auroville is a secular undertaking, and later claim that both are religious institutions. The Government of India had accepted the former claims and acted upon them.

The majority opinion accepted the Charter of Auroville as given by the Mother as evidence that Auroville is not a religious institution. Though the Charter requires each one who lives in Auroville to be "the willing servitor of the Divine consciousness," though it calls for the use of "all discoveries from without and within," and though it describes Auroville as the site of both "material and spiritual research," the majority of the justices had no trouble seeing these by its own definition as non-religious. Thus, they took the Charter as proof that Auroville is a secular institution.[13]

---

[11]*Ibid.*, p. 27. From *M. Giasuddin* v. *State of A. P.*, AIR 1977 SC 1935.

[12]*Ibid.*

[13]The above quotations are from the Court's version in *Ibid.*, 28. The full Charter of Auroville as set down by the Mother and quoted with some apparently unconscious minor changes by the Court reads:

As expected, the majority opinion begins with a discussion of the meaning of the term "religion." Reviewing the fact that the words "religion" and "religious denomination" are undefined in the Constitution, and quoting the *Mahābhārata* regarding the term *dharma* to support the ambiguity of "religion," it asserts that the term has no clear meaning: "it is a term which is hardly susceptible of any rigid definition."[14] It then treats as its basic definitional assumption five "propositions of law" which it distills from the judgment of the Court in the 1954 case *Commissioner, Hindu Religious Endowments, Madras v. Sirur Mutt*. The Court, it says, has "consistently followed" this definition of "religion" in later cases:

> (1) Religion means "a system of beliefs and doctrines which are regarded by those who profess that religion as conducive to their spiritual well-being."
> (2) A religion is not merely an opinion, doctrine or belief. It has its outward expression in acts as well.
> (3) Religion need not be theistic.
> (4) "Religious denomination" means a religious sect or body having a common faith and organisation and designated by a distinctive name.
> (5) A law which takes away the rights of administration from the hands of a religious denomination altogether and vests [it] in another authority would amount to violation of the right guaranteed under Clause (d) of Art 26.[15]

The opinion then examined the teachings of Sri Aurobindo "to see whether they constitute a religion." Its summary recognizes that Aurobindo pro-

---

> Auroville belongs to nobody in particular. Auroville belongs to humanity as a whole. But to live in Auroville one must be the willing servitor of the Divine Consciousness.
>
> Auroville will be the place of an unending education, of constant progress, and a youth that never ages.
>
> Auroville wants to be the bridge between the past and future. Taking advantage of all discoveries from without and within, Auroville will boldly spring toward future realisations.
>
> Auroville will be a site of material and spiritual researches for a living embodiment of an actual human unity.

The Mother, *Collected Works* (Pondicherry, 1980), XIII, pp. 199–201.

[14] *Ibid.*, p. 19. The Court is actually quoting from its 1954 judgment in *Commissioner, Hindu Religious Endowments, Madras v. Shirur Mutt*, p. 348.

[15] *Ibid.*, p. 20.

fessed "a divine consciousness pervading the whole universe"; an evolution of this Divine which will lead humanity "back to all pervading divine consciousness" in which humanity and the universe "are destined to become divine"; a path leading to "union with Brahman," freeing "the individual from the hands of individuality and by exclusion of all mankind, will eventually achieve Mukti or liberation"; and a universality of appeal and explanation in terms of "the subtle worlds working behind" the surface and a "spark of divinity within which is one everywhere." The opinion makes no attempt to related these to its own definition of "religion" but concludes that Aurobindo's beliefs constitute a philosophy of "cosmic salvation through spiritual evolution" with its "distinctive feature" being that it is universal.

It is the claim that Aurobindo's teaching can include people from all the religions, and it is this inclusivism that the majority opinion is convinced is its "distinctive feature." This claim of inclusivism is similar to that made by "Hindu" apologists who espouse a Neo-Advaita position, a position particularly made popular by Swami Vivekananda and S. Radhakrishnan. The majority of the judges, however, accepted Aurobindo's claim of universality and thereby assumed his position to be one encompassing all religions. By such an assumption, it cannot be one of the religions. "Any one born in any part of the world, born of parents professing any religion can accept his yoga."[16] Among the modern Hindu apologists, however, this all-inclusive characteristic is a claim made of "Hinduism," even giving it superiority over the other religions which are exclusivistic.

Though their summary of persuasive evidence refers to the totality of the arguments in a general manner, the acceptance of the claim of universality by Sri Aurobindo and the Mother seems to constitute an important element for the majority of the justices as they side with the respondents. In fact, the majority opinion does not comment on any other doctrine it cites. Only the claim to universality is discussed as an important claim in the evidence the Court cites to judge that Aurobindo's vies is non-religious and that the Society is not a religious denomination.

This would seem to be the end of the discussion on the basis of what the Court considers now an established definition of religion with "propositions of law laid down" by the Court. However, in his minority opinion Justice Chinnappa Reddy does not feel compelled to accept any previous definitions given by the Court. In his opinion judicial definitions are "explanatory not

---

[16]*Ibid.*, p. 21. The above discussion of the position by the majority opinion is on *Ibid.*, pages 21–22. For an analysis of how President Radhakrishnan affirmed that the state could promote his position, which he called "the religion of the spirit" and still be "secular," because not promoting one of the "religions," see Robert N. Minor, *Radhakrishnan: A Religious Biography* (Albany, 1987), pp. 120–123.

Auroville and the Courts

definitive." They are not statutory in themselves, deciding what the only legal definition of a term is, but merely attempts to explain what was meant in a particular statute. A new statute by its very intentions may include new definitions.

Unfortunately, he says, judicial definitions are often mistakenly taken as statutory themselves.

> Law has a tendency to harden with the passage of time and judicial pronouncements are made to assume the form of statutory pronouncements. So soon as a word or expression occur[ing] in the statute is judicially defined, the tendency is to try to interpret the language employed by the judges in the judicial definition as if it has been transformed into a statutory definition. That is wrong. Always words and expressions to be interpreted are those employed in the statute and not those used by judges for felicitous explanation.[17]

With this assumption as his starting point, he was free to reexamine the intended meaning of the term and to range through the problems involved in defining "religion" with the intention of struggling anew with the matter.

His opinion began with a reminder to the Court similar to that of the majority though in more precise terms. The issue surrounding the term "religion" is that different people define the word differently, not that the word cannot be defined or cannot be given a rigid definition. "Religion like 'democracy' and 'equality' is an elusive expression, which everyone understands according to his preconceptions. What is religion to some is pure dogma to others and what is religion to others is pure superstition to some others."[18] But, he says, the appropriate approach to the question of definition here is explanatory, to explain what was and is meant. One must not only ask what the experts say but what do the people of "the Socialist, Secular, Democratic Republic of India" mean by "religion" and "religious denomination"? On the basis of the fact that India is a democracy the appropriate approach to the question, then, is to determine what the people of India mean by "religion." Since the Constitution says this involves the conscience, "religion" must be taken in "no narrow, stifling sense but in a liberal, expansive way."

Though he calls for a broad definition, Justice Reddy has limits in mind. Thus, he says, etymology is of no help because it provides too broad a meaning: "to bind." Every bond would be called "religion" on that definition. On the one hand for Justice Reddy one cannot "obviously" confine "religion" to the

---

[17]*Ibid.*, p. 9.

[18]*Ibid.*, p. 3.

traditional religions (Hinduism, Islam, Buddhism, Christianity, etc.): "A religion may not be widespread. It may have little following. It may not have even a name, as indeed most tribal religions do not have." But few doubt that these are "religions" as well.

On the other hand there are further limits to the definition, for, he says, groups may be dedicated to "secular" tasks but lack "the 'spiritual connection.'"

> Again, a band of persons, large or small, may not be said to be adherents of a religion merely because they share some common beliefs and common interests and practise common rites and ceremonies; nor can pietistic recitation and solemn ritual combine to produce religion on that account only. Secret societies dedicated to secular tasks and indulging in queer oaths and observances, guilds and groups of persons who meet but to dine and wine but who subject their members to extravagant initiation ceremonies, village and tribal sorcerers and coven of witches who chant, rant and dance in the most weird way possible are all far removed from religion. They appear to lack the 'spiritual connection'.[19]

Justice Reddy's opinion assumes that one can distinguish secular tasks; indeed, past Supreme Court decisions have done this through the imposition of a new religious model that conflicts with traditional models in which religion encompasses all of life. And the Courts have shown that these "secular" activities can be associated with "religion." But for Justice Reddy, in the question of whether or not a community constitutes a religion, what cannot be lacking is "the spiritual connection." That "spiritual" element is what would distinguish a "religious" group from a "secular" one. He moves on without offering a definition of that element.

Justice Reddy surveys the Constitutional discussions of religion by examining the language surrounding it in Articles 25 and 26 of the Constitution itself. He concludes that "the Constitution considers Religion as a matter of thought, expression, belief, faith and worship, a matter involving the conscience and a matter which may be professed, practised and propagated by anyone and which may even have some secular activity associated with it." He surveys past court decisions, and concludes that they also evidence that "religion" is "incapable of precise judicial definition...." Yet, based upon the Constitution and these past decisions, he sums up: "So, religion is a matter of belief and

---

[19]*Ibid.*, p. 4.

doctrine, concerning the human spirit, expressed overtly in the form of ritual and worship."[20]

Armed with this definition distilled from the Constitution and, thus, representing the view of the people of India, he finds that the definition is easily applied in some cases. In others a religion may not be easily identified by the definition. As a result, for these exceptional cases he recommends that the Court fall back upon the claims of the community and the viewpoints of outsiders about the institution in question.

> There is no formula of general application. There is no knife-edge test. Primarily, it is a question of the consciousness of the community, how does the fraternity or sodality (if it is permissible to use the word without confining it to Roman Catholic groups) regard itself, how do others regard the fraternity or sodality.[21]

Justice Reddy proposes that in cases where a community does not clearly fit into a general definition of religion, the community itself and the perceptions of outsiders should be the test of whether or not a community constitutes a religion.

He suggests that a community may be a religion if the founder of the community did not intend to found a religion.

> In origin, the founder may not have intended to found a religion at all. He may have merely protested against some rituals and observances, he may have disagreed with the interpretation of some earlier religious tenets. What he said, what he preached and what he taught, his protest, his dissent, his disagreement might have developed into a religion in the course of time, even during his lifetime. He may be against religion itself, yet history and the perception of the community may make a religion out of what was not intended to be a religion and he may be hailed as the founder of a new religion.[22]

In fact, he points out, at the beginning of many of the accepted religions themselves there are examples of individuals who did not think that they were founding a new religion.

As to the phrase "religious denomination," Justice Reddy rejects the Oxford dictionary definition borrowed by Justice Mukerjea in the Sirur Mutt

---

[20]*Ibid.*, p. 8.
[21]*Ibid.*
[22]*Ibid.*, pp. 8–9

case: "a collection of individuals classed together under the same name; a religious sect or body having a common faith and organisation and designated by a distinctive name."[23] Since judicial definitions are explanatory not statutory, he says, the Court is under no obligation to continue to use it. Many accepted groups possessed no distinctive name or special organisation.

In applying these thoughts to what Justice Reddy calls "Aurobindoism," the Justice does not cite Aurobindo's followers but outside experts who observed Aurobindo and the movement. He finds numerous cases in encyclopedia and other secondary literature to support the contention that "the world and India treated and respected Shri Aurobindo as a religious teacher and the founder of a new religious movement whose principal thesis was the evolution or transformation of humanity into divinity through the practice of Integral Yoga."[24] Of course, as other great religious teachers, Aurobindo denied that he was founding a religion. But his disciples and religious leaders all over the world thought that he was. Arguments, then, that Aurobindoism is not a religion are unconvincing, and he concludes that there is no reason why "'Aurobindoism' cannot be classified, if not as new religion, as a new sect of Hinduism and why the followers of Shri Aurobindo cannot be termed a religious denomination."[25] Since the Society stands before the Court making the same claim to religious status, he allows them their claim. Past claims by the Society that it was a non-religious organization notwithstanding; the fact is that these merely indicate that a religious denomination was engaged in non-religious activities.

Though the two opinions differed over the nature of "Aurobindoism" as a religion, they agreed that the Act was constitutional. The majority opinion, "even assuming but not holding the Society or Auroville were a religious denomination," follows the standard procedure of the Court for dealing with such matters. The Act, it said, only takes over "the management of the Auroville by the Society in respect of the secular matters."[26] The Act deals with the administration of property, and property management is "a purely secular matter," as consistently held precious decisions.

The minority opinion agrees. It holds that the Aurobindo Society is a section of a religious denomination. But the Act provides for the management of Auroville, and that is a secular institution.

> Auroville is a township and not a place of worship. It is a township dedicated not to the practice and propagation of any religious

---

[23]*Commissioner, Hindu Religious Endowments, Madras* v. *Sirur Mutt*, pp. 347–348

[24]*S. P. Mittal* v. *Union of India*, p. 10.

[25]*Ibid.*, p. 11.

[26]*Ibid.*, p. 30.

doctrine but to promote international understanding and world peace, surely a secular and not a religious activity.[27]

Promotion of international understanding and world peace is defined as a secular undertaking, "by no means a religious ideal." Since that was Auroville's purpose, the Government of India and UNESCO had adopted the project. In the minority opinion, then, this is another example of secular activity of a religion. Hence it is not protected by the Articles 25 and 26 of the Constitution.

Furthering the "Secular"

It is clear that the assumption that there are two realms designated "religion" and "secular" is firmly established. These are taken for granted by the Constitution and the Supreme Court, not argued for nor definitively defined. It is clear that this assumption is accepted even by those who argue that the State is interfering with religion. That traditional religious views of reality have not distinguished these categorized but treated all of life as one, is also clear. From the Constitutional model of "religion," this traditional lack of distinction is a false claim, an encroachment of "religion" on the "secular."[28]

The Supreme Court of India has accepted the responsibility of determining what falls within these two categories, while continuing to admit that the determination is difficult. From its earliest case, it has noted that the Constitution allow the state to regulate and even administer properties of a religion, that is clearly acceptable. The Court acts thereby as the authority that promotes religious change. If the "secular" is a new category, its progressive definition is an expansion of the power of the State to make what from a traditional view are religious pronouncements.

In its attempt to define "religion" the Court has introduced further categories, as Baird has shown. The Court advanced "essentiality" as a category and said it was important to decide whether an activity was "essential to a religion." At first it stated that what was essential would be determined in terms of the religion itself, but when a religious institution explicitly claimed that how income from a temple should be spent was a religious matter, the Court refused that claim. The religious community's explicit statement of "essentiality" was

---

[27]*Ibid.*, p. 12.

[28]Besides the discussion in Baird, "Religion and the Secular...." and "'Secular State' and the Indian Constitution," from the perspective of the historian of religion, see also Donald Eugene Smith, *India as a Secular State* (Princeton, 1963) and Ved Prakash Luthera, *The Concept of the Secular State and India* (Calcutta, 1964) for the perspectives of two political scientists.

not taken as a basis for accepting whether an activity was religious or essential to the religion.

Likewise other claims of religious individuals and communities have been rejected and the realm of the "secular" has appeared to expand. The Court declared that the scale of expenses and the provisions of proper materials for rituals are "secular" matters, that the actual determination of which priestly duties are "religious" is a "secular" task, and that the appointment of a priest is "secular." It appears to have had little trouble doing this without clear definition of the categories, but in the process it has, from a traditional standpoint, expanded the realm of the "secular" at the expense of more traditional views. Historically the Court by doing so has enforced religious change.

By 1980 and the Auroville case, the majority of the Court had adopted a definition of "religion" which it said it would use in this new case to decide whether an entire system which is professed, practiced, and even propagated is a religion. There is nothing, however, in the majority opinion itself which actually argues in terms of a comparison between the Court's definition of religion and Aurobindo's beliefs and practices. The opinion proposes that the Court examine "the teachings of Sri Aurobindo to see whether they constitute a religion."[29] Aurobindo's teachings are understood by the Court as a "system of beliefs and doctrines" that are meant to produce "spiritual well-being." Though these beliefs also involve "outward expression" in meditation and devotion and though "religion need not be theistic," there is no attempt to address these specific elements of the accepted definition. Aurobindo's beliefs are presented without argument or comment except for the reference to "the distinctive feature" of these beliefs: its universality.

This characteristic, however, is unhelpful. Universality is as noted above, an important characteristic of "Hinduism" in the minds of modern Hindu apologists who argue that universality often sets "Hinduism" apart from the other religions. The Court itself actually identified this as a characteristic of "Hindu religion" in *Sastri Yagnapurushadji* v. *Muldas Bhudardas Vaishya* (1966), quoting S. Radhakrishnan. It repeated the quotation of Radhakrishnan in the Auroville Case when referencing the 1966 decision:

> Naturally it was realised by Hindu religion from the very beginning of its career that truth was many-sided and different views contained different aspects of truth which no one could fully express. This knowledge inevitable bred a spirit of tolerance and willingness to understand and appreciate the opponent's point of view. Because of this broad sweep of Hindu philosophic concepts under Hindu

---

[29] *S. P. Mittal* v. *Union of India*, p. 21.

philosophy, there is no scope for excommunicating any notion or principle as heretical and rejecting it as such.[30]

"Universality," it would appear from the Court's own discussions, can therefore be a claim of a religion as much as a claim of a non-religious institution.

The introduction of the category "spiritual" by Justice Reddy in the minority opinion without further explanation draws attention to another ambiguous term which has often been used in the discussion of the definition of "religion." The manner in which he used the term in the writing of his opinion seems to assume that all people understand the meaning of the word "spiritual." In other legal contexts, however, "the spiritual dimension" seems to be taken as "secular." For the Supreme Court in its 1977 decision "spiritual" was "secular." There the Court referred to a "spiritual dimension to the first page of our Constitution...."[31] The secular state's founding document which protects its secularity had, the Court said, a spiritual dimension. In the majority opinion in the Auroville case the use of the term "spiritual" in Auroville's Charter is not considered an indication of religion. Even in parliamentary debates some ministers see no problem with a secular state supporting a "spiritual" institution.[32]

The ambiguity of the term "spiritual" is clear. And Justice Reddy offers no definition of it either. He had noted that the category "superstition," was inadequate as well, though the Court used it in *Yagnapurusdasji* v. *Muldas*,[33] to attempt to distinguish non-religious beliefs from religious ones. "What is religion to others is pure superstition to some others," Justice Reddy noted. His use of the term "spiritual" assumes that it is somehow less ambiguous, and so he moves on as do others who use the term.

Finally, Justice Reddy reintroduces the notion of self-definition by the religious community. For the Court, the idea that a religious community itself can define which of its elements are religious is not new. In March, 1954, in *Panachand Gandhi* v. *State of Bombay*, and institution the Court accepted as religious attempted to argue that activities to be regulated by the State of Madras were religious and, thus, protected. The Court, in an earlier case the same month, *Commissioner, Hindu Religious Endowments, Madras* v. *Sirur Mutt*, had said that a religious institution has the right to determine its own affairs in matters of

---

[30]*Ibid.*, p. 31. Quoting *Yagnapurushdasji* v. *Muldas*, p. 1129, which is a paraphrase of S. Radhakrishnan, *Indian Philosophy* (London, 1929), I, p. 48.

[31]*M. Giasuddin* v. *A. P. State*, p. 1935.

[32]For example, see the speech by Karan Singh, then Minister from Udhampur, concerning "The Auroville (Emergency Provisions) Act, 1980," *Lok Sabha Debates, 4th Session* (New Delhi, 1980), X, No. 11 (December 17, 1980), pp. 367–74.

[33]*Yagnapurusdasji* v. *Muldas*, p. 1135.

"religion," and that what constitutes "religion" is ascertained with reference to the doctrines of the religion itself. In spite of this statement, in *Panachand Gandhi* v. *State of Bombay* the Court rejected the claims of an accepted "religious" institution that the activity in question was "religious." What this indicated was that given the Court's definition of "religious" and "secular," the religious institution was attempting to extend the "religious" into an area of its activities which the Court already considered "secular."[34] It was, therefore, unacceptable to the Court, even it the self-definition of the community was otherwise.

A further question in any self-definition is who speaks authoritatively for the community when its members disagree? How does the Court, therefore, know which evidence is best in determining a community's self-definition? Two further complications arise. First, if the community identifies with a historical tradition of any length in which various opinions exist, which opinion is authoritative? Is it the position of the founder or one in a line of gurus? Is it the current community or a previous representative? Do previous statements of the same organization take precedence over present ones?

Second, if the community denies that there is such an authority, where does one seek the self-definition? Is there a pope or an authoritative religious leader to whom the members surrender? Is there a scripture upon which they agree, and is there an authoritative interpreter? According to members of the Aurobindo movement, following the Mother, authority is now left with the inner Spirit which indwells each individual. What if these inner spirits appear to disagree? Do members of the Sri Aurobindo Society or the Aurovillians now speak with that authority?

Justice Reddy does not mention those followers who would deny that "Aurobindoism" is a religion. In their Counter Affidavit to the Court, followers of Aurobindo in Auroville did not speak to the issue of whether or not "Aurobindoism" is a religion. Their claim was that Auroville was not a religious institution or denomination. Their petition spoke more in terms of the issue of previous Court judgments: whether or not an institution or activity of a "religion" was religious. As their lawyer summarized their claim:

> It is in this most profound sense that I, speaking on behalf of the Auroville residents, feel this assertion by the Society that Auroville constitutes a religious denomination to be the perpetration of an immense fraud which falsifies the very reasons and understanding which led us all to come here and invest our lives towards the realization of Auroville as a research experiment for the "living embodiment of and actual human unity." And I pray that this false

---

[34]*Supreme Court Journal*, XVII, 1954, p. 486. See also Baird, "Religion and the Secular....," p. 52–53, for an analysis.

assertion will not be allowed to hinder the unfolding of the Mother's 'Dream'.[35]

Interviews with many followers of Aurobindo indicate that they deny that his viewpoint constitutes a "religion."

Justice Reddy does not ask who in a community speaks for the community on the issue of whether or not it is a religion. What if the whole community or its authoritative voices deny that it is a religion? Even within the accepted religions (Christianity, Islam, Hinduism, etc.) religious thinkers and others will often deny that their beliefs and practices constitute a religion.[36]

In the past the Court has used reification, that is treating as a single entity a collection of historical facts which are characterized by diversity and change, to its advantage in order to solve this problem. In 1958 in *M. H. Quareshi* v. *State of Bihar*, the Court treated Islam, a category which includes a multitude of varied communities geographically and historically throughout the world, as a reified entity. Instead of asking whether it is essential to the community of believers before the Court, the judges asked whether it was essential to "Islam." Surveying "Islam" as a reification, they found within that category an opinion that the sacrifice of a cow on Bakr Id Day was unessential.

> It has also been pointed out that from time immemorial the Indian Mussalmans have been sacrificing cows and this practice, if not enjoined, is certainly sanctioned by their religion and it amounts to their practice of religion protected by Article 25. While the petitioners claim that the sacrifice of a cow is essential, the State denies the obligatory nature of the religious practice. The face emphasised by the respondents [the State], cannot be disputed, namely that many Mussalmans do not sacrifice a cow on the Bakr Id Day.[37]

Hence, using reification, "Islam" taught that it was unessential even though the members of the present community claimed it was an essential and traditional element of their faith. They misunderstood the essentials of their religion, the Court declared.

---

[35] From Counter Affidavit INCA W. P. No. 5879 submitted by K. Tewari on behalf of the residents of Auroville, filed in the Supreme Court, January, 1981.

[36] For examples which Wilfred Cantwell Smith has used to argue for the end of the use of the term "religion" altogether since he believes no truly religious person calls his beliefs a religion, see his *The Meaning and End of Religion* (New York, 1963), pp. 114–115.

[37] *Supreme Court Journal*, XXI, 1958, pp. 984–985.

The Court has similarly thought of Aurobindoism as a reified entity with an assumed unity. This method for the majority of the Court has enabled the judges to quote Aurobindo and the Mother: "There can be no better proof than what Sri Aurobindo and the Mother themselves thought of their teachings and their institutions to find out whether the teachings of Sri Aurobindo and his integral Yoga constitute a religion or a philosophy."[38] This and previous declarations of the Society for purposes of government support, the judges conclude, mean that: "there is no room for doubt that neither the Society nor Auroville constitute a religious denomination and the teachings of Sri Aurobindo only represent his philosophy and not a religion."[39]

In the minority opinion, reification enables the conclusion that Aurobindoism is a religion. Founder's opinions are of little use and the Society's past claims merely indicate "that it is engaged in several secular activities...." However, the people of India and the world treated Sri Aurobindo as a religious teacher. Justice Reddy actually quotes no members of the movement *per se*, though some of the experts may be. In any case, he concludes, that "we must hold, the Aurobindo Society is a section of a religious denomination within the meaning of the expression in Art. 26 of the Constitution."

The determination of the definition of "religion" and "secular" is no easier than it was in the earliest cases which came before the Supreme Court. What has been consistent is the expansion of the category of "secular" and the fact that in all but two of the cases that have come before the Supreme Court of India, one before and one after the Auroville case,[40] the Court has supported the State in legislation which limits the scope of religion and increases the realm over which the legislation may be passed. The Supreme Court's disposition of Auroville, then, whether it is in fact a religious or secular institution, is consistent with the Court's preference for the expansion of the "secular" over the "religious" and evidence that what appears to be a settled judicial definition of "religion" is still problematic for members of the Court.

---

[38]*S. P. Mittal* v. *Union of India*, 1958, p. 29.

[39]*Ibid.*, p. 30.

[40]See *Saifuddin Saheb* v. *State of Bombay* (AIR 1962 SC 853–876), where the Court upholds the right of the Dai-ul-Mutlaq to excommunicate a member of the Dawoodi Bohra community, against the Bombay Prevention of Excommunication Act of 1949; and *Bihore Emmanuel* v. *State of Kerala* (SCJ, II 1986, 395–412), where the Court upholds the right of Jehovah's Witness children to refrain from singing the National Anthem in school ceremonies though they "do stand up respectfully" during the singing.

17

To Convert or Not To Convert: Legal and Political Dimensions of Conversion in Independent India

Ronald W. Neufeldt

Introduction

In discussing religion and religious affiliation in India the noted legal scholar, J. Duncan M. Derrett, has this to say:

> Religious affiliation is not a question of an individual's belief, for on that footing he is free to believe or not believe in anything he wishes, but of social *belonging*. The Muslims belonged to a nation different from their predecessors. The Christians, for the most part, decided to detach themselves from their parent Hindu society (which in fact placed most of them in a low prestige position) and to become a new society by being accepted by people who at the time had a high prestige-rating....Hinduism has no objection to castes hiving off and developing new communities: but they cannot, in social terms, have their cake and eat it![1]

Hindu resistance to conversion, he goes on to argue, is based squarely on the view that a "change of personal belief does not automatically mean a change in social belonging."[2]

D. E. Smith, in his discussion of India as a secular State, supports this view and adds other considerations. Conversions are opposed, he argues, because: they are seen to be disruptive of family, caste and village social life; they are seen as an abandonment of Indian culture; they are seen as motivated by political considerations; they are seen as promoted by unethical and questionable

---

[1] J. Duncan M. Derrett, *Religion Law and the State in India* (New York, 1968), p. 58.
[2] *Ibid.*

methods; they are opposed to universalism as expressed by Gandhi and Radhakrishnan.[3]

As both of these scholars indicate, conversion has been and continues to be a thorny issue for governments and legislators in India. And as Smith indicates, conversion was a subject of legislation for Indian governments well before independence and the colonial period.[4] That the subject continues to exercise the minds of politicians and legislators is seen quite clearly in the remarks of former Chief Justice P. B. Gajendragadkar on the constitutional right to propagate religion.

> Apropos this right to propagate, I would like to suggest that since conversion leads to complaints about the adoption of unfair, illegal or unworthy means or methods in bringing about conversion, it is desirable that the appropriate legislatures may consider the reasonableness and the feasibility of requiring all conversions to be registered before prescribed authorities. Speaking for myself I am inclined to think that concerted and deliberate attempts at conversion are inappropriate in a truly secular society.[5]

As we shall see, some legislatures have attempted—with some success—to do exactly what Gajendragadkar suggested, and that, in spite of the fact, that the issues raised in the quotation received considerable attention during the Constituent Assembly Debates. The success has important and potentially surprising implications for future discussions of religious freedom in general and conversion in particular within India.

The discussion in this paper will by no means be exhaustive. To focus the analysis somewhat, I propose to deal with the Constituent Assembly Debates, Freedom of Religion Acts in Orissa, Madhya Pradesh and Arunachal Pradesh, and court cases focusing on propagation and conversion. Some mention will also be made of developments in the Lok Sabha, particularly those following the 1978 Arunachal Pradesh Freedom of Religion Act. Throughout the concern will be with Article 25 which grants freedom of religion, specifically the freedom of conscience and the right freely to profess, practice and propogate. More specifically, at issue is the right to propogate and the concerns that have been raised with respect to this right.

---

[3] Donald Eugene Smith, *India as a Secular State* (Princeton, 1963), pp. 165–168.

[4] See Smith's discussion of laws under the Sultantate, Akbar, and Aurangzeb, and the Caste Disabilities Removal Act of 1850 in *India as a Secular State*, pp. 63–71.

[5] P. B. Gajendragadkar, *Secularism and the Constitution of India* (Bombay, 1971), p. 72.

Constituent Assembly Debates

From the beginning of the preparations for the Constituent Assembly Debates, and throughout the Debates for that matter, attention was paid to the issue of religious freedom, including the right to expression. The Experts Committee, appointed to prepare the materials for the Constituent Assembly, decided in 1946 that there should be a resolution outlining the objectives of the Assembly. This resolution, adopted in January 1947, contained a statement that the future Constitution should guarantee freedom of thought, expression, belief, faith, and worship.[6] Prior to this, in December 1946, K. T. Shah, a member of the Fundamental Rights Subcommittee, sent a note on fundamental rights to the Assembly President. Included in the note was an article insisting on the "right to freedom of conscience, which includes freedom of belief, worship, or profession of any religion, faith, or doctrine, as well as the negation of any such belief...."[7] This, along with the resolution of January 1947, set the stage for the Debates on religious freedom in the Constituent Assembly.

Of importance is the recognition that from the beginning of the Debates the rights relating directly to conversion were front and centre in the discussion of religious freedom, namely the right to free expression or profession of any religion. That these rights were discussed alongside the right to practice seems to suggest that early on the framers of the Constitution were quite aware of the connection between expression or profession, and the possibility of conversions. This connection is signalled by the draft articles presented by members of the Subcommittee on Fundamental Rights during March 1947. K. M. Munshi, for example, proposed that "freedom of conscience and the right freely to profess and practise religion" be subject to "public order, morality, or health" that persons under eighteen should not be free to change religion without parental consent, and that conversion brought about by coercion, undue influence, or material inducement be punishable by law.[8] Harnam Singh wanted to restrict freedom to preaching which does not offend the sentiment of other communities, while B. R. Ambedkar proposed the right to profess, preach, and convert subject to public order and morality.[9]

The Subcommittee, in preparing its first draft report submitted on April 3, 1947, opted essentially for a revised version of Munshi's draft articles.[10] The

---

[6] *The Framing of India's Constitution, Select Documents*, Vol. II (New Delhi, 1967), pp. 3–4. Hereafter referred to as *Framing*.

[7] *Framing*, Vol. II, p. 50.

[8] *Framing*, Vol. II, p. 76.

[9] *Framing*, Vol. II, pp. 81 and 87.

[10] *Framing*, Vol. II, pp. 122–126.

second draft report submitted on April 16, 1947, changed the prohibition of conversion for those under 18 to the prohibition of forcing anyone under the age of 18 to join or profess a religion other than the one in which he or she was born.[11] The Subcommittee on Minorities recommended further changes, that the right to propagate be included in the list of rights, that children under the age of 18 be allowed to change religion if the parents are converted, and that conversions be recognized only if changes are attested by a magistrate following a proper inquiry.[12]

The Advisory Committee on Minorities and Fundamental Rights in reviewing the draft and the recommendations of the Subcommittee on Minorities paid considerable attention to the word "propagation." In spite of suggestions that the word is superfluous and pernicious, it was allowed to stand. The argument that it is superfluous had to do with the fact that freedom of expression had already been conceded in other Articles. Those who saw it as pernicious, argued that it would simply be quite divisive. The clause dealing with change of religion for persons under 18 was dropped entirely, but the clause prohibiting conversion brought about by undue influence and coercion was retained.[13] Accordingly the interim report of the Advisory Committee, issued on April 3, 1947 included the right to propagate alongside the right to profess and practise and the prohibition of conversion brought about by coercion or undue influence. Any mention of minors was dropped.[14]

The Constituent Assembly, in considering the interim report, accepted the clause granting freedom of conscience and the right to profess, practise and propagate and referred the statement on conversion brought about by coercion and undue influence back to the Advisory Committee, but not before considerable discussion of an amendment proposed by Munshi to prohibit conversion of minors.[15] Some of the arguments are significant in that they reappear later but in changed contexts. F. R. Anthony was vocal in his opposition to Munshi's proposed amendment arguing that the force of the reference to minors was to nullify the right to practice and propagate.

> I say that if you have this particular provision, or if you place an absolute embargo on the conversion of a minor, you will place an

---

[11] *Framing*, Vol. II, pp. 173–174.

[12] *Framing*, Vol. II, pp. 208–209.

[13] *Framing*, Vol. II, pp. 265–272.

[14] *Framing*, Vol. II, p. 298.

[15] *Framing*, Vol. II, p. 302. It is interesting to note that the right to propagate was accepted without comment. See *Constituent Assembly of India*, Vol. III, 1947, p. 485. Hereafter referred to as *Debates*.

Law and Conversion

> embargo absolutely on the right of conversion....Not a single adult who is a parent, however deeply he may feel, however deeply he may be convinced, will ever adopt Christianity, because by this clause you will be cutting off that parent from his children.[16]

He went on to argue that the provision cut at the root of family life, of the parents' right to raise children in the religion of their choice. Similar arguments were put forward by Rev. Jerome D'Souza and B. R. Ambedkar.[17] The language used by Anthony is instructive. He speaks of conversion as a right.

Rev. J. J. M. Nichols-Ray opposed the amendment on other grounds. He argued that there is a spiritual role to conversions which must be taken into account.

> I myself was converted when I was about fifteen years old when I heard the voice of God calling me....I did not care for anything save to obey and follow the voice of God in my soul. Why should a youth who has such a call of God be prevented by law from changing his religion and calling himself by another name when he feels before God that he is influenced by the Spirit of God to do that and is ready even to sacrifice his life for that.[18]

A number of arguments were put forward in favour of Munshi's amendments. Purushottamdas Tandon took the position that conversions in any context should not be encouraged and that in the case of minors they are quite improper for two reasons. A minor is easily persuaded. If a minor is not recognized by law to be able to transact transfers of deeds, the law should not recognize the conversion of a minor. The conversion of minors, he argued, "is coercion and undue influence in all circumstances."[19] Algu Rai Shastri questioned the nature of missionary activity suggesting that it is exploitative and therefore an injustice to the majority community.

> The consequence is that grown-up people in such castes as the *Bhangies* and *Chamars* are converted, and with them their children also go into the fold of the new religion. They should be affectionately asked to live as brothers. This is what has been taught by prophets, angels and leaders. But this is not being practised today.

---

[16] *Debates*, Vol. III, 1947, pp. 489–90.

[17] *Debates*, Vol. III, 1947, pp. 496 and 502.

[18] *Debates*, Vol. III, 1947, p. 491.

[19] *Debates*, Vol. III, 1947, p. 492.

> We are in search of opportunities to indulge in underhand dealings.... Thus everybody can realize how all possible unfair means have been adopted to trample the majority community [20]

When the Advisory Committee brought back unchanged the clause dealing with coercion and undue influence, two further arguments were put forward against conversion, one involving an interesting view of secularism and the other involving a sinister view of the purpose of all conversions. Both arguments have in common a clear concern for the position of the majority community. M. Ananthasayanam Ayyangar appealed to the concept of secularism.

> Our minorities are communal minorities for which we have made provision. Do you want an opportunity to be given for numbers to be increased for the purpose of getting more seats in the Legislatures?... All people have come to the same opinion that there should be a secular State here; so we should not allow conversion from one community to another.[21]

R. V. Dhulekar asserted that conversions lead to separatist tendencies and diminish the numerical strength of Hindus and other communities. He went so far as to imply that all conversions of Hindus to Islam had been conversions by fraud or coercion and not conversions based on reason.[22] Since the clause was removed from the Fundamental Rights section, it effectively died at this point, as far as the Constitution was concerned.

A draft Constitution prepared by the Constitutional Advisor was submitted to the Drafting Committee in October 1947. It is interesting to note that there is, in the draft, no explicit mention of conversion, although the possibility of conversion is implicit in the right to propagate. The draft was submitted to the Constituent Assembly on February 28, 1948. The right to propagate elicited considerable discussion, including motions to remove the right. At issue in the calls to eliminate the right to propagate was anxiety over conversion. Tajamul Husain argued that religion as a private affair ought not to be disturbed through propagation in a secular state.

> Supposing I honestly believe that I will attain salvation according to my way of thinking, and according to my religion, and you, Sir, honestly believe that you will attain salvation according to your way,

---

[20] *Debates*, Vol. III, 1947, p. 498.

[21] *Debates*, Vol. V, 1947, p. 364.

[22] *Debates*, Vol. V, 1947, pp. 364–365.

> then why should I ask you to attain salvation according to my way, or why should you ask me to attain salvation according to your way? If you accept this proposition, then, why propagate religion? As I said, religion is between oneself and his God. Thus honestly profess religion and practice it at home. Do not demonstrate it for the sake of propagating....If you start propagating you will become a nuisance to others. So far it has been a nuisance.[23]

Lokanath Misra raised the spectre of Hindu enslavement and the eventual annihilation of Hindu culture and therefore the innate secularism in Hinduism.

> To my mood Vedic culture excludes nothing. Every philosophy and culture has its place but now the cry of religion is a dangerous cry. It denominates, it divides and encamps people to warring ways. In the present context what can this word 'propagation' in Article 19 mean? It can only mean paving the way for the complete annihilation of Hindu culture, the Hindu way of life and manners....Hinduism is just an integrated vision and a philosophy of life and cosmos....But Hindu generosity has been misused and politics has overrun Hindu culture.[24]

Clearly Misra did not see religion as simply a private affair as did Husain. Hinduism, he argued, is a total way of life, but secular in that it gives a place to every philosophy and culture. One finds a similar theme in the arguments of K. V. Kamath, directed not at the issue of propagation *per se*, but at clauses dealing with religious instruction in schools. The State, he argued, should not be prevented from imputing spiritual training in the comprehensive sense of *dharma*, or eternal values found in Hinduism, Sufism, and Christianity. Indeed, India has a spiritual mission to perform, to rescue the world from a loss of eternal values. In a sense, then, the State has the right to propagate and to convert. Not surprisingly he appealed to the writings of both Aurobindo and Radhakrishnan.[25]

None of the proposals designed to curtail or remove the right to propagate, or to give power to the State for general spiritual training, were supported by the Assembly. Indeed, those who argued for the right to propagate insisted that this was merely according to minority communities a right practised by the majority community. Pandit L. K. Maitra, appealing to the words of Vivekanan-

---

[23] *Debates*, Vol. VII, 1948, pp. 817–818.

[24] *Debates*, Vol. VII, 1948, p. 824.

[25] *Debates*, Vol. VII, 1948, pp. 824–826.

da, argued that if India is to fulfil her mission to provide the world with the spiritual culture that is India's heritage, the right to propagate must be seen to be inherent.[26] L. Krishnaswami Bharati went as far as to suggest that Hindus ought to practice propagation in order to educate people in the religious tenets and doctrines of Hinduism. Other communities should emulate the Christian community for in the end "it is all God, though under different names."[27] T. T. Krishnamachari was even more explicit pointing out that since members of the majority community were already propagating, the issue should not be the elimination of propagation but appropriate propagation.

> It is perfectly open to the Hindus and the Arya Samajists to carry on their Suddhi propaganda as it is open to the Christians, the Muslims, the Jains and the Buddhists and to every other religionist, so long as he does it is subject to public order, morality and the other conditions that have to be observed in my civilized government.[28]

It is important to note this admission of missionary activity by Hindus, given ongoing resistance to conversion from Hinduism and some of the traditional arguments used to support that resistance.

A new draft was submitted to the President of the Assembly on November 3, 1949. The Article on religious rights, Article 25, contained freedom of conscience and the right freely to profess, practise and propagate religion subject to: public order, morality and health, and laws regulating economic, finances, political or other secular activity and providing for social welfare and reform and throwing open Hindu religious institutions. An explanation regarding the meaning of Hindu with respect to issues of reform, social welfare and throwing open Hindu temples was added. It states "In Subclause (b) of Clause (2) the reference to Hindus shall be construed as including a reference to persons professing Sikh, Jaina or Buddhist religion, and the reference to Hindu institutions shall be construed accordingly."[29]

State Laws

The Constituent Assembly devoted considerable time to the issues of conversions of minors and conversions brought about by undue influence, coercion, and fraud, and the business of registering conversions. In the initial

---

[26] *Debates*, Vol. VII, 1948, p. 832.

[27] *Debates*, Vol. VII, 1948, p. 833.

[28] *Debates*, Vol. VII, 1948, p. 836.

[29] *Framing*, Vol. IV, p. 758.

drafts on freedom of religion, Clauses directed to those issues were included. In later and final drafts these Clauses were dropped, although there was considerable pressure to retain them. As far as the Constitution is concerned, we are left with an Article providing for freedom of belief and conscience and the rights freely to profess, practise and propagate religion. The dropped Clauses do not, however, fade from memory. Attempts have, from time to time, been made in the Lok Sabha to reintroduce forms of these Clauses through private members bills. These attempts have been largely unsuccessful.

On the level of State Legislation, however, the picture is different. In 1967, the State of Orissa enacted the Orissa Freedom of Religion Act, the first of three such State Acts. As might be expected the explanation for the Act appeals to maladjustments in social life and to law and order. There is, however, an understanding of conversion in the explanation which may allow for extraordinary interference in the right to propagate.

> Conversion in its very process involves an act of undermining another's faith. The process becomes all the more objectionable when this is brought about by recourse to methods like force, fraud, material inducements and exploitation of one's poverty, simplicity and ignorance. Conversion or attempt at conversion in the above manner, besides creating various maladjustments in social life, also give rise to problems of law and order. It is therefore important to provide measures to check such activities which also directly impinge on the freedom of religion.[30]

While the Act at first glance appears to be directed simply to conversions by force, fraud, material inducements, and exploitation, the punishments make it clear that the law makers had in mind conversions of minors and others who were thought to need special protection. The penalty for unlawful conversion of a minor, a woman and a member of a scheduled caste was much more severe than the penalty for the unlawful conversion of an adult.[31]

A similar Act was passed by the Madhya Pradesh Legislature in 1968, in this case called the Madhya Pradesh Dharma Swatantrya Adhiniyam. Again, in the interests of public order and concern for threat to community life, conversions by "force or allurement or by fraudulent means, and matters incidental thereto"

---

[30] Lalit Mohan Suri, ed., *The Current Indian Statutes* (Chandigarh, 1968), p. 5.
[31] *Ibid.*

were prohibited.[32] In addition the Act also required registering conversions with the District Magistrate.[33]

The Act appears to be the culmination of two previous events, the appointment of the Niyogi Commission in 1954 to enquire into Christian missionary activity in Madhya Pradesh and the Madhya Pradesh Conversion Bill of 1963, a private Member's Bill, which raised some of the concerns expressed in the Niyogi Commission Report. The report tended to question the sincerity of conversions and to see conversions as contributing to undermining traditional values and structures and to the denationalization of Indians.[34]

In 1978, the third such Act was passed by the Arunachal Pradesh Legislature. Originally labelled the Arunachal Pradesh Freedom of Indigenous Faith Bill, it was renamed the Freedom of Religion Act on the advice of the President, who recommended that the protection sought by the Bill be afforded to persons of any faith.[35] In some respects this Act is similar to the Orissa and Madhya Pradesh Acts, but in important ways it goes considerably beyond those Acts. Aimed specifically at conversions from indigenous faiths, it is described as

> A Bill to provide prohibition of conversion from indigenous faith of Arunachal Pradesh to any other faith or religion by use of force or inducement or by fraudulent means and for such matters connected therewith.[36]

The definitions underline the emphasis on indigenous faith. Conversion is defined as "renouncing an indigenous faith and adopting another faith or religion."[37] Indigenous is defined as

> such religious beliefs and practices including rites, rituals, festivals, observances, performances, abstinence, customs, as have been found sanctioned, approved, performed by the indigenous communities of Arunachal Pradesh from the time these communities have been

---

[32] *The Yearly Digest of Indian and Select English Cases* (Madras, 1977), p. 2092.

[33] Brojendra Nath Banerjee, *Religious Conversions in India* (New Delhi, Harnam Publications), p. 246.

[34] For a description of the report see Moin Shakir, ed., *Religion, State and Politics in India* (Delhi, 1989), pp. 281–282, and D. E. Smith, *India as a Secular State*, pp. 208–214.

[35] *Lok Sabha Debates*, Vol. XXII, February 29, 1979, p. 115.

[36] Banerjee, *Loc. cit.*, p. 261.

[37] *Ibid.*, p. 262.

Law and Conversion

known and includes Buddhism..., Vaishnavism..., and Nature worship....[38]

In some respects the definition of indigenous is reminscent of the definition of Hindu in the Constitutional provision for religious freedom. Force includes "show of force or a threat of injury of any kind including threat of divine displeasure or social excommunication."[39] The prohibition in the Act also makes reference to indigenous faith.

> No person shall convert or attempt to convert, either directly or otherwise any person from indigenous faith by use of force or by inducement or any fraudulent means nor shall any person abet any such conversion.[40]

Finally the Act required that conversions from indigenous faith be registered with the District Deputy Commissioner by the person doing the converting.[41]

The architects of the Act cited the issue of public order, morality and health as the primary concern behind the Act.

> The problem of conversion from one indigenous faith to any other faith or religion by use of force or by inducement or by fraudulent means has been creating unhealthy and undesirable friction in the unsophisticated and simple tribal communities of Arunachal Pradesh threatening social peace and public order.[42]

The appeal to public order aside, the implications of the Act are obvious. Non-indigenous faiths are regarded as alien and therefore as endangering national interests.[43] Conversion from indigenous faith is not only to be discouraged, but, as far as is possible, prevented. Indigenous faith and nationalism are in some respects then to be seen as synonymous. While conversions from indigenous faith are not welcome, no such attitude to conversions back to indigenous faith is expressed. The content of sermons, exhortations, or religious literature can be

---

[38] *Ibid.*
[39] *Ibid.*
[40] *Ibid.*
[41] *Ibid.*, p. 263.
[42] *Ibid.*
[43] *Ibid.*, p. 264.

deemed to be unlawful if these include references to divine displeasure. Presumably this would apply only to sermons, exhortations, and literature in the context of non-indigenous faith. The threat of excommunication cannot be used to convert people to non-indigenous faiths. Presumably it could be used in the other direction.

Lok Sabha

Bills, similar to the three State Acts have been attempted in the Lok Sabha from time to time, but without the success experienced at the State level. As early as 1954, Jethalal Joshi, a member of parliament for the Congress Party, introduced the Indian Converts (Regulation and Registration) Bill. Had the Bill been passed it would have required licensing those engaged in converting, registering converts, and a declaration of intent by prospective converts.[44] In 1960 Prakash Vir Shastri of the Swantantra Party moved the Backward Communities (Religious Protection) Bill aimed at regulating conversions from backward communities to Christianity, Islam, Judaism, and Zoroastrianism.[45] In 1978 O. P. Tyagi, a member of parliament for the Janata Party, introduced the Freedom of Religion Bill designed to prohibit conversions by force, inducement, or fraud in order to protect scheduled castes, tribes, minors, and women. In effect, it was designed to foist onto the whole nation elements of the Orissa, Madhya Pradesh, and Arunachal Pradesh Acts. While Nehru had helped to scuttle the Bill proposed in 1954, in the case of Tyagi's Bill, the then Prime Minister, Morarji Desai, supported the Bill.[46]

Tyagi's Bill included a number of the potentially problematic aspects of the Arunachal Pradesh Act. Conversion by force is defined as including "show of force or threat of injury of any kind including threat of divine displeasure or social excommunication."[47] Inducement is said to include "the offer of any gift or gratifications either in cash or in kind and shall also include the grant of any benefit, either pecuniary or otherwise."[48] The fines for unlawful conversion of minors, women, and members of scheduled castes or tribes are double the fines for unlawful conversion of others.

---

[44] Smith, *Loc. cit.*, p. 184.

[45] *Ibid.*, p. 186.

[46] Shakir, ed., *Loc. cit.*, p. 283.

[47] Banerjee, *Loc. cit.*, p. 281.

[48] *Ibid.*

Law and Conversion

The implications of these aspect of the Bill are similar to the implications of the Arunachal Pradesh Act. Banerjee in his discussion of conversions in India makes the statement that

> words "force, fraud and inducement" have not been given their obvious and natural meaning....The meaning of the words in the Bill has been stretched beyond their normal meaning and any charitable act done in the preservance or benefitting members of any other religious community resulting in a change of religion could be construed as coming within the scope and ambit of this Bill.[49]

He also raises the question whether providing privileges for members of scheduled castes on reconversion to Hinduism could be construed as inducement.[50] Tyagi's Bill died with the demise of the Janata government.

In 1981 two further Bills were introduced, both of which received scathing criticism. On September 4, B. V. Desai, member from Raichur, introduced a Bill to prohibit all foreign missionaries from functioning in India on a religious basis. Clause 3 of the Bill aimed specifically at preaching: "Preaching of all religions and helping in conversion of the poor from one religion to another shall be banned."[51]

Among arguments brought against the Bill were the following: preaching and propagation are for the express purpose of convincing others to join a religion (this is reminiscent of the connection made between propagation and conversion in the Constituent Assembly Debates), it contravenes Articles 25 and 26 of the Constitution, it places restrictions on helping the poor, and it perpetuates the false impression that the poor convert for material gain.[52] Eduardo Faleiro, member from Mormugao, in particular, argued that mass conversions occur because the poor want to get away from the social disadvantages inherent in Hinduism, but that this does not necessarily result in material gain since the benefits of reservations are frequently lost.[53]

On December 11, 1981, Vasant Kumar Pandit, member from Rajgarh introduced a Bill asking for compulsory registration of conversions. Eduardo Faleiro compared the requirements of the Bill as analogous to Hitler's requirements that the Jews display the Star of David. G. M. Banatwalla, member from

---

[49] *Ibid.*, p 286.

[50] *Ibid.*, pp. 286–287.

[51] *Lok Sabha Debates*, Vol. XIX, September 4, 1981, p. 364.

[52] *Ibid.*, pp. 365–368.

[53] *Ibid.*, pp. 367–368.

Ponani, argued that the requirement to register a conversion and the requirement of a subsequent memorandum to the community from which the person was converting would be an invitation to anti-social elements to create disorder. He also accused the mover of engaging in speculation about foreign money and doubtful conversions.[54] Vasant Kumar's response provides in capsule form much of the anti-conversion propaganda, and is reminiscent of elements of anti-conversion arguments in the Constituent Assembly Debates.

> We have a registrar of births, marriages, and a registrar of deaths. The change of faith means almost a rebirth of a person. I do not know why so much objection is being taken. I think the question of law and order will arise—and it has arose—when there are doubts that the conversions were not of a free conscience but were made through compulsion and enticement....In recent years, particularly from the new census figures, we do see that large numbers of people are changing their faith. By this Bill I merely want to give the person a full chance to think over the whole thing, because mass conversions are now taking place. If it is a question of one or two individuals I do not mind. But when mass conversions take place it definitely leaves a doubt whether it is really the result of true change of faith.[55]

It should be noted that the appeal to law and order made in objections to the Bill are similar to appeals made in support of the State Acts. It is also the central issue in the Supreme Court judgment in response to the challenges to the State Acts.

The Courts

Conversion in the period under discussion, does not appear to be dealt with directly in many High Court or Supreme Court cases. One finds many cases dealing with the meaning of and limits to religious liberty and these have obvious importance for the discussion of the right to profess and to propagate. A number of cases in which Article 25 is cited, tend to deal with challenges to State Laws which affect the administration of religious trusts. Important in the judgments of such cases are the limits to be set on religious rights including the right to propagate.

---

[54] *Ibid.*, Vol. XXII, December 11, 1981, pp. 402–404.

[55] *Ibid.*, pp. 404–405.

In 1953, for example, the provisions of the Bombay Public Trusts Act of 1950 were challenged in the High Court in Bombay in *Ratilal* vs *State of Bombay*. The petitioners claimed that the provisions of the Bombay Public Trust Act contravened Articles 25 and 26 of the Constitution in that the Act allows for the State to meddle in the administration of a religious trust, and allows for a non-Jain to administer a Jain trust. In his judgment Chief Justice Chagla speaking for the court argued that the exercise of religious freedom cannot be unlimited.

> Article 25 protects religious freedom as far as individuals are concerned. The right is not only given to citizens of India but to all persons, and the right is to profess, practise and propagate religion. But here again, the right is not an unrestricted right. It is a right subject to public order, morality, and health, and further it permits the State to make any law regulating or restricting any economic, financial, political or other secular activity, although it may be associated with religious practice, and there is a further right given to the State and that is that the State can legislate for social welfare and reform even though in doing so it may interfere with the profession and propagation of religion by an individual.[56]

The case was appealed to the Supreme Court in 1954. In his interpretation of Article 25, Justice B. K. Mukherjea speaking for the court appears, at first glance, to repeat arguments made by the Chief Justice of the High Court. There is, however, an important statement made with reference to the purpose of propagation, a statement which surfaces later in the 1977 challenge to the Freedom of Religion Acts in Orissa and Madhya Pradesh. Commenting on Article 25, Justice Mukherjea says,

> Thus, subject to the restrictions which this Article imposes, every person has a fundamental right under our Constitution not merely to entertain such religious belief as may be approved of by his judgement or conscience but to exhibit his belief and ideas in such overt acts as are enjoined or sanctioned by his religion and further to *propagate his religious views for the edification of others.*[57]

The wording is essentially the same as the wording used in Justice Mukherjea's judgment in the Shirur Math case in which he states that Article 25 guarantees the

---

[56] *Ratilal* vs *State of Bombay*, Bombay, 1952 AIR Bombay 244.

[57] *Ratilal* vs *State of Bombay*, 1954 AIR S.C. 391. My emphasis.

right for a person "to exhibit his belief in such outward acts as he thinks proper and to propagate or disseminate his ideas for the edification of others."[58]

Important in setting limits to the right to propagation in the interests of law and order are cases dealing with alleged insult to religion. In 1954 in *Mohammed Siddiqui* vs *State of Uttar Pradesh* heard in the High Court in Allahabad, Mohammed Siddiqui protested the refusal of a Lucknow Magistrate to issue a permit for a procession. The Court upheld the action of the Magistrate, arguing that public profession and practice can hurt religious susceptibilities and therefore be a threat to peace.[59] In the 1964 case *Public Prosecutor* vs *Ramaswami*, heard before the High Court in Madras, Ramaswami, the publisher of the Tamil weekly *Nathikan*, was accused of deliberate and malicious intent to outrage the feelings of Muslims through the publication of two articles critical of Muslims. In issuing the judgment of the court Justice Kailasam spoke directly to the issue of conversion.

> In this case the respondent is a non-believer in God (*Nathikan*) and claimed the right to propagate his views and convert others to his own views....The appellant is entitled to express and propagate his own views as long as he does not affect public order, morality and health....The question that has to be considered is whether the two articles were written with a deliberate and malicious intention of outraging the religious feelings of Muslims.[60]

In this judgment we have the seeming admission that propagation for the purpose of conversion is a Constitutional right. Of course, the right is not absolute since the act of propagation impacts upon the life of the community and must therefore be subject to considerations of law and order. This is, it would seem, an understanding of the right to propagate different from that put forward by Justice Mukherjea in *Ratilal* vs *State of Bombay*. But, it is Mukherjea's view which seems to hold sway in the challenge to the Freedom of Religion Acts of Orissa and Madhya Pradesh.

Rev. Stanislaus of Raipur, Madhya Pradesh had chosen to challenge the Dharma Swatantrya Adhinayam through refusing to register conversions. In his arguments, before the High Court, he had challenged the Act on two points. The first was that Parliament, and not the Madhya Pradesh Legislature had the power

---

[58] *Commr. H.R.E.* vs. *L.T. Swamiar*, 1954 AIR S.C. 289.

[59] *Mohammed Siddigui* vs *State of Uttar Pradesh*, 1954 AIR Allahbad 757.

[60] *Public Prosecutor* vs *Ramaswami*, 1964 AIR Madras 259.

to make the law. The second was that the Act attacked Article 25 of the Constitution.[61] The High Court upholding the Act responded as follows:

> What is penalised is conversion by force, fraud or by allurement. The other element is that every person has the right to profess his own religion and to act according to it. Any other interference with that right of the person by resorting to conversion by force, fraud or allurement cannot, in our opinion, be said to contravene Article 25(b) of the Constitution of India as the Article guarantees religious freedom subject to public health. As such we do not find that the provisions...of the M.P. Dharma Swantantrya Adhinayam 1968 are violations of Article 25 (1) of the Constitution of India. On the other hand, it guarantees that religious freedom to one and all including those who might be amenable to conversion by force, fraud or allurement.[62]

The High Court of Orissa, in a challenge to the Orissa Freedom of Religion Act ruled in the opposite direction. It held that Article 25(1) guarantees the right to conversion, that the prohibition is covered by limitations placed on Article 25(1), that the definition of inducement is too wide to be covered by the limitations to Article 25(1), and that the State has no power to enact the legislation since the power to do so belongs to Parliament.[63]

Both cases went to the Supreme Court and, since both Acts were similar, the Court decided to hear the two cases together. In both cases the Court found that the Acts fell within the purview of the State in that the object of the Acts is to prohibit forcible conversion in order to avoid disturbances to public order.[64] In delivering the judgment of the court, Chief Justice Ray argued that Article 25(1) guarantees the right to propagate, but not to convert. Using what appears to be a novel argument, Justice Ray stated that to insist on the right to convert is to impinge on the freedom of conscience also guaranteed by the Constitution.

> What the Article grants is not the right to convert another person to one's own religion, but to transmit or spread one's religion by an exposition of its tenets. It has to be remembered that Article 25(1) guarantees "freedom of conscience" to every citizen, and not merely to the followers of one particular religion and that, in turn, postulates

---

[61] *Rev. Stanislaus* vs *M.P.*, 1977 AIR S.C. 909.

[62] *Ibid.*, p. 910.

[63] *Ibid.*

[64] *Ibid.*, p. 908.

that there is no fundamental right to convert another person to one's own religion because if a person purposely undertakes the conversion of another person to his religion, as distinguished from his effort to transmit or spread the tenets of his religion, that would impinge on the "freedom of conscience" guaranteed to all the citizens of the country alike.[65]

In his judgment Justice Ray referred for support to the judgment delivered by Justice Mukherjea in *Ratilal* vs *State of Bombay*, 1954, in which Mukherjea had stated that individuals have the right to propagation "for the edification of others." Presumably Ray's judgment is an expansion of the idea that conversion is to be for the purpose of edification only, for it attempts to drive a wedge between propagation and conversion. One has the right to propagate, but not to propagate in order to convert another. The issue from Justice Ray's perspective is not simply law and order but freedom of conscience. Intent to convert impinges on this freedom. If freedom of conscience is to be observed in equal measure for all, then conversion cannot be claimed as a right in the view of the Justice. Presumably this means that since some religious communities do not see conversion as a duty, equal treatment of all means that conversion cannot or should not be the object of propagation even if another community or tradition calls its adherents to propogate in order to convert others.

Conclusions

As the developments in this paper and more recent events would indicate, conversion remains a troublesome issue for India legally and politically. In the wisdom of the framers of the Constitution, it was eventually seen as unnecessary to include Clauses dealing with conversions brought about by coercion, fraud, or undue influence and the conversion of minors largely on arguments that existing laws were adequate to handle such issues. While, from time to time, members of the Lok Sabha have, through private members' Bills, attempted to reintroduce such Clauses, these attempts have met with failure, at least for the time period under discussion. Such attempts have, however, been quite successful at the State level, particularly in the form of the three Freedom of Religion Acts discussed in this paper. This success has been achieved largely through appeals to public peace and law and order. Apparently, what is good for the States is not good for the whole of the country.

The outcome is problematic on a number of levels. First, there is considerable confusion over the purpose of propagation. The makers of the

---

[65] *Ibid.*, p. 911.

Law and Conversion

Constitution seem to recognize an obvious link between propagation and conversion. The arguments that win the day are the arguments that recognize conversion as a primary object of propagation. By implication, at least, conversion is a right. This connection was recognized explicitly by Justice Kailasam in *Public Prosecutor* vs *Ramaswami*, 1964, speaking for the High Court in Madras. Pertinent Supreme Court decisions however, seem to run in another direction. That is, the primary purpose of propagation is edification, not conversion. As Justice Ray argued in *Rev. Stanislaus* vs *M.P.*, propagation for the sake of conversion impinges on "freedom of conscience." This leads to the second observation. On the levels of the Supreme Court and the State Acts it is, in my view, the majority view on conversion and not the minority view which is being upheld. In other words, the majority community will be much more comfortable with the idea of propagation for the sake of edification than it will be with propagation for the sake of conversion. Third, at least in the arena of the State Acts, the majority commonly enjoys rights not accorded to the minorities, or in the case of Arunachal Pradesh, the non-indigenous religions. Specifically, there appear to be no limitations placed on reconversion to Hinduism or on Hindu missionary activity. Indeed, Hindu missionary activity was already recognized as a fact at the time of the framing of the Constitution. Inducement may be available to reconversion to Hinduism, but not to conversion from Hinduism. Finally, it could be argued, as Christians did in the case of the State Acts, that limitations placed on propagation in the State Acts and upheld by the Supreme Court, are stretched beyond what was intended by the framers of the Constitutions, or beyond the obvious and natural meanings of the words. This is the position taken by the High Court of Orissa with respect to the definition of inducement in the Orissa Act. The same case might be made for the definition of force, and fraud in the State Acts, and for the understanding of the intent of freedom of conscience in Chief Justice Ray's decision to overturn the judgment of the High Court of Orissa.

18

Conflict in the Courts: Caste and Religious Conversion in the Indian Secular State

Robert J. Stephens

In one of his many statements regarding the significance of the caste "system" to "Hinduism," B.R. Ambedkar wrote:

> It is the cardinal faith of every Hindu that the Hindu Social Order is a Divine Order. The prescriptions of the Divine Order are three. *First* Society is permanently divided into four classes namely (1) Brahmins, (2) Kshatriyas, (3) Vaishyas, (4) Shudras. *Second* the four classes in point of their mutual status are linked together in an order of graded inequality.... *Third* the occupations of the four classes are fixed.... This is called by the Hindus the *Varna Vevastha*. It is the very soul of Hinduism. Without *Varna Vevastha* there is nothing else in Hinduism to distinguish it from other religions.[1]

Ambedkar is not alone in identifying caste as an essential element in "Hinduism." From modern Indian thinkers as diverse as Sarvepalli Radhakrishnan to Dayananda Saraswati, the centrality of caste to "Hinduism" has been affirmed. Indeed the problem of the relationship between caste and "Hinduism" has engaged a variety of thinkers from both religious and legal disciplines on a number of levels. Recently an important discussion has focused on the issue of religious conversion to "non-Hindu" traditions, especially Chris-

---

[1] *Dr. Babasaheb Ambedkar: Writings and Speeches*, Vol. 4, ed. Vasant Moon (Bombay: Department of Education, Government of Maharashtra, 1987), p. 189.

tianity and Islam, and what changes conversion might entail regarding the new convert's caste status and legal identity.

In light of the Constitution of the modern, secular state of India, issues which involve caste status and religious and legal identity remain a vexing problem. An explicitly stated goal of the Indian Constitution is to insure "equality of status and opportunity" among all citizens. Indeed Article 15(1) states that "The State shall not discriminate against any citizen on the grounds only of religion, race, caste, sex, place of birth or any of them." Discrimination on the basis of religion or caste is then, in Article 15, declared to be illegal. Yet "Hinduism," as it has been variously defined in the courts and by certain scholars of religion, has been said to affirm and uphold caste as one of its defining characteristics. This paper explores the key definitional issues relevant to the ongoing discussions of "Hinduism," caste, and religious conversion, within the "secular state" of modern India. I will analyze those religious concerns which the courts have upheld in their adherence to what has been identified as the "constitutional religious model."[2] The focus will be on the loss of certain rights and privileges afforded to persons deemed to be members of the Scheduled Castes (SC), Scheduled Tribes (ST), or Other Backward Castes (OBC) upon conversion to religions other than "Hinduism."

The Problem of Definitions

In a recent article, "On Defining 'Hinduism' as a Religious and Legal Category," Robert Baird argues for the necessity of distinguishing between "Hinduism" in a legal sense and "Hinduism" in a religious sense within the context of the Indian Constitution.[3] Here a recognition is made that within Article 25 of the Indian Constitution, persons who profess the Sikh, Buddhist, or Jain religion, for legal purposes, may be considered to be Hindus. Legal definitions, which state what a given term means within the context of the law differ

---

[2] See Robert D. Baird, "Religion and the Secular: Categories for Religious Conflict and Religious Change in Independent India," in R.D. Baird, *Essays in the History of Religions* (New York: Peter Lang, 1991), pp. 95-118. The highest concerns of the state are listed in the preamble of the Constitution. They include the Enlightenment ideals of justice, liberty, equality, and fraternity.

[3] *Religion and Law in Independent India*, ed. R.D. Baird (New Delhi: Manohar, 2004), pp. 69-86.

Conflict in the Courts: Caste and Religious Conversion 403

from real definitions, which state what a given thing *really is* regardless of how it is legally defined. As Robert Minor points out, "legal definitions, like stipulative definitions" are "functional ... their purpose is to enable a state to establish and maintain its ultimate concern."[4] Definitions of religious "Hinduism" have been used by the courts to determine who counts in a legal sense as belonging to or as professing the Hindu religion. This is a particularly salient issue for persons who wish to be counted as "Hindus" for the purpose of obtaining special benefits or reservations made for the Scheduled Castes (SC).

The recent history of setting up special provisions for depressed classes (now called SC) among the Hindu fold can be traced back to Gandhi's *harijan* movement of the 1930s and following. In 1931 at the second Round Table Conference in London, Gandhi, as the sole representative of the Indian National Congress, announced his intentions "to resist with his life" Ambedkar's plan of introducing separate electorates for the untouchables.[5] Ambedkar's efforts toward establishing a separate electorate resulted in the communal award of 1932 in which the depressed classes were granted a double vote, one in a special constituency and one in the general electorate.

True to his word, Gandhi responded to the communal award by entering a "fast unto death" later that same year. The British response to Gandhi's fast sets the tone for how the issue of the depressed classes would be defined and handled in the future. As Eleanor Zelliot points out, "The British Government's response to Gandhi's fast was to declare that a solution to the representation of the Depressed Classes had to be settled within the Hindu community."[6] Indeed Gandhi's subsequent *harijan* campaign proceeded on the primary assumption that the untouchables (whom he called *harijans*—literally "those born of the god Hari," i.e. Vishnu) were *Hindus* who needed nothing more than reintegration

---

[4] *The Religious, the Spiritual, and the Secular: Auroville and Secular India* (Albany: SUNY Press, 1999), p. 162.

[5] Dieter Conrad, "The Personal Law Question and Hindu Nationalism," in *Representing Hinduism*, ed. V. Dalmia and H. von Stietencron (New Delhi: Sage, 1995), pp. 306-337, p. 315.

[6] "Gandhi and Ambedkar: A Study in Leadership," in Eleanor Zelliot, *From Untouchable to Dalit: Essays on the Ambedkar Movement*, 2nd rev. edn. (New Delhi: Manohar, 1996), pp. 150-183, p. 167.

into caste Hinduism.[7] In Gandhi's view, separate electorates would only foster a divisiveness within Hinduism and would not alleviate the essentially Hindu problem of untouchability. This understanding of untouchables *as Hindus*, an understanding which is both historically and presently highly contested, was "incorporated into the Presidential Order defining and enumerating the Scheduled Castes."[8]

To be counted as a member of a SC between the years of 1950 through 1990, one was required to prove membership in a depressed caste of the Hindu religion.[9] In 1990 the Presidential Order regarding SC was amended such that paragraph three now reads: "... no person who professes a religion different from the Hindu, the Sikh or the Buddhist religion shall be deemed to be a member of a Scheduled Caste."[10] Several important Supreme Court and High Court

---

[7] See Boyd H. Wilson's article "Ultimacy as a Unifier in Gandhi," in *Religion in Modern India*, 3rd edn., ed. R.D. Baird (New Delhi: Manohar, 1995), pp. 402-421, p. 404, where he writes, "Gandhi says that he is a Hindu because he believes in the Vedas, *varnāśrama dharma*, in cow protection, in idol worship, in the *śāstras*, and in the oneness of God."

[8] Conrad, *op. cit.*, 317. In writing on the connection between religious conversion and political sensibilities, Jose Kananaikil writes: "The dominant Hindu Community in India has become exercised over the conversion of large number [*sic*] of Scheduled Castes to Islam and Christianity. The concern has been shown in different ways such as claiming the Scheduled Castes as part of the Hindu society, reconverting those who have joined other religions and restricting welfare programmes and other government benefits to those who profess Hinduism.... All this has seriously affected the functioning of secular democracy in India," in *Scheduled Castes and the Struggle Against Inequality: Strategies to Empower the Marginalized* (New Delhi: Indian Social Institute, 1983), pp. 8-9.

[9] The Constitution (Scheduled Castes) Order (1950), paragraph 3 reads: "... no person who professes a religion different from Hinduism shall be deemed to be a member of a Scheduled Caste."

[10] See Marc Galanter's essay "Group Membership and Group Preferences in India," in *Law and Society in Modern India* (Delhi: Oxford University Press, 1989), pp. 103-140, p. 129: "The religious requirement is an expression of the power which Art. 341 confers on the President and Parliament to determine which 'caste, race or tribe or *part of or group within* any caste, race or tribe' shall be included in the list of Scheduled Castes." This religious qualification within the Scheduled Castes Order has been extended twice since its inception. In 1956 Sikhs were admitted and in 1990, following much protest, certain Buddhists were allowed SC status. See Conrad, *op. cit.*, p. 320. The 1956 Order had been amended from the 1936 Order which included that "No Indian Christian shall be deemed a member of a Scheduled Caste."

cases reveal how "Hinduism" has been defined, both religiously and legally, as well as how caste has been understood as being especially associated with "Hinduism." Non-indigenous religions have been perceived by the Indian judiciary at certain times as lacking the feature of caste. Therefore persons who profess these religions are not granted the financial benefits of the SC nor reservations in educational, medical or political institutions.

That the courts have defined "Hinduism" as the *religion of the caste system* is surely not surprising. Caste, a word from the Latin *castus* and later the Portugese/Spanish *casta* meaning "properly, chaste, or something not mixed," was originally applied to the social organization that the Portugese found upon their arrival in India.[11] Since its inception on Indian soil, the concept of "the caste system" has been construed as an essential element of another originally European term, "Hinduism," among Western onlookers and eventually among Indians alike. This reification of the "heterogeneous customs and rituals" of India into *the caste system*, (notice that the singular is almost always used), is perhaps most evident in the Western, scholarly appropriation of the Sanskrit terms *varnāśrama dharma*.[12] In explaining the origins of caste groupings in modern India, notable Indologists such as Max Müller, P.V. Kane and later Louis Dumont and Robert Lingat looked to the classical Sanskrit texts for answers.[13] According to the Brahmanical texts which they were reading, such as the *Rigveda* and certain *dharmasūtras*, Orientalist scholars found a religious model which posited a static social order which had been established on *Bharata* since time immemorial. *Rigveda* 10.90, the famous *Purusha Sūkta,* verses 11-12 describe the creation of Brahmans, Kshatriyas, Vaishyas and Shudras from the primeval sacrificial victim:

---

[11] Louis Dumont, *Homo Hierarchicus: The Caste System and Its Implications*, rev. English edition (Chicago: University of Chicago, 1980), p. 21.

[12] See Gita Dharampal-Frick, "Shifting Categories in the Discourse on Caste: Some Historical Observations," in *Representing Hinduism, op. cit.*, pp. 82-100, p. 82.

[13] Cf. Müller's famous Sacred Books of the East series which translates the "classics," especially G. Bühler's translation of the *Manusmriti, The Laws of Manu*, SBE, Vol. 25 (Oxford: Clarendon Press, 1886), Kane's *History of the Dharmaśāstra*, 4 vols. (Bombay: Bhandarkar Oriental Research Institute, 1930-53), Louis Dumont's *Homo Hierarchicus, op. cit.* and Robert Lingat's *The Classical Law of India*, trans., J.D.M. Derrett (Delhi: Oxford University Press, rpt. 1998).

> When they divided *Purusha* how many portions did they make? What do they call his mouth, his arms? What do they call his thighs and feet? The *Brāhman* was his mouth, of both his arms was the *Rājanya* made. His thighs became the *Vaiśya*, from his feet the *Śūdra* was produced.[14]

The theory of the four *varnas* (literally "colors") and the four *āśramas* or life-stages is further spelled out in the *dharmasūtras* of Baudhāyana and Āpastamba and in the *dharmaśāstras* such as the *Manusmriti*.[15] In the Brahmanical view of the cosmos, each male has certain social responsibilities and religious duties by virtue of his stage in life (*āśrama*) and by virtue of his birth group (*jati*) within one of the four *varnas*. Brahmans perform sacerdotal functions and are responsible for religious teaching, Kshatriyas protect social welfare through military and political functions, Vaishyas oversee economic and commercial affairs, and "the duty of the Shudras is to serve the superior *varnas*."[16] The orientalist perspective in the study of "Hinduism," which adopted this "classical" Brahmanical picture of a static Indian, "Hindu" society can be faulted on several fronts.[17] As Peter van der Veer points out:

> There are several objections to be raised against this orientalist perspective....The first is that the structures of power and changing power relations are separated from the production and management of meaning....This implies the relative neglect both of the politics of religious organization and the relation between on the one hand changing religious orientations and experiences

---

[14] R.T.H. Griffith, trans., *The Hymns of the Rig Veda*, (1889), reprinted in *The Sacred Writings of Hinduism*, ed. Jaraslov Pelikan (New York: Book-of-the-Month Club, 1992), p. 603.

[15] See Lingat, *op. cit.*, especially Chapters 2 and 4.

[16] *Ibid.*, 31.

[17] As I am using "orientalist perspective" in the Indian context, I am referring to those views of India which developed primarily in 19th century Western scholarship which posit an identifiable religious essence, i.e. "Hinduism" and rely upon Brahmanically sanctioned texts to construct and reinforce these views. For an extended discussion of "orientalism" see Edward Said's *Orientalism* (New York: Vintage, 1978), especially Chapter one, "The Scope of Orientalism."

Conflict in the Courts: Caste and Religious Conversion

and on the other hand economic and political processes.... The orientalist perspective is a theological rather than an anthropological or historical one. The other major objection concerns the use of an ideological model derived from the indological interpretation of Sanskrit text.... The idea that a model derived from these texts can be applied to Indian civilization and society of all times and places is based upon the assumption that 'traditional' Hindu society was and is a kind of 'frozen' social reality. This assumption is clearly mistaken.[18]

Upon examining recent Supreme Court cases involving definitional issues of caste and "Hinduism," one sees that the work of scholars on Indian religions has been frequently consulted. In *Yagnapurushdasji* v. *Muldas* the court cites the historian Arnold Toynbee, the philosopher/politician Sarvepalli Radhakrishnan and the Indologists Max Müller and Monier Williams in arriving at its understanding of religious "Hinduism."[19] "Hinduism" is described by the court as a tolerant "monistic idealism" which includes "an acceptance of the Veda as the highest authority," belief in a "great world rhythm," the belief in "rebirth and pre-existence," and has as its goal "release and freedom from the unceasing cycle of births and rebirths; *Moksha* or *Nirvana* which is the ultimate

---

[18] "The Concept of the Ideal Brahman as an Indological Construct," in *Hinduism Reconsidered*, ed. G.D. Sontheimer and H. Kulke (New Delhi: Manohar, 1997), pp. 153-172, p. 154. In his chapter on "Vedic" views of caste, Wilhelm Halbfass admits to the theoretical and abstract nature of his discussion of caste which focuses on Sanskrit literary traditions: "The present chapter deals with theoretical concepts and constructs. It does not address the question to what extent these concepts correspond to social and historical realities; i.e. it does not deal with caste as an actual phenomenon. What this chapter discusses may, in fact, seem even more theoretical, abstract and removed from the realities of social life than what we find in the *Dharmaśāstra* literature. The critique of brahminical schemes and constructions which É. Senart and many others have raised with regard to the *Dharmaśāstras* may seem to be even more appropriate when it comes to the philosophical reconstructions of the *varna* structure." In "Homo *Hierarchicus*: The Conceptualization of the *Varna* System in Indian Thought," in his *Tradition and Reflection: Explorations in Indian Thought* (Albany: SUNY Press, 1991), pp. 347-405, pp. 348-349.

[19] AIR 1966 SC 1119.

aim of Hindu religion and philosophy."[20] In *Punjabrao* v. *Meshram*, the court explains that in its definition of "Hinduism," the "word 'Hindu' is used in ... the sense of the orthodox Hindu religion which recognizes castes and contains injunctions based on caste distinctions."[21] The court posits that this view of "Hinduism" or "Hindu society" is commensurate with the view of B.R. Ambedkar:

> The main object of Dr. Ambedkar was to secure for the members of the Scheduled Castes an honorable place in society and he felt that the various disabilities placed upon members of these castes were due to the fact that in Hindu religion, to which they belonged, they had been accorded the lowest rank in society with the result that they had come to be regarded as untouchables. Undoubtedly, the caste system has virtually come to be regarded as an *essential feature of Hindu society* and, therefore, Dr. Ambedkar felt that the only way open to members belonging to the lowest group was to sever their connection completely from such a society.[22]

Other legal definitions of "Hinduism" have relied upon outside experts and secondary literature as well. In his analysis of *S.P. Mittal* v. *Union of India* (1983) which determined the status of the township of Auroville in the courts, Robert Minor states:

> In applying these thought[s] to what Justice Reddy called 'Aurobindoism,' the justice did not cite Aurobindo's followers but outside experts who have observed Aurobindo and the movement. He discovered numerous cases in encyclopedias and other secondary literature to support the contention that 'the world

---

[20] *Ibid.*, 1129-1130.

[21] AIR 1965 SC 1179 at 1184.

[22] *Ibid.*, 1181, emphasis added. Only a year later in *Yagnapurushdasji, op. cit.*, 1135, certain members of the same court argued that the apprehension regarding the entrance of untouchables into Hindu temples on the part of the Swaminarayan sect is "founded on superstition, ignorance and complete misunderstanding of the true teachings of the Hindu religion...."

and India treated and respected Shri Aurobindo as a religious teacher and the founder of a new religious movement whose principal thesis was the evolution or transformation of humanity into divinity through the practice of Integral Yoga'.... and he concluded that there is no reason why 'Aurobindoism' cannot be classified, if not as a new religion, as a sect of Hinduism and why the followers of Shri Aurobindo cannot be termed a religious denomination.[23]

Although in this case, the court ultimately decided that Auroville's institutions are "spiritual," and hence "secular" but not "religious," it is interesting to note where the court looked in order to determine what "Hinduism" is. The Calcutta High Court's decision regarding the "non-Hindu" status of the Ramakrishna Mission relied upon similar types of evidence. In his analysis of this case, Brian K. Smith writes:

> The case of the Ramakrishna Mission provides us with some insights into what the Indian court, at least, regards as distinctively and definitionally Hindu. A Hindu is one who affirms the absolute authority of the Vedas—a definition of Hinduism that I myself, among many others, have put forward in somewhat different terms. A Hindu is also one, according to the court, who subscribes to the "Hindu moral code" of *varnāśrama dharma* and to the caste system that is guided by that moral code, and this too is a definitional trait noted by scholars as well as the court. The fact that academic definitions and legal ones here overlap is not coincidental. The judges ruling in this case quoted liberally from scholarly works to back up their opinions, as did the lawyers in their petitions—a sobering and perhaps disturbing thought for Indologists accustomed to assuming that learned trea-

---

[23] *The Religious, the Spiritual, and the Secular: Auroville and Secular India, op. cit.,* p. 122.

tises are read only by academic colleagues and overheard only by fellow conventioneers.[24]

In other cases which have involved definitional issues, the courts have proceeded without specifically defining "Hinduism" but have assumed nonetheless that caste is a defining characteristic of "the Hindu religion." In these cases the courts have pronounced judgements on the basis of an established understanding of "Hinduism" without citing expert opinions.[25] In certain judgements, caste has been assumed to be a particular characteristic of "Hinduism," and, more importantly, as a characteristic *not* observed in non-Hindu religions.

Conversion in the Courts

In *Rajagopal* v. *Arumugam* the issue at stake was whether Rajagopal could take a reserved seat in the Mysore Legislative Assembly as a member of a SC.[26] Arumugam claimed that Rajagopal should not be allowed to stand as a candidate for a reserved seat because he was not an Adi Dravida Hindu but rather an Indian Christian. He had been converted, it was claimed, in 1949 shortly

---

[24] "How Not to Be a Hindu: The Case of the Ramakrishna Mission," in *Religion and Law in Independent India, op. cit.*, pp. 425-442, pp. 441-442. Smith joins the ranks of the many Indologists before him who have posited an essential definition of "Hinduism." In his reading of Brahmanical literature, Smith agrees with the Indological construct which identifies "Hinduism" as "the religion of those humans who create, perpetuate, and transform traditions with legitimizing reference to the authority of the Veda" (p. 349 n. 57).

[25] C.f. *Jagdishwaranand* v. *Police Commissioner, Calcutta* A.I.R. 1984 SC 51 at 55 where Justice Ranganath indicates that upon examining "... the writings of Shri Ananda Murti in books like *Carya-Carya, Nama Shivaya Shantaya, A Guide to Human Conduct,* and *Ananda Vachanamritam*," the court understood these writings to be "essentially founded upon the essence of Hindu philosophy." Thus the Ananda Margis "belong to the Shaivite order ..." and hence "belong to the Hindu religion."

[26] AIR 1969 SC 101. For more on the religious and legal issues surrounding conversion in modern India see Ronald Neufeldt, "To Convert or Not to Covert: Legal and Political Dimensions of Conversion in Independent India," in *Religion and Law in Independent India, op. cit.*, pp. 381-399 and R.D. Baird "Traditional Values, Governmental Values, and Religious Conflict in Contemporary India", *Brigham Young University Law Review* 2 (1998): 337-356.

before he entered Woorhees Christian High School. The election proceeded with Rajagopal ineligible to run for a reserved seat. In the suit that followed, Rajagopal claimed that even if he had once been a Christian, nonetheless, since that time he had been reconverted to "Hinduism" and was thereby readmitted to his caste. The High Court considered certain documentary evidence such as the correction of his service records, the declaration of his sons as "Hindu," and his marriage to an Adi Dravida woman and concluded that Rajagopal had indeed been reconverted to "Hinduism" and thus the election results were invalid. In justifying the court's decision to scrutinize the issue of caste membership as a Hindu phenomenon, G.S. Sharma writes:

> We agree with the High Court that, when the appellant embraced Christianity in 1949, he lost the membership of the Adi Dravida Hindu caste. The Christian religion does not recognize any caste classifications. All Christians are treated as equal and there is no distinction between one Christian and another of the type that is recognized between members of different castes belonging to the Hindu religion. In fact, [the] caste system prevails only amongst Hindus or possibly in some religions closely allied to the Hindu religion like Sikhism. Christianity is prevalent not only in India, but almost all over the world and nowhere does Christianity recognize caste division. The tenets of Christianity militate against persons professing Christian faith being divided or discriminated on the basis of any such classification as the caste system. It must, therefore, be held that, when the appellant got converted to Christianity in 1949, he ceased to belong to the Adi Dravida caste.[27]

The emphasis on caste status as a Hindu phenomenon which one may lose upon conversion to another religion is also evident in *Michael* v. *Venkataswaran* where the religious requirement was upheld against a Paraiyan convert to Christianity.[28] In this case the convert and his fellow caste members

---

[27] *Legislation and Cases on Untouchability and Scheduled Castes in India* (New Delhi: Indian Council of Social Science Research, 1975), p. 132.
[28] AIR 1952 Madras 474.

considered him to be a member of the caste even after his conversion to Christianity. In spite of this, the court held that "the general rule is ... conversion operates as an expulsion from the caste ... a convert ceases to have any caste."[29] In a 1953 case from Madras, the court likewise held that conversion from "Hinduism" results in a loss of caste:

> In *In re Thomas* another bench of the Madras court considered a convert case which did not involve the presidential order. The Madras government had extended school-fee concessions to converts from the Scheduled Castes 'provided ... that the conversion was of the ... student or of his parent....' A Christian student whose grandfather had converted could not, it was held, complain of discrimination, since converts did not belong to the Harijan community. By conversion they had 'ceased to belong to any caste because the Christian religion does not recognize a system of castes.' The concessions to recent converts were merely an indulgence, and the state could determine the extent of this indulgence.[30]

In a similar case from 1969, *Goka Ramalingam* v. *Boddu Abraham*, a church register was entered into evidence to demonstrate that the respondents were ineligible to stand for a reserved seat. While the respondents' names were not included in the register, it was discovered that their parents' names were.

---

[29] *Ibid.*, 478.

[30] Cited in Marc Galanter, "Changing Legal Conceptions of Caste," in *Law and Society in Modern India, op. cit.*, pp. 141-181, p. 171. This decision is in keeping with an early decision from the Madras High Court involving the lack of caste in Christianity. In *Michael Pilla* v. *Barthe* A.I.R. 1917 Madras 431, certain "high caste" Christians petitioned for the restoration of a wall which served to separate them from "low caste" Christians during church services. In addition they petitioned that "low caste" Christians not be allowed to perform certain ceremonial actions at the front of the church as their presence there would pollute the religious implements. The court rejected their claim because they could find no precedence for enforcing caste distinctions among Christians. Caste, it was held, is based on Hindu notions of purity and pollution and is thus not a part of the Christian religion. Cf. Galanter, "Group Membership and Group Preferences in India," *op. cit.*, p. 129.

Thus it was held that by virtue of their parents' conversion to Christianity, the respondents were "born Christians" and thus could not occupy reserved seats.[31]

Since its establishment in 1950, membership in the SC has been restricted to members of the Hindu community. In 1956, certain Sikh groups were named among the SC. Other indigenous religious groups who theoretically repudiate caste, such as the Arya Samaj, have been understood as nonetheless having caste. In 1957 Shankar Deo was elected to fill a reserved seat from the State of Mysore. By birth he was a member of the Samgar caste which had been specified in the Presidential Order of 1950 as a SC. In his nomination papers, Shankar described himself as a member of this caste. The election tribunal rejected his claim on the basis that on the date the papers were filed, Shankar was an Arya Samajist "by creed, belief, and profession."[32] The High Court held that despite his membership in the Arya Samaj, he retained his caste standing. It was held that the Arya Samaj, unlike Christianity or Islam, is not a "new religion entirely distinct from Hinduism." Hence one does not cease to be a Hindu when one professes belief in the Arya Samaj creed.

In *Jasani* v. *Parashram* persons born into the Mahar caste later in life joined the Mahanubhava Panth, a religious group which, like the Arya Samaj, also repudiates caste.[33] For this reason their nomination papers for reserved seats were rejected. Here the court sought to determine the "social and political consequences" of such a conversion and sought to settle the issue of caste membership in a "commonsense practical way rather than on theoretical and theocratic grounds."[34] The court's concern was not with the theology of the group in question but with the consequences of the act of conversion:

---

[31] 1969 (1) S.C.C. 24.

[32] A.I.R. 1960 Mysore 27.

[33] For Dayananda Saraswati, who founded the Arya Samaj in Bombay in 1875, caste was considered to be "Vedic" and thus an essential part of "Hinduism." However, caste was not something to be determined by one's birth but rather by one's innate abilities, skills and proclivities as these were developed and displayed in life. Some modern Aryas, such as those who filed the suit in the *Jasani* case, deny that caste is a feature of the Arya Samaj.

[34] 1954 SCJ 315 at 326.

> Conversion brings many complexities in its train, for it imports a complex composite composed of many ingredients. Religious beliefs, spiritual experience and emotion and intellectual conviction mingle with more material considerations such as severance of family and social ties and the casting off of or the retention of old customs and observances. The exact proportions of the mixture vary from person to person. At one extreme there is bigoted fanaticism bitterly hostile towards the old order and at the other an easy going laxness and tolerance which makes the conversion only nominal. There is no clear cut dividing line and it is not a matter which can be viewed from only one angle.[35]

The court spelled out three factors to be considered in judging the social consequences of conversion:

> Looked at from the secular point of view, there are three factors which have to be considered: (1) the reactions of the old body, (2) the intentions of the individual himself, and (3) the rules of the new order. If the old order is tolerant of the new faith and sees no reason to outcaste or excommunicate the convert and the individual himself desires and intends to retain his old social and political ties the conversion is only nominal for all practical purposes and when we have to consider the legal and political rights of the old body the views of the new faith hardly matter.[36]

The court held that despite their conversion to a religious sect which denies caste, the respondents remained members of the Mahar caste.

In other cases involving an indigenous Indian religion which also repudiates caste, Buddhist converts were said to have lost their SC status upon conversion. In *Punjabrao* v. *Meshram* certain evidence was brought before the Bombay High Court and the Supreme Court to the effect that Dr. D.P. Meshram and others had ceased to be Hindus and had been converted to Buddhism.

---

[35] *Ibid.*, 326.
[36] *Ibid.*, 326-327.

Meshram did not deny before the court that included on his daughters' wedding invitations were the words "Subh *Lagna*" (auspicious wedding) followed by a picture of Lord Buddha and the inscription "May victory and prosperity be yours—Obeisances to Buddha."[37] In his response, Justice Mudholkar writes:

> It is well known that in Hindu weddings the invitations issued in an Indian language the picture of the *Kuladaivata* is generally printed and the blessings of the *Kuladaivata* are invoked. Had respondent No. 1 considered himself to be a Hindu he would have followed the usual practice. No doubt, sophisticated people, though still belonging to the Hindu religion, have discarded the practice of printing the picture of the family deity on wedding invitations and of invoking the blessings of the deity. Respondent No. 1 does not suggest that he belongs to that class. Indeed if it were so, there would have been no occasion to print the picture of Lord Buddha and seek his blessings. In this invitation the picture of the *Kuladaivata* was substituted by that of Lord Buddha. This is more consistent with respondent No. 1 having become a Buddhist than with his remaining a Hindu.[38]

Likewise, the Justice finds it unlikely that Meshram would have married his daughters to Buddhist bridegrooms were he still a Hindu belonging to the SC. In countering these claims, Meshram stated that it was not until a week before the wedding ceremony and well after the traditional period of engagement (*sakshyagandh*) had ended that he found out that his two daughters would be marrying Buddhists and that the wedding would be performed according to Buddhist customs. As for the picture of the Buddha printed on the wedding invitations, "... he tried to give an explanation for this curious conduct by saying that he treated Lord Buddha as the '11th [sic] incarnation' and that is why he had Lord Buddha's picture printed on the wedding invitation."[39] Needless to say, the court was not convinced by these measures.

---

[37] *Op. cit.*, 1182.
[38] *Ibid.*, 1182.
[39] *Ibid.*, 1182.

In addition, evidence was advanced regarding the usage of a plot of land belonging to the defendant. On a plot of land one house away from Meshram's residence there had previously stood a Śiva temple which housed a *lingam* and other Śaivite relics. On June 6, 1959 none other than B.R. Ambedkar himself installed an image of Lord Buddha in the place where the *lingam* had once been in this temple. Meshram, who owned the land on which the temple stood, was accused of being a principle actor in the conversion of the *mandir* into a Buddhist *vihar*. The court concluded that "however great the admiration or regard a Hindu may have for Lord Buddha, he would shudder at the idea of desecrating a Shiva Linga in this manner or even of converting what was once a Shiva temple into a Buddhist temple."[40] Thus Meshram in his actions "professed" in a public manner the Buddhist religion and as a result forfeited his SC status.[41]

The issue of reconversion to Hinduism has also been addressed by the courts. In a 1983 case involving an Adi Dravida twice elected to the Lok Sabha, Justice Reddy writes that no specific ceremony is required for one to be reconverted back to Hinduism and to his caste.[42] Following the 1976 *Arumugam* decision that stated that reconversion to Hinduism *may* result in the reinstatement into one's previous caste, the court found that the actions of Devarajan's fellow caste members indicated that he was "treated by everyone concerned as an Adi Dravida." Furthermore, his actions were consistent with how a true "Hindu" behaves: "He never attended a church. On the other hand, there is acceptable evidence to show that he was offering worship to Hindu deities in Hindu temples and that his marriage was performed according to Hindu custom and rites."[43] While a formal ceremony of reconversion (*shuddhi*) is not required, intentions as expressed in behavior must be consistent with "the Hindu faith":

---

[40] *Ibid.*, 1183.

[41] *Ibid.*, 1184. The court cites Webster's Dictionary definition of "profess" as "to avow publicly, to make an open declaration of, to declare one's belief in: as, to profess Christ. To accept into a religious order." They further hold that "the word 'profess' in the Presidential Order appears to have been used in the sense of an open declaration or practice by a person of the Hindu (or the Sikh) religion. Where, therefore, a persons says, on the contrary that he has ceased to be a Hindu he cannot derive any benefit from that Order" (1184).

[42] *Anbalagan* v. *Devarajan* A.I.R. 1984 SC 411.

[43] *Ibid.*, 415.

A person may be a Hindu by birth or by conversion. A mere theoretical allegiance to the Hindu faith by a person born in another faith does not convert him into a Hindu, nor is a bare declaration that he is a Hindu sufficient to convert him to Hinduism. But a bona fide intention to be converted to the Hindu faith, accompanied by conduct unequivocally expressing that intention may be sufficient evidence of conversion. No formal ceremony of purification or expiation is necessary to effectuate conversion.[44]

In *Guntur Medical College* v. *Mohan Rao*, a student's application for a reserved medical seat was rejected despite his having performed a *shuddhi* reconversion ceremony.[45] Mohan Rao was born to parents of the Madiga SC in Andhra Pradesh who, prior to his birth, had converted to Christianity. He applied for a reserved admission to medical school but was rejected because the school held that no candidate can claim to belong to the SC except by birth. This rule was overturned in the Supreme Court since it was held to go beyond the parameters of the Presidential SC Order of 1950. The only requirement at that time was that a person should "profess the Hindu or Sikh religion," not that one must necessarily be a Hindu by birth. The decisive factor for this court was that the Madiga caste had accepted Mohan as a member despite his family's conversion.[46]

---

[44] *Ibid.*, 414. The court is quoting here the earlier decision found in *Perumal Nadar* v. *Ponnuswami* A.I.R. 1971 SC 2352 at 2353.

[45] A.I.R. 1976 SC 1904.

[46] See M.J. Anthony, *Dalit Rights: Landmark Judgements on SC/ST/Backward Classes* (New Delhi: Indian Social Institute, 1997), p. 36, where he writes: "It is for the members of the caste to decide whether or not to admit a person within the caste. Since caste is a social combination of persons governed by its rules and regulations, it may, if its rules so provide, admit a new member just as it may expel an existing member. Their acceptance is the key test." Anthony is referring here to the caste *panchayats* (literally the "council of five") who make determinations, which are legally binding, regarding caste membership and excommunication. See Marc Galanter and Upendra Baxi, "Panchayat Justice: An Indian Experiment in Legal Access," in M. Galanter, *Law and Society in Modern India, op. cit.*, 54-91.

In a 1986 ruling the Supreme Court held that caste identity was subordinate to religious identity in determining SC benefits.[47] A cobbler named Soosai claimed to be a member of the Adi Dravida caste despite his having openly been converted to Christianity. The Tamil Nadu Village Industries Board conducted a survey of cobblers' work sites and found that they deserved the benefit of free bunks as members of a SC. Soosai was not given a bunk because the government order specifically stated that those persons who had been converted to the Christian religion were not eligible for the benefit.

Soosai brought a suit in which he argued that this was a direct violation of the equality guaranteed him in Articles 14 and 15 as well as a violation of his religious freedom guaranteed in Article 25. While he openly admitted his conversion to Christianity, nonetheless, he claimed to have retained his old caste status. The court found that regardless of his caste identity, the Presidential SC Order applies only to the Hindu community. His membership in a caste was immaterial to this case. The deciding factor for the court was his membership in a non-Hindu religious tradition. Soosai, as a Christian, could not, by definition, receive SC benefits. The court argued that:

> To establish that the order discriminated against Christians, it must be shown that they suffer from a comparable depth of social, cultural and educational backwardness within the Christian community necessitating intervention by the state. It was not enough to show that the same caste continued after conversion. It must be established further that the disabilities they suffered under Hinduism continued in their oppressive severity in the new environment.[48]

Only one year after the *Soosai* case, the Bombay High Court found that backwardness may continue even after a SC member converts from Hinduism to a non-Hindu religion. In *Gopalkrishna* v. *State of Maharashtra* a Buddhist convert sought promotion in the police force of the greater Bombay area as a member of the SC.[49] The court held that any member of a SC who renounces Hinduism and embraces Buddhism ceases to be a member of the SC. The question before the court, however, involved the degree to which converts remain

---

[47] *Soosai* v. *Union of India* A.I.R. 1986 SC 733.

[48] M.J. Anthony, *Dalit Rights, op. cit.*, 63-64.

[49] A.I.R. 1987 Bombay 123.

"backward" after their conversion to a non-Hindu religion. The court found that "backwardness" transcends any one religious community. Hindu untouchables who convert to Buddhism remain untouchables. Therefore the reservation in favor of Buddhist converts was upheld. In a similar case from the Supreme Court, Justice Reddy stated: "The practice of caste however irrational it may appear to our reason and however repugnant it may appear to our moral and social sense, is so deeprooted in the Indian people that its mark does not seem to disappear on conversion to a different religion."[50] As a result of these recent decisions in the courts involving the persistence of "backwardness" despite religious conversion, as well as the political pressure exerted by the Mandal Commission Report, certain Buddhist castes were enumerated on the list of SC beginning in 1990.[51]

Conclusion

The issue of caste identity and religious conversion has been approached in at least two distinctive ways which have had a direct impact on the Indian judiciary. The primary way in which caste has been understood is in terms of a *theoretical* and *theological* equation which posits caste as a defining characteristic of "Hinduism." This understanding of caste as the pivotal element around which "Hinduism" is framed and through which "Hinduism" must be interpreted informed the views of Gandhi, Ambedkar, Nehru, and Radhakrishnan, among Indian nationalists, as well as Müller, Kane, Dumont, and Lingat to name only a few Western Indologists. Likewise this view of caste as a special problem of "Hinduism" lays behind the Presidential Order on Scheduled Castes of 1950.

In his book, *Imagining India*, Ronald Inden traces the history of Western depictions of India in which European self-discovery takes place through describing the "otherness" of India. In the 18th and 19th century construction of identities, which took place both ways between India and Europe, the primary

---

[50] *Anbalagan v. Devarajan, op. cit.*, 414.

[51] Originally established in 1979, the Mandal Commission issued a report in 1980 that classified 3,743 castes as "backward," this was equivalent to around 53 per cent of the population. In the 1991 parliamentary election campaigns, the Janata Dal political party made the Mandal Report one of its primary platforms, much to the dislike of the BJP and its "upper caste" Hindu constituency. See Ranbir Vohra, *The Making of India: A Historical Survey* (Armonk, NY: M.E. Sharpe, 1997), pp. 272-287.

defining characteristics attributed to India were none other than "Hinduism" and "the caste system."[52] In Inden's assessment, scholars imagined India by means of various essences attributed to it, most notably "the caste system."[53] Inden further breaks down this essentialist, Indological discourse on caste into the "empiricist/realist" approach and the "romantic/idealist" approach.

Early commentators on India, such as the historian James Mill, conflated the observations of European travelers with the then newly translated "classical" texts of India like *The Laws of Manu* in order to arrive at an "essence" of India. This mixture of empirical observation with Brahmanically constructed history allowed Mill and others to posit caste as the primary identifying characteristic of Hindu India. What Inden identifies as the empirical approach reached its zenith with the advent of the British census in India. What emerged with the census was a "hegemonic discourse on caste": "Previous accounts of caste had been drawn from texts composed by self-serving Brahmans or had been anecdotal, penned by Western travelers, missionaries, or revenue collectors. Now we were to have truly systematic and scientific, that is, quantitative knowledge of India's essence.[54]

---

[52] See also Gita Dharampal-Frick, "Shifting Categories in the Discourse on Caste: Some Historical Observations," *op. cit.*, where she describes "Hinduism" and caste as 18th and 19th century hypothetical constructions which were given life as distinctive social institutions, which were reified and essentialized, and were understood as static, universal, and univocal entities. She finds this ideology present as well in the Mandal Commission Report which presupposes that caste is the central issue in "Hinduism" to be addressed.

[53] *Imagining India* (Oxford: Basil Blackwell, 1990), see generally the introduction and Chapter 2 on caste as the essence of "Hinduism" and India. Regarding the history of "Hinduism" and caste within the discipline of Indology, Inden writes: "One of the major purposes of Indological discourses has been to give the impression that the world was ordered in a natural, stable way. Scholarly writing achieved this by building 'essences' into its metaphors" (2).

[54] *Ibid.*, 58-59. Cf. also D.E. Smith's *India as a Secular State* (Princeton: Princeton University Press, 1963), p. 304, where he writes: "Another British practice which frequently came under fire was that of recording caste in the decennial census. At each recurring census the authorities received innumerable petitions from different castes requesting the government to recognize their claims to higher rank. The practice of recording caste clearly provided a new field for caste conflict and tended to perpetuate caste consciousness. The British census commissioner eliminated the return of caste in the 1941 census schedule, but more because of the questionable accuracy of such returns than because of their harmful social consequences."

What Inden identifies as the romantic/idealist approach was found among philosophers such as G.W.F. Hegel and Indologists such as Max Müller. For these thinkers India was Europe's opposite. The West was imagined as rational, reformist, the very home and birth place of *homo aequalis*, India with its caste system was superstitious, stifling toward individual initiative, exploitative, and static. The sociologist Max Weber went so far as to argue that, given India's extreme traditionalism in the form of the caste system, "modern capitalism" as we know it would never have developed there. While Europe had notions of class, it did not have a "caste system" which was so integral to India. For Hegel, caste was construed as the "necessary and distinctive nucleus of India, logically integral to the whole of Indian civilization."[55] Later Indian nationalists like Gandhi, Nehru, and Radhakrishnan reacted to, and were influenced by, Western perceptions of caste:

> Probably the most important Romantic idealist writings from 1875 to Independence are not those of Western scholars but of the many Indian nationalists, including Gandhi and Nehru themselves.... The philosopher Radhakrishnan's discussion of caste under the rubric of the individual and social order is an excellent example of this Indian nationalist stance. He emphasizes the scheme of the four *varnas*, which he calls classes rather than castes, over the myriad smaller groups fetishized by the empiricists. That model of order was a logical and complete system for the division of labour and, even more, of man's nature. It was also one of organic solidarity and universal, applying to all mankind and not just to India; and Radhakrishnan argues that for many centuries foreigners were accepted into its folds....Yet Radhakrishnan does not escape from the world of essences. Far from it. By essentializing his version of caste, by making it an unchanging ideal that precedes human history and stands outside it, he too makes it into a substantialized agent, one that not only made India but that could or can make the whole of humanity in its image.[56]

---

[55]*Ibid.*, 71.

[56]Ibid., 72-73. See also Robert N. Minor, *Radhakrishnan: A Religious Biography* (Albany: SUNY Press, 1987), p. 48, where he writes: "The critics' arguments have been

Another way in which caste has been understood, especially more recently in the Indian judiciary, has been informed by a *sociological* inquiry regarding the way in which "backwardness" and caste works "on the ground" among SC Indians. While the evidence from court cases shows that this approach has been taken far less than the theoretical/theological approach, nonetheless, evidence from a sociological perspective regarding the continuance of "backwardness" after religious conversion has been heard by the courts. In addition, the rather diffuse nature of caste practices has not escaped the attention of some scholars. Thus Ainslie Embree has pointed out that:

> As far as traditional Indian social structure is concerned, the basic point to stress is that caste is not a system, as it is so often called, but a useful descriptive rubric covering two rather different aspects of traditional Indian society. First of all, caste implies a concept, or a theory, deeply imbedded in Indian thought, of how a good society works. But, since it is a theory, one will not expect to find social practice always conforming to it any more than one will expect to find that the injunction 'Thou shall not kill' is always obeyed by Christians.[57]

---

reversed in Radhakrishnan's mind. Instead of criticisms about caste inequalities which exist on the level of caste as it is practiced in India, Radhakrishnan defines an ideal system. He argues for this system on the basis of what in his interpretation is its inherent equality and its democratic function in society. This, he says, is what caste really means."

[57] *Utopias in Conflict: Religion and Nationalism in Modern India* (Berkeley: University of California Press, 1990), p. 65. See also Robert Stern's ethnographic/social scientific work entitled *Changing India* (Cambridge: Cambridge University Press, 1993), pp. 52-83. In his chapter on caste, Stern points out the unlikely nature of classical formulations of caste: "We have no idea whether *varna dharma* ever really existed as a hierarchy of social groups, based upon skin color or anything else. It doesn't now and even if it did sometime in the dim past, that would be quite irrelevant to its importance in India today" (54). He goes on to point out that the "importance" of caste and *jatis* in India today lies not in its Hindu-based ideology but in its widespread and diffuse nature: "The ideologies are Hindu, but *jatis* are Indian. Groups convert from Hinduism, change their faith; but in the ideology of *varna dharma* they cannot change their breed" (60). Hence the categorization by birth group (*jati*) occurs among Indian Jews, Christians, Muslims, etc., whether recent converts or not, and not simply among Hindus alone.

Likewise Justice Reddy has recognized that the "deeprootedness" of caste within the Indian people appears to affect all Indian religious communities and not just "Hinduism." Justice Reddy goes so far as to quote an earlier High Court judgement to the effect that conversion to non-indigenous religions, such as Christianity, does not always negate caste membership: The Court ... noticed that it was not an infrequent phenomenon in South India for a person to continue to be regarded as belonging to his original caste even after conversion to Christianity.... It cannot, therefore, be laid down as an absolute rule uniformly applicable in all cases that whenever a member of a caste is converted from Hinduism to Christianity, he loses his membership of the caste. It is true that ordinarily that on conversion to Christianity, he would cease to be a member of the caste, but that is not an invariable rule. It would depend on the structure of the caste and its rules and regulations. There are castes, particularly in South India, where the consequence does not follow on conversion since such castes comprise from Hindus and Christians.[58]

This of course raises the issue of SC benefits to a new level. If castes which have been historically considered "backward" are deserving of SC awards, and one retains one's caste identity even upon conversion to Christianity, then it only follows that some Christians (and Muslims) should also be eligible to receive SC benefits. After all, it is lists of the various castes themselves which are enumerated on the Presidential Order. Thus, regardless of one's religious affiliation, membership in one of the enumerated castes, by the Court's own logic, should qualify one for SC benefits. However, the courts cannot make new laws, they can only interpret and enforce existing ones. They are thus required to award SC benefits only to persons professing the Hindu, Sikh or Buddhist religions. While other indigenous religious traditions, i.e., "Sikhism" and "Buddhism," have been added to the 1950 Presidential Order, the exclusion of non-indigenous religions betrays what Marc Gallanter has called a "sacral view of caste" on the part of the constitutional provision enumerating scheduled castes.

As indicated above, the Presidential Order of 1950 would seem to point to the notion that caste and "Hinduism" are coterminous, essentially related elements, bound together in a vision of an idealized Hindu society. To deem conversion to a non-indigenous religious tradition as an automatic disqualification for SC benefits violates the prohibition in Article 15 against discrimination

---

[58]*Anbalagan v. Devarajan, op. cit.*, 412-413.

solely on the bases of caste or religion. As Galanter points out, "It also restricts freedom of religion, which would seem to require that government refrain from administering its welfare schemes so as to put a heavy price tag on its exercise. The Hindu requirement seems to reflect a hostility toward conversions which is anachronistic."[59]

The courts are in a sense required to give legal effect to a picture of "Hinduism" (and related indigenous religious traditions—even those which ostensibly repudiate caste) as the religion(s) of the caste system and of "Hindu society" as a society which is composed of the four *varnas*. This essentializing picture of caste as a Hindu phenomenon ignores the practice of caste distinctions as it has historically and continues presently to take place among *non-Hindu* Indians. The purpose behind the SC Order is to promote the goal of equality of opportunity as it is found in the constitutional religious model. The extent to which this goal has been reached is called into question when religious qualifications are allowed to determine eligibility for SC benefits. While the Constitution of India forbids discrimination solely on the basis of caste, and purveyors of the constitutional religious model seek to eradicate discriminatory caste mentality altogether, it is perhaps inevitable that caste identity will continue to be reinforced when benefits are allotted on the basis of membership in a disadvantaged caste. However, it would not seem to be necessary to discriminate on the basis of religion, in addition to caste, to further the secular state's goal of equality. By removing the religious qualification from the SC Order, the state of India will be taking a step toward recognizing need where it exists among Indian citizens regardless of their religious or communal identities.

---

[59] "Group Membership and Group Preferences in India," *op. cit.*, 133. See also in the same volume "Changing Legal Conceptions of Caste," pp. 141-181.

19

How Not to be a Hindu:
The Case of the Ramakrishna Mission

Brian K. Smith

"Hinduism" is, according to most recent definitions of it, notoriously difficult to define.[1] According to some, in fact, Hinduism probably does not exist at all. Robert Frykenberg argues in a recent and influential article that

> there has never been any such a thing as a single 'Hinduism' or any single 'Hindu community' for all of India. Nor, for that matter, can one find any such thing as a single 'Hinduism' or 'Hindu community' even for any one socio-cultural region of the continent. Furthermore, there has never been any one religion—nor even one system of religions—to which the term 'Hindu' can accurately be applied. No one so-called religion, moreover, can lay exclusive claim to or be defined by the term 'Hinduism.'

"The very notion of the existence of any single religious community by this name," Frykenberg concludes, "has been falsely conceived."[2]

Both outsiders and insiders (i.e. "Hindus") over the past two centuries have found it advantageous (for different reasons) to envision Hinduism as resistant to, if not transcendent of, precise definition. Outsiders found it easier to compare unfavorably such an amorphous entity to the more discriminating and bounded religions of the West. Hindus, conversely, could capitalize on

---

[1] For recent discussions of the definitional problems, see Gunther D. Sontheimer and Hermann Kulke (editors), *Hinduism Reconsidered* (New Delhi, 1989); and especially the symposium, with articles by John Stratton Hawley, Alf Hiltebeitel, Wendy Doniger, Prasenjit Duara, et al., entitled "Hinduism and the Fate of India," *The Wilson Quarterly* (Summer 1991), pp. 20–52.

[2] Robert E. Frykenberg, "The Emergence of Modern 'Hinduism' as a Concept and as an Institution: A Reappraisal with Special Reference to South India," in Sontheimer & Kulke, *Loc. cit.*, p. 29.

Hinduism's supposed tolerance and inclusiveness in order to claim universality; Hinduism was, it could be and is sometimes said, all religions in one.

For scholars the assumed indefiniteness of Hinduism has in the past often meant conceiving of the religion in metaphorical terms. Hinduism, as Ronald Inden has noted in his recently published book *Imagining India*, has been constituted by Westerners as "a *female* presence who is able, through her very amorphousness and absorptive powers, to baffle and perhaps even threaten Western rationality, clearly a male in this encounter."[3] Hinduism, according to Monier-Williams, is like an Indian banyan tree whose "single stem sends out numerous branches destined to send roots to the ground and become trees themselves, till the parent stock is lost in a dense forest of its own offshoots."[4] Alternatively, Hinduism is likened to an excessively fecund and chaotic jungle. The following is from the authoritative three-volume work of Charles Eliot entitled *Hinduism and Buddhism*:

> Hinduism has often and justly been compared to a jungle. As in the jungle every particle of soil seems to put forth its spirit in vegetable life and plants grown on plants, creepers and parasites on their more stalwart brethren, so in India art, commerce, warfare and crime, every human interest and aspiration seek for a manifestation in religion, and since men and women of all classes and occupations, all stages of education and civilization, have contributed to Hinduism, much of it seems low, foolish and even immoral. The jungle is not a park or garden. Whatever can grow in it, does grow. The Brahmans are not gardeners but forest officers....Here and there in a tropical forest some well-grown tree or brilliant flower attracts attention, but the general impression left on the traveller by the vegetation as he passes through it mile after mile is infinite repetition as well as infinite luxuriance. And so it is in Hinduism.[5]

"Hinduism" by definition, these scholars claim, cannot be defined. It is too fluid, too all-encompassing, and most of all too "tolerant" to be subjected to a concept like "orthodoxy," or even "orthopraxy."[6] "Hinduism," wrote Nehru, "is

---

[3] Ronald Inden, *Imagining India* (Oxford, 1990), p. 86.

[4] Monier-Williams, cited in John Stratton Hawley, "Naming Hinduism," *Wilson Quarterly* 15, 3 (Summer 1991) p. 22.

[5] Cited in Inden, *Loc. cit.*, pp. 86–87.

[6] Among the very few people who find it difficult to maintain the stereotype of Hinduism as "tolerant" in light of past, recent, and ongoing daily evidence to the contrary, is Nirad C. Chaudhuri. "If the familiar words about tolerance and capacity for synthesis of the Hindus

vague, amorphous, many-sided, all things to all men. It is hardly possible to define it, or indeed to say precisely whether it is a religion or not, in the usual sense of the word."[7] Govinda Das has written that Hinduism "rejects nothing. It is all-comprehensive, all-compliant."[8] Others such as S. Radhakrishna insist that Hinduism is an equally indefinable "mode of life," and thus also not a religion *per se*.[9] A Hindu, writes yet another scholar, is one who "does not repudiate that designation" or, more positively, a Hindu is someone who "says he is a Hindu."[10]

The school of nondefinition perhaps reached its apex with Percival Spear's remarkable "sponge theory." Throwing up one's hands in despair of ever delimiting Hinduism, one returns to the realm of metaphor to characterize a religion this indiscriminate and all-consuming:

> Hinduism has been likened to a vast sponge, which absorbs all that enters it without ceasing to be itself. The simile is not quite exact, because Hinduism has shown a remarkable power of assimilating as well as absorbing; the water becomes part of the sponge. Like a sponge it has no very clear outline on its borders and no apparent core at its centre. An approach to Hinduism provides a first lesson in the 'otherness' of Hindu ideas from those of Europe. The Western love of definition and neat pigeon-holing receives its first shock...[11]

Many Indologists have thus declared Hinduism either too disorganized and exotically other, or too complex and recondite, to be subjected to the definitional strictures applicable to other religions and cultures. One wonders if

---

were true, one would be hard put to explain why there are endemic outbursts of murderous ferocity." *The Continent of Circe* (Bombay, 1965), p. 33. A study of what factors contributed to the generation of this supposedly essential feature of Hinduism in both Western constructions of Indian religion and in South Asian political and religious discourse remains a desideratum. For the present, see Arvind Sharma, "Some Misunderstandings of the Hindu Approach to Religious Plurality," *Religion* 8 (Autumn 1978), pp. 133–54; Kaisa Puhakka, "The Roots of Religious Tolerance in Hinduism and Buddhism," *Temenos* 12 (1976), pp. 50–61; Paul Hacker, "Zur Geschichte und Beurteilung des Hinduismus," in *Kleine Schriften*, edited by Lanbert Schmithausen (Weisbaden, 1978); and Frits Staal.

[7] Jawaharlal Nehru, *The Discovery of India* (London, 1960), p. 63.

[8] Quoted in Hervey DeWitt Griswold, *Insights into Modern Hinduism* (New York, 1934), p. 15. Cf. T. G. Percival Spear: "Hinduism rests essentially on public opinion. Not to be a Hindu means simply not being thought to be a Hindu." *India, Pakistan and the West* (Oxford, 1958), p. 58.

[9] S. Radhakrishnan, *The Hindu View of Life* (New York, 1973).

[10] Govinda Das, *Loc. cit.*

[11] Spear, *Loc. cit.*, p. 57.

such radical antipathy to definition stems from a kind of paranoic sense of professional self-interest: it is as if Indologists worry that should a definition of their object of study actually be generated, the need for experts in the field would somehow be compromised, or even vanish. This, of course, would be to misunderstand the function of definition in the pursuit of knowledge; but the almost pathological aversion to definition in the study of Hinduism seems to call for some explanation.

In any event, Hinduism, we are told, can be and is virtually everything; indeed, it appears difficult *not* to be a Hindu. And there are some Hindus who find this notion quite appealing. For Hindus, a nondefinition of Hinduism has played a somewhat different role than it has for Indologists and Comparative Religionists. Hinduism is represented as all religions in one rather than one religion among all others. Hinduism has been portrayed by Hindus as tolerant, universalistic, and even nonsectarian—in part in order to soft-peddle its socio-political status as the dominant and dominating religion of "secular" modern India. An Indian "senior civilian official," quoted by Mark Fineman in a story published in *The Los Angeles Times* on Oct. 31, 1990, concerning yet another bout of Hindu-Muslim riots, "insisted that the confrontation is at least as much a political as a religious issue.... 'Hinduism by definition is secular. It embraces all religions,' the official continued. 'I just hope that what the country is witnessing now is not a redefinition of Hinduism itself'"—a "redefinition" here meaning nothing more than a "definition" of Hinduism as one religion or a group of religions, and not *all* religions (or no religion at all).[12]

Philosophers and religious leaders, in addition to Indian civil administrators, have also regarded the supposed all-inclusiveness of Hinduism as a laudable trait. When, in the late 18th century, Warren Hastings invited pundits from all over India to draw up a summary of Hindu beliefs, here is, in part, what the native theologians submitted as typically a "Hindu" doctrine:

> He [the Supreme Being] appointed to each race its own faith, and to every sect its own religion; and having introduced a multiplicity of different customs He views in each place the mode of worship respectively appointed to it. Sometimes He is with the attendants upon the mosque; sometimes in the temple at the adoration of

---

[12] In a subsequent story by the same reporter, "Hindu Throng Demands Temple on Muslim Shrine Site," *The Los Angeles Times*, April 5, 1991, the Shankaracharya Divyanandaji Bhanpurapeeth was quoted as saying, "Hinduism, you see, is not a religion. Hinduism is a way of life. The relationship between husband and wife is the same as the relationship between religion and politics."

idols— the intimate of the Musalman, the friend of the Hindu, the companion of the Christian, the confidant of the Jew.[13]

Such statements of one-world-religionism have continually received philosophical backup from the Vedantins, who for many centuries have tended to regard all other competitors, both inside and outside the overgrown jungle or saturated sponge that is Hinduism, as versions of themselves—perhaps slightly off-base, certainly focused on the part rather than the whole, incomplete in their vision, but nevertheless all somehow "saying the same thing" and therefore really Vedantins after all. All is One, as the slogan goes. (Certain ecumenically minded dialogical Christians, perennial philosophers, and crypto-theologians in Religious Studies Departments, have recently reinvented this polemical wheel with the notion that all religions share some sort of underlying unity. One might also mention in this context those Western rock stars and their fans who naively announce that "we are the world.")

Hindu "tolerance," however, is not toothless; encompassment of others, as Louis Dumont has taught us, entails hierarchical ranking.[14] Those who create the auspices under which such tolerance, inclusiveness, and universalism may proceed—and, again, I speak here not only of certain Hindus but all such universalists—also create an oftentimes unacknowledged hierarchical scale whereby some truths are truer than other truths. Those, for example, who *do not* espouse the values of tolerance, inclusiveness, unity and so forth will not be accorded the same status as those who do. Hinduism's superiority is implicitly but nevertheless emphatically asserted through the very notion that Hinduism is, by definition, infinitely tolerant. The proclamation of the all-encompassing nature of Hinduism might also very well function as a subtle, perhaps wishful, but nevertheless ideologically potent strategy of hegemonic expansion, comparable to somewhat cruder strategies practiced by other religions— missionary ventures, the holy war or *jihad*, imperialism and colonialism, foreign trade and commerce, *et al*.

Despite the claim by scholars of Hinduism as well as by certain Hindus themselves that Hinduism cannot be delimited by virtue of its fluidity and all-embracing (non)essence, the history of that thing we call Hinduism suggests otherwise. To argue that there is no Hindu "orthodoxy" is also to deny that Hindus can have a sense of "heresy," which ignores abundant historical evidence to the contrary. Beginning with the Hindu reaction, in texts like the *Manu Smrti*,

---

[13] Cited in Ram Gopal, "Hinduism, Islam, and Christianity," *Indian Express*, Sept. 20, 1990.

[14] Louis Dumont, *Homo Hierarchicus: The Caste System and Its Implications*, complete rev. English ed., trans. by Mark Saisbury, Louis Dumont, and Basia Gulati (Chicago, 1980).

to Buddhists, Jains, and others who denied the absolute authority of the Veda and of the Brahmins who brokered that canon, and continuing among those contemporary Hindus we are all too ready to label, and dismiss, as "fundamentalists," Hindus have defined themselves in the same moment that they have defined others as *not Hindus*.

Furthermore, while it may be possible, if not entirely unobjectionable, for scholars to envision the object of their research as a chaotic jumble of beliefs and practices without discernable boundaries of either orthodoxy or orthopraxy; and while it may be strategic for some Hindu polemicists to champion their tradition by denying its particularity[15]—while such indulgences might be the privilege of some, those charged with running the legal machinery of present-day pluralistic India cannot afford them. The law must go where academic angels too often fear to tread, and its explorations of this terrain may be of some interest to those of us in the academy concerned, in one way or another, with an entity called "Hinduism."

In 1983, a case was brought before Justice B. C. Ray in Calcutta by attorneys representing the teachers of the Vivekananda Centenary College at Rahara, an institution controlled by the Ramakrishna Mission Society. The teachers contended that the College they worked for had been established by the government and was therefore being illegally adminstered by the Ramakrishna Mission. Furthermore, as a public institution the College was subject to govermental guidelines—including, most relevantly, the West Bengal College Teachers Act which legislates higher salaries and greater benefits and job security than the teachers were receiving.

The defense argued that not only had the Ramakrishna Mission established the College (the Mission had in fact donated the land, although the buildings were built with the aid of governmental funds), but more shockingly also declared that Ramakrishnaism is not a sect of Hinduism but a distinct minority religion with all the constitutional protection religious minorities receive

---

[15] The continuing search for authenticity and self-identity among Indian intellectuals in the post-colonial era has sometimes returned to the notion that Hinduism is, or should be, infinitely encompassing. See, for example, T.N. Madan's, "The Quest for Hinduism," in *Non-Renunciation: Themes and Interpretations of Hindu Culture* (Delhi, 1987); and especially Ashis Nandy, *The Intimate Enemy: Loss and Recovery of Self Under Colonialism* (Delhi, 1983). Many such ponderings are sophisticated efforts to deconstruct older constructs and recapture fluidity; as Nandy writes, "The alternative to Hindu nationalism is the peculiar mix of classical and folk Hinduism and the unselfconscious Hinduism by which most Indians, Hindus as well as non-Hindus, live" (p. 104). Others in contemporary India, i.e. the Hindu nationalists Nandy opposes, increasingly move toward a concretized and exclusivistic notion of "Hinduism"—perhaps a localized reflex of the worldwide inclination toward fundamentalism in the face of the disturbing reality of pluralism and multiculturalism.

The Ramakrishna Mission

in India. In a case still pending before the Indian Supreme Court, lawyers for the newly dubbed "Ramakrishnaites" have persuaded the judiciary that the Mission need not follow state law determining the payment and benefits of teachers at the Vivekananda Centenary College since "Ramakrishnaism" is a minority religious organization with all the "special rights and privileges guaranteed under Articles 26 and 30 of the Constitution"[16] (including, among other of perquisites, the right and privilege to pay employees less than mandated by the state for institutions of the majority religion). As a result of the legal proceedings, Ramakrishnaites are no longer Hindus.[17]

"During the hearing of the case," Ram Swarup has noted, "the court faced some intricate questions: What is religion in its essence and accidents?....

---

[16] Article 26 reads as follows

> Subject to public order, morality and health, every religious denomination or any section thereof shall have the right
> (a) to establish and maintain institutions for religious and charitable purposes;
> (b) to manage its own affairs in matters of religion;
> (c) to own and acquire movable and immovable property; and
> (d) to administer such property in accordance with law.

Article 30 states

> (1) All minorities, whether based on religion or language, shall have the right to establish and administer educational institutions of their choice.
> (2) The State shall not, in granting aid to educational institutions, discriminate against any educational institution on the ground that it is under the management of a minority, whether based on religion or language.

[17] In the wake of the considerable controversy generated by this case, officials of the Ramakrishna Mission have contended that this drastic step was necessary in order to stop interference in their affairs by the communist government of West Bengal. Brahmachari Chaitanya Jagannath of the Chicago Vivekananda Vedanta Society, for example, is quoted as saying "When I was there [in India] I got an earful of the kind of harrassment that was being perpetrated against the so-called private schools. The swamis were being forced out of positions of responsibility and authority by the state government and the teachers. They felt it was religious persecution, and there was no recourse to protect themselves other than if they got this special status." Others attempt to separate the political and religious aspects of the case. Major T. R. Vedantham of the Ramakrishna Mission of Madras has said that "They have only gotten minority status given to them in legal terms. What is involved is politics and not religion." Swami Bhasyananda, head of the Vivekananda Vedanta Society of Chicago reportedly has taken an even more cynical view: "I personally feel they have done it to get the advantage, the same advantage which Muslims are getting and other minority communities are getting. We are proud that we are Hindus. We would not say that we are not Hindus. We are Hindus, no doubt. It was just to get that advantage. If we can get those advantages as a minority, then why should we not do so?" All the above quotations are from *Hinduism Today*, Vol. 8, no. 2 (March 1, 1986), p. 1.

When does an old religion become new?"[18] For to claim a sect is *not* Hindu necessarily entails a delineation of what Hinduism *is*, of why and when the sect ceases to be Hindu and becomes something else, and of what features make this "something else" an independent religion. In what follows, I will briefly trace the arguments offered in the case as to why Ramakrishnaism should be regarded as a separate religion and the criteria presented for what counts as "Hinduism" according to the courts of India.

The case, it would seem, would not be easy to make. The Ramakrishna Mission—a neo-Vedantic reformist organization founded nearly a hundred years ago by Swami Vivekananda, the principal disciple of a somewhat eccentric Hindu temple priest named Ramakrishna—is widely viewed as the quintessence of "high church" or intellectual Hinduism. The membership of the Mission has always been, and remains, overwhelmingly comprised of individuals who identify themselves as Hindus (many of whom were quite dismayed to learn that overnight they had legally ceased to be what they thought they were). And what's more, the two major figures in the movement, Ramakrishna and Vivekananda, both seem to have stated repeatedly and rather unequivocally their allegiance to Hinduism.[19]

The last of these apparent objections to the argument that there is such a thing as "Ramakrishnaism" distinct from Hinduism was, it turns out, the easiest to combat. Just as Jesus did not know that he was founding a religion called "Christianity," just as Gautama did not realize he was bringing into existence something called "Buddhism," just as Mahavira did not perceive himself as the founder of a tradition labelled "Jainism," so too, the lawyers argued, Ramakrishna did not understand that he was the first "Ramakrishnaite." The judge concurred:

> In origin the founder may not have intended to found any religion at all. He may have merely protested against some rituals and observances; he may have disagreed with the interpretation of some earlier

---

[18] "Quest for a Non-Hindu Identity," *Indian Express*, Sept. 19, 1990.

[19] The opposition (i.e. lawyers representing the teachers at the College) made all these points and more. The arguments presented against the Mission's claim to be non-Hindu are summarized in the following: "Thakur Sri Sri Ramkrishna did not profess or preach any religion. He was a Hindu which religion he never gave up by proselytisation. He merely explained Vedanta in his own simple language and he propagated Neo Adityavad treating all beings as God and preaching the cult of service not on compassionate ground but treating 'Jiba as Shiva" i.e. God and discarding any sort of sectarianism. This is nothing but a philosophy based on the Jana Kanda of Veda i.e. Upanishads and not a religion different from Hindu religion. So Ramakrishnaism or the cult of Thakur Sri Sri Ramkrishna is not a religion but a mere philosophy. It cannot be termed as a minority religion different from Hindu religion." 2 *Calcutta L. J.* 366 (1983).

religous tenets. What he said, what he preached and what he thought, his protest, his dissent, his disagreement might have developed into a religion in the course of time or even during his life time. History and perception of the community may make a religion out of what was not intended to be a religion and he may be held as the founder of the new religion.....Neither Buddha, nor Mahavir nor the Christ ever thought of founding a new religion, yet three great religions bear their names...The above observations...would equally apply to the teachings of Sri Ramkrishna and his followers.[20]

Founders of religion, the court noted with all the acumen of good historians of religion, do not know that they are founding a religion; founders of religion become so only retroactively.[21] "The fact that Sri Ramakrishna never expressly abjured Hindu religion, and had sometimes described his disciples as Hindu monks, would not be decisive," declared the court;[22] while "Ramakrishnaism was no doubt born out of Hinduism...for that reason it need not be buried in it."[23]

But why are the doctrines and practices of Ramakrishna, regardless of what *he* thought they were, not in fact Hindu doctrines and practices? Here the case turned, paradoxically enough, on the very universalism that some Hindus and many scholars of Hinduism believe to be at the heart of Hinduism. Ramakrishnaism is *not* Hinduism, the attorneys successfully argued, because Ramakrishna taught a doctrine that transcended the particularities of Hinduism, or any existing religion for that matter. While other religions, including Hinduism, are exclusive, Ramakrishnaism is uniquely and truly all-inclusive:

> The cult or religion of Shri Ramakrishna Paramahansadeb is that all beings are the manifestations of God and all religions are but different paths of reaching God. No religion should be condemned and that to attain spiritual salvation or to reach divinity the paths prescribed by the tenets and dogmas, religious practices of different

---

[20] 1 Calcutta L. J. 150 (1986).

[21] Or as the Ramakrishnaites have put it, "It is to be appreciated that these were the formative days of the Math and the Mission, and Ramakrishnaism could not then be considered to be so widely accepted as to constitute a religion by itself for official use. Again having regard to the facts that Ramakrishna himself never declared to give or establish a religion of his own and that at that stage the implications of his teachings could not be fully worked out, it was but natural for his disciples to describe themselves by their religion of birth [i.e. Hindus]." Cited in Jagtiani, *Loc. cit.*, p. 73.

[22] Cited in *Hinduism Today*, Vol. 8, no. 2 (1 March 1986), p. 1.

[23] Cited in Jagtiani, *Loc. cit.*, p. 78.

religions are equally good. The divinity of 'Jiva Shiva' has to be practised, that is, service to the human beings is to be made treating him as manifestation of God and serving him in a spirit of worship. There is no necessity of one surrendering his own religion, be he a Hindu or a Christian or Muslim or Jew in order to be a follower of the cult or religion of Shri Ramkrishna.... Thus in fact, Thakur Shri Ramkrishna preached a World Religion which is quite different from all other religions including Hindu Religion.[24]

As the harmonizer of all religions, Ramakrishna reputedly founded a new "world" or "universal" religion that claims to be, as the affidavit ingenuously puts it, a "sectless sect." The teachings of Ramakrishna "were meant not for the members of any particular caste, creed or religion but for the entire mankind."[25] Ramakrishnaism, it is now asserted, "never equated itself with any other religion and such equation, instead of promoting its purpose, will prevent it from acheiving its mission,"[26] Therefore, "Any attempt to equate [the] religion of Ramakrishna with the Hindu religion, as professed and practised, will be to defeat that very object of Ramakrishnaism and to deny his gospel. Ramakrishnaism includes the basic virtues of Hinduism and particularly the Hindu spirit, but does not exhaust itself in the Hindu Religion."[27]

Moreover, Ramakrishna's non-Hindu universalism was not just a matter of doctrine; it was also borne out in practice. Lawyers pointed out that the guru had in the course of his life tried out many different *sadhanas*, experimented with many different paths to the truth:

> Sri Ramakrishna practised Hinduism and particularly Bhakti Yoga— the Path of Love. He, however, did not stop there and instead of confining himself within Hinduism and experimenting with other paths according to the tenets of Hinduism, embarked upon altogether novel experiments in accordance with the principles of other religions. He practised Islam as a devout Muslim, read Koran and [performed] *namaj* in [the] mosque and proclaimed to have realised the supreme according to Islamic faith. It is also well known that Sri

---

[24] 2 Calcutta L. J. 348 (1983).

[25] Cited in Jagtiani, *Loc. cit.*, p. 73.

[26] *Ibid.*, p. 75.

[27] *Ibid.*, p. 78.

The Ramakrishna Mission

Ramakrishna experienced with [sic] Christianity and claimed to have attained the same height.[28]

Ramakrishna indeed claimed that "During my sadhana period I had all kinds of amazing visions....I have practised all religions—Hinduism, Islam, Christianity—and I have also followed the paths of the different Hindu sects."[29] In this "sadhana period," the founder of Ramakrishnaism successively adopted the five modes of the Vaishnava *sadhana*; he perfectly realized the ways of *tantra*, *bhakti*, and *jñāna*; he "accepted the divinity of the Buddha" and "showed great respect for" the founders of Jainism and Sikhism;[30] and, most importantly for the case, he purportedly had mystical experiences which "verified the truth" of Christianity and Islam in the course of adopting, for a period lasting all of three days for each, the lifestyle characteristic of those two religions.

Ramakrishna became a Muslim for three days under the guidance of one Govinda Ray, a convert from Hinduism to Islam who was especially attracted to Sufism.[31] During this time Ramakrishna says he "devotionally repeated the holy syllable 'Allah,' wore cloth like the Muslims, said Namaz thrice daily and felt disinclined even to see Hindu deities, not to speak of saluting them, inasmuch as the Hindu mode of thought vanished altogether from my mind." As part of this *sadhana*, Ramakrishna also developed a taste for Muslim food. A Muslim cook was sent for, but disciples prevented him from defiling the kitchen; the *mleccha* chef reputedly stood outside the kitchen giving directions to the Brahmin cook who "prepared the food in the Muslim manner."

According to a later hagiographical work by Akshoy Sen,[32] the formerly Hindu Ramakrishna even had the urge to eat beef while he was in this manner plumbing the essence of Islam. This desire could have raised the problem of contradictory doctrines and practices among religions that all purportedly "say the same thing." Happily, Ramakrishna was able to overcome this false paradox by astrally taking the body of a dog (the implication here that to assume fully the life of a Muslim means becoming a dog is noteworthy) and indulging in the meat of a dead cow (the Hindu doctrine of *ahiṃsā* or "non-violence" was in this way

---

[28] *Ibid.*, p. 72.

[29] *The Gospel According to Sri Ramakrishna*, trans. into English with an Introduction by Swami Nikhilananda (New York, 1952), pp. 744, 35.

[30] *Ibid.*, p. 34.

[31] The following is taken from Swami Saradananda's biography, *Sri Ramakrishna, The Great Master*, trans. by Swami Jagadananda (Madras, 1952), pp. 259-61. Cf. Nikhilananda's version, *Ibid.*, pp. 33-34.

[32] Ramakrishna Punthie, cited in Ram Swarup, *Ramakrishna Mission: In Search of a New Identity*, pp. 9–10.

preserved) that was floating down the Ganges (a river sacred to Hindus, and not to Muslims).

The three days of Ramakrishna's Islamic *sadhana* culminated in a vision of what Saradananda, Ramakrishna's biographer, describes in vague terms as a radiant, luminous figure: "At the time of practising Islam, the Master at first had the vision of an effulgent, impressive personage with a long beard." The story was subsequently embellished by Nikhilananda in his introduction to *The Gospel of Sri Ramakrishna*: the apparition was identified as "perhaps Muhammad."[33] The specter "gently approached him and finally lost himself in Sri Ramakrishna. Thus he realized the Mussalman God."[34] So much for Ramakrishna the Muslim.

Verifying the truth of Christianity entailed listening to some readings from the Bible at the home of one Jadunath Mallick (the exact passages are unspecified), and contemplating a painting of the Madonna and Child found on the wall there. The latter launched Ramakrishna into another ecstatic fit:

> [H]e felt that the picture came to life, and effulgent rays of light, coming out from the bodies of the mother and the Child, entered into his heart and changed radically all the ideas of his mind! On finding that all the inborn Hindu impressions disappeared into a secluded corner of his mind and that different ones arose in it, he tried in various ways to control himself.... But nothing availed. Rising with a great force, the waves of those impressions completely submerged the Hindu ideas in his mind. His love and devotion to the Devas and Devis vanished, and in their stead, a great faith in and reverence for Jesus and his religion occupied his mind, and began to show him Christian padres offering incense and light before the image of Jesus in the Church and to reveal to him the eagerness of their hearts as is seen in their earnest prayers.[35]

---

[33] Nikhilananda, *op. cit.*, p. 34. The story has been filled out in other ways as time has gone on. In the Written Argument, the Ramakrishnaite lawyers quote S. C. Chatterjee as saying that Ramakrishna read the Qur'an during his Islamic *sadhana* (although it is unspecified in which language he read that text); Nehru is cited to the effect that Ramakrishna "went to Muslim and Christian mystics and lived with them for years, following their strict routine"; and Radhakrishna is quoted as saying that Ramakrishna "meditated on the Quran and practised the prescribed rites," and that he "studied Christianity and lived like a Christian anchorite." See Ram Swarup, "Hinduism, Islam & Christianity," *Indian Express*, Sept. 20, 1990.

[34] *Ibid.*

[35] Swami Saradananda, *Loc. cit.*, p. 295.

The Ramakrishna Mission

Forgetting all about his erstwhile devotion to the Hindu Mother Goddess, Ramakrishna's Christian trance, which lasted, again and coincidentally, three days, climaxed in the appearance of still another luminous figure. This time it was Christ. The figure approached him and at that moment he realized the very essence of the Christian doctrine: "Jesus! Jesus the Christ, the great Yogi, the loving Son of God, one with the Father, who gave his heart's blood and put up with endless torture in order to deliver men from sorrow and misery!"[36] Jesus "then embraced the Master and disappeared into his body and the Master entered into ecstasy, lost normal consciousness and remained identified for some time with the Omnipresent Brahman with attributes."[37] Nikhilananda, comments in a rather nonegalitarian fashion that "the effect of this experience was stronger than that of the vision of Muhammad."[38] Be that as it may, according to Saradananda's account, "Having attained the vision of Jesus thus, the Master became free from the slightest doubt about Christ's having been an incarnation of God."[39]

Such incidents were recounted in court to demonstrate that Ramakrishna did not just advocate the truth of all religions but actually experienced and embodied those truths in his own person and life.[40] Ramkrishnaism, the court

---

[36] *Ibid.*, p. 296. Nikhilananda's version is similiar: "As the two faced each other, a voice rang out in the depths of Sri Ramakrishna's soul: 'Behold the Christ, who shed His heart's blood for the redemption of the world, who suffered a sea of anguish for love of men. It is He, the Master Yogi, who is in eternal union with God. It is Jesus, Love Incarnate.'"

[37] *Ibid.*, p. 296. Cf. Nikhilananda, p. 34: "The Son of Man embraced the Son of the Divine Mother and merged in him. Sri Ramakrishna realized his identity with Christ, as he had already realized his identity with Kali, Rama, Hanuman, Radha, Krishna, Brahman, and Mohammed."

[38] Nikhilananda, *Loc. cit.*, p.34. As critic Ram Swarup caustically observes, "This difference could provide much scope for future disputants. One school may hold that while all prophets are equal, some are more equal than others." Swarup's observation may be even more accurate than he intends. One Ramakrishnaite has recently said that the Koran, though true, must be understood "with the proper interpretation of the Vedas." Furthermore, because of the somewhat lesser status of the Islamic prophet ("Vivekananda said, 'Mohammed was a prophet but he stumbled on the truth. He did not get an experience.'"), "Islam has created a lot of trouble in the whole of the world. And it is not stopping...This fanaticism nobody can tolerate." Swami Bhasyananda, quoted in *Hinduism Today*, *Loc. cit.*, p. 11.

[39] Swami Saradananda, *Loc. cit.*, p. 296.

[40] "The Master" is said "to have been perfected according to all the main religions prevalent in the world." *Ibid.*, p. 296. This tradition of worship of all religions and religious figures supposedly continues in the present. Swami Bhaskarananda of the Seattle Vedanta Society has been quoted as saying, "Nothing has changed....[W]e adore and worship Jesus as a divine incarnation. We adore and worship Buddha also...Yes, traditionally we are Hindus. We could be called Sufis also, because Sri Ramakrishna also practiced Sufism and is called a Sufi saint." Quoted in *Hinduism Today*, *Loc. cit.*, p. 11.

ruled, "now not only consists of opinions and doctrines about the Ultimate Reality but it indicates the outward expressions and acts which are necessary to be performed for achieving their goal. Ramkrishnaism has now become a cult or a religion."[41] Ramakrishna's life, opined a judge who closely followed the case and wrote an editorial about it, "was a confirmation of unity of religions by spiritual experiences. He realised unity by practising different religions. It was left to his disciples to spread his religion universal which they named 'vedanta.'"[42]

The "religion universal" the disciples of Ramakrishna spread was, despite the name given to it, not Hinduism or even Hindu Vedanta. In the course of ruling that Ramakrishnaism was different from Hinduism, the court had to say what counts as "Hindu." Ramakrishnaism is not legally Hinduism for the following reasons.

First, Hinduism is declared to be founded on the Vedas which are believed to be the sum total of "divine revelations and accordingly their authority is beyond all question and above all disputes." "The Hindu religion, as it is now professed, practised and propagated," claimed the Ramakrishnaites, "takes its start from the Vedas which are held to be sacred. According to the Hindus, the Vedas contain the entire mass of spiritual truths whether discovered or not. Whenever any spiritual truth is discovered, it becomes part of the Vedas."[43] Ramakrishnaism, despite the fact that its teachings are called "Vedanta," is not, it was argued, based on the Vedas or Vedanta as Hinduism is:

> This religion is founded neither upon the whole of the Vedas nor even the whole of Vedanta with all their ancient and sacred interpretation but only upon the Vedanta and its principles as propounded by Shri Ramkrishna and practically illustrated by his own life....The mere fact that Thakur Sri Ramakrishna's Neo-Adyaitabad is based on Vedanta does not go to establish that Ramkrishnaism or the cult

---

[41] 1 *Calcutta L. J.* 144 (1986).

[42] R. M. Datta, "Legal Status of Ramakrishna Mission," *Times of India*, 22 December 1986.

[43] Cited in Jagtiani, *Loc. cit.*, p. 76. Apparently, some Ramakrishnaites continue to adhere to much the same notion concerning the authority of the Vedas: "We are staunch Hindus, but we are not fanatic Hindus. We belong to all. And that is what the Vedic dharma is...We want to bring all the communities of the world into the fold of the Vedas. What is wrong then? Then you can say this means we want to make all the people of the world Hindus. Hindu means that individual who accepts the universal laws given by the Vedas. Ultimately people will understand those laws even though everybody is sitting tightly on their own dogma. I say no, there is no dogma in Hinduism." Swami Bhasyananda, quoted in *Hinduism Today*, *Loc. cit.*, p. 11.

of Shri Ramkrishna is a part of Hindu religion and identical with it....[44]

Ramakrishnaism, argued its lawyers, "has its own philosophical basis" which may "flow from the Vedas, yet it is founded neither upon the whole of the Vedas nor even the whole of Vedanta," but only "upon the Vedanta and its principles as propounded by Sri Ramakrishna and practically illustrated by his own life."[45] (Thus, ironically, the Ramakrishnaite understanding of *vedanta* is actually more exclusionary than the Hindu version thereof.) Furthermore, whereas Hindus are supposed to believe in the absolute authority of only the Vedas, Ramakrishnaism affirms the truth of all scriptures:

> A traditional Hindu claims to be a Hindu and Hindu only, and believes in the Vedas only, and not in the scriptures of any other religion; he is at most indifferent to, or even tolerant of, but has no respect for the other scriptures. But a follower of the cult or religion of Shri Ramakrishna, coming originally from the Hindu fold, though a Hindu, claims to be something more at the same time. As a follower of Shri Ramkrishna's Religion Universal, along with the Vedas, he accepts also the Holy Koran, the Holy Bible and all other religious scriptures to be true.[46]

Secondly, Ramakrishnaism is not Hinduism because the latter is distinguished by a particular "moral code" (i.e. *varnāśrama dharma*) and especially by the institution of caste. "The caste system (*varna*)," claimed the Ramakrishnaites, "is a distinctive feature of the Hindu religion and it has been so recognised by the courts in India. The caste system has become an integral feature of Hindu society and is bound up with the practise of Hindu religion."[47] "A man who is a member of a caste is a Hindu," maintained the lawyers, and "he who is not, is not a Hindu"; thus, a "Hindu without a caste is a contradiction in terms."[48] And the court in this case agreed:

> It cannot be denied that whatever may be the philosophy, the doctrine of what we called Hinduism so far as social and usages

---

[44] 2 Calcutta L.J. 337.

[45] *Ibid.*, p. 349.

[46] *Ibid*, p. 337.

[47] Cited in Jagtiani, *Loc. cit.*, p. 76.

[48] Both quotations are cited in Ram Swarup, "Service of God in Man," *Indian Express*, Nov. 16, 1990.

went, [the] caste system became an integral part of Hindu religion....[The] caste system has become an integral feature of Hindu Society and is bound up with the practice of Hindu religion. The well-accepted scriptures of the Hindus contain reference to caste as having even a divine origin.[49]

According to the division bench, however, Ramakrishnaites "do not follow Hindu moral code or accept the caste system....Ramkrishnaism does not prescribe such [a] code of life [as that] laid down by Hindu Religion."[50] In other words, Ramakrishnaism does not require its adherents to abide by the supposedly essential Hindu concept of *varnāśrama dharma* —a Hindu "moral code" tailored to caste and stage of life.

Thirdly, and perhaps most interestingly, Hinduism was distinguished by its exclusivity—one is a Hindu at the exclusion of being something else. Furthermore, and again according to the division bench, non-Hindus could also be Ramakrishnaites, and could do so without undergoing the supposedly typical Hindu rites of purification preliminary to conversion:

> In order to be a follower of Sri Ramkrishna, non-Hindus are not required to embrace Hinduism and to undergo Suddhi or other form of purification. He could continue to profess and practice his own religion and at the same time be a follower of Sri Ramkrishna's faith. Thus there is no necessity of surrendering one's own religion.[51]

Ramakrishnaites "recruit" (but don't "convert") their followers from other religions, which is really the transition from a particular religion to a position beyond sectarian "compartments" altogether:

> The [Ramakrishna] Order is concerned only with "recruitment" of suitable members into its fold and not really with any "conversion." All recruits, no doubt, embrace the religion of Ramakrishna but this is not conversion as it is commonly understood. It is not the movement from one compartment into another but a movement out of all compartmentalism in order to have a comprehensive view of all the compartments together with their foundation.[52]

---

[49] 2 *Calcutta L.J.* 394.

[50] 1 *Calcutta L.J.* 155.

[51] *Ibid.*, p. 151.

[52] From the Written Arguments submitted by the Ramakrishna Mission lawyers, cited in Jagtiani, *Loc. cit.*, p. 74.

By way of contrast, the court declared that the "Hindu religion does never admit any person professing another faith and religion such as Muslim, Christian or Buddhism etc. in it unless such person gives up his religion to embrace Hinduism."[53]

In sum, the Ramakrishnaites successfully argued that they were a religion "separate and different from the religion of the Hindus. Ramakrishnaism has its separate God [i.e. Ramakrishna himself who is an avatar and "treated as the deity and worshipped as such by the members of the Order"[54]], separate name, separate church, separate worship, separate community, separate Organisation and, above all, separate philosophy."[55] Hinduism may be a particularistic religion as opposed to the universalistic Ramakrishnaism, but Hinduism is also according to the Ramakrishnaites (and to Percival Spear, quoted above) a "sponge religion" which "absorbs all shocks." But, to mix the metaphor, its "wide open doors are meant not only for entry but also for exit."[56]

The case of the Ramakrishna Mission provides us with some insights into what the Indian court, at least, regards as distinctively and definitionally Hindu. A Hindu is one who affirms the absolute authority of the Vedas—a definition of Hinduism that I myself, among many others, have put forward in somewhat different terms.[57] A Hindu is also one, according to the court, who subscribes to the "Hindu moral code" of *varnāśrama dharma* and to the caste system that is guided by that "moral code," and this too is a definitional trait

---

[53] 2 *Calcutta L. J.* 348. Other "broad concepts" supposedly distinctive of Hinduism were also cited. See pp. 147-48 of the 1986 decision, where the judge quotes Chief Justice Gajendragadkar in the case of *Yagnapurush Dasji* v. *Muldas,* AIR 1966 S.C. 1119, who "held that beneath the diversity of philsophic thoughts, concepts and ideas expressed by Hindu philosophers, lie certain broad concepts which could be treated as basic. The first among these was the acceptance of the Vedas as the highest authority in religious and philsophical matters. Other basic concepts were acceptance of the view of the great world rhythm, vast periods of creation, maintenance and dissolution follow each other in endless succession. We also add that Varnasharma (caste system) theory of re-birth, etc. are the other salient features of Hinduism. The learned Judge observed that all systems of Hindu philosophy believe in re-birth and pre-existence."

[54] Ram Swarup comments on the basis of this citation from the Written Arguments that "It is obvious that the RKM's problem is not some irresistible call of a new-fangled universalism, but the usual time-honoured malady of sectarianism to which most organisations succumb." "Service of God in Man," *Indian Express,* 16 November 1990.

[55] Cited in Jagtiani, *Loc. cit.,* pp. 78–79.

[56] *Ibid.,* p. 79.

[57] See Brian K. Smith, *Reflections on Resemblance, Ritual, and Religion* (New York, 1989), pp. 13-14: "Hinduism is the religion of those humans who create, perpetuate, and transform traditions with legitimizing reference to the authority of the Veda."

noted by scholars as well as the court.[58] The fact that academic definitions and legal ones here overlap is not coincidental. The judges ruling in this case quoted liberally from scholarly works to back up their opinions, as did the lawyers in their petitions—a sobering and perhaps disturbing thought for Indologists accustomed to assuming that learned treatises are read only by academic colleagues and overheard only by fellow conventioneers.

The Indian court also noted in this case what many of us too often forget or do not care, for one reason or another, to acknowledge: Hinduism is one religion among many, and not all religions rolled together. Unfortunately, by isolating "universalism" and the belief and practice in the "truth of all religions" as characteristic of the new religion of Ramakrishnaism, the court has ignored the conundrums which have always been attendent upon such conceptions.

Do the Ramakrishnaites, or anyone else for that matter, really believe that *all* religions and *all* scriptures are "true?" What would such a thing mean? Are there absolutely no boundaries, nothing that would not count? Are there no recognized contradictions in "universal truth" as one moves from the doctrines of one faith to those of another? Are all "religious" teachers—Mohammad, Jesus, Krishna and the Buddha; but also Rajneesh and Jim Jones, let alone less "tolerant" figures such as the Ayatollah Khomeini and Muammar Kaddafi—to be embraced as "equally valid"?

By ruling that Ramakrishnaism is a "universal religion," the court simply displaced the claims sometimes made for Hinduism as a whole onto what was once, up until 1983, considered one of its parts. While criteria were put forward for what counts as "Hinduism" (primarily the authority of the Veda and the institution of caste), it is not clear what criteria there could be for delimiting Ramakrishnaism. Such all-inclusive "we are the worldism" will ultimately be as problematic a claim to sustain for the Ramakrishnaites as it has been for scholars of Hinduism, certain Hindus, World Council of Churches liberals, dialogers, and rock stars.

---

[58] For references, see *Ibid.*, pp. 10–12.

20

Recognition and Legislation of Private Religious Endowments in Indian Law

Michael C. Baltutis

Introduction

  The practice of endowing religious institutions—temples as places for worship and maths as places for religious instruction—dates back to the origin of the institutions themselves. References to temples exist in documents dating from approximately 500 B.C.E.;[1] temples containing images of the deities (these images referred to hereafter in this paper, as in other academic literature, as "idols") became prevalent in the centuries following the commencement of the common era;[2] and Sankara is said to have established the first four *maths* in the 8th century C.E.[3] A tradition of gift-giving (*dana*) in India as a means of distributing wealth and attaining fame and prestige extends back through the Vedic period and is imbued with a legal format before the turn of the Common Era.[4] By this time, *dana* is being applied in the form of land grants to *brahmanas*,[5] large gifts of cash to religious beneficiaries, and the building of alms-houses for distribution of food and clothing to the city's needy.[6] Nath says of *dana*:

---

[1] B.K. Mukherjea, *The Hindu Law of Religious and Charitable Trust* (Calcutta, 1983), p. 16.
[2] *Ibid.*, p. 25.
[3] *Ibid.*, pp. 22-23.
[4] Vijay Nath, *Dana: Gift System in Ancient India* (New Delhi, 1987), p. 14.
[5] *Ibid.*, p. 19.
[6] *Ibid.*, p. 58.

"Its unilateral and predominantly religious aspect clearly distinguished it from spontaneous or ceremonial gifts (*priti dana*) exchanged by friends and relatives."[7] These religious gifts of money or land, called "endowments", are given to existing religious institutions or are used to found new institutions for any number of purposes: Furthering the goals of the institution, undergoing personal penance, giving for purely altruistic purposes, and establishing and improving one's reputation.

From very early on, local governments began to take notice of and oversee the endowments received by its institutions. Reddy discusses the existence of a separate Religious Endowment Department in 15th century Andhra Desa, which supervised the functioning of religious institutions and maintained copies of the original grants; similar arrangements were also made in other Hindu kingdoms.[8] These examples lend credence to the position of Indian legal scholar J. Duncan M. Derrett, who maintains that the modern government of India, the setting of this paper, in regulating the existence and implementation of religious endowments, is acting in consonance with its own traditions and not "in conscious or unconscious imitation of the West."[9] These regulations have been implemented through individual states' religious and charitable endowment acts, income tax laws (the most recent Act passed in 1961), and the courts, and have been analyzed and reinforced by the Hindu Religious Endowment Commission's Report of 1962. Through these first three mechanisms, the government has been able to define, categorize and regulate endowments, Hindu and otherwise. "Religious" and "charitable", "temple" and "*math*", "absolute" and "partial", and "public" and "private" have all proved effectively manageable categories for state and national governments. Through this process of definition and categorization, governments have mandated that endowments meet certain requirements in order to retain their valid status. Part I of this paper will deal with the validity of endowments, their publicity and privacy, and historical benefits; Part II will offer a brief history of the regulation of religious endowments from 1810 and will discuss the manner in which these benefits have been removed. State legislation since 1927 has explicitly defined

---

[7] *Ibid.*, p. 13.

[8] Soma Reddy, *Hindu and Muslim Religious Institutions: Andhra Desa, 1300-1600*, (Madras, 1984), p. 124.

[9] J.D.M. Derrett, *Religion, Law and the State in India* (New York, 1968), p. 482.

endowments so as to exclude private religious endowments, assuming regulatory duties for public endowments while allowing private endowments nearly absolute autonomy; numerous High and Supreme Court cases have strained to define the boundary between public and private endowments, ensuring the constitutionality of endowment acts and the proper administration of the endowments themselves, while presenting decisions allowing for the existence of private endowments; income tax codes have addressed the tax-exempt status of each, excluding private endowments from the benefits accrued by their public counterparts; and the Report of the Hindu Religious Endowment Commission of 1962 has put forth recommendations whose goals mirror those of the states' legislation.

One of the main reasons for this difference between the courts, state endowment acts, and income tax law stems from the actual operation of each. The courts hear cases on a regular basis and are exposed to the wide variety of existing endowments. They allow oral and documentary evidence to establish the "custom and usage" of an endowment, of the region, or of the religion or sect; the relevant "customs and usages", as opposed to a universal endowment law, assist the courts in making their decisions. Endowment acts and income tax laws, on the other hand, do not look at every case; their goal is to establish general policies pertaining to each and every religious endowment, thereby simplifying their regulatory duties. (Interestingly, the Commission also looked at individual cases, yet sided with the state acts and income tax law.) Franklin Presler, in his book *Religion Under Bureaucracy*, notices this difference and proceeds a step further:

> The court's orientation is basically conservative: to preserve the past and to administer as much as possible by reference to the specific customs of each temple.... The HRCE [Hindu Religious and Charitable Endowment Department], for its part, does not believe that long and complicated hearings on the specific nature of each temple are necessary; the important things are already known. Temples are "public" and "religious" and their problems stem primarily from "politics" and mismanagement. To address these problems in the most efficient way possible does not necessarily or even usually mean following local practices or "custom and usage." It means the hard-headed and consistent application of general rules and regulations, for

which, if anything, detailed and intimate knowledge of a temple's local circumstance is often a hindrance.[10]

Presler tends to romanticize the traditional "organic link between public authority and temples"; he sees the HRCE as "a bureaucratic organization designed specifically to eliminate all signs of personal, patrimonial-like interests on the part of those with authority in temples, whether they be trustees, EOs [Executive Officers], or commissioners";[11] he does not, however, credit the HRCE for ensuring that the endowments are being managed according to the grantor's intention; nor does he draw an analogy between the HRCE and similar departments in India's past. One with such a view of temple management will tend to also favor the view of the courts, which readily allow for the existence of privately-managed temples.

PART I: ENDOWMENTS

Religious Endowments

A valid charitable or religious endowment must possess certain characteristics. The donor must first ensure that the endowment is for a truly charitable or religious purpose. Examples of charitable purposes have been listed in various acts and court cases and include: Health, education, relief of the poor, and preservation of sciences and literature. Examples of religious purposes are rarely if ever provided for in the Acts; such examples can, however, be drawn from actual practice: The establishment of an idol, the maintenance of an idol, the building of a temple or *math*, performances of *shraddha* and endowments for periodic *pujas*. While charitable purposes are defined by the benefits bestowed upon the public, religious purposes have no such necessary "public" corollary. A privately endowed family idol, then, constitutes a valid religious endowment just as much as a *math* established for the religious education of the general public.

Valid endowments have certain other legal requirements. The donor must be legally competent to create such a trust; at the very least, this means

---

[10] Presler, *Loc. cit.*, p. 61.

[11] *Ibid.*, p. 164.

that the donor must be of legal age and of sound mind. No ceremony is necessary to create the endowment itself as it was centuries ago. Formerly, two formalities signaled the transfer of endowed property: Through *sankalpa*, one indicated the purpose and direction of the property, and through *utsarga*, one renounced all ownership of the property. While these ceremonies are presently unnecessary, the donor must still uphold the spirit of them by showing that he has explicitly and completely divested himself of the ownership of the endowed property and all its directly resulting financial benefits; through this renunciation, often in a will, the donor avoids any confusion over the reality of the endowment and any possible accusation that the property was merely being tied up to avoid financial liability.[12] A written document detailing the origin and nature of the endowment is also unnecessary. Mukherjea gives the donor's "intention" as the real test for an endowment's validity; this intention must be shown through the donor's (and trustees', upon the death of the donor) application of profits from the endowment to the religious purpose under which the endowment was created. (In *Shri Ram Kishan Mission* v. *Dogar Singh*, The Allahabad High Court quotes Mukherjea on this point: "The real test is furnished by the intention of the grantor.")[13] An endowment will be judged invalid if shown that, even though dedication was made to an idol, the intention of the donor was to tie up the dedicated money in the family.[14] Most states also require that the trust or endowment be registered; such a register would contain information regarding such details as: The endowment's origin, denomination, paid employees, wealth, idol(s), legends, and a list of its regular services and festivals.[15] The final necessity for the creation of a valid endowment is a concrete object of endowment. Endowments which have been created for unspecified purposes, for idols of unspecified deity, for "*dharma*", or without the provision of a specific amount of money have all been judged invalid. The individual who would have inherited the property, had it not been endowed, may appeal the validity of an endowment for any of these reasons; if the appeal is upheld,

---

[12] Paras Diwan, *Law of Endowments, Wakfs and Trusts* (Allahabad, 1992), p. 47.
[13] AIR 1984 All 72 at 75.
[14] Mukherjea, *Loc. cit.*, pp. 107-108.
[15] V.K. Varadachari, *Law of Hindu Religious and Charitable Endowments* (Lalbagh, 1985), p. 572.

the now-invalidly endowed money or property will devolve according to laws of succession like any other property.

Different court cases, state acts, and income tax laws may have as their object either "endowments", "temples", or "trusts." While these terms cannot be used absolutely interchangeably, they are all related. Section 2(13) of the Bombay Public Trusts Act of 1950 relates all three of these terms in its definition of public trust:

> "[P]ublic trust" means an express or constructive trust for either a public religious or charitable purpose or both and includes a temple, a math, a wakf, [church, synagogue, agiary or other place of public religious worship,] [a dharmada] or any other religious or charitable endowment and a society formed either for a religious or charitable purpose or for both and registered under the Societies Registration Act, 1860 [XXI of 1860].[16]

Religious endowments, then, are instances of trusts, which can be applied for the creation of a temple. A definition of "religious endowments" is given by the Orissa Hindu Religious Endowments Act of 1951:

> "[R]eligious endowment" or "endowment" means all property belonging to or given or endowed for the support of maths or temples or given or endowed for the performance of any service or charity connected therewith or of any other religious charity, and includes the institution concerned and the premises thereof and also all properties used for the purpose or benefit of the institution and includes all properties acquired from the income of the endowed property.[17]

Each state's act begins with a set of definitions that includes the term relevant to the act: "trust", "religious trust", or "endowment"; these terms denote the property initially given for a religious purpose—the corpus—and all properties (and income) derived from it.

---

[16] *Ibid.*, p. 649.
[17] *Ibid.*, p. 835.

Recognition and Legislation of Private Religious Endowments

Public and Private Religious Endowments

There are two fundamentally structural differences between public and private endowments: owner and beneficiaries. In a public temple, the installed idol itself is held to be the temple's legal owner, and the beneficiaries—those to whom the endowment is dedicated—are the general public. In a private temple, the owner is the individual who endowed the idol, and the beneficiaries are the family members.

The definition of "public endowment" used by the courts and in the Income Tax Act of 1961 is taken from the definition for "endowment" used in the states' trust and endowment acts; similarly, the definition used for "public temple" in the Supreme Court comes from the definition for "temple" given in the endowment acts; private trusts, however, are defined in neither the Income Tax Act or the endowment acts. The Income Tax Act says only of private endowments that they do "not enure for the benefit of the public."[18] Section 2 of the Orissa Act reads: "It (this Act) extends to the whole of the State of Orissa and applies to all Hindu public religious institutions and endowments."[19] The Bihar Hindu Religious Trusts Act of 1950, however, makes its sole application to public trusts very explicit:

> "[R]eligious trust" means any express or constructive trust created or existing for any purpose recognised by Hindu Law to be religious, pious or charitable but shall not include ... a private endowment created for the worship of a family idol in which the public are not interested.[20]

The Bihar Trust Act is the only state act which mentions private endowments by name; in fact, it is the only act which uses the word "private." This Act clearly states that the numerous private endowments in Bihar—including family idols, the buildings in which they reside, and the income earned from them—do not fall within its jurisdiction. The Bihar Act's description of a private endowment—"created for the worship of a family idol"—seems to be quite

---

[18] *Income Tax Act 1961*, p. 103.
[19] Varadachari, *Loc. cit.*, p. 833.
[20] *Ibid.*, p. 614.

clear until we look at the last part of the definition—"in which the public are not interested." The Act elaborates further by including a definition of "person interested in a religious trust":

> any person who is entitled to receive any pecuniary or other benefit from a religious trust and includes—
> (i) any person who has a right to worship or to perform any rite, or to attend at the performance of any worship or rite, in any religious institution connected with such trust or to participate in any religious or charitable administration under such trust....[21]

The Bombay Public Trusts Act of 1950 defines the "person having interest" more loosely:

> (a) in the case of a temple, person who is entitled to attend at or is *in the habit of attending* the performance of worship or service in the temple, or who is entitled to partake or is *in that habit of partaking* in the distribution of gifts thereof,
> (b) in the case of a math, a disciple of the math or a person of the religious persuasion to which the math belongs ... (emphasis added). [22]

A person, then, could be said to be *interested* in a temple, according to Bombay's Act, who regularly attends a particular temple; Bihar's Act mandates that this person possess a *right* to attend. Through the interest of the devotee, as a member of the public and not of the family that established the idol, the temple could lose its "private" designation and become a public temple, thus falling within the jurisdiction of the state.

The Supreme Court has shied away from offering a strict distinction between public and private endowments. The court stated in *Radhakanta Deb v. Commr., Hindu Religions Endowments, Orissa*: "The question as to whether the religious endowment is of a private nature or of a public nature has to be decided with reference to the facts proved in each case and it is difficult to lay

---

[21] *Ibid.*, p. 614.
[22] *Ibid.*, pp. 648-649.

down any test or tests which may be of universal application."[23] The court has applied some tests inconsistently and sporadically: Size of temple, manner of worship, and structure and location of temple. In *Profulla Chorone* v. *Satya Choron*, it offered a general guideline affirming that a private temple is dedicated to the worship of an idol, while a public temple is dedicated for the use of the public.[24] In *G.S. Mahalaxmi* v. *Shah Ranchhoddas*,[25] the Supreme Court provided several tests specifically for public temples: "Public temples are generally built or raised by the public and the deity installed to enable the members of the public or a section thereof to offer worship";[26] also, "The devotees as well as the Maharaj were treating that temple as a public temple."[27] A private temple would be one that is not raised by the public, not open to worship by at least a section of the public, and not treated as a public temple. According to the last test, the court sees the general public as having a role in determining the publicity or privacy of a temple not only through the temple being dedicated for them but also through the court's perception that they acted as though it was dedicated for them. This latter test, while difficult to discern its evidence, would help to establish the temple's "custom and usage."

Other factors have been consistently applied by the court in a majority of cases. In *Deoki* v. *Murlidhar*, the Supreme Court established a key distinction between public and private trusts. Private trusts are those in which the beneficiaries are comprised of an ascertainable group of specific individuals; in public trusts, the beneficiaries are the "general public or a class thereof."[28] This decision appears to agree with the Bihar Act's distinction based on *interest*. This ascertainable group of individuals, usually the members of the immediate family, need not be the only people who benefit from the endowment, however. In *Bihar State Board of Religious Trust* v. *Biseshwar Das*[29] the Supreme Court appears to undermine the rigidity of the states' laws—and

---

[23] AIR 1981 SC 798 at 800.
[24] AIR 1979 SC 1682 at 1687.
[25] AIR 1970 SC 2025 at 2031.
[26] *Ibid.*, p. 2031
[27] *Ibid.*, p. 2035.
[28] AIR 1957 SC 133 (cf. Diwan, *Law of Endowments* ..., p. 53).
[29] AIR 1971 SC 2057.

perhaps even the *Deoki* decision—explaining that the general public *can* attend private temples when participating in festivals and receiving *darshan*, and it can present offerings; the general public cannot, however, use the temple "as of right."[30] The public may have some interest in a private temple. *Biseshwar* maintains that a truly private temple will have the right at any time to refuse entry to any member of the general public, and the temple will be judged to be public only when it has been shown that the *shebaits* have not refused entry to or offerings from the general public. Through these decisions, the courts have shown that even the most crucial test for determining the nature of an endowment—the public's use—cannot be applied universally. The Court has thus drawn a fine line between the public's worship in private temples and the public's right to worship in public temples.

Historical Benefits of Religious Endowments

As noted in the introduction, there are many possible reasons for one to create an endowment: Furthering the goals of the institution, continuing the worship of the family idol, giving for purely altruistic purposes, or improving one's reputation. Others have been encouraged to create an endowment for more practical purposes. There have been three major financial benefits associated with religious endowments: Exemptions from the payment of income taxes, exemptions from laws against wealth accumulation and trust perpetuity, and the rights of property. After a brief history of endowment regulation later in this paper, we will examine how the first and second of these benefits have been eroded through income tax laws and how the third has been challenged by the Endowment Commission.

(1) *Income tax exemption.* The issue of income-tax exemption can be stated simply and quickly: The income derived from a religious or charitable endowment established for public purposes is not to be included in the total income of the tax year and is, thus, tax-exempt.[31] Income resulting from a private religious endowment is not given a similar, or any other, income-tax exemption.

(2) *Perpetuities and accumulation.* The laws against perpetuities and accumulation stem from their English counterparts, which prevented individu-

---

[30] *Ibid.*, pp. 2061-2062.
[31] *Income Tax Act 1961*, p. 99.

als from tying up personal wealth in order to avoid paying income taxes and other creditors. Sections 14 and 17 of the Transfer of Property Act of 1882 deal with perpetuities and accumulation, respectively. Section 14 states:

> No transfer of property can operate to create an interest which is to take effect after the lifetime of one or more persons living at the date of such transfer, and the minority of some person who shall be in existence at the expiration of that period, and to whom, if he attains full age, the interest created is to belong.[32]

A perpetuity, then, involves a transfer of property—not by traditional means of inheritance—that extends beyond the lives of the primary beneficiaries to their offspring. For such a trust to remain valid, the offspring of the primary beneficiaries, after the death of the latter, must attain "full age"—the age specified in the will (e.g. "property to be given when first child turns 25")—within eighteen years of the deaths of all primary beneficiaries. In other words, a trust, once enacted, may not sit idle for more than eighteen years following the deaths of the primary beneficiaries and before the second generation of beneficiary comes of age.

An accumulation takes place when a grantor does not immediately will money or property but delays the transfer until a certain future time; the law allows for two lengths of accumulation: The lifetime of the transferor and eighteen years from the date of the transfer, whichever is longer. Any stated period beyond these will cause the transfer to be automatically void. In cases which violate either rule against perpetuity or accumulation, the property will, after the given time, devolve upon the testator's heirs according to regular rules of inheritance. Mitra explains the object of Section 17, the second half of which has also been used to explain the English rule against perpetuities:

> The object of this section is to fix a time-limit for accumulation and thus to prevent the hardship which would have been caused to heirs and descendants if unlimited accumulations were allowed, and also to prevent the property being for ever locked up, which would be a menace to the trade of the country.[33]

---

[32] B.B. Mitra, *Transfer of Property Act, 1882* (Calcutta, 1996), p. 147.
[33] *Ibid.*, p. 163.

For the financial well-being of the grantor's family (accumulations) and country (accumulations and perpetuities), these withholdings of money and property are not permitted.

The relevance of these provisions for religious endowments follows immediately in Section 18, which reads:

> The restrictions in sections 14, 16, and 17 shall not apply in the case of a transfer of property for the benefit of the public in the advancement of religion, knowledge, commerce, health, safety, or any other object beneficial to mankind.[34]

Religious endowments are permitted to circumvent the laws to which non-publically beneficial trusts must adhere. If not already obvious, these rules also do not apply to private religious endowments. Trusts for public religious endowments are allowed to accumulate for, in theory, an unlimited amount of time before being applied and, once created, are allowed to provide benefits to countless generations of the public. This latter point is not only legally valid but has a sort of ontological value as well. One of the very few necessities in establishing a religious endowment is the endower's renunciation of the property—in either ceremony, writing, or intention. This renunciation follows a dedication to the new owner; in a temple, the owner is the installed idol, in a *math*, the purpose for which the property is dedicated.[35] These respective entities are considered property of the endowment vests; "they" own the property, not the *mahant* (head of the *math*), nor the *shebait*, nor the endower's heirs. As the endowment, in the form of the temple or *math*, is dedicated immediately, and the juristic person is one who cannot die (nor have offspring), the rule against perpetuities cannot be effected.[36]

---

[34] *Ibid.*, pp. 167-168.

[35] Mukherjea, *Loc. cit.*, p. 339.

[36] Derrett includes the exemption from an estate duty upon transfer of property as an additional benefit, due to the immortality of the deity (*Religion, Law* ..., p. 491). The Wealth-Tax Act, 1957, originally exempted both public and private religious trusts from this annual tax, but a later amendment denied this exemption to endowments that forfeit income-tax exemption according to the Income Tax Act, 1961 (Diwan, *Tax Planning* ..., p. 402).

(3) *Property rights.* The landmark *Shirur Math* [37] case established the foundation for property ownership within religious endowments. It established that the *mahant* (like the *shebait* of the temple) is more than just a servant of the *math* but is something less than the property owner. Both *mahants* and *shebaits* have rights over the disposition of the institution's property and are to be compensated for their services; they may receive personal donations but are not legally entitled to offerings made to the temple itself. Similar to the *Shirur Math* ruling, the Supreme Court noted in *Profullo Chorone* v. *Satya Chorone*, that while the property does not vest in the *shebait*, this manager still "has a right to a part of the usufruct".[38]

There is essentially no legal difference in the property rights of public and private endowments. In both cases, ownership of the endowed property resides in the idol (or purpose), and the profits of each must be put back into the institution, according to the original endowment. The identities of the beneficiaries and the direction of the dedication provide the only differences. Derrett notices the practical differences, lauding the usage of the private family idol for personal financial gain:

> If one thing is certain it is that making a personal profit out of possessing an idol is as old as the Vedic age, and perfectly legitimate. A man should be able to make a living out of possessing ancestral charms and potions; why not out of an idol which could perform miracles?[39]

While the owners of both public and private temples have renounced ownership in their endowments, the status of private temples seem advantageous. That, at least, seems to be the case when observing that temples that have been operating "for the benefit of the public" while treating the profits as private gifts will, when challenged in the courts, claim a private status. If judged to be a private temple, it will continue to operate without regulation, checked only by

---

[37] SCJ 1954 335.

[38] AIR 1979 SC 1682 at 1686.

[39] J.D.M. Derrett, "The Reform of Hindu Religious Endowments," in *South Asian Politics and Religion*, ed. Donald E. Smith (Princeton, 1966), pp. 311-336, pp. 319-320.

the retrospective lawsuits of family members; if judged to be public, however, accusations of "mismanagement of funds" will hold, and laws that have been enacted to regulate endowments will be enforced.

PART II: ENDOWMENT REGULATION

Central Endowment Regulations (1810-1920)

Reaping lucrative financial benefits through the mismanagement of an endowment's funds has occurred since the origin of endowments themselves (see Introduction above). Appendix XIII of the Report of the Hindu Religious Endowment Commission (HREC) 1960-62 recites a list of complaints brought before the Commission regarding mismanagement:

> The Executive Officer does not maintain accounts. Funds are being misappropriated and temple articles are being pilfered and sold.
>
> The head of one of the temples at Beyt Dwarka, is alleged to have lost Rs. 11,000/- of the trust in speculation.
>
> The members of the Board are alleged to be drawing travelling allowances out of all proportion to the salaries they earn. The Chairman of the Devasthanam is alleged to be drawing fifteen to twenty thousand rupees per year as travelling and other allowances.[40]

It is against these types of complaint that even ancient kings would intervene. The history of modern endowment regulation begins with the passage of Regulation XIX of 1810 of Bengal, in which the British assumed supervision over charitable and religious trusts. Following Bengal's regulation, Madras passed Regulation VII of 1817, and Bombay passed Regulation XVII of 1827, all three for the explicit purpose of regulating endowments. The preamble to Regulation XIX states the reason for its implementation:

---

[40] *Report 1962*, pp. 382-384.

Whereas considerable endowments have been granted in land by the preceding Governments of this country [Regulation XVII adds: "as well as by the British government"], and by individuals, for the support of mosques, Hindu temples, colleges and other pious and beneficial purposes, and whereas there are grounds to suppose that the produce of such land is used in many instances contrary to the intentions of the donors ... and whereas it is an important duty of every government to provide that all such endowments be applied to the real intent and will of the grantor ... the following rules have been framed.[41]

Under these regulations, the states' Boards of Revenue (BOR) acquired ultimate responsibility for the regulation of endowments. In addition to providing for the proper application of endowments according to the will of the grantor, the BOR had also to provide for repairs and maintenance of buildings, appoint trustees for non-hereditary temples, supervise trustees of hereditary temples, and ensure that the endowments were not used for any private purpose. Subordinate to the BOR were district-level Local Agents who supplied the Board with information on the temples (e.g. names and numbers of endowments, names of trustees, method of trustee election for each temple). The appointed trustees themselves comprised the third level of the regulatory hierarchy, who directly managed the religious institutions, collecting and appropriating land and cash revenue.[42] These services were financially supported by a fee taken out of temple funds–kept in the government's treasuries.[43] Singh gives the sole purpose of these regulations as ensuring the proper administration of endowments and not for the possibility of governmental resumption of any part of the misappropriated endowed property,[44] but Presler states that a power of the BOR's Collector was to resume misused or uncared for land, resulting in a new source of governmental income. Presler quotes the BOR Procedures from 1838: "From these causes [of mismanagement] it has been found absolutely necessary to

---

[41] Kashmir Singh, *Law of Religious Institutions—Sikh Gurdwaras* (Amritsar, 1989), pp. 64-65.
[42] *Ibid.*, p. 41.
[43] Presler, *Loc. cit.*, p. 17.
[44] Singh, *Loc. cit.*, p. 42.

interfere summarily and eject the managers ... and to entrust the Native Revenue Officers with the direct administration of the lands."[45]

The British continued their regulation of religious endowments until the 1830s, when religious groups in England began to protest their government's involvement in non-Christian institutions. This involvement included not only the auditing of financial documents and upkeep of the buildings themselves, but also payments to temples whose endowments had lapsed.[46] In 1843, the British government began its withdrawal from endowment regulation; all management was given over to local *rajas*, *panchayats*, newly-formed committees, or existing temple priests and trustees.[47] This withdrawal produced a vacuum of authority in endowment regulation, producing mismanagement on a scale rivaling, and possibly surpassing, that of any prior period. The British severed all ties between the BOR and endowment regulation in the Religious Endowment Act of 1863 (Act XX), which provided for the appointment of Local Committees to replace the BOR. These Committees exercised supervision only over those temples whose trustees were appointed; temples whose trustees were hereditary were left wholly unmanaged until 1920. This policy has been described as "a horrid failure ... that has been responsible for causing the ruin of several important Hindu religious endowments and irreparable damage to many others."[48] The Charitable and Religious Trusts Act of 1920 (Act XIV)—passed almost 60 years later—allowed an interested party to apply to a court "for the obtaining of information regarding trusts created for public purposes of a charitable or religious nature."[49] This "information" specifically includes the financial dealings of a trust. And like all the preceding acts—Regulation XIX of 1810, VII of 1817, XVII of 1827, and XX of 1863—Act XIV of 1920 operates only for *public* charitable and religious trusts; private religious endowments were still wholly unregulated.[50] Act XIV operated within the existing frame-

---

[45] Presler, *Loc. cit.*, p. 18.

[46] *Ibid.*, p. 18.

[47] *Ibid.*, p. 20.

[48] *Report 1931*, p. 25.

[49] Varadachari, *Loc. cit.*, p. 541.

[50] To add to the list of regulatory acts which do *not* apply to private religious endowments and trusts, we can add the Indian Trusts Act of 1882. Its Preamble mentions the expediency "to define and amend the law relating to private trusts and trustees." We need go no further than Section 1 to notice that "nothing herein contained ... applies to public or private religious or charitable endowments...." (Mukherjea, pp. 1, 5).

work of Article 92 of the Civil Procedure Code of 1908, the combination of which allowed "interested parties" to hold trustees responsible for alleged mismanagement by forcing them to open their books and file suit in cases of mismanagement; beginning with Madras in 1925, state governments, under continued local pressure, began to eschew the four pages of Act XIV creating more proactive and cost-effective legislation, allowing the states themselves to hold public endowments responsible for their financial dealings, instead of forcing devotees to bring their own suits against wealthy temples.

State Trust and Endowment Acts (1927 - present)

The HRE Act (Madras Act II of 1927) marked the government's first attempt to proactively address the issue of temple mis-administration. The Act's proactivity was effected by a shift from a court-based system to an executive-based system, signaling a departure from the long-standing British policy of non-interference.[51] Most states have also created their own public trust and endowment acts since the adoption of the Constitution. The Acts, whose purposes are similar—"An Act to provide for the better Administration and Governance of Hindu Religious Institutions and Endowments in the State of Orissa", for example [52]—fall within the limits of regulation prescribed by the Indian Constitution. Article 25(2)(a) allows the State to regulate or restrict "any economic, financial, political or other secular activity which may be associated with religious practice",[53] while leaving all religious activities to the administration of the temples themselves. The "secular" duties assumed include: Preparing codes of conduct for endowment staff, appointing a Board of Trustees, inspecting ledgers, removing the head of the institution for various reasons, and assessing fees (called "contributions").[54]

While these acts do not pertain to private endowments at all, they are still relevant here, as a private endowment later judged to be public will be subject to the Act of its respective state. In the same way that governmentally-appointed trustees claimed hereditary status following the passage of Act XX

---

[51] Presler, *Loc. cit.*, p. 28.

[52] Varadachari, *Loc. cit.*, p. 832.

[53] V. N. Shukla, *Constitution of India* (Lalbagh, 1982), p. 143.

[54] The Andhra Pradesh Charitable and Hindu Religious Institutions and Endowments Act, 1966.

of 1863 to avoid further regulation, endowment managers have claimed a private status for their endowments to prevent the loss of these traditional freedoms. I will deal with specific related court cases in a later section.

Income Tax Regulation

Earlier, I listed three financial benefits associated with religious endowments: Exemption from income tax, exemption from laws against perpetuity and accumulation, and property rights. These first two benefits have been eroded by the Income Tax Act of 1961 (referred to as "the Act"), and suggestions have been offered by the Hindu Religious Endowment Commission against the third.

A public religious endowment receives income from several sources, its two primary ones being rental property and donations. These two sources are taxed differently. Section 11 of the Act addresses income from property, breaking it down into two more categories: applied and accumulated. Applied funds are those spent during the tax-year; these are tax-exempt. Of those funds accumulated, or unspent, only the first 25 per cent is exempt. The endowment can delay taxation on the remaining 75 per cent for up to ten years, if it discloses the intention behind its accumulation to the Income-Tax Officer and invests the accumulated funds in certain approved investments.[55] Section 12 addresses income derived from contributions, dividing them into two different categories as well. Sub-section 1 allows voluntary contributions from the general public applied solely to religious purposes to be excluded for the income for that year; an amendment was passed in 1973, however, making these voluntary contributions taxable as of April 1, 1973.[56] Under sub-section 2, contributions made by another "trust or charitable or religious institution to which the provisions of section 11 apply." will be treated as income for that year and will not be tax-exempt.

Section 13(a) follows all of the other regulations, laws, acts, and bills we have seen.

---

[55] *Income Tax Act 1961*, pp. 99-100. These approved investments include: government savings certificates; immovable property; Post Office; Savings Bank; the Unit Trust of India; any government company; National or State Bank; Scheduled Bank, Cooperative Bank, or government financial institutions, Industrial Development Bank of India (Devadason 4).

[56] E.D. Devadason, *Taxation of Charitable and Religious Trusts & Institutions Under Direct Taxation Laws* (Madras, 1986), pp. 31-32.

> Nothing contained in section 11 shall operate so as to exclude from the total income of the previous year of the person in receipt thereof—
> (a) any part of the income from the property held under a trust for private religious purposes which does not enure for the benefit of the public.[57]

This non-exemption of income tax for private trusts was not new. It had existed in the previous Act of 1922, its logic explained by the Supreme Court in *Jogendra Nath* v. *Income-tax Commissioner*: As the idol being a juristic person can hold property, file a suit to defend such property, and receive rent from its property, it can also, through its *shebaits*, be taxed for its property.[58] Section 13(b)(1) and (2) of the Act, the last sub-section of which is new, does not exempt trusts created for a particular religious communities, for castes, or for one whose income "enures directly or indirectly for the benefit" of the trust's founder or relatives.[59] While the Income Tax Act of 1961 does not affect the religious endowment's exemption from the law against perpetuity, it does restrict and complicate the endowments' former exemptions from income tax and the law against accumulation. Derrett, speaking of the restrictions in Section 13(b), could just as well be speaking of all of those in Sections 11 through 13(a): "This does not, of course, in any way hinder the dedication of property to a deity, but it does tend to remove one of the main incentives for such dedications." He does not see India as a state that will "subsidize sectarian foundations nor shelter sources of income which masquerade as endowments, i.e. establishments for idols."[60]

---

[57] *Income Tax Act 1961*, p. 103.
[58] AIR 1969 SC 1089 at 1093.
[59] *Income Tax Act 1961*, p. 104.
[60] Derrett, *Religion, Law*..., p. 486. The Estate Duty Act, 1953, denies another benefit to private endowments. This one-time tax charged to beneficiaries upon the death of the property owner is exempted for public endowments, whose "owner" is the religious purpose—a non-taxable "individual"—to which it is dedicated, but refuses the exemption for private temples whose "real owners are the beneficiaries" (*Tax Planning* ..., p. 415).

The Courts and the Hindu Religious Endowment Commission

The third benefit associated with religious endowments is the right of owning property.[61] This right has not been removed and has even been reasserted by the Supreme Court as recently as 1979, but the HREC, after visiting 232 temples in north and south India between 1960 and 1962, saw claims to ownership as a recurring example of mismanagement, which needed to be addressed. Personal ownership cannot occur in the case of *mahants*, as the Commission suggests that all *maths* be considered public religious endowments; at its fourth of 114 suggestions, it offers that *shebaits* "not be allowed to claim any personal or proprietary interest in the management of the institution" or in the offerings and donations made to the temple. Members of the Commission themselves even had a "divergence of opinion" amongst them regarding the rights of the *shebait* to donations expressly intended for them; the Commission decided that they could keep these donations, as long as there was no confusion over the object of the donation; the donation was marked in a separate ledger; and the donation, upon the death of the receiver, would revert back to the institution.[62] The consolidation of funds in an institution seems less threatening to the Commission than that in the individuals managing the institution.

The Report of the HREC is the only primary government document among those examined in this paper that deals with private religious endowments.[63] The state endowment acts and income-tax act mentioned them only so far as to assert that they would not deal with them. Only in court cases and the Report have government officials detailed personal contact with private religious endowments—their "custom and usage"—on any regular basis. The similarities of these documents, however, end there.

In the past 30 years, the Supreme Court has heard approximately twenty cases involving disputes over the publicity/privacy of a religious institution. In

---

[61] In "A Note on the Report of the Hindu Religious Endowments Commission," in *AIR Journal*, v. 51 (Oct. 1964), pp. 98-99, Sumantrao C. Bhat refers to the "evil" of property rights as a "specific problem" of Hindu Endowments, as opposed to the "general problems" that afflict endowments of all religious communities.

[62] *Report 1962*, p. 37.

[63] The Bihar Hindu Religious Trusts Act, 1950, uses the phrase "private endowment" but, as mentioned earlier, does not consider it to be a "religious trust" according to its definition.

six of these cases, the court has ruled that the institutions—five temples and one *math*—were private, in each case overturning the prior judgement of the respective High Court. I will briefly outline three of these cases here.

Radhakanta Deb v. *Commr., Hindu Religious Endowments, Orissa* (1981), involves an appeal to the Supreme Court by the trustees of a temple against the Commissioner of Hindu Religious Endowments of Orissa.[64] Two documents were brought in as exhibits in this case to prove the privacy of the temple. The first is an "ancient" document from 1895, which did not itself create the endowment but was execute shortly thereafter. The second is a settlement deed for the family's property from 1932. The Court understood both of these documents, which include phrases such as, "for the good of our family", "the family deity", "as a mark of pride of our family", together and as clearly stating private dedication, ownership and administration by the family. While the public regularly attended worship at the temple, the public's *right* to worship there was denied by witnesses and extant documents.[65]

Haribhanu Maharaj, Baroda v. *Charity Commissioner, Ahmedabad* (1986), presents the final case in a string of appeals. The Charity Commissioner had ruled the property in question—in this case a *math*—public, the Assistant Judge reversed the Commissioner's ruling, the High Court reversed the Judge's ruling, and this appeal, in which the *math* stands as a public institution, is brought before the Supreme Court. Laxman Maharaj Math was constructed in 1835 by, as the Court rules, "members of the family for showing their reverence to their ancestors".[66] Two features that weigh heavily on the Court in this case are location and size. The *math* was located within the residential quarters of the appellant; the Supreme Court, citing several precedent-setting cases regarding location, chides the High Court for not taking this fact into account. The Supreme Court ruled also that the size of the institution did not lend itself

---

[64] AIR 1981 SC 798.

[65] The Supreme Court also criticizes the Orissa High Court, whose judgement of publicity was based partially on the fact that the seventy-five foot tall temple implied the public's right to worship. (AIR SC 1981 804) The temple's physical prominence comes into play in *Ramaswami* v. *Commissioner, Hindu Religious and Charitable Endowments Administration, Madras*, in which the Madras High Court also rules that the temple in question is public: "If it is a family temple it would not have been built at such a distance [from the family home] and on a hillock over 2000 ft high."

[66] AIR 1986 SC 2139 at 2142.

to being public; the total size of the property is 150′ × 170′, while the *math* measures only 16′ × 12′. In spite of additional evidence showing cash grants from local rulers and documents listing "Ramji Mandir" as the owner of the *math*, a *Sanad* issued by Shrimant Sarkar Maharaj Saheb in 1912 explicitly stating the privacy of the *math* "sets at rest any doubt about the private character of the Math."[67]

The final case is *The Bihar State Board of Religious Trust* v. *Ramsubaran Das* (1996). The respondent in the case inherited property from his uncle after the latter's death in 1959. The uncle had been claiming annuities and submitting returns, accounts and expenditures to the Bihar State Board, as he had to do for public properties. The nephew claimed that his uncle had filed these documents "under misapprehension of fact and law" and that "the said actions are not binding on the plaintiff."[68] The Trial Court ruled that as the public had no hand in the construction of the temple, as the property had, many years before, passed from a Muslim to a Hindu, and as the revenue records show the owner to be the respondent's uncle and not the deities, the temple must be private. The High Court reversed the Trial Court's decision, basing its own decision on two factors. First, the uncle's claims on the property, shown through the lengthy exchange of paperwork with the Bihar State Board (1951-59) are not "mistaken" and, by themselves, show that he treated the properties as public. Second, in 1916, one Hulasbati Devi filed a deed of endowment, dedicating "certain properties" to the temple—specifically, to Laxmi Narainjee, a deity. The High Court ruled that such an "accretion" can only be made to deities themselves in a public temple; in a private institution, the dedication would be made to its human owner. The Supreme Court quickly brushes aside this contention, stating that while the dedication was made to the deities, it was the *mahants* who would be dealing with the property on the deities' behalf. On this basis, the Supreme Court allows the appeal, declaring the privacy of the respondent's temple.

In these cases, the Supreme Court relies upon "custom and usage", as given through verbal testimony, tendencies of religious institutions in different geographical regions, and any extant documents. The goal of the HREC could be seen as similar to that of the courts: "[T]o examine generally the institutions of Hindu religious endowments and to recommend the classes of such endow-

---

[67] *Ibid.*, p. 2145.
[68] AIR 1996 SC 3354.

ments which should be treated as public religious endowments".[69] Unlike the state endowment acts, the Commission would examine individual institutions and make recommendations as to which ones, and which types, are to be classed as public and private; the endowment acts would take over at that point, enforcing its regulations against those considered public and generally ignoring those considered private.

Although the Report describes private endowments in much the same way as the courts, it soon becomes apparent that opinions of the Commission and the courts on private endowments differ markedly. The Commission mentions as crucial for determining the nature of a temple the object of dedication, beneficiaries, and scope of worshipers. Before offering its own suggestions, the Report recalls the answers it received on the questionnaires it distributed to the question of the distinction between public and private temples; the answers listed come not from the general public, but from the current and former government officials who responded:

> [O]nly private places of puja kept in residential houses and meant for personal and family use and not open to the public and not deriving benefit from public endowments, should be treated as private endowments.
> [A] public religious endowment is one which is founded by public donation and is meant for the entire Hindu community without reservations and receives offerings from the public and that where an endowment is founded for his own family and the public has no right of entry or worship, it should be treated as a private one.
> [A]ll endowments should generally be presumed to be public endowments.[70]

The most popular idea gleaned from the surveys seems to be that a private endowment is one to which the public is not allowed. It has been, however, the court's prerogative to prove just the opposite, that public attendance not only does not prove the publicity of an endowment, but that to refuse worship to a member of the public is "a heresy which is scarcely expected in Hindus

---

[69] *Report 1962*, p. 1.
[70] *Ibid.*, p. 40.

who are by and large constitutionally reverent and prone to worship."[71] The Commission offers 114 suggestions covering many aspects of religious and charitable endowments; a paragraph of the fourth suggestion directly pertaining to private endowments is worth quoting in full:

> It is essential to lay down that where the public or a section of the public have traditional, customary and unrestricted access to a temple, it should be treated as a public one and that even in cases where a temple is maintained within residential premises if offerings and gifts are received by the temple authorities from the public or a section thereof at the time of worship or other religious service, it should be treated as a public temple and should cease to be treated as private one.[72]

The Commission, then, while claiming to account for "custom and usage", operates more like the endowment acts, offering a single universal (yet still vague) definition of public and private endowments—"public attendance" means "public temple." It is to the courts' rulings in favor of the privacy of temples as in those mentioned above that the HREC responds:

> [C]ourts and tribunals have refrained in most cases from investigating and taking into account the basic idea underlying the dedication of temples and mutts. They have too often taken for granted that there can be private temples to which the public contribute by way of offerings and donations.[73]

It is this fundamental difference over the "basic idea" of dedication—presumably, the idea that a private temple is dedicated to the idol and its beneficiaries should be only family members—that the Commission sees as comprising the conflict between itself and endowment acts on one side and the courts on the other.

---

[71] AIR 1979 All 74 at 79-80.
[72] *Report 1962*, p. 173.
[73] *Ibid.*, p. 40.

Conclusion

I have attempted in this paper to outline the differential treatment of private endowments among various governmental bodies and documents. This difference in treatment takes place on two levels: of legislation and of recognition. On the legislative level, state endowment acts have ignored, while income-tax law and the HREC have worked to prevent the continued existence of unregulated private endowments; the courts have freely allowed private endowments, where they fit the court's working description. On the level of recognition, however, the HREC sides with the courts, both of which take into account the "custom and usage" of the private endowments they personally encountered. The state endowment acts never examined "custom and usage", did not define private endowments and, hence, never considered them a legal entity; they are little more than legal loopholes—at best deviations from public endowments deserving only nominal support, at worst their virtual opposites sorely in need of reconception and immediate regulation.

While private endowments are not presently open to regulation, many of their former pecuniary benefits have been disposed of so that they are now treated as little more than regular private property, legally possessing very little religious, and no charitable, purpose. This treatment as private property, however, still does not provide them with immunity to the accusation of "mismanagement of funds", a charge more commonly brought against the *shebaits* of the publicly-dedicated temples.[74] The court's application of "custom and usage" will allow for the continued existence of private temples, while the government's continued withholding of benefits to such private property may assist in a decline in their creation and maintenance. Strict application of the HREC's definitions of "publicity" and "privacy" and the resulting re-categorization of every private religious endowment accepting entry and offerings from the public as "public"— a nearly impossible task—will provide the final step in the construction of state authority over unregulated and "mismanaged" endowments and the prevention of the consolidation of wealth, power, and influence in private hands.

---

[74] AIR 1968 SC 915.

21

A Persistent Disjunction:
Parallel Realms of Law in India

Richard W. Lariviere

A problem faced by every legal system is the disparity between the law at the upper end of the legal hierarchy—the law at the top—and the law as actually interpreted and implemented locally. The judicial reasoning of Sandra Day O'Connor and the official acts of the Justice of the Peace in Dime Box, Texas are all part of the same judicial landscape. This is a large landscape, however, and many miles and twists of logic separate Justice O'Connor and the Justice of the Peace. The same is true of the judicial landscape in independent India. What Chief Justice Bhagwati said the law was and what the police in Bhagalpur say the law is can be very different matters.

India is different from the United States in this matter of the continuum of the legal landscape. In India there is a disjunction between the law at the top and the local law that is part of the history of law in the subcontinent. There is a distrust of state courts and state legal apparatus that is pervasive. In every modern Indian language I know, litigation is referred to as a disease. Anecdotal evidence indicates a profound distrust of courts and the legal processes they represent.[1] Anecdotal evidence is all that we have, because there is no scientific

---

[1] Bernard S. Cohn, "Some Notes on Law and Change in North India," *Economic Development and Cultural Change*, Vol. 8, (1959–60), pp. 79-93; "Anthropological Note on Disputes and Law in India," *American Anthropologist*, Vol. 67, n. 2 (1965), pp. 85–122; Lucy Carroll, "Muslim Family Law in India: law, custom, and empirical research," *Contributions to Indian Sociology*, (n.s.) Vol. 17 (1983) pp. 205–22; Marc Galanter, "Justice in Many Rooms: Courts, Private Ordering, and Indigenous Law," *Journal of Legal Pluralism* Vol. 19 (1987), pp. 1–47; R.M. Hayden, "A Note on Caste Panchayats and Government Courts in India," *Journal of Legal Pluralism* Vol. 22 (1984), pp. 43–52, and "Excommunication as Everyday Event and Ultimate Sanction: The Nature of Suspension from an Indian Caste," *Journal of Asian Studies*, Vol. 3 (1983), pp. 291–307; M. N. Shrinivas, "A Caste Dispute Among Washermen of Mysore," *Eastern Anthropologist*, Vol. 6–7 (1952/54), pp. 148–68.

study of attitudes toward the courts among India's citizenry. In the wonderful film *Courts and Councils: Dispute Settlement in India*,[2] which looks at dispute settlement in India, there is a haunting interview with the headman of the Nandiwalla caste. In this interview the headman describes the disdain he and his fellow caste members feel for the government courts. He vows that he will never have recourse to those courts since they make the truth into a lie and a lie into the truth, and he asserts that he and his castemates have no need for the government's courts. They can handle dispute settlement very well amongst themselves. For me, the image of the resolve in his voice and on his face is the mental picture that I have of the disjunction between law at the top and local law.

In India, the common law tradition has been imposed from the top down onto a variety of traditions. This fact of history is well known, and has been repeatedly analyzed and discussed by scholars.[3] It is not my intention to go over this old ground yet again. What I want to suggest today is that our understanding of certain aspects of the *uniqueness* of this event in Indian history is probably wrong. It is my view that the tension—the disjunction—between the law at the top and the local traditions in India was a familiar feature of Indian legal history.

To prove such a sweeping observation conclusively is beyond the scope of this paper. Given the nature of the evidence, conclusive proof may not even be possible, but the question is important in that it may help to explain some of the attitudes one finds among the citizens of India, such as that of the headman of the Nandiwallas.

Where shall we look for historical evidence of the disjunction between law at the top and local law? The earliest sources for such a question are the *dharmaśāstras*. It is well-known that these texts are deliberately ahistorical and thus annoyingly uncooperative in yielding answers to historical questions. At first glance this would seem to make the *dharmaśāstra* texts of little value for investigating the possibility of a disjunction between levels of law in society. After all, it is the claim of these texts to be presenting the eternal and immutable dharma. To admit any disagreement or disjunction is to deny the very immutability of dharma which is central to the world view of the authors of these texts. It is

---

[2] A production of World View Productions, produced by Michael Camerini and James Macdonald, directed by Ron Hess, distributed by the South Asia Center, University of Wisconsin.

[3] Upendra Baxi, "People's Law in India—The Hindu Society," in M. Chiba *Asian Indigenous Law* (London, 1986), pp. 216–66; Marc Galanter, "The Aborted Restoration of 'Inidigenous' Law in India," *Comparative Studies in Society and History*, Vol. 14 (1972), pp. 53–70.; edited by K. Ewing, *Shari'at and Ambiguity in South Asian Islam* (Berkeley, 1988); R. W. Lariviere, "Justices and Panditas: Some Ironies in Contemporary Readings of the Hindu Legal Past," *Journal of Asian Studies* Vol. 48 (1989), pp. 757–69; W.F. Menski, "Solemnisation of Hindu Marriages: The Law and Reality," *Kerala Law Times* (J) 1985, pp. 1–9.

true that disagreements are theoretically allowed for under *mīmāṁsā* rules of interpretation. Should there be disagreement, *śruti* always overrules *smṛti*, Manu overrules all other *smṛtis*, and when texts of equal authority disagree, then one is free to choose.[4] The fact is, however, any commentator worth his salt explains away *apparent* contradictions and inconsistencies within the texts. The commentators are compelled to do so by their beliefs in the nature of the texts. We are not so compelled. It is in the very contradictions and inconsistencies that broad strokes of the historical canvas are revealed to us.

I have for some time been wondering about the relationship between the ideas of sin/crime and penance/punishment as articulated in the *dharmaśāstras*. This is one of those topics that is full of contradictions in the basic texts, yet they are only rarely addressed directly by commentators. In the matter of the relationship between crime/sin and punishment/penance we find some hints of the disjunction between the law at the top and local law.

The problem in the broadest terms is this. If there is a moral universe where what we call the "law of karma" is at work, why should it be necessary for the king to punish any wrong-doer? The wrong-doer will get his just punishment in due course either in this life or the next. Yet the very texts which tell us about how "the law of karma" works also demand that the king punish wrong-doers in various ways. These same texts also prescribe penances which will undo the pernicious karmic effects of certain deeds. Sometimes both punishment and penance are prescribed. Why? Is this a form of double jeopardy? Can the king's punishment be seen as a substitute for or a part of the penance? Or do we have a vestige here of parallel legal systems?

Let's look at the oldest sources on this subject. First it is worthy of note that the literature on penances was enormous: out of 28 chapters in the *Gautamadharmasūtra*, ten were devoted to penance. The same proportions apply to *Vasiṣṭhadharmasūtra*. Several *smṛtis* are devoted exclusively to the subject.[5] Many other *smṛtis* and several *purāṇās* have hundreds of verses on penances. In addition there are many digests which are dedicated to the treatment of penance.[6] The early *dharmasūtra* text of *Āpastamba* says that when someone deviated from the correct path in performing prescribed rituals, then a "disciplinarian" (*śāstṛ*) prescribed an appropriate penance for him. The commentators tell us that this "disciplinarian" should be someone like the man's teacher (ācāryādi). If the transgressor did not perform the penance, the disciplinarian could take him before the king. The king would send him to his personal priest (*purohita*) who then

---

[4] A. S. Nataraja Ayyar, *Mimamsa Jurisprudence (The Sources of Hindu Law)* (Allahabad, 1952).

[5] For example, Atrismṛti, Devalasmṛti, Bṛhadyamasmṛti, and Sātātapasmṛti.

[6] *See* P.V. Kane, *History of Dharmaśāstra* Vol. 4 (Poona, 1973), p. 77.

prescribed a penance and forced him to perform it if he continued to be recalcitrant.[7] We learn elsewhere that the king could, on his own, initiate an action against a subject who had not properly fulfilled a penance.[8] In all cases, however, the penance was not determined by the king, but by *brāhmaṇas* who were expert in such matters. It was the responsibility of a collection of *brāhmaṇas* known as a *pariṣad* to determine the penance appropriate to specific breaches of good conduct. The *pariṣad* made its own rules about penances. It was the court for settling spiritual debts.

Why should the king be involved in matters of penance? In the first place, it is doubtful whether the king was involved very frequently. As P.V.Kane has pointed, out the guidelines for the *pariṣad* were clear, and their procedures were well established.[9] Their authority, too, was well established and included sanctions. The sanction for not performing the penance was a formidable one: the ritual of the *ghaṭasphoṭa*.[10] This was a ritual in which the offender's relatives made a slave girl face the south and kick over a jar filled with water so that all the water flowed out of it. After this the relatives entered a period of mourning for the now "officially dead" offender. At this point they were to stop sitting with him, speaking to him, or engaging in any other type of social intercourse with him. Nevertheless, from time to time a very important matter or a particularly recalcitrant case apparently required the aid of the king. This is explained to us by the famous commentator on Manu, Medhātithi.[11] Medhātithi tells us that the king's role with regard to his subjects is that of protector. He is to protect them from harm, and harm is of two types, literally "visible" and "invisible," i.e. harm in a physical sense and harm in a spiritual sense. Medhātithi says that the king is to protect people from the visible harm of, for example, having their possessions stolen, but he should also protect them from the future sorrows of the next world (*amutrikaduḥkha*) which arise when rules are violated (*vidhyatikrama*).

What is clearly happening here is that the king was appealed to in order to enforce a penance which the people could not enforce themselves through the usual methods. The penance was important for its cosmic significance. Without performing a penance for specific wrongs, the individual would suffer in a future

---

[7] *Āpastambadharmasūtram* 2.5.10.12–16, edited by Georg Buhler *Bombay Sanskrit and Prakrit Series* nos. 45 and 50 3rd edition (Poona, 1932) p. 68.

[8] *Nāradasmṛti* 18.3, edited by R.W. Lariviere, *University of Pennsylvania Studies on South Asia* no. 4 and 5 (Philadelphia 1989). *Kātyāyayanasmṛti*, 949 compiled by P.V. Kane (Poona, n.d.); and *Bṛhaspatismṛti (reconstructed)* 29.13 compiled by K.V. Rangaswami Aiyangar, *Gaekwad's Oriental Series* no. 85 (Baroda, 1941).

[9] P.V. Kane, *op. cit.*, volume 2, pp. 966–74.

[10] *Ibid.*, p. 388.

[11] In his commentary on *Manu* 8.1.

life, but the community in which he lived would also suffer the stigma of having such an unmitigated sinner in its midst. Only penance would allow a wrong-doer back into full membership in society. Until penance was performed, such a wrong-doer was not afforded normal interaction with the other members of his community. This was a burden and inconvenience for everyone, and if left unresolved could result in a debilitating split in the community. The king was asked to force a resolution to such a matter.

This reasoning clearly establishes the king's role in the enforcement of penance. The determination of penance was left to the spiritual authorities, but seeing to it that the penance is performed was the king's job. Scholars such as Heesterman and Lingat have made much of the delineation between the spiritual realm of the *brāhmaṇa* and the temporal realm of the king. These scholars have built elaborate theories of religion and social order in classical India around this relationship.[12] Yet the line is not clear in many aspects of legal administration. The relationship between penance and punishment is just such a case.

The relationship between penance and punishment becomes very murky in cases where the sin for which a penance was prescribed was also a crime which required a punishment to be inflicted by the king. These included the crimes of murder, theft, incest, and perjury. The writers of Sanskrit legal texts had difficulty with these instances. Some of the basic *smṛtis*[13] say explicitly that when a king punished a man that man's ritual status became as pure as anyone else's, and that no further penance was necessary beyond the royal punishment. In this view it would seem that the king was endowed with the authority to prescribe penance. The commentators would not allow the king to have this power. They said that penance and punishment were simultaneous only in those cases where the punishment was death—after the king had the accused put to death, there was no need for further penance on his part—a brilliant bit of panditic insight if ever there was one.[14] Medhatithi differed slightly with this position. He said that *any* corporal punishment also served as a penance. He explained his view as follows: there is an invisible effect on the perpetrator when he undergoes punishment, and this effect is similar to the effects of a penance.

Manu 8.314–316 says :

---

[12] Robert Lingat, *The Classical Law of India* (Berkeley, 1973), pp. 232-37; Jan Heesterman, *Inner Conflict of Tradition* (Chicago, 1985), pp. 108–27, 141–57.

[13] *Vasiṣṭhasmṛti* edited by A.A. Fuhrer *Bombay Sanskrit and Prakrit Series* no. 23 (Bombay, 1916), 19.45, *Manu* 8.318, and *Nārada* 19.55 (both *ed. cit.*).

[14] Vijñaneśvara on *Yājñavalkyasmṛti* edited by Narayan Ram Acharya 5th edition (Bombay, 1949), 3.359.

A thief should untie his hair, present himself in haste before the king and confess the theft saying, "I have done this. Punish me." He should be carrying on his shoulders a stake or club of khadira wood, or a spear pointed at both ends, or an iron rod. The thief is freed from sin of the crime whether he is punished or released, but if the king doesn't punish him, he takes the sin on himself.

In *Yājñavalkya* 3.257 we read a similar statement, but this one is very specific: it speaks of the theft of a *brāhmaṇa's* gold. Here, too, the king had an "option" of punishing or not, but in either case the confession was adequate to purify the perpetrator. We are told elsewhere that the the spear or rod was used by the king to punish the thief. The king was to strike the thief with the weapon, but only once.[15] To fail to do so meant that the king took on the sin.

This is the textual way of obliquely demanding that the king perform the punishment. Why is the king only obliquely requested to punish a thief? The texts do not anywhere else hesitate to tell a king explicitly what his obligation was. This is peculiar in the extreme. It would seem logical that a king should be required to punish a perpetrator of such a serious crime as stealing a *brāhmaṇa's* gold—remember that this is one of the *mahāpātakas*. Why is there such uncertainty and ambivalence in the texts? Lingat's explanation is that the *brāhmaṇas* were reluctant to endow the king with the power of prescribing and administering penance.[16] Punishment was one thing; that was clearly the king's province. But to give the king the authority to administer penance was to give him a place in the realm of spiritual matters that was reserved exclusively to the council of *brāhmaṇa* leaders known as the *pariṣad*. This was a blurring of roles and responsibilities that many commentators found odious. For this reason many of them wanted to confine the simultaneity of penance and punishment only to those cases where the death penalty was involved. The very finality of that punishment made penance a moot point. There, and there only were these commentators comfortable obviating penance in favor of a king's punishment.

This is evidence, it seems to me, of parallel realms of law: what we might call the royal and the sacerdotal. These were not necessarily in competition, although, for the authors of the *dharmaśāstras* there is an apparent concern to delimit the king's authority in specific matters to that of a final enforcer. There is other explicit evidence of parallel realms of law where the texts discuss courts other than the king's. In the *Nāradasmṛti*, for example, we are told that there were courts for caste organizations, for guilds, and for other types of associations. Each of these groups had their own rules which took precedence over other

---

[15] Commentators on *Manu* 8.316.

[16] Lingat, *Loc. cit.*, 235–37.

Parallel Realms of Law

laws—even the king's laws. The king's only responsibility with regard to these courts was to use his influence, when called upon, to enforce the customs and rulings of these bodies.[17] In these cases, what we have can only be described as a local law tradition which is parallel to the legal system of the king. There are points of intersection, but they are apparently limited. I say "apparently" because the evidence about the true relationship between the king's courts and the *brāhmaṇa pariṣad*, the caste courts, the guild courts, and so on is very meagre. The peculiar nature of the accounts of the relationship between punishment and penance, however, leads me to suspect that what we have here is an attempt on the part of the *smṛti* writers to integrate these various legal realms into one, but with limited success.

Fortunately, in later periods we have more explicit information about this issue of the relation between the king's courts and other courts. One of the best documented periods in Hindu legal history is that of the Maratha era. The evidence that survives from this region represents a very late period in Indian legal history, but the legal administration of the period and region is untainted by contacts with European legal systems. I want to turn to the evidence from this region to see what light it can shed on the question of the relationship between law at the top and local law.

Before the time of Shivajī (d. 1680) the relationship between the local traditions and those of the king share the same misty uncertainty of the *dharmaśāstras*. We know something of the relationship from the time of the Delhi Sultanates, but not a great deal. The consensus of scholars of the period is that for the early period—1300–1347—the legal institutions of the Sultans, specifically Muhammad bin Tughluq, did not penetrate to the local village level. By the end of this period there were two classes of officers—one class representing the new Muslim appointees and the other the old local Hindu system.[18] Under the Bahmanis and the later Sultans there came to be greater integration of the Muslim systems and the indigenous judicial institutions. The exact role and function of the various officers cannot detain us here. The period is marked by fluctuations in political power and allegiances which affected the relationship between the sultans and the local administrative systems. Until the time of Shivajī and his successors, the Peshwas, there was a gradual coming together of the two systems with both Muslim appointees and local Hindu representatives sitting together to hear cases in a Majlis.[19] With the ascension of Shivajī many of the institutions which evolved under the Sultans were retained,

---

[17] Narada 10.1–7 (*ed. cit.*).

[18] V.T. Gune, "The Judicial System of the Marathas," *Deccan College Dissertation Series*, no. 12 (Poona, 1953), p. 8.

[19] *Ibid.*

but given a distinctly Hindu character. Holders of Muslim offices, such as the *qazi* were reduced in importance and came to be looked upon as merely the head of the local Muslim religious community.[20]

If we look at how our subject of sin/crime and punishment/penance was treated in this region and this period, we get a clearer feel for the relationship between the law at the top and the local law. Luckily the Maratha state kept remarkably good records. Many of these records have survived and been published. Thus for the first time we have clear records of how a Hindu kingdom administered justice, and what the relationship between the king's law and the local law was.

In the period of the Peshwas (1750–1818) there was a three-fold punishment for any crime: a royal punishment (*diwāndaṇḍa*), religious punishment (*devadaṇḍa*), and a caste punishment (*jātidaṇḍa*).[21] In each realm of punishment there was a separate juridical body. In the case of the royal punishment the Peshwa was the highest judicial authority. The Peshwas had deputies who could substitute for them. They also had a Chief Justice who had jurisdiction over all cases referred to them by the Peshwa. Local representatives of the Peshwa consisted of several classes of officers who had wide discretionary powers in the local setting. In serious cases these local officers referred the case to the Peshwa's court. In most cases the local officers executed the punishments handed down by their superiors in the Peshwa's court. This included executions (being stomped by elephants, beheading, being blown from guns, branding, amputation and the like). Such powers and responsibilities were a mark of the trust the Peshwa had in them and must have placed these individuals in a position of considerable stature at the local level.[22]

In all cases except capital crimes, after the Peshwa's court or his agents at the local level had exacted their punishment, the convicted party had to undergo a separate punishment which would re–admit the culprit to a ritual status which would enable him to take part in religious rituals. The court that administered these penances and had the right to hear religious and caste disputes was the *Brahmasabhā*. The rights of this court were explicitly recognized by the Maratha rulers.[23] At the same time, incidents which affected a particular caste's integrity such as adultery, assault, and other forms of misconduct were adjudicated in a court called the *jātisabhā*.

We know from surviving records how these courts worked. The *Brahmasabhā* was held at places of religious importance, temples, and the like.

---

[20] *Ibid.*, p. 36.

[21] *Ibid.*, p. 102.

[22] *Ibid.*, pp. 102–08.

[23] *Ibid.*, p. 112.

The accused was required to have a letter from his caste or from some other officer requesting that a penance be prescribed for a particular offence. The accused then had to get the permission of the *brāhmaṇas* at that place to actually perform the penance, and he had to pay prescribed fees for the right to perform the penance. At the end of the penance, a document entitle a *śuddhipattra* was given to him certifying his re-established ritual purity. This was the *devadaṇḍa*. After going through this process in the *Brahmasabhā*, the accused returned to his village where he had to certify his purity to the caste members there. He had to show the *śuddhipattra* to the local caste authorities. Its authenticity had to be examined, and then the accused was subjected to an odd sort of jury: he had to offer a feast to his fellow caste members; if they would agree to eat with him, it was the final certification of his re-admission to what was technically called *paṅktipāvana*, or suitability for commensality.[24]

What is interesting about this evidence from the Maratha records, is that in each of these cases the adjudication and certification of three different levels had to be gone through in order to fully regain one's status in the community. If any one of these was to be denied or foregone, the consequences for the accused were severe. These levels of "legal" administration were sequential—one might even say interdependent—but they are clearly separate with their own criteria for resolving a matter and their own concerns for doing so. Moreover, what the king did was of little or no consequence for the lower levels. Similarly, what the lower levels did had no effect on the legal administration of the king. This is clearly evidence for more or less isolated levels of legal administration.

There is considerable evidence that for a significant part of contemporary India's population the state courts are seen as a morass of incomprehensible activity which is costly, disruptive and ultimately unjust. These courts are to be avoided if possible. It has been implied that this is because there has been an overlaying of the alien, colonial, common-law tradition onto the indigenous, traditional law, that there is a pathology about the relationship between these realms of law that is new or unprecedented in Indian history.[25] I think that this is wrong; there has always been a disjunction between the state government and the local government in regions of India. What is unusual about the contemporary situation is that the reach of the law at the top is greater and

---

[24] *Ibid.*, pp. 112–14.

[25] Oliver Mendelsohn, "The Pathology of the Indian Legal System," *Modern Asian Studies* Vol. 15 (1981), pp. 823–63; Marc Galanter, "The Displacement of Traditional Law in Modern India," *Journal of Social Issues* Vol. 24 (1968), pp. 65–91; David A. Washbrook, "Law State and Agrarian Society," *Modern Asian Studies* Vol. 15 (1981), pp. 649–721; *See* Dinesh Khosla, *Myth and Reality of the Protection of Civil Rights Law: A Case Study of Untouchability in Rural India* (Delhi, 1987) for a fine study of how "the law" is actually percieved in a village setting.

more pervasive than in any previous epoch. This has to do with the fact that communications technology is greater than in any previous epoch. People understand how the various levels of law can be harnessed in their own interests, and they have become adept at manipulating "the systems" to their advantage.[26] Experience has shown an ever larger set of clients of these systems where the ultimate power lies and how to gain access to that power: which courts to petition, which strategies to use, how to appeal to superior courts, etc. This ever-widening circle of legal savvy has not completely displaced traditional modes of dispute settlement, however. Traditional society has certainly suffered changes since 1947, but to the extent that India remains a predominantly rural, predominantly village society it will continue to have parallel realms of law. As long as there continues to be a castes structure to any parts of society there will be parallel realms of law.

These parallel realms of law have always existed, and the ambivalence of India's citizens to those realms of law with which they do not have immediate experience or close familiarity is nothing new. It is the same situation as has existed since recorded time in the subcontinent.

---

[26] Richard K. Gordon, Jr. & Jonathan M. Lindsay, "Law and the Poor in Rural India: The Prospects for Legal Aid," *The American Journal of International Law and Policy* Vol. 5 (1990), pp. 655–772, see especially p. 723.

22

Reflections on Law and Meaningfulness in a North Indian Hindu Village

Jonathan M. Lindsay and Richard Gordon[1]

Introduction

One evening in the mid-eighties, a *barat* (marriage procession) was approaching the village of Kisanpur[2] in western Uttar Pradesh when it found its way blocked by immense puddles, caused by heavy rain the night before. The *barat* consisted of *Jatavs* (also known as *Chamars*, the untouchable leatherworker caste), and its destination was the *Jatav* neighborhood on the west side of Kisanpur. Rather than wade through deep water and mud, the *barat* decided to approach its destination via an alternate route, a lane through a part of town dominated by *Kirar Rajput Thakurs* (a middling high *Kshatriya* caste). Here, however, the procession was met by lathi-wielding *Thakurs* who unceremoniously informed the *Jatavs* that the *barat* could not proceed further and would have to retrace its steps. Rather than risk a physical altercation with the *Thakurs*, the *barat* turned back and found its way to the marriage site by a circuitous route through fields and puddles on the periphery of the village.

There is nothing remarkable about the general features of this story. No doubt similar instances occur frequently in villages throughout India. Recently a particularly violent version of this type of encounter attracted national headlines in Agra district, not far from Kisanpur. But there are interesting aspects to the language with which the Kisanpur participants described the incident. The chief instigator among the *Thakurs* defended the action of his community not on religious grounds or on the basis of protecting the *Thakur* neighborhood from pollution, but on the grounds that the lane was *niji*, or private property. The

---

[1] The authors wish to thank Professor V. S. Rekhi, Professor John Mansfield, Professor Marc Galanter, Mr. Zubair Khan, Mr. Gaurav Singh, and Mr. Harilal Dhingra for their invaluable assistance and coments on earlier versions of this paper.

[2] Kisanpur is a fictional name for an actual village. Throughout this article, all names of villagers from Kisanpur have been changed. Fieldwork for this article was carried out in Kisanpur in 1983, 1985 and 1991.

Thakurs didn't have documents to prove it, but "everyone in the village knew" that they "owned" the lane by virtue of generations of occupation and use. The *Jatavs* confirmed this version of the story. The *Thakurs* turned them back, they said, because they claimed the lane was "private," a designation that the *Jatavs* disputed vigorously: the lane was not private, they said, but one that belonged to the village. Similar arguments surfaced in the case of the Agra incident.

Of course, it is difficult to know what internalized beliefs motivated the *Thakurs* to behave as they did. It is possible that they felt on some level that they were protecting their neighborhood and families from the polluting presence of untouchables. The motivation may in fact be grounded in the local varieties of Hindu tradition. But the language used to describe and defend it has the flavor of modern legal terminology. Traditional concerns in Kisanpur about pollution and hierarchy, it seems, are sometimes put in the language of private property rights and adverse possession.

Typically, the story of law in rural India has been told as a story of the failure of law as an instrument of social change. Critiques have focused on the failure of political will to enforce laws designed to redress inequalities, the failure of the secular court system to provide a meaningful alternative to local dispute-settling forums, and the persisting dissonance between the egalitarian ideology of modern law and the ideology of local religious tradition.

In his study of the Protection of Civil Rights Act and its perception and use by Bihari villagers,[3] Dinesh Khosla provides an example of such a critique. Khosla chronicles the dismal performance of the statute in altering the practice of untouchability in rural areas. The law, which, like many examples of modern social legislation, "aimed at delegitimizing institutionalized, traditionally-sanctioned, and in many cases deeply internalized social practices and values,"[4] was greeted with enthusiasm by its intended beneficiaries and alarm by the upper castes. But within a short period of time, the law came to be viewed by Khosla's respondents with cynicism, resignation, and contempt as being largely irrelevant to village life. As Khosla puts it, his respondents felt that "the goals of the law were so divorced from the dynamics, intricacies, currents and cross-currents of rural reality that it could not find its execution in the rural setting."[5] Prosecutions under the act were reduced to a trickle, and scheduled castes came to see the law as the "artifact of politicians"[6] eager to capitalize on the legacy of Gandhi. Social

---

[3] Khosla, "Untouchability—A Case Study of Law in Life," in Podgorecki, Whelan and Khosla, *Legal Systems and Social Systems* (London, 1985), 126–173.

[4] *Ibid.*, p. 127.

[5] *Ibid.*, p. 148.

[6] *Ibid.*, p. 138.

activists saw the bill as an impediment to reform, a way of subverting their struggle by entangling it in labyrinthine legalities.

At the outset of his argument, Khosla offers the following proposition: "a law is not meaningful unless its intended beneficiaries can use the legal structures to achieve its ideals."[7] It is perhaps unfair to seize upon this narrow definition of "meaningfulness," a narrowness which is belied by Khosla's own rich evidence and analysis. His data suggests that the law may have had important symbolic significance, and may also have had the perverse effect of exacerbating feelings of hostility and mistrust between upper and scheduled castes. But his ultimate conclusion is dictated by his view of what is meaningful—since law has failed in achieving its direct instrumental aims, law has for all intents and purposes, stopped at the "boundaries of the village."[8]

It is impossible to disagree with Khosla and others that law of the secular state has in practice fallen far short of its goals of transforming local patterns of dominance and hierarchy. But this is not to say that those aspects of modern law and legal institutions which are designed to affect social hierarchy have not penetrated rural Hindu society in certain profound and "meaningful" ways. In this paper, we provide some reflections on the manner in which such penetration has occurred in a particular north Indian village.

Our work in Kisanpur originally grew out of an effort to understand in a specific social setting the potential benefits to the rural poor of free legal aid schemes, the provision of which was given much vocal support by jurists, academics, and politicians in India during the early 1980s.[9] Our primary focus was not on the logistical, financial, political or institutional problems facing the implementation of such programs, which in any event are formidable and perhaps insurmountable. Instead, struck by the lack of attention paid to local social realities in those debates, we focused on the conditions and needs of intended beneficiaries. What are the types of problems faced by the poor in a village that could be profitably addressed by easier access to the legal system? What are the day to day realities of power and dominance in Kisanpur that appeals to outside law and legal institutions would inevitably encounter and perhaps founder upon? What "meaning" does law have in the life of this community?

In attempting to answer these questions, few safe conclusions emerged. It became clear to us, however, that in the case of Kisanpur, those aspects of law which are designed to affect social dominance and hierarchy have not simply stopped at the "boundaries of the village." Some have crept across the line,

---

[7] *Ibid.*, p. 130.

[8] *Ibid.*, p. 162.

[9] Gordon and Lindsay, "Law and the Poor in Rural India: the Prospects for Legal Aid," *American University Journal of International Law and Policy* (1990), pp. 655–772.

leaving others behind. Law, legal language, and legal institutions are understood and misunderstood, adapted, abused, ignored, transformed and enmeshed with local traditions in oblique and contradictory ways. To understand the "failure" of law, as well as to appreciate it's potential, requires an effort to come to grips with such local meanings.

The Setting[10]

Kisanpur is a village of about 2500 in Aligarh District in western Uttar Pradesh. The village is located about 40 kilometers from the district headquarters in Aligarh. From the nearest metalled road and bus stop, one approaches Kisanpur over 4 kilometers of largely *kuccha* road, a road entirely unimproved until two years ago when some sections of it were paved with brick. Similarly, until two years ago the village was without electricity. Now electricity is available on a sporadic basis for lighting the homes of those who can afford the cost of the connection, and for running tubewell motors. Economic activity is almost entirely focused on agriculture. There is no market in Kisanpur, and with the exception of a few very small shops and some small cottage industries, commercial activity is largely absent or is carried on in the nearby market towns. The quality of the agricultural land is generally high and the region has been under intense irrigation since early in the British era.

Kisanpur is overwhelmingly Hindu; there are only a few Muslim families in the village. All told, there are 18 *jatis* represented in Kisanpur, including two Muslim *jatis*, as set forth in the following table:

Jati Structure in Kisanpur

Varna[a]	Jati[b]	Population[c] (percent)	Traditional Occupation[d]
Brahmin	Brahmar	3	priest
	Mahabrahmin [e]	1	cremator
Ksatriya	Rajput Thakur	36	prince/warrior
	Jat	6	landowner
Vaisya	Bania	2	shopkeeper
	Baghaili [f]	13	shepherd

---

[10] Much of the material in Sections 2 and 3 of this article is based upon research first presented by the authors in Gordon & Lindsay, *Ibid*.

Sudra	Barhai	1	carpenter
	Kumhar	1	potter
(Backward)[g]			
	Lohar	1	ironmonger
	Kohar	6	bearer
	Nai	2	barber
	Teli	1	oil presser
Untouchables[h]	Jatav [i]	16	leatherworker
(Scheduled Castes)			
	Dhobi	2	clothes washer
	Dom	1	pigherder
	Bhangi	4	sweeper
Muslims [j]	Julaha	1	weaver
	Manihar	2	bangle seller

a. *Brahmin, ksatriya* and *vaisya* categories are relatively well agreed upon by all *jatis*, though see comment below on *Baghailis*. *Sudra* and untouchable categories are agreed upon by upper *varna jatis*. *Jatis* from these *varnas* tend not to refer to themselves as belonging to *varnas*.

b. *Jati* designations have been obtained from members of those communities. Ranking is our best estimate, arrived at by asking each person to rank *jatis* hierarchically.

c. Population percentages are approximate.

d. Traditional occupations taken from the Hindi meanings of *jati* names, though see comment 9 below on *Jatavs*. With the exception of *Brahmars* and *Rajput Thakurs,* at least some members of each *jati* practiced the traditional occupation at least part-time.

e. *Mahabrahmins*, though a type of priest and agreed to be *brahmins*, were traditionally considered to be untouchable due to their profession of handling corpses.

f. *Baghailis* appear to have been considered *sudras* at one time, but had recently managed to gain acceptance by most *jatis* as *vaisyas*.

g. These *jatis* identified themselves as being backward classes.

h. These *jatis* identified themselves as being scheduled castes. Higher *jatis* identified them as being either lower *jatis* or "scheduled castes."

i. *Jatav* is a *jati* name designed to support the *jati's* claim to *ksatriya* status (the full name is sometimes given as *Rajput Jatav*). However, *Jatavs* claim *jati* kinship to *Chamars*, or leather workers.

j. Though Muslims are not properly part of the *varna* and *jati* system, they do display some aspects of it.

The most important *jatis*, both numerically and in terms of power and wealth, were the *Rajput Thakurs* and *Jats*, who during interviews often reminded us of their *kshatriya* status and of their descent from warriors and kings. While *Jats* held themselves equal to *Rajputs* (and while intermarriage between the two *jatis* had been recently generally sanctioned by both communities), *Rajputs* were united in their opinion that the *Jats* were inferior. Both made reference to the relatively lower status of the *Brahmars* in the village. One larger farmer noted that "*brahmins* are supposed to be scholars, but these *Brahmars* in Kisanpur aren't scholars, so they aren't real *brahmins*. We have to go outside of the village to get *brahmins* for weddings."

Some of the *jatis* in Kisanpur continue to perform their traditional *jajmani* tasks. Many *Nais*, for example, act as barbers both on a daily basis and for religious ceremonies, while a majority of *Bagailis* are engaged in goat herding. But in general, the main economic activity of virtually everyone in the village was either the cultivation of one's own fields, or laboring on the fields of others.

Kisanpur exhibits many of the characteristics of a Srinivasian "dominant caste" village.[11] The *Thakur* community dominates in all of the seven categories enunciated by Srinivas. Numerically, they are by far the largest single caste group, comprising 36% of the total population of the village. Economically, they own approximately 75% of the land in the village, as well as the most advanced equipment and housing. The *pradhan* of the village *panchayat* is invariably a *Thakur*, and political control of the village revolves around the competition between factions within the *Thakur* community, with participants from other *jatis* largely reacting to or playing off of this central competition. The *Thakurs* reinforce their strength by virtue of their ability to secure good educations for their children, and by placing their children in government postings. Finally, they dominate when it comes to displays of physical strength.

At the opposite end of the spectrum, the largest grouping among the scheduled castes of Kisanpur were the *Jatavs*. *Jatav* (or, according to the Jatavs themselves, more properly "*Rajput Jatav*") is a name adopted in the 1930's by *Chamars* (leatherworkers) in this part of Uttar Pradesh in a classically sanscritiz-

---

[11] M.N. Srinivas, *Social Change in Modern India* (Berkeley, 1966). See T.K. Oommen, *Social Structure and Politics: Studies in Independent India* (New Delhi, 1984), pp. 69–80, for an interesting critique of the concept of dominant caste.

Law and Meaningfulness

ing attempt to improve their caste standing.[12] The *Jatavs* are primarily landless laborers, although a few families own some land. However, of all the scheduled castes in Kisanpur, the *Jatavs* exhibit the most determined desire to improve their conditions, as will be evident from some of the material that follows in Part III. Perhaps this is a result of a long organizational tradition among Aligarh *Jatavs* dating back to the independence movement. In recent years, while the condition of the *Jatavs* in Kisanpur is still quite poor and vulnerable, a number of processes have been set in motion which have provided a modicum of improvement. First, the *Jatavs* are relatively well-informed about the various economic schemes established by the government to promote the uplift of the scheduled castes. While frequently complaining that such schemes often do not reach the intended beneficiaries, the *Jatavs* have nevertheless been able to take advantage of at least some of them. The key to freedom from domination by the *Thakurs*, they told us, was in establishing some economic independence so that "we are not just slaves who work on the lands of the *Thakurs* and have to beg for them to give us their old clothes." In pursuit of this independence, they have for the last decade been involved in village handicrafts, principally making locks in their homes as piecework for a factory in Aligarh.

With the evolution of democracy at the village level, intra-*jati* factionalism has become endemic, particularly among the larger and more powerful *jatis*. Much of the intra-*jati* competition of the dominant *Rajput jati*, and much of the somewhat tenuous solidarity of the lower *jatis*, is played out in the arena of elective politics, particularly the politics of the statutory village *panchayat*.[13] The *panchayat* in Kisanpur is headed by a *pradhan*, or president, who calls meetings, whose signature is required for the disbursement of funds, and who is viewed by outsiders (including government officials) as the representative of the village.[14] There is an *up-pradhan* or vice-president, and seven other members, with scheduled castes holding, at least in theory, the same percentage of seats as they do in the village population.[15] The *panchayat* controls or influences the control of numerous scarce resources. Among the most important are the management of village lands,[16] of drought relief and certain public works programs

---

[12] Government of India, *Census of India, United Provinces of Agra and Oudh*, Vol. 18, p. 530 (1931).

[13] U.P. *Panchayati Raj Act (Act 26 of 1947)*; see K. Van DeSand, *Foundations and Problems of Local Government in Rural India* (Mainz, 1980).

[14] U.P. *Panchayati Raj Act (Act 26 of 1947)*, Rule 47.

[15] *Ibid.*, Rules 7, 9.

[16] Acting as the *Bhumi Prabandhak Samiti*. Id, Section 28; *U.P. Zamindari Abolition and Land Reforms Act (Act 1 of 1951)*, Sections 117 and 122.

funded by higher levels of government;[17] influence over the allocation of benefits under the Integrated Rural Development Programme;[18] and in general, relations with the outside world. Because control of the *panchayat* can mean control over substantial benefits, elections to and control of the *panchayat* are among the most potent sources of competition within a dominant *jati*.

Traditional *jajmani* ties can often form the basis of inter-*jati* factional alliances. But with the evolution of democracy at the village level, the factions among the larger and more powerful *jatis* often seek what are essentially electoral alliances with lower *jatis*. Of course, even factionalism at the village level often gives way to unity when a particular *jati* is under intense pressure, and often disappears as politics moves up from the village level. Nevertheless, this source of *jati* disunity is an important force. Often entire lower *jatis* may form alliances with one or another faction, based either on implicit or explicit promises from a faction within the dominant *jati*. As such, inter-*jati* cooperation in factional struggles may be bought and kept only so long as the alliance is beneficial to the nondominant *jati*, and only for so long as the rival faction does not hold out the promise of greater benefits if allegiance is switched.

At the time of this study, the *Rajput* community, though dominant, was firmly split into two factions, one led by the former *pradhan* who had recently (in 1991) been returned as *pradhan*, Jaswant Singh, the other led by the person who had served as *pradhan* when Jaswant Singh was out of office, whose name was Dev Singh. Jaswant Singh was the largest landholder in the village, and his supporters were in control of the *panchayat* before the schism of the *Rajputs* into two clearly defined factions. Dev Singh's faction seemed to evolve from those who were disgruntled with Jaswant Singh's first period as *pradhan*. Each faction alleged that the other's leader had been corrupt while acting as *pradhan*; each accused the other of using the office to help family and faction members by selling village land and pocketing the money. It does appear that during his first term as *pradhan*, Jaswant Singh had been involved in turning over village common lands to his relatives, and had used certain drought relief funds to build a road to one of his fields. Since that time, factions had become increasingly active, and the search for allies among the lower *jatis* had become vigorously competitive. In a number of instances, for example, people supported fellow faction members of different *jatis* in land and boundary claims against *jati*-mates who were members of the other faction.

The method of participation in village factionalism varied from *jati* to *jati*. For example, the *Brahmar jati*, which lies ritually above the *Rajputs* and the

---

[17] *U.P. Panchayati Raj Act (Act 26 of 1947)*, Section 15.

[18] Government of Uttar Pradesh, *U.P. Integrated Rural Development Programme Manual* (Lucknow, 1983).

Law and Meaningfulness

majority of whose members owned land, seemed largely above the factional fray, although there was one politically active *Brahmar* family which tended to side with the Jaswant Singh faction. The *Kohars* (bearers) had sided primarily with the Dev Singh faction, apparently because he was perceived by them to be less corrupt than Jaswant Singh, and because he was less likely to favor *Rajputs* from other factions over non-*Rajput* members of his own faction. The *jati panchayat* of the *Baghailis* had, we were told, formally decided not to participate in the factions.

By contrast, the *Jatavs*, the second largest *jati* numerically, had become deeply involved in village politics and had become important players in the *panchayat* elections. As a result, their position within the village had been affected by the role they played in the dynamics of factionalism among the *Thakurs*. The importance of the *Jatavs* in these contexts has given them some minimal leverage to secure benefits for their community that would not have been available otherwise. As we will describe in greater detail below, *Jatavs* have been promised, and have sometimes received, financial and other support in exchange for their loyalty at elections.

Law as Process

We start by exploring the Khosla notion of meaningfulness: are the poor in Kisanpur able to use legal structures to achieve the ideals set forth in laws designed for their benefit? Unlike Khosla, to approach this question, we have started not with any substantive law in mind but instead have tried to understand the extent to which such structures are made use of and in what contexts. However, exploring the meaning of the process for the lower castes also gives us entry into their thinking about the relative value of various enactments in their lives.

Scholars have disagreed on the extent to which courts, with their emphasis on equality of status, have been accepted by village society as a method of adjudicating disputes, although virtually all studies have enumerated pathologies and dysfunctions that have rendered courts unrecognizable from a western, liberal perspective.

Cohn has suggested that, due to the continuing clash of values between village and court, Indians have used the courts not to solve disputes, but to further them.[19] Mendelsohn has suggested that the use of legal process as one of many weapons brought to bear upon an opponent, rather than a device to settle disputes,

---

[19] B. Cohn, "Some notes on Law and Change in North India," *Economic Development & Cultural Change*, Vol. 8, p. 91.

is due to the fact that the vast majority of legal cases have involved land.[20] In this view, the courts are only a part of a larger administrative system dealing with the vast complexities of land ownership, and cannot be expected to handle these issues in a simple, adjudicatory manner. Other scholars have suggested that "lawyer's law" would be accepted only in very limited circumstances where there was no deep conflict in traditional values. Cases involving family disputes, for example, or ones in which Hindu beliefs were paramount, would remain within the traditional system.[21]

In short, the literature on courts is marked by a litany of structural flaws and a bemoaning of the fact that courts are little more than arenas for manipulation, deceit and game-playing. But (to play a variation on our more general quibble with Khosla), to acknowledge the myriad flaws in the system is not the same as concluding that the process is meaningless in the village context. Perhaps courts and access to courts play a role vastly at odds with the western liberal model, but that does not render them irrelevant. Indeed, our evidence from Kisanpur suggests just the opposite. However alien their origins and their philosophical underpinnings, courts are an integral part of village life.

In Kisanpur, the most common types of lawsuit are those brought by the male offspring of large landowners, mostly *Rajputs* and *Jats*, concerning the partition of land between them.[22] There are two types of partition battles. The first involves inheritance. Because there is no tradition of primogeniture in Hinduism, assets are divided up evenly among all male children. Traditionally such divisions were simple; families normally lived together and divided up the land's produce evenly. However, because land ownership is now legally recorded, and because brothers may wish to leave the village, there is a greater interest in making certain that one's inheritance is reflected in a legally recorded, equal share in land. That can lead to major court disputes over the relative size and quality of each inheritance.

---

[20] Mendelsohn, "The Pathology of the Indian Legal System," *Modern Asian Studies*, Vol. 15, p. 824 (1981).

[21] Singh, "Legal Perceptions and Usages in North Indian Village Disputes," *Journal Of Social Research*, Vol. 19, p. 26 (1976).

[22] See M. Sharma, *The Politics of Inequality: Competition and Control in an Indian Village* (Honolulu, 1979), p. 136–38. In the principal village of Professor Sharma's research, a lack of funds to pay lawyers prevented intra-*jati* disputes over land from going to court. She discovered that mediators or "big men" resolved these disputes. Only inter-*jati* disputes went to court. This is not the case in Kisanpur. In one instance, a particularly litigious *Rajput* landowner had instituted over fifty lawsuits, almost all against his *Rajput* neighbors. While faction leaders often resolved intra-*jati* conflicts, conflicts involving land often went to court, particularly when such conflicts were inter-factional.

The second involves land ceiling legislation, and is a sort of permutation of the first. In Kisanpur, the state government has set a limit of a little over seven hectares per family.[23] In order to stay under the limit and not forfeit land to the state, it often becomes necessary to make a legal partition; such partitions often turn into bitter court battles.[24] Fictional divisions between relatives often become real ones.

Land reform in India is often described as a failure, and with regard to any stated aim of transferring land from the wealthy to the landless, it has largely earned such a description. But it has had a perhaps unintended consequence. Increasing land partitions due to ever bigger populations and ever lower land ceilings has resulted in two things: ever smaller holdings (often meaning reduced wealth and power for any one individual or family) and increased battles among members of the same extended family.[25]

Another common form of legal action involves disputes among neighbors. Surveying and the legal recording of land ownership is imperfect. A common feature of land disputes is the subtle moving of irrigation barriers (often at night) onto neighboring pieces of land in an attempt to claim portions of that land as one's own. These claims frequently wind up in court. Because such actions usually involve *Rajputs* or *Jats*, these disputes often reinforce factional divisions or create new ones.

At least among those upper *jatis* who own land, courts have become familiar allies in the context of local power struggles. Almost all of these families have a passing acquaintance with the courts, and look to them as a way of furthering their disputes. One of the most important effects of legal process appears to be its usefulness in the harassment of one's opponents. Being dragged into court over periods of months or years to give testimony can be a very expensive, time-consuming and degrading experience. But this is not all. The ability to secure interim orders and temporary injunctions, though subject to appeal, are also powerful weapons. What was less clear to us was the effect of legal judgments (both interim and final) in these cases. In most instances, the mere threat of police action to enforce eviction seemed to be sufficient to end the dispute, although it also appeared that this threat was more a tool to assist the

---

[23] *U.P. Imposition of Ceiling on Land Holdings Act (1960) (Act 1 of 1961)*, Sections 3, 4 & 5. A family of more than five members is allowed an additional eight acres per child, with a maximum of twenty-four acres extra.

[24] See O. Mendelsohn, "The Role of the Courts in the Failure of Indian Land Reform," unpublished manuscript on file with the authors, presented at "The Career and Prospects of Law in Modern India" Conference, University of Wisconsin, Madison, June, 1982.

[25] Vyas, "Changes in Land Ownership Pattern: Structural Change in Indian Agriculture," in Hobsbawm, ed., *Peasants in History: Essays in Honor of Daniel Thorner* (Calcutta, 1980), p. 187–88.

legal victor in negotiating a better compromise outside of the court. Criminal trespass could result in the actual arrest of an individual, which in India can be quite terrifying. In addition, the ability of the victor to register land with the Land Office seemed to be important, in that only land that was registered could be effectively sold or used as collateral for a loan.

Courts therefore have clearly had a role to play in the battles between individuals and factions drawn from the ranks of the dominant castes. But how, if at all, have courts affected the interplay between high and low in the Hindu social structure? The judicial system, as flawed as it may be, has at least the theoretical potential to be less affected by *jati* status or hierarchy then would be a village forum for dispute settlement. In addition, as an arm of the liberal state, the courts might provide a better opportunity for the enforcement of new rights accorded lower *jatis* by that state. Appeal to an outside forum would represent a "searching for a means to escape the disabilities and coercions of traditional village society...an effort to unravel [oneself] from traditional moral and social orders."[26]

In discussions about the poor and the Indian legal system, it is often taken as a given that the poor, especially in distant rural areas, are ignorant of their rights and mystified by the complexities and alien forms of the system. Again, among the scheduled castes of Kisanpur, we were struck by the fact that knowledge about rights and courts are part of local folk knowledge. This is not to say that such knowledge is free from confusion and misunderstanding. Accurate understandings coexist with distortions and mystification. Similarly, feelings expressed to us about the efficacy of courts often seemed marked by contradictions: the impulse to appeal to outside forums when possible coexists with a profound cynicism about the value of doing so. Some of these conflicting meanings reveal themselves in the following cases.

Case of The Road

A road has always run out from the village proper, past a small separate colony of *Jatav* families, toward the principal metalled road. During land consolidation, the Land Officer recorded that the land under the road actually belonged to a neighboring *Rajput*. The Land Officer then recorded that the road itself lay through some land belonging to one of the *Jatavs*. The *Rajput* started to construct the road through the *Jatav* property, and began to cultivate the actual road.

---

[26] Rudolph & Rudolph, *The Modernity of Tradition* (Chicago, 1967), p. 267.

The *Jatav* who owned the property through which the new road lay went to see a lawyer in the nearest market town. The lawyer was a *Bania*. Soon afterward the *Bania* referred the case to another lawyer, who was also a *Jatav*. Apparently the *Jatav* lawyer and the landowner went to see the Land Officer. However, the Land Officer refused to see them. It is not clear if he asked for a bribe, or if he simply refused to talk to them.

The two then went to see the Sub-Divisional Magistrate (S.D.M.), a member of the state administrative service who oversees all local civil affairs, including the police. The S.D.M., who was also a *Rajput*, agreed to come to the village to make an investigation. While there, he went to visit the *Rajput* who now claimed title to the land where the road had been. The *Rajput* landowner knew a *jati*-mate in the same market town where the S.D.M.'s office was located. That *Rajput* was apparently engaged in the business of prostitution, and sent a prostitute to see the S.D.M. The prostitute spent three or four days with the S.D.M. The S.D.M. then refused to act on the case.

The two *Jatavs*, landowner and lawyer, then went to see the Collector, who is the chief local tax official and the direct superior of the Land Officer. The Collector also presides over the Land Court. Although the Collector did not send someone out to see the village, the same prostitute was sent to the Collector for a period of four days. The Collector then refused to act on the case. The lawyer never filed a formal case before the Collector's Court. "What would be the point? We have no money to fight a court case."

The Capture of the Village Lands

This case involves a wealthy *Rajput* family whose farm abutted the commons, and their "grabbing" of village common lands. The *Rajput* family was closely related to Jaswant Singh and they had acquired the land during his tenure as village president. In theory, village commons are under control of the entire panchayat as the *bhumi samiti*, or "land committee." Land ownership, however, is registered with a state records office.[27] The Registrar presides over the state records and is under the supervision of the District Land

---

[27] The Registrar is known in English as well as in Hindi by the vernacular name Lekhbal.

Officer.[28] The *Rajput*'s possession of the common lands caused particular hardship to one *Bhangi* (sweeper) named Ram Das. The amount taken was not large, perhaps only an acre, but it was on this particular section of land that Ram Das had usually grazed his animals.

Ram Das performed the traditional services of a *Bhangi* for a *Rajput*, a member of the Dev Singh faction. Ram Das complained about the land capture to his patron who directed him to the District Land Officer. The District Officer ordered the Registrar to make an investigation into the complaint. While traditionally most government officials from outside the village report directly to the *pradhan*, the Registrar went directly to the *Rajput* who had captured the land. There he secured a bribe, returned to the Land Officer, and reported that the land was private property. It turned out that the Registrar was also a *Rajput* of the same *gotra*.

After hearing the Land Officer's decision, Ram Das went to Dev Singh, the *pradhan*. Ram explained that the decision was improper and threatened to file a lawsuit. Dev Singh knew that Ram Das was a member of his faction and that the Rajput who had captured the land was a member of the Jaswant Singh faction. Dev Singh summoned the Registrar back to the village and ordered the recordation of the land as common. As president of the *panchayat*, he then ordered the offending *Rajput* to vacate the land and threatened that the *panchayat* would take legal action if he did not. Faced with these prospects, the *Rajput* relented and returned the captured land.

The Capture of Consolidation Land

This case involved the capture by several *Rajput* families of certain lands after the completion of "land consolidation." Consolidation was a statutory program which reconfigured property ownership so that landowners would no longer have numerous, noncontiguous pieces of land. For their old, scattered properties owners were given new, undivided lands equal in agricultural output to their original holdings. The purpose of consolidation was to make cultivation more efficient, and to pave the way for mechanization. Because of increased efficiency and because of the contemplated enforcement of land ceiling legislation, consolidation usually resulted

---

[28] The District Land Officer is known in English as well as in Hindi by the vernacular name Tehsildar.

in a small surplus of land after all holdings had been reassigned. According to the statute, this land was supposed to be distributed to landless villagers, beginning with the scheduled castes.

During Jaswant Singh's tenure as president, title to this land was instead transferred to a number of his relatives. Jaswant Singh saw to it that the Registrar, who was from the same *jati* and *gotra*, recorded title in the names of his relatives, who apparently also paid the Registrar hefty bribes. A significant amount of land was involved—around forty acres or so—and a number of *Rajput* families had benefitted.

Krishna Singh, the leader of the Kisanpur *Jatavs*, heard about the statutory distribution scheme for scheduled castes from a *Jatav* who was lawyer in a nearby town. Krishna Singh was aware of the numerous court cases involving land partition among the upper *jati* landowners. In addition, he had earlier spent three years in Delhi working as a brick kiln worker. While there, he had been involved in litigation concerning back pay due to kiln workers under the state minimum wage act. The litigation, taken on behalf of all kiln workers (most of whom were scheduled caste members from different *jatis*), was prosecuted by a Delhi *Jatav* lawyer. The case was successful, and Krishna Singh and his fellow workers received a substantial financial settlement. Krishna Singh felt that a court case might work here to force the *Rajput* "land grabbers" to return the land, and force the *panchayat* to distribute it to the scheduled castes in the village. He organized a committee, including members from each of the other scheduled caste *jatis* to fight the case. The majority *Jatavs* decided at a *jati panchayat* to support the suit. The other scheduled caste *jatis* were not unanimous; a small number of families split on factional lines and declined to become involved, while most of the others decided to support the committee even though they had ties to patrons associated with Jaswant Singh's faction.

The committee collected a small fund from each family and engaged a local *Jatav* lawyer to prosecute the case. The *Jatav* lawyer filed suit before the District Magistrate, who ordered the Registrar and the District Land Officer to make an investigation and report back to him. The Registrar arrived in the village and went directly to see Jaswant Singh, the *pradhan*, who had made the initial arrangements for the land to be registered in his name. The Registrar agreed to drop the investigation.

Soon after, one of the *Rajputs* who had captured some land stopped Krishna Singh on the road and told him that if he did not stop the lawsuit, he would be killed. After this threat was given, the committee decided to wait. They did not go to the police because they feared that the police would only go to the *pradhan*, who would send them away. In the next election for president of the *panchayat*, the committee decided to support Dev Singh, who won. Then Krishna Singh went to Dev Singh and asked for his help. Dev Singh said that he would not oppose the filing of the case or the decision of the court.

The case continued for a number of years without a disposition. Dev Singh apparently lost interest in the case, and refused to help prosecute it. Before the most recent election in 1991, Jaswant Singh promised Krishna Singh that, in return for *Jatav* support, he would agree to help retrieve some misappropriated land. Krishna Singh agreed, and Dev Singh was defeated. Since the election, Jaswant Singh has officially supported the lawsuit, agreeing that some land was misregistered under his previous tenure as *pradhan*.

Since the filing of the testimony of Jaswant Singh, the *Jatavs* have run out of money to pay their lawyer, and Jaswant Singh has displayed no interest in helping them financially. As a result, the case has not been prosecuted, and has remained dormant. Attempts are continuing to raise enough money to continue the suit.

These cases, like virtually every other case we heard in Kisanpur, demonstrate the connection between factionalism and the courts, and the potential, albeit modest, for the lower castes to use the second to exploit the first for their own benefit. The frustrations encountered by the *Jatav* litigant in the first case—a lack of resources to follow through on a legal challenge, and a feeling that outside authorities were easily manipulated by the upper *jatis*—were not atypical of the stories related to us when we raised the question of the use of courts.

But existing side by side with this frequently expressed cynicism about the value of pursuing legal strategies was a countervailing perception that there was something to be gained by greater use of courts by the lower *jatis*. Often, it seemed, this belief was expressed in the same breath by those who most effectively articulated the frustrations. While the first case was described to us as an example of the failure of courts to accomplish anything positive, the second was was held up as evidence that the threat of legal action, combined with the use of caste connections and a factional dispute, could actually result in a benefit realized by a lower *jati* member.

The third case, while not yet settled, at least showed that courts could influence electoral politics, and the potential distribution of benefits by the *panchayat*. However, nine years after its commencement, the suit still languishes

Law and Meaningfulness

in court. It is impossible for us to tell whether community interest in the case had flagged, thus making it difficult to repeat the remarkable money-raising effort undertaken at the outset of the case. In conditions of extreme poverty, forgoing even a small amount of income to pursue a strategy of highly uncertain outcome may be unattractive. In any event, it remains the position of the *Jatavs* that what stands between them and the resumption of the case is a lack of financial resources. In fact, although it was not clear exactly how they had benefitted, there appeared to be a conviction among the scheduled castes with respect to Case No. 3 that they had gained something real simply by asserting their power in the elections. Legal process, combined with the electoral process, had empowered them in some way. There may even have been actual practical benefits in the form of more access to benefits administered by the *panchayat*, although these were not specifically enumerated for us. But it may be sufficient to say that, without winning the case, they had gained something from the battle.

We were also told with enthusiasm of a number of additional cases the *Jatavs* would like to pursue if only the money to do so were available. The cases were of three types, although all of them involve programs that are administered by the *panchayat*. The first and most important type of case involved, like the first two case studies presented above, control by the *panchayat* over use, allocation, and distribution of village land to lower *jatis*. The second concerned other government benefits, usually in cash but sometimes in the form of food, controlled by the *panchayat* and earmarked for the lower *jatis*. These ranged from the failure of the *pradhan* to release funds that were supposed to be distributed to scheduled caste widows, to allegations that free wheat for the poor had been expropriated by *Thakur* members of the *panchayat*. The third type, not surprisingly, concerned who got to sit on the *panchayat* (each village election seemed to involve an appeal). Failure to bring these cases so far, we were told, had nothing to do with a lack of *vishwas* (trust) in the courts, but a simple lack of money.

Such views were offered along with frank acknowledgement of the many inadequacies of the legal system. We were given detailed complaints about the poor quality of lawyers, the length of legal proceedings and the difficulty of enforcing judgments. But at the same time, we were told that such problems were not sufficient to warrant abandoning appeals to outside forums. For example, the substantial delays involved in litigation, plus the necessity of repeatedly travelling to court over long periods of time, did not seem to bother the members of the committee in Case No. 3. Because of cooperation among members of the committee, and because of the high level of underemployment, finding someone who could take the time to travel to court was not seen as too much of a burden. It was generally viewed that the greater burden would be born by the defendant, who would not only lose time but prestige in being repeatedly dragged to court by a member of a lower *jati*. When we asked about the problem of delay, the committee members noted that this was annoying, but not enough to prevent them from fighting the case. Once again, members noted that dragging the defendants into court was part of the battle. "It gives us some power over them."

Such balanced and realistic appraisals of legal processes underscores the surprising depth of the knowledge achieved by the *Jatavs* of law and courts. They understand the benefits of appealing to the legal system in certain specific situations, and yet they know how limited those benefits are likely to be. They appear to know what soft spots in the hierarchy can be used to their advantage, what pressure points will set off unpleasant reactions, what solutions will cause what new problems. Clearly, not all scheduled caste *jatis* in Kisanpur match the relative sophistication of the *Jatavs* in these matters. Nevertheless, one of the more striking aspects of life in Kisanpur is the extent to which the poor are aware of their legal rights and privileges. Such legal knowledge is due in great part to the increasing presence of lower *jatis* in legal and bureaucratic professions (a presence brought about in part by reservation policies) and the nature of *jati* communication. While this was clear primarily in the case of the *Jatavs*, the information provided by *Jatav* lawyers from outside the village has been communicated among all lower *jatis*. Scheduled caste leaders were also aware of the importance of courts in village land disputes; we often heard stories concerning legal battles among the upper *jatis* from lower-*jati* faction members.

Indeed, the notion expressed by some that the Indian legal system is alien, inscrutable and mysterious to the rural poor must be discarded, or at least regionally confined. To the extent that it is a puzzle to the Indian peasant, it partakes of the universal characteristics of legal systems throughout the world. A tendency to be put off by the complexity of a system is *not* evidence of the inability of one culture to function within the confines of imported institutions. It is merely evidence of a tendency to be put off by complexity. Without exception, every one of our respondents knew someone who had been involved in the system and who could be relied upon to provide the type of information and informal assessment of a particular case necessary to get started.

However, the cases described above also expose the inevitable commingling of law and village politics in Kisanpur. Looking for help from an outside authority is not enough to remove the case from the purview of local power struggles and the continuing vulnerability of the scheduled castes to upper caste pressure. For example, bringing the case in the first instant was perceived as requiring the enlistment of some support among one of the prominent *Thakur* factions, and the promise of political support to its candidate. This need to rely upon the opportunistic indulgence of *Thakur* leaders gave rise to skepticism about the final effects of a positive judgment. One *Jatav* stated that "the new president is going along with [the Court petition] because it is harassing a member of the opposing faction. But if anything ever comes of it, then the facts will disappear and the *Thakurs* will stand together against the scheduled castes."

The fact is that the coercive power of outside courts themselves can be greatly attenuated in the village setting. Assuming for the moment that a poor litigant can expect to win judgments in court if his statutory or constitutional rights are being trampled by local elites or local officials of the state, what solace is there in victory? The distance between court and village can be a great one, both physically and psychologically. A winner in court must often return to a setting where the coercive power of village elites is greater than the strength of a court writ, and where the police are unwilling or unable to help. This perceived irrelevance of having one's rights vindicated in court has led many social activists to the conclusion that pursuing a legal strategy is at best a waste of time, and at worst, a cooption by a corrupt and slow behemoth, lulling the poor to sleep with false promises. Certainly Kisanpur suggests that the attempt to vindicate certain rights in court will not necessarily turn those rights into a reality.

It must be admitted that the vigorous pursuit of legal rights in Kisanpur remains a risky and dangerous proposition. As long as the upper *jatis* continue to control socially, economically, and often numerically, there will be a limit to their tolerance for change. Thomas Sowell's argument about how American affirmative action laws have created greater antagonism toward the disadvantaged among the advantaged[29] has proven itself true in India time and again; legal benefits provided for the have-nots can often result in a revolt by the haves. The caste riots in a number of states, particularly in this era of the Mandal Commission report, have been in large part reactions by upper-*jatis* against what they see as overly preferential treatment, enacted by the state and enforced through the legal system, for lower *jatis*.

Thus, one's relative enthusiasm for the use of outside forums is in part a factor of one's sense of vulnerability. Different communities among the scheduled castes apparently perceived this vulnerability differently. Unlike the scheduled caste members who live in the heart of the village, the *Jatav* residents of a separate colony near the entrance to the village proper reacted negatively to the idea of using legal strategies. They were, they said, too vulnerable to physical attack; prosecuting cases would incite violence against them.

Furthermore, any appraisal of the use of courts by the poor must take into account the relationship of the scheduled castes and the larger community with the Indian police, as the supposed enforcers of legal judgments. It must also take into account that the Indian police are noted primarily for their high level of corruption, their use of impermissible force, and their repeated violations of civil and human rights. The alleged corruption of many members of the police, and

---

[29] T. Sowell, *Civil Rights: Rhetoric or Reality* (New York, 1984), p. 90.

often their simple physical inability to control or coerce powerful lawbreakers, greatly affect the practical importance of court decrees. Victories to the landless in court may result only in further violence against them at home.

Still, while there is a strong basis for pessimism about the direct effect legal action might have on village patterns of domination, the Kisanpur example suggests that this pessimism should not be overdrawn. One conclusion we can draw from the Kisanpur example is that the meaningfulness of legal action by the lower *jatis* cannot be measured strictly in terms of winning in court or getting a victory enforced. As we have noted, scholars have long observed that court settlements are seldom considered a full resolution of the underlying dispute by village litigants, even when (as is the case in most village lawsuits) the dispute is between members of the same *jati*. Instead, appeal to the legal system is often viewed as an elaborate method of increasing one's bargaining position in the local arena. In this sense, greater access to courts for the lower jatis at the very least gives them a tool by which they can more effectively play the game of village politics.

We have presented a somewhat detailed discussion of attitudes toward legal process among the poor of Kisanpur because it is in this realm that we found the most articulate descriptions of the meaning of law in the village. Process by its nature involves dealing with the practical and the day-to-day. But discussions of process not only give us access to ideas about outside forums, lawyers, police and the efficacy of judgments. They also provide clues as to the relative importance of various substantive provisions of law in the minds of our respondents.

For example, it is instructive to note the types of legal rights that were and weren't implicated either in the context of actual cases or in the context of describing cases that would be desirable to fight if the resources were available. The discussions reveal a strong emphasis on government distribution programs that are supposed to be administered by the *panchayat*. Thus, the situations most frequently cited had to do with the improper siphoning off of benefits earmarked for the scheduled castes by the *pradhan*, the ex-*pradhan*, or their cronies. The *Jatavs* in particular could describe in great detail laws pertaining to the distribution of land rendered excess by land consolidation, the distribution of pension money for scheduled caste widows, the obligations of the *panchayat* with respect to common lands, the obligation of the *pradhan* with respect to the use of rural development funds such as the Jawahar Scheme, etc. Not only was knowledge of the law most detailed in these areas, it was here that the admittedly fragile aspirations of the scheduled castes were focussed with respect to the possible vindication of their rights through outside legal processes.

By way of contrast, it is interesting to note what types of legal rights are treated with less enthusiasm, either because the possibility of realizing them seems too remote, or because such rights for one reason or another have not been conceptualized as "legal." In the latter category falls a whole range of laws designed to provide economic resources to the poor such as concessional agricultural loans, loans or grants for small-scale businesses, and similar programs. Again, knowledge of the existence of such programs and the benefits they could provide was quite high. But so was knowledge of the obstacles that stood in the way of taking advantage of these programs—numerous stories were recounted to us of demands for bribes by officials in rural development institutions and other forms of corrupt behavior that often discouraged the scheduled castes from participating in these programs. But interestingly enough, the corruption of officials, as opposed to the malpractices of fellow villagers, was not seen as a phenomenon where appeals to courts or other forms of outside authority might help. It is difficult to explain this difference in perception—perhaps the blurring of legal process with village politics described above has fostered the perception that such activity has no real meaning *outside* the context of political life.

There was also little enthusiasm among the scheduled castes about trying to vindicate their rights under the classic statutes designed to attack directly the evils of caste discrimination; enactments, for example, such as the Protection of Civil Rights Act and temple-entry legislation. Here, the Kisanpur scheduled castes echoed the sentiments of Khosla's respondents with remarkable faithfulness. While generally knowledgeable about the PCRA, and supportive of its goals, our scheduled caste respondents felt that invoking it would only exacerbate tensions between upper and lower castes and do nothing to change behavior and attitudes. But perhaps more importantly, whatever the continuing indignities of the caste system, there was a perception among the lower castes that the way to escape those indignities was to pursue economic betterment and the self-respect that comes from a modicum of financial independence. Given that perception, to focus directly on such problems as untouchability or entry to village temples was a waste of time and resources and disruptive to the political give-and-take that is the key to securing improvements in the life of the community.

Law as Ideology and Law as Silence

When we move beyond the realm of law as a concrete process, meanings become more elusive. In a number of contexts, scholars have alluded to the symbolic power of law, particularly in situations where the direct consequences of an enactment have been minimal. Thus, P. C. Joshi[30] in his study of land reform legislation notes that most appraisals of the legislation focus only on the successful resistance by landowners, and the subversion of the goals of the act.

---

[30] P. C. Joshi, *Land Reform in India: Trends and Perspectives* (Bombay, 1975), p. 92.

Such appraisals fail to take into account the fact that the passage of such policies, however dismal their implementation has led to a "growing awareness of the deprived sections." Similarly, Barbara Joshi[31] argues that the egalitarian social policies of the state have a force of their own, independent of the reluctance and weak personal commitment of state actors to these policies. People find meanings in the words of such policies. They play a role in the creation of solidarity around a cause, they lend legitimacy to a struggle and they help in the establishment of self-identity.

Of course, such alleged power of legal pronouncements is notoriously difficult to prove, or "to disentangle from the plethora of surrounding variables."[32] The Protection of Civil Rights Act may have had a powerful emotive effect on the self-perception of former "untouchables," but how do we distinguish this from the effect, say, of the teachings of Gandhi and other reformers, or of the establishment of democracy, or the widening of economic opportunities beyond the village or of modern education? In the context of Kisanpur, all we can really do is point to the language used by the villagers to suggest that legal ideology among other influences has played a role. Complaints by the scheduled castes about their lot in life are peppered with references to constitutional and statutory rights. There may be accompanying cynical expressions about such rights "not being worth the paper they are printed on"; one Jatav spokesman told us that the Constitution had been written by Dr. Ambedkar, but had subsequently been appropriated by the rich and the mighty and used for their purposes only. "It belongs to the Thakurs now," he said. But the fact remains that to bolster their arguments, the scheduled castes draw heavily from these sources.

Pauline Kolenda[33] has recently described her attempts to discover how attitudes toward caste have changed in a village in Western Uttar Pradesh in which she had first worked nearly 30 years ago. Kolenda found that at least among younger, educated segments of the village, attitudes have changed considerably regarding the origins, justifications and desirability of the *jati* system. Education, politics, the increasing interaction of the village with urban centers where *jati* distinctions are less pronounced, and the promulgation of egalitarian state policies, have all contributed to what Kolenda calls a "new ideology" among younger villagers that *jati* is not a good system. The ideology may at best have been only partially internalized by those that profess to follow it,

---

[31] B. Joshi, "Whose Law, Whose Order: 'Untouchables,' Social Violence and the State in India." *Asian Survey*, vol. 22, page 678 (1982).

[32] U. Baxi, *Toward a Sociology of Indian Law* (New Delhi, 1986), p. 72.

[33] P. Kolenda, "Micro-Ideology and Micro-Utopia in Khalapur: Changes in the Discourse on Caste over 30 Years." *Economic and Political Weekly*, Vol. XXIV, No. 32 (August 12, 1989), p. 1831.

Law and Meaningfulness

but it is significant that to hold such opinions is considered the "correct" thing to do.

Without historical data like that used by Kolenda, we cannot state with certainty whether attitudinal change in Kisanpur has followed the same course. However, like Kolenda, we also discovered that at least at a high level of generality, it was considered correct among the younger, more outward looking and better educated sections in all *jatis* to say that the *jati* system is bad. Of course, such opinions coexist with day to day practices that perpetuate the injustices of the system. *Thakur* respondents may in one breath explain that untouchability has been abolished by law and by the teachings of Mahatma Gandhi; they may in the next defend attacking a *Jatav barat* moving through a *Thakur* part of town, or explain that *Jatavs* are not allowed in the new temple. But the new ideology has had the effect of prompting many such persons to construct new justifications for their actions. Thus we find in the *barat* example presented at the beginning of this paper, that a spurious argument about private property rights surfaces in the midst of a classic inter-*jati* confrontation. Similarly, exclusion of *Jatavs* from the new temple is defended on the grounds that it is a "private" temple, overlooking the fact that the temple had been constructed on common property near the village school. One suspects that such arguments were not necessary in an era when attitudes toward *jati* as a system were not marked by the degree of ambivalence that is present today.

The ambivalence, to be sure, should not be overstated. There are still strong sentiments openly expressed by some among the upper castes in Kisanpur that *jati* hierarchy is a good thing and that modern attempts to weaken it through law are either irrelevant or pernicious. Respondents in the village were generally aware that efforts had been made in the constitution and in statutes to promote equality and to eradicate such practices as untouchability and the prevention of temple entry. We tried to get people to reflect upon what such measures meant for the continued validity of the *jati* system. As with Khosla's respondents, there was little recognition among the upper castes that such laws had any direct relevance. As was stated to us several times by *Thakur* interviewees, such laws and "village law" are "*alug-alug*" (separate). State efforts to address these practices may apply outside the village, but they stop at the border. An interesting wrinkle appeared in the form of answers relating to reservations. Several *Thakurs* made the point that how could one say that the Constitution had made all *jatis* equal when the government, in promulgating reservations policies, was in fact emphasizing the inequality of *jatis*? It is also interesting to note that most respondents attributed the existence of the *jati* system to "*samaj*" (society) and not to religion. Frequently, reference might be made initially to the four parts of the body of God in the *Vedas*, but even in such instances, the modern form of the system was attributed to societal norms. Nothing in religion says that a

Bagaili is higher than a *Dhobi*, one *Thakur* pointed out. The origin of this ranking lies in tradition.

Finally, law has meaning as silence, where, echoing Khosla, it stops at "the boundaries of the village." In Kisanpur, as elsewhere, law has had the least visible impact in areas of domestic relations, where villagers tend to see traditional arrangements as beyond the pale of the law. Indeed, our respondents seemed either utterly unaware of most family law legislation, or, in the case of particularly famous legislation such as the anti-dowry statute, simply feel that it is irrelevant. Especially among the higher *jatis*, there is some sentiment that dowry is a bad thing, and perhaps to some extent the passage of the dowry legislation has had an educative effect in the emergence of this attitude. More likely is that those voicing anti-dowry opinions have observed what rapidly escalating prices can do to the economic well being of a family, perhaps their own. In any case, the notion that law could put a stop to the practice was viewed with derision by our respondents. Judges themselves ask for dowry for their sons, said one *Thakur*.

Similarly, the fact that law allows inter-*jati* marriage is deemed to be perhaps fine outside the village context, but again, simply pointless in the village. One might contenance such intermingling of the castes in a court marriage in the city, but it is wrong to expect that such a marriage would be accepted were the couple to try to return to the village. State law, we were told, is for the city, not the village. The village was recently scandalized by the marriage of the youngest son of the *pradhan* to a *Dhobi* girl in the city of Aligarh. *Thakurs* stated that the girl would never be fully accepted into village life, although they admitted that a family as influential and well-connected as the *pradhan*'s could violate such laws without real sanction.

By contrast, the ultimate sanction was adopted in an inter-*jati* marriage recently in a village in nearby Mathura district. In that incident, a *Jat* girl was "married" to two *Jatav* boys. The dominant *Jat* community *panchayat* allegedly condemned the three to death for violating the norms of the village and the *Jat* caste, and executed this sentence by burning them alive. When this story was related to villagers from each of the major *jatis* in Kisanpur, there was an almost uniform response that it was entirely proper for a community to punish those who transgress traditional laws regarding such matters as marriage. Repeatedly, reference was made to the possibility that a curse would fall upon the village otherwise. This response was ironically strongest among the scheduled castes, presented vehemently by some of those who previously had lectured us on the injustices of the *jati* system and the lack of justification for that system in either state or religious law. Opinions varied about whether the severity of the punishment was excessive or not. Some felt that in Kisanpur such an incident would be dealt with through social boycott rather than violence. Again, perhaps the most startling response was from the *Jatavs*, who told us that killing might be justified in such a situation, so long as both upper *jati* and lower *jati* participants were punished in the same manner. That being the case in the Mathura incident, they had no objection to the deaths.

Can we characterize these attitudes as an instance of the simple rejection of state law in favor of local "religious" law? One might have expected these attitudes to be justified by reference to religious tenets, whether folk or brahmanical, and whether clearly or vaguely understood. Interestingly, none of our respondents adopted such a rationale. Repeatedly, we were told that the strict rules concerning marriage or other family matters were not derived from God but were laws developed by society. Nothing in religion compelled the adoption of such laws, we were told. Nevertheless, it is interesting to note, first, that the allegedly "secular" origins of such laws has done nothing to diminish their power, and secondly, even if developed by society over the ages rather than ordained by God, violations of these rules are often seen as subject to supernatural consequences, such as curses.

Conclusion

We have attempted to show in the above discussion how law has meaning for the inhabitants of Kisanpur both as a process and as ideology, and both with respect to those parts of law that are accepted and those that are ignored. The portrait that emerges is admittedly an impressionistic one; to an extent it evades the daunting task of weighing the relative importance of such meanings against other influences on village life. But it is useful to remember how attenuated the connection is, even in western societies, between legal processes and meanings on the one hand, and, on the other, the web of relationships that constitute everyday life. As Stewart Macauley puts it:

> We are all subject to many private governments where the influence of the legal system is problematic. Long term continuing relationships have their own norms and sanctions, often far more powerful than anything the legal system has to offer. [However], sometimes individuals and groups seek to affect the balance of power within these private governments by appeal to courts, administrative agencies and legislatures.[34]

If such difficulties exist in evaluating legal systems in western liberal democratic societies, then to pinpoint the precise effect legal processes have on social relations in Kisanpur poses insurmountable challenges. But the fact

---

[34] S. Macauley, "Law and the Behavioral Sciences: Is There Any There There?" *Law and Policy*, Vol. 6, (1984), p. 148.

remains that such processes are an established part of village life. They are perceived as meaningful to the people who use them as being one way to affect the balance of local power, however disfunctional or pathological they may appear in operation. Similarly, the stories told to us by by the inhabitants of Kisanpur suggest that law has an elliptical meaningfulness in their lives not necessarily related to the "success" of law in a strictly instrumental sense. Much of the meaningfulness of social legislation in Kisanpur lies in the ways—often distorted, exaggerated or contradictory—in which the language of law enters into local discourse and percolates into local ideologies.

Index of Cases

A.S.E. Trust v. Director, Education 77
Abdul Husain v. Shamsul Huda 258
Abdul Jabiy v. State of U.P. 137
Adelaide Company v. Commonwealth 271
Ahmedalli Mohammad Hanif Makandar v. Rabiya 114
Ambika Sharan Singh v. Mahant Mahadevanand 257
Anbalagan v. Devarajan 419
Arya Samaj Education Trust v. The Director of Education 86
Asbestos Cement Ltd. v. Sawarkar 139
Avadhani v. Religious Endowments Board 350

B. Mokhtar Pasha v. The General Manager, Personnel and Administration, Bharat Heavy Electricals Ltd. 141
Bali Tahira v. Ali Fissali 318
Bechi v. Ahsan-ullah Khan 135
Bihar State Board of Religious Trust v. Biseshwar Das 451-2
Bihar State Board of Religious Trusts v. Ramsubaran Das 464
Bijore Emmanuel v. State of Kerala 124, 380
Biju Uthup v. Fr. George Manjunkal 239-41
Bira Kishore Deb v. State of Orissa 26

Chandanwal Chopra v. State of West Bengal 133
Comm. H.R.E. v. L.T. Swamiar 271
Commissioner for Hindu Religious and Charitable Endowments, Mysore v. Ratnavarma Heggade 83
Commissioner of Wealth Tax v. Abdul H.M.M. Ali 242
Commissioner, Hindu Religious Endowments,

Madras v. Sirur Mutt 25-6, 366, 369, 377

D.A.V. College, Batinda v. State of Punjab 77
Damodar Tatyaba v. Vamanrao Mahadik 264
Davis v. Benson 25, 45
Deoki v. Murlidhar 451
Dharamapuram Pandarasannadhi v. Virapandian 354
Domino's Pizza v. Praabhjot S. Kholi 198 n
Durgah Committee v. Hussain Ali 31

Ebrahim Sulaiman Sait v. M.C. Mohammad 261

Fowler v. Rhode Island 271
Fuzlunbi v. Khader Vali 107

G.S. Mahalaxmi v. Shah Ranchhoddas 451
Ganpar v. Returning Officer 82
Gogireddi Sambireddy v. Gogireddi Jayamma 76, 217, 224
Goka Ramalingam v. Boddu Abraham 412-13
Goli Eswariah v. Commissioner of Gift Tax 241
Gopal Narhar Safray v. Hanumant Ganesh Safray 75
Gopalakrishnan v. State of Maharashtra 418-19
Gouri v. Niader 356
Guntur Medical College v. Mohan Rao 417
Guramma v. Mallappa 75-6
Gurdial Kaur v. Manghal Singh 222

Haji Mohammad Sayeed and others v. Abdul Ghafoor and others 140

Harcharan Singh v. *S. Sajjan Singh* 263
Hari Singh v. *Popatlal* 261
Haribhanu Maharaj, Baroda v. *Charity Commissioner, Ahmedabad* 463
Hiralal Mallick v. *State of Bihar* 367

Jagdev Sidhanti v. *Pratap Singh* 256
Jagdishwaranand v. *Police Commissioner, Calcutta* 410
Jasani v. *Parashram* 413-14
Jiwan Khan and others v. *Habib and others* 135
Joshua v. *Geevarghese Mar Diocorus* 240

Khizer Basha v. *Indian Airlines Corporates* 212
Krishna Singh v. *Mathura Ahir* 350, 354-7, 359
Krishnaji v. *Hanmaraddi* 354
Kultar Singh v. *Mukhtiar Singh* 256

Laxmi Raman v. *Chandan Singh* 261-2

M. Giasuddin v. *State of A.P.* 368, 377
M. Peeran Saheb v. *Special Officer, Punganur Municipality* 143
M.H. Quareshi v. *State of Bihar* 30, 379
M.K. Stremann v. *Commissioner of Income Tax* 242
Madhab Chandra Bandopadhya and others v. *State of West Bengal* 84, 85
Maneka Gandhi v. *Indira Gandhi* 238
Masud Alam and others v. *Commissioner of Police and others* 127
Michael v. *Venkateswaran* 122, 411-12
Mohammad Ali Khan v. *Zucknow Municipality* 138, 139
Mohammed Ahmed Khan v. *Shah Bano Begum* 115, 208, 318
Mohammad Sayeed and others v. *Abdul Ghafoor and others* 140
Mohammed Siddiqui v. *State of Uttar Pradesh* 396
Mohd. Fasi v. *Superintendent of Police, Alleppy and others* 141

Mohd. Wasi and others v. *Bachchan Sahib and others* 140
Moonshee Buzloor Ruheem v. *Shumsoonnissa Begum* 216

N.K. Sikdar v. *Chief Election Officer* 142
Narantakath Avullah v. *Parakkal Mammu and others* 135, 197, 199
Narsu Appa and Emperor v. *Kalidas Amtharam* 311
Ningol Angothi v. *Nangmaijing Sharma* 355

Ontario Human Rights Commission and Harbhajan Singh Pandori v. *Peel Board of Education* 195

Panachand Gandhi v. *State of Bombay* 26, 366, 378
Pandit Parma Nand v. *Nihat Chand* 356
Pathanamthitta Majilissae Islamia v. *Nagoor Meeran Sheik Muhammad* 126
Peeran Saheb v. *Special Officer, Punganur Municipality* 224
Perumal Nadar v. *Ponnuswami* 417
Presbyterian Church in the United States v. *Mary Elizabeth Blue Hull Memorial Presbyterian Church* 241
Profulla Chorone v. *Satya Choron* 451
Public Prosecutor v. *Ramaswami* 396, 399
Punjabrao v. *Meshram* 408, 414-15

R.C. Cooper v. *Union of India* 262
Radhakanta Deb v. *Commr. Hindu Religious Endowmetns, Orissa* 450-1, 463
Rajagopal v. *Aurumugham* 410-11
Raman Bhai v. *Dabhi* 254
Rangachariar v. *Yegna Dikshatur* 357
Ratilal v. *State of Bombay* 395, 396, 398
Rev. Stanlislaus v. *M.P.* 397, 399
Rosanna v. *Subanna* 355

S.P. Mittal v. *Union of India* 408-9
Saifuddin Saheb v. *Sate of Bombay* 28, 136, 312

Index of Cases

Sangannagouda v. *Kalkangouda* 75
Sankarakinga Nadam v. *Raja Rajeswara Dorai* 32-3
Sardar Syedna Taher Saifuddin Saheb v. *State of Bombay* 136, 224, 240
Sastri Yagnapurushadji v. *Muldas Bhudardas Vaishya* 376, 377
School District of Abington Town v. *Edward Lewis* 42
Seshammal and others v. *State of Tamil Nadu* 366
Shihabuddin v. *K.P. Ahammed* 123
Shri Govindlalji v. *State of Rajasthan* 272, 366
Shri Ram Kishan Mission v. *Dogar Singh* 447
Shubh Nath v. *Ram Narain* 252
Shuganchand v. *Prakash Chand* 76
Shyamsunder v. *Shankar Deo* 76-7
Srinivasa Aiyar v. *Saraswathi Ammal* 224
State of Bihar v. *Zuberi* 343
State of Bombay v. *Narasu Appa Mali* 215, 217, 218, 219, 220, 222, 223, 310

Sudha v. *Sankappa Rai* 223
Sughani v. *Nawab* 355
Syedna Taher Saifuddin v. *Tyabbhai Mousaji* 311

Teeluch Chunder v. *Shyamachurn* 356
Tejraj v. *State of Madhya Bharat* 140
Tirkangauda Mallangauda v. *Shivappa Patel* 75

Venkataraman Devaru v. *State of Mysore* 32
Venkata Subbiah v. *Bhujangayya* 355

Wealth-tax Comm. Bhopal v. *Abhdul Hssain Mulla Muhammad Ali* 203

Yagnapurushdasji v. *Muldas* 31, 59, 77, 78, 79, 83, 273, 366, 376, 377, 441

Z.B. Bukhari v. *Brij Mohan Mehra* 259
Zohara Khatoon v. *Mohammad Ibrahim* 107

Index

Adi Granth 169
adivasi 252, 254
adoption 61, 75, 76, 162, 207, 217, 236, 303, 313, 315, 327, 328, 329, 344, 356
Adoption Bill 237, 315-16
advaita 79, 84
Advisory Committee on Minorities and Fundamental Rights 384
agamas 27
ahimsa 65
Ahmadiya 124, 125, 140, 142
Ahmed Khan, Shah Bano and Supreme Court 151-2
Akal Takht, Ranjit Singh and excommunication 200
Akali Dal 172, *see also* Tat Khalsa; and gurdwara reform movement 174; and Nehru 183; and SGPC and Malcolm Hailey's positive steps 173; its leader Prakash Singh Badal 182, 189; Master Tara Singh as its leader 183
Akalis denounciation of Indian Constitution 180
Ali, Fazal, Justice 318
Ambedkar, B.R. 15; and untouchability 298; as Union Law Minister 303; on Hindu Code and Uniform Civil Code 305-7; on Hinduism and Islam in India 43; on Hinduism or Hindu society 408; on right to profess, preach and convert 383; on Uniform Civil Code 288-9
Amendment Act (1994) 178
Anand Marga cult and Supreme Court judgement 83
Anand Margis, garland of human skills and Supreme Court 46
Anand Marriage Act (1908) 171

Anglo-Hindu case law 231-2, 236
Anthony, F.R. and Munshi on conversion 384-5
anti-*sati* legislation 209
Anti Untouchability Act 309
apastamba 471
archaka 27-8
Archeological Sites and Remains Act (1958) 139
Article 1 37
Article 8 (renumbered as Article 14) 293
Article 13 (renumbered as Article 19) 13; and Fundamental Rights 283-4, 290
Article 13(1) 217, 218
Article 13(3)(a) 219
Article 14 63, 65, 220, 221, 222, 293, 310, 321
Articles 14 and 15 221-2
Articles 14 and 15(1) 310
Articles 14, 17 and 25 65
Article 15 (renumbered as Article 21) 293
Article 15 402
Article 15(1) 402
Article 16(4) and backward classes reservation 15
Article 17 197-8
Article 17 and abolishing of untouchability 15
Article 19(2)(a) 296-7
Article 19 (renumbered as Article 25) 297
Article 22(1) 299
Articles 23-24 301
Article 25(2) 61
Article 25(2)(b) 69-70
Article 25 and freedom of religion 181; freedom of conscience and free profession 284

Article 25(1) 61
Article 25(2) 64
Article 25(2)(a) 311
Article 25(2)(b) 33, 34
Articles 25 and 26 43-7, 139, 221, 224, 361 & *n*; and religious freedom and restriction 17-18
Articles 25-28 and right to freedom of religion 283
Article 26 43, 45, 46, 136, 139, 221, 224, 227, 270, 272, 285, 311, 361, 364, 365, 368, 372, 375, 380, 393, 395, 431
Article 26(b) 27, 33, 312
Article 27 47-8, 285
Article 28 48, 285
Article 29 224
Articles 29 and 30 48, 285
Article 30 47, 229
Article 30(1) 84
Article 31A 139
Article 35 (renumbered as Article 44) 285, 289; and Muslim members of Constituent Assembly members opposition to 286-7
Article 36 286
Article 372(1) 216
Article 372(3) 216
Article 39 (renumbered as Article 48) 289-90
Article 44 (Article 35 of the Draft Commission and personal law) 19-20
Article 44 224, 243; of Directive Principles of State Policy 106, 218-19; on Uniform Civil Code 20
Arunachal Pradesh Freedom of Indigenous Faith Bill renamed as Freedom of Religion Act 390
Arunachal Pradesh Freedom of Religion Act 382
Arya Samaj 212; against caste by birth 77
Arya Samaj movement 47
Ascetics and renunciants 356-9
asrams or monasteries 55
Aurobindo, Sri (1872-1950) 363; as religious teacher 374, 409
Aurobindoism 374, 378, 408
Auroville (Emergency Provisions) Act (1980) 361; and violation of Articles 25 and 26 364
Auroville conflict 47, 363-75
Auroville project as 'International cultural township' and UNESCO 363, 368; as secular undertakings 375

Babar 116, 117, 131, 154
Babri Masjid-Ramjanmabhoomi controversy 91-2 *n*
Backward Classes Commission, Report of 90-2
Backward Communities (Religious Protection) Bill 392
Baird, Robert D. 59, 161, 362, 375
Bakr Id day and cow sacrifice 30-1
Banatwalla, G.M. 393-4
Banerjee on conversions 393
Bengal as creature of colonial power 269
Bengal Regulations of 1781 215
Bentham, founder of British Utilitarian movement 61; Mill and Locke 66-7
Bhagavadgita 11, 53; its moral explanation of caste 54
Bhagwati, Chief Justice 469
"bhakti Hinduism" 73
Bhrigu, sage 9
Bihar Trust Act 449-50
Biju Uthup case 244
Bharatiya Janata Party (BJP) 212; and election propaganda 264-5
"Blind Darkness" 13
Boards of Revenue 457
Bombay Prohibition of Devadasi Dedication Act (1934) 333, 340
Bombay Excommunication Act (BEA) 136, 311
Bombay Hindu Places of Public Worship (Entry Authorization) Act (1956) 31, 77-8
Bombay Prevention of Excommunication Act (1949) and Articles 25 and 26 28

Index

Bombay Public Trusts Act (1950) 395, 448
brahmana 10, 89, 259, 329, 334, 335, 336, 337, 426, 430, 435, 463
brāhmaṇas 472, 473, 474, 477; *karma* and rebirth 13
Brahmasabha 476-7
bride price 151, 158, 320
British Columbia, Sikh communities in 193
Buddha 66, 80, 85, 435, 441
Buddhism 12, 80, 97, 372, 432, 441
Buddhist, Jain, and Sikhs as Hindus 402-3

Canada, and Ishar Singh case 193-4; Karnail Singh Bhinder and turban wearing case 194; Sikh cases in 193-9
Canadian Human Rights Act and Sikhs 193
caste 3, 503; as classification of persons 63; kinds of view 96; meaning of 405; system in Hinduism and Ambedkar 401; Western perceptions of 421
Caste Disabilities Act (1850) and Bengal Code 29
Central Bureau of Investigation 364
Central Endowment Regulations (1810-1920) 456-9
Chagla, Chief Justice 217, 219, 220, 310, 311, 395
Chief Khalsa Divan (CKD) 170-2
child marriage, Bagawati on 43
Chisti, Moinuddin saint shrine, Ajmer 138
Christianity 82, 84, 295, 328, 372, 379, 387, 392, 432, 435, 436
Christian(s) 11, 14, 32; and bigamy 223; Parsis and Uniform Civil Code 163
Church and the State and Article 27 47-8
citta or mind 63, *see also manas*
Civil Code Bill 22
civil law 20
communal riots 246
communal violence in India, theories of 248-9
Communalism 103
Constitution makers and freedom of religion 43
Constitution (42nd Amendment) Act 1976)

and word "secular" inclusion of 37
Constitution of India 3-4, 7-8, 14-19; and egalitarian presuppositions 59-64; and freedom of religion 29; and *guna* theory 60; and *karma* and *guna* theory 51; and kinds of promises 284; and Personal Law 213-25; and religious freedom 17; and secularism 36, 121; as modern human rights document 15; equality in 283; religion and state 41-2; v. *Manusmriti* 15-19
constitutional vision, inadequacy of 270-1;
Contract Act 211
conversion 4, 140, 213, 315, 381, 383, 384, 385, 386, 388, 389, 390, 391, 392, 394, 395, 396, 440; and Constituent Assembly Debate 303, 321, 325-6, 382-8; and Lok Sabha 392; and the courts 394-8; and the courts 410-19; Hindu resistance to 381
"corrupt practice" 251, 264
Criminal Procedure Code (1973) 317
Criminal Procedure Code (1898) 317

Dalal Bill 188
Dalal draft and "Central Religious Body" 188, 190
dana 443-5, 446, *see also* endowments
dar al-amn 121, 122
dar al-harb 121, 122
dar al-Islam 121, 122
Darbar Sahib 174
Dawoodi Bohra Community and religious excommunication 28-9
Dayabhaga school 20
Dayanand Saraswati 47
De, Krishna Prasad on Constitution and freedom of religion 51-2
Delhi riots 247
Delhi Sikh Gurdwara Act (Act 82 of 1971) 183
Derrett, J.D.M., Hindu Code and Uniform Civil Code 22
Deshmukh Bill 270
desocialization 278

devadasi 4, 5, 325-44; and British Indian government 328-30; and caste exploitation 339; and property rights 327; as 'basavis' 337-8; as Hindu priestesses 325; as *nityasumangali* (ever-auspicious women) 325; as prostitutes 325; Bagwati on 43; dedicated to Yellamma 338; economics as reason for dedication as 339-40; her dedication to and religious belief 339; in colonial India 327-33; in independent India 333-44; its customs and court recognition of 327-8; Karnataka government and rehabilitation of 330; known as 326; lack of education as reason for dedication as 340; meaning of 338; translated as "maidservant of the god" 325

Devadasi Reform and Andhra Pradesh 342; and Central Government 328-31; and deprived of religious status 334-6; and local legislatures 331-3; and new reform legislations 336-8; and reform legislation of Karnataka 340-2; and religious freedom 342-4

dharma 53, 54, 55, 101, 348, 349, 369, 387

dharmashastras 55, 212, 236, 358-9, 404-5, 470-1; and kings authority 474

Directive Principles of State Policy, Part IV of Constitution 19, 40, 106, 144, 208, 218, 243, 283, 284, 285, 286, 287, 321, 344

"disciplinarian" (*śāstṛ*) 471

divorce 61, 62, 65, 111, 112, 114, 151, 152, 156, 160, 161, 169, 175, 179, 183, 184, 185, 190, 195, 197, 198, 200, 294, 308, 309, 310, 316, 317, 318, 319, 320

doctrine, development of 250-6

Domino Pizza, Prabhjot Kholi and Maryland Human Relations Commission 198

Durkheim and religion 74-80

Durr-ul-Mukhtar as Urdu version of Quran 143

education, free and compulsory for children 284

election, use of religion in 249
Emergency (1975) 260
endowment regulations 456-66
endowments (*waqf*) 444; private 467; public and private 449-52; use of 108
England and Sikhs as ethnic origins 193; Sikhs in 192-3
excommunication in Encyclopedia of Social Sciences 29-30; practice of 28-30

Family Courts Act 234
faqirs 137
faraiz 132
farida 128
farq 147
farz 132
fatz 122
female renunciation *see* women and renunciation
fiqh 106, 107, 108
freedom of conscience, Article 25
Freedom of Religion Acts 382
freedom of religion as fundamental rights (Article 25) 64
Fundamental Duties 15, 219, 221
fundamentalism *v.* secularism 48

Gajendragadkar, Chagla and Personal Law 220
Gandhi, Indira and Brahmans support 259; assassination of 184
Gandhi, M.K. 39; and Bentham and Mill 66-7; and traditional presuppositions 65; his *harijan* movement 403; theory of 66-7
Gautamadharmasutra 471
Golden Temple Complex, Akali Takht in 175
Golden Temple name in Amritsar massacre 175
Gowda Saraswat Brahman sect 32
"Great Tadition" 60
guna theory 57, 58, 60
Gurdwara, take over issues 201-2
Gurdwaras Act 174, 177; nature of 178; politics of 187

Index

Guru Granth Sahib, Sri 177, 187, 203
Guru tradition 255-6
Gurudwara Election Commission 183

Habermas, Weber, Durkheim and religion 280-2
Haj and Id al-Adha 130-2
haram 143, 144, 145
Harijan Act of Bombay State 311
harijans see untouchables 404
harm, types of 472
hell as process of *karma* and rebirth 13
Hindu 70-1; "tolerance" 429
Hindu Adoption and Maintenance Act 181
Hindu Adoption and Maintenance Act (1956) 70
Hindu Adoption and Maintenance Bill 23
Hindu Bigamous Marriage Act (BGBMA) 310
Hindu Castes and Sects 357
Hindu Ceremonial law 32
Hindu Code (1951) 311
Hindu Code 67, 212, 229, 231, 236, 239, 304, 305, 306, 307, 309, 310
Hindu Code Bill 19, 22-3, 60, 62, 65, 70, 156, 303, 309; Congress government introduction of 303
Hindu Code in 1955-6 229, 231-2, 236, 239
Hindu fundamentalists 116
Hindu Law Committee 22, 24
"Hindu Law" or *dharmashastra* 8, 55, 212, 236, 358, 359, 362, 363
Hindu Maha Sabha 303, 308
Hindu majority 92-3
Hindu Marriage Act (1955) 70, 76, 181
Hindu Marriage Act 316
Hindu Marriage Bill 23
Hindu Minority and Guardianship Act (1956) 70
Hindu Minority and Guardianship Act 181
Hindu Minority and Guardianship Bill 23
Hindu religion 39
Hindu Religious Endowment Commission (HREC), report of 444-5, 456; and courts 462-7

Hindu Succession Act 181
Hindu Succession Bill 23
Hindu Undivided Family (HUF) 130
Hindu, definition of 409-10
Hinduism 229, 442; and ambiguity of 71; and justification of inequality 51; defining as 402; definition of 405, 425-6, 428, 430; ideas of 74; models of 73; religious and legal 69-71, 75-85; religious and legal base Risley's definition of 267
Hindu 44, 70, 71, 73, 75, 78, 83, 85, 92, 93, 98, 124, 154, 229, 256, 292, 425-6, 428; and bigamy 223-4
hindutava 264-5
human sacrifice, Bagawati on 43

Id 126, 139
Id-al-Adha (locally called *Baqrid*) 131
Id-ul-Fitr 129
iddat 151, 158, 317
idgahs 139
iftar 128
Income Tax Act (1961) 449
India as multi-religious pluralist society 37-8; as secular state 69
Indian Adoption Bill 313-15
Indian Converts (Regulation and Registration) Bill 392
Indian Succession Act (ISA) 238, 316
International Convention for the Suppression of Traffic in Women and Girls 320
inequality 10-12
Islam 14, 82, 84, 97, 122, 123, 124, 125, 126, 127, 128, 129, 130, 131, 372, 379, 392, 435, 436, as code of life 122; freedom of private life style and Constitution in 141-4; its beliefs and practices and Indian public law 122-3; mandatory don'ts of 144-6; sectarian beliefs and practices of 134-5
Islamic Guide to Conscience (*shariahi*) 105-6
Islamic Personal Law and Common Civil Code 155

J. Gupta, Das on excommunication 312-13
Jain, Sikhs, and Buddhist as Hindus 402-3
jati system *see* caste
Jehovah's Witness, singing of national anthem and Supreme Court 46
jethedar 175, 190
Jethedar Manjit Singh 202
jnana 57

Kailasa on conversion 396
kaivaliya 57
Kamat, H.V. on minority institutions 301
kamyakarmas 55
Kanwar, Roop and *sati* 319-20, *see also* widow burning
karma and essentials of justice 14; and Patanjali 56; and rebirth 12-14; doctrine of 55; Farquahar, J.N. on 52; *guna* theory, presupposition of 52-9
karma-samsara and equality 59
Kaur, Rajkumari Amrit, Constituent Assembly member 286
Kazis Act (1880) 232
Khalistan 203
Khalsa 169
Khojas ahd Cutchi Memons and minority rights 21
Kisanpur 482-7, cases of 490-4; *jati* structure in 482-3; law as ideology and silence 499-503; law as process 487-90
Kishwar, Madhu, editor of *Manushi* 160
Krishnamachari, T.T. on propagating 388
kshatriya (ruler) 8, 10; and punishment 12

langar case in British Columbia 200
law and religion in ancient India 9-10; in independent India 14-34; study of 3
law, meaning of 24
"law of *karma*" 471
Laws of Manu 8, *see also Manusmriti*
Laxman Maharaj Math 463
Legislation by Parliament 19-24
Literati doctrine, hegemony of 272-3
Locke, John and his theory of human nature

63; his view on equality at birth 63

Madan, T.N. 97, 99, 210
Madholkar, secular and religious matters 255
Madras (Prevention) Act (1947) 340
Madras Hindu Religious Endowments Act (2 of 1927) 83
Madras Prohibition of Devadasi Dedication Act (1947) 333
Madras Temple Entry Authorization Act (1947) 32
madrasahs (theological schools) 109
manas (mind) 55
Mandal Commission recommendations 90-1 *n*
Mandal, B.P. Chairman of Mandal Commission 90
mandir, mosque and politics 116-18
Manu 473-4; and classes 11
Manusmriti and brahmans (priests) 8-10; principles of 8, 9; and justice 10-11; and law of *karma* 12-13
Marx and religion 274-5
Masani, Minoo, Constituent Assembly member 286
maths 443-4, *see also* temple
meat eating 13
Medhatithi 472
Medical Termination of Pregnancy Act (1971) 145
Mehta, Hansa, Constituent Assembly member 286, 292
Michigan, Sikh Centre of 203; Sikhs in 203
Mill's essay on Liberty 62
Mimamsa and Yoga *darshanas* 55
Minority Commission Report 316
Misra, Lokanath on propagation 387; on Sikhs kirpan wearing 296
Mitakshara school 20
Mohani, Maulana Hasrat on Muslim Personal Law 294-5
monism 79-80, 123, 137
mosque, mandir and politics 116-18
mufti 110-12

Index

Muhammad, Hazrat as prophet 124
Mukherjea, B.K. on Freedom of Religion Acts 395-6
Müller, Max 80, 267; on religious Hinduism 407
Munshi, K.M. on Directive Principles and Uniform Civil Code 287-8; on "freedom of conscience" 383-4
Muslim law and divorce 221
Muslim law and marriage 21
Muslim Marriage Act (1939), dissolution of 235-6
Muslim minority 92-3
Muslim Personal Law (Shariat) Application Act (1937) 318
Muslim Personal Law 105 107-10, 115, 118, 119, 120, 121, 122, 150, 151, 155, 158, 162, 259, 287, 288, 314, 318; fundamentals of 295
Muslim Shrines Act 1942 139
Muslim Women's (Protection of Rights on Divorce) Bill 115-16
Muslim Women's (Protection of Rights on Divorce) Bill 1986 and her rights 319
Muslims 235; and bigamy 223; in India 14

namaz, Islamic prayer 125-8, 132, 140, 435
Nandy, Ashis 210
Nehru, Jawaharlal and Gandhi's resolution 67; and secular state 16; as Architect of Modern India 38-9
"neo Hinduism" 73
"New Great Tradition" 34
New York, Sikhs in 196
Nichols, J.J.M. on conversion 385
Nirvachanapaddathi and worship 32
nityakarmas 55
non-Sikh elements 175
North America, and Gurdwara disputes in 204; and Sikh identity in 199

Ohio, and Harjinder Singh guilty of wearing kirpan 198
Om as religious symbol 256

Ontario, and Sikh wearing kirpan 195-6
Oommen, T.K. 210; and religious pluralism 211; on religious reform 212
Operation Blue Star 179, 184
Orissa Freedom of Religion Act 389
Orissa Hindu Religious Endowments Act (1951) 448
Other Backward Classes (OBCs) 90-2, 98-9

panchayat 484, 485, 486, 490, 491, 492, 493, 496, 500
"*Panth*" 257
Parsi Marriage and Divorce Act (1936) 233-4
Parsi Memorial Courts 233-4
Parsis 233-4
Parsis and bigamy 223
Parsi-Zoroastrians and Adoption Bill 315
"*patit*" or fallen Sikh 191
"persistent centrism" and Rudolph 100
personal from cultural, disassociation of 257-66
Personal Law 20; after adoption of Uniform Civil Code 239-41; and Constitution 213-25; and Fundamental Rights 220; and Muslim resistance 20-1; and optional future 236-9; and other bodies relation between 241-7; during British period 213-15; systems 225-39
Peshwas (1750-1818), types of punishments 476
polygamy and Hindus 23
polygamy and Muslims 23
"popular Hinduism" 73
prakrit 57, 59
Prataskar, Law Minister on Indian Succession Act 307-8
pratisiddhakarmas 56
Preamble of Consitution 16, 40, 59-60, 283
Protection of Civil Rights Act 480
Protestants 47
Public Gambling Act (1867) 144
Punjab Gurdwaras Act (1925) 172
purdah, practice of 142-3
puruṣa 59, 60, 61, 63

Qadhi 108
Qadiyani, Mirza Ghulam Ahmad as prophet 124
Quran 108, 114, 131, 132, 133, 140, 141, 142, 143, 213, 215, 318, 320; Islamic scripture 132-4
qurbani (ceremonial slaughter) 131

Race Relations Act (1976) 193
Radhakrishnan, S. and Hinduism as movement 39; and his "The Hindu view of life" 73-4; on secularism 37, 64-5
rajasi 57
Ram Janmabhoomi-Babri Masjid controversy 209
Ramakrishna and "religion universal" 438; as worshipper of Kali 84; became Muslim 435-6; his Christian trance 436-7; his Islamic *sadhana* 435-6; his teachings 84-5; on *sadhana* 434
Ramakrishna cult as religious minority 86
Ramakrishna Mission case and Calcutta High Court 4, 5, 409
Ramakrishnaism 430-4, distinct from Hinduism 432-4
Ramakrishnaites 440-4; as minority 84-6; "world religion" 86
Ramanuja 347-8; renunciation of world 348-9; his cousin Govinda Perumal story 351-2
Ramayana 53; and Sita's purity 53
Rashtriya Swayamsevak Sangh (RSS) 212
Ray, Justice on freedom of conscience 397-8
Reddy, S. Muthulakshmi, India's first female legislator and abolishing of *devadasi* system 331-2
religion and law in ancient India 9-10; in independent India 14-34; definition of 371-2; Supreme Court definition on 25; secularism and Indian Constitution 40-1
religion, conceptualization of 266-8; definition of 266-7; in colonial society 268-70; nature of right to 270-2
"religion" and "secular" 18-19, 25; definition of 380; as superstition 31
Religionssoziologie 274
religious endowments 446-56; freedom and dependency of 268-70; historical benefits of 452-6; symbol and myth, distinction between 252-3; toleration 39-40, 42
Religious Freedom Restoration Act (1994) America 196
renunciation 5; and caste issues 354; and *dharmashastras* 358; and question of authority 355-6; and women 349-54; in Srivaisnava tradition 348; meaning of 350; of women as civil death 350
Representation of Peoples Act (1952) 250-6
Republic Day 26th January, 1950 303
right to practice and propagate religion 44-5
Rigveda 405-6
Roman Catholics 47
roza, Islamic fast 128-30

sahajdhari Sikhs 178
Sahib, Damdama as fifth takht 187
Sahib, Ismail on religious education in State schools 298-30
Sahib, Mohammed Ismail on Uniform Civil Code 290-3, 295
Saivite in Vaishnava Temple 27
Samkhya guna theory 57
samskaras 55-7
sanctum sanctorum entry 27
sankalpa 447
sannyasis (renuncient) 348
"*Sarbat Khalsa*" 190
Sati (Prevention) Act (1987) 320 *see also* Kanwar, Roop
Satsangis 78, *see also* Swaminarayanan sect; as Hindus 81
sattva 57
Saxena and Article 22 299
Scheduled Castes 404, *see also* untouchables 404
secularism, Indian concept of 48-9; meaning of 35-6

Index

"secularization" 326-7
sevapuja, aspects of 26-7
Seventh Schedule to the Constitution 217, 224
Shah Bano Act 236-8
Shah Bano case 4, 5, 46, 113-16, 149-63, 232, 319; and Congress party 157-8; and Indian secularism 161-3; and Rajiv Gandhi's response 160; and views on Supreme Court judgement 156-7, 208; its judgement and government stand 155-6; its judgement and Muslim woman's right to maintenance 244; Muslim reaction to the Supreme Court judgement 152-5; Section 125 of Criminal Procedure Code 158
Shah, K.T., Ambedkar and constitutional amendment 37; on Fundamental Rights 383; on religious education in Schools 300
shahada 122, 123, 124, 132
shariah and *fiqh* and government courts 110-13
Shariat Act (1937) 21, 234-5, 287; and optional features in 237
shrines and mosques 138-41
Shromani Gurdwara Parbandhak Committee (SGPC) 172; and Congress taken control 182
shudra (servant) 10-12; and punishments 12; *karma* and rebirth 14
Sikh as not *kesdhari* 204; identity 204-5
Sikh Gurdwaras and Shrines Act (VI of 1922) 172-3
Sikh Gurdwaras Appellate Judicial Authority 189
Sikh Gurdwaras Tribunal 173, 188,
Sikh identity, renewal of 199
"Sikh *maryada*" 189
Sikh Parliament 189
Sikh Personal Law 184-6
Sikh Rahit Maryada 191-2, 202
Sikh Review, The 186
Sikh Society Working Committee 203
Sikh symbols, protection of 192

Sikh(s) and law in Independent India 179-91; and *nisacha rakhda* (to believe in) 177; and politics 174, and protection of untouchables 179; as global community 167-8; attack on militants in Golden Temple Complex 179; Buddhist and Jain as Hindus 402-3; definition of 176-8; identity 181; its affirmation 173; its castes and reservations 180-1; its identity, politics and law in colonial Punjab 168-9; its marriage ceremony (*anand*) 171; its opposition to Article 25 182; Kashmir Singh on its identity 181; kirpan wearing as religious symbol 181, 185; legal issues, identity and diaspora 191-206; political manifesto and elimination of Hindu status 184; practicing of 5 Ks 171-2; pro-Khalistan or militant Sikhs 192; radical Sikhs uprising and prevention of Maharajah Duleep Singh return to Punjab 169; riots (anti-Sikh) 179, 184; terms of controversy 173
Sikhism as Hindu sect 170; and 'rahit maryada' 171; as separate from Hinduism 176; meaning of *amritdhari* and *patit* in 178; and antagonism towards Hinduism 179; and Sikh Rahit Maryada 185; as a separate religion 181
Singh Sabha movement 170
Singh, Gurmukh and excommunication of 175
Singh, Harnam on freedom to preach 383
Singh, V.P., Prime Minister and Mandal Commission 91
Singhvi, L.M. on Uniform Civil Code 20
Socially and Educationally Backward Classes (SEBCs) 90-2, 98-9
Sociological theory 273-82
Special Marriage Act 1872 238
Special Marriage Act (1954) 238
Special Marriage Act (SMA) 305, 314, 316, 320
Sri Aurobindo Society and Union of India cases 361, 364

Stanislaus, Rev. on registration of conversions 396-7
State Trust and Endowment Acts (1927-present) 459-60
Subramaniam, C. on personal liberty 293
Supreme Court cases 25-34
Supreme Court of India on religion 45-6
Swaminarayanan as God 81
Swaminarayanan sect and claims of non-Hinduism 78-9; Hindu 85

tamas 57
tantra 435
Tamil Nadu Hindu Religious and Charitable Endowments (Amendment) Act (1970) 27
Tat Khalsa 170-3; and "Hum Hindu Nahin" 170; and voting rights to *amritdhari* Sikhs 173; movement 175; network and Gurdwara Act 175-6
temple entry 32-3
"temple Hinduism" 73
temple or *math* 446
Tora, Gurcharan Singh as President of SGPC 189
traffic in women and girls, suppression of and *devadasi* in India 330
Transfer of Property Act 211
"tribal Hinduism" 73
turban as central to Sikh identity 195
Tyagi, P. on Freedom of Religion Bill 392

U.S. Constitution, Church and state 41-3
ulama as guardians of *shariah* 109
Uniform Civil Code (Article 44) 284
Uniform Civil Code 5, 10, 207-9, 225, 286; *v.* personal laws 218
United Minorities Front (UMF) 157
untouchability 64; Bhagwati on 43
untouchables, as *harijan*, meaning of 403; separate electorate for and Ambedkar 403

upanishads 52, 71, 84
utsarga 447

Vacaspatimisra 59
Vaishnavite in Saivite Temple 27
vaishya (commoner) 10
Vancouver events and Sikhs 200-1
varna (classes) 10, 54; as obsolete 23; theory of 405-6, *see also* caste
varnashrama dharma 53, 54, 73, 74, 439, 440, 441
Vedas 53, 56, 70, 74, 77, 80, 84, 348, 353, 430, 438, 439, 441, 442, 499
Vasisthadharmasutra 471
"village Hinduism" 73
Vishva Hindu Parishad (VHP) 212; and Hindu code 229
"voluntary civil code" 238

Webber, Max on India 421; and religion 74-5, 79
West Bengal College Service Commission Act (1978) 84
West Bengal College Teachers (Security and Service) Act (1975) 84
widows burning, Bhagwati on 43, *see also sati*
Williams, Monier on religious Hinduism 407
women 11; and renunciation 349-54; of renouncement as "auspicious women" 350; *sannyasinis* in Srivaisnava movement 352-3; *shudras* and renunciation 353-4; of unfaithful and rebirth 13

Yajnavalkya 474
Yellamma, women dedication to as *devadasis* or *jogtis* 338
yoga sutras 58; and *karma* 55
yogangas 57

Zaehner, R.C. 71
zakat, Islamic charity tax 122, 128, 129, 130, 132